BATMAN
LEGACY

VOLUME TWO

BATMAN
LEGACY

VOLUME TWO

CHUCK DIXON
DOUG MOENCH
ALAN GRANT
Writers

GRAHAM NOLAN
JIM APARO
JIM BALENT
STAZ JOHNSON
DAVE TAYLOR
RICK BURCHETT
Pencillers

SCOTT HANNA
BOB SMITH
RAY McCARTHY
STAN WOCH
BILL SIENKIEWICZ
ROB LEIGH
TOM PALMER
RICK BURCHETT
Inkers

GLORIA VASQUEZ
BUZZ SETZER
ADRIENNE ROY
PAMELA RAMBO
LEE LOUGHRIDGE
NOELLE GIDDINGS
DAVID HORNUNG
Colorists

JOHN COSTANZA
ALBERT DeGUZMAN
TIM HARKINS
TODD KLEIN
BILL OAKLEY
Letterers

GRAHAM NOLAN and BILL SIENKIEWICZ
Collection cover artists

BATMAN created by BOB KANE
with BILL FINGER

BANE created by CHUCK DIXON,
DOUG MOENCH and GRAHAM NOLAN

SCOTT PETERSON | DENNIS O'NEIL Editors– Original Series
DARREN J. VINCENZO | JORDAN B. GORFINKEL Associate Editors – Original Series
JEB WOODARD Group Editor – Collected Editions
PAUL SANTOS Editor – Collected Edition
STEVE COOK Design Director – Books
MONIQUE NARBONETA Publication Design

BOB HARRAS Senior VP – Editor-in-Chief, DC Comics
PAT McCALLUM Executive Editor, DC Comics

DIANE NELSON President
DAN DiDIO Publisher
JIM LEE Publisher
GEOFF JOHNS President & Chief Creative Officer
AMIT DESAI Executive VP – Business & Marketing Strategy,
        Direct to Consumer & Global Franchise Management
SAM ADES Senior VP & General Manager, Digital Services
BOBBIE CHASE VP & Executive Editor, Young Reader & Talent Development
MARK CHIARELLO Senior VP – Art, Design & Collected Editions
JOHN CUNNINGHAM Senior VP – Sales & Trade Marketing
ANNE DePIES Senior VP – Business Strategy, Finance & Administration
DON FALLETTI VP – Manufacturing Operations
LAWRENCE GANEM VP – Editorial Administration & Talent Relations
ALISON GILL Senior VP – Manufacturing & Operations
HANK KANALZ Senior VP – Editorial Strategy & Administration
JAY KOGAN VP – Legal Affairs
JACK MAHAN VP – Business Affairs
NICK J. NAPOLITANO VP – Manufacturing Administration
EDDIE SCANNELL VP – Consumer Marketing
COURTNEY SIMMONS Senior VP – Publicity & Communications
JIM (SKI) SOKOLOWSKI VP – Comic Book Specialty Sales & Trade Marketing
NANCY SPEARS VP – Mass, Book, Digital Sales & Trade Marketing
MICHELE R. WELLS VP – Content Strategy

BATMAN: LEGACY VOLUME TWO

Published by DC Comics. Compilation and all new material Copyright © 2018 DC Comics.
All Rights Reserved.

Originally published in single magazine form in BATMAN 534, BATMAN: BANE 1,
BATMAN: BANE OF THE DEMON 1-4, BATMAN: SHADOW OF THE BAT 54, CATWOMAN
36, DETECTIVE COMICS 701-702, ROBIN 32-33. Copyright © 1996, 1997, 1998 DC
Comics. All Rights Reserved. All characters, their distinctive likenesses and related
elements featured in this publication are trademarks of DC Comics. The stories,
characters and incidents featured in this publication are entirely fictional. DC Comics
does not read or accept unsolicited submissions of ideas, stories or artwork.

DC Comics, 2900 West Alameda Avenue, Burbank, CA 91505
Printed by Solisco Printers, Scott. QC, Canada. 1/12/18. First printing.
ISBN: 978-1-4012-7761-1

Cataloging-in-Publication Data is available.

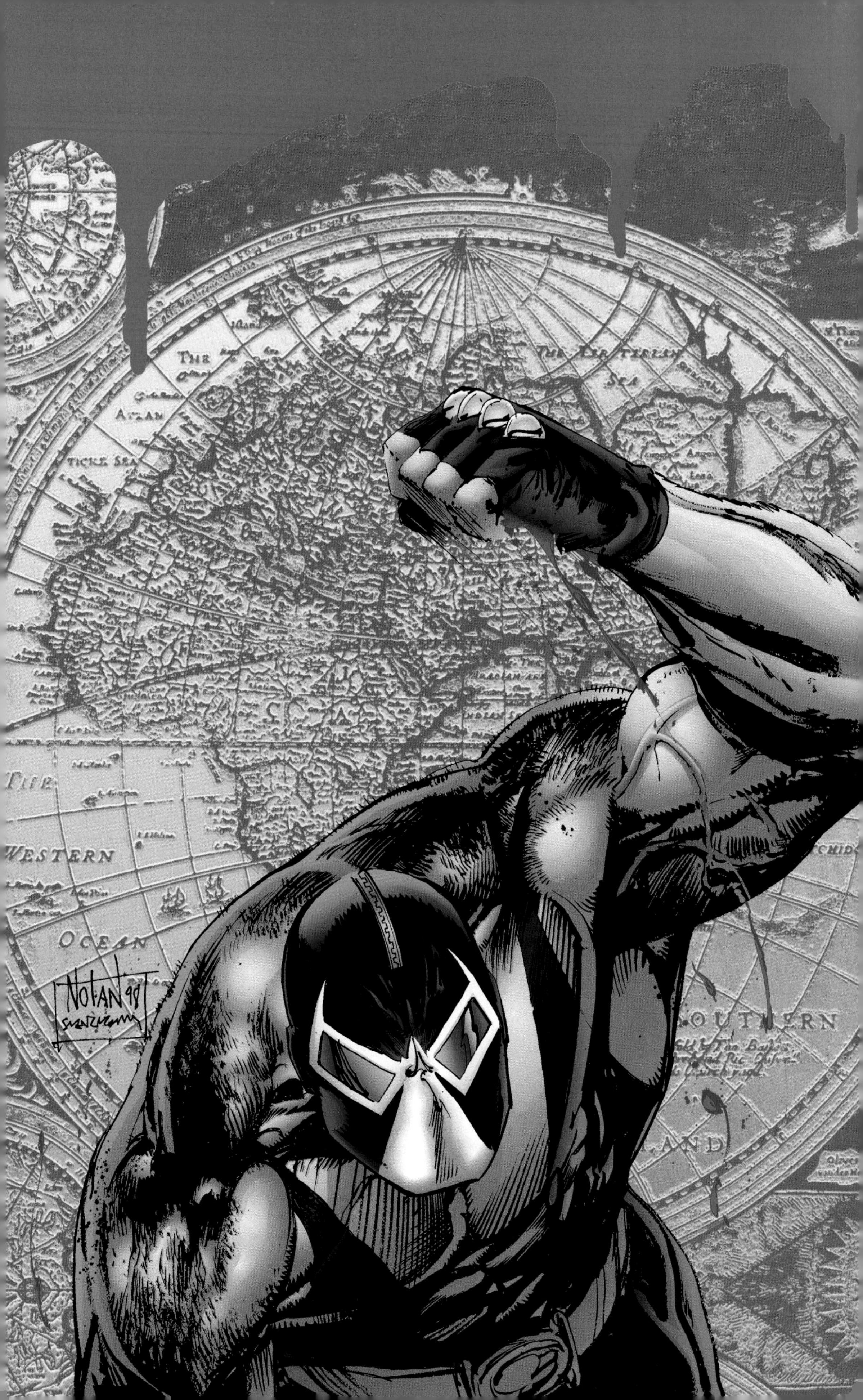

THE
WESTERN
OCEAN
SOUTHERN
NOLAN 98

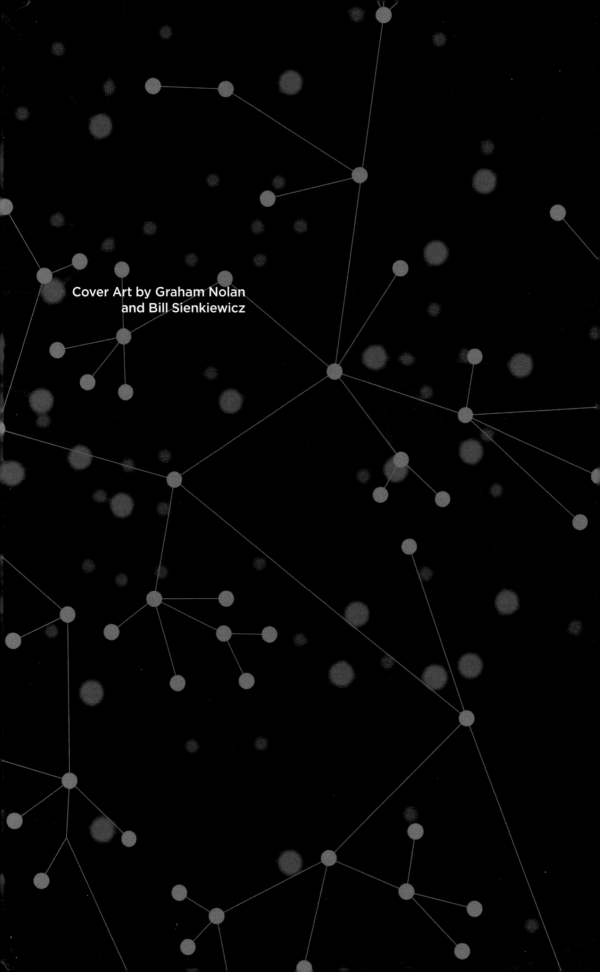

Cover Art by Graham Nolan
and Bill Sienkiewicz

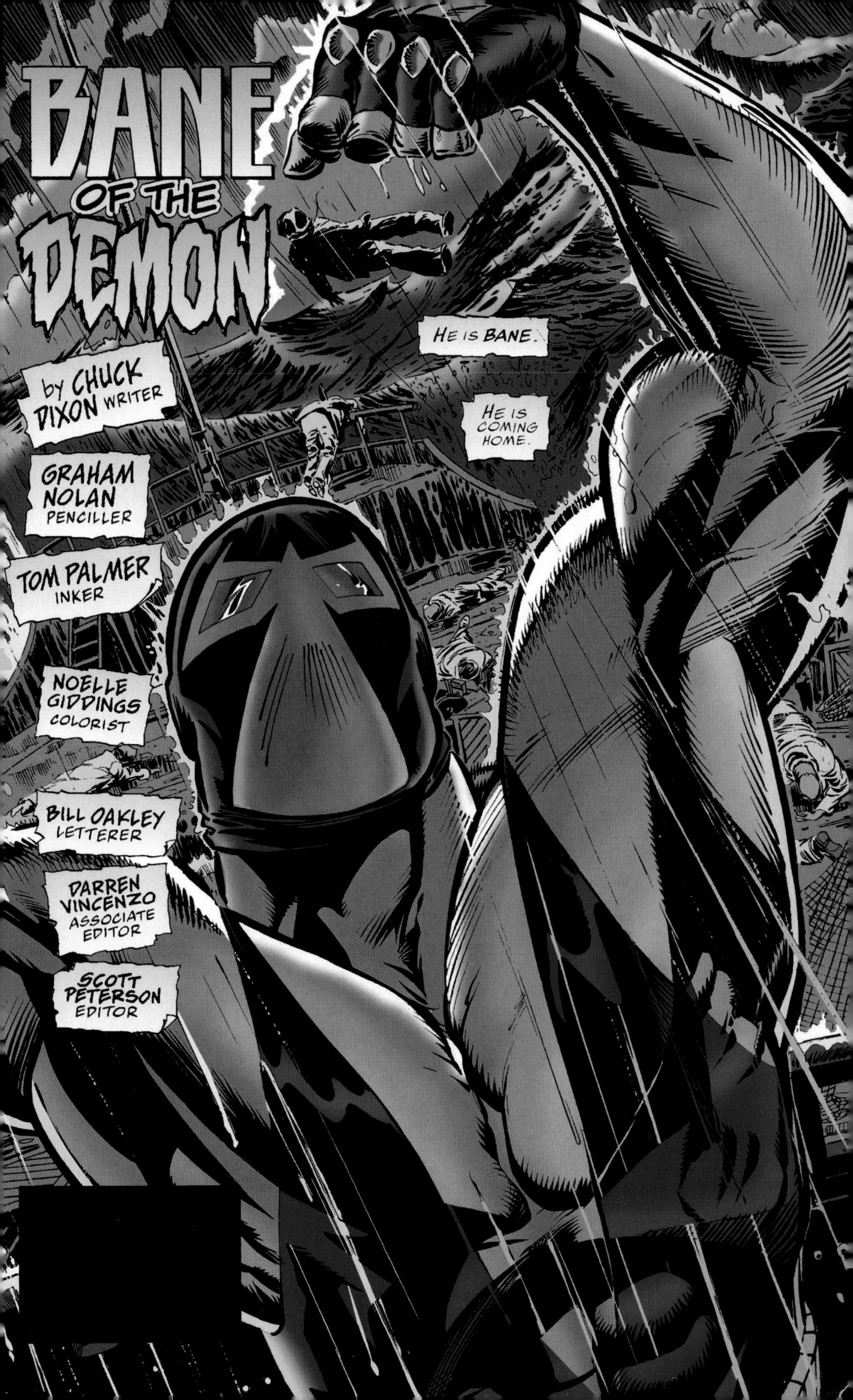
BANE OF THE DEMON
HE IS BANE.
HE IS COMING HOME.
by CHUCK DIXON WRITER
GRAHAM NOLAN PENCILLER
TOM PALMER INKER
NOELLE GIDDINGS COLORIST
BILL OAKLEY LETTERER
DARREN VINCENZO ASSOCIATE EDITOR
SCOTT PETERSON EDITOR

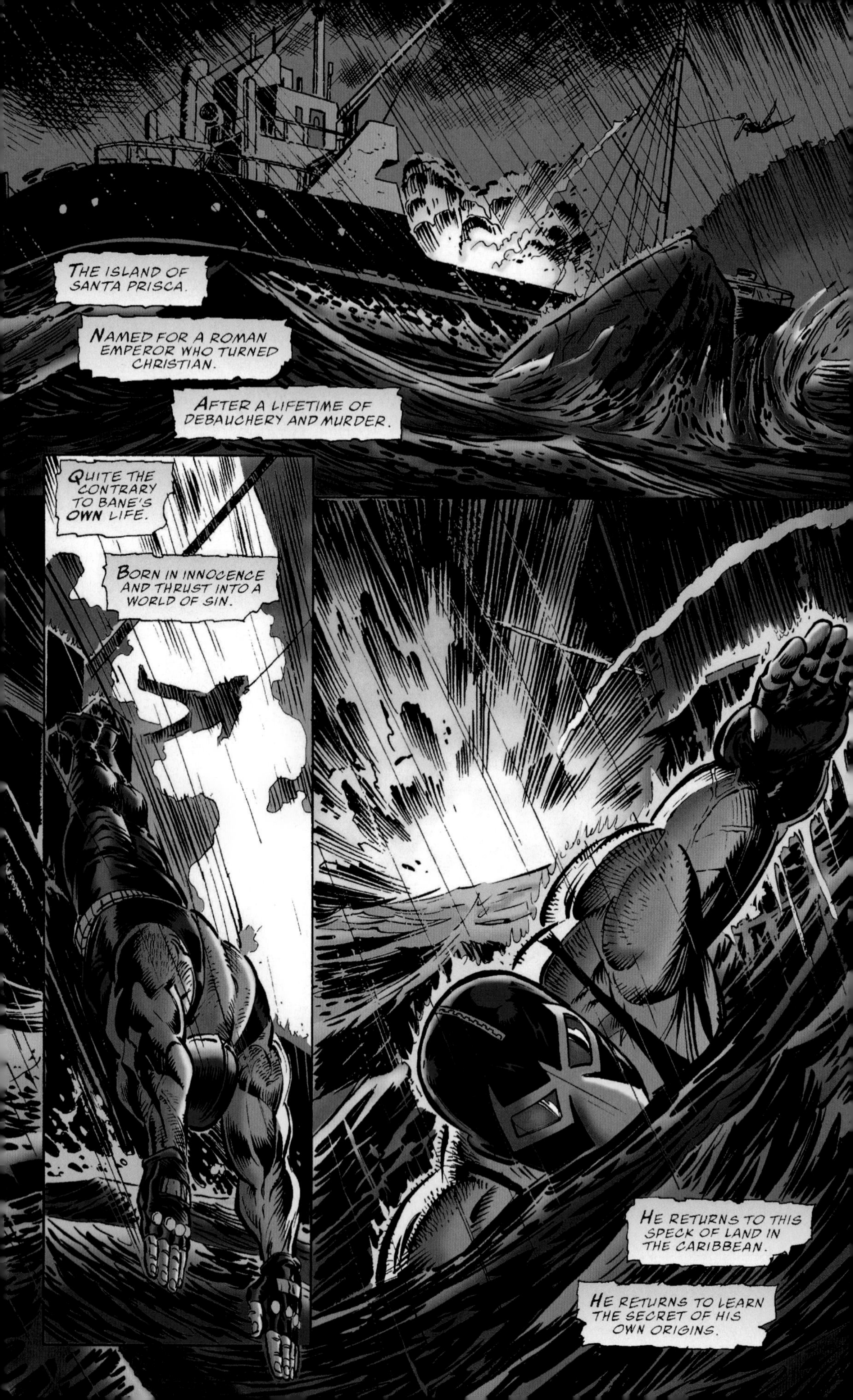
THE ISLAND OF SANTA PRISCA.
NAMED FOR A ROMAN EMPEROR WHO TURNED CHRISTIAN.
AFTER A LIFETIME OF DEBAUCHERY AND MURDER.
QUITE THE CONTRARY TO BANE'S OWN LIFE.
BORN IN INNOCENCE AND THRUST INTO A WORLD OF SIN.
HE RETURNS TO THIS SPECK OF LAND IN THE CARIBBEAN.
HE RETURNS TO LEARN THE SECRET OF HIS OWN ORIGINS.

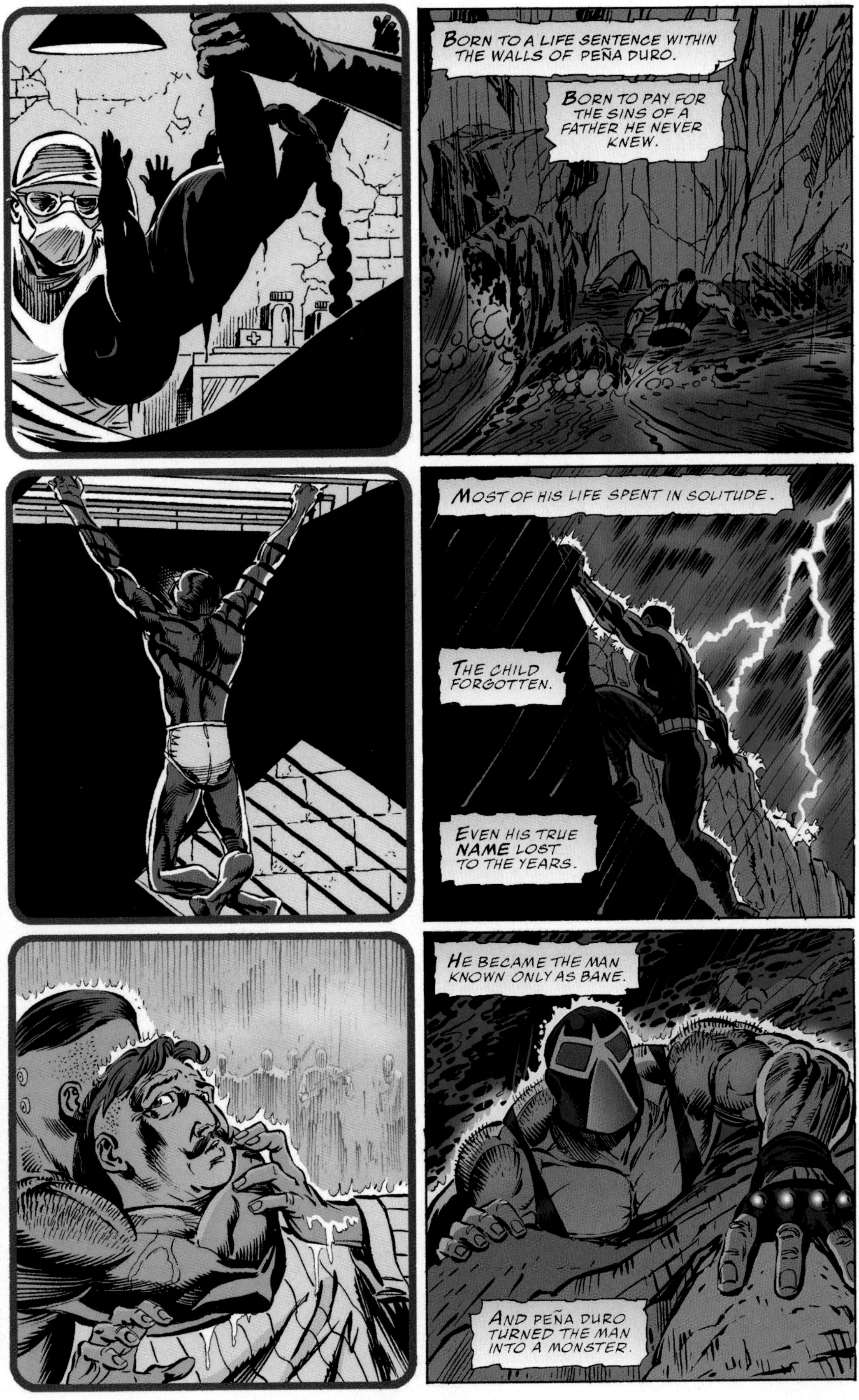
BORN TO A LIFE SENTENCE WITHIN THE WALLS OF PEÑA DURO.
BORN TO PAY FOR THE SINS OF A FATHER HE NEVER KNEW.
MOST OF HIS LIFE SPENT IN SOLITUDE.
THE CHILD FORGOTTEN.
EVEN HIS TRUE NAME LOST TO THE YEARS.
HE BECAME THE MAN KNOWN ONLY AS BANE.
AND PEÑA DURO TURNED THE MAN INTO A MONSTER.

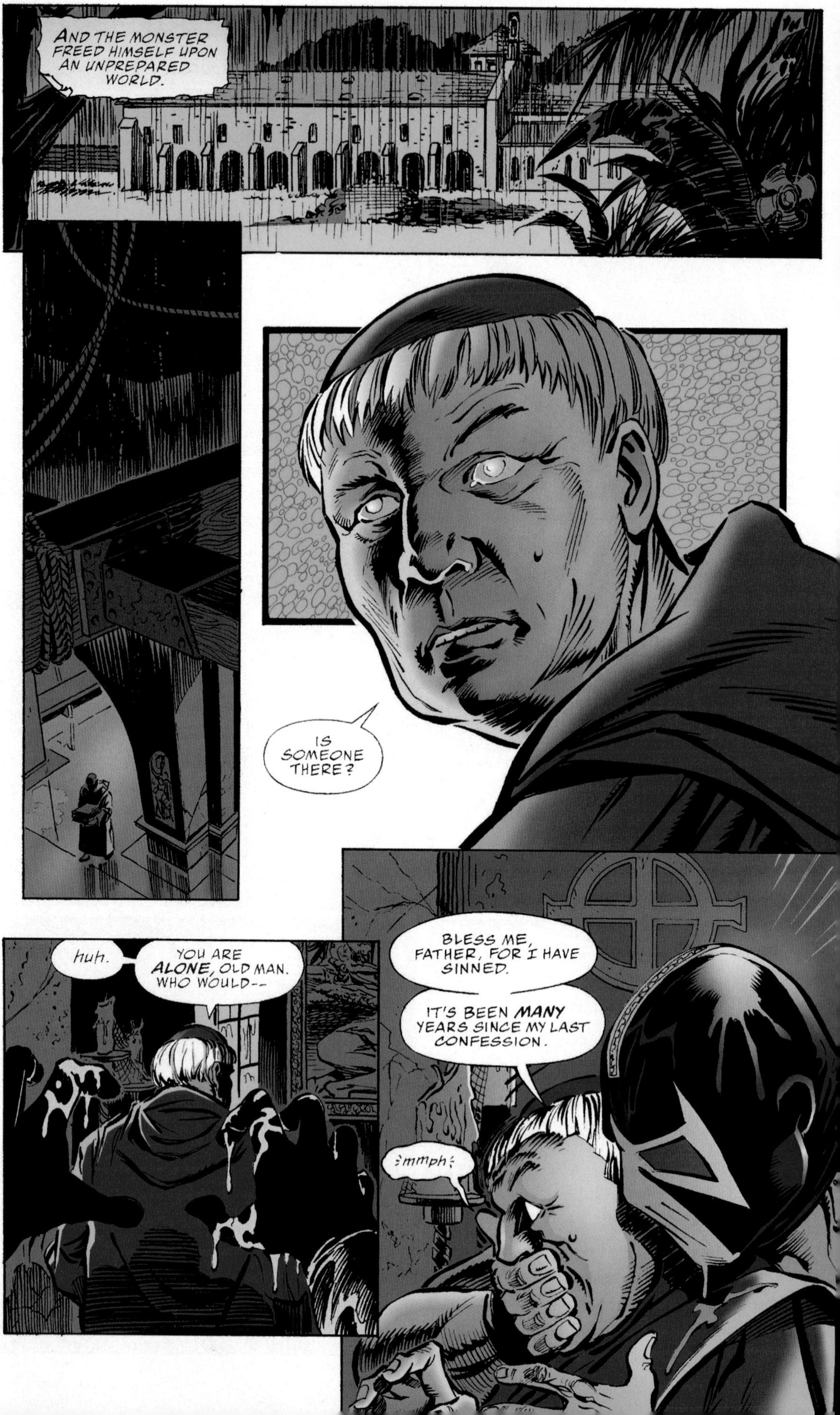
AND THE MONSTER FREED HIMSELF UPON AN UNPREPARED WORLD.
IS SOMEONE THERE?
huh.
YOU ARE ALONE, OLD MAN. WHO WOULD--
BLESS ME, FATHER, FOR I HAVE SINNED.
IT'S BEEN MANY YEARS SINCE MY LAST CONFESSION.
mmph

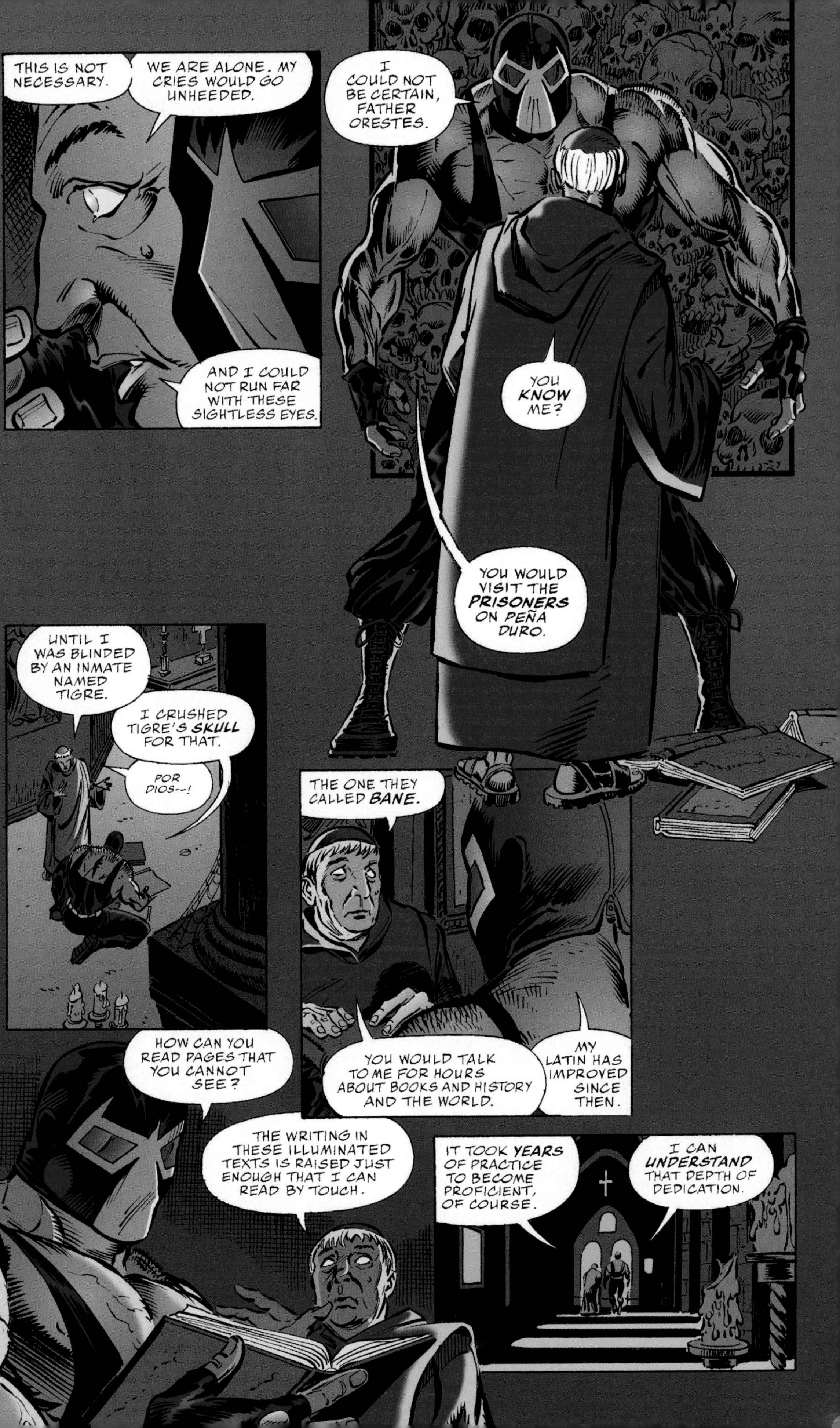
THIS IS NOT NECESSARY.
WE ARE ALONE. MY CRIES WOULD GO UNHEEDED.
AND I COULD NOT RUN FAR WITH THESE SIGHTLESS EYES.
I COULD NOT BE CERTAIN, FATHER ORESTES.
YOU KNOW ME?
YOU WOULD VISIT THE PRISONERS ON PEÑA DURO.
UNTIL I WAS BLINDED BY AN INMATE NAMED TIGRE.
I CRUSHED TIGRE'S SKULL FOR THAT.
POR DIOS--!
THE ONE THEY CALLED BANE.
YOU WOULD TALK TO ME FOR HOURS ABOUT BOOKS AND HISTORY AND THE WORLD.
MY LATIN HAS IMPROVED SINCE THEN.
HOW CAN YOU READ PAGES THAT YOU CANNOT SEE?
THE WRITING IN THESE ILLUMINATED TEXTS IS RAISED JUST ENOUGH THAT I CAN READ BY TOUCH.
IT TOOK YEARS OF PRACTICE TO BECOME PROFICIENT, OF COURSE.
I CAN UNDERSTAND THAT DEPTH OF DEDICATION.

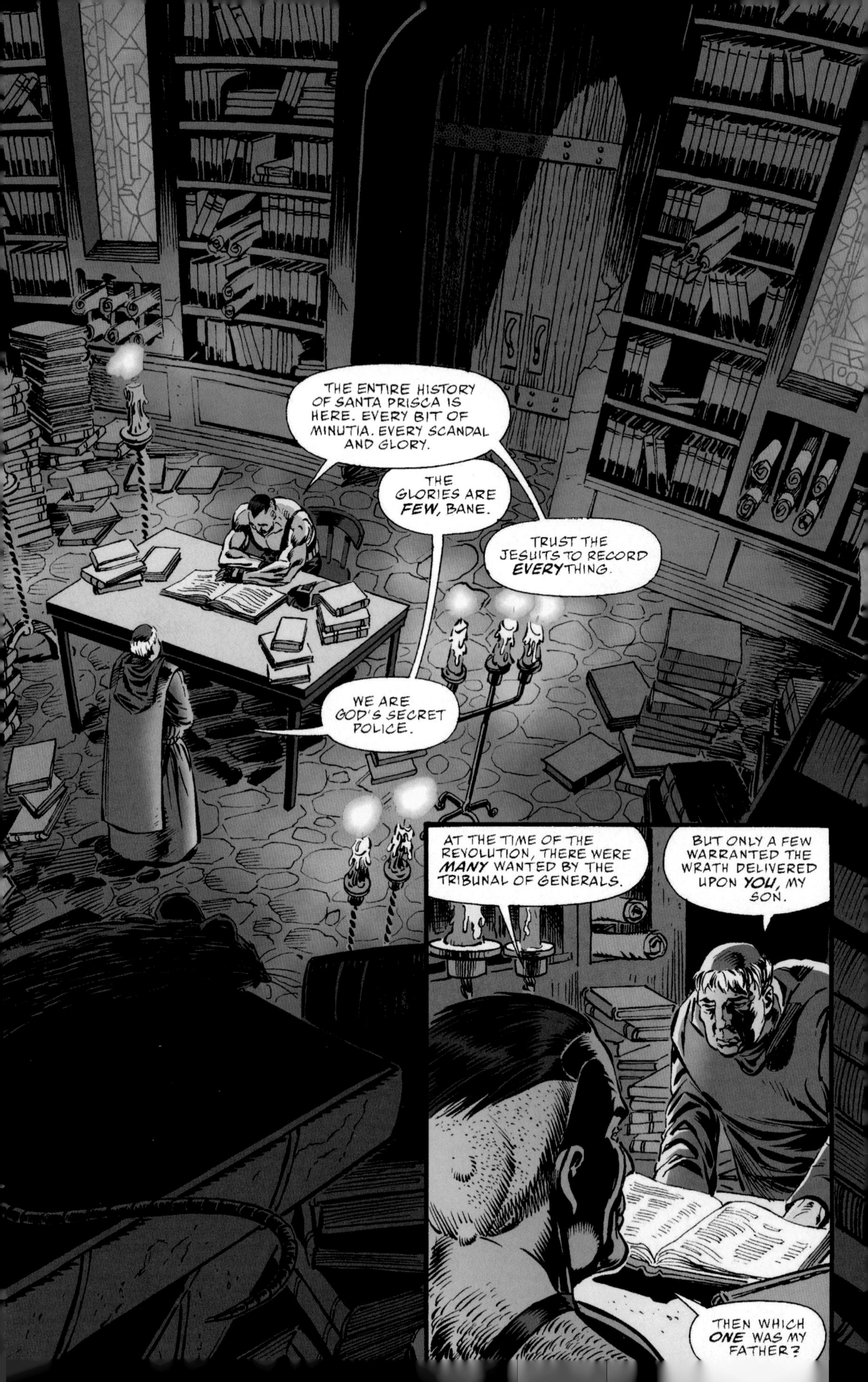

THE ENTIRE HISTORY OF SANTA PRISCA IS HERE. EVERY BIT OF MINUTIA. EVERY SCANDAL AND GLORY.
THE GLORIES ARE FEW, BANE.
TRUST THE JESUITS TO RECORD EVERYTHING.
WE ARE GOD'S SECRET POLICE.
AT THE TIME OF THE REVOLUTION, THERE WERE MANY WANTED BY THE TRIBUNAL OF GENERALS.
BUT ONLY A FEW WARRANTED THE WRATH DELIVERED UPON YOU, MY SON.
THEN WHICH ONE WAS MY FATHER?

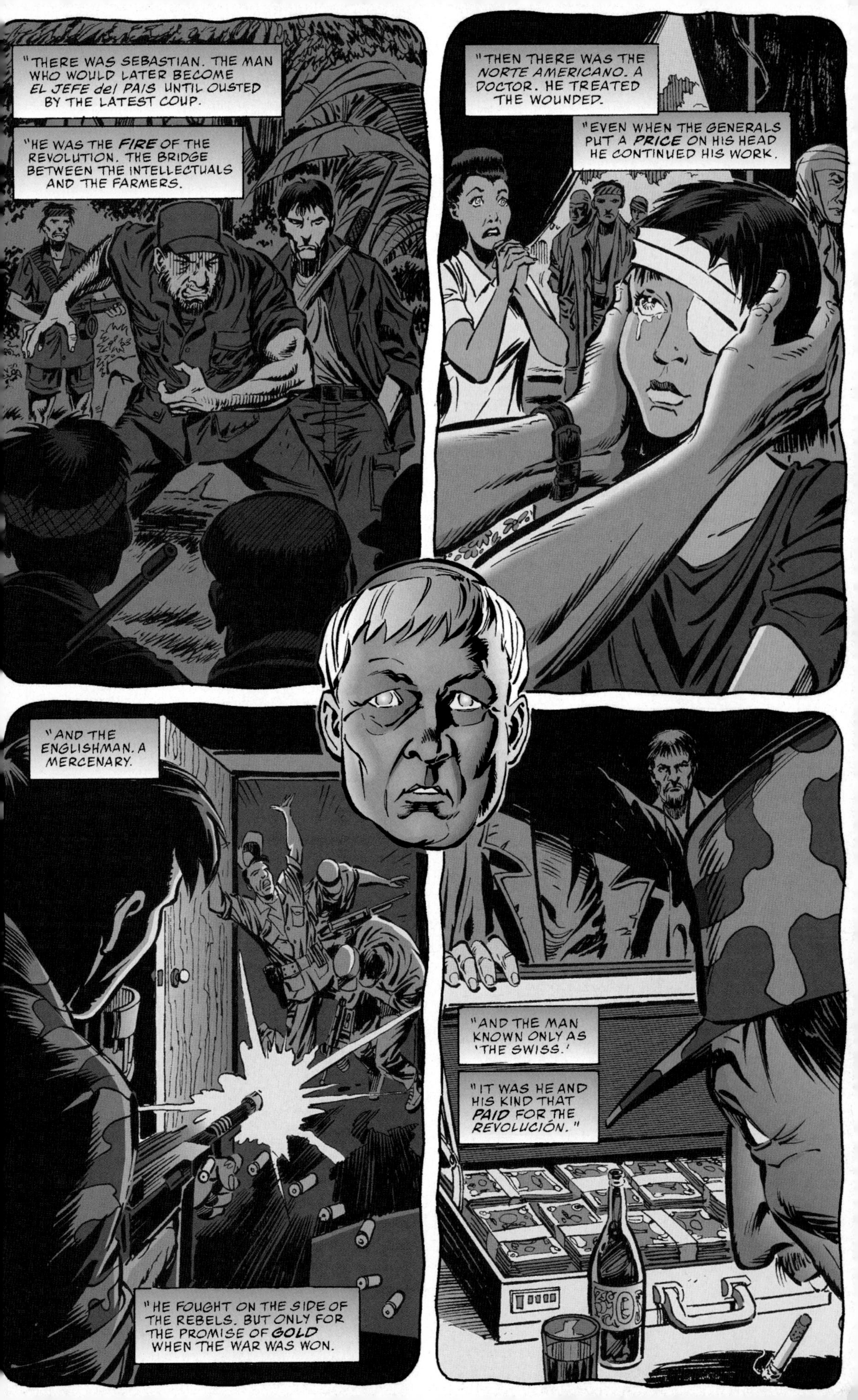
"THERE WAS SEBASTIAN. THE MAN WHO WOULD LATER BECOME *EL JEFE del PAIS* UNTIL OUSTED BY THE LATEST COUP.
"HE WAS THE ***FIRE*** OF THE REVOLUTION. THE BRIDGE BETWEEN THE INTELLECTUALS AND THE FARMERS.
"THEN THERE WAS THE *NORTE AMERICANO*. A DOCTOR. HE TREATED THE WOUNDED.
"EVEN WHEN THE GENERALS PUT A ***PRICE*** ON HIS HEAD HE CONTINUED HIS WORK.
"AND THE ENGLISHMAN. A MERCENARY.
"HE FOUGHT ON THE SIDE OF THE REBELS. BUT ONLY FOR THE PROMISE OF ***GOLD*** WHEN THE WAR WAS WON.
"AND THE MAN KNOWN ONLY AS 'THE SWISS.'
"IT WAS HE AND HIS KIND THAT ***PAID*** FOR THE ***REVOLUCIÓN.***"

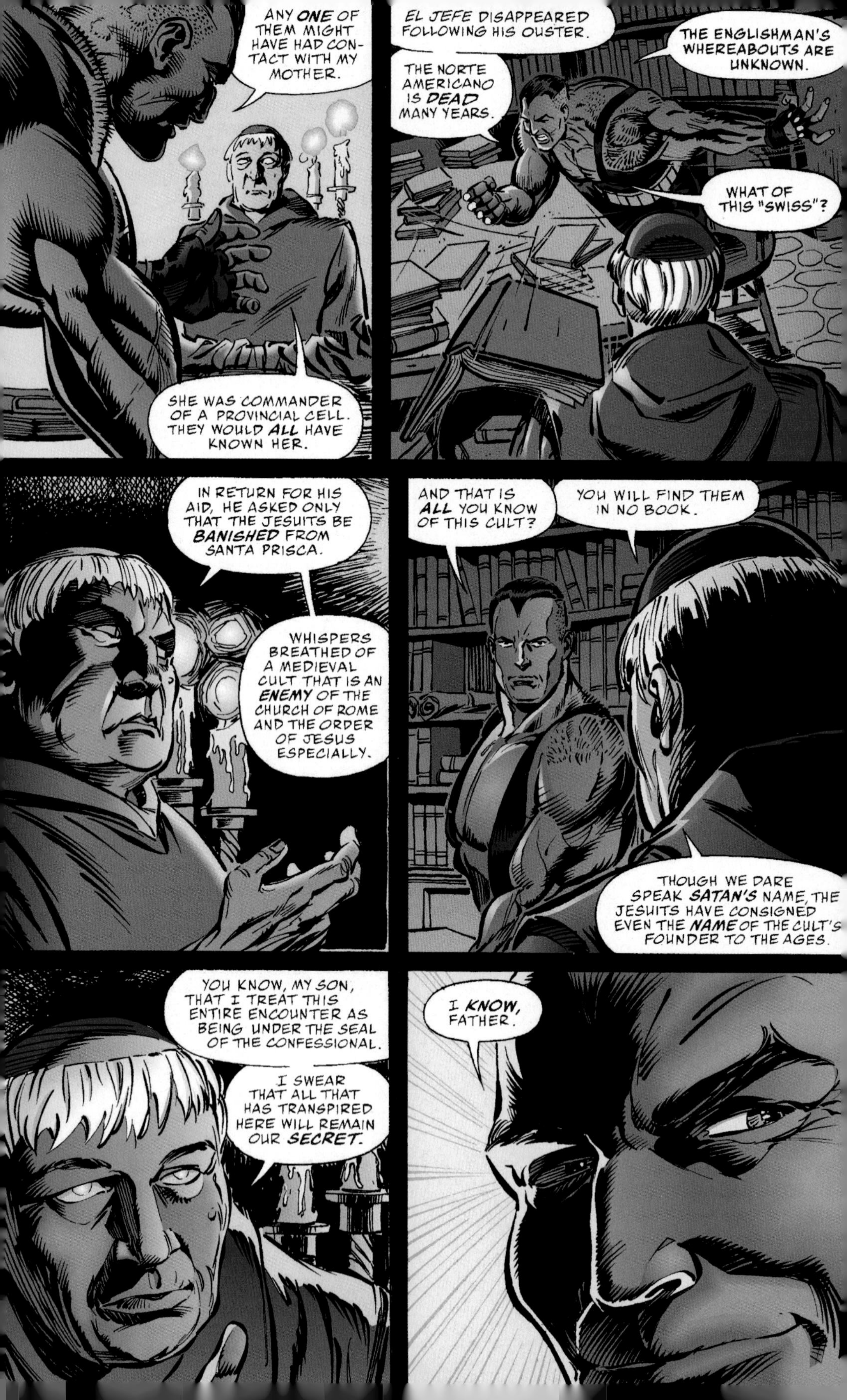
ANY ONE OF THEM MIGHT HAVE HAD CONTACT WITH MY MOTHER.
SHE WAS COMMANDER OF A PROVINCIAL CELL. THEY WOULD ALL HAVE KNOWN HER.
EL JEFE DISAPPEARED FOLLOWING HIS OUSTER.
THE NORTE AMERICANO IS DEAD MANY YEARS.
THE ENGLISHMAN'S WHEREABOUTS ARE UNKNOWN.
WHAT OF THIS "SWISS"?
IN RETURN FOR HIS AID, HE ASKED ONLY THAT THE JESUITS BE BANISHED FROM SANTA PRISCA.
WHISPERS BREATHED OF A MEDIEVAL CULT THAT IS AN ENEMY OF THE CHURCH OF ROME AND THE ORDER OF JESUS ESPECIALLY.
AND THAT IS ALL YOU KNOW OF THIS CULT?
YOU WILL FIND THEM IN NO BOOK.
THOUGH WE DARE SPEAK SATAN'S NAME, THE JESUITS HAVE CONSIGNED EVEN THE NAME OF THE CULT'S FOUNDER TO THE AGES.
YOU KNOW, MY SON, THAT I TREAT THIS ENTIRE ENCOUNTER AS BEING UNDER THE SEAL OF THE CONFESSIONAL.
I SWEAR THAT ALL THAT HAS TRANSPIRED HERE WILL REMAIN OUR SECRET.
I KNOW, FATHER.

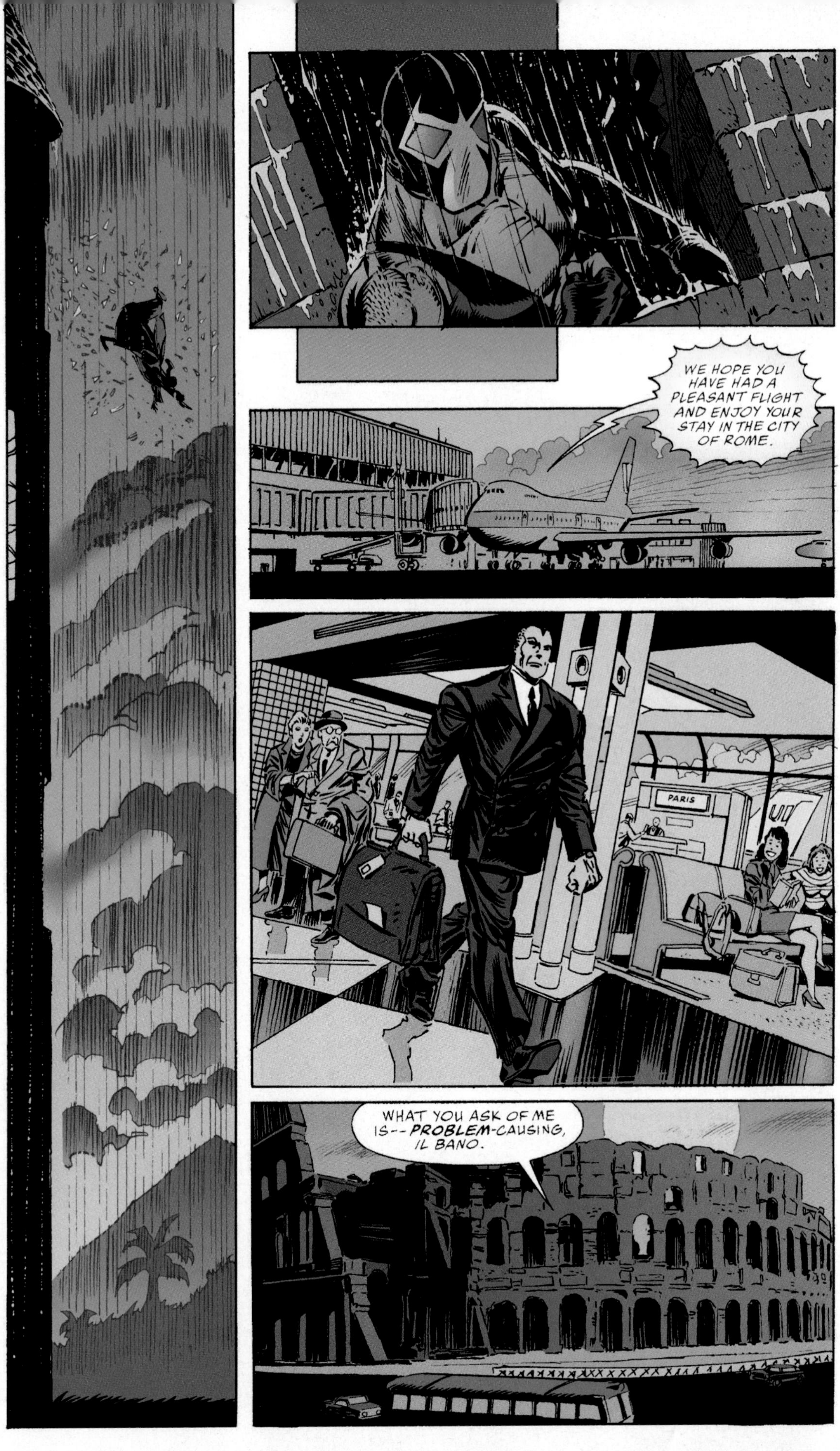
WE HOPE YOU HAVE HAD A PLEASANT FLIGHT AND ENJOY YOUR STAY IN THE CITY OF ROME.
PARIS
WHAT YOU ASK OF ME IS--PROBLEM-CAUSING, IL BANO.

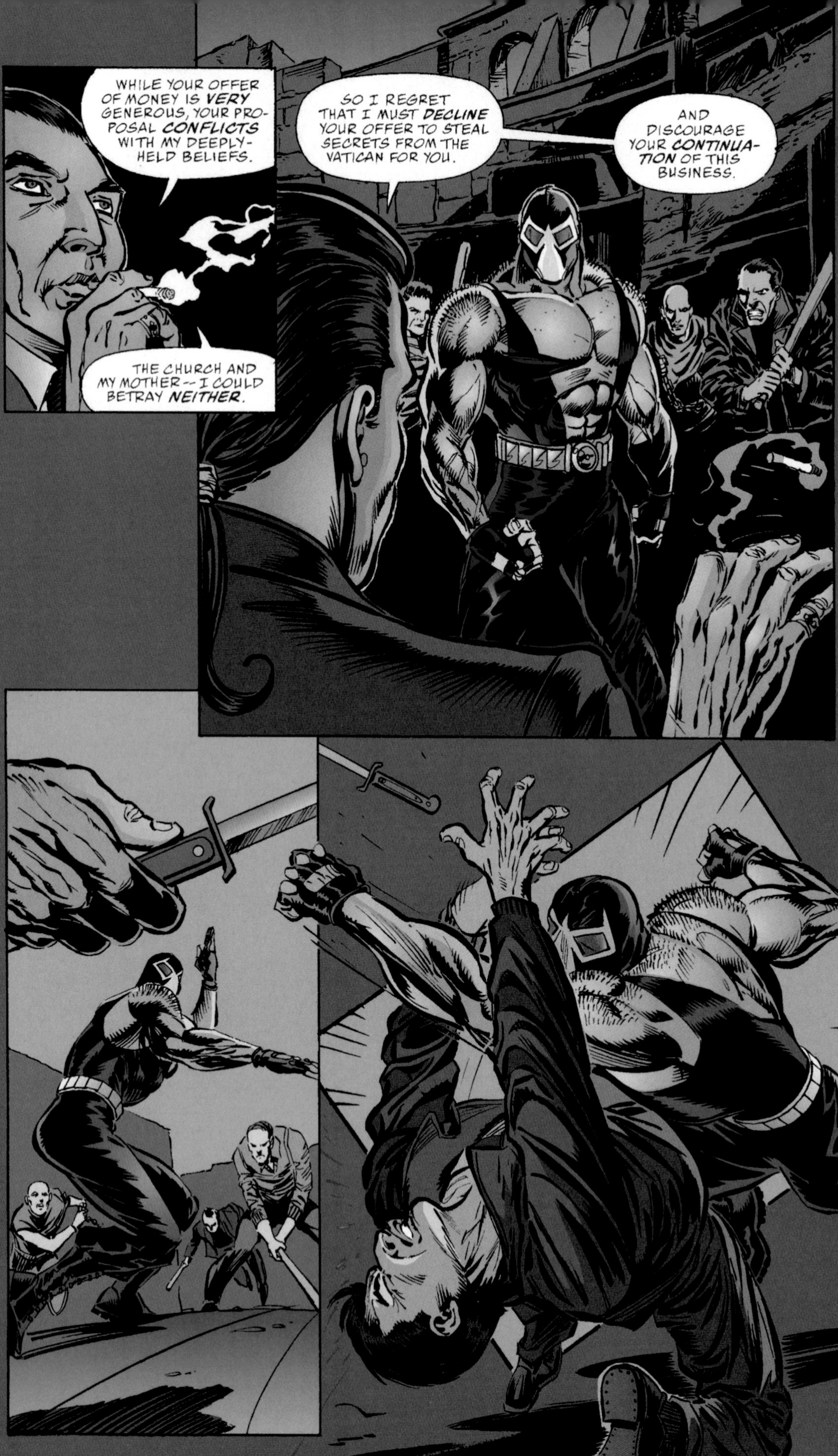
WHILE YOUR OFFER OF MONEY IS VERY GENEROUS, YOUR PROPOSAL CONFLICTS WITH MY DEEPLY-HELD BELIEFS.
THE CHURCH AND MY MOTHER -- I COULD BETRAY NEITHER.
SO I REGRET THAT I MUST DECLINE YOUR OFFER TO STEAL SECRETS FROM THE VATICAN FOR YOU.
AND DISCOURAGE YOUR CONTINUATION OF THIS BUSINESS.

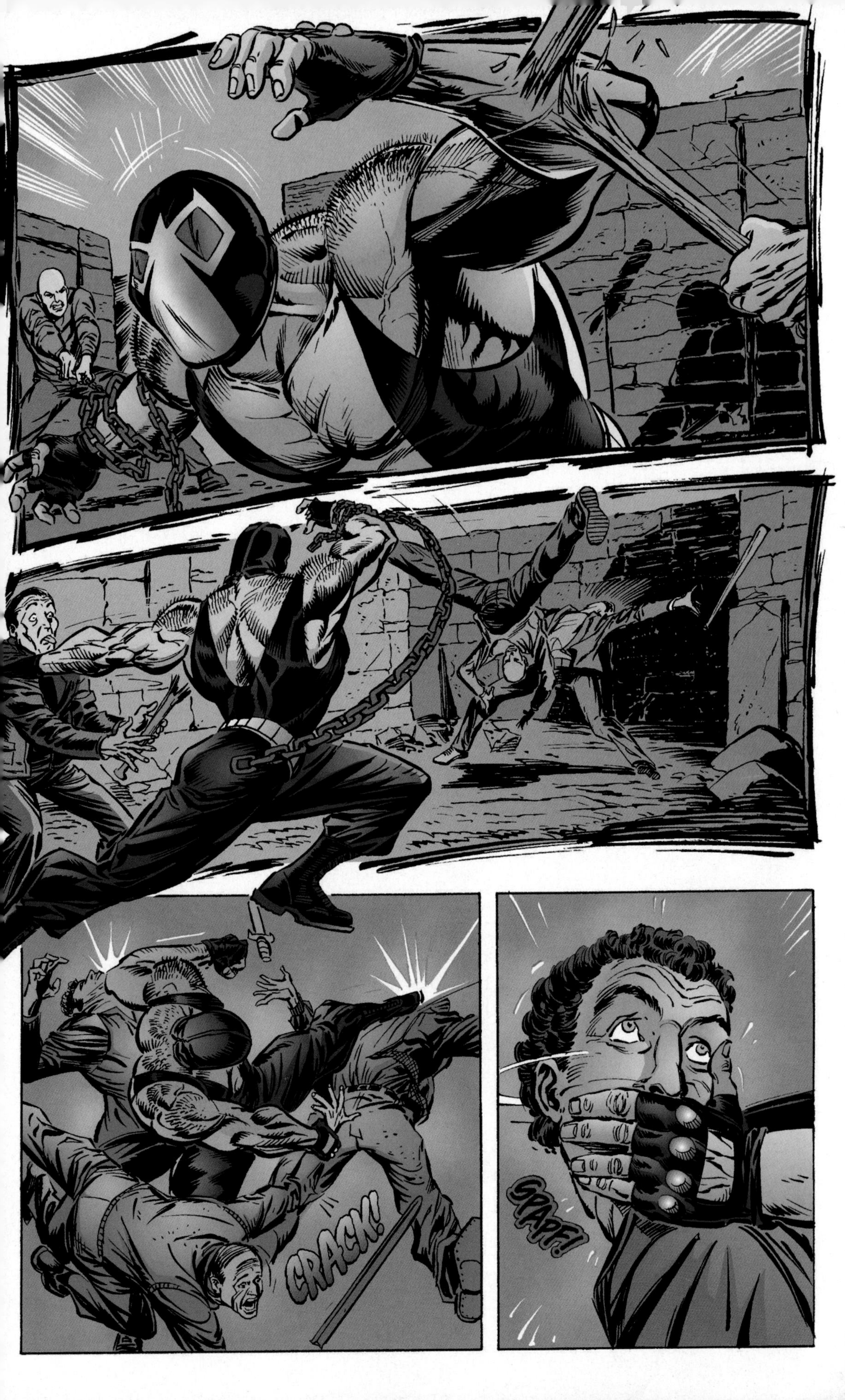
CRACK!
GRAPF!

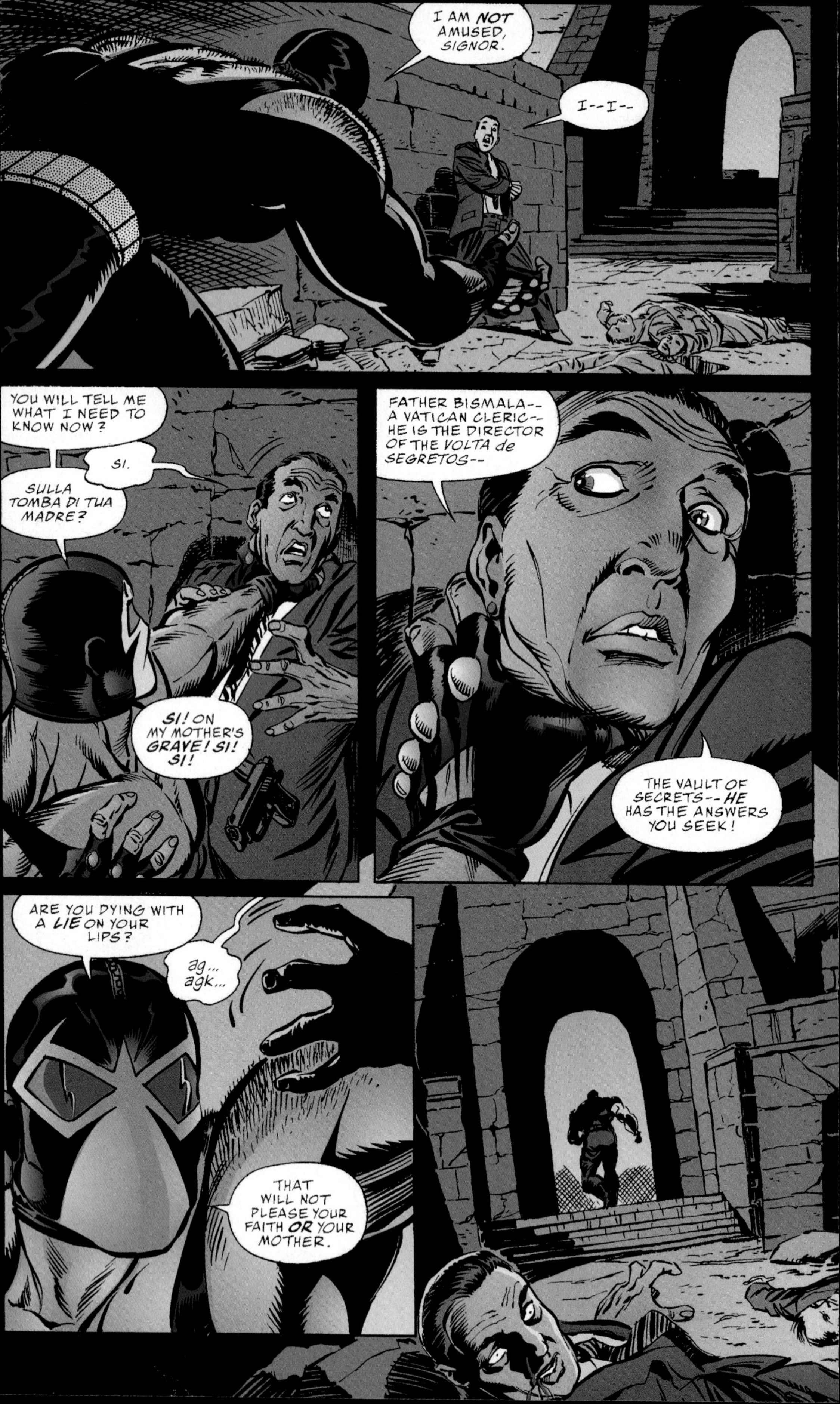
I AM NOT AMUSED, SIGNOR.
I--I--
YOU WILL TELL ME WHAT I NEED TO KNOW NOW?
SI.
SULLA TOMBA DI TUA MADRE?
SI! ON MY MOTHER'S GRAVE! SI! SI!
FATHER BISMALA-- A VATICAN CLERIC-- HE IS THE DIRECTOR OF THE VOLTA de SEGRETOS--
THE VAULT OF SECRETS--HE HAS THE ANSWERS YOU SEEK!
ARE YOU DYING WITH A LIE ON YOUR LIPS?
ag... agk...
THAT WILL NOT PLEASE YOUR FAITH OR YOUR MOTHER.

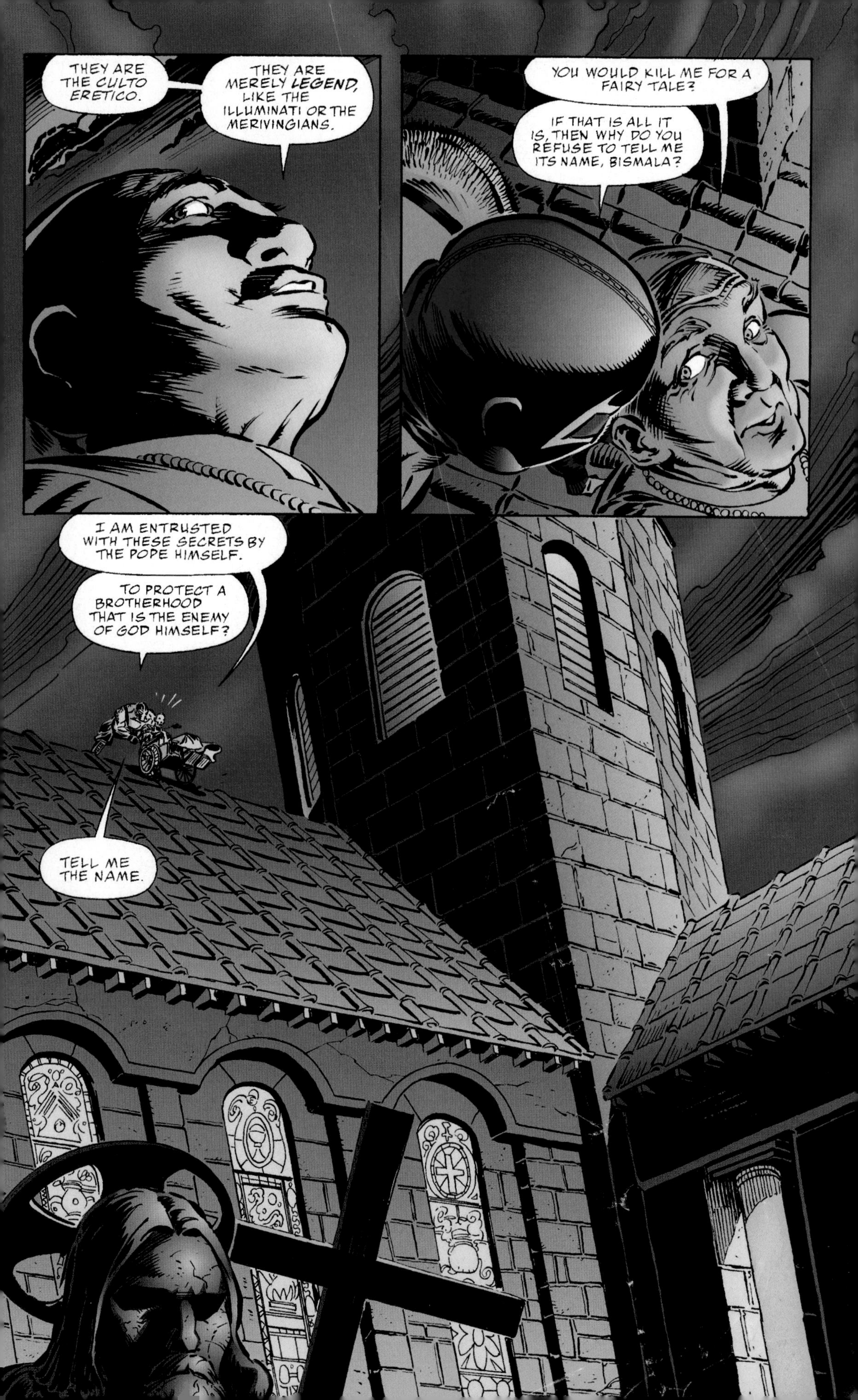
THEY ARE THE CULTO ERETICO.
THEY ARE MERELY LEGEND, LIKE THE ILLUMINATI OR THE MERIVINGIANS.
YOU WOULD KILL ME FOR A FAIRY TALE?
IF THAT IS ALL IT IS, THEN WHY DO YOU REFUSE TO TELL ME ITS NAME, BISMALA?
I AM ENTRUSTED WITH THESE SECRETS BY THE POPE HIMSELF.
TO PROTECT A BROTHERHOOD THAT IS THE ENEMY OF GOD HIMSELF?
TELL ME THE NAME.

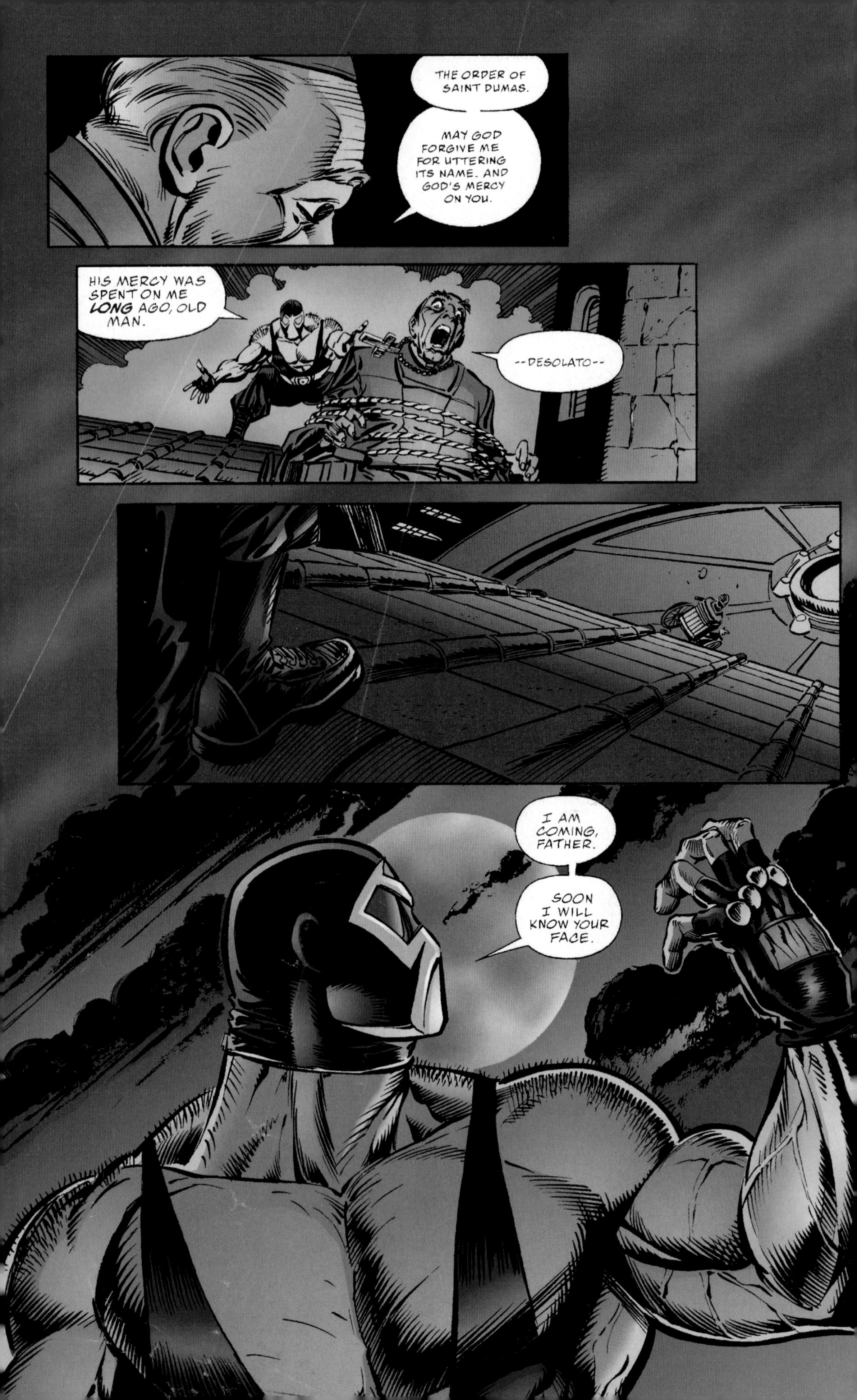
THE ORDER OF SAINT DUMAS.
MAY GOD FORGIVE ME FOR UTTERING ITS NAME. AND GOD'S MERCY ON YOU.
HIS MERCY WAS SPENT ON ME **LONG** AGO, OLD MAN.
--DESOLATO--
I AM COMING, FATHER.
SOON I WILL KNOW YOUR FACE.

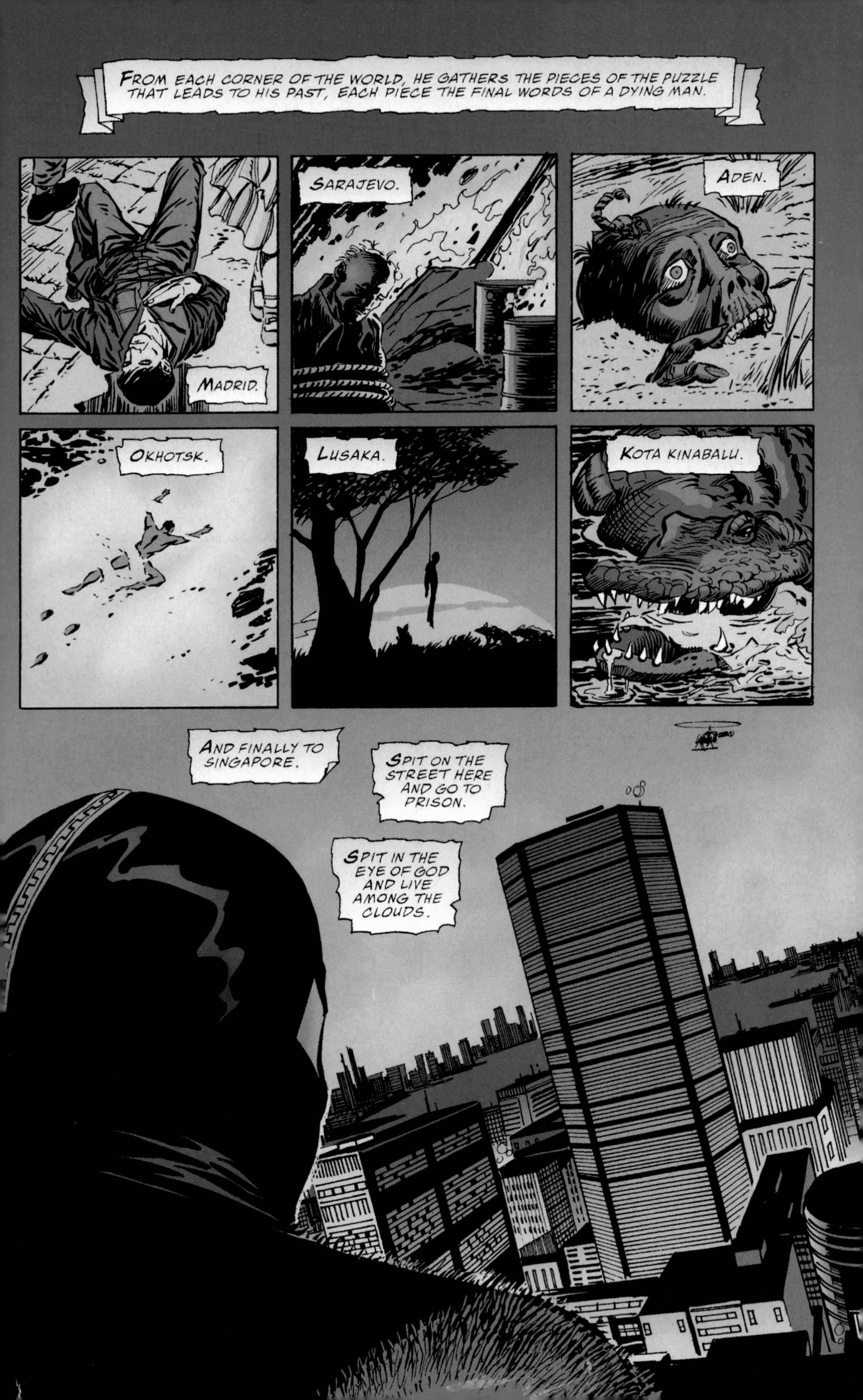
FROM EACH CORNER OF THE WORLD, HE GATHERS THE PIECES OF THE PUZZLE THAT LEADS TO HIS PAST, EACH PIECE THE FINAL WORDS OF A DYING MAN.
MADRID.
SARAJEVO.
ADEN.
OKHOTSK.
LUSAKA.
KOTA KINABALU.
AND FINALLY TO SINGAPORE.
SPIT ON THE STREET HERE AND GO TO PRISON.
SPIT IN THE EYE OF GOD AND LIVE AMONG THE CLOUDS.

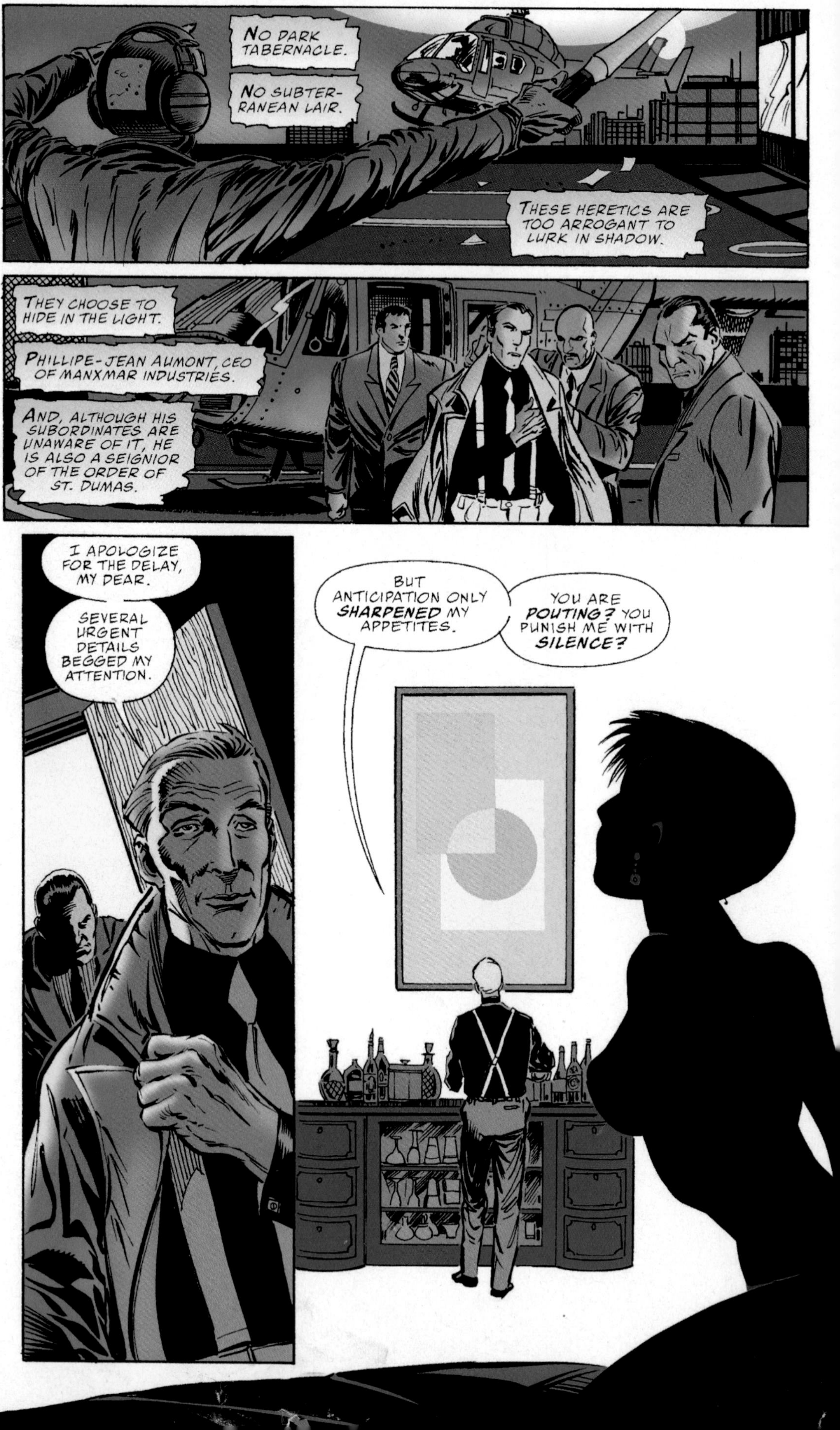
NO DARK TABERNACLE.
NO SUBTERRANEAN LAIR.
THESE HERETICS ARE TOO ARROGANT TO LURK IN SHADOW.
THEY CHOOSE TO HIDE IN THE LIGHT.
PHILLIPE-JEAN AUMONT, CEO OF MANXMAR INDUSTRIES.
AND, ALTHOUGH HIS SUBORDINATES ARE UNAWARE OF IT, HE IS ALSO A SEIGNIOR OF THE ORDER OF ST. DUMAS.
I APOLOGIZE FOR THE DELAY, MY DEAR.
SEVERAL URGENT DETAILS BEGGED MY ATTENTION.
BUT ANTICIPATION ONLY SHARPENED MY APPETITES.
YOU ARE POUTING? YOU PUNISH ME WITH SILENCE?

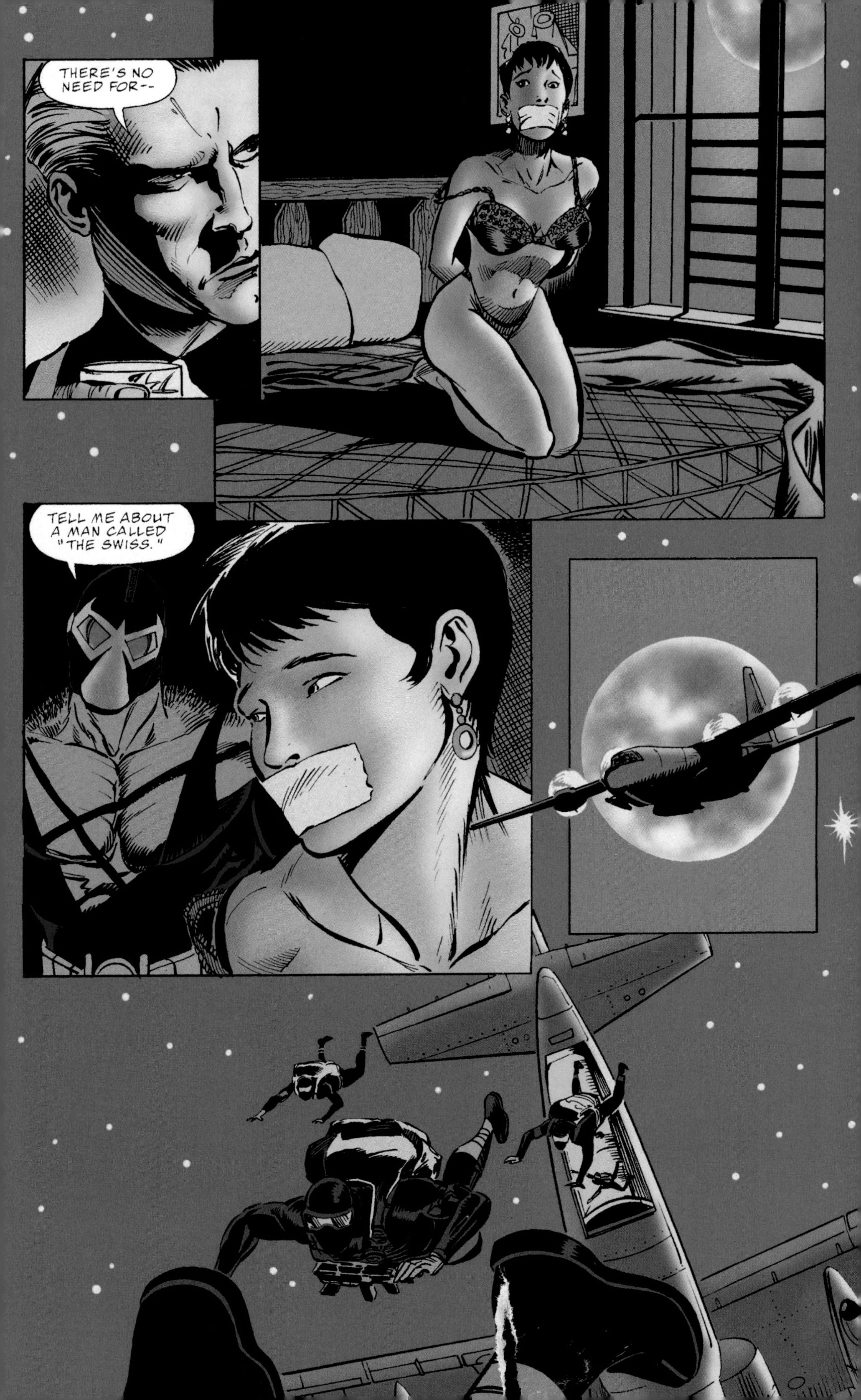
THERE'S NO NEED FOR--
TELL ME ABOUT A MAN CALLED "THE SWISS."

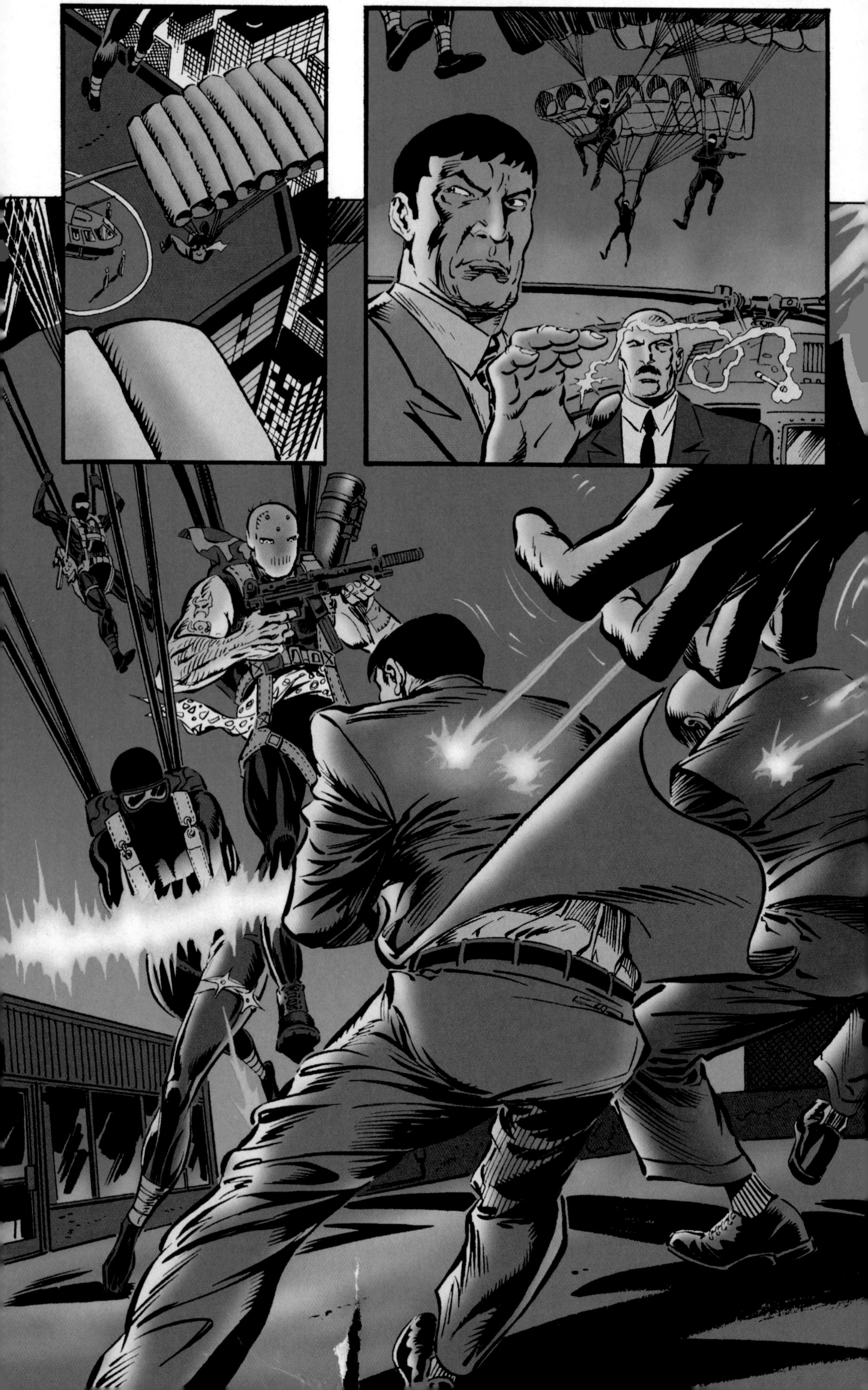

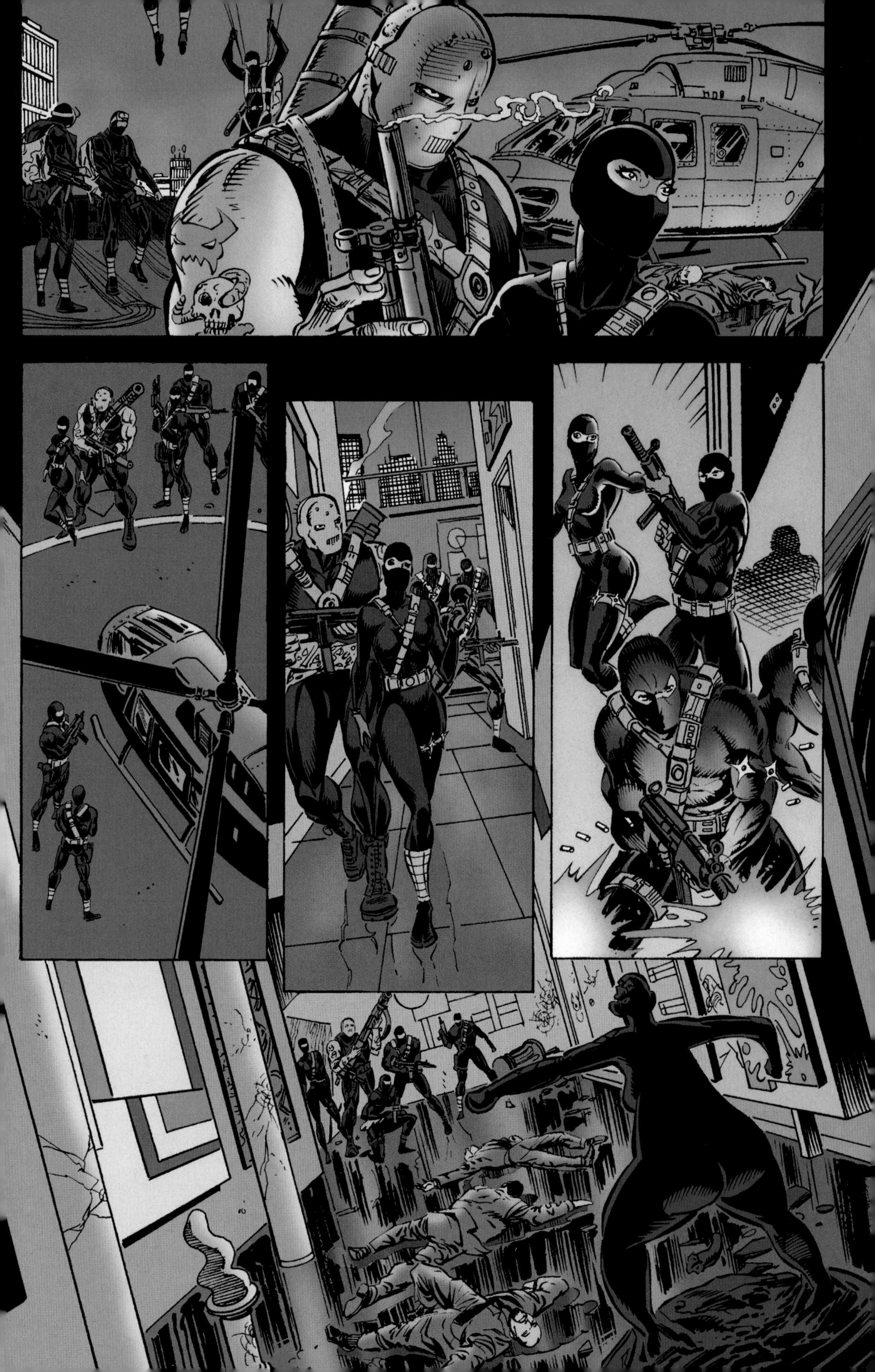

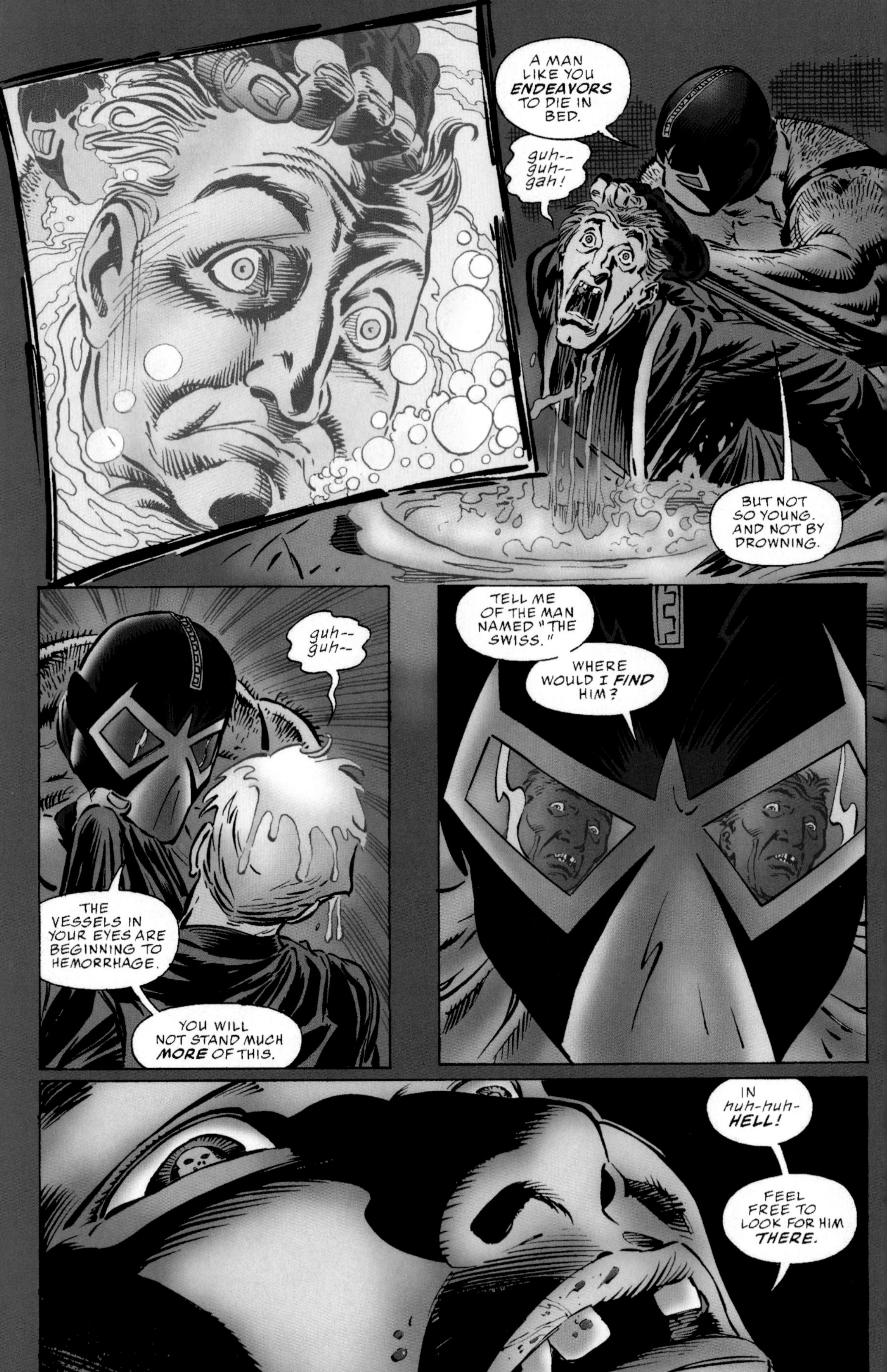
A MAN LIKE YOU ENDEAVORS TO DIE IN BED.
guh-- guh-- gah!
BUT NOT SO YOUNG. AND NOT BY DROWNING.
guh-- guh--
THE VESSELS IN YOUR EYES ARE BEGINNING TO HEMORRHAGE.
YOU WILL NOT STAND MUCH MORE OF THIS.
TELL ME OF THE MAN NAMED "THE SWISS."
WHERE WOULD I FIND HIM?
IN huh-huh-HELL!
FEEL FREE TO LOOK FOR HIM THERE.

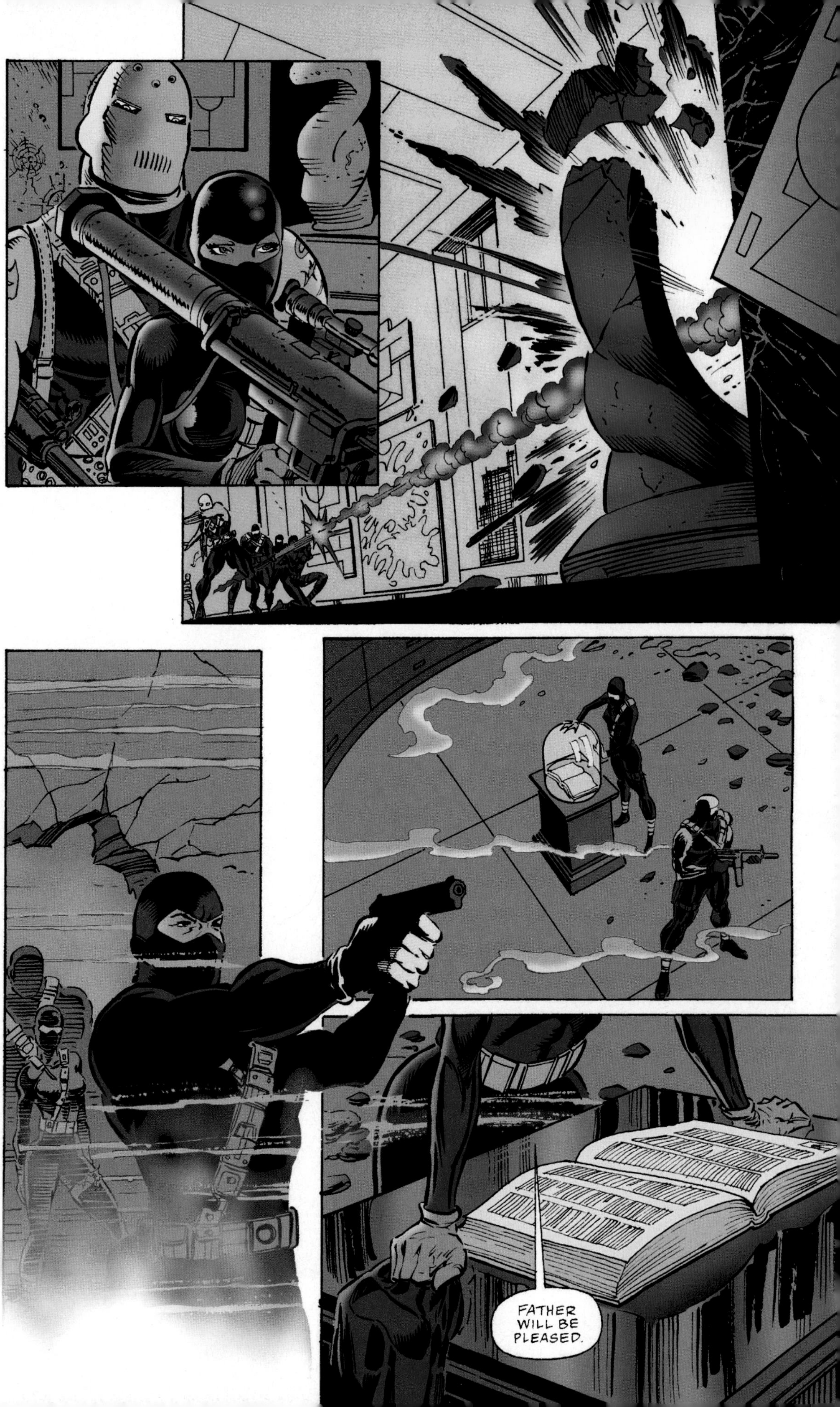
FATHER WILL BE PLEASED.

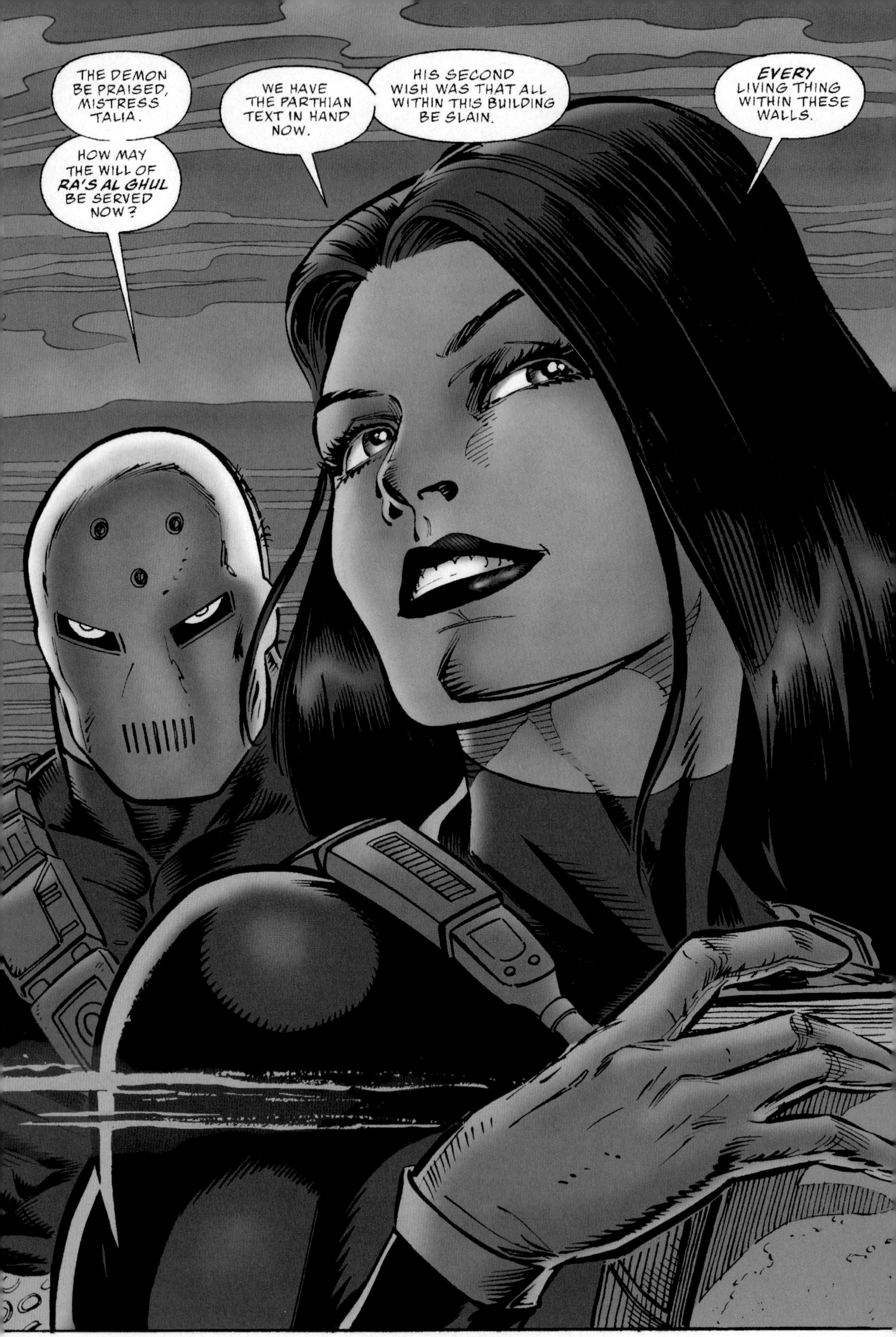
THE DEMON BE PRAISED, MISTRESS TALIA.
HOW MAY THE WILL OF RA'S AL GHUL BE SERVED NOW?
WE HAVE THE PARTHIAN TEXT IN HAND NOW.
HIS SECOND WISH WAS THAT ALL WITHIN THIS BUILDING BE SLAIN.
EVERY LIVING THING WITHIN THESE WALLS.

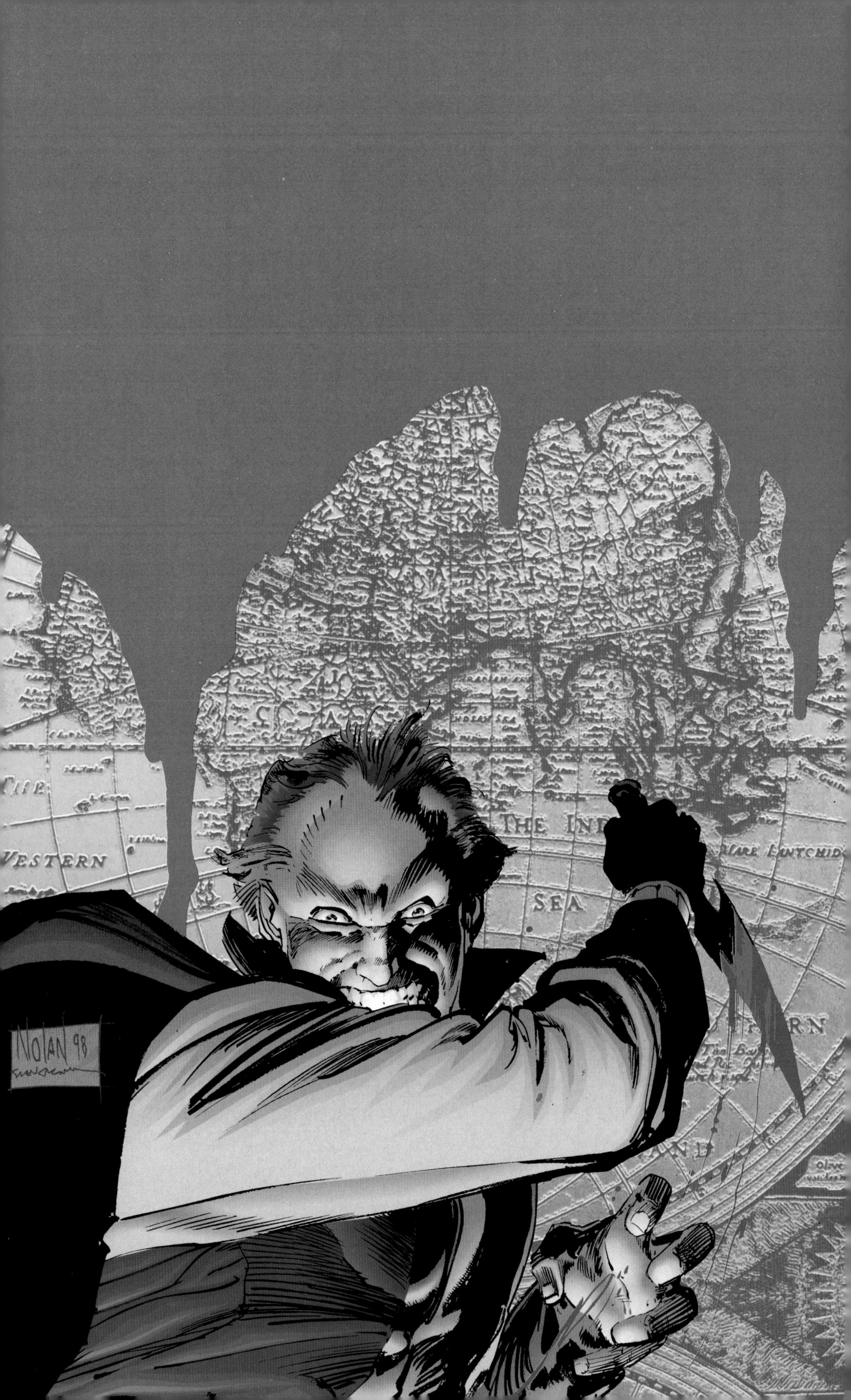
VESTERN
THE IN
SEA
NOLAN 98

Cover Art by Graham Nolan
and Bill Sienkiewicz

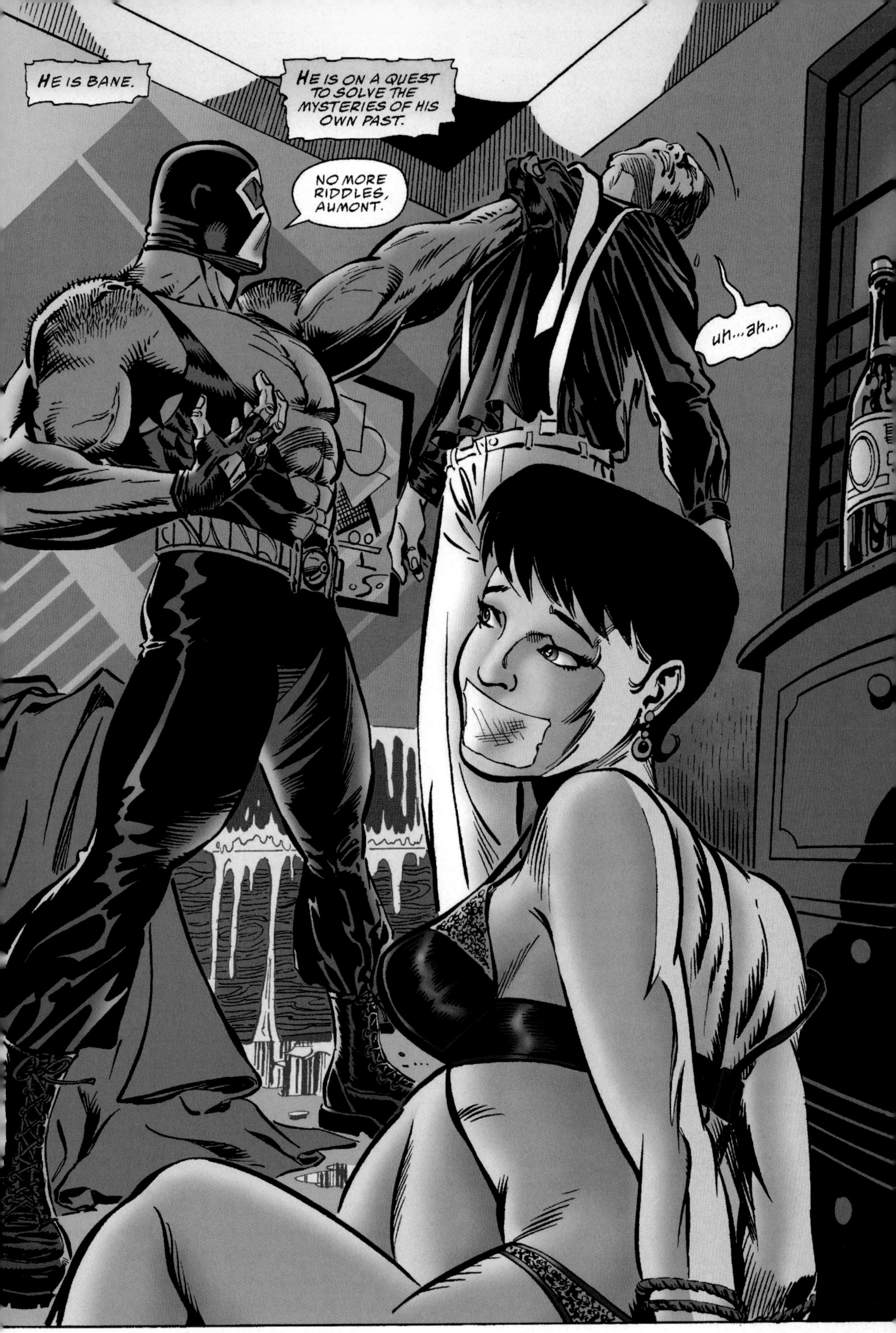
HE IS BANE.
HE IS ON A QUEST TO SOLVE THE MYSTERIES OF HIS OWN PAST.
NO MORE RIDDLES, AUMONT.
uh...ah...

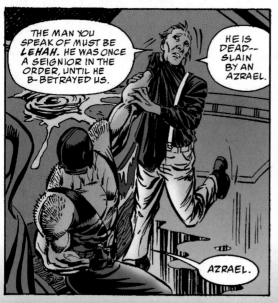

THE MAN YOU SPEAK OF MUST BE *LEHAH*. HE WAS ONCE A SEIGNIOR IN THE ORDER, UNTIL HE B- BETRAYED US.

HE IS DEAD-- SLAIN BY AN AZRAEL.

AZRAEL.

THE AVENGING ANGEL.

ALL WHO DEFY SAINT DUMAS ARE SEARED BY THE SWORD OF THE AZRAEL.

THEN *THIS* LEG OF MY QUEST IS ENDED.

AS IS YOUR *USE* TO ME.

puh- please...

NO-- NO!

≈wurrrghh!≈

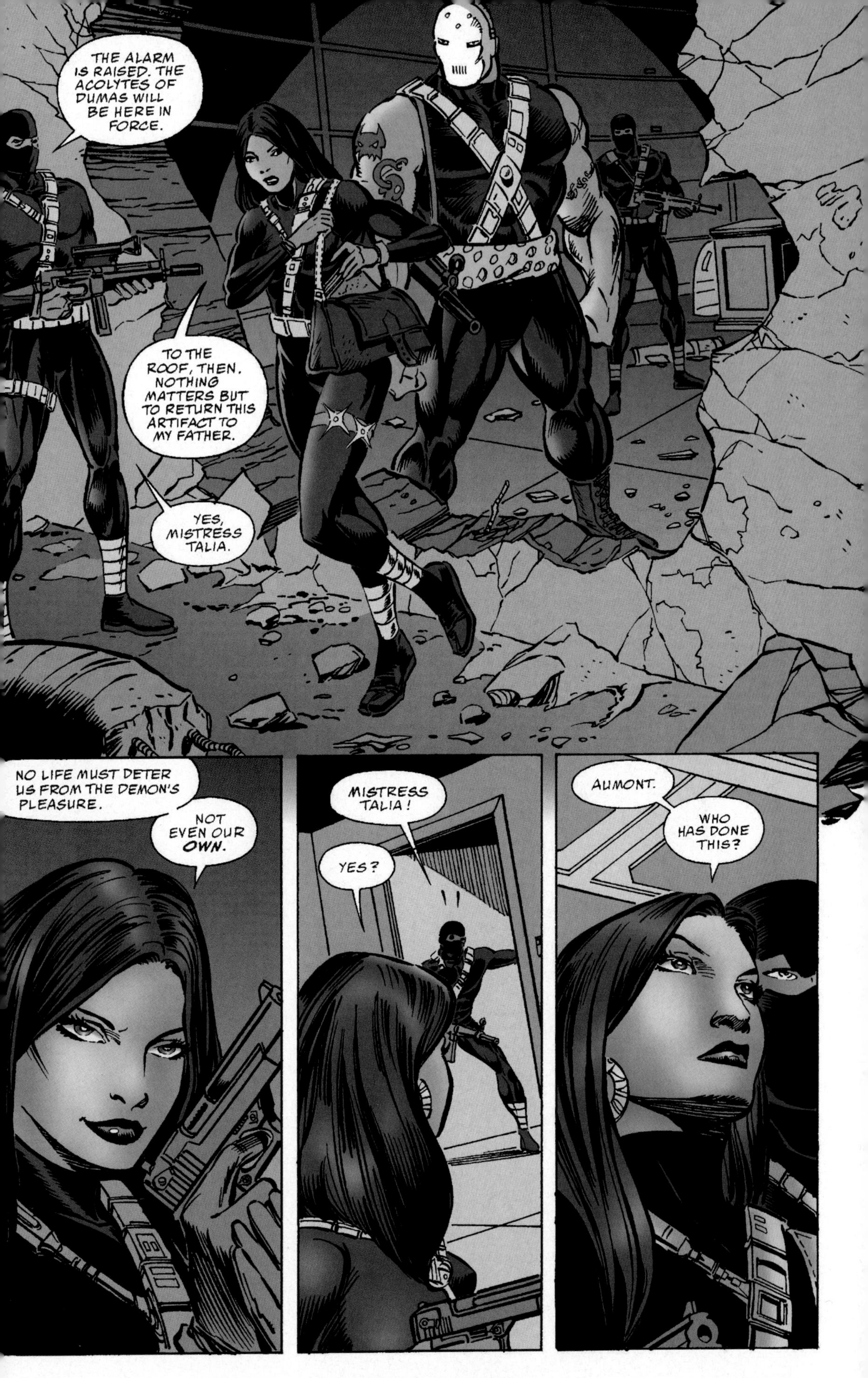
THE ALARM IS RAISED. THE ACOLYTES OF DUMAS WILL BE HERE IN FORCE.
TO THE ROOF, THEN. NOTHING MATTERS BUT TO RETURN THIS ARTIFACT TO MY FATHER.
YES, MISTRESS TALIA.
NO LIFE MUST DETER US FROM THE DEMON'S PLEASURE.
NOT EVEN OUR *OWN*.
MISTRESS TALIA!
YES?
AUMONT.
WHO HAS DONE THIS?

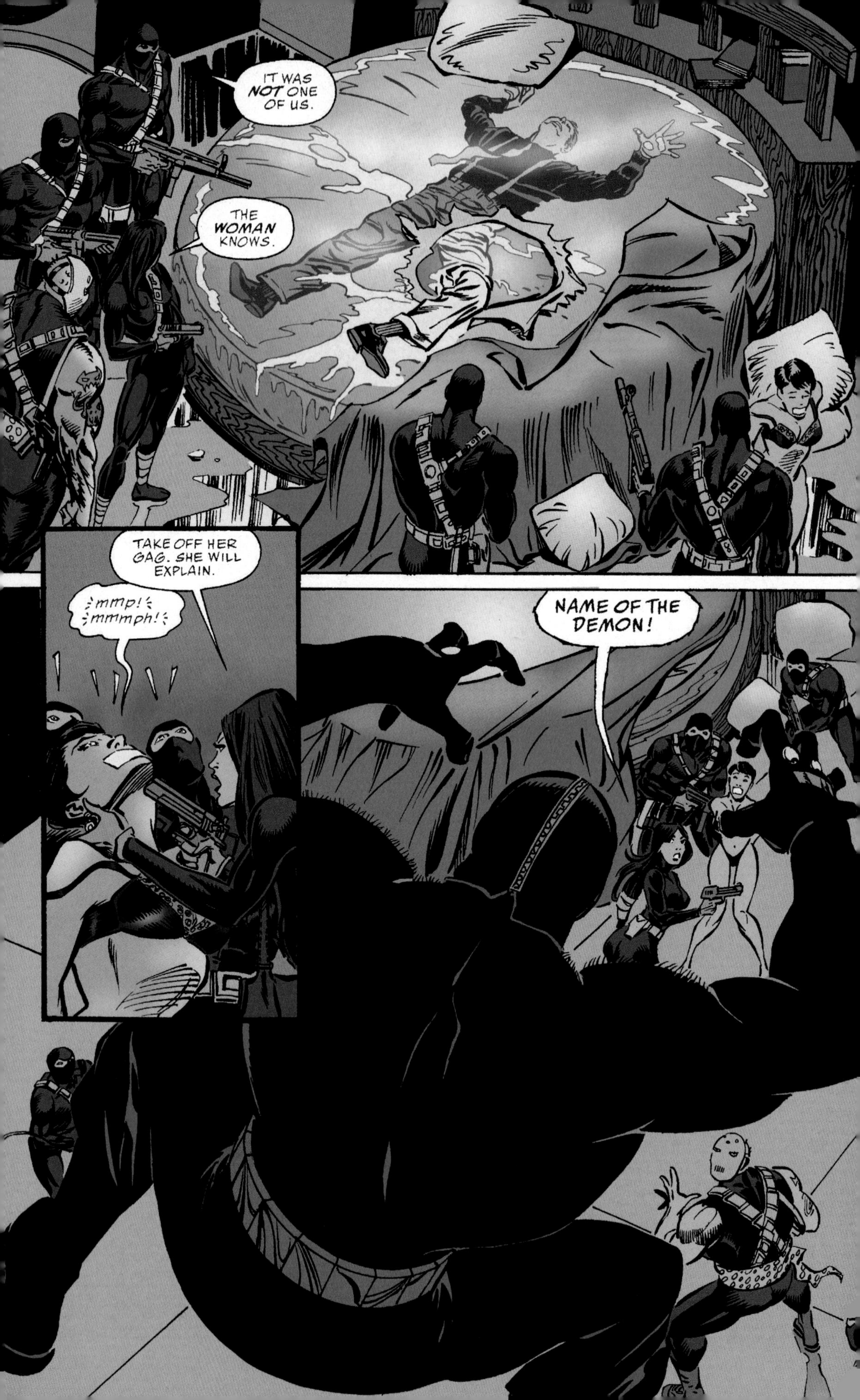
IT WAS NOT ONE OF US.
THE WOMAN KNOWS.
TAKE OFF HER GAG. SHE WILL EXPLAIN.
mmp! mmmph!
NAME OF THE DEMON!

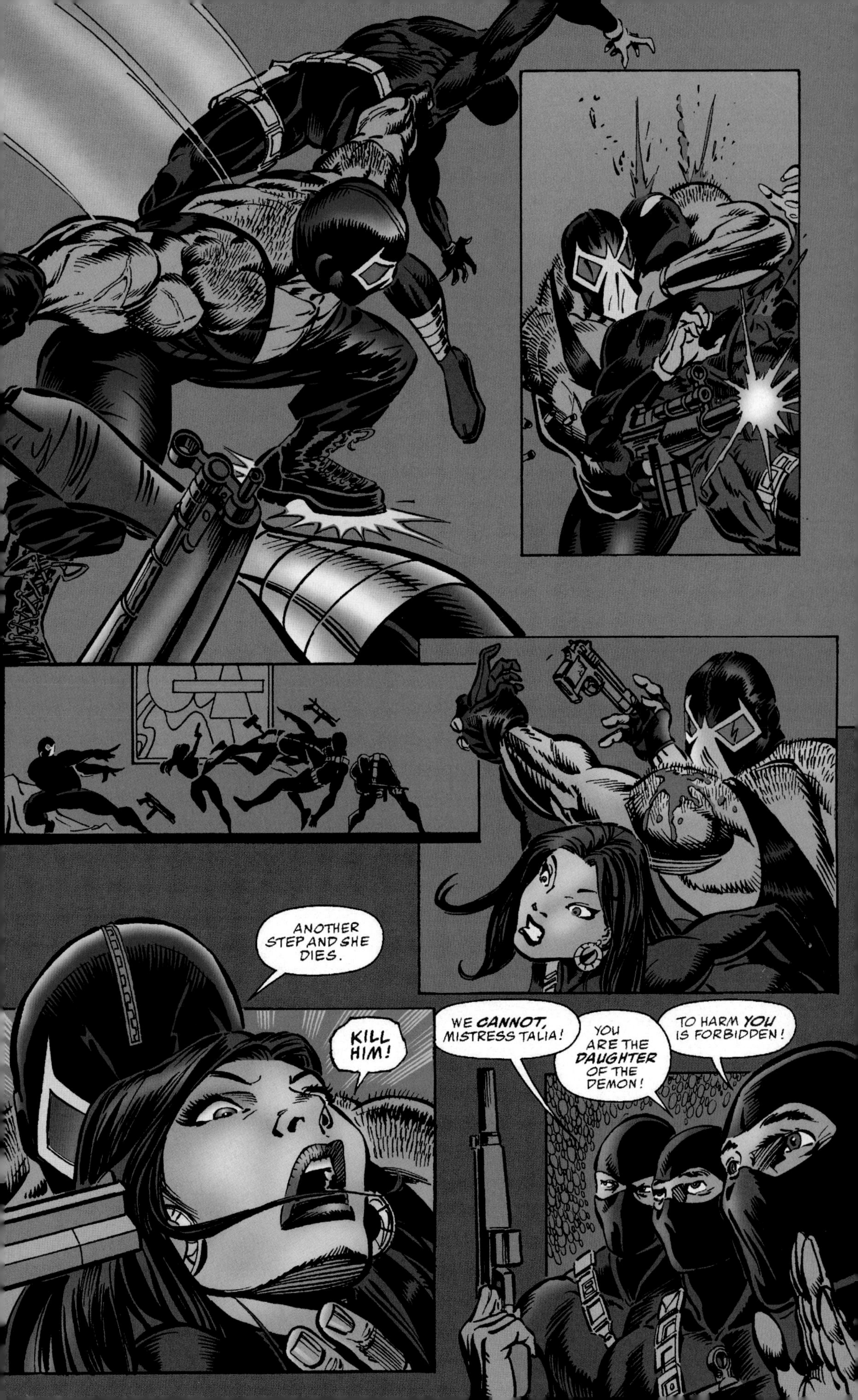
ANOTHER STEP AND SHE DIES.
KILL HIM!
WE CANNOT, MISTRESS TALIA!
YOU ARE THE DAUGHTER OF THE DEMON!
TO HARM YOU IS FORBIDDEN!

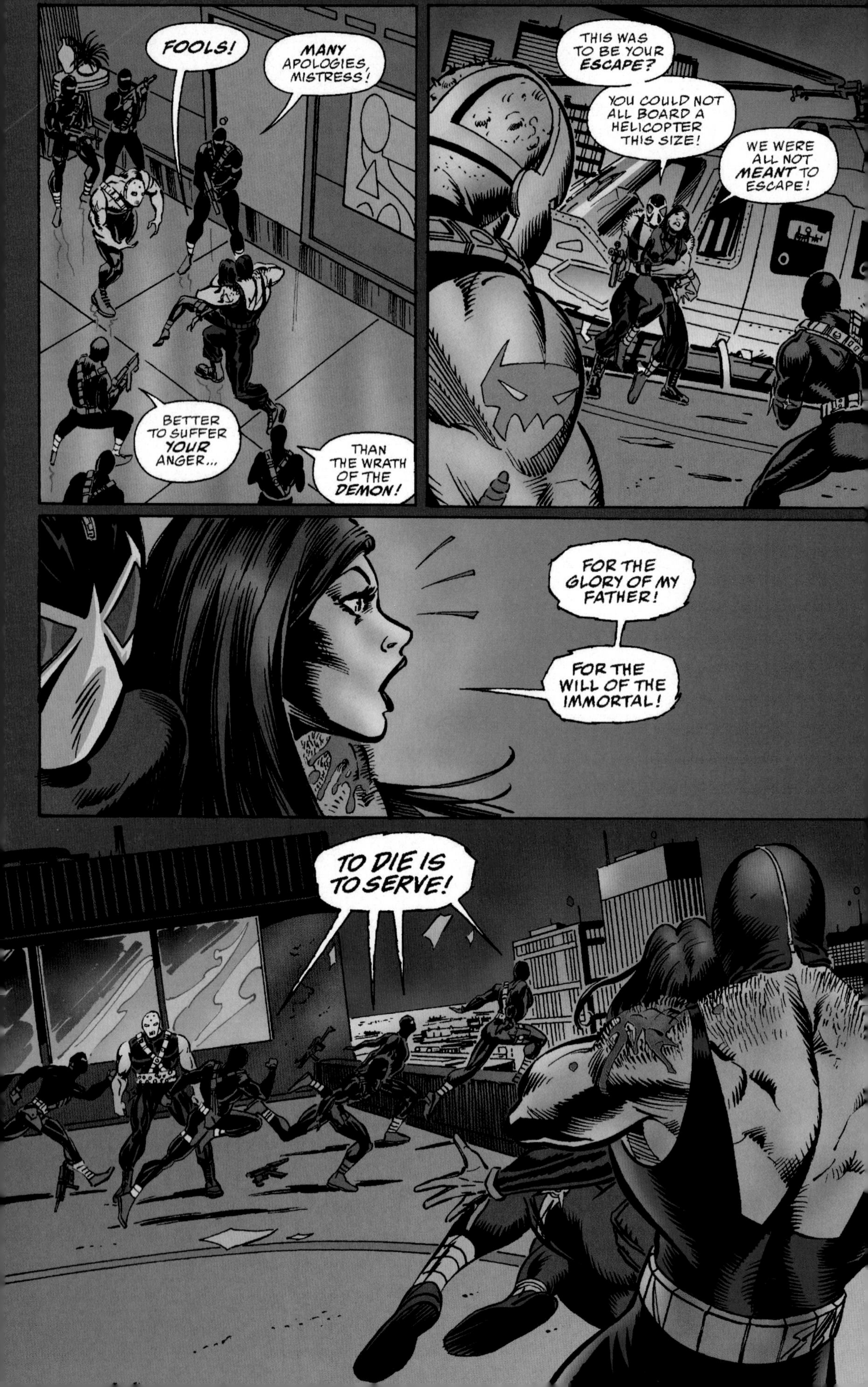
FOOLS!
MANY APOLOGIES, MISTRESS!
BETTER TO SUFFER YOUR ANGER...
THAN THE WRATH OF THE DEMON!
THIS WAS TO BE YOUR ESCAPE?
YOU COULD NOT ALL BOARD A HELICOPTER THIS SIZE!
WE WERE ALL NOT MEANT TO ESCAPE!
FOR THE GLORY OF MY FATHER!
FOR THE WILL OF THE IMMORTAL!
TO DIE IS TO SERVE!

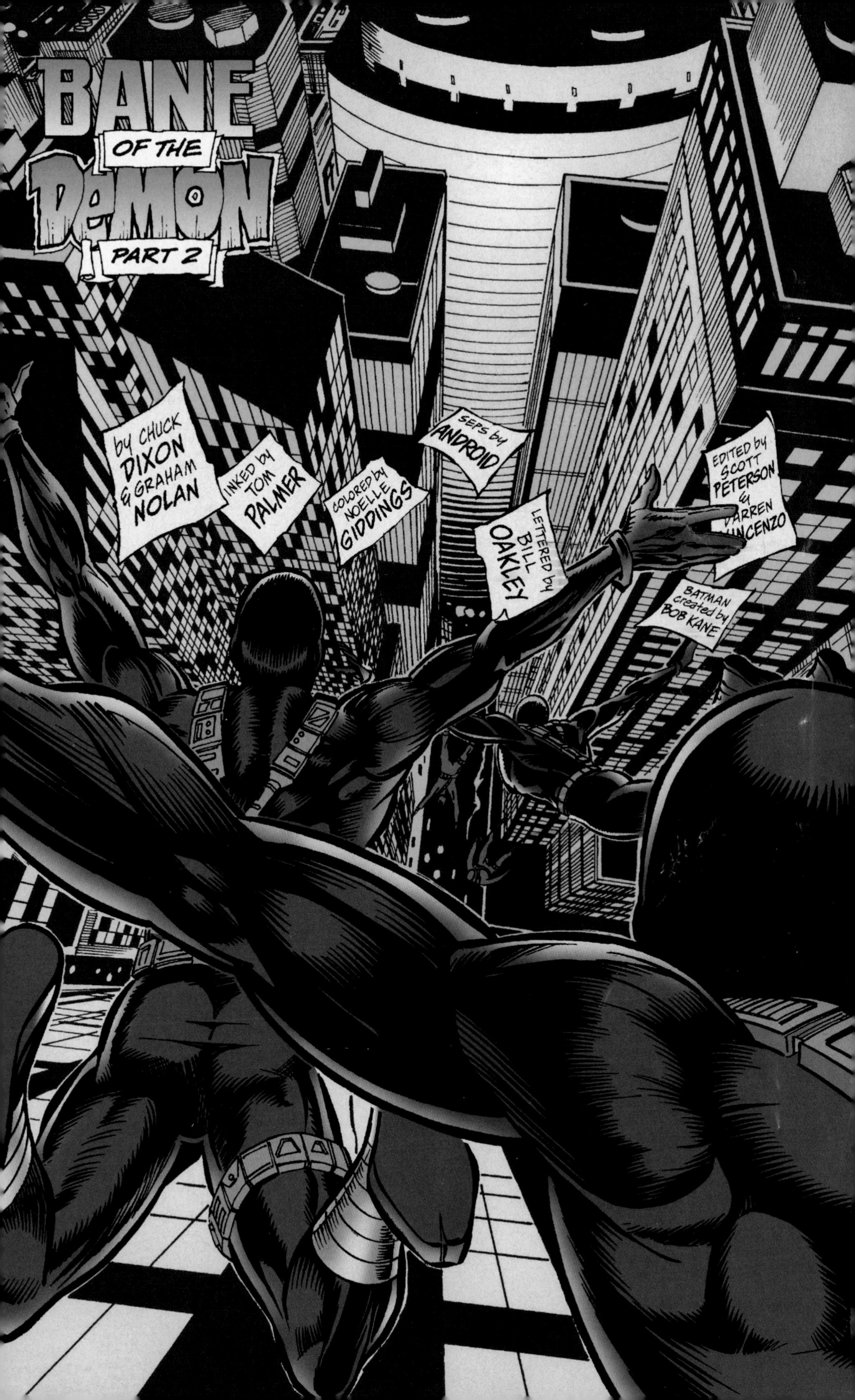
BANE
OF THE
DEMON
PART 2
by CHUCK DIXON & GRAHAM NOLAN
INKED by TOM PALMER
COLORED by NOELLE GIDDINGS
SEPS by ANDROID
LETTERED by BILL OAKLEY
EDITED by SCOTT PETERSON & ARREN NCENZO
BATMAN created by BOB KANE

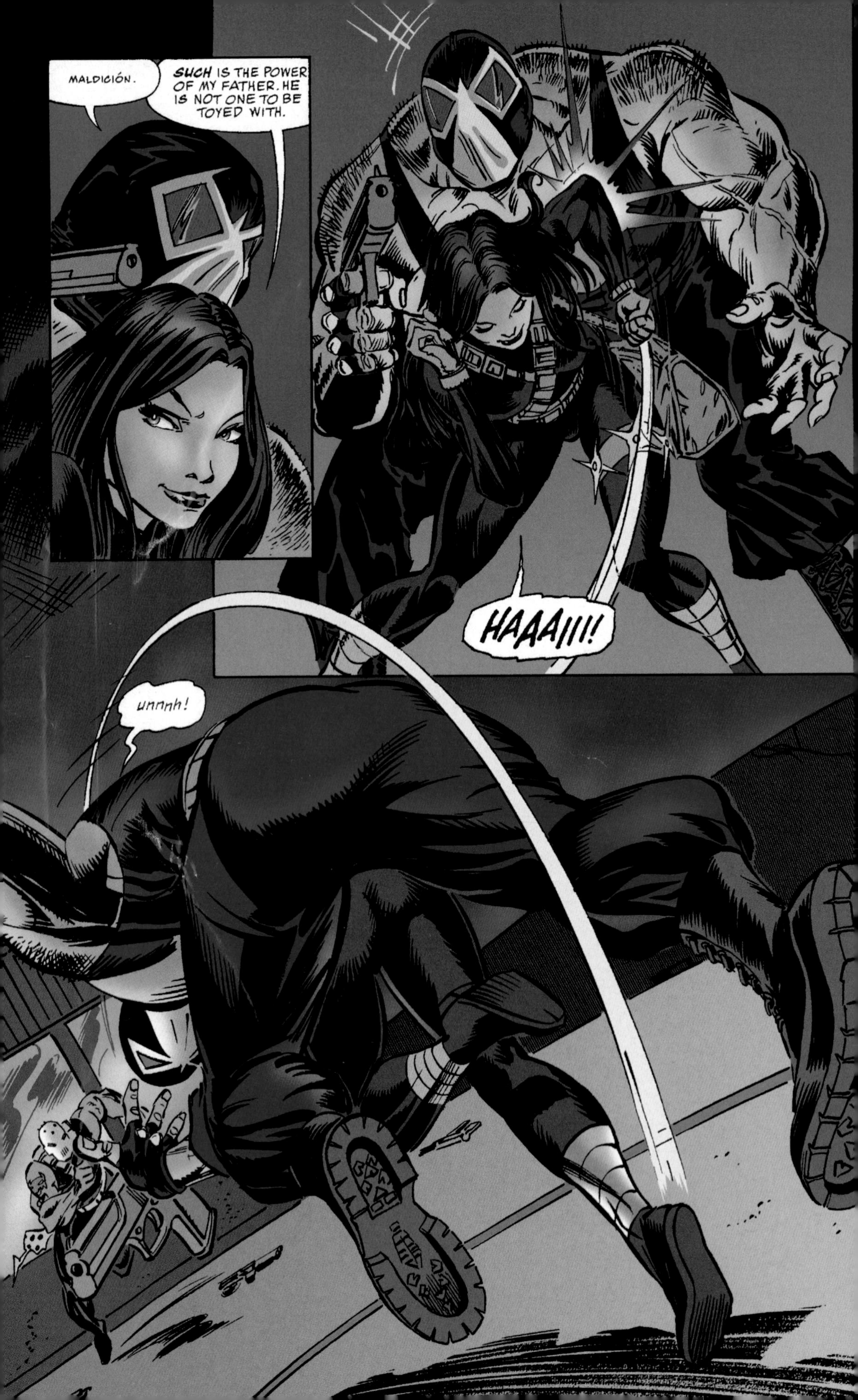
MALDICIÓN.
SUCH IS THE POWER OF MY FATHER. HE IS NOT ONE TO BE TOYED WITH.
HAAAIII!
unnnh!

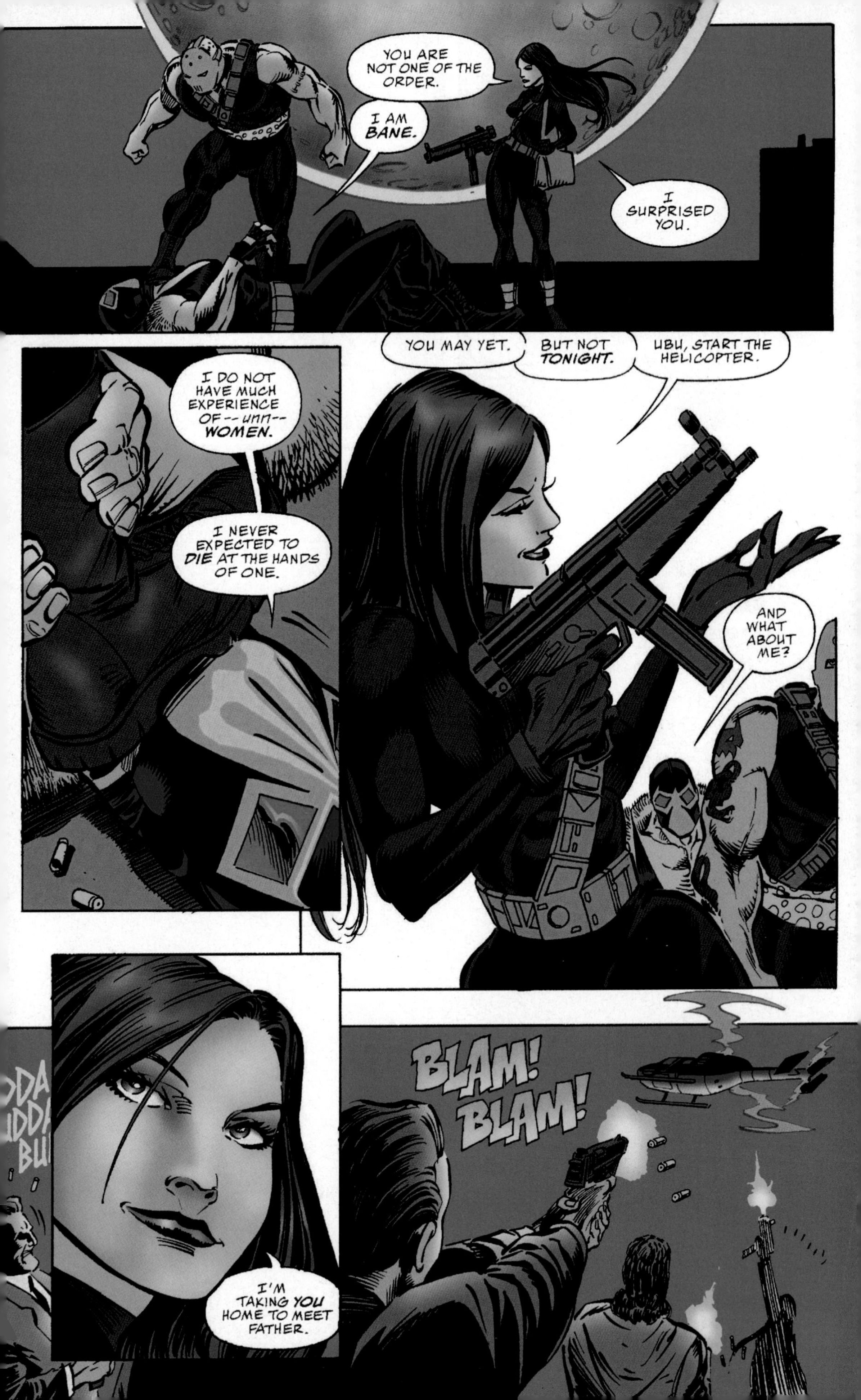
YOU ARE NOT ONE OF THE ORDER.
I AM BANE.
I SURPRISED YOU.
I DO NOT HAVE MUCH EXPERIENCE OF -- UNN-- WOMEN.
I NEVER EXPECTED TO DIE AT THE HANDS OF ONE.
YOU MAY YET.
BUT NOT TONIGHT.
UBU, START THE HELICOPTER.
AND WHAT ABOUT ME?
I'M TAKING YOU HOME TO MEET FATHER.
BLAM! BLAM!

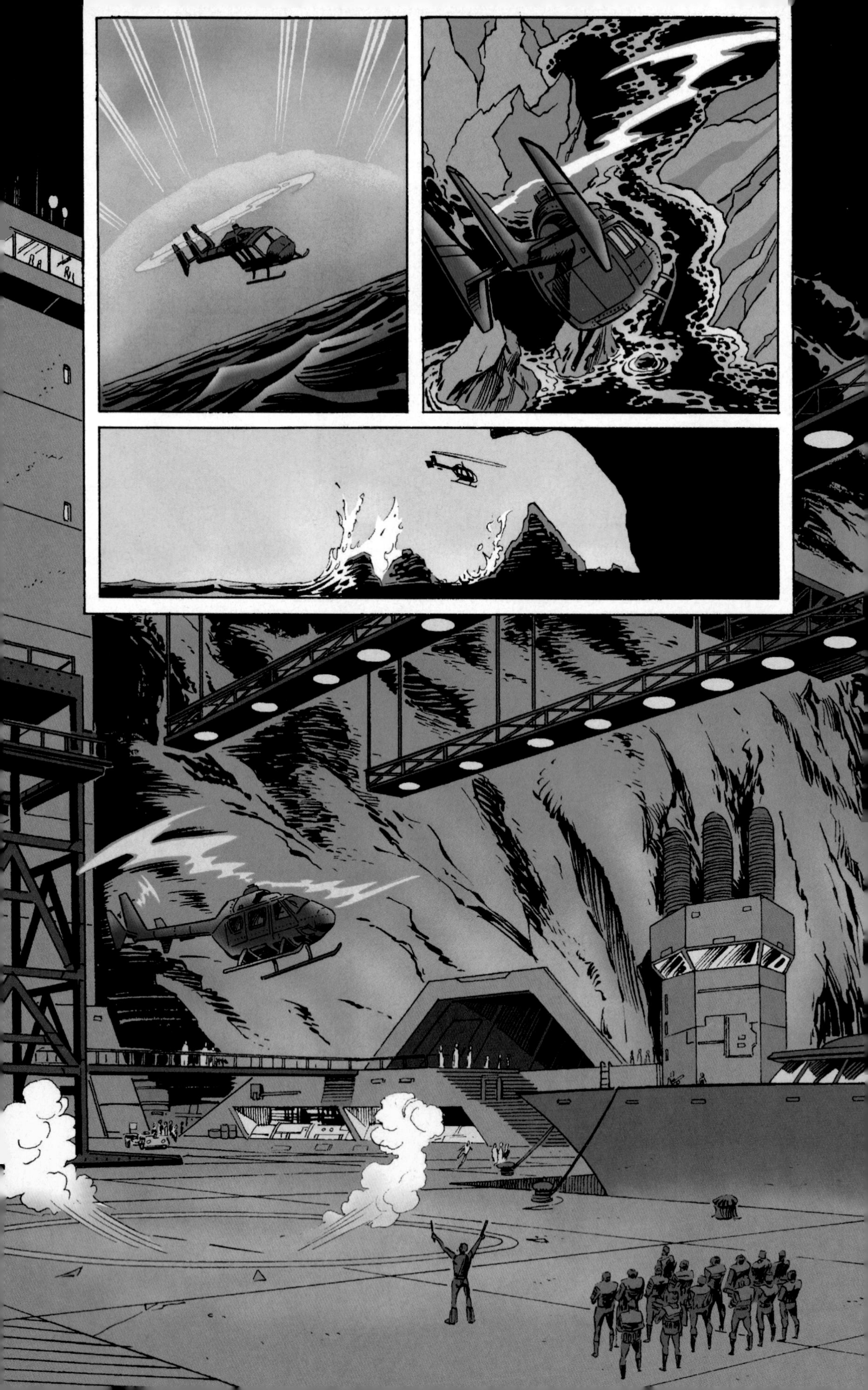

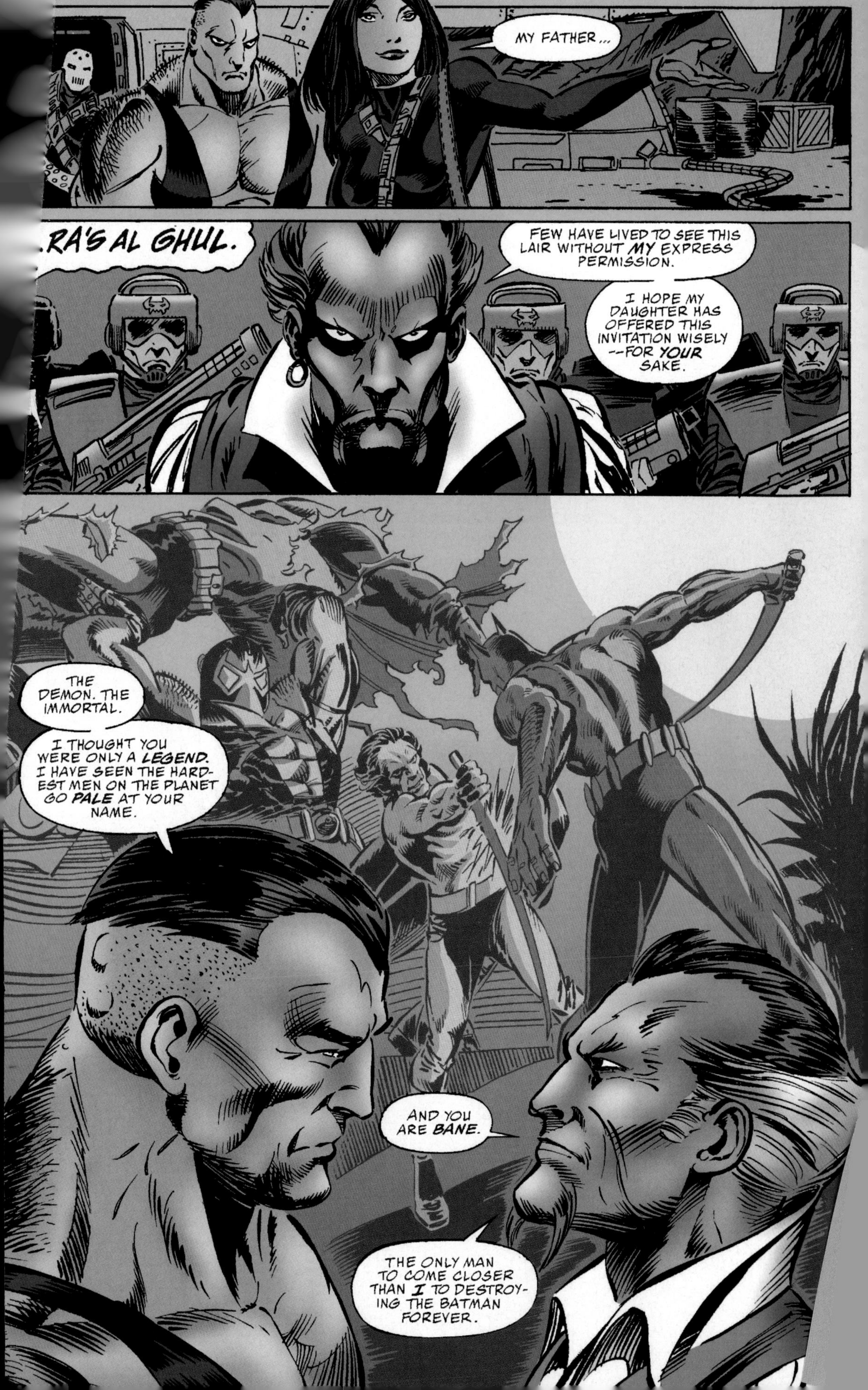
MY FATHER...
...RA'S AL GHUL.
FEW HAVE LIVED TO SEE THIS LAIR WITHOUT MY EXPRESS PERMISSION.
I HOPE MY DAUGHTER HAS OFFERED THIS INVITATION WISELY --FOR YOUR SAKE.
THE DEMON. THE IMMORTAL.
I THOUGHT YOU WERE ONLY A LEGEND. I HAVE SEEN THE HARD-EST MEN ON THE PLANET GO PALE AT YOUR NAME.
AND YOU ARE BANE.
THE ONLY MAN TO COME CLOSER THAN I TO DESTROY-ING THE BATMAN FOREVER.

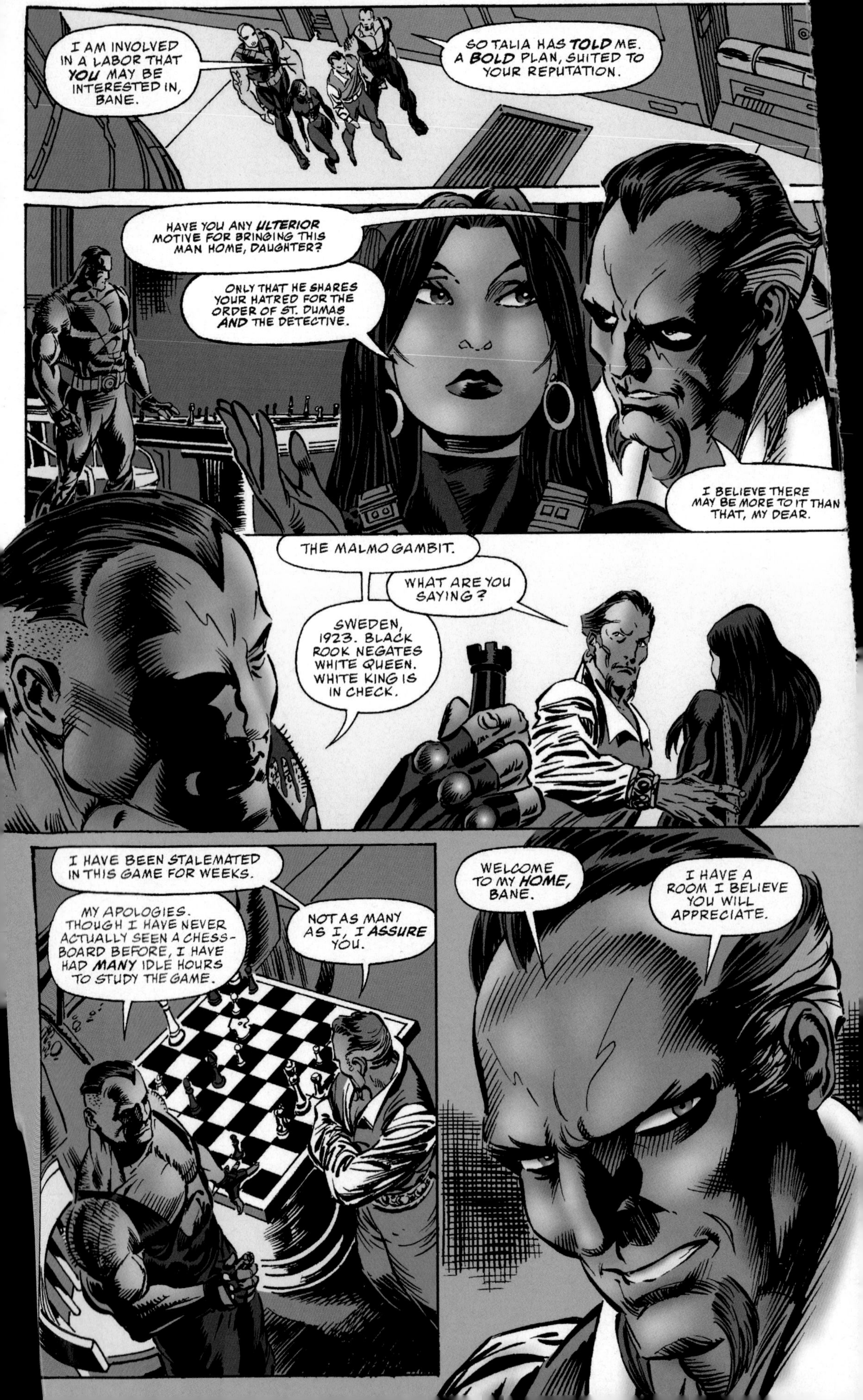
I AM INVOLVED IN A LABOR THAT YOU MAY BE INTERESTED IN, BANE.
SO TALIA HAS TOLD ME. A BOLD PLAN, SUITED TO YOUR REPUTATION.
HAVE YOU ANY ULTERIOR MOTIVE FOR BRINGING THIS MAN HOME, DAUGHTER?
ONLY THAT HE SHARES YOUR HATRED FOR THE ORDER OF ST. DUMAS AND THE DETECTIVE.
I BELIEVE THERE MAY BE MORE TO IT THAN THAT, MY DEAR.
THE MALMO GAMBIT.
WHAT ARE YOU SAYING?
SWEDEN, 1923. BLACK ROOK NEGATES WHITE QUEEN. WHITE KING IS IN CHECK.
I HAVE BEEN STALEMATED IN THIS GAME FOR WEEKS.
MY APOLOGIES. THOUGH I HAVE NEVER ACTUALLY SEEN A CHESS-BOARD BEFORE, I HAVE HAD MANY IDLE HOURS TO STUDY THE GAME.
NOT AS MANY AS I, I ASSURE YOU.
WELCOME TO MY HOME, BANE.
I HAVE A ROOM I BELIEVE YOU WILL APPRECIATE.

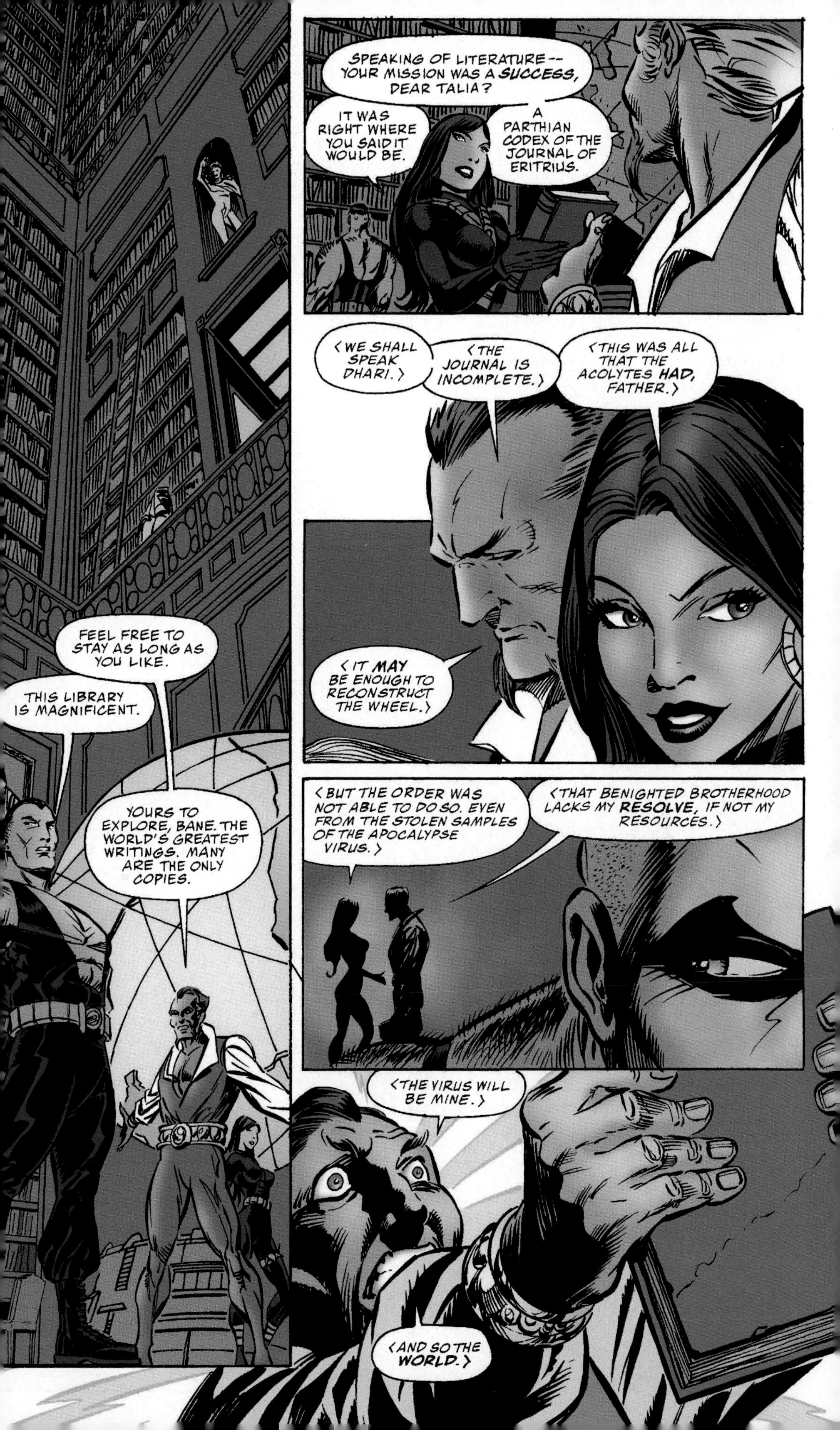
SPEAKING OF LITERATURE-- YOUR MISSION WAS A SUCCESS, DEAR TALIA?
IT WAS RIGHT WHERE YOU SAID IT WOULD BE.
A PARTHIAN CODEX OF THE JOURNAL OF ERITRIUS.
FEEL FREE TO STAY AS LONG AS YOU LIKE.
THIS LIBRARY IS MAGNIFICENT.
YOURS TO EXPLORE, BANE. THE WORLD'S GREATEST WRITINGS. MANY ARE THE ONLY COPIES.
<WE SHALL SPEAK DHARI.>
<THE JOURNAL IS INCOMPLETE.>
<THIS WAS ALL THAT THE ACOLYTES HAD, FATHER.>
<IT MAY BE ENOUGH TO RECONSTRUCT THE WHEEL.>
<BUT THE ORDER WAS NOT ABLE TO DO SO. EVEN FROM THE STOLEN SAMPLES OF THE APOCALYPSE VIRUS.>
<THAT BENIGHTED BROTHERHOOD LACKS MY RESOLVE, IF NOT MY RESOURCES.>
<THE VIRUS WILL BE MINE.>
<AND SO THE WORLD.>

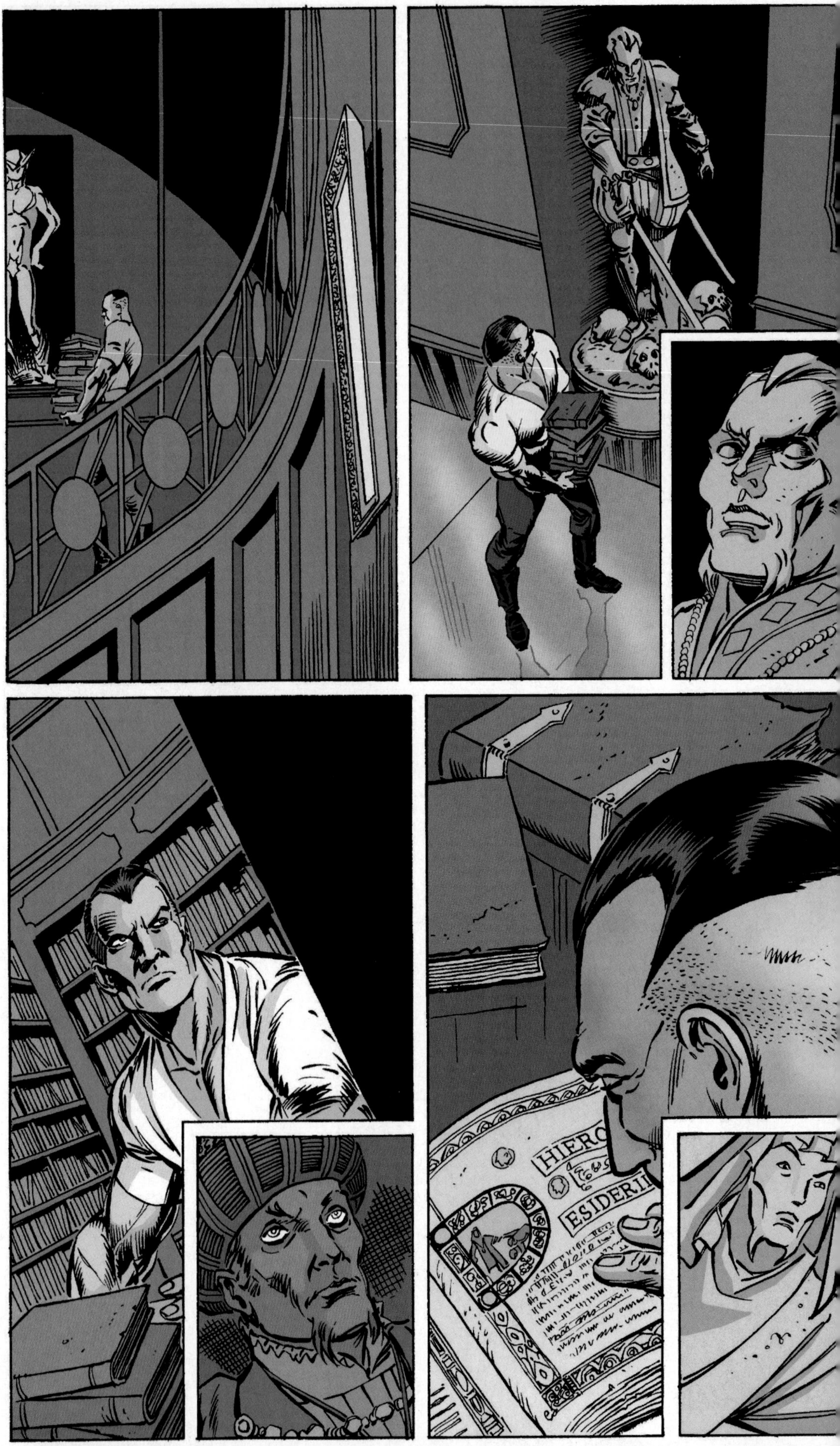
HIERO
ESIDERII

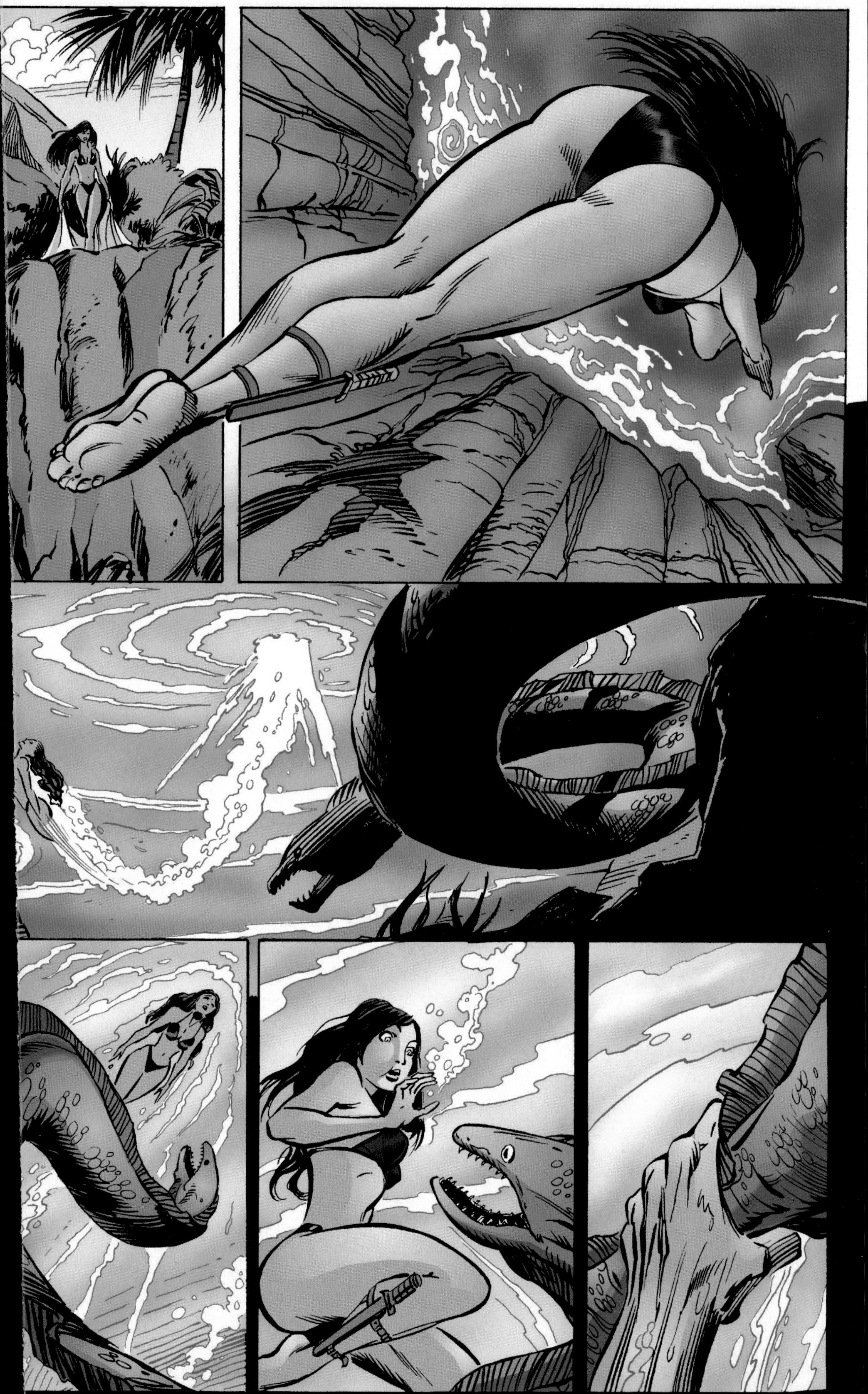

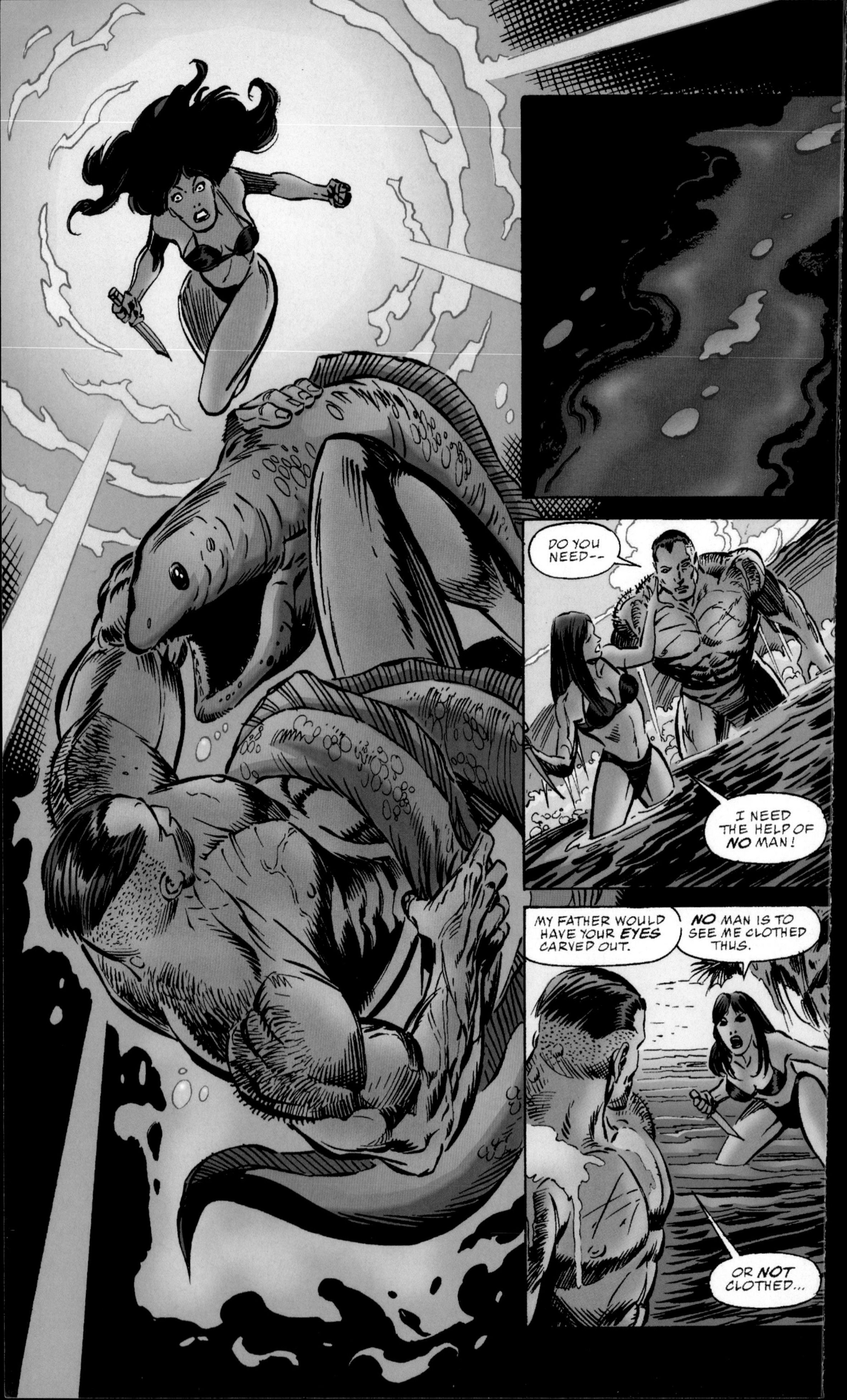
DO YOU NEED--
I NEED THE HELP OF NO MAN!
MY FATHER WOULD HAVE YOUR EYES CARVED OUT.
NO MAN IS TO SEE ME CLOTHED THUS.
OR NOT CLOTHED...

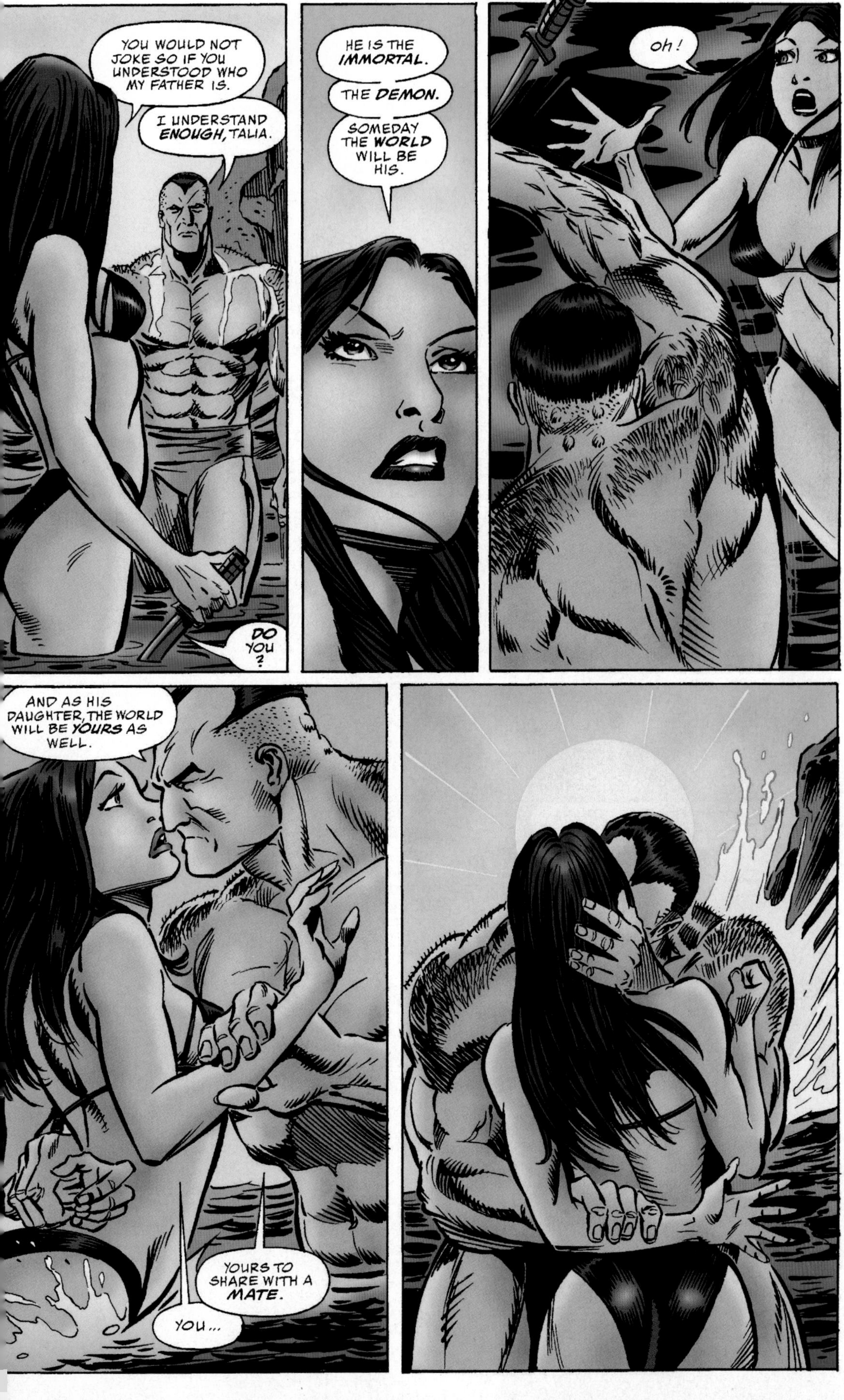
YOU WOULD NOT JOKE SO IF YOU UNDERSTOOD WHO MY FATHER IS.
I UNDERSTAND ENOUGH, TALIA.
DO YOU?
HE IS THE IMMORTAL.
THE DEMON.
SOMEDAY THE WORLD WILL BE HIS.
oh!
AND AS HIS DAUGHTER, THE WORLD WILL BE YOURS AS WELL.
YOURS TO SHARE WITH A MATE.
YOU...

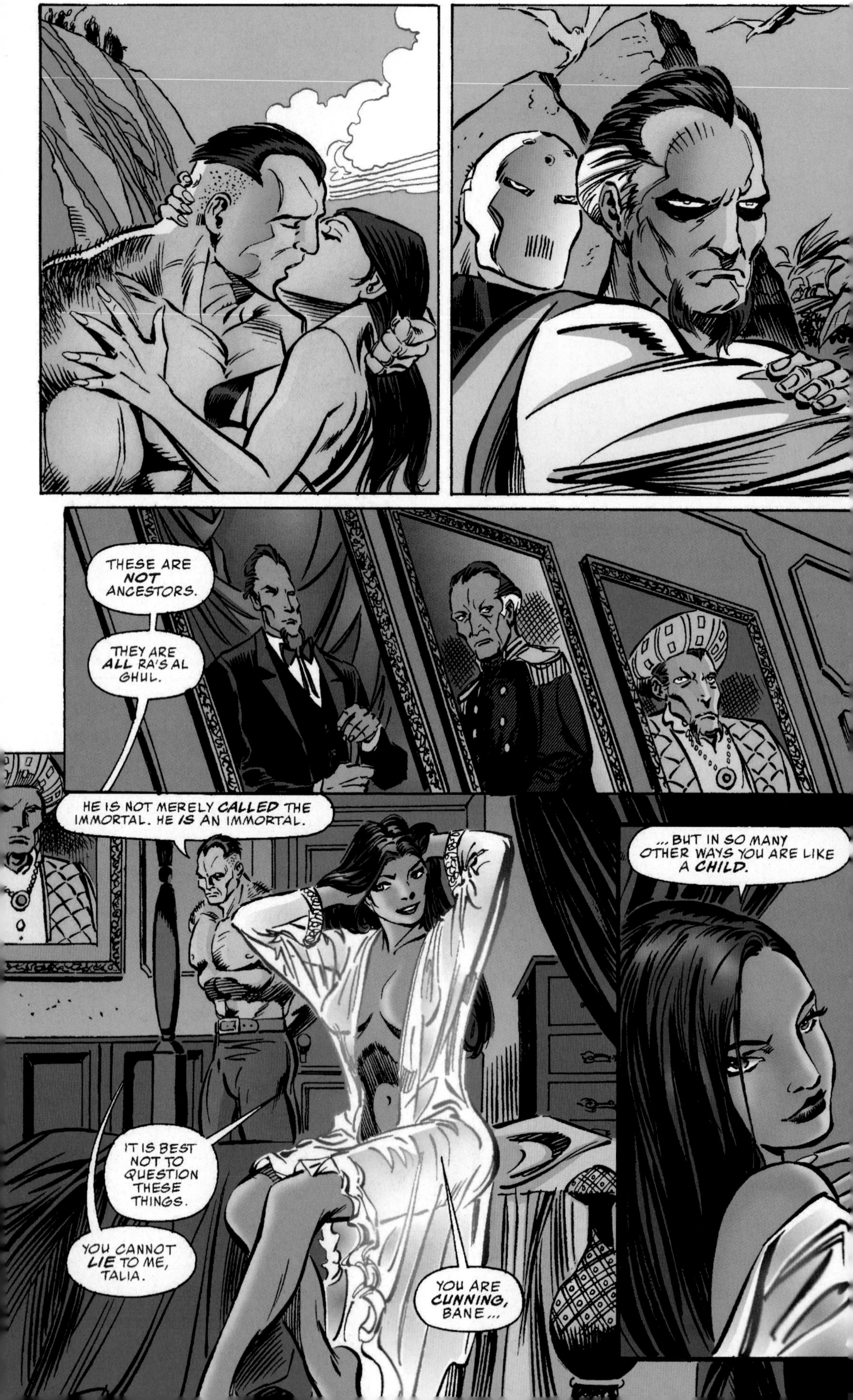

THESE ARE NOT ANCESTORS.
THEY ARE ALL RA'S AL GHUL.
HE IS NOT MERELY CALLED THE IMMORTAL. HE IS AN IMMORTAL.
IT IS BEST NOT TO QUESTION THESE THINGS.
YOU CANNOT LIE TO ME, TALIA.
YOU ARE CUNNING, BANE...
...BUT IN SO MANY OTHER WAYS YOU ARE LIKE A CHILD.

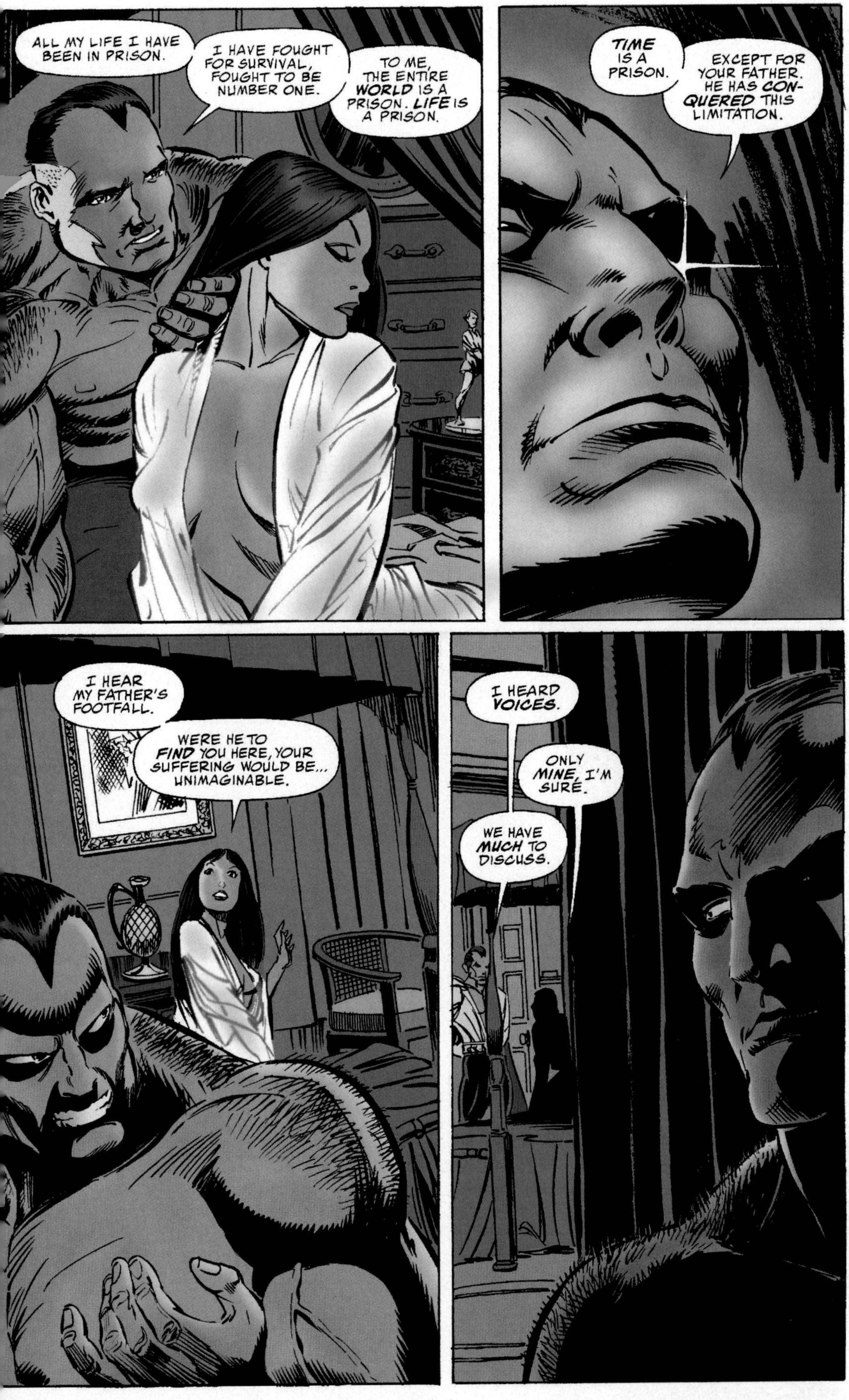
ALL MY LIFE I HAVE BEEN IN PRISON.
I HAVE FOUGHT FOR SURVIVAL, FOUGHT TO BE NUMBER ONE.
TO ME, THE ENTIRE WORLD IS A PRISON. LIFE IS A PRISON.
TIME IS A PRISON.
EXCEPT FOR YOUR FATHER. HE HAS CONQUERED THIS LIMITATION.
I HEAR MY FATHER'S FOOTFALL.
WERE HE TO FIND YOU HERE, YOUR SUFFERING WOULD BE... UNIMAGINABLE.
I HEARD VOICES.
ONLY MINE, I'M SURE.
WE HAVE MUCH TO DISCUSS.

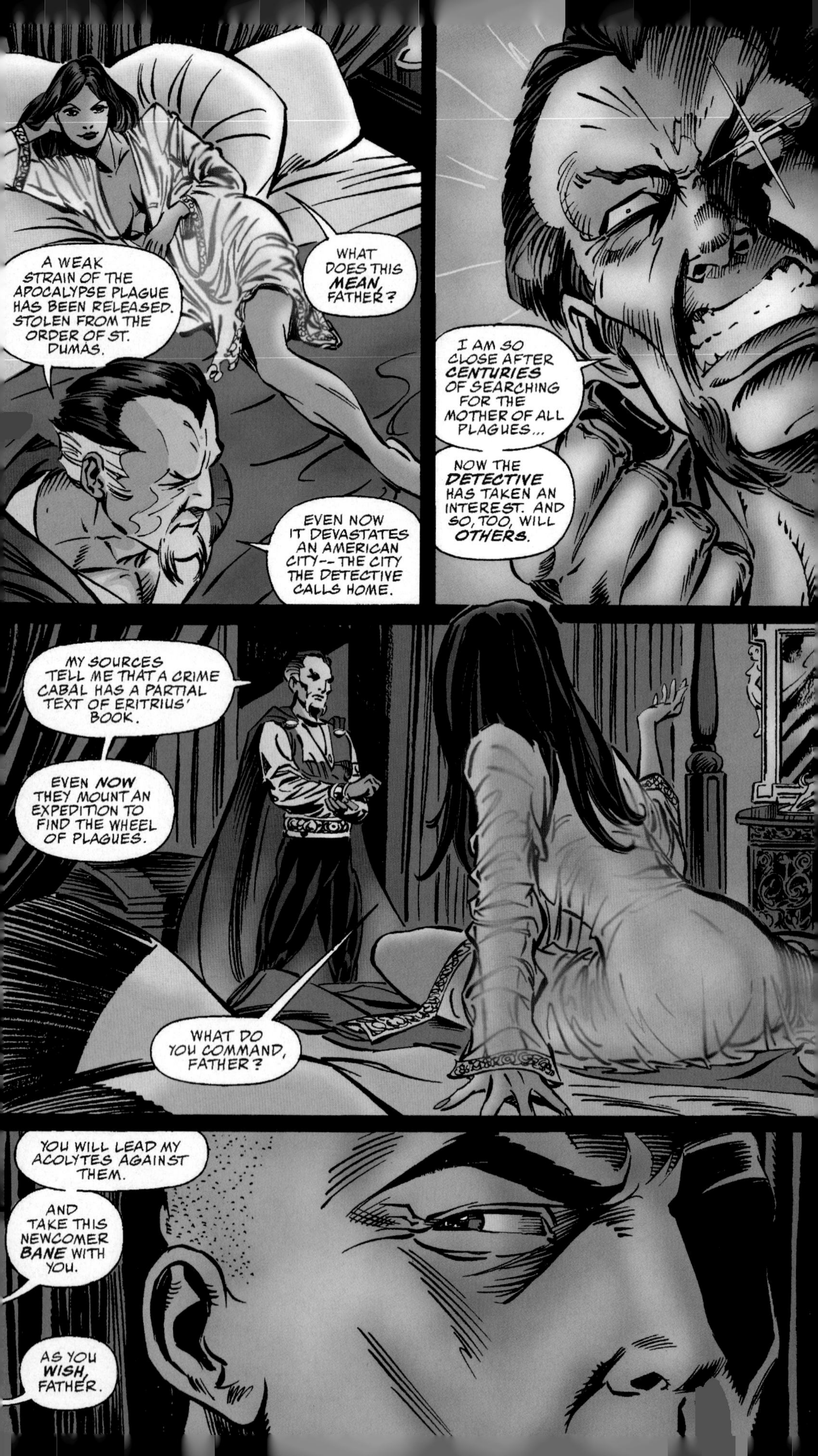
A WEAK STRAIN OF THE APOCALYPSE PLAGUE HAS BEEN RELEASED. STOLEN FROM THE ORDER OF ST. DUMAS.
WHAT DOES THIS MEAN, FATHER?
EVEN NOW IT DEVASTATES AN AMERICAN CITY-- THE CITY THE DETECTIVE CALLS HOME.
I AM SO CLOSE AFTER CENTURIES OF SEARCHING FOR THE MOTHER OF ALL PLAGUES...
NOW THE DETECTIVE HAS TAKEN AN INTEREST. AND SO, TOO, WILL OTHERS.
MY SOURCES TELL ME THAT A CRIME CABAL HAS A PARTIAL TEXT OF ERITRIUS' BOOK.
EVEN NOW THEY MOUNT AN EXPEDITION TO FIND THE WHEEL OF PLAGUES.
WHAT DO YOU COMMAND, FATHER?
YOU WILL LEAD MY ACOLYTES AGAINST THEM.
AND TAKE THIS NEWCOMER BANE WITH YOU.
AS YOU WISH, FATHER.

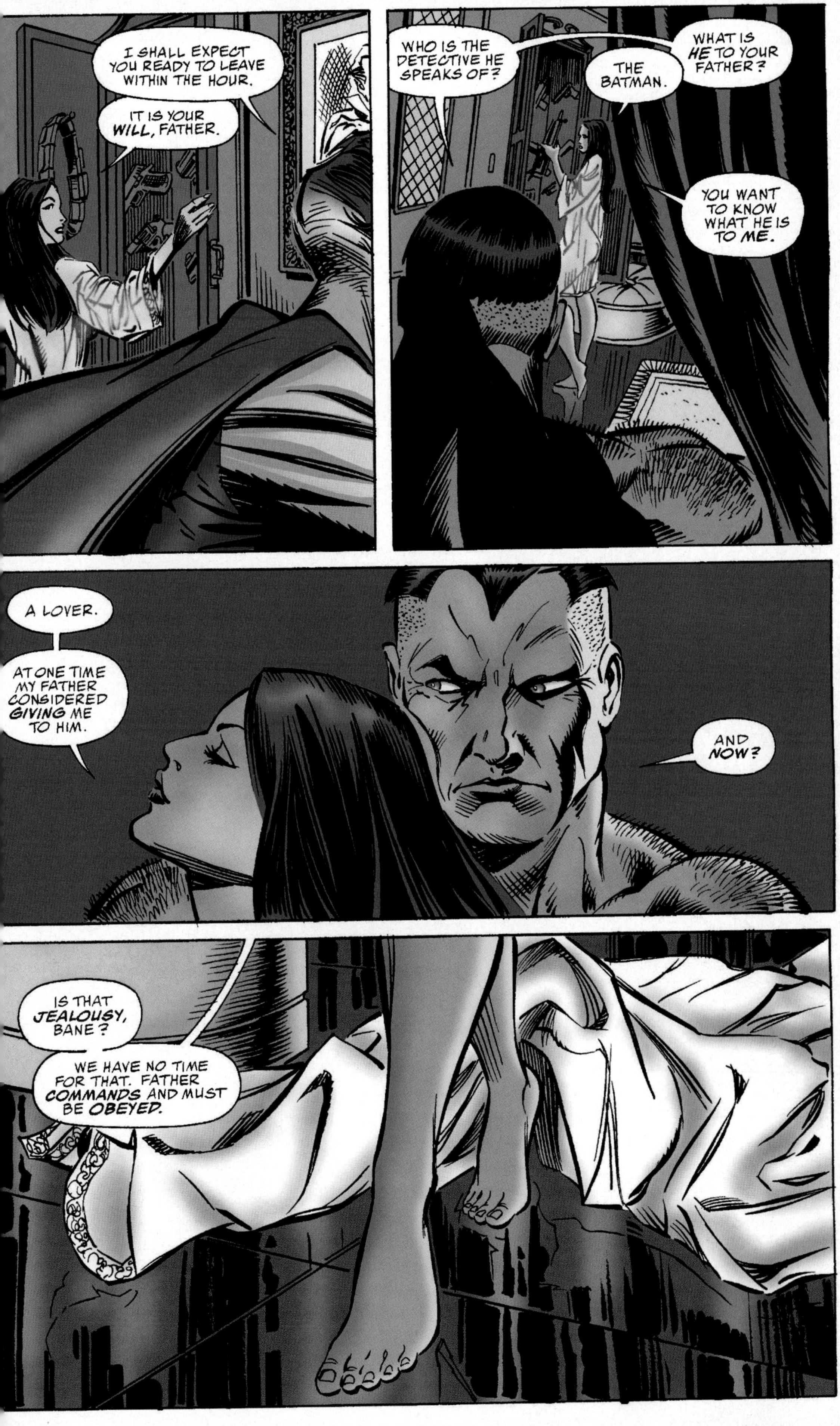
I SHALL EXPECT YOU READY TO LEAVE WITHIN THE HOUR.
IT IS YOUR WILL, FATHER.
WHO IS THE DETECTIVE HE SPEAKS OF?
THE BATMAN.
WHAT IS HE TO YOUR FATHER?
YOU WANT TO KNOW WHAT HE IS TO ME.
A LOVER.
AT ONE TIME MY FATHER CONSIDERED GIVING ME TO HIM.
AND NOW?
IS THAT JEALOUSY, BANE?
WE HAVE NO TIME FOR THAT. FATHER COMMANDS AND MUST BE OBEYED.

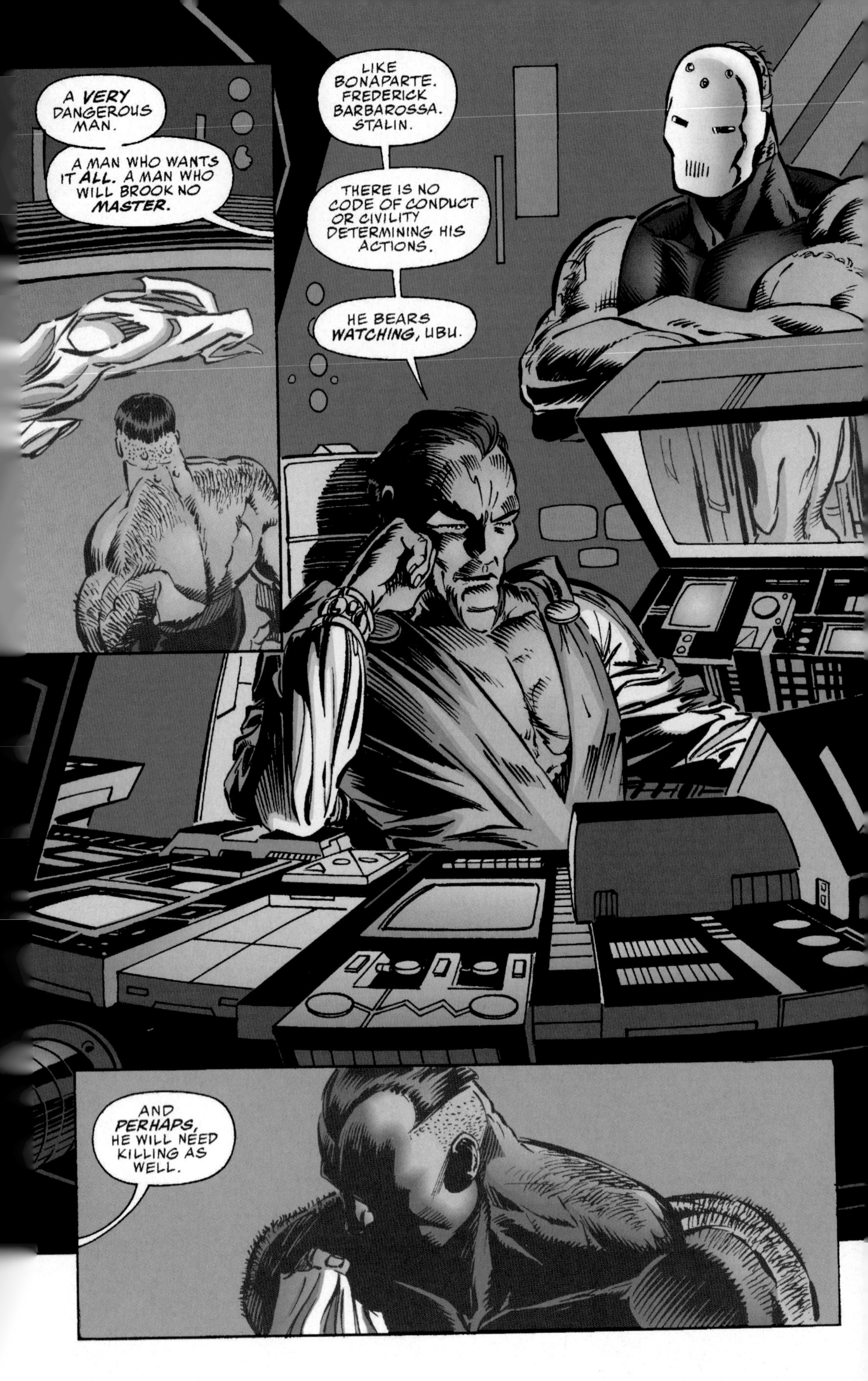
A VERY DANGEROUS MAN.
A MAN WHO WANTS IT ALL. A MAN WHO WILL BROOK NO MASTER.
LIKE BONAPARTE. FREDERICK BARBAROSSA. STALIN.
THERE IS NO CODE OF CONDUCT OR CIVILITY DETERMINING HIS ACTIONS.
HE BEARS WATCHING, UBU.
AND PERHAPS, HE WILL NEED KILLING AS WELL.

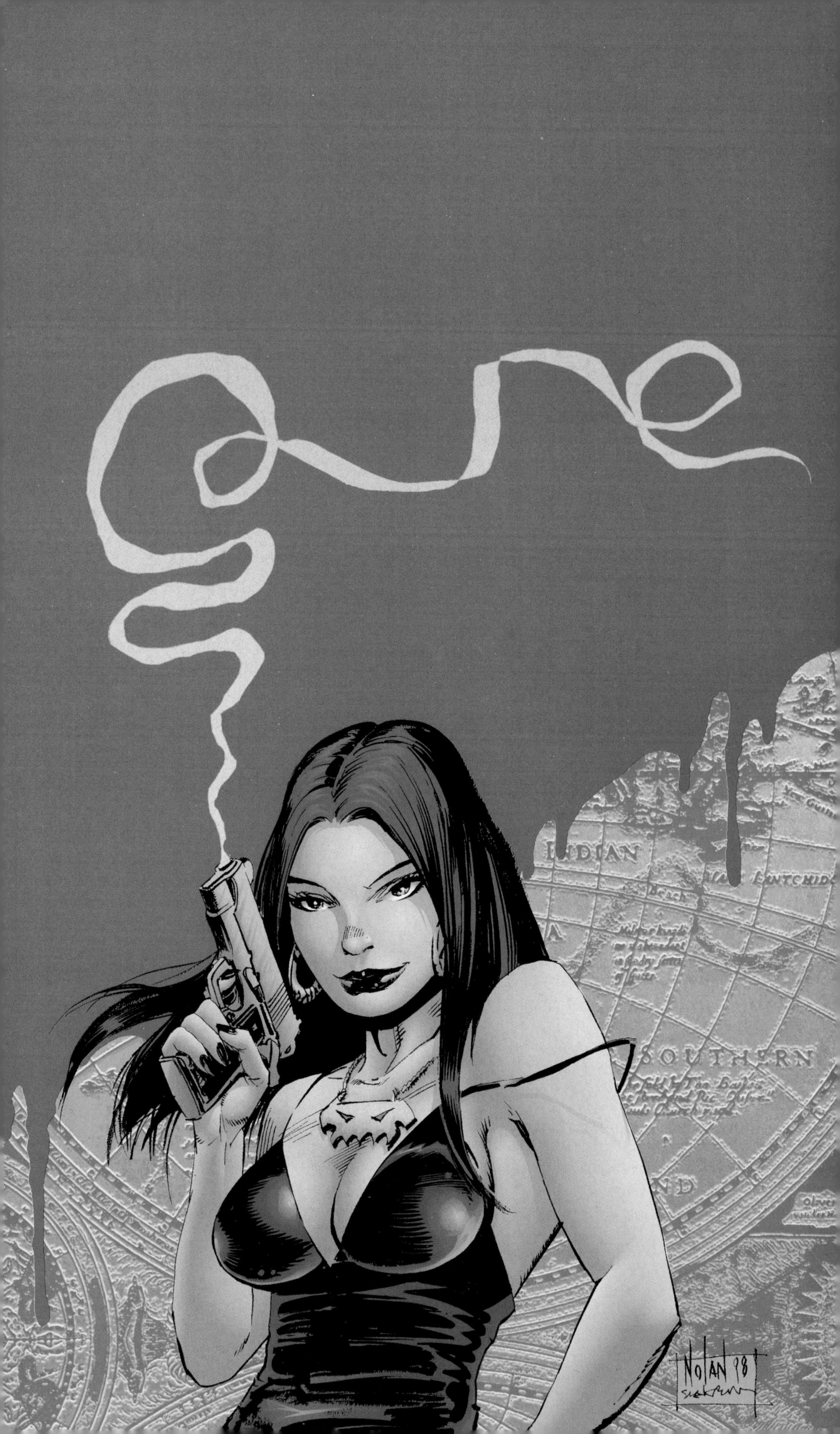
one
INDIAN
SOUTHERN
NOLAN 98

Cover Art by Graham Nolan
and Bill Sienkiewicz

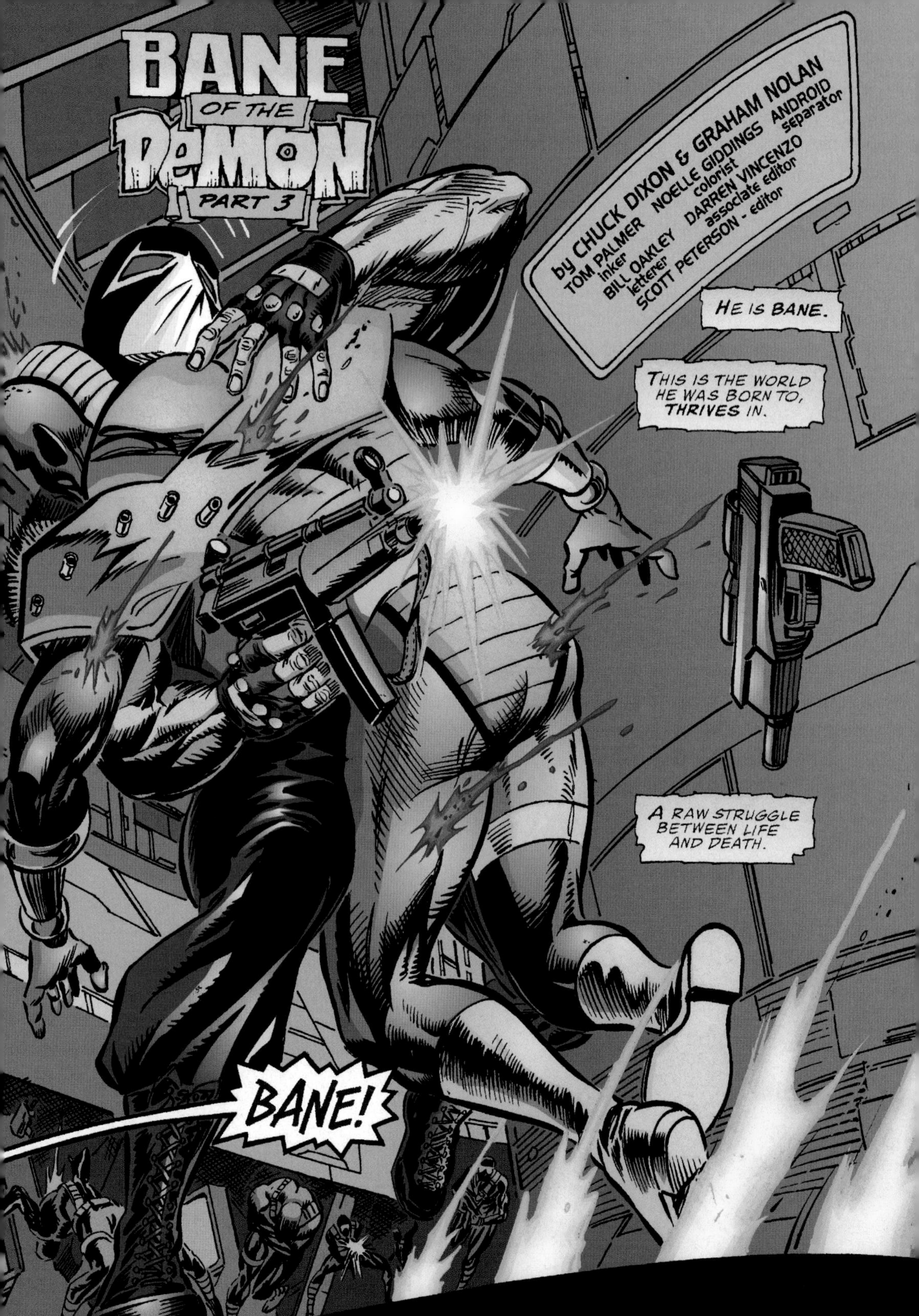
BANE OF THE DEMON
PART 3
by CHUCK DIXON & GRAHAM NOLAN
TOM PALMER inker NOELLE GIDDINGS colorist ANDROID separator
BILL OAKLEY letterer DARREN VINCENZO associate editor
SCOTT PETERSON - editor
HE IS BANE.
THIS IS THE WORLD HE WAS BORN TO, THRIVES IN.
A RAW STRUGGLE BETWEEN LIFE AND DEATH.
BANE!

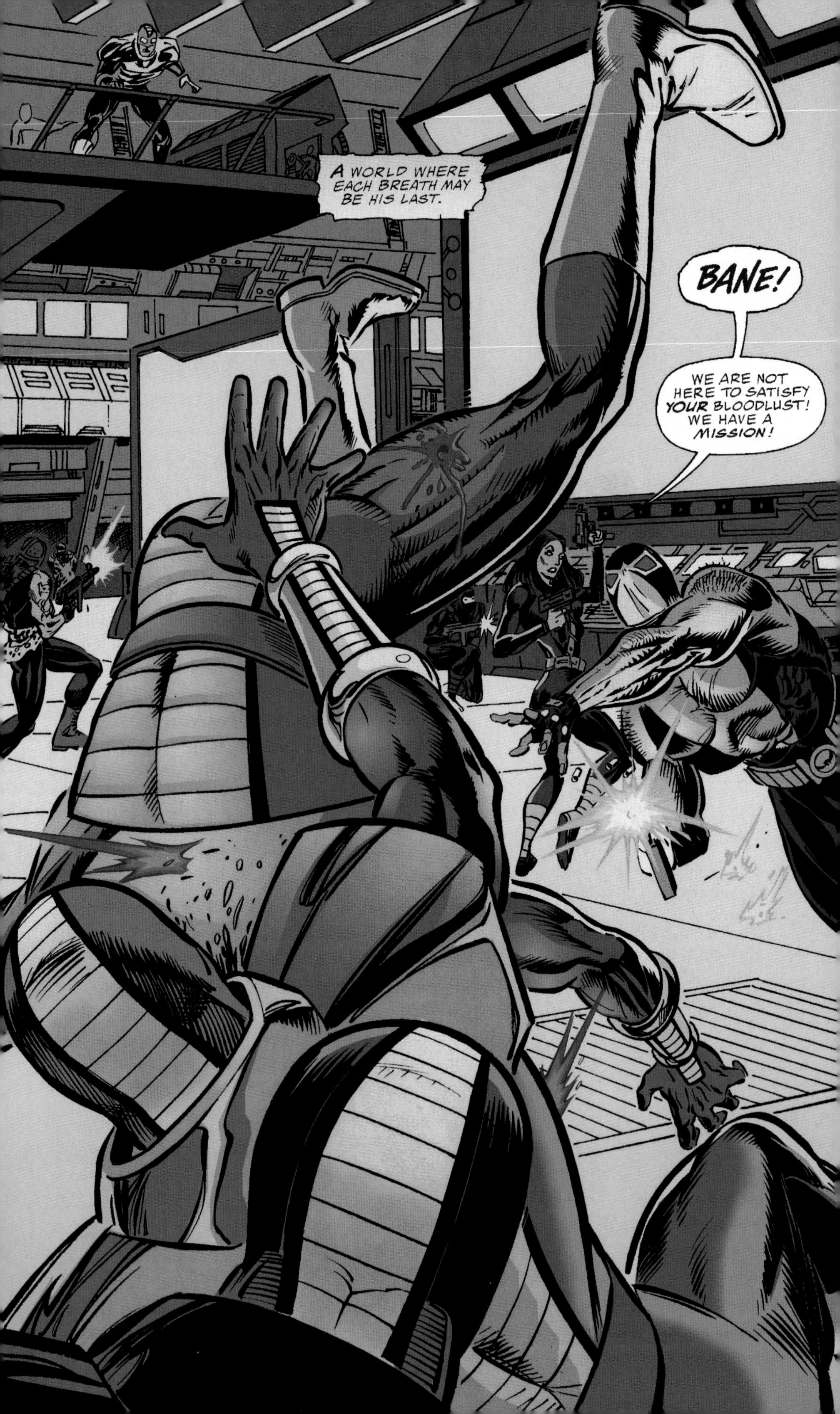
A WORLD WHERE EACH BREATH MAY BE HIS LAST.
BANE!
WE ARE NOT HERE TO SATISFY YOUR BLOODLUST! WE HAVE A MISSION!

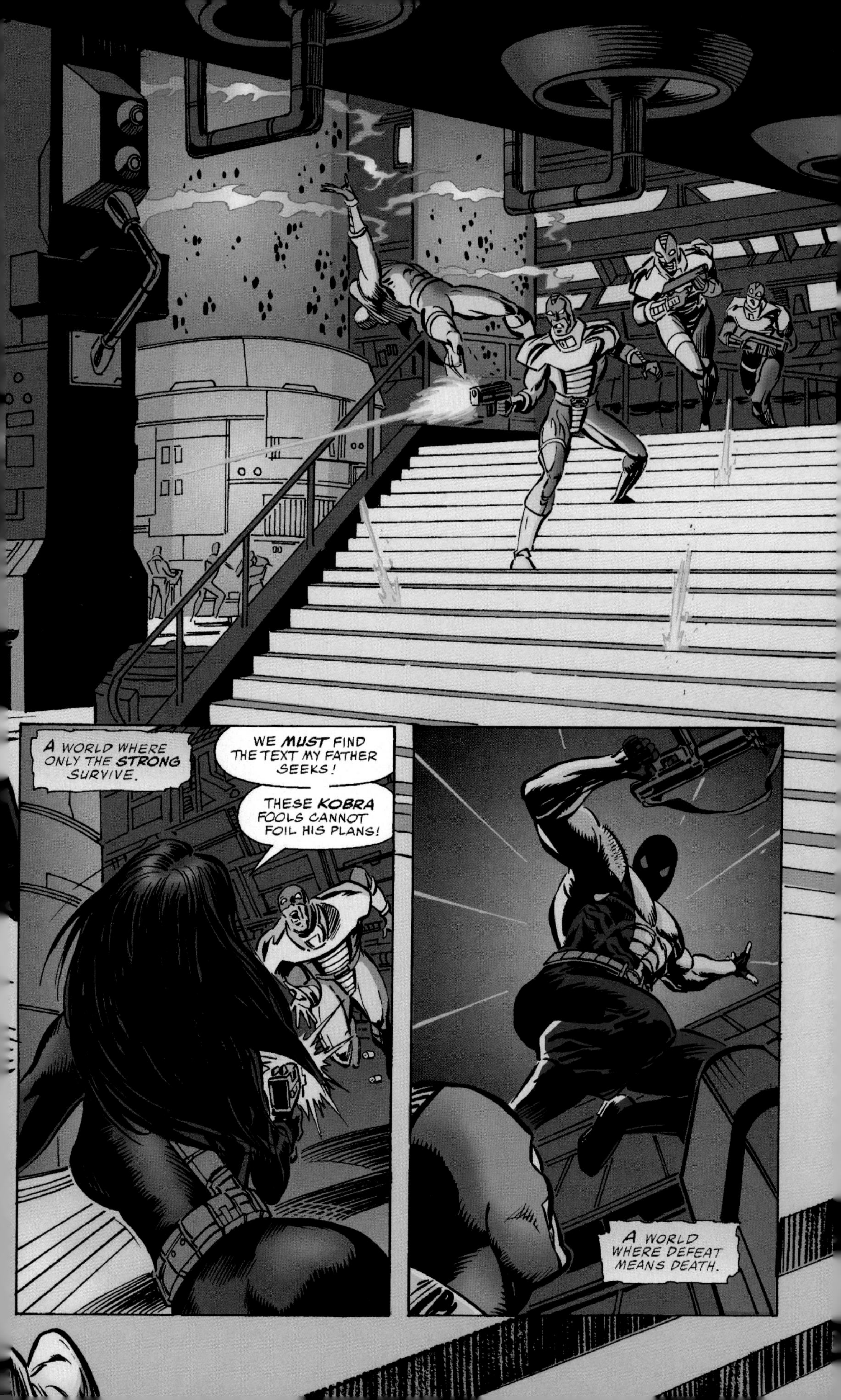

A WORLD WHERE ONLY THE STRONG SURVIVE.
WE MUST FIND THE TEXT MY FATHER SEEKS!
THESE KOBRA FOOLS CANNOT FOIL HIS PLANS!
A WORLD WHERE DEFEAT MEANS DEATH.

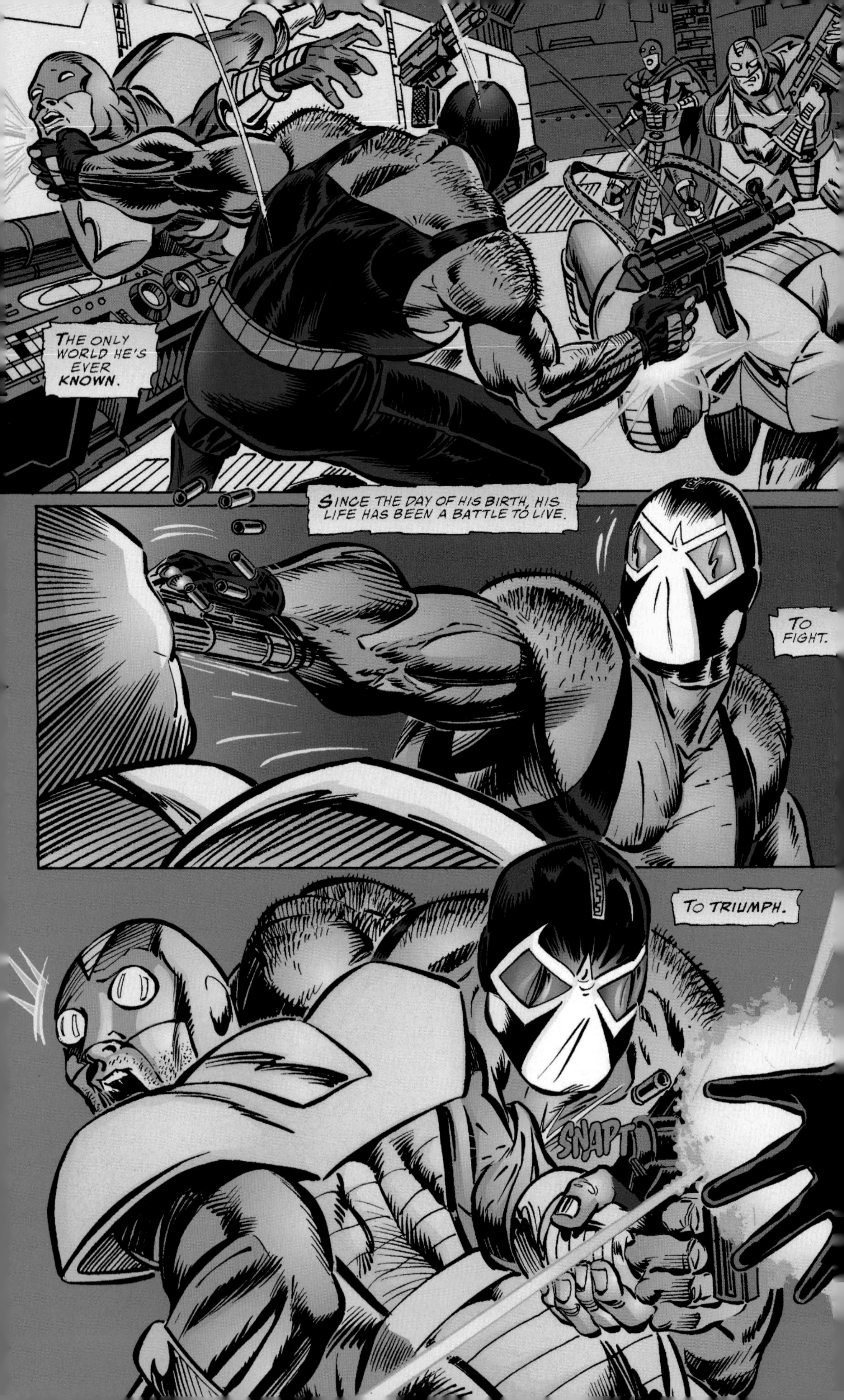

THE ONLY WORLD HE'S EVER KNOWN.
SINCE THE DAY OF HIS BIRTH, HIS LIFE HAS BEEN A BATTLE TO LIVE.
TO FIGHT.
TO TRIUMPH.
SNAP

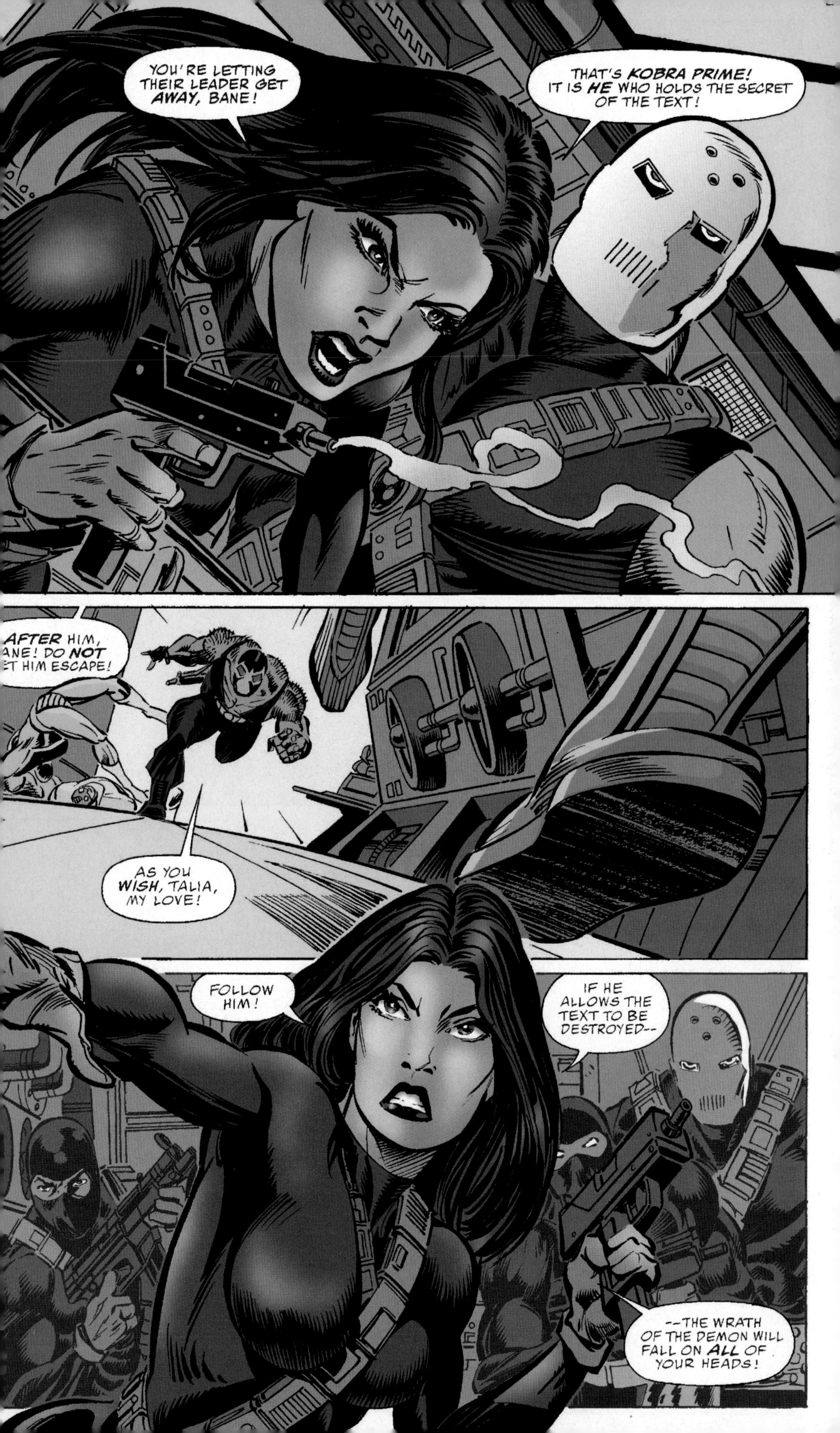
YOU'RE LETTING THEIR LEADER GET AWAY, BANE!
THAT'S KOBRA PRIME! IT IS HE WHO HOLDS THE SECRET OF THE TEXT!
AFTER HIM, ANE! DO NOT ET HIM ESCAPE!
AS YOU WISH, TALIA, MY LOVE!
FOLLOW HIM!
IF HE ALLOWS THE TEXT TO BE DESTROYED--
--THE WRATH OF THE DEMON WILL FALL ON ALL OF YOUR HEADS!

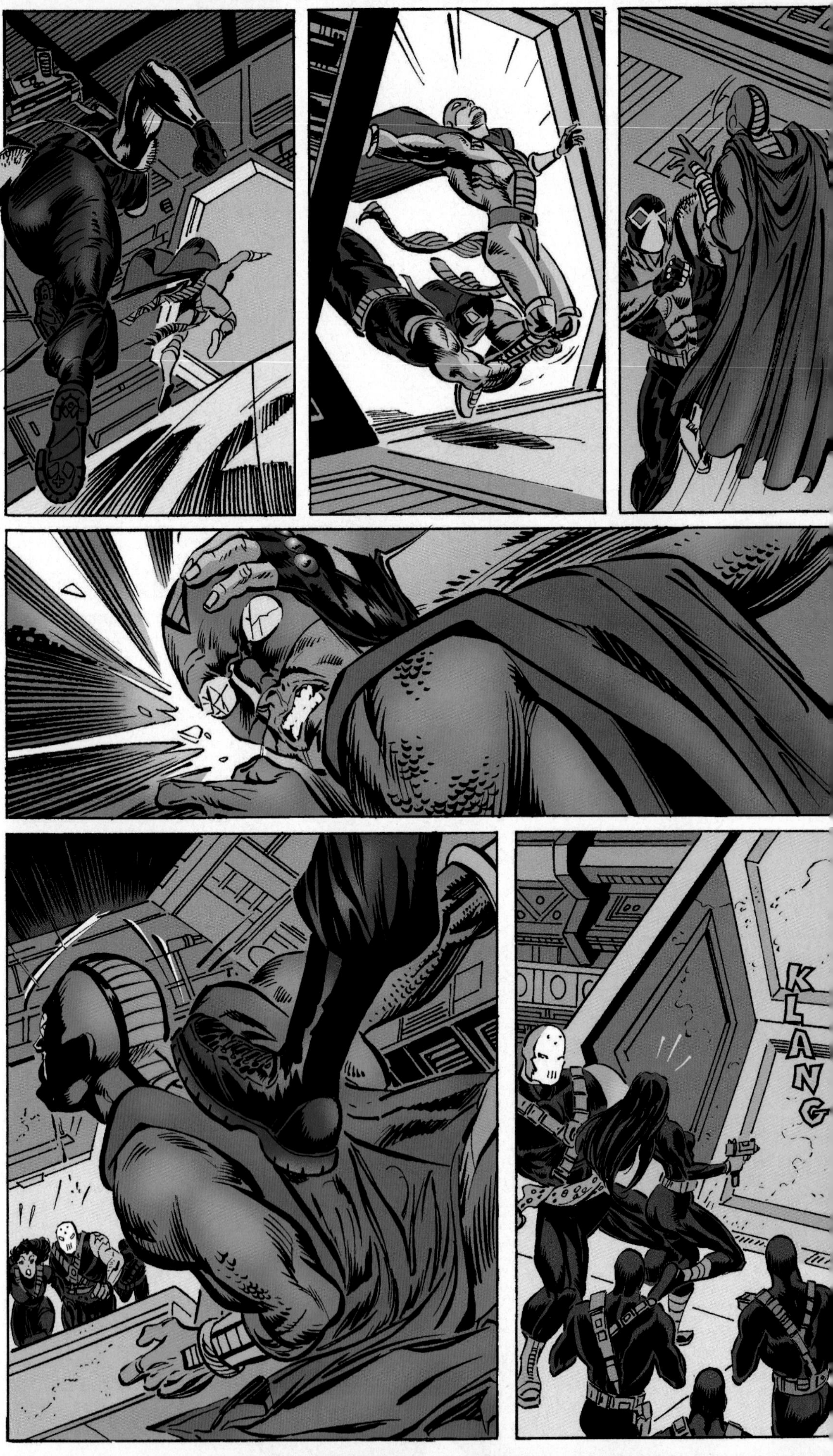
KLANG

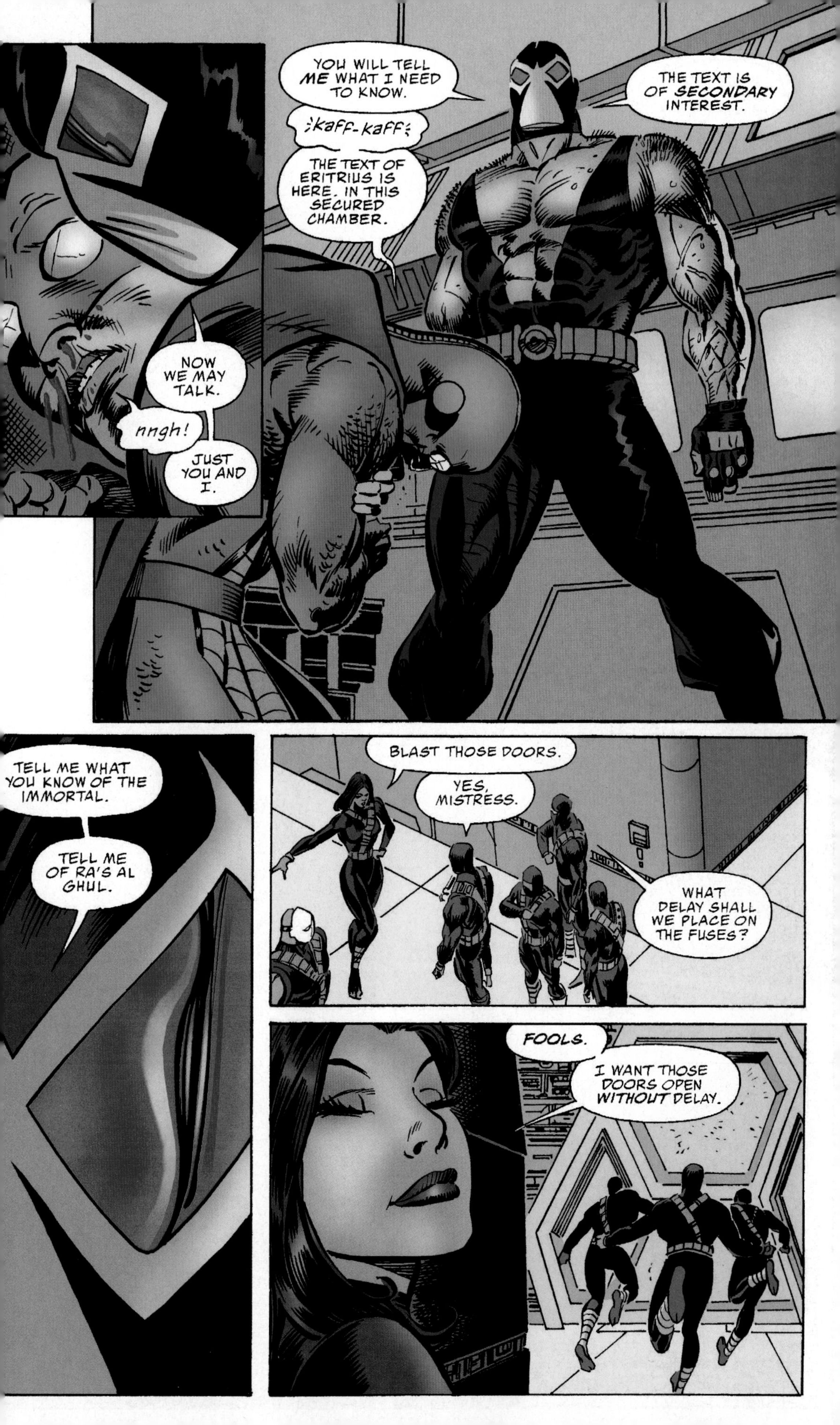
YOU WILL TELL ME WHAT I NEED TO KNOW.
;kaff-kaff;
THE TEXT OF ERITRIUS IS HERE. IN THIS SECURED CHAMBER.
THE TEXT IS OF SECONDARY INTEREST.
NOW WE MAY TALK.
nngh!
JUST YOU AND I.
TELL ME WHAT YOU KNOW OF THE IMMORTAL.
TELL ME OF RA'S AL GHUL.
BLAST THOSE DOORS.
YES, MISTRESS.
WHAT DELAY SHALL WE PLACE ON THE FUSES?
FOOLS.
I WANT THOSE DOORS OPEN WITHOUT DELAY.

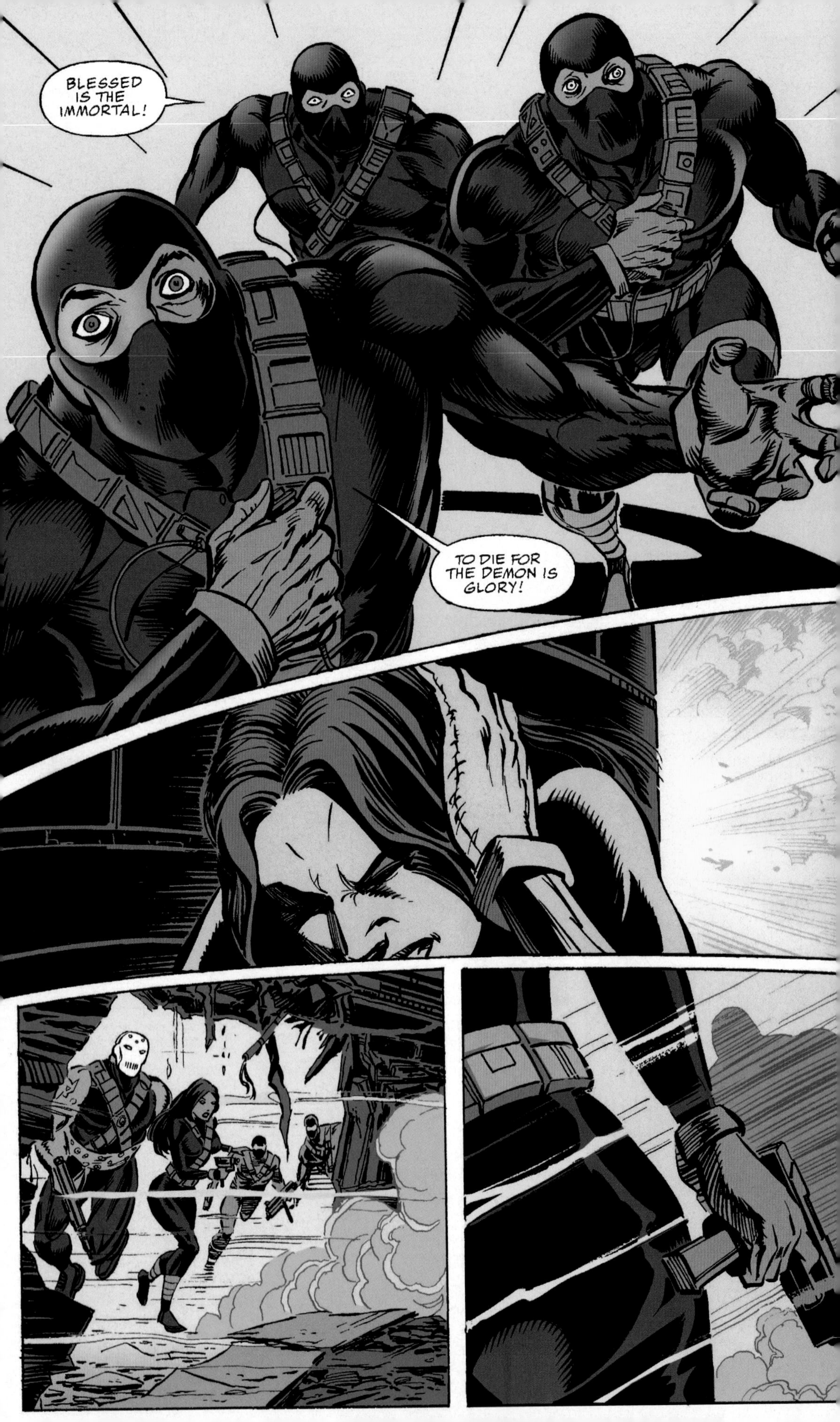
BLESSED IS THE IMMORTAL!
TO DIE FOR THE DEMON IS GLORY!

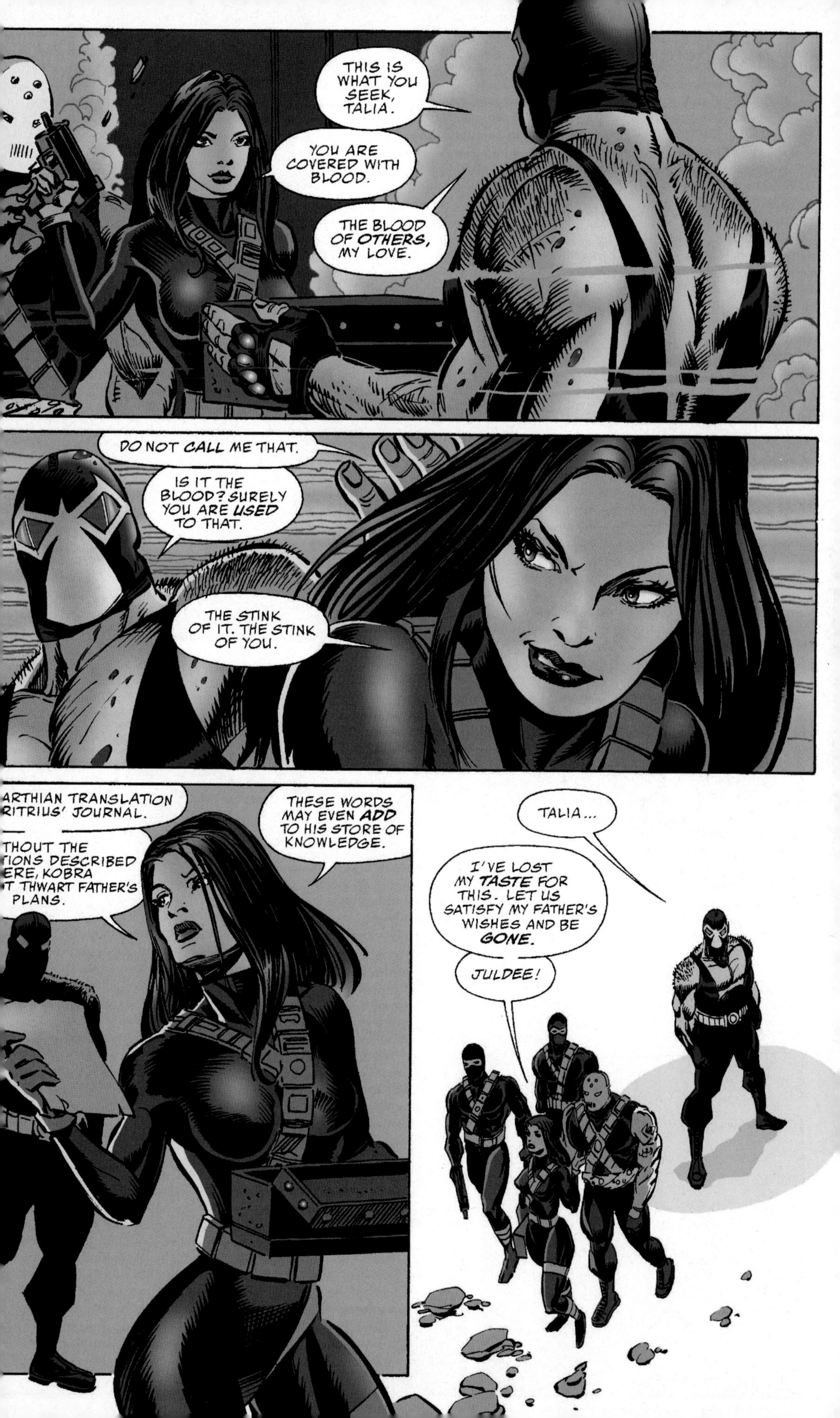
THIS IS WHAT YOU SEEK, TALIA.
YOU ARE COVERED WITH BLOOD.
THE BLOOD OF OTHERS, MY LOVE.
DO NOT CALL ME THAT.
IS IT THE BLOOD? SURELY YOU ARE USED TO THAT.
THE STINK OF IT. THE STINK OF YOU.
ARTHIAN TRANSLATION RITRIUS' JOURNAL.
THOUT THE TIONS DESCRIBED ERE, KOBRA T THWART FATHER'S PLANS.
THESE WORDS MAY EVEN ADD TO HIS STORE OF KNOWLEDGE.
TALIA...
I'VE LOST MY TASTE FOR THIS. LET US SATISFY MY FATHER'S WISHES AND BE GONE.
JULDEE!

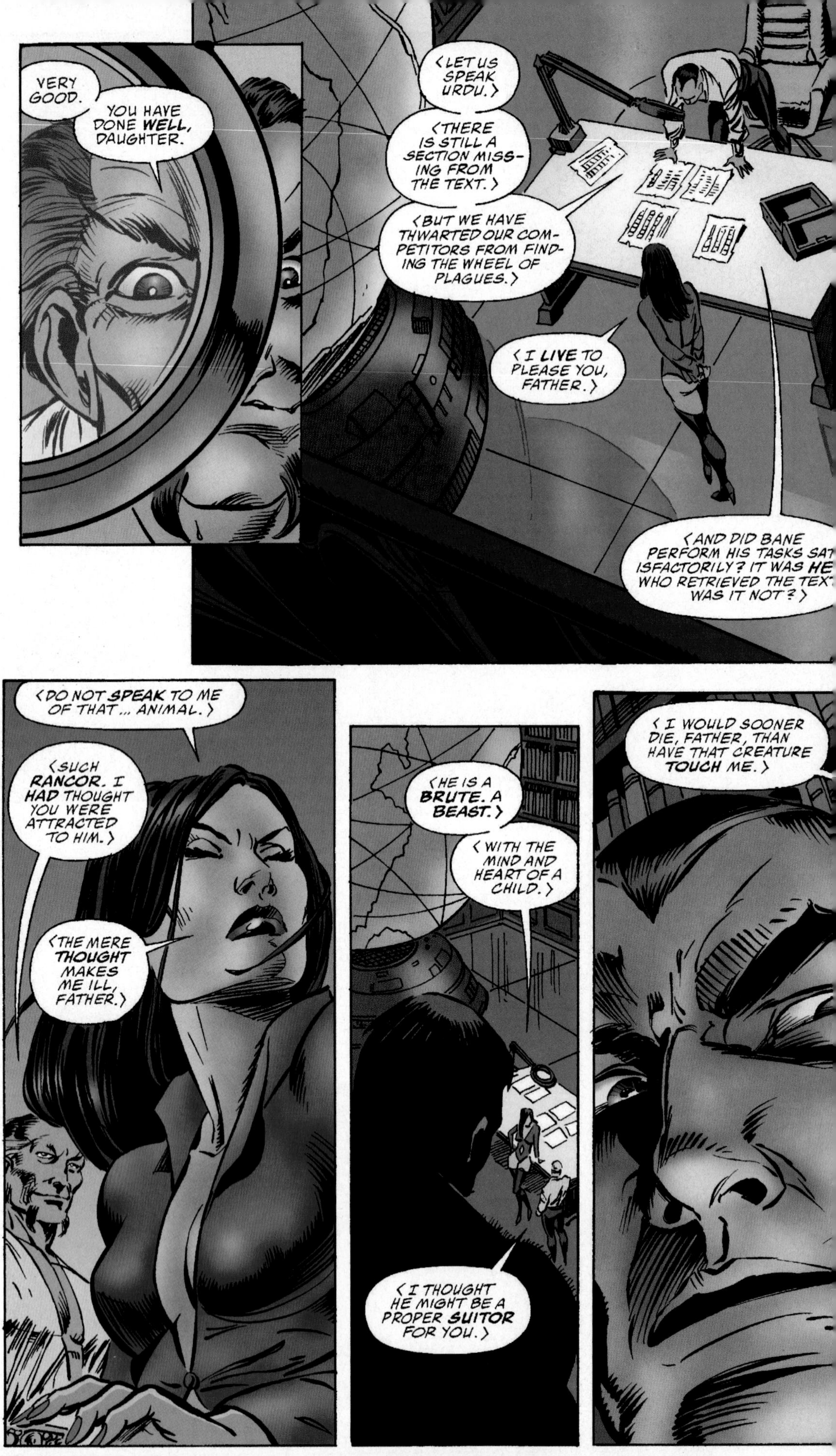
VERY GOOD.
YOU HAVE DONE WELL, DAUGHTER.
<LET US SPEAK URDU.>
<THERE IS STILL A SECTION MISSING FROM THE TEXT.>
<BUT WE HAVE THWARTED OUR COMPETITORS FROM FINDING THE WHEEL OF PLAGUES.>
<I LIVE TO PLEASE YOU, FATHER.>
<AND DID BANE PERFORM HIS TASKS SAT-ISFACTORILY? IT WAS HE WHO RETRIEVED THE TEXT WAS IT NOT?>
<DO NOT SPEAK TO ME OF THAT... ANIMAL.>
<SUCH RANCOR. I HAD THOUGHT YOU WERE ATTRACTED TO HIM.>
<THE MERE THOUGHT MAKES ME ILL, FATHER.>
<HE IS A BRUTE. A BEAST.>
<WITH THE MIND AND HEART OF A CHILD.>
<I THOUGHT HE MIGHT BE A PROPER SUITOR FOR YOU.>
<I WOULD SOONER DIE, FATHER, THAN HAVE THAT CREATURE TOUCH ME.>

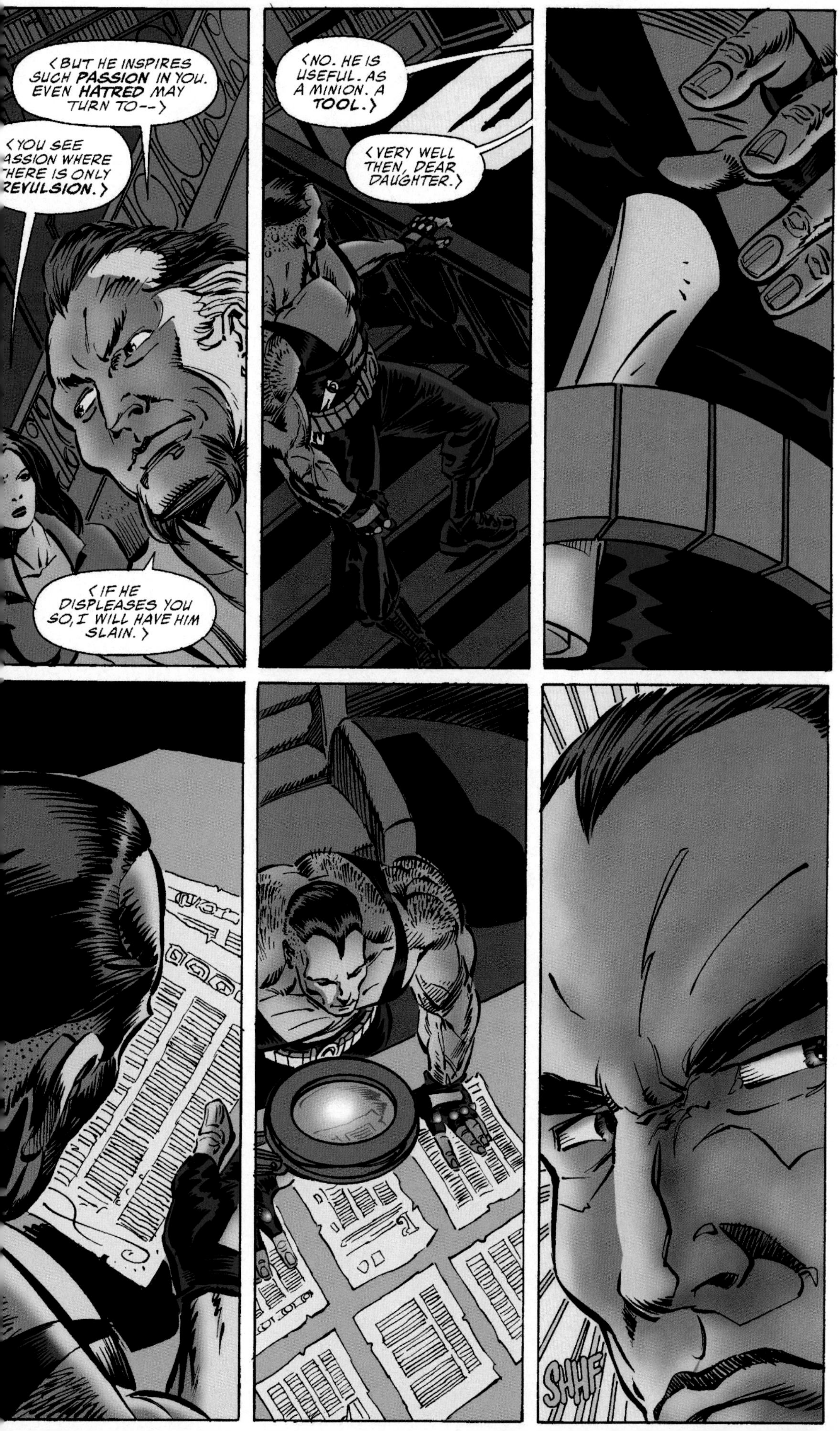

<BUT HE INSPIRES SUCH PASSION IN YOU. EVEN HATRED MAY TURN TO-->
<YOU SEE ASSION WHERE THERE IS ONLY REVULSION.>
<IF HE DISPLEASES YOU SO, I WILL HAVE HIM SLAIN.>
<NO. HE IS USEFUL. AS A MINION. A TOOL.>
<VERY WELL THEN, DEAR DAUGHTER.>
SHHF

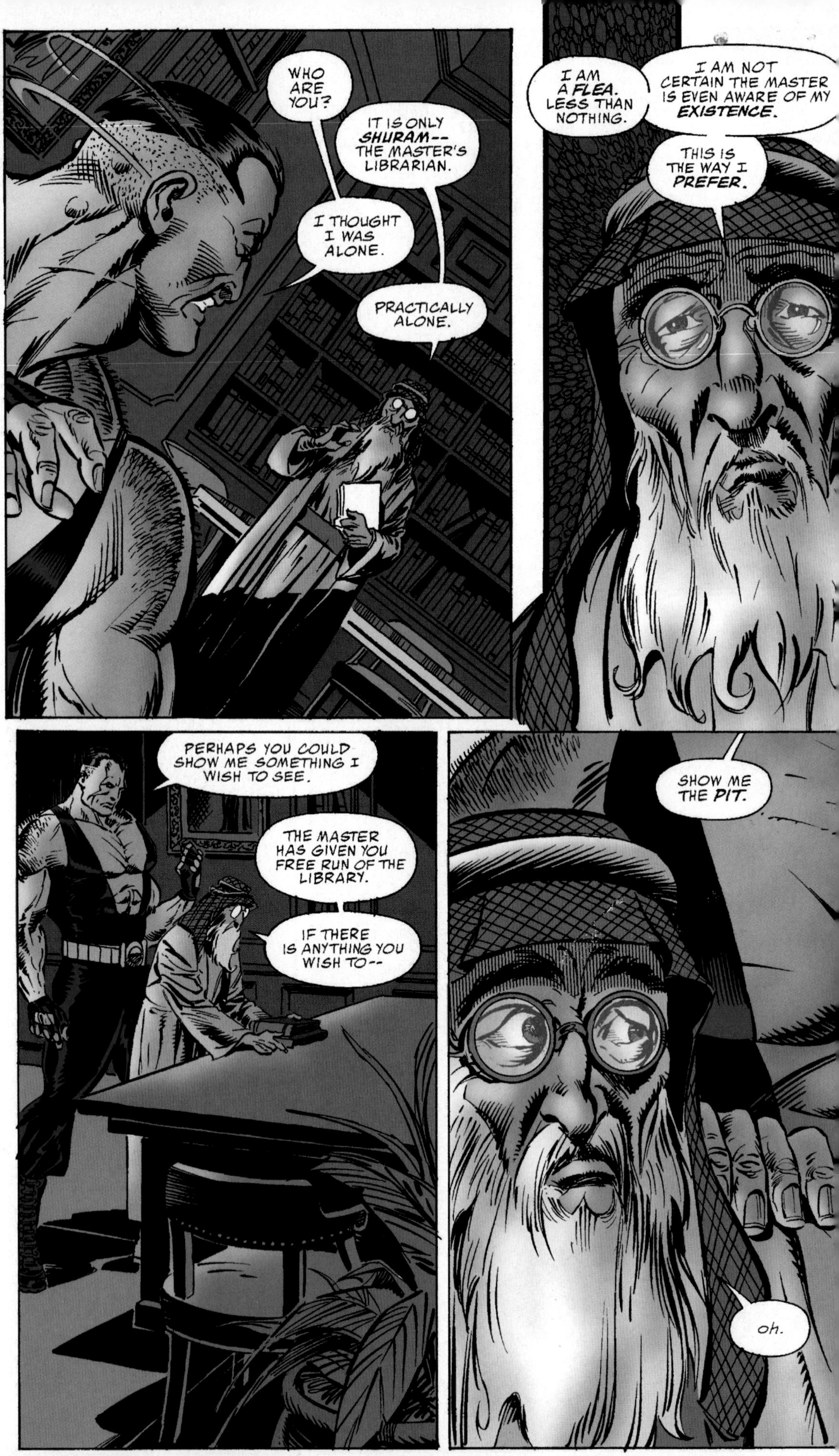
WHO ARE YOU?
IT IS ONLY SHURAM-- THE MASTER'S LIBRARIAN.
I THOUGHT I WAS ALONE.
PRACTICALLY ALONE.
I AM A FLEA. LESS THAN NOTHING.
I AM NOT CERTAIN THE MASTER IS EVEN AWARE OF MY EXISTENCE.
THIS IS THE WAY I PREFER.
PERHAPS YOU COULD SHOW ME SOMETHING I WISH TO SEE.
THE MASTER HAS GIVEN YOU FREE RUN OF THE LIBRARY.
IF THERE IS ANYTHING YOU WISH TO--
SHOW ME THE PIT.
oh.

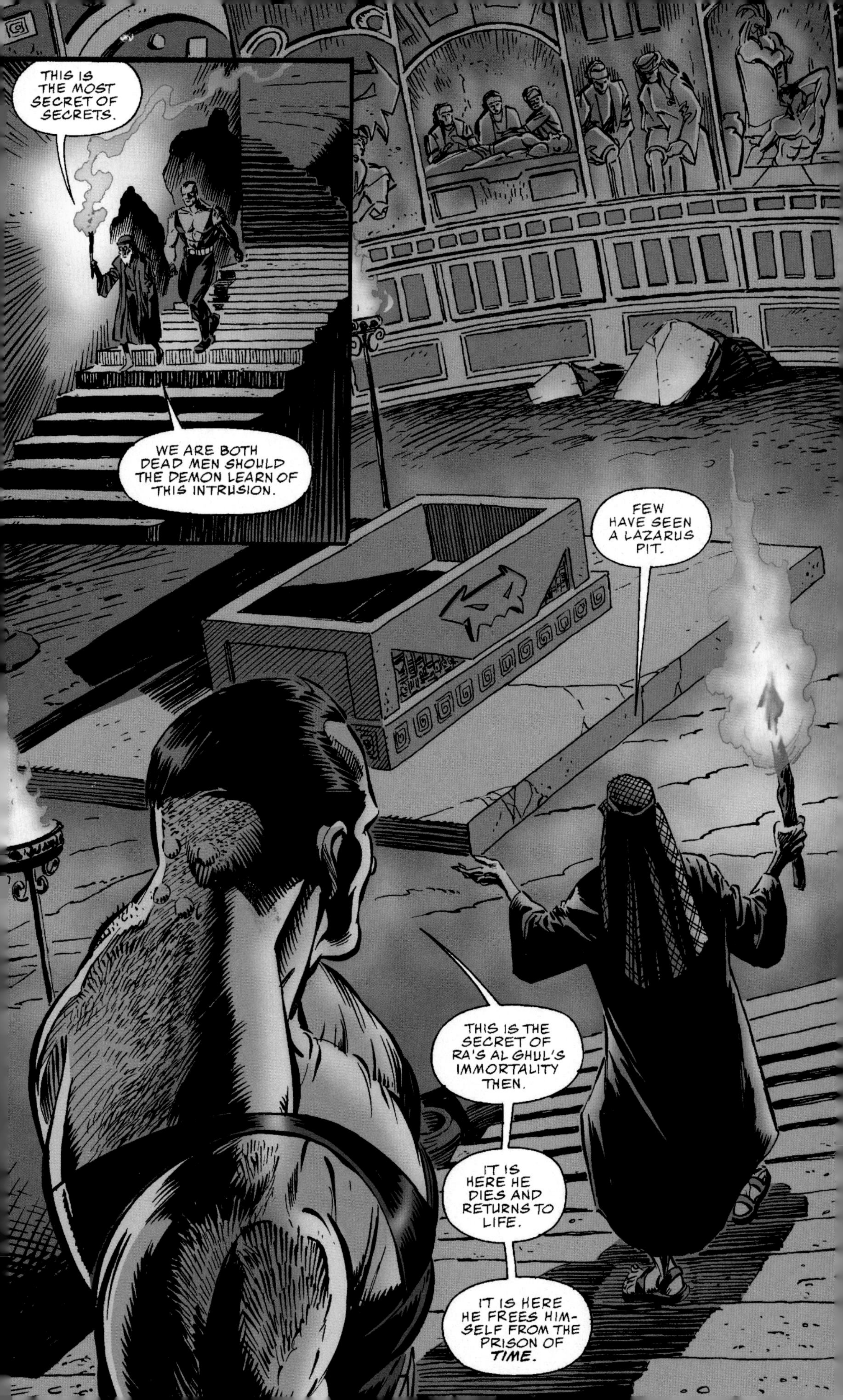
THIS IS THE MOST SECRET OF SECRETS.
WE ARE BOTH DEAD MEN SHOULD THE DEMON LEARN OF THIS INTRUSION.
FEW HAVE SEEN A LAZARUS PIT.
THIS IS THE SECRET OF RA'S AL GHUL'S IMMORTALITY THEN.
IT IS HERE HE DIES AND RETURNS TO LIFE.
IT IS HERE HE FREES HIM-SELF FROM THE PRISON OF *TIME*.

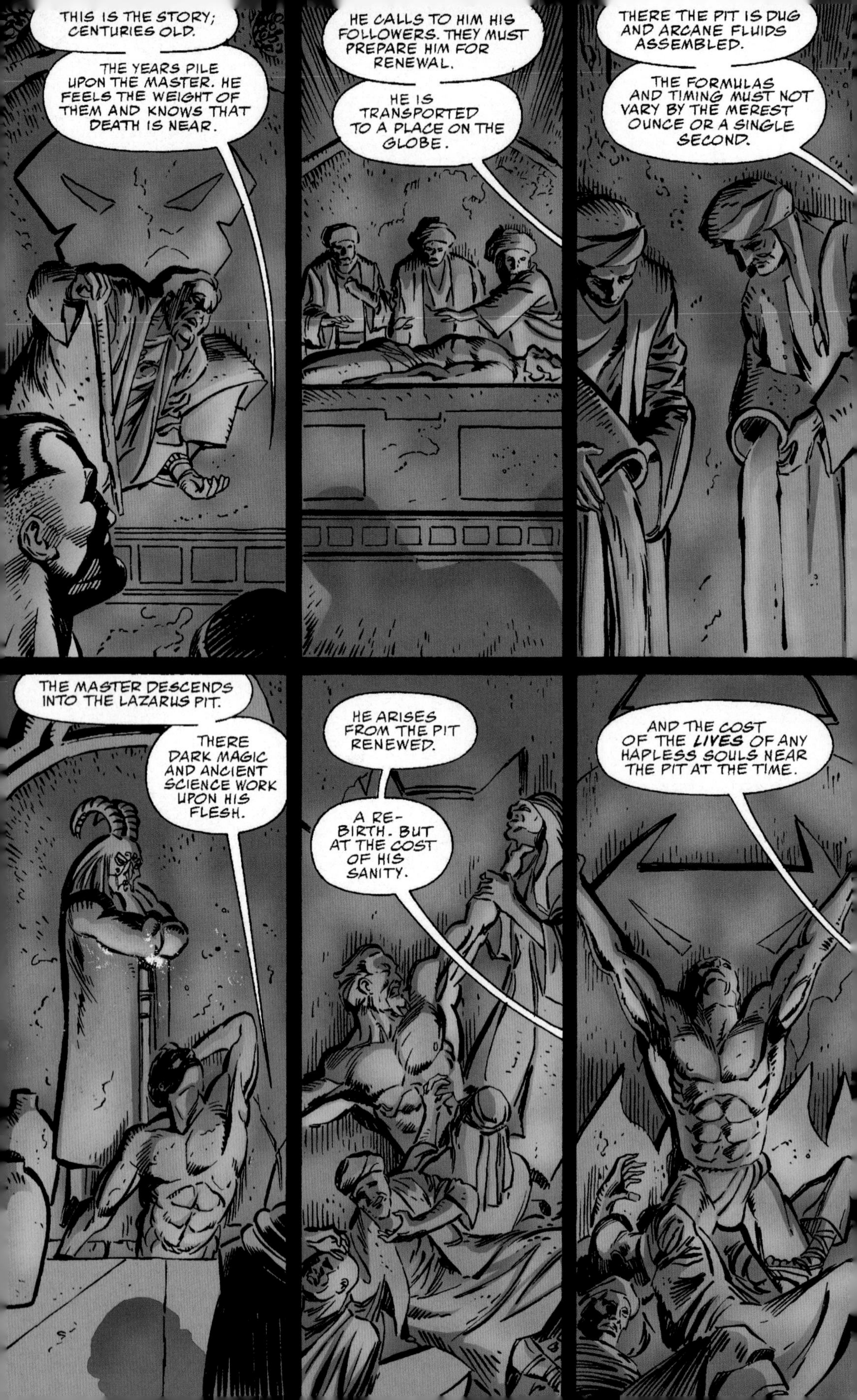
THIS IS THE STORY; CENTURIES OLD.
THE YEARS PILE UPON THE MASTER. HE FEELS THE WEIGHT OF THEM AND KNOWS THAT DEATH IS NEAR.
HE CALLS TO HIM HIS FOLLOWERS. THEY MUST PREPARE HIM FOR RENEWAL.
HE IS TRANSPORTED TO A PLACE ON THE GLOBE.
THERE THE PIT IS DUG AND ARCANE FLUIDS ASSEMBLED.
THE FORMULAS AND TIMING MUST NOT VARY BY THE MEREST OUNCE OR A SINGLE SECOND.
THE MASTER DESCENDS INTO THE LAZARUS PIT.
THERE DARK MAGIC AND ANCIENT SCIENCE WORK UPON HIS FLESH.
HE ARISES FROM THE PIT RENEWED.
A RE-BIRTH. BUT AT THE COST OF HIS SANITY.
AND THE COST OF THE LIVES OF ANY HAPLESS SOULS NEAR THE PIT AT THE TIME.

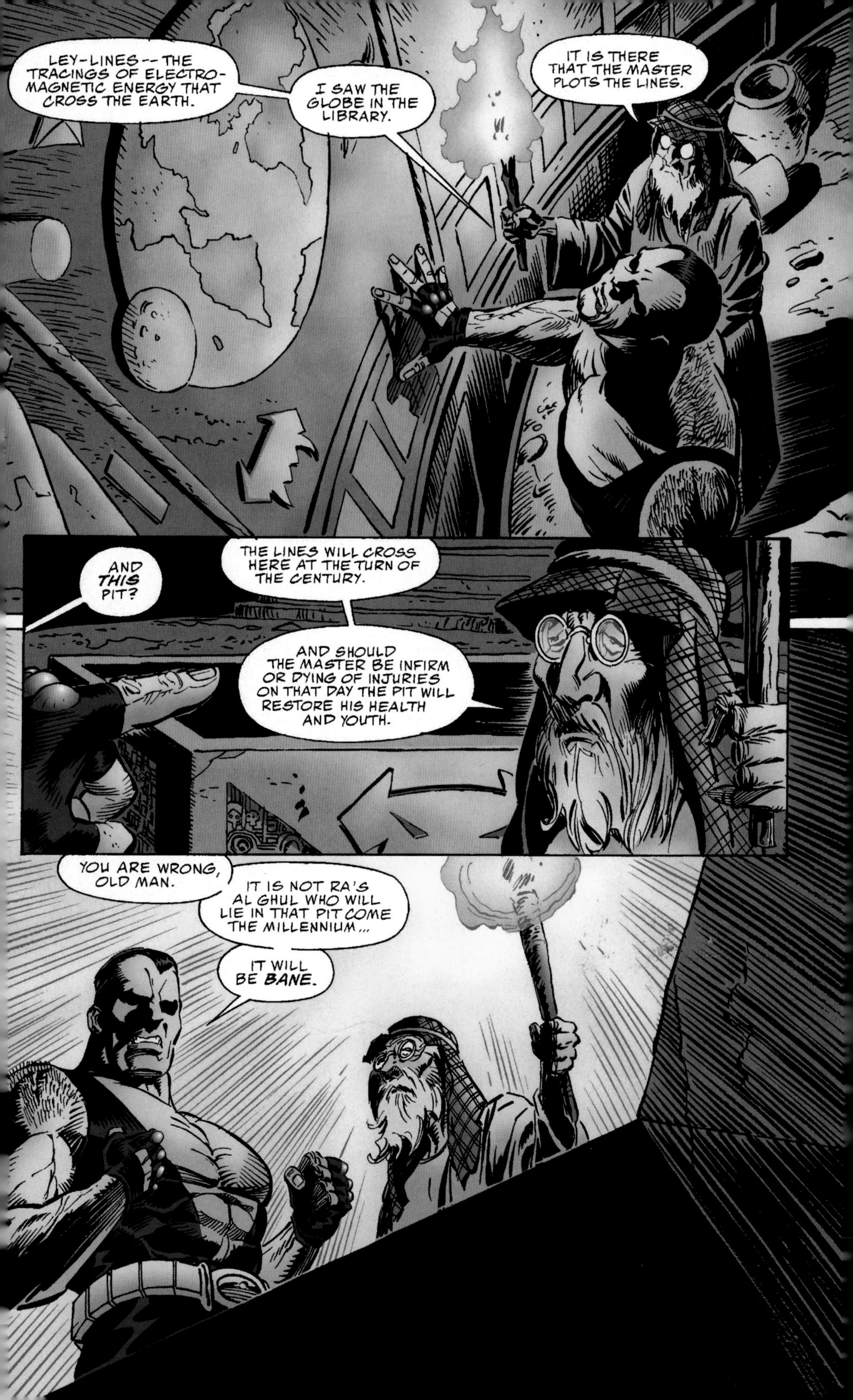
LEY-LINES -- THE TRACINGS OF ELECTRO-MAGNETIC ENERGY THAT CROSS THE EARTH.
I SAW THE GLOBE IN THE LIBRARY.
IT IS THERE THAT THE MASTER PLOTS THE LINES.
AND THIS PIT?
THE LINES WILL CROSS HERE AT THE TURN OF THE CENTURY.
AND SHOULD THE MASTER BE INFIRM OR DYING OF INJURIES ON THAT DAY THE PIT WILL RESTORE HIS HEALTH AND YOUTH.
YOU ARE WRONG, OLD MAN.
IT IS NOT RA'S AL GHUL WHO WILL LIE IN THAT PIT COME THE MILLENNIUM...
IT WILL BE BANE.

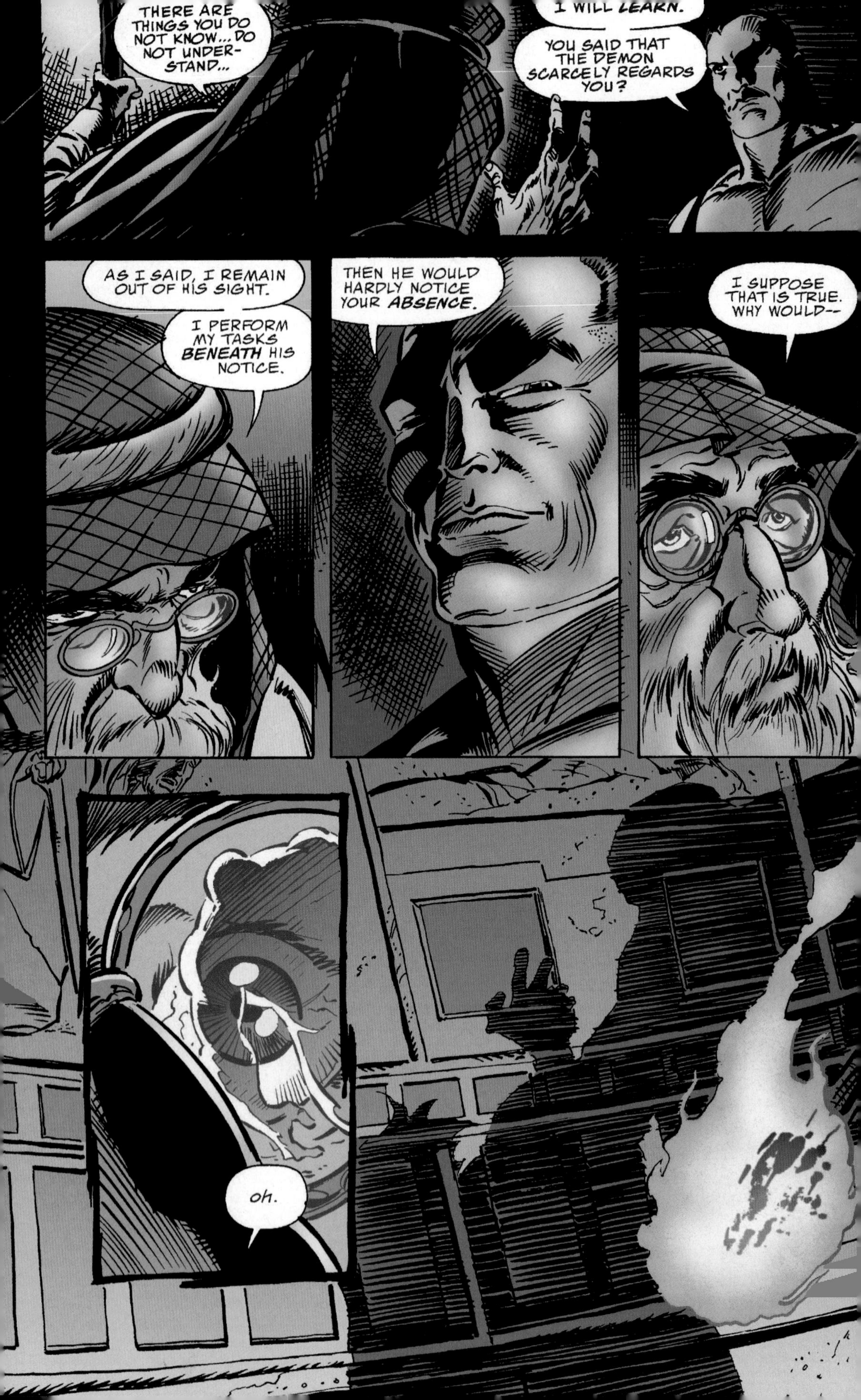

THERE ARE THINGS YOU DO NOT KNOW... DO NOT UNDER-STAND...
I WILL LEARN.
YOU SAID THAT THE DEMON SCARCELY REGARDS YOU?
AS I SAID, I REMAIN OUT OF HIS SIGHT.
I PERFORM MY TASKS BENEATH HIS NOTICE.
THEN HE WOULD HARDLY NOTICE YOUR ABSENCE.
I SUPPOSE THAT IS TRUE. WHY WOULD--
oh.

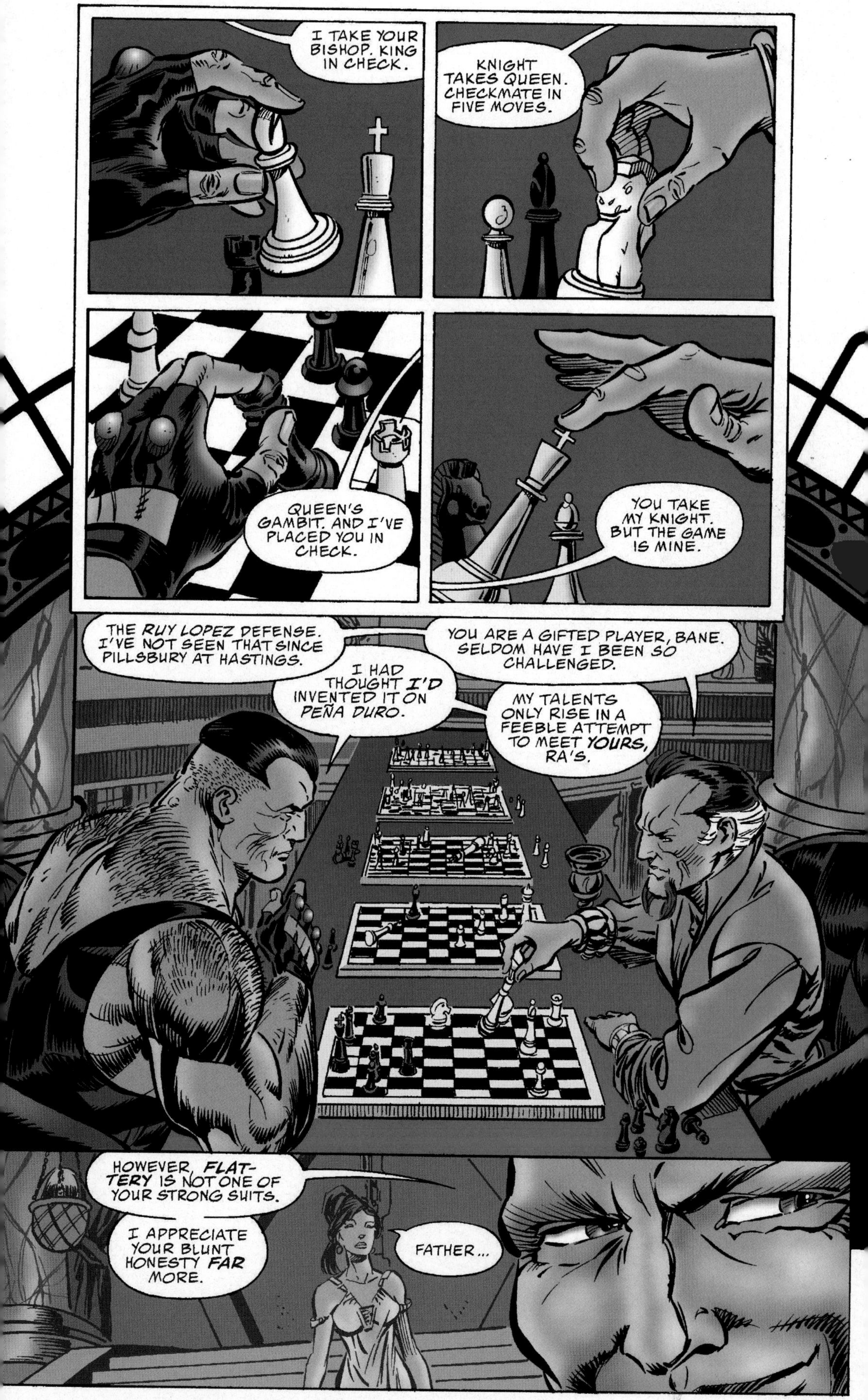
I TAKE YOUR BISHOP. KING IN CHECK.
KNIGHT TAKES QUEEN. CHECKMATE IN FIVE MOVES.
QUEEN'S GAMBIT. AND I'VE PLACED YOU IN CHECK.
YOU TAKE MY KNIGHT. BUT THE GAME IS MINE.
THE RUY LOPEZ DEFENSE. I'VE NOT SEEN THAT SINCE PILLSBURY AT HASTINGS.
I HAD THOUGHT I'D INVENTED IT ON PEÑA DURO.
YOU ARE A GIFTED PLAYER, BANE. SELDOM HAVE I BEEN SO CHALLENGED.
MY TALENTS ONLY RISE IN A FEEBLE ATTEMPT TO MEET YOURS, RA'S.
HOWEVER, FLATTERY IS NOT ONE OF YOUR STRONG SUITS.
I APPRECIATE YOUR BLUNT HONESTY FAR MORE.
FATHER...

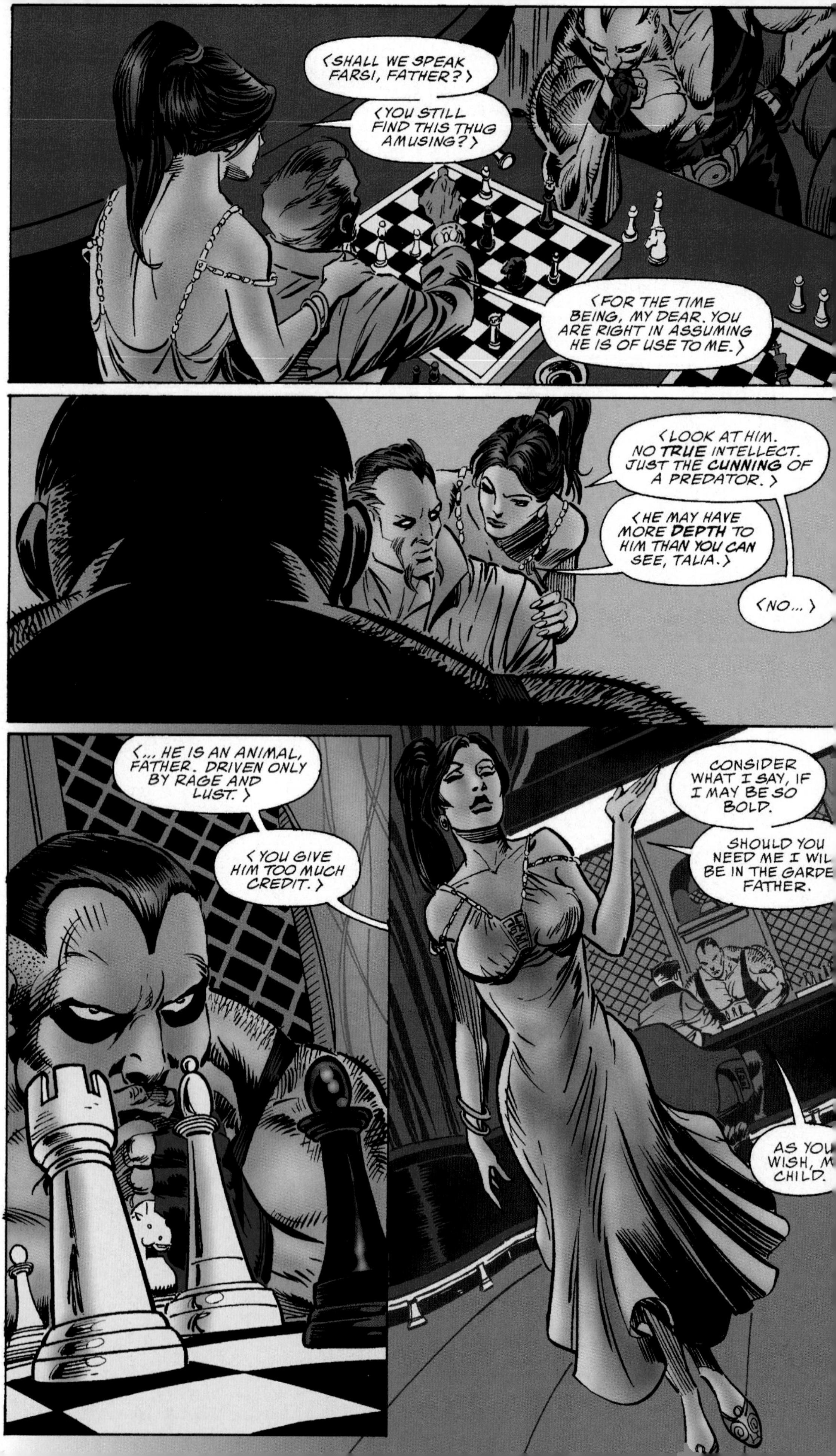

‹SHALL WE SPEAK FARSI, FATHER?›
‹YOU STILL FIND THIS THUG AMUSING?›
‹FOR THE TIME BEING, MY DEAR. YOU ARE RIGHT IN ASSUMING HE IS OF USE TO ME.›
‹LOOK AT HIM. NO TRUE INTELLECT. JUST THE CUNNING OF A PREDATOR.›
‹HE MAY HAVE MORE DEPTH TO HIM THAN YOU CAN SEE, TALIA.›
‹NO...›
‹... HE IS AN ANIMAL, FATHER. DRIVEN ONLY BY RAGE AND LUST.›
‹YOU GIVE HIM TOO MUCH CREDIT.›
CONSIDER WHAT I SAY, IF I MAY BE SO BOLD.
SHOULD YOU NEED ME I WIL BE IN THE GARDE FATHER.
AS YOU WISH, M CHILD.

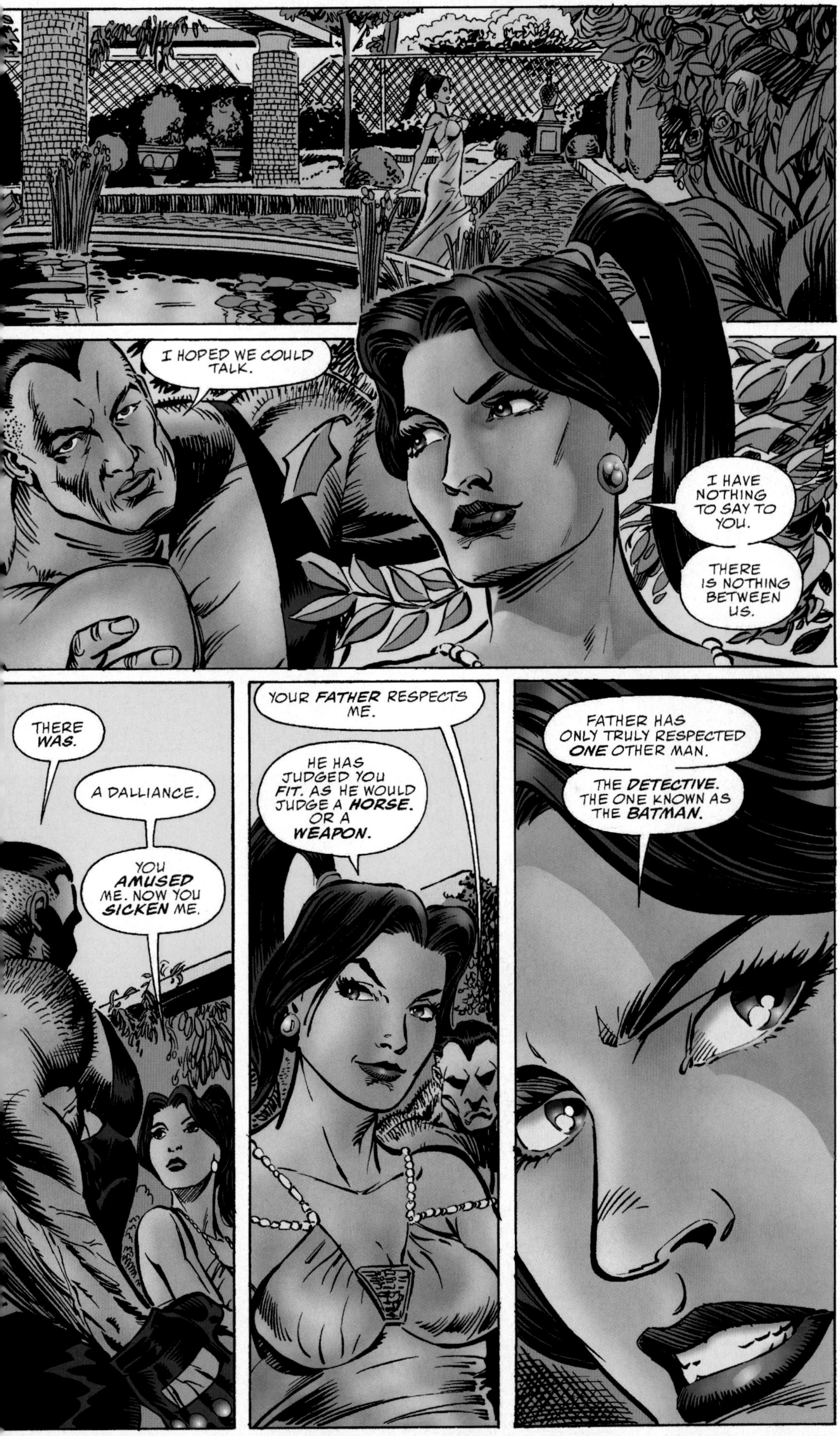
I HOPED WE COULD TALK.
I HAVE NOTHING TO SAY TO YOU.
THERE IS NOTHING BETWEEN US.
THERE ***WAS***.
A DALLIANCE.
YOU ***AMUSED*** ME. NOW YOU ***SICKEN*** ME.
YOUR ***FATHER*** RESPECTS ME.
HE HAS JUDGED YOU ***FIT***. AS HE WOULD JUDGE A ***HORSE***. OR A ***WEAPON***.
FATHER HAS ONLY TRULY RESPECTED ***ONE*** OTHER MAN.
THE ***DETECTIVE***. THE ONE KNOWN AS THE ***BATMAN***.

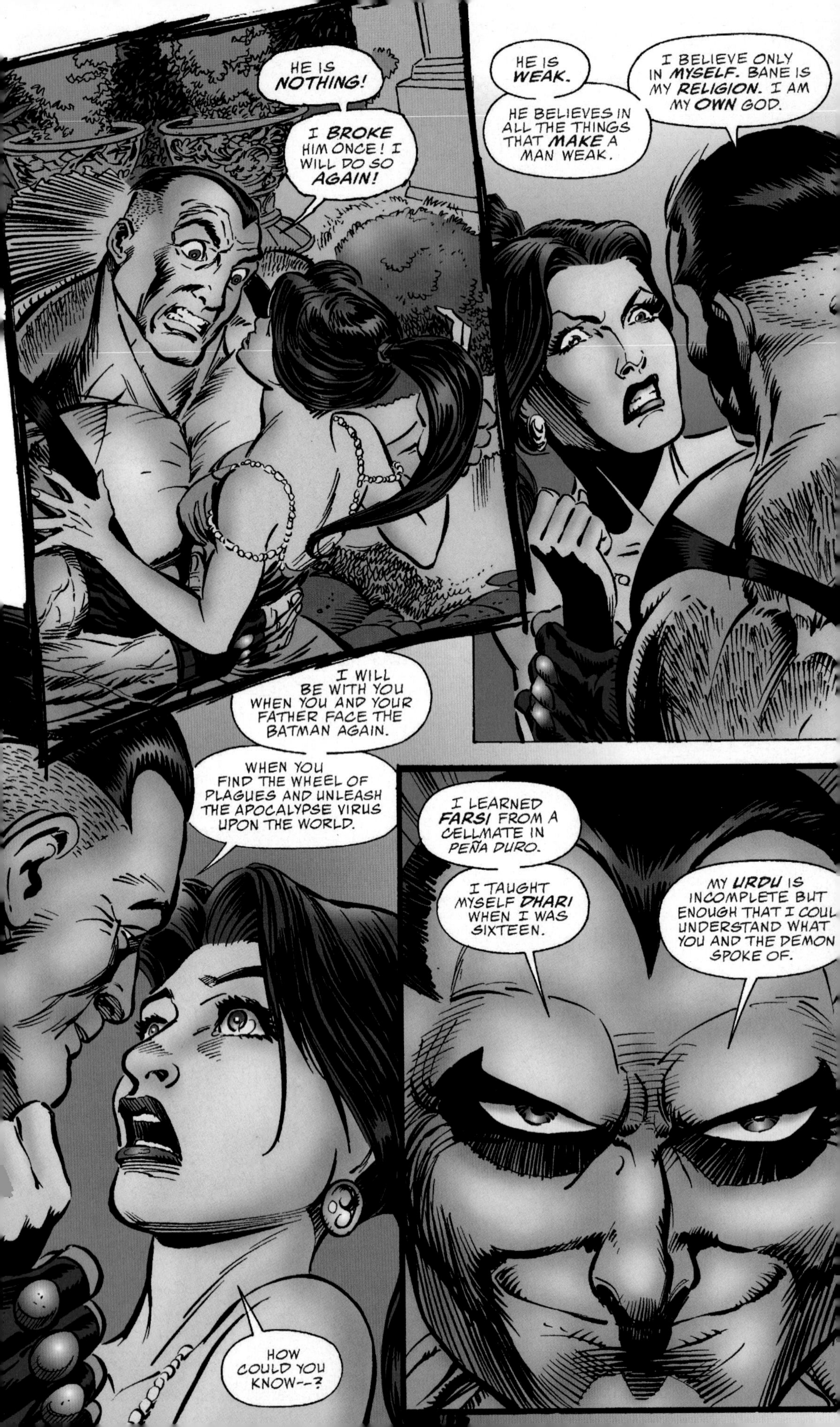

HE IS NOTHING!
I BROKE HIM ONCE! I WILL DO SO AGAIN!
HE IS WEAK.
HE BELIEVES IN ALL THE THINGS THAT MAKE A MAN WEAK.
I BELIEVE ONLY IN MYSELF. BANE IS MY RELIGION. I AM MY OWN GOD.
I WILL BE WITH YOU WHEN YOU AND YOUR FATHER FACE THE BATMAN AGAIN.
WHEN YOU FIND THE WHEEL OF PLAGUES AND UNLEASH THE APOCALYPSE VIRUS UPON THE WORLD.
HOW COULD YOU KNOW--?
I LEARNED FARSI FROM A CELLMATE IN PEÑA DURO.
I TAUGHT MYSELF DHARI WHEN I WAS SIXTEEN.
MY URDU IS INCOMPLETE BUT ENOUGH THAT I COUL UNDERSTAND WHAT YOU AND THE DEMON SPOKE OF.

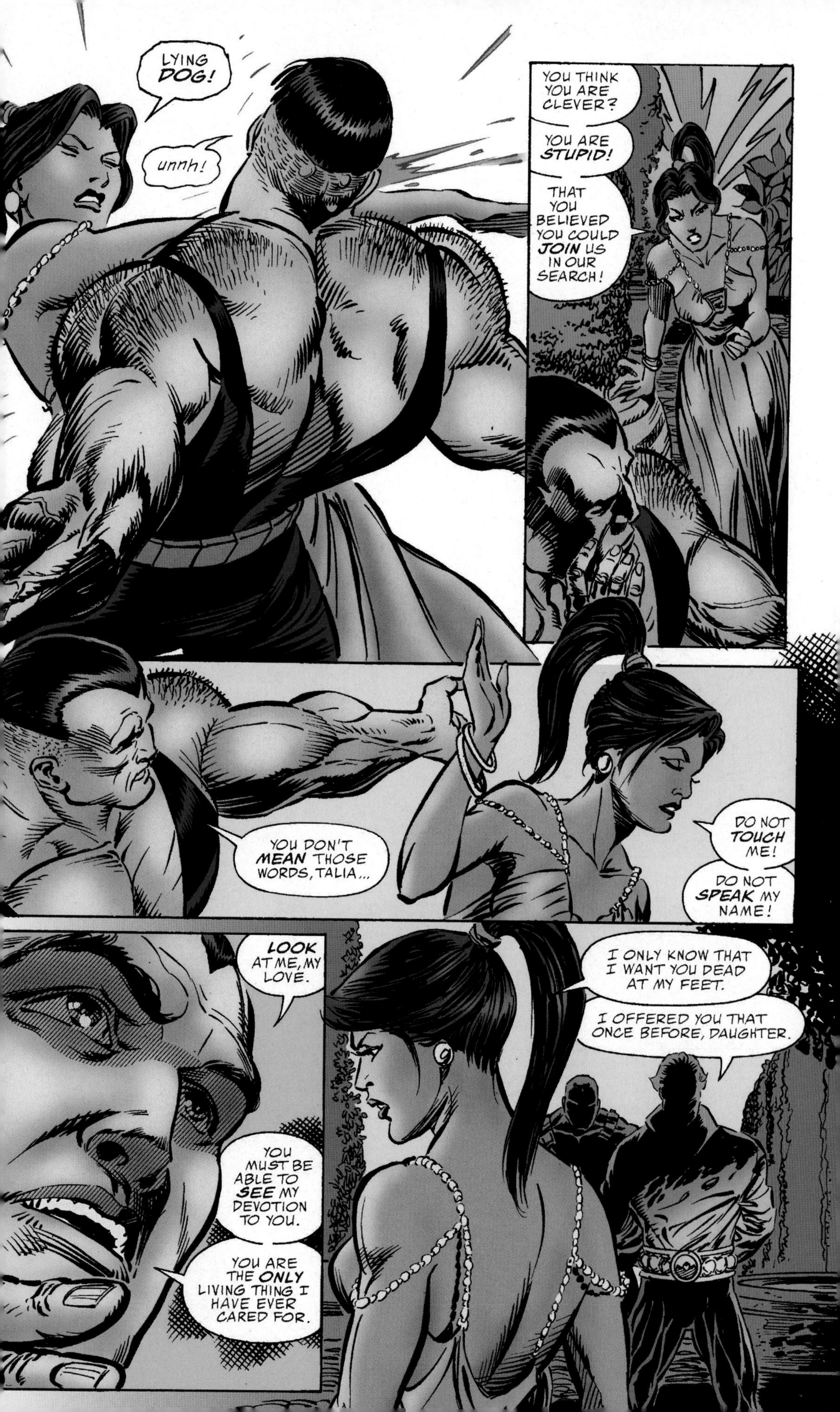
LYING DOG!
unnh!
YOU THINK YOU ARE CLEVER?
YOU ARE STUPID!
THAT YOU BELIEVED YOU COULD JOIN US IN OUR SEARCH!
YOU DON'T MEAN THOSE WORDS, TALIA...
DO NOT TOUCH ME!
DO NOT SPEAK MY NAME!
LOOK AT ME, MY LOVE.
YOU MUST BE ABLE TO SEE MY DEVOTION TO YOU.
YOU ARE THE ONLY LIVING THING I HAVE EVER CARED FOR.
I ONLY KNOW THAT I WANT YOU DEAD AT MY FEET.
I OFFERED YOU THAT ONCE BEFORE, DAUGHTER.

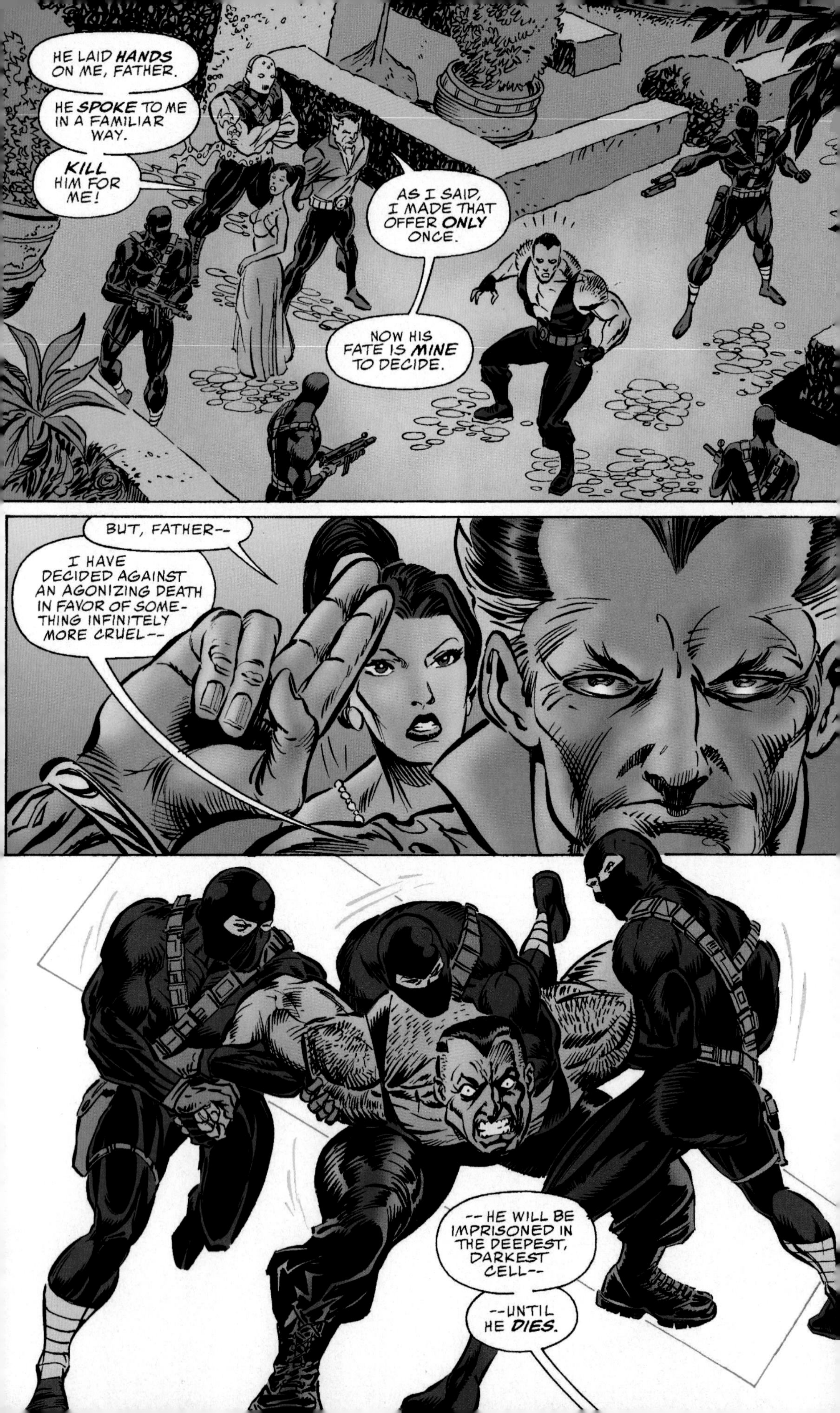
HE LAID HANDS ON ME, FATHER.
HE SPOKE TO ME IN A FAMILIAR WAY.
KILL HIM FOR ME!
AS I SAID, I MADE THAT OFFER ONLY ONCE.
NOW HIS FATE IS MINE TO DECIDE.
BUT, FATHER--
I HAVE DECIDED AGAINST AN AGONIZING DEATH IN FAVOR OF SOME-THING INFINITELY MORE CRUEL--
--HE WILL BE IMPRISONED IN THE DEEPEST, DARKEST CELL--
--UNTIL HE DIES.

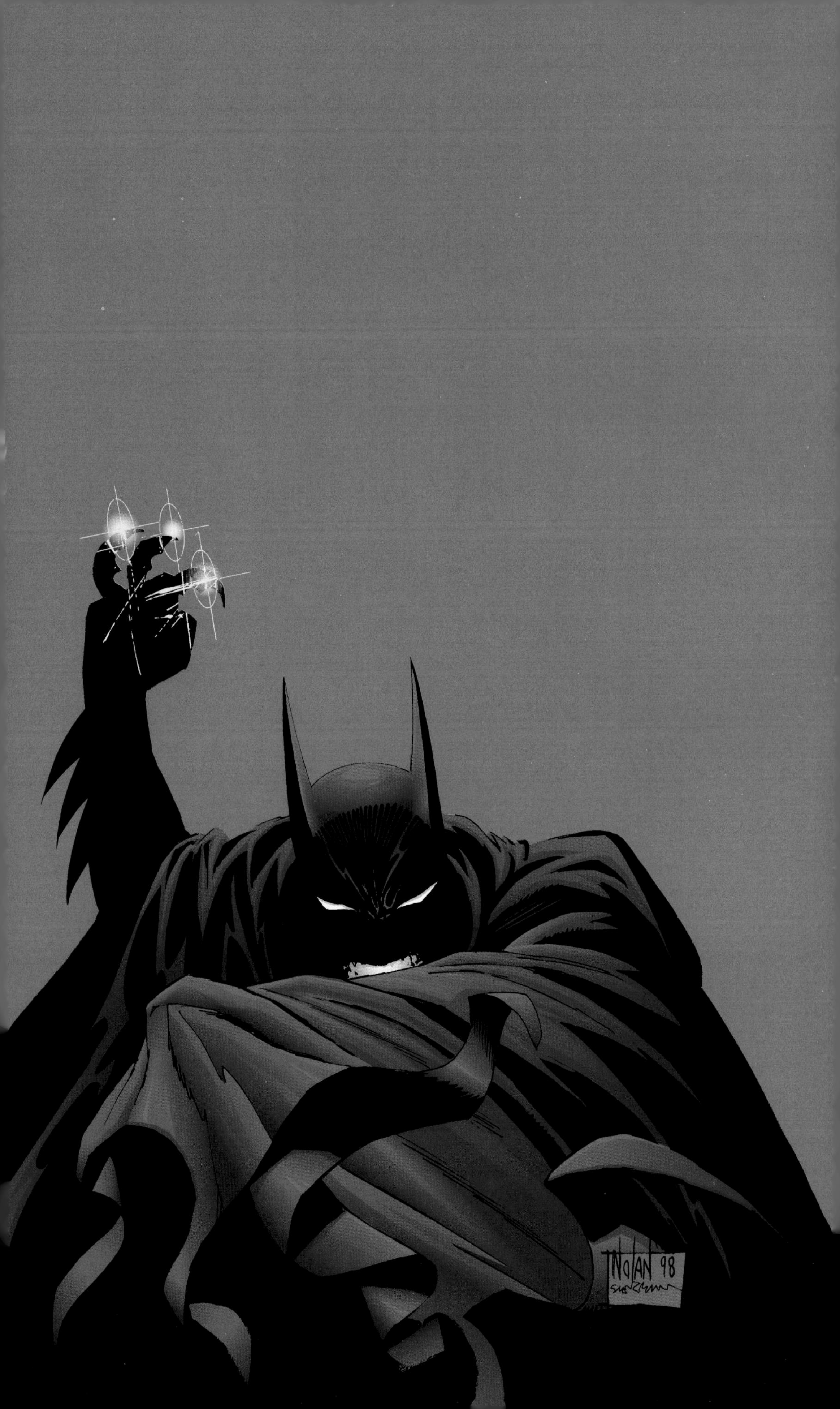
NOLAN '98

Cover Art by Graham Nolan
and Bill Sienkiewicz

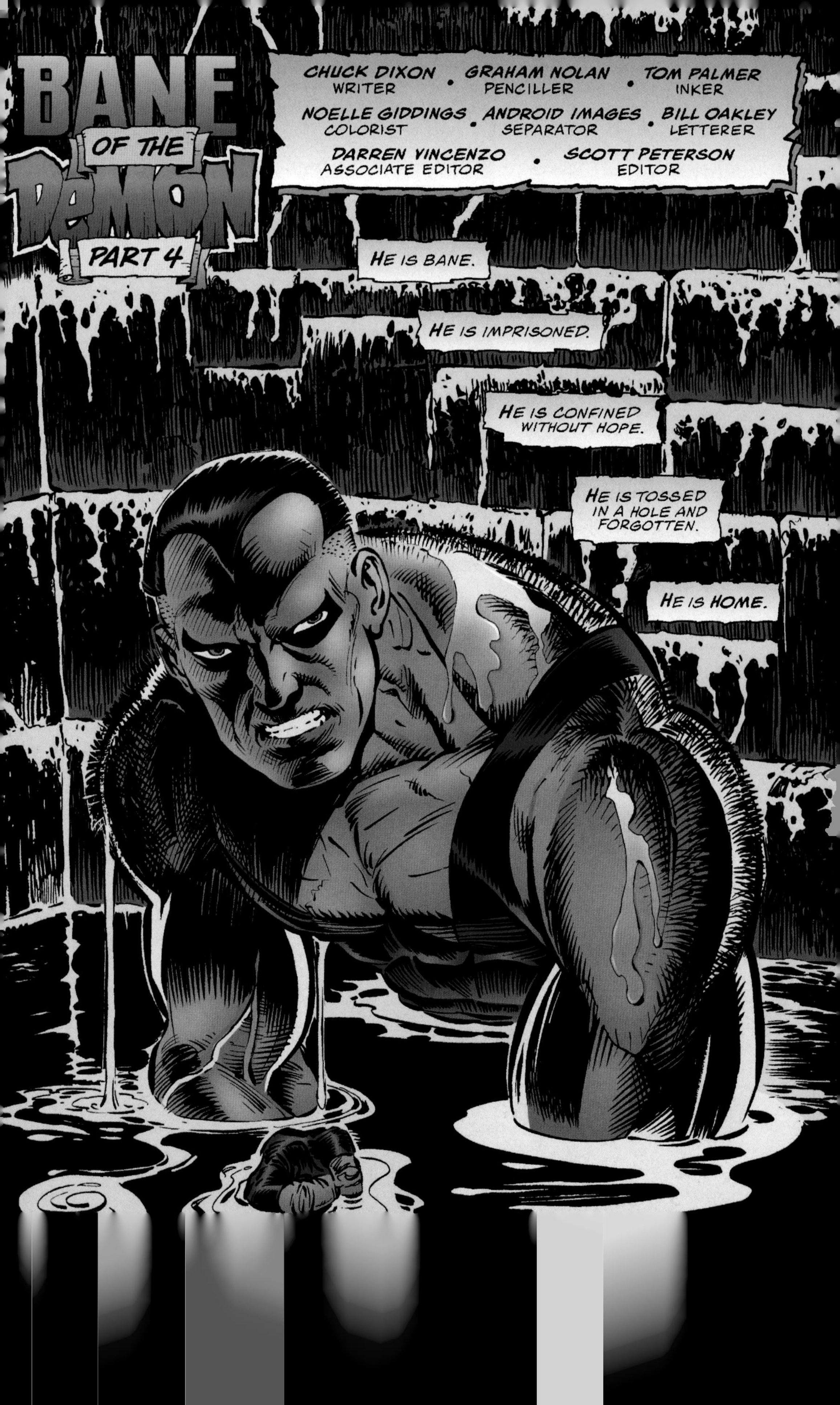

BANE OF THE DEMON
PART 4
CHUCK DIXON WRITER • GRAHAM NOLAN PENCILLER • TOM PALMER INKER
NOELLE GIDDINGS COLORIST • ANDROID IMAGES SEPARATOR • BILL OAKLEY LETTERER
DARREN VINCENZO ASSOCIATE EDITOR • SCOTT PETERSON EDITOR
HE IS BANE.
HE IS IMPRISONED.
HE IS CONFINED WITHOUT HOPE.
HE IS TOSSED IN A HOLE AND FORGOTTEN.
HE IS HOME.

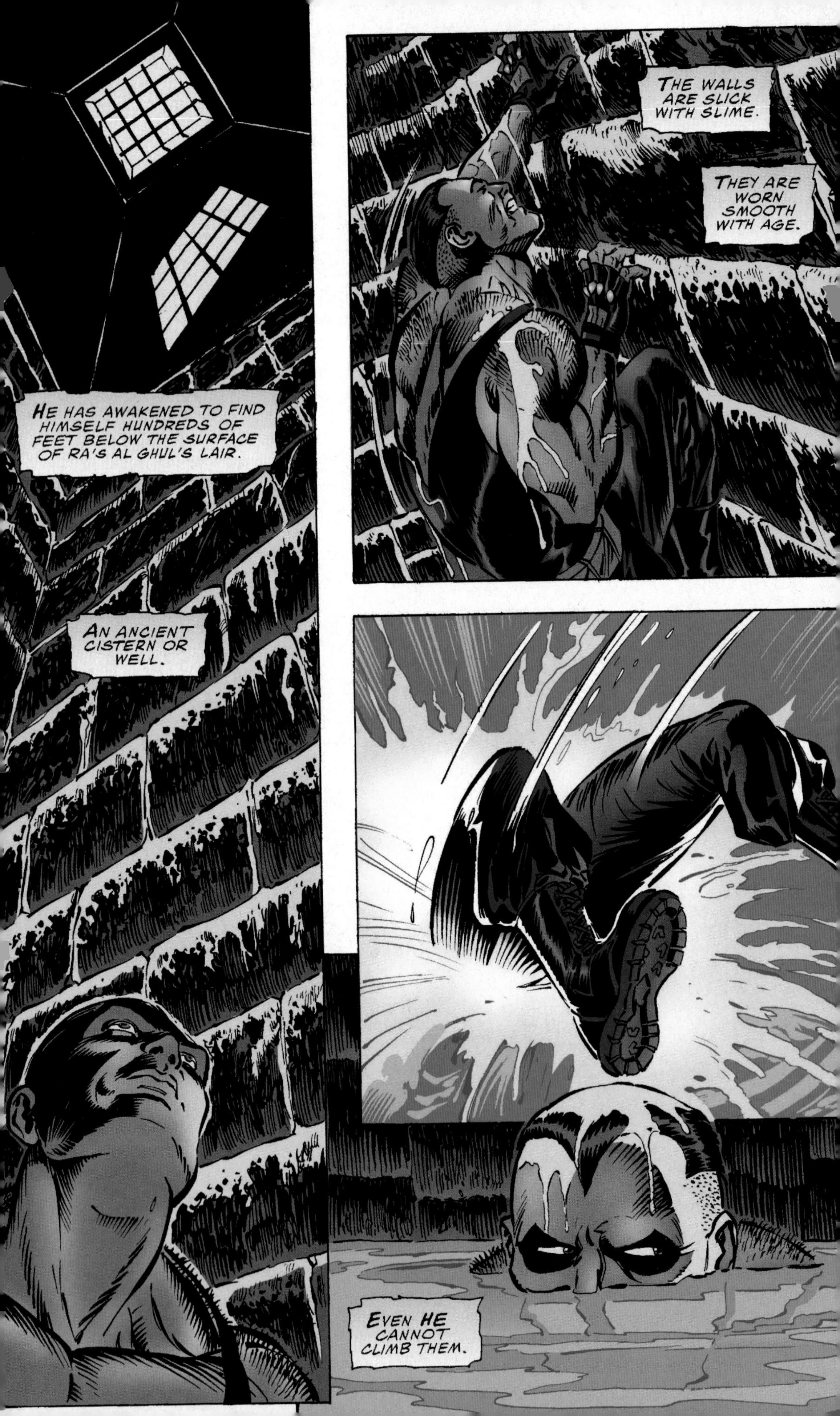
HE HAS AWAKENED TO FIND HIMSELF HUNDREDS OF FEET BELOW THE SURFACE OF RA'S AL GHUL'S LAIR.
AN ANCIENT CISTERN OR WELL.
THE WALLS ARE SLICK WITH SLIME.
THEY ARE WORN SMOOTH WITH AGE.
EVEN HE CANNOT CLIMB THEM.

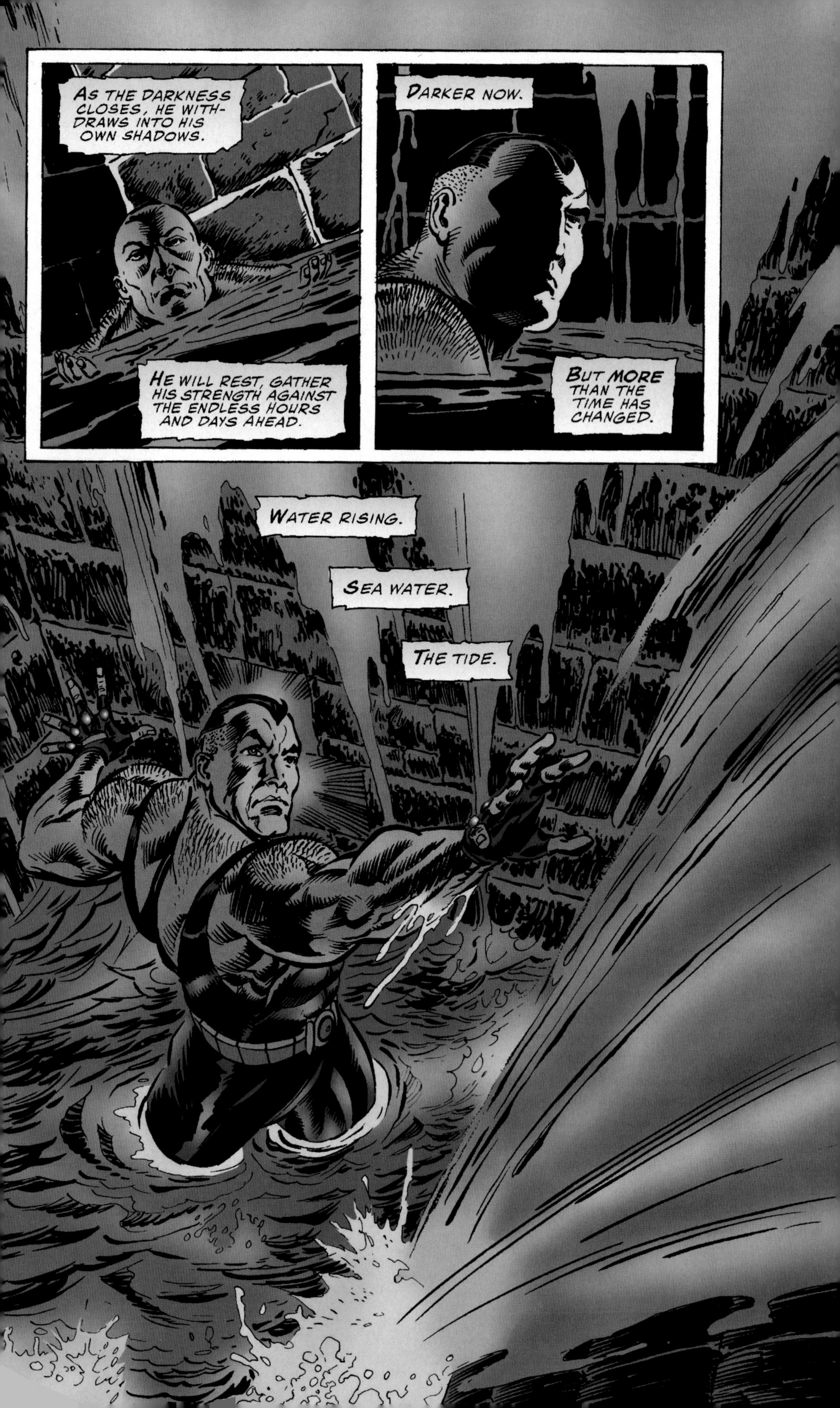

As the darkness closes, he with-draws into his own shadows.
He will rest, gather his strength against the endless hours and days ahead.
Darker now.
But more than the time has changed.
Water rising.
Sea water.
The tide.

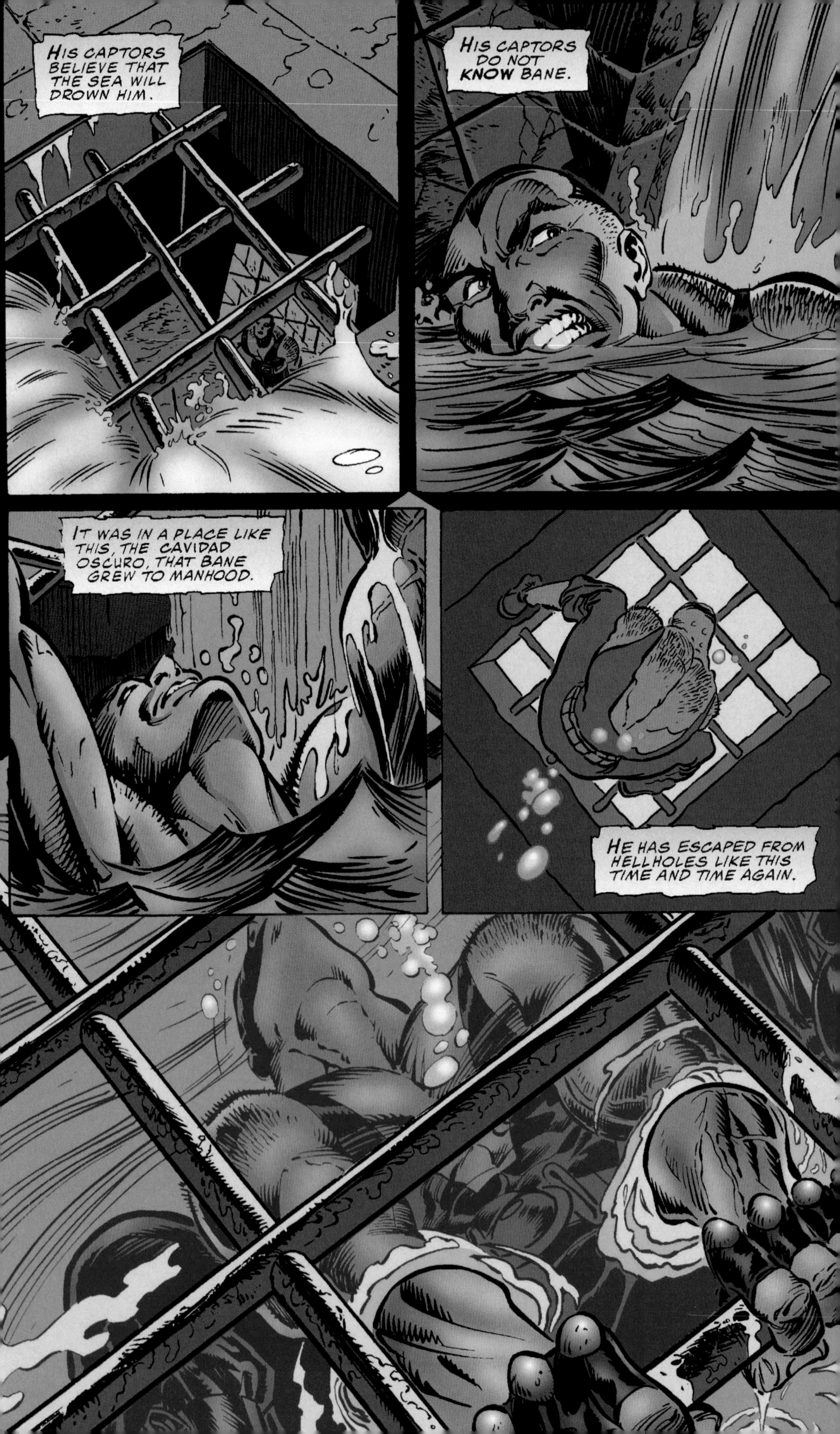
HIS CAPTORS BELIEVE THAT THE SEA WILL DROWN HIM.
HIS CAPTORS DO NOT KNOW BANE.
IT WAS IN A PLACE LIKE THIS, THE CAVIDAD OSCURO, THAT BANE GREW TO MANHOOD.
HE HAS ESCAPED FROM HELLHOLES LIKE THIS TIME AND TIME AGAIN.

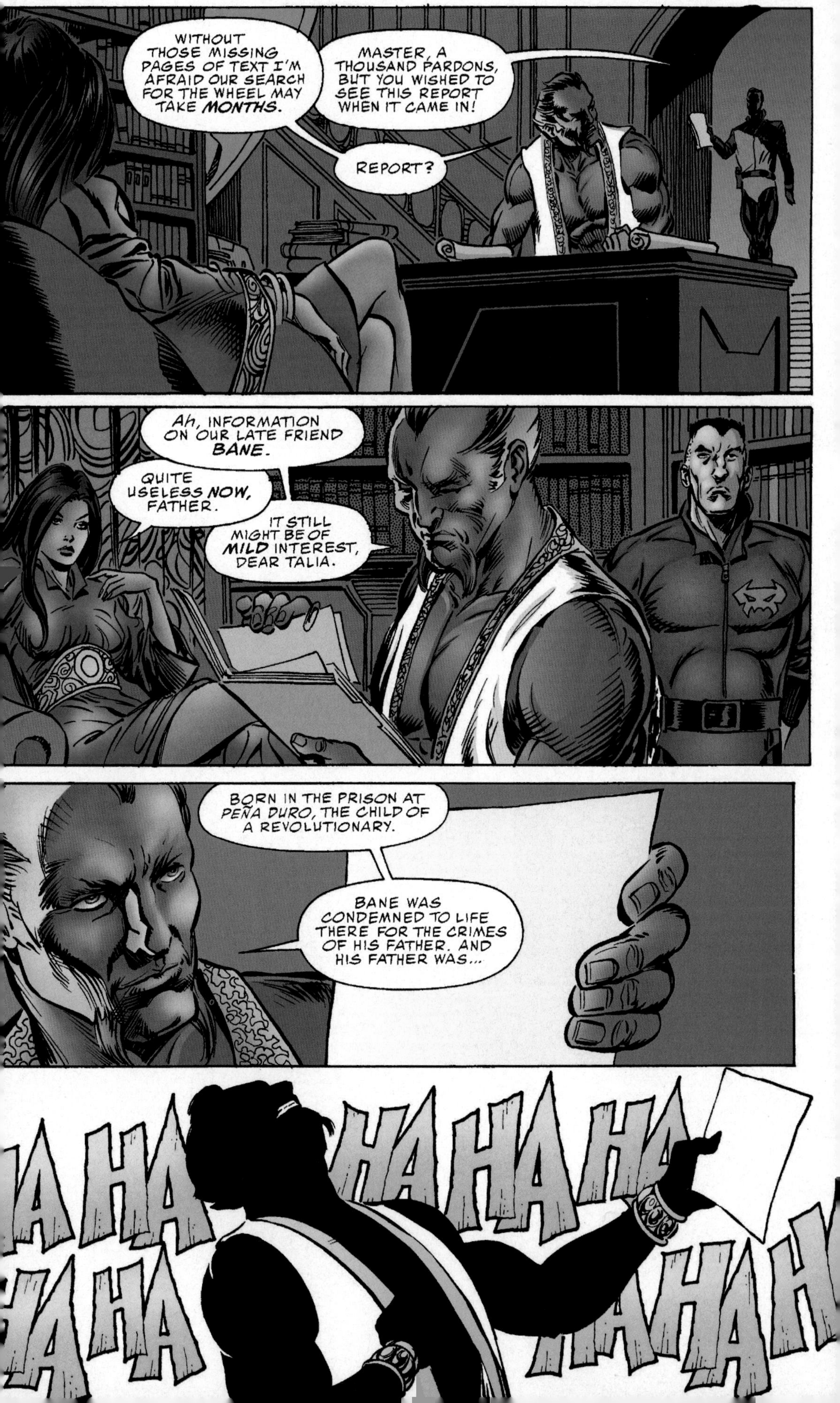
WITHOUT THOSE MISSING PAGES OF TEXT I'M AFRAID OUR SEARCH FOR THE WHEEL MAY TAKE MONTHS.
MASTER, A THOUSAND PARDONS, BUT YOU WISHED TO SEE THIS REPORT WHEN IT CAME IN!
REPORT?
Ah, INFORMATION ON OUR LATE FRIEND BANE.
QUITE USELESS NOW, FATHER.
IT STILL MIGHT BE OF MILD INTEREST, DEAR TALIA.
BORN IN THE PRISON AT PEÑA DURO, THE CHILD OF A REVOLUTIONARY.
BANE WAS CONDEMNED TO LIFE THERE FOR THE CRIMES OF HIS FATHER. AND HIS FATHER WAS...
HAHAHAHAHA HAHAHAHAH

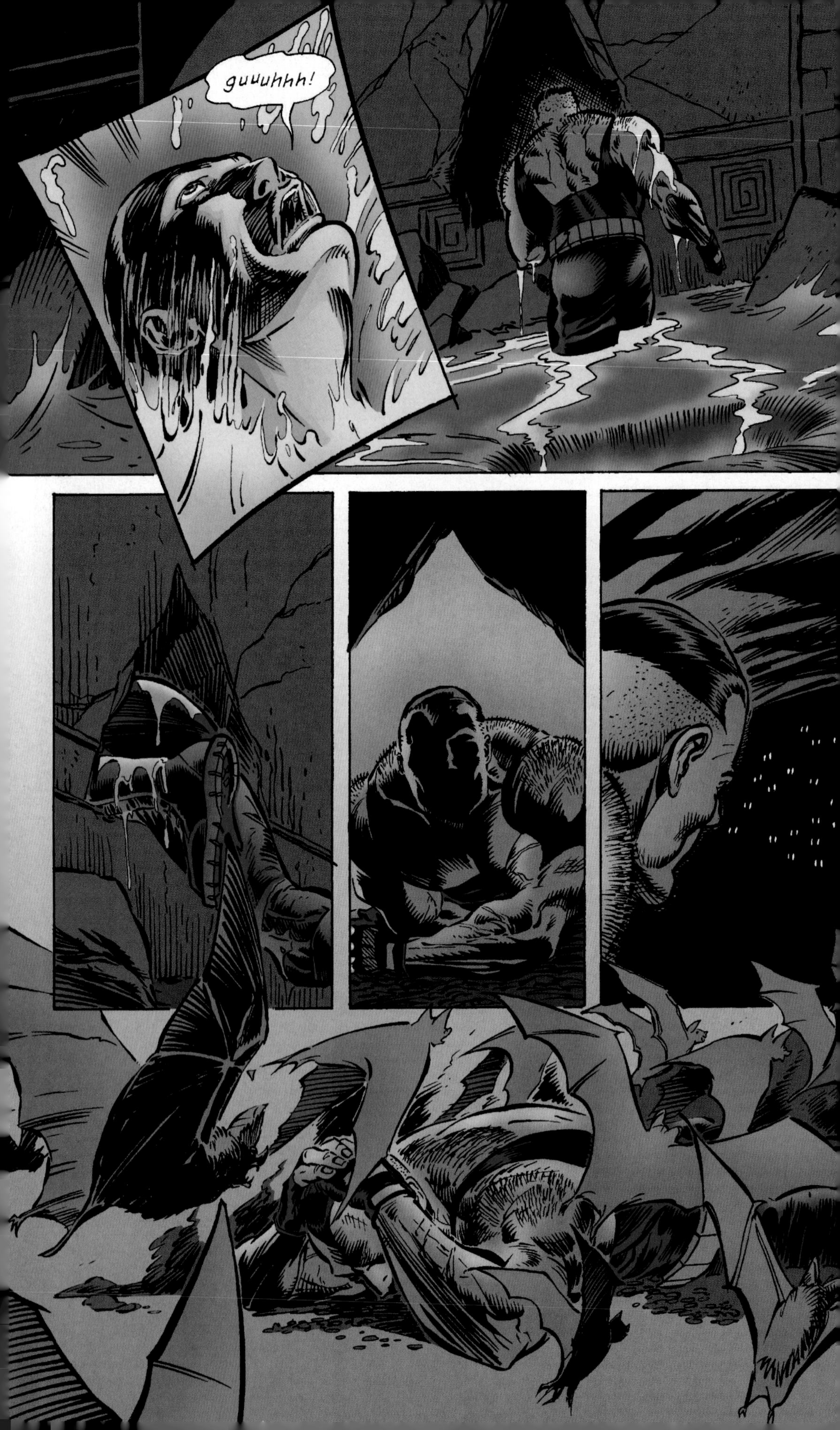
guuuhhh!

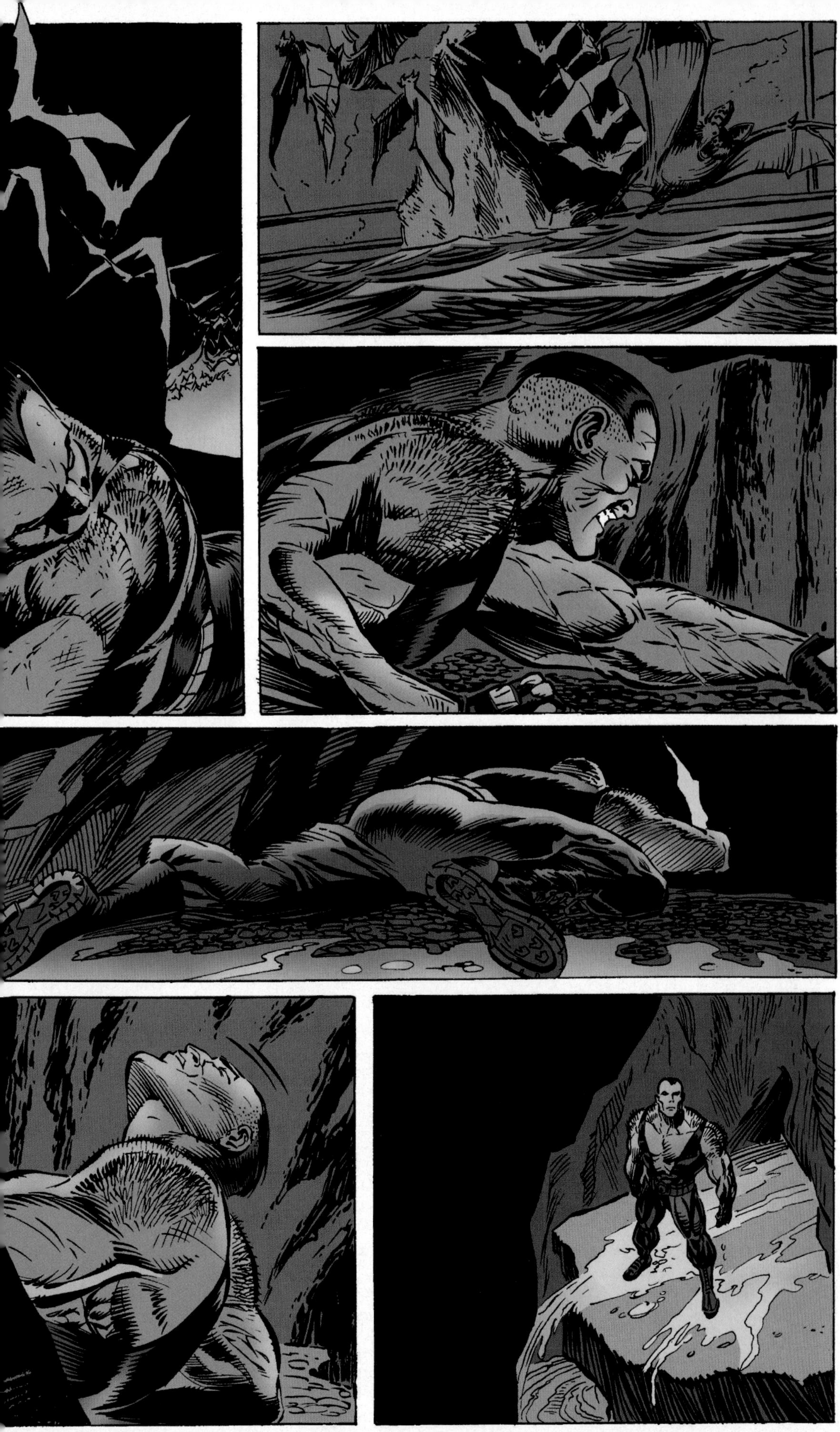

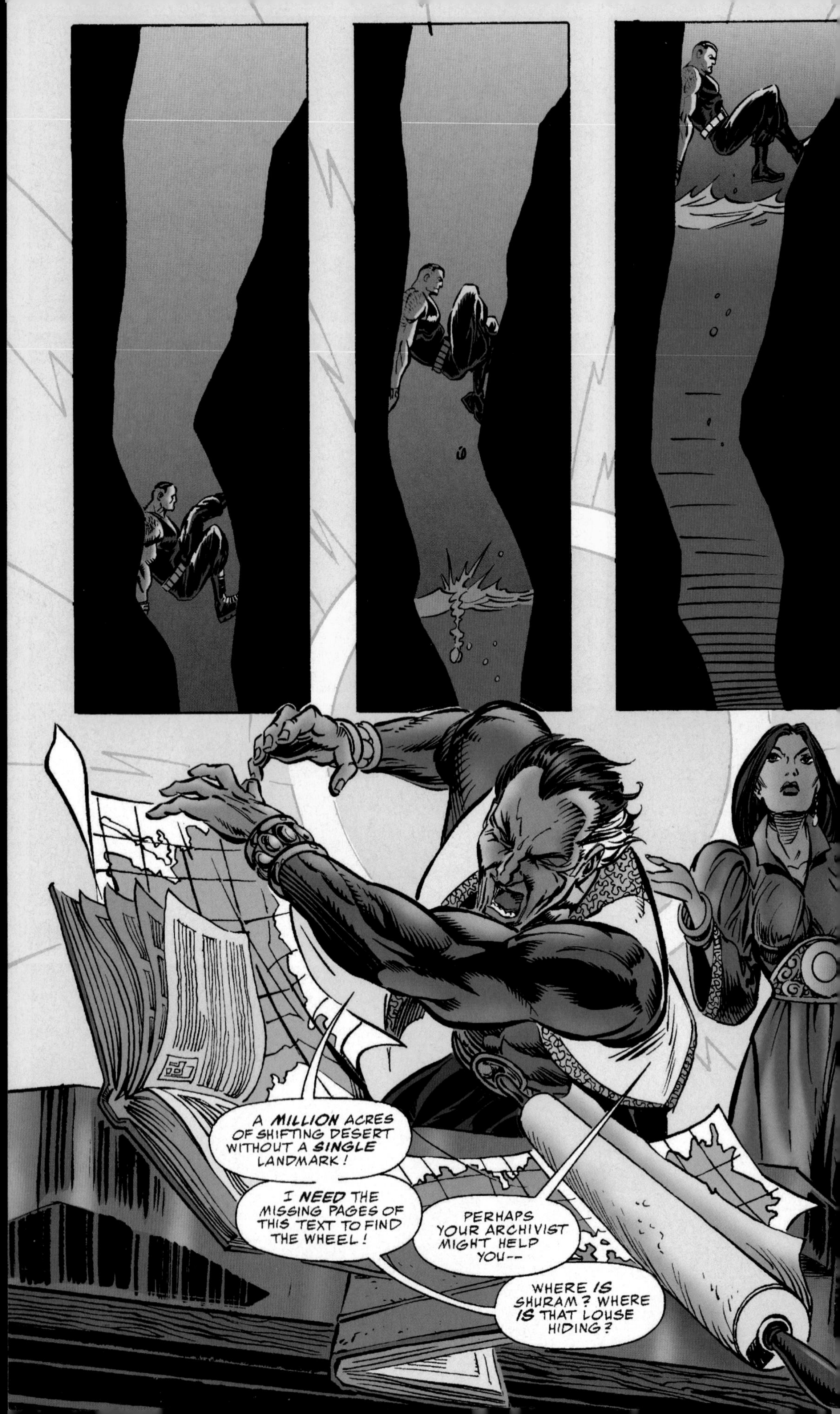
A MILLION ACRES OF SHIFTING DESERT WITHOUT A SINGLE LANDMARK!
I NEED THE MISSING PAGES OF THIS TEXT TO FIND THE WHEEL!
PERHAPS YOUR ARCHIVIST MIGHT HELP YOU--
WHERE IS SHURAM? WHERE IS THAT LOUSE HIDING?

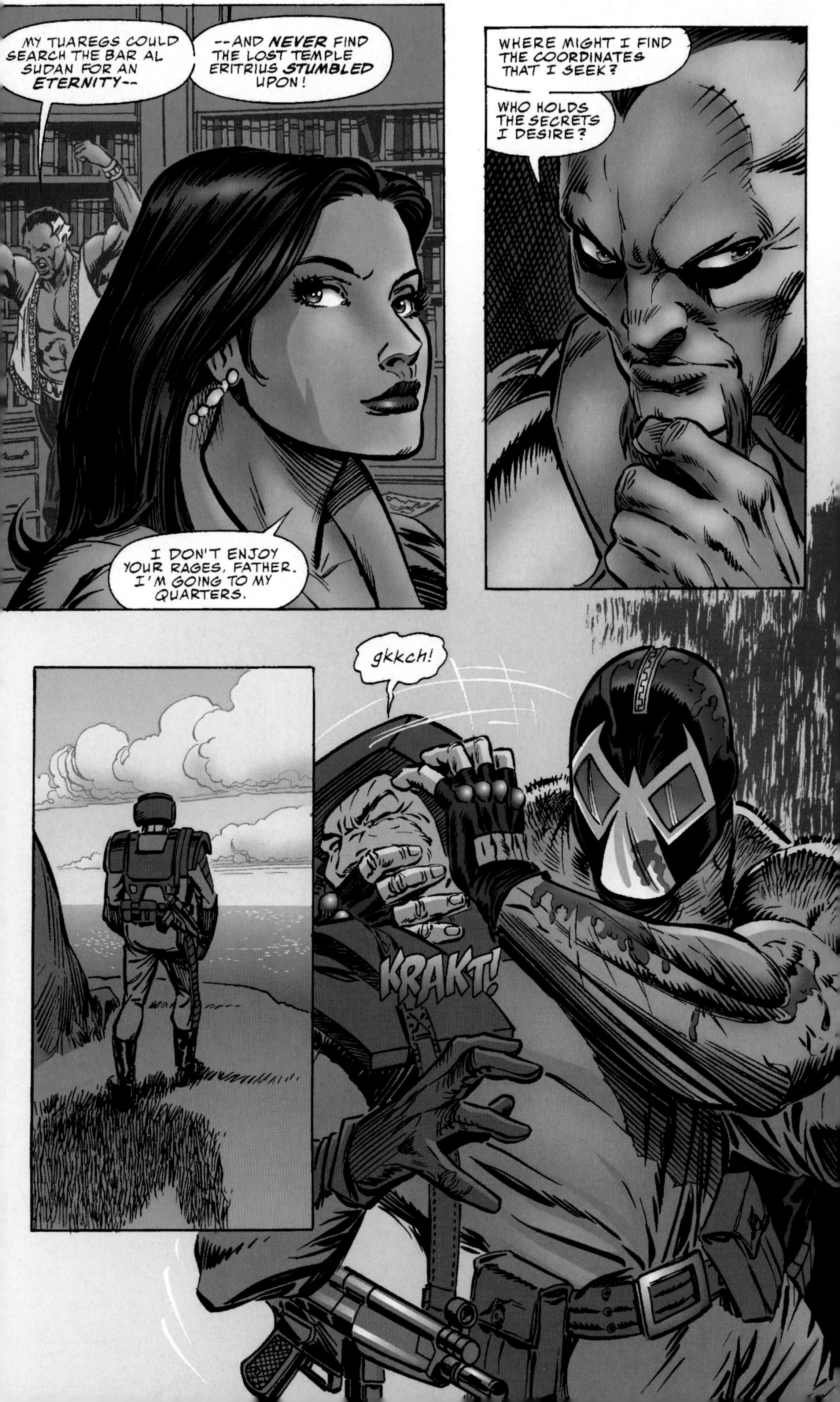
MY TUAREGS COULD SEARCH THE BAR AL SUDAN FOR AN ETERNITY--
--AND NEVER FIND THE LOST TEMPLE ERITRIUS STUMBLED UPON!
I DON'T ENJOY YOUR RAGES, FATHER. I'M GOING TO MY QUARTERS.
WHERE MIGHT I FIND THE COORDINATES THAT I SEEK?
WHO HOLDS THE SECRETS I DESIRE?
gkkch!
KRAKT!

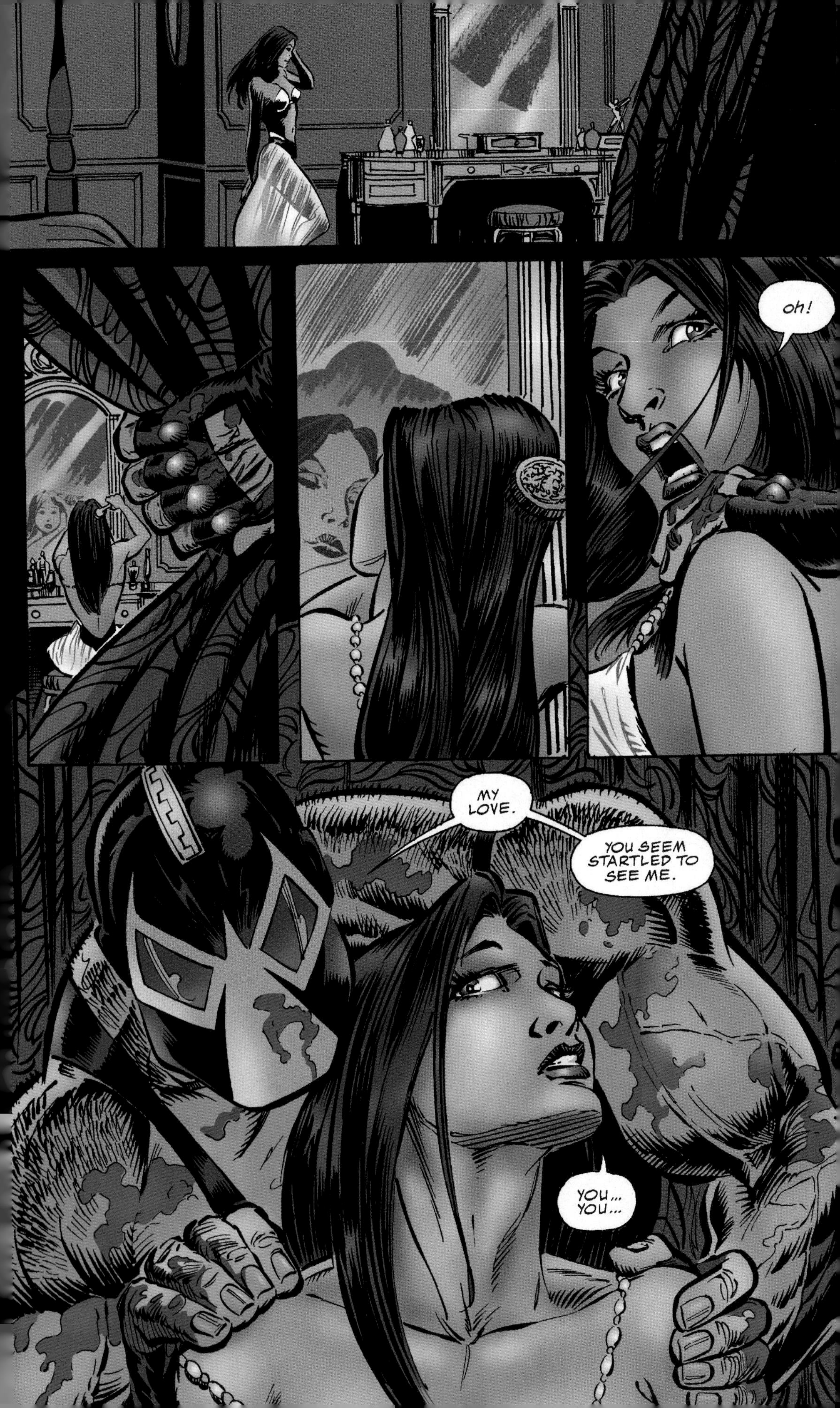
oh!
MY LOVE.
YOU SEEM STARTLED TO SEE ME.
YOU... YOU...

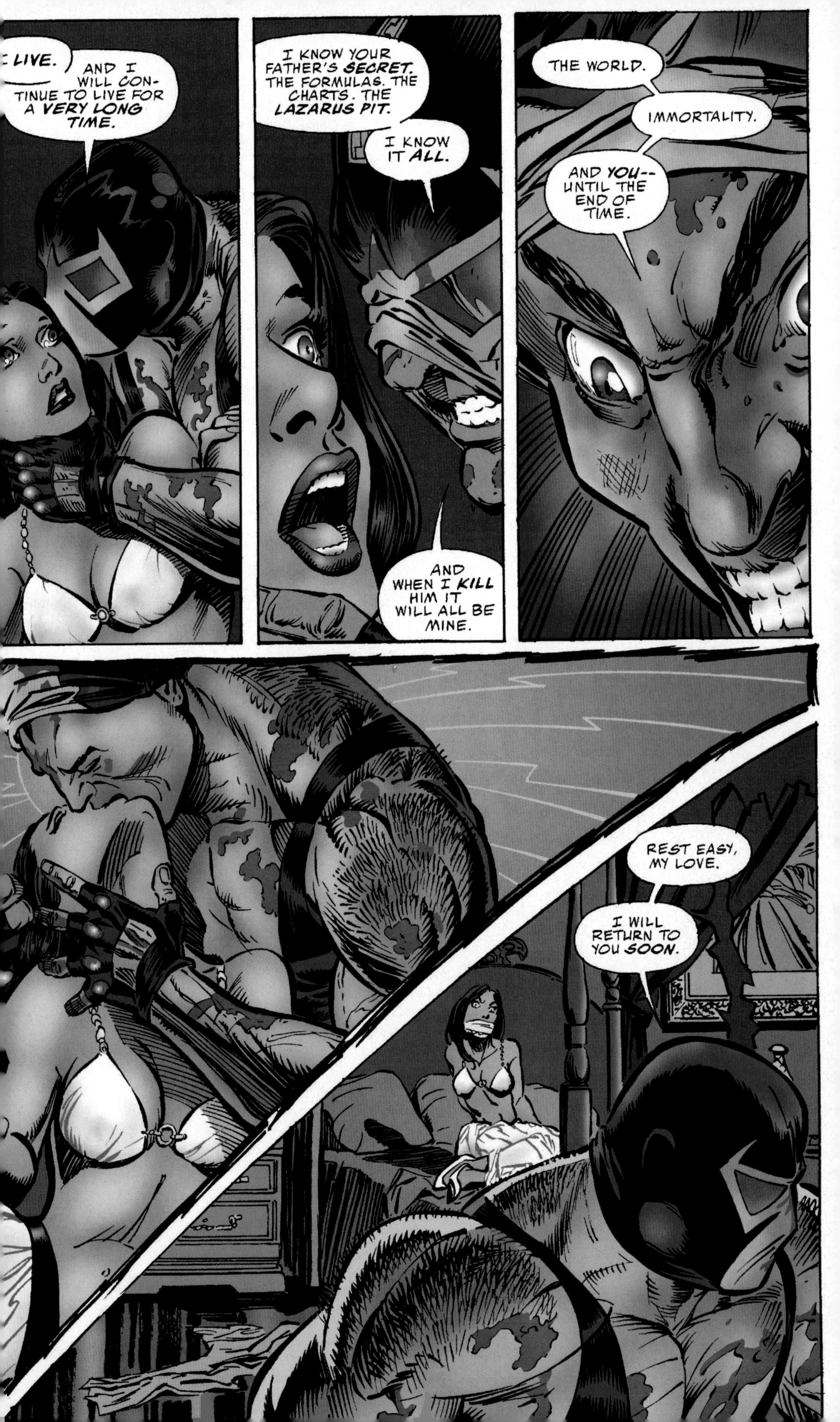

LIVE.
AND I WILL CONTINUE TO LIVE FOR A VERY LONG TIME.
I KNOW YOUR FATHER'S SECRET. THE FORMULAS. THE CHARTS. THE LAZARUS PIT.
I KNOW IT ALL.
AND WHEN I KILL HIM IT WILL ALL BE MINE.
THE WORLD.
IMMORTALITY.
AND YOU-- UNTIL THE END OF TIME.
REST EASY, MY LOVE.
I WILL RETURN TO YOU SOON.

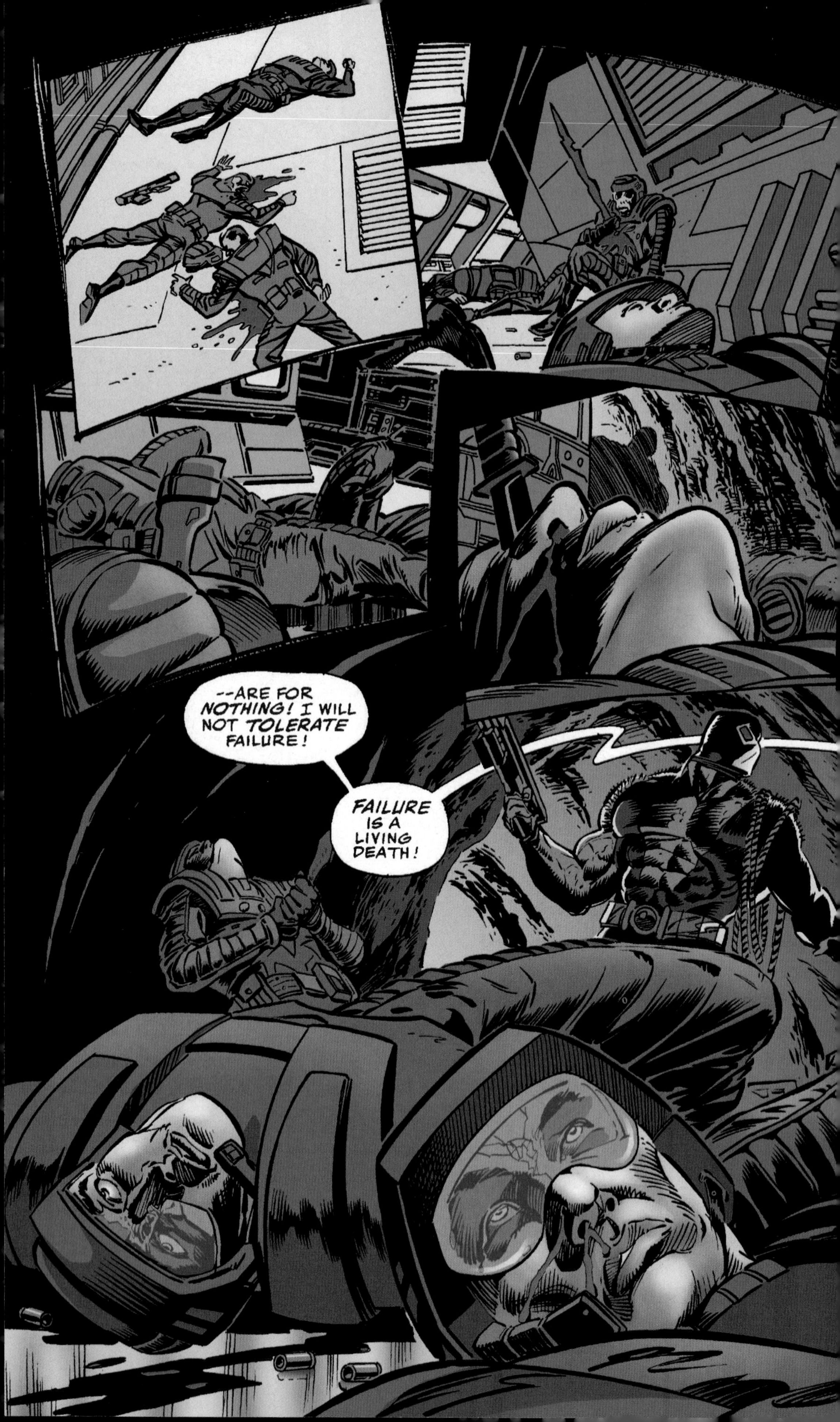
--ARE FOR NOTHING! I WILL NOT TOLERATE FAILURE!
FAILURE IS A LIVING DEATH!

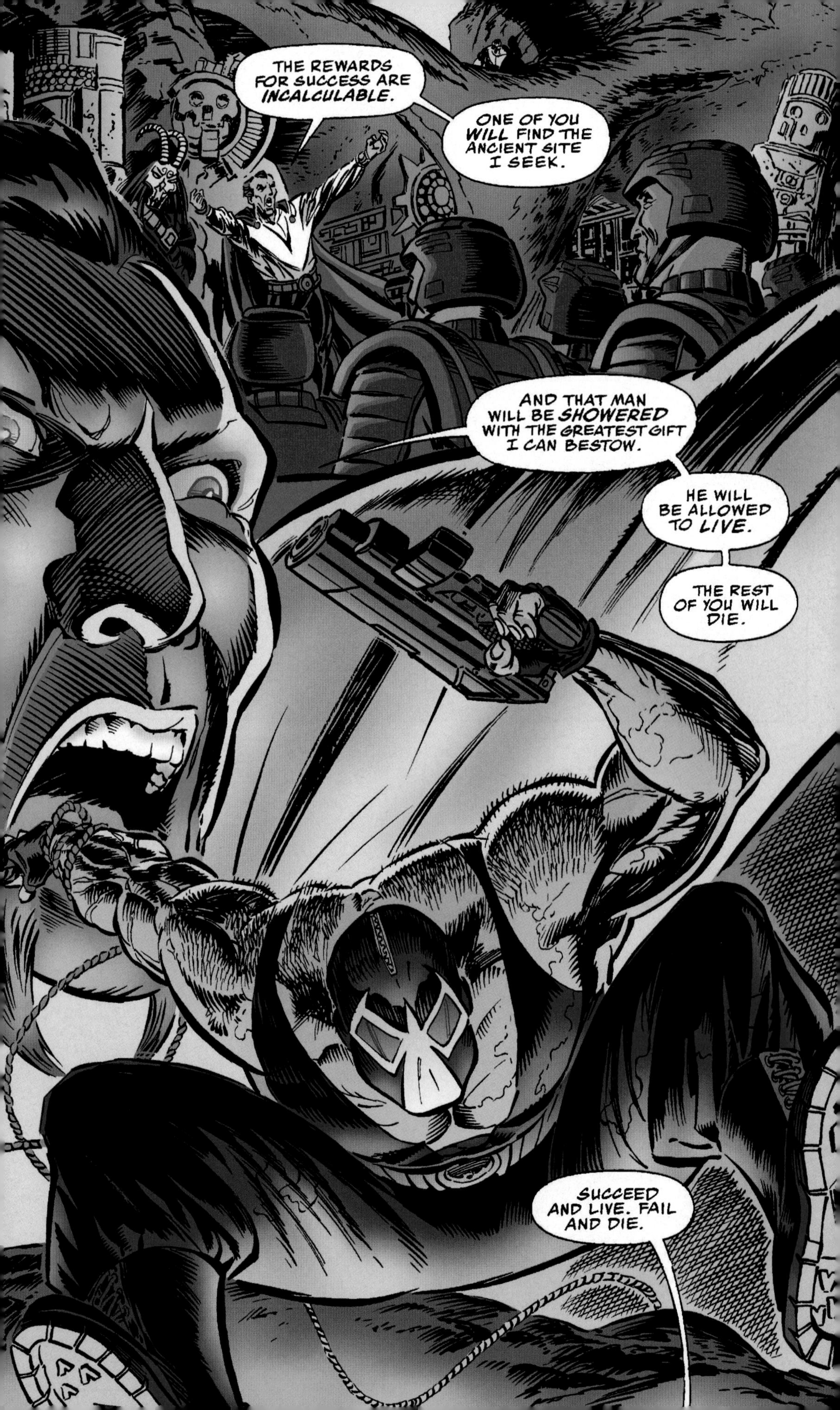

THE REWARDS FOR SUCCESS ARE INCALCULABLE.
ONE OF YOU WILL FIND THE ANCIENT SITE I SEEK.
AND THAT MAN WILL BE SHOWERED WITH THE GREATEST GIFT I CAN BESTOW.
HE WILL BE ALLOWED TO LIVE.
THE REST OF YOU WILL DIE.
SUCCEED AND LIVE. FAIL AND DIE.

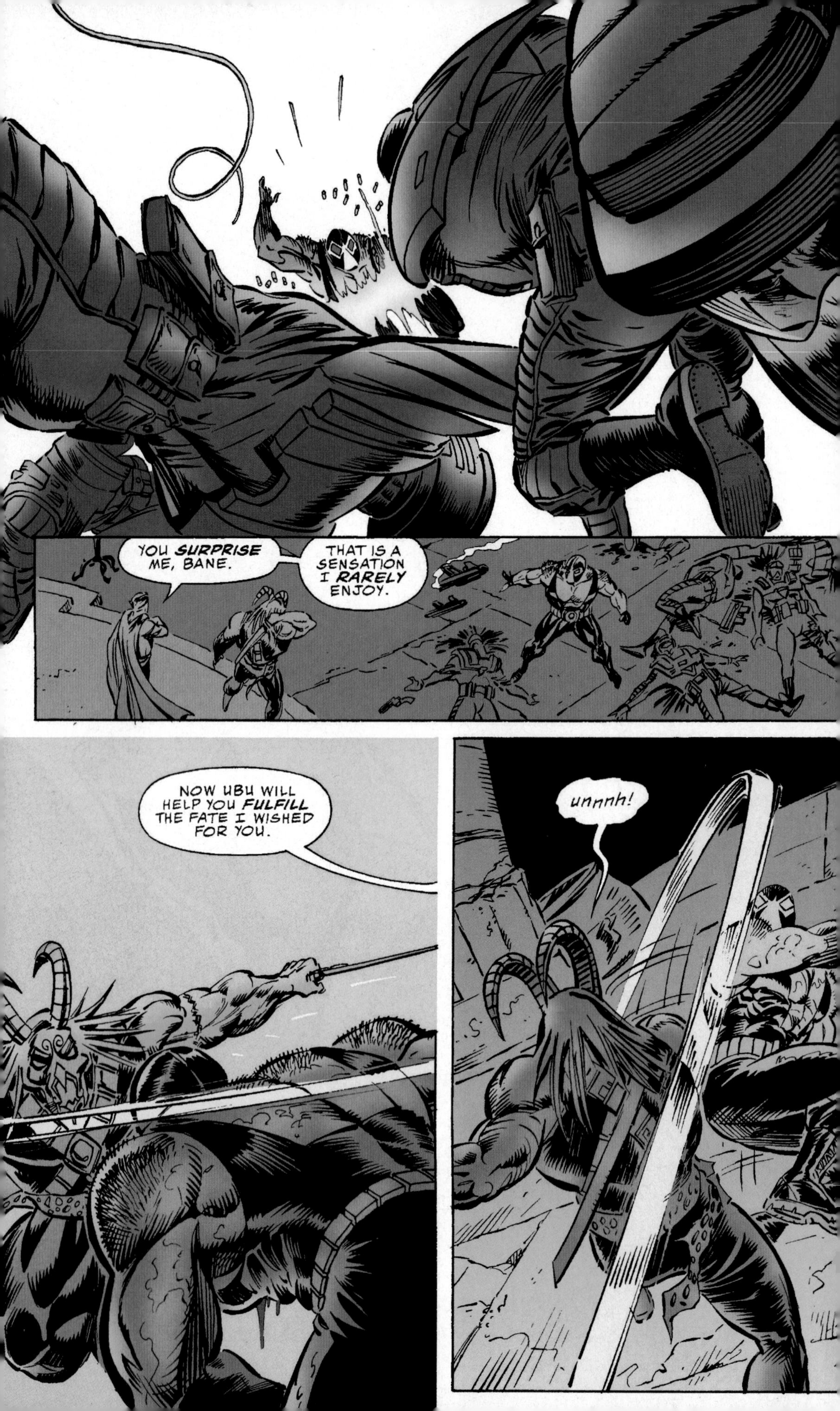
YOU SURPRISE ME, BANE.
THAT IS A SENSATION I RARELY ENJOY.
NOW UBU WILL HELP YOU FULFILL THE FATE I WISHED FOR YOU.
unnnh!

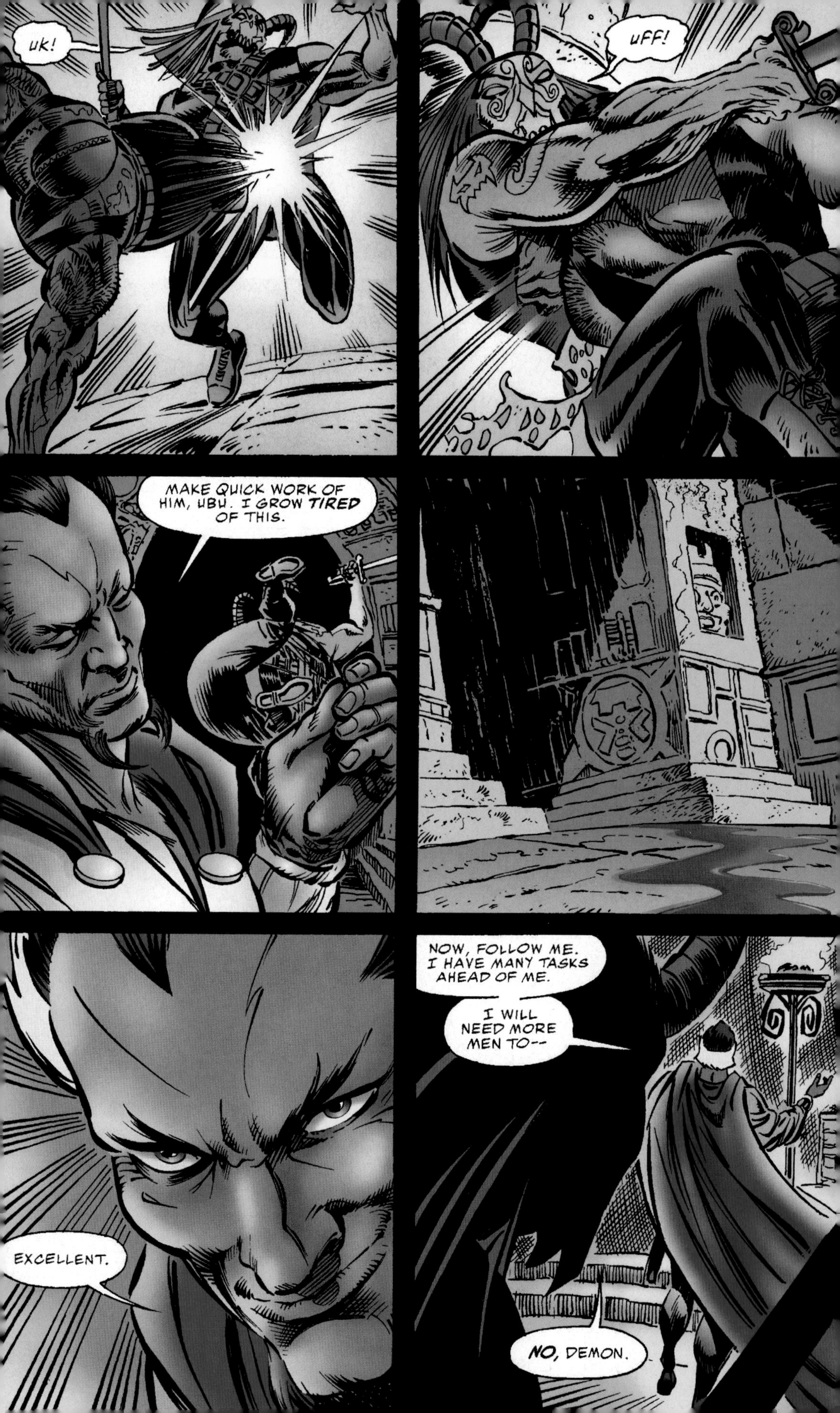
UK!
UFF!
MAKE QUICK WORK OF HIM, UBU. I GROW TIRED OF THIS.
EXCELLENT.
NOW, FOLLOW ME. I HAVE MANY TASKS AHEAD OF ME.
I WILL NEED MORE MEN TO--
NO, DEMON.

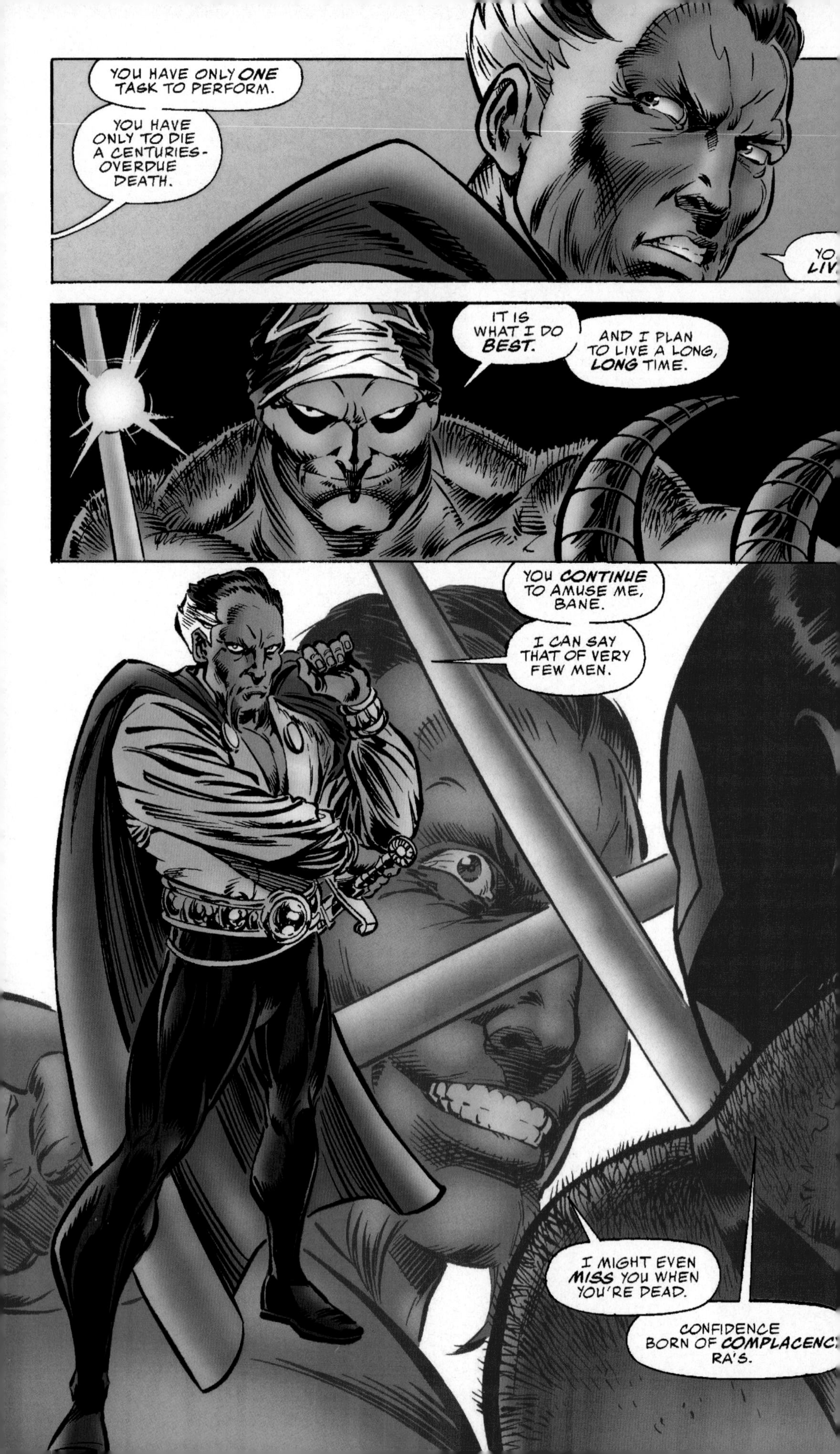
YOU HAVE ONLY **ONE** TASK TO PERFORM.
YOU HAVE ONLY TO DIE A CENTURIES-OVERDUE DEATH.
IT IS WHAT I DO **BEST**.
AND I PLAN TO LIVE A LONG, **LONG** TIME.
YOU **CONTINUE** TO AMUSE ME, BANE.
I CAN SAY THAT OF VERY FEW MEN.
I MIGHT EVEN **MISS** YOU WHEN YOU'RE DEAD.
CONFIDENCE BORN OF **COMPLACENC** RA'S.

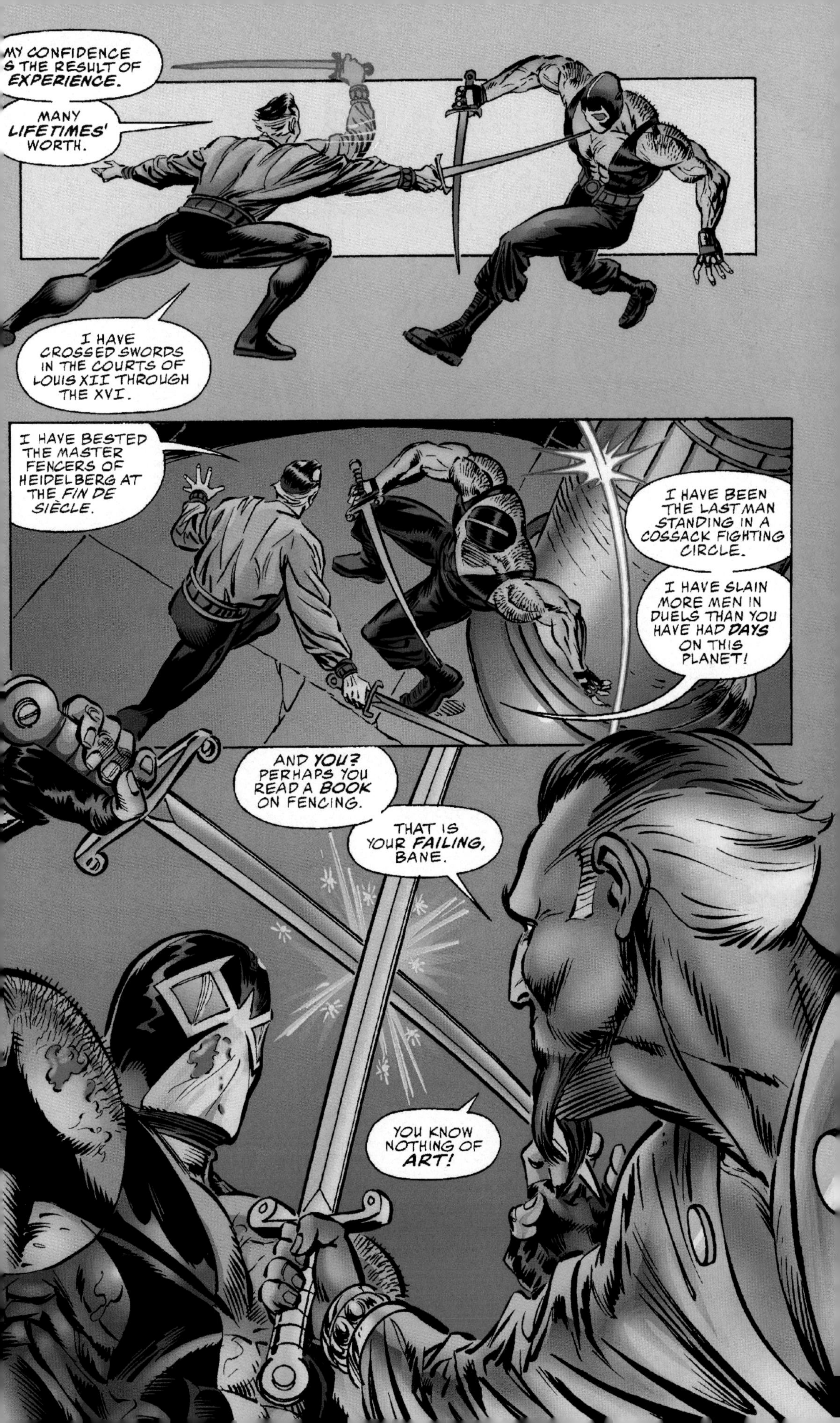
MY CONFIDENCE IS THE RESULT OF EXPERIENCE.
MANY LIFETIMES' WORTH.
I HAVE CROSSED SWORDS IN THE COURTS OF LOUIS XII THROUGH THE XVI.
I HAVE BESTED THE MASTER FENCERS OF HEIDELBERG AT THE FIN DE SIÈCLE.
I HAVE BEEN THE LAST MAN STANDING IN A COSSACK FIGHTING CIRCLE.
I HAVE SLAIN MORE MEN IN DUELS THAN YOU HAVE HAD DAYS ON THIS PLANET!
AND YOU? PERHAPS YOU READ A BOOK ON FENCING.
THAT IS YOUR FAILING, BANE.
YOU KNOW NOTHING OF ART!

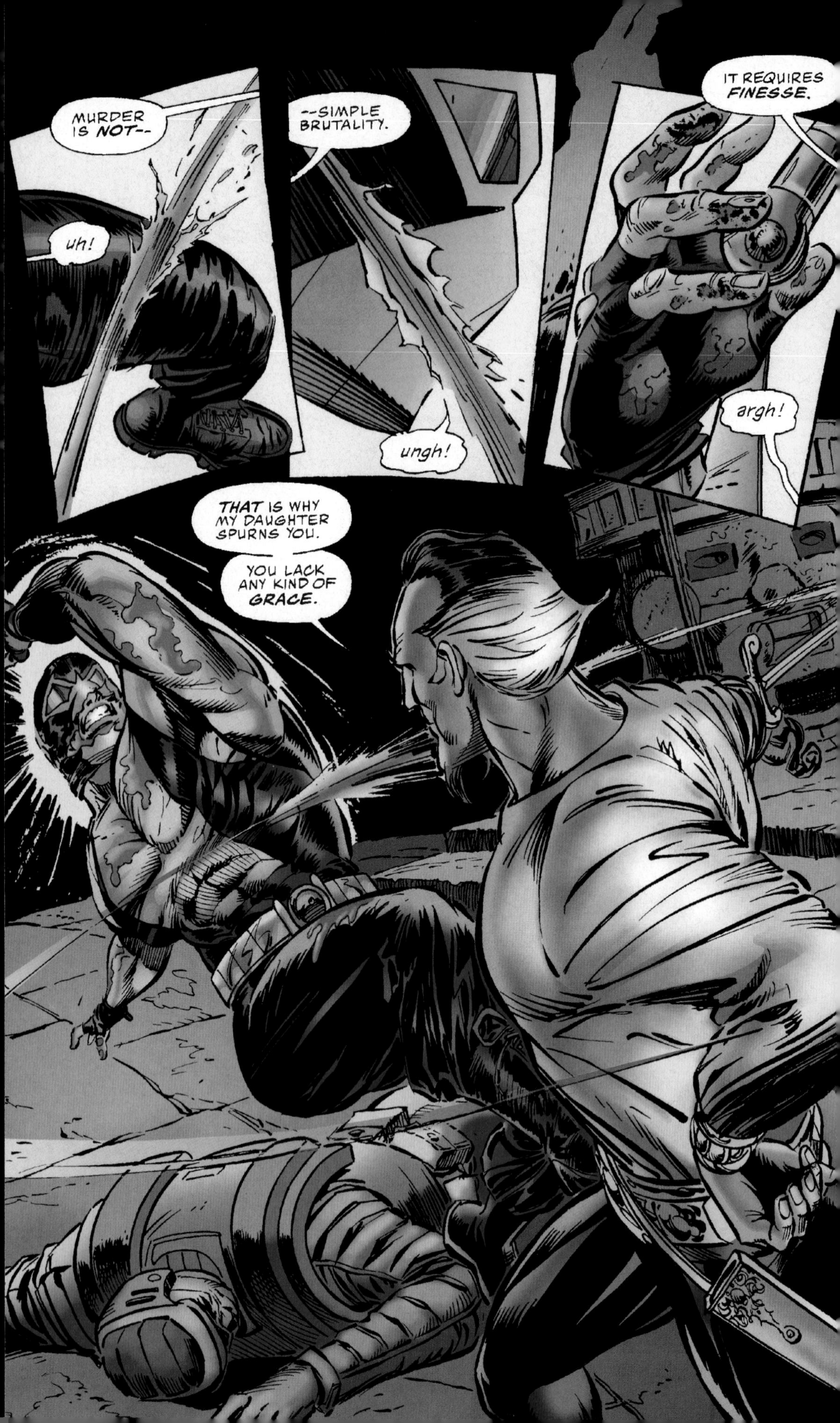

MURDER IS NOT--
uh!
--SIMPLE BRUTALITY.
ungh!
IT REQUIRES FINESSE.
argh!
THAT IS WHY MY DAUGHTER SPURNS YOU.
YOU LACK ANY KIND OF GRACE.

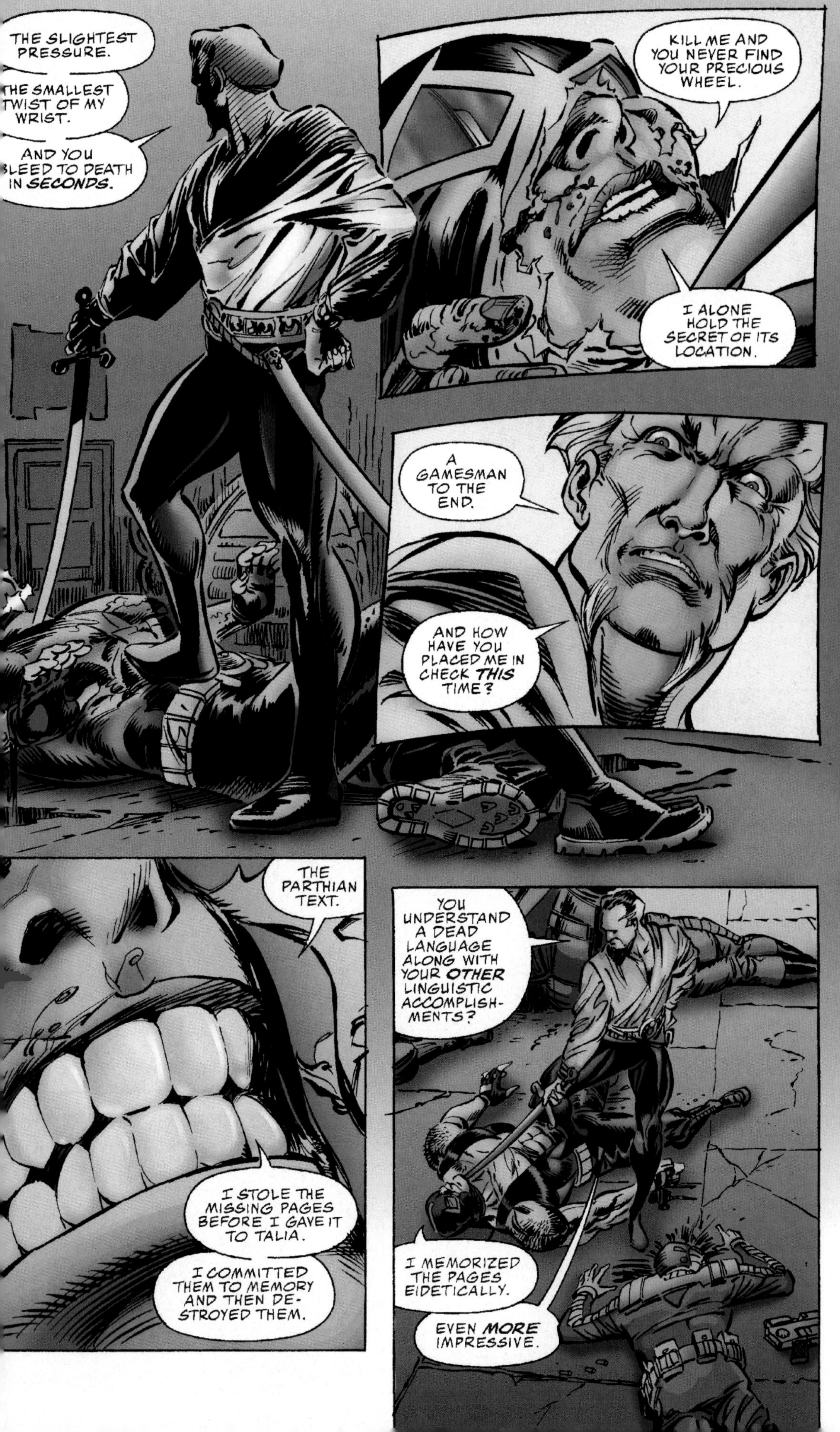
THE SLIGHTEST PRESSURE.
THE SMALLEST TWIST OF MY WRIST.
AND YOU BLEED TO DEATH IN *SECONDS*.
KILL ME AND YOU NEVER FIND YOUR PRECIOUS WHEEL.
I ALONE HOLD THE SECRET OF ITS LOCATION.
A GAMESMAN TO THE END.
AND HOW HAVE YOU PLACED ME IN CHECK *THIS* TIME?
THE PARTHIAN TEXT.
I STOLE THE MISSING PAGES BEFORE I GAVE IT TO TALIA.
I COMMITTED THEM TO MEMORY AND THEN DE-STROYED THEM.
YOU UNDERSTAND A DEAD LANGUAGE ALONG WITH YOUR *OTHER* LINGUISTIC ACCOMPLISH-MENTS?
I MEMORIZED THE PAGES EIDETICALLY.
EVEN *MORE* IMPRESSIVE.

YOU ARE FAR TOO DANGEROUS TO *LIVE,* BANE.

YOU HAVE DONE WHAT FEW MEN IN A THOUSAND YEARS HAVE ACCOMPLISHED.

YOU HAVE *DEFIED* ME. YOU HAVE *THWARTED* ME. YOU HAVE *BETRAYED* ME.

YOU HAVE A MIND *EQUAL* TO THE GREATEST I HAVE KNOWN, EVEN IF IT IS INFERIOR TO MY *OWN.*

YOU ARE TREACHEROUS AND VAIN. LOYALTY MEANS NOTHING. YOU ARE A BEING OF PURE *SELF.*

YOU ARE *ENTIRELY* WITHOUT MORALS OR ANY VIRTUE SAVE COURAGE.

YOU MAY JUST BE THE *SECOND* MOST DANGEROUS MAN ALIVE.

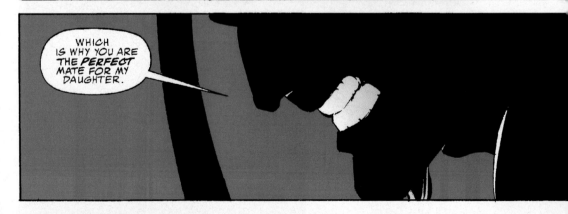

WHICH IS WHY YOU ARE THE *PERFECT* MATE FOR MY DAUGHTER.

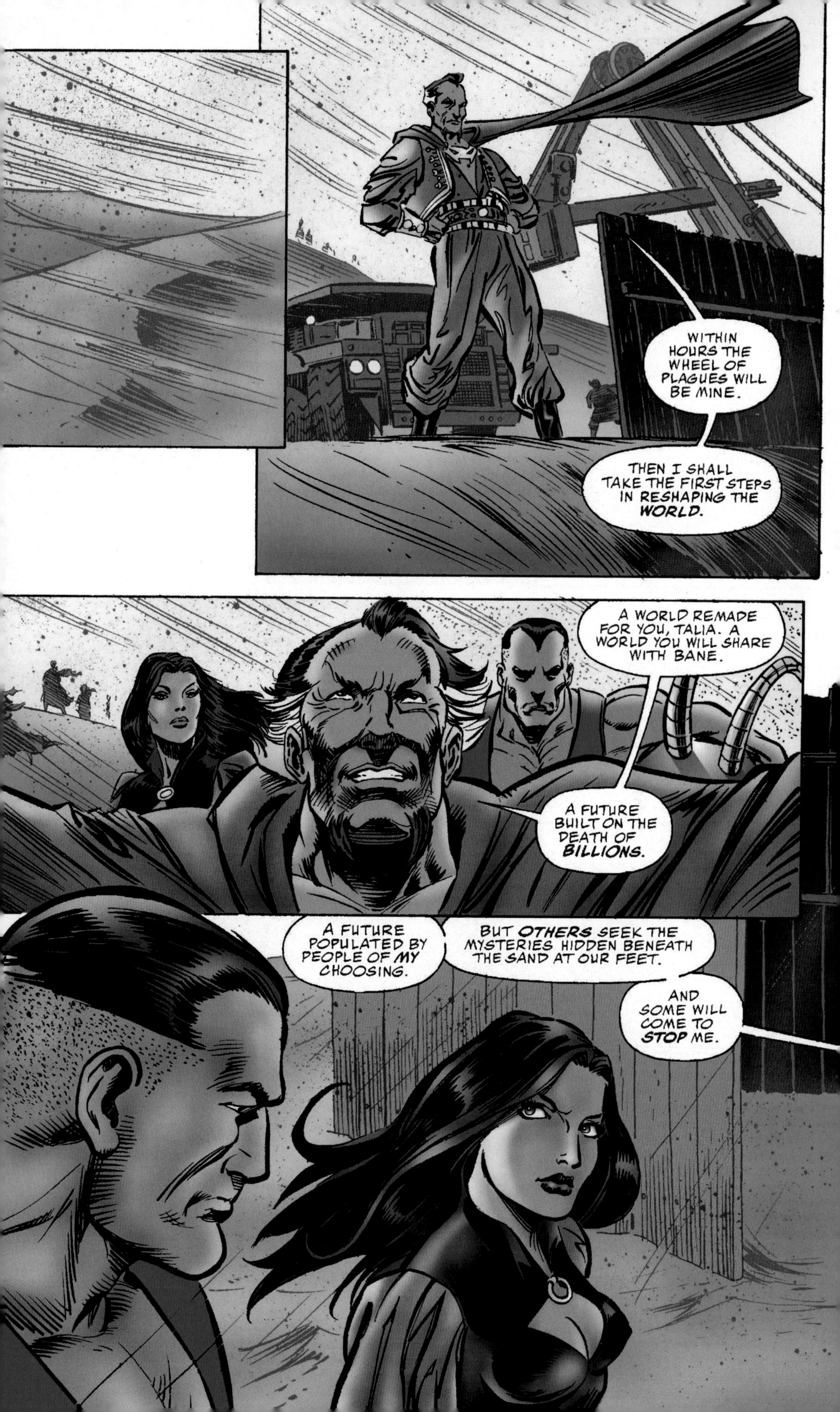
WITHIN HOURS THE WHEEL OF PLAGUES WILL BE MINE.
THEN I SHALL TAKE THE FIRST STEPS IN RESHAPING THE WORLD.
A WORLD REMADE FOR YOU, TALIA. A WORLD YOU WILL SHARE WITH BANE.
A FUTURE BUILT ON THE DEATH OF BILLIONS.
A FUTURE POPULATED BY PEOPLE OF MY CHOOSING.
BUT OTHERS SEEK THE MYSTERIES HIDDEN BENEATH THE SAND AT OUR FEET.
AND SOME WILL COME TO STOP ME.

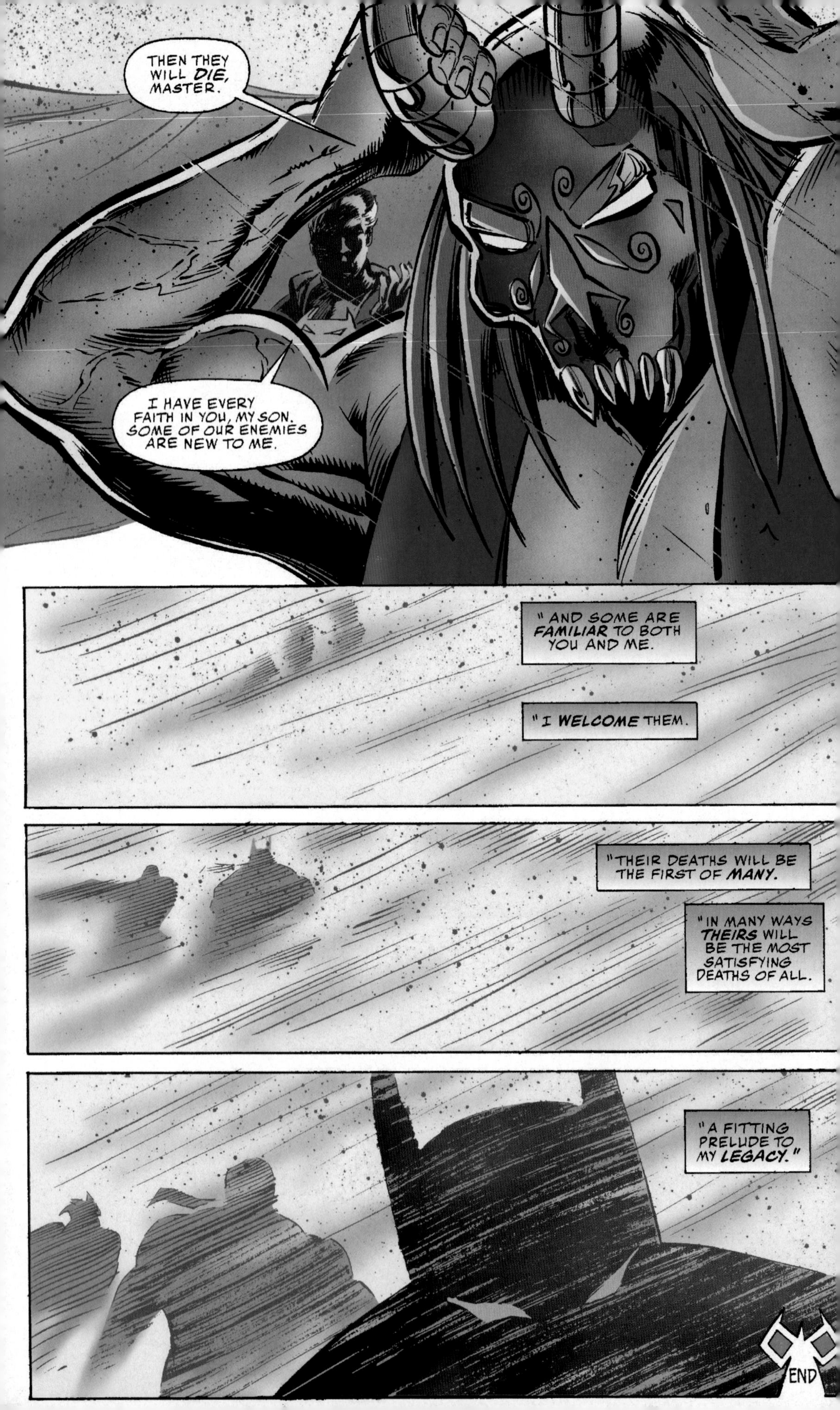
THEN THEY WILL DIE, MASTER.
I HAVE EVERY FAITH IN YOU, MY SON. SOME OF OUR ENEMIES ARE NEW TO ME.
"AND SOME ARE FAMILIAR TO BOTH YOU AND ME.
"I WELCOME THEM.
"THEIR DEATHS WILL BE THE FIRST OF MANY.
"IN MANY WAYS THEIRS WILL BE THE MOST SATISFYING DEATHS OF ALL.
"A FITTING PRELUDE TO MY LEGACY."
END

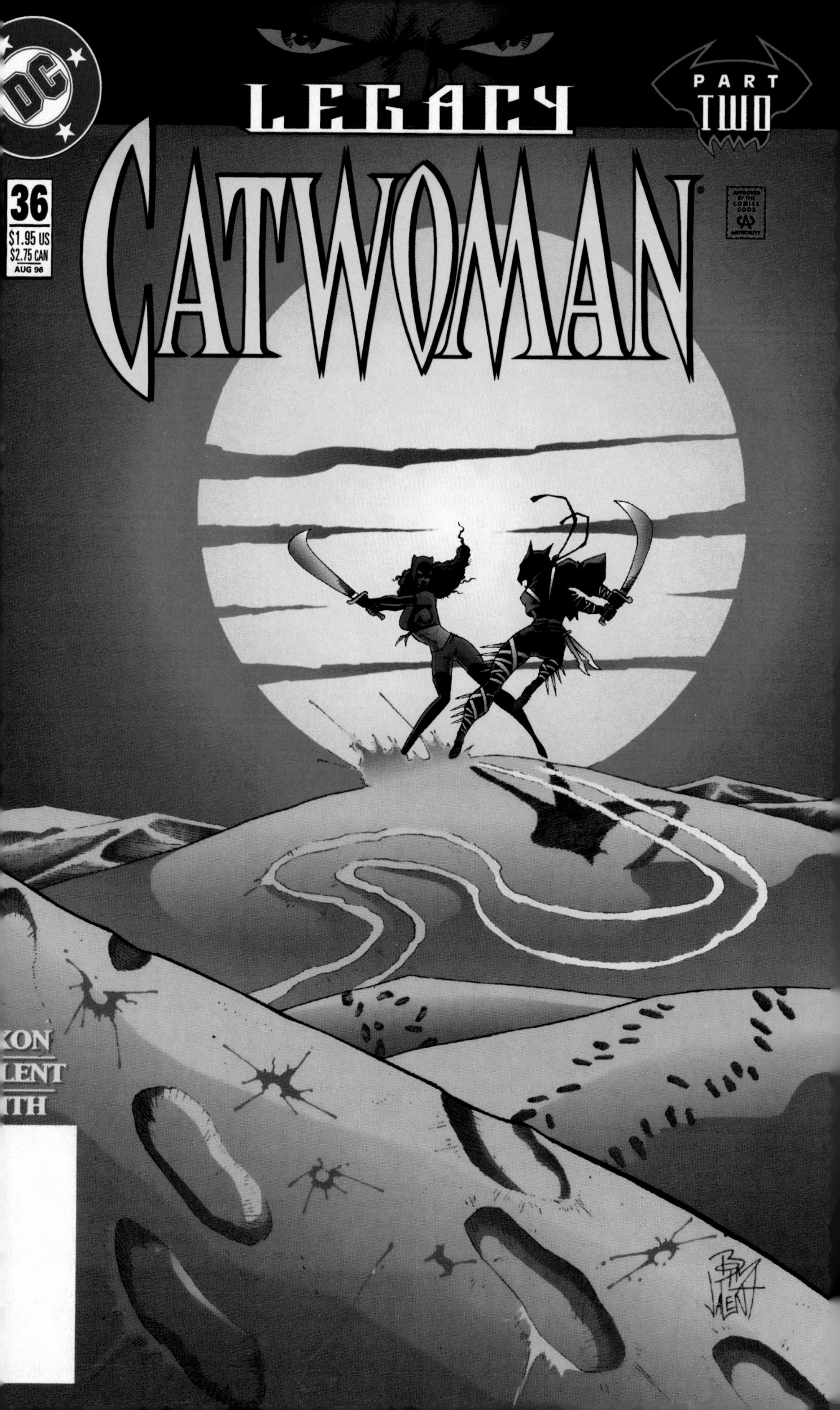

DC
LEGACY
PART TWO
CATWOMAN
36
$1.95 US
$2.75 CAN
AUG 96
APPROVED BY THE COMICS CODE AUTHORITY
KON
LENT
ITH

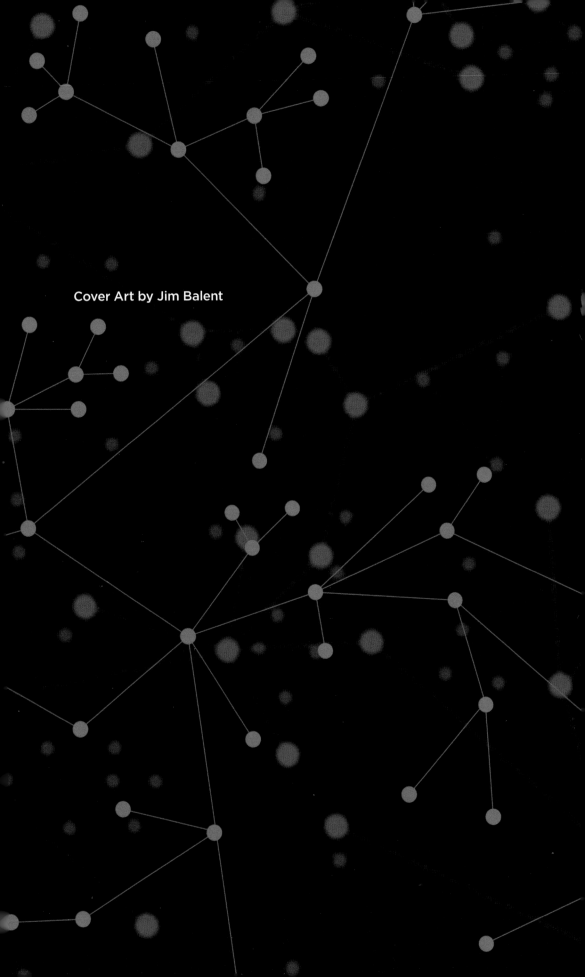

Cover Art by Jim Balent

THE BEST OF ENEMIES
I'M ABOUT TO DROWN IN A DESERT.
I'D STOP TO APPRECIATE THE IRONY IF I WASN'T IN SUCH A PANIC.
IRONY'S WASTED ON ME, I GUESS.
STORY-CHUCK DIXON
ARTISTS-JIM BALENT & BOB SMITH
COLORIST-BUZZ SETZER
LETTERER-ALBERT DE GUZMAN
ASSOCIATE EDITOR-JORDAN B. GORFINKEL
EDITOR-DENNY O'NEIL

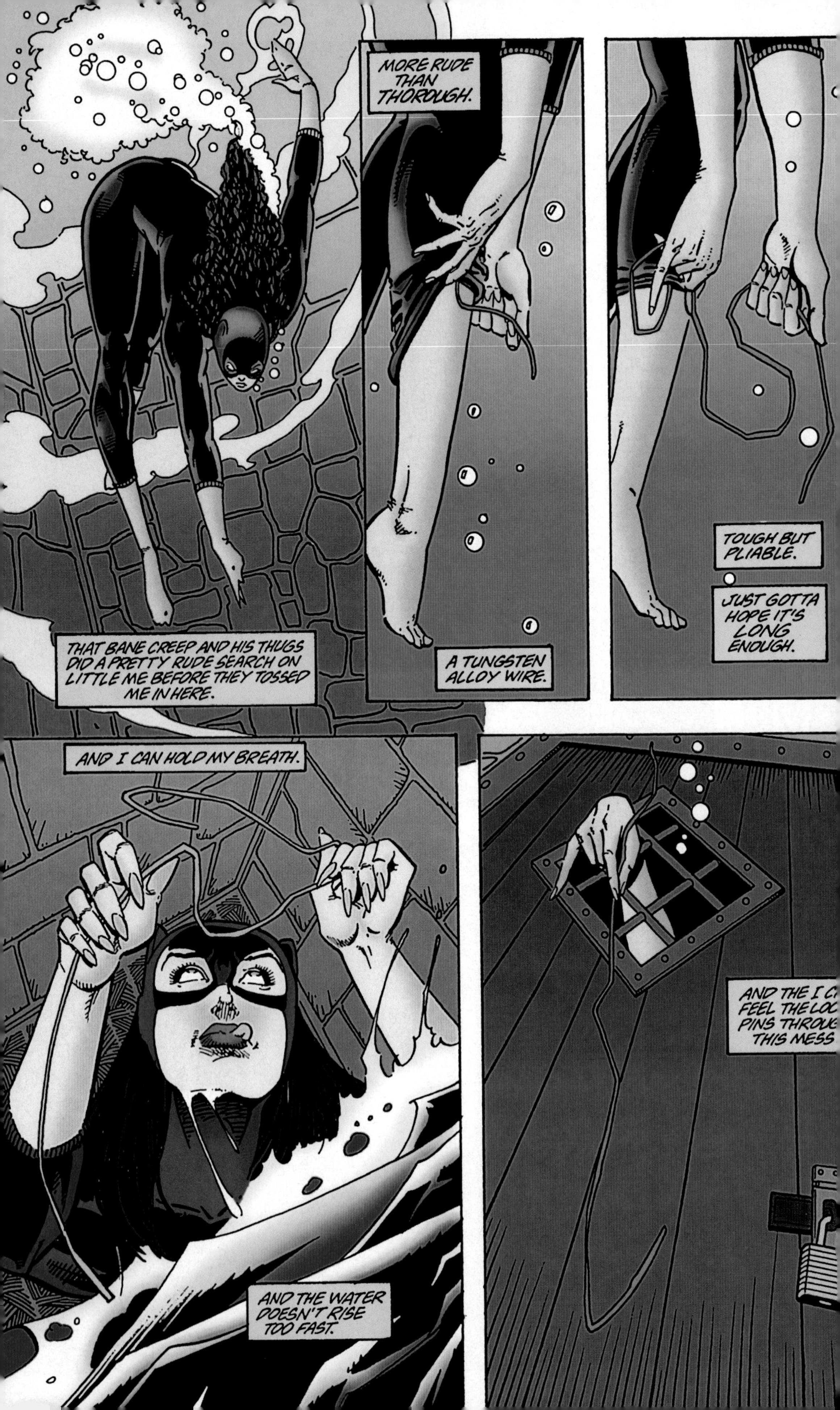

THAT BANE CREEP AND HIS THUGS DID A PRETTY RUDE SEARCH ON LITTLE ME BEFORE THEY TOSSED ME IN HERE.
MORE RUDE THAN THOROUGH.
A TUNGSTEN ALLOY WIRE.
TOUGH BUT PLIABLE.
JUST GOTTA HOPE IT'S LONG ENOUGH.
AND I CAN HOLD MY BREATH.
AND THE WATER DOESN'T RISE TOO FAST.
AND THE I C
FEEL THE LOC
PINS THROU
THIS MESS

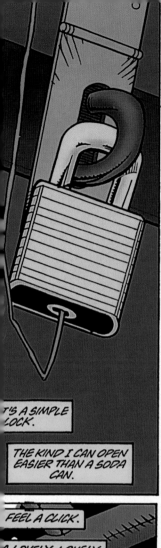

IT'S A SIMPLE
LOCK.

THE KIND I CAN OPEN
EASIER THAN A SODA
CAN.

BUT THAT'S UNDER
OPTIMUM CONDITIONS.

AND THIS SITUATION AIN'T
OPTIMUM, CHARLIE.

AND THE ANGEL'S
ALL WRONG.

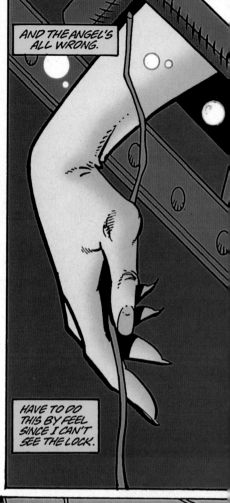

HAVE TO DO
THIS BY FEEL
SINCE I CAN'T
SEE THE LOCK.

FEEL A CLICK.

A LOVELY, LOVELY
CLICK.

AND IT'S
CLEAR.

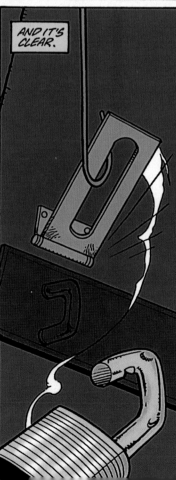

A LUNGFUL OF
SWEET AIR.

MIGHT BE
MY LAST.

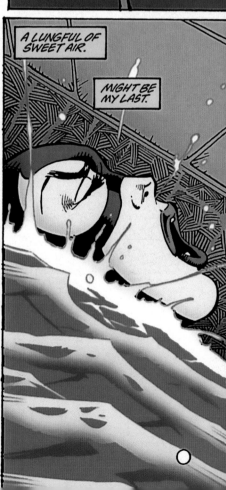

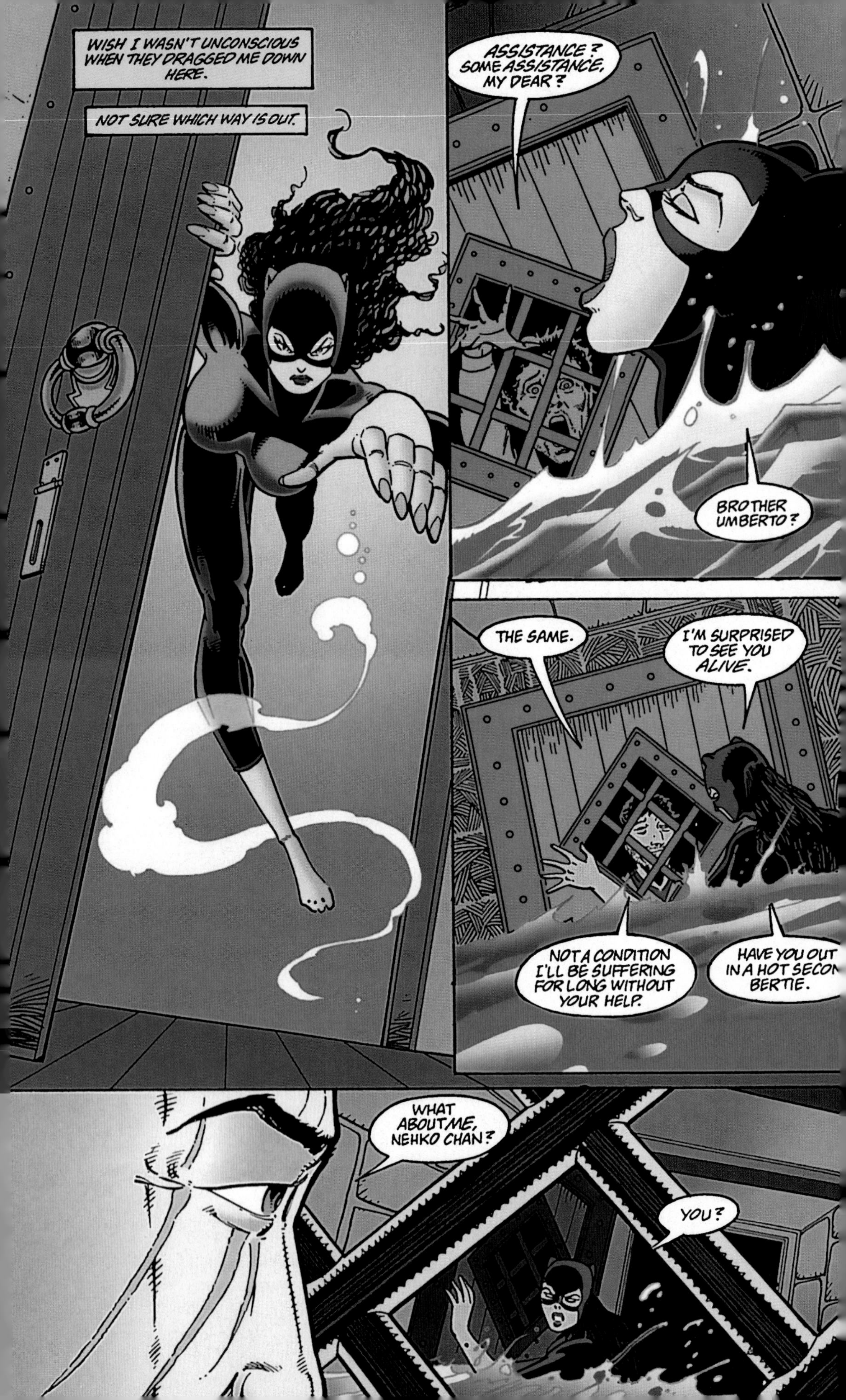
WISH I WASN'T UNCONSCIOUS WHEN THEY DRAGGED ME DOWN HERE.
NOT SURE WHICH WAY IS OUT.
ASSISTANCE? SOME ASSISTANCE, MY DEAR?
BROTHER UMBERTO?
THE SAME.
I'M SURPRISED TO SEE YOU ALIVE.
NOT A CONDITION I'LL BE SUFFERING FOR LONG WITHOUT YOUR HELP.
HAVE YOU OUT IN A HOT SECON
BERTIE.
WHAT ABOUT ME, NEHKO CHAN?
YOU?

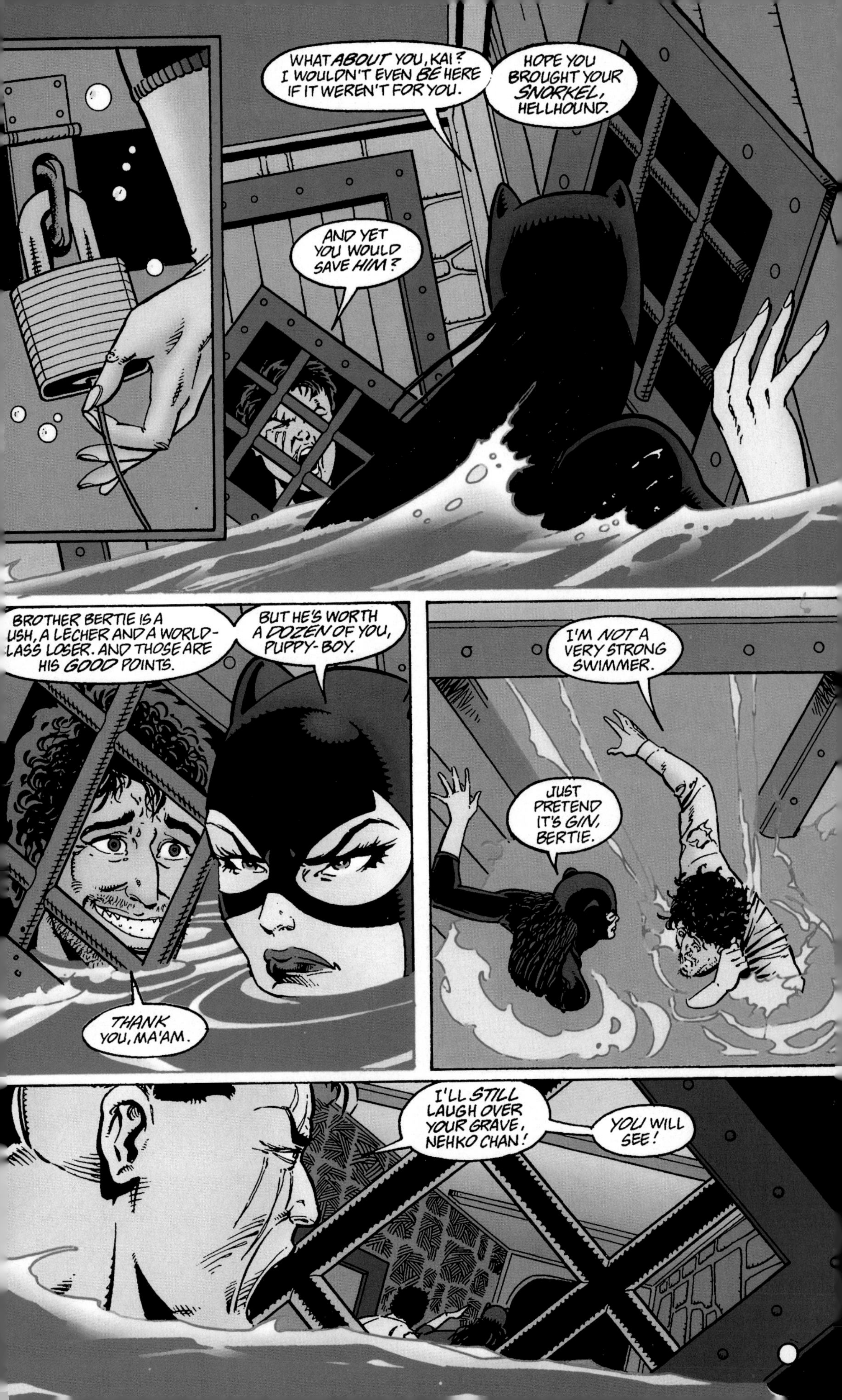
WHAT ABOUT YOU, KAI? I WOULDN'T EVEN BE HERE IF IT WEREN'T FOR YOU.
HOPE YOU BROUGHT YOUR SNORKEL, HELLHOUND.
AND YET YOU WOULD SAVE HIM?
BROTHER BERTIE IS A LUSH, A LECHER AND A WORLD-CLASS LOSER. AND THOSE ARE HIS GOOD POINTS.
BUT HE'S WORTH A DOZEN OF YOU, PUPPY-BOY.
THANK YOU, MA'AM.
I'M NOT A VERY STRONG SWIMMER.
JUST PRETEND IT'S GIN, BERTIE.
I'LL STILL LAUGH OVER YOUR GRAVE, NEHKO CHAN!
YOU WILL SEE!

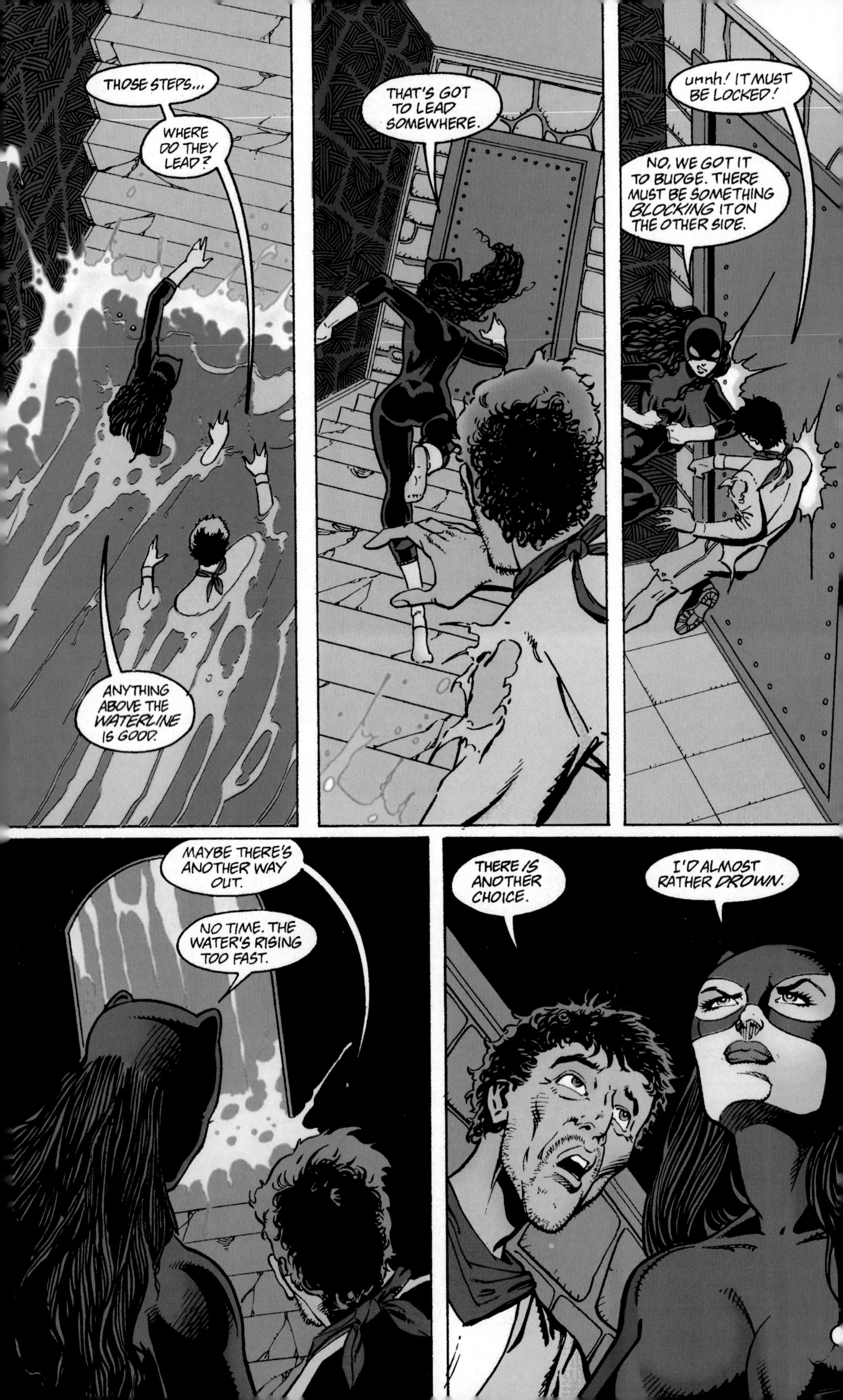
THOSE STEPS...
WHERE DO THEY LEAD?
ANYTHING ABOVE THE WATERLINE IS GOOD.
THAT'S GOT TO LEAD SOMEWHERE.
unnh! IT MUST BE LOCKED!
NO, WE GOT IT TO BUDGE. THERE MUST BE SOMETHING BLOCKING IT ON THE OTHER SIDE.
MAYBE THERE'S ANOTHER WAY OUT.
NO TIME. THE WATER'S RISING TOO FAST.
THERE IS ANOTHER CHOICE.
I'D ALMOST RATHER DROWN.

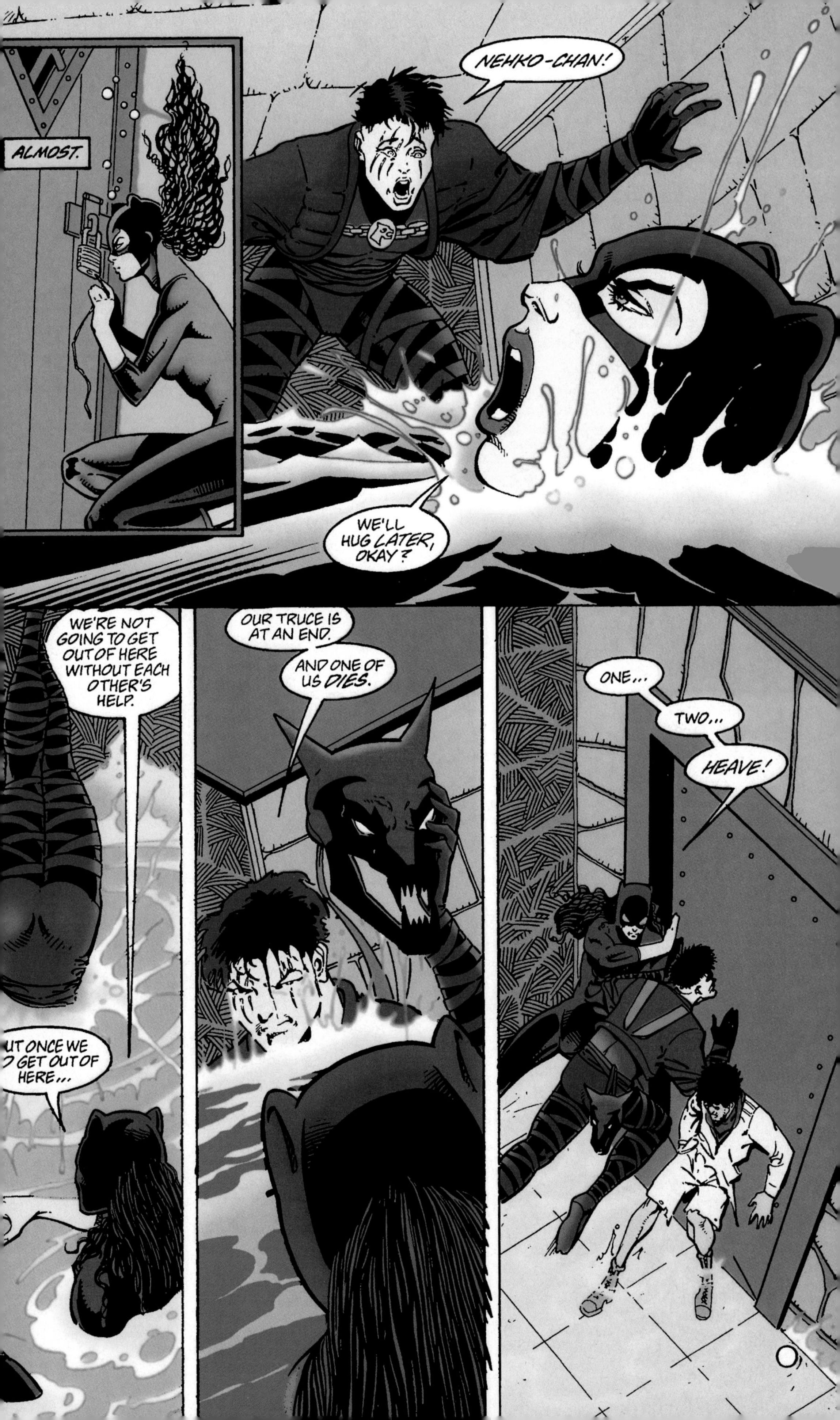
ALMOST.
NEHKO-CHAN!
WE'LL HUG LATER, OKAY?
WE'RE NOT GOING TO GET OUT OF HERE WITHOUT EACH OTHER'S HELP.
UT ONCE WE O GET OUT OF HERE...
OUR TRUCE IS AT AN END.
AND ONE OF US DIES.
ONE...
TWO...
HEAVE!

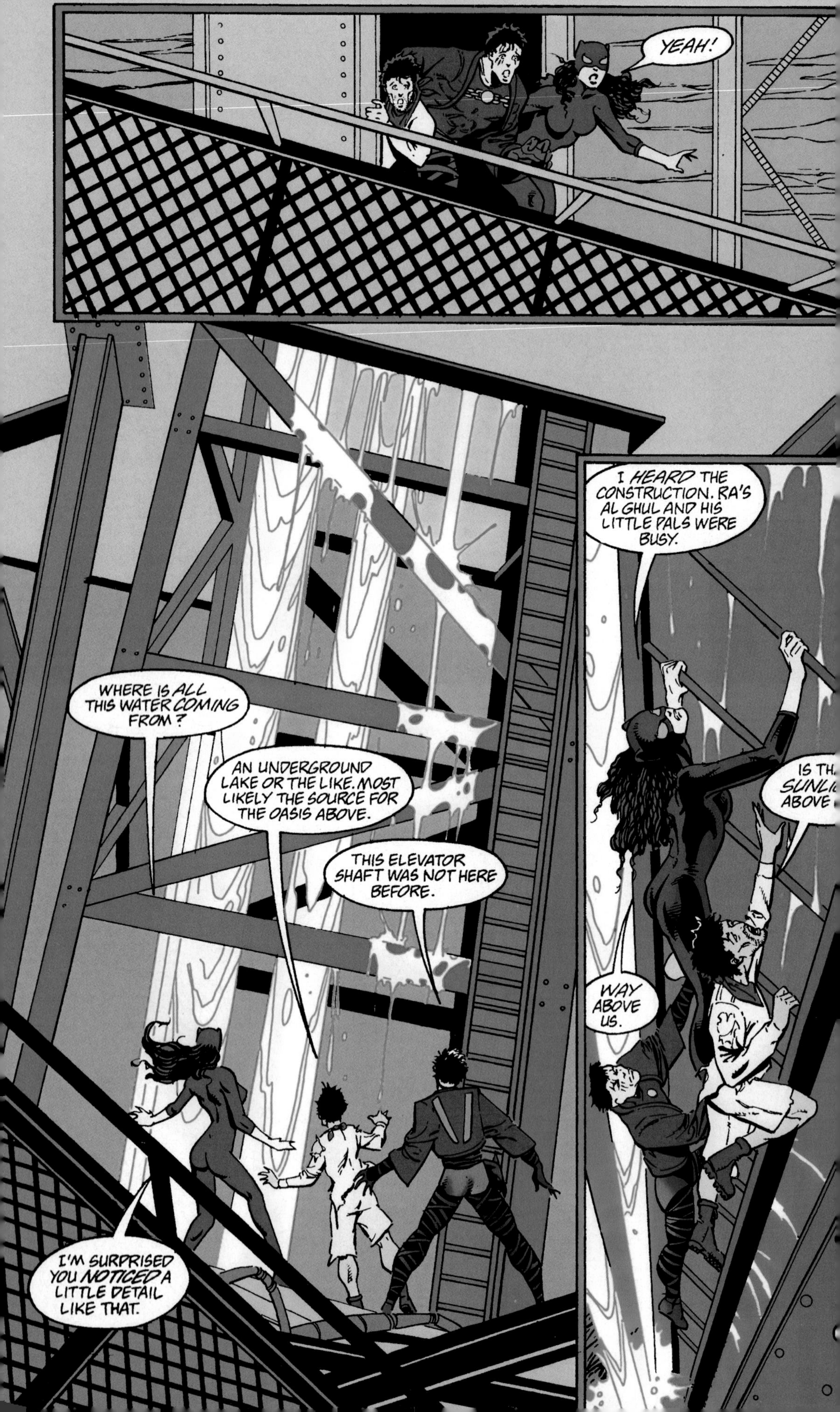
YEAH!
WHERE IS ALL THIS WATER COMING FROM?
AN UNDERGROUND LAKE OR THE LIKE. MOST LIKELY THE SOURCE FOR THE OASIS ABOVE.
THIS ELEVATOR SHAFT WAS NOT HERE BEFORE.
I'M SURPRISED YOU NOTICED A LITTLE DETAIL LIKE THAT.
I HEARD THE CONSTRUCTION. RA'S AL GHUL AND HIS LITTLE PALS WERE BUSY.
WAY ABOVE US.

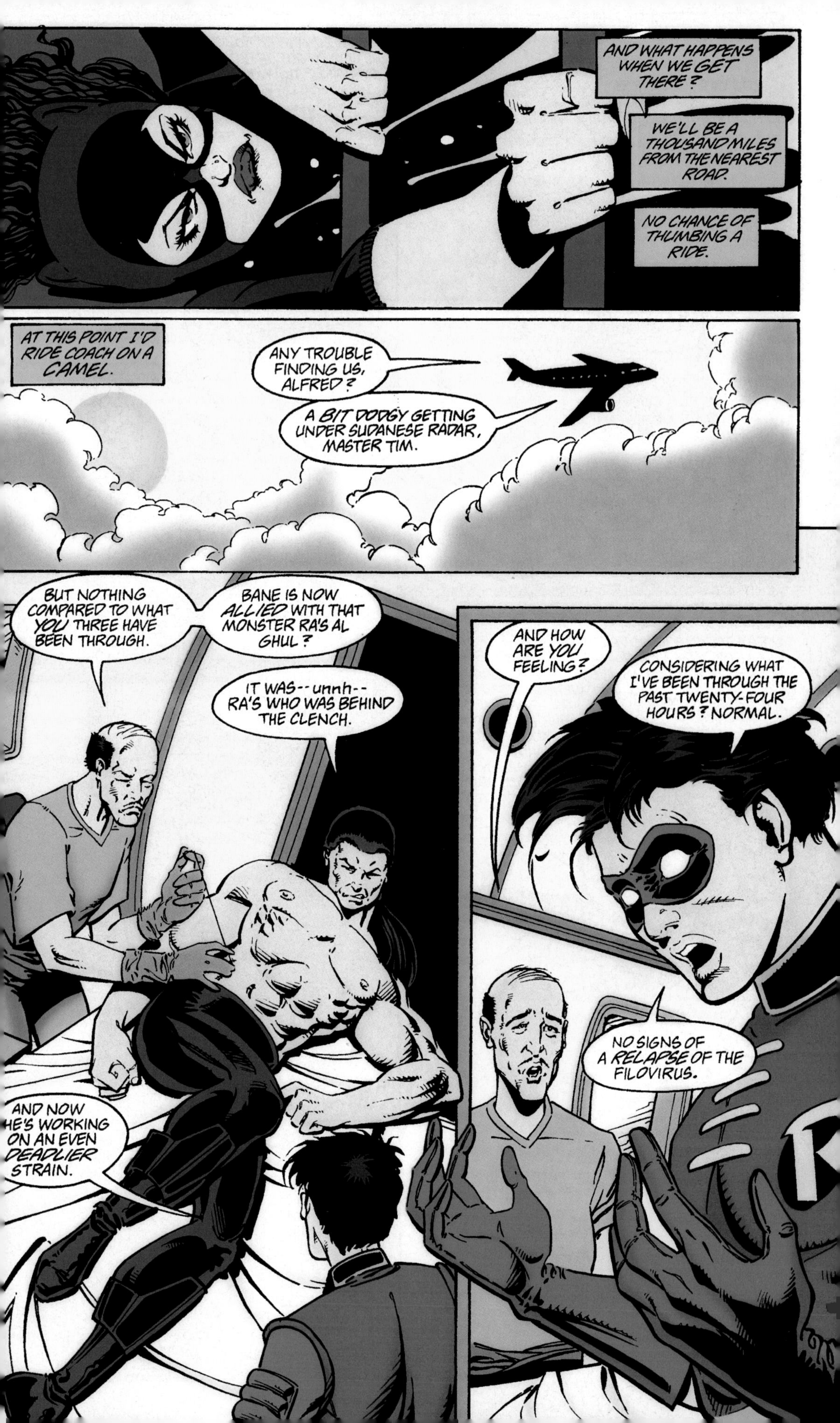

AND WHAT HAPPENS WHEN WE GET THERE?
WE'LL BE A THOUSAND MILES FROM THE NEAREST ROAD.
NO CHANCE OF THUMBING A RIDE.
AT THIS POINT I'D RIDE COACH ON A CAMEL.
ANY TROUBLE FINDING US, ALFRED?
A BIT DODGY GETTING UNDER SUDANESE RADAR, MASTER TIM.
BUT NOTHING COMPARED TO WHAT YOU THREE HAVE BEEN THROUGH.
BANE IS NOW ALLIED WITH THAT MONSTER RA'S AL GHUL?
IT WAS--unnh--RA'S WHO WAS BEHIND THE CLENCH.
AND NOW HE'S WORKING ON AN EVEN DEADLIER STRAIN.
AND HOW ARE YOU FEELING?
CONSIDERING WHAT I'VE BEEN THROUGH THE PAST TWENTY-FOUR HOURS? NORMAL.
NO SIGNS OF A RELAPSE OF THE FILOVIRUS.

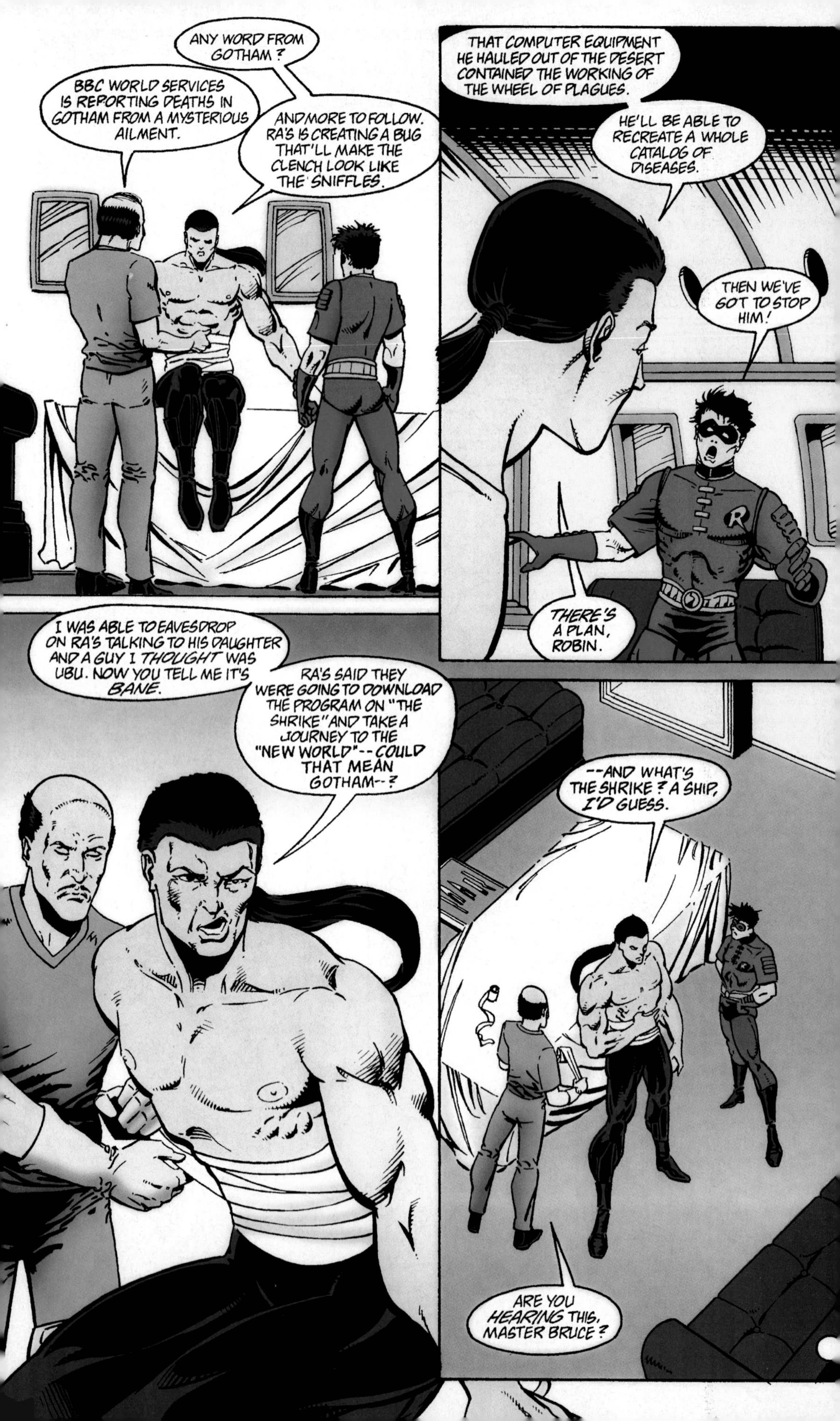
ANY WORD FROM GOTHAM?
BBC WORLD SERVICES IS REPORTING DEATHS IN GOTHAM FROM A MYSTERIOUS AILMENT.
AND MORE TO FOLLOW. RA'S IS CREATING A BUG THAT'LL MAKE THE CLENCH LOOK LIKE THE SNIFFLES.
THAT COMPUTER EQUIPMENT HE HAULED OUT OF THE DESERT CONTAINED THE WORKING OF THE WHEEL OF PLAGUES.
HE'LL BE ABLE TO RECREATE A WHOLE CATALOG OF DISEASES.
THEN WE'VE GOT TO STOP HIM!
THERE'S A PLAN, ROBIN.
I WAS ABLE TO EAVESDROP ON RA'S TALKING TO HIS DAUGHTER AND A GUY I THOUGHT WAS UBU. NOW YOU TELL ME IT'S BANE.
RA'S SAID THEY WERE GOING TO DOWNLOAD THE PROGRAM ON "THE SHRIKE" AND TAKE A JOURNEY TO THE "NEW WORLD"-- COULD THAT MEAN GOTHAM--?
--AND WHAT'S THE SHRIKE? A SHIP, I'D GUESS.
ARE YOU HEARING THIS, MASTER BRUCE?

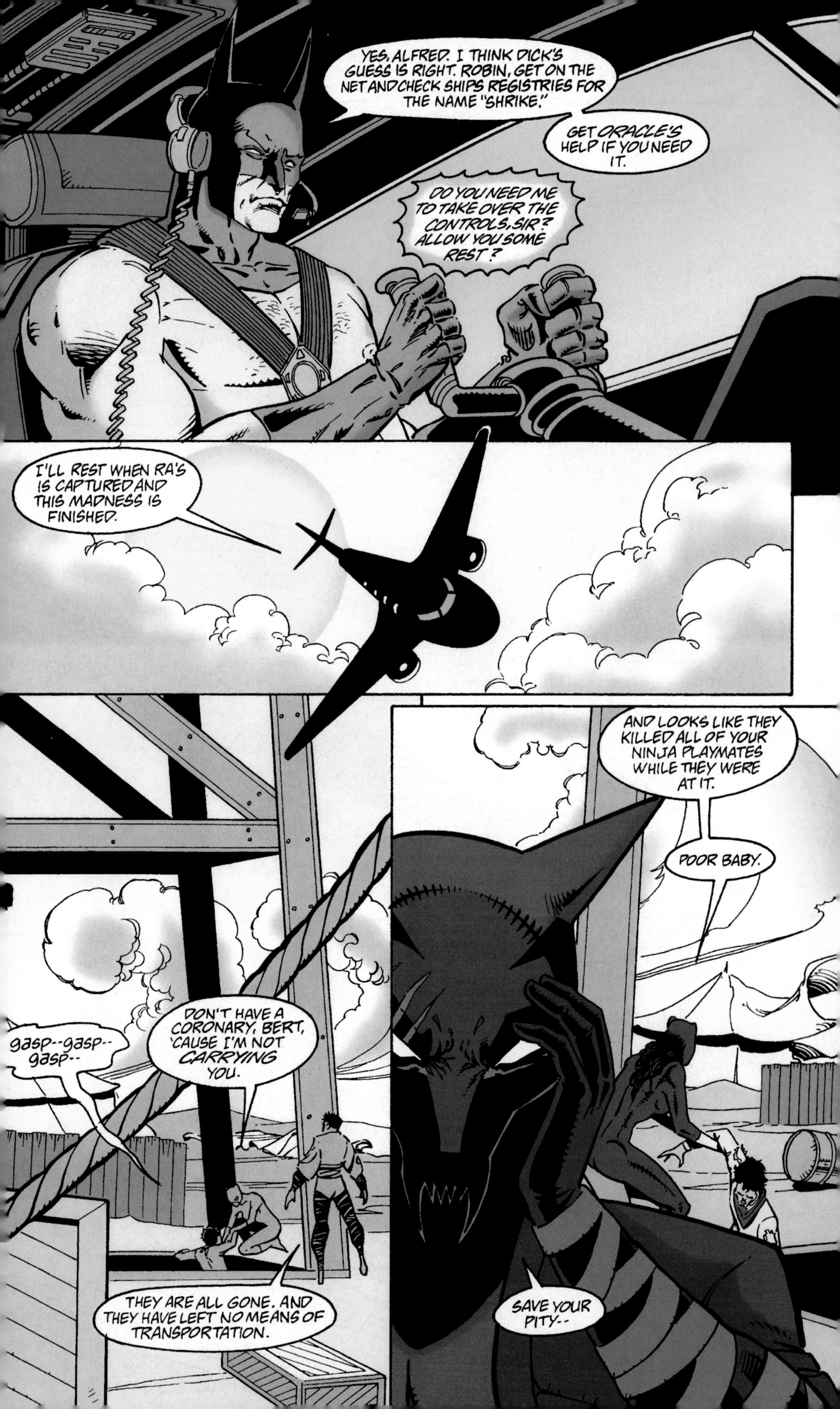

YES, ALFRED. I THINK DICK'S GUESS IS RIGHT. ROBIN, GET ON THE NET AND CHECK SHIPS REGISTRIES FOR THE NAME "SHRIKE."
GET ORACLE'S HELP IF YOU NEED IT.
DO YOU NEED ME TO TAKE OVER THE CONTROLS, SIR? ALLOW YOU SOME REST?
I'LL REST WHEN RA'S IS CAPTURED AND THIS MADNESS IS FINISHED.
AND LOOKS LIKE THEY KILLED ALL OF YOUR NINJA PLAYMATES WHILE THEY WERE AT IT.
POOR BABY.
gasp--gasp--gasp--
DON'T HAVE A CORONARY, BERT, 'CAUSE I'M NOT CARRYING YOU.
THEY ARE ALL GONE. AND THEY HAVE LEFT NO MEANS OF TRANSPORTATION.
SAVE YOUR PITY--

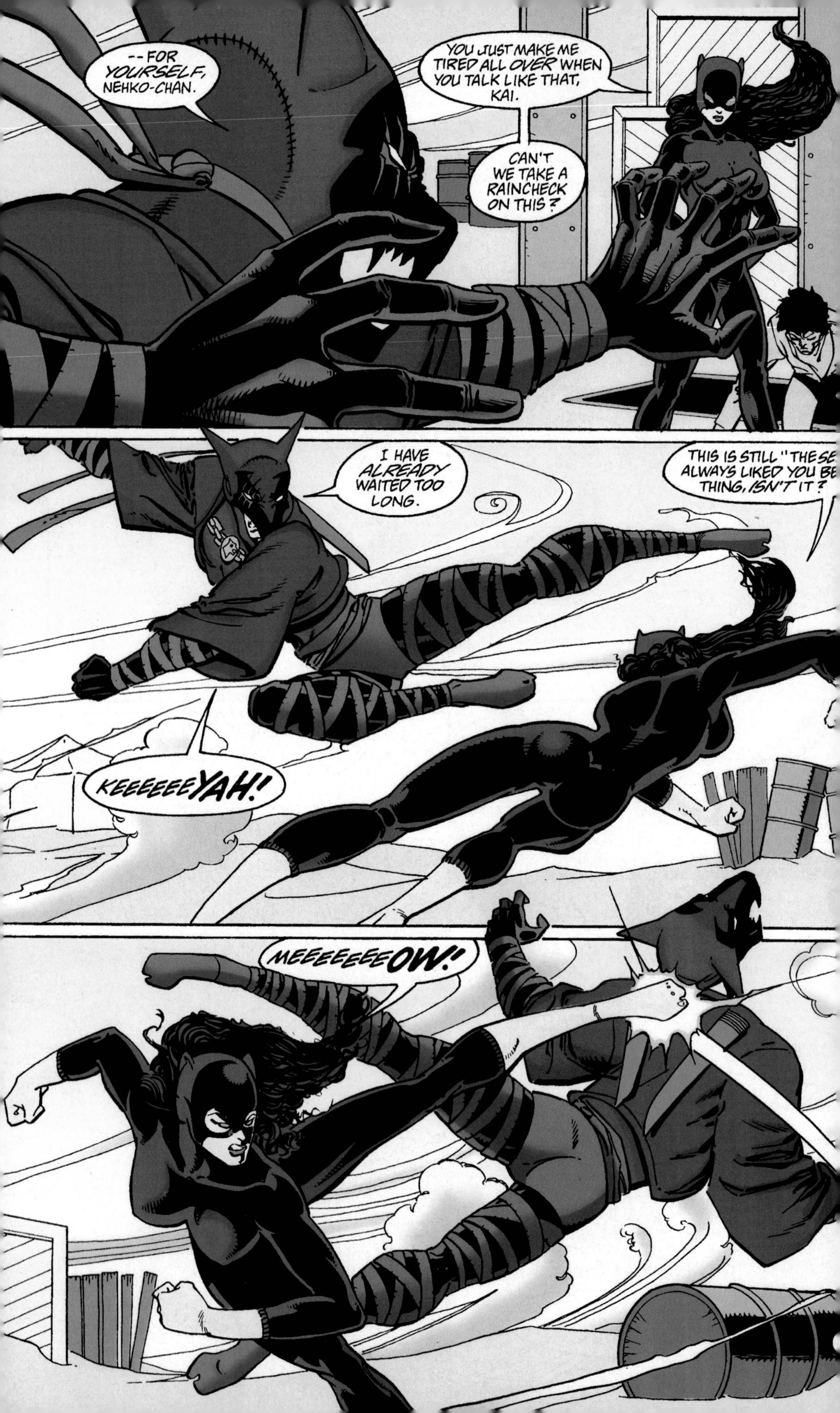
--FOR *YOURSELF,* NEHKO-CHAN.
YOU JUST MAKE ME TIRED ALL *OVER* WHEN YOU TALK LIKE THAT, KAI.
CAN'T WE TAKE A RAINCHECK ON THIS?
I HAVE *ALREADY* WAITED TOO LONG.
THIS IS STILL "THE SE
ALWAYS LIKED YOU BE
THING, *ISN'T* IT?
KEEEEEEE*YAH!*
MEEEEEEEE*OW!*

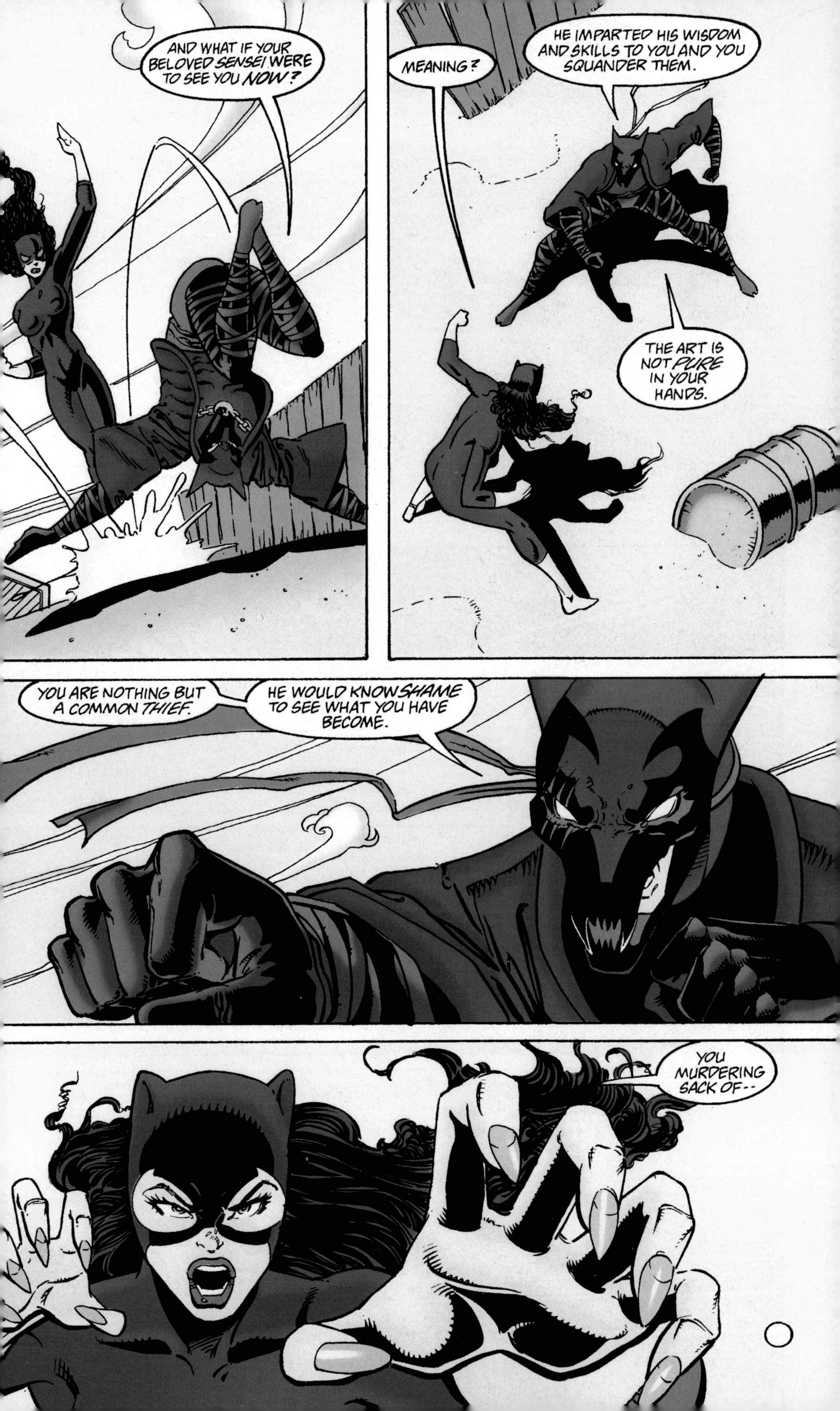
AND WHAT IF YOUR BELOVED SENSEI WERE TO SEE YOU NOW?
MEANING?
HE IMPARTED HIS WISDOM AND SKILLS TO YOU AND YOU SQUANDER THEM.
THE ART IS NOT PURE IN YOUR HANDS.
YOU ARE NOTHING BUT A COMMON THIEF.
HE WOULD KNOW SHAME TO SEE WHAT YOU HAVE BECOME.
YOU MURDERING SACK OF--

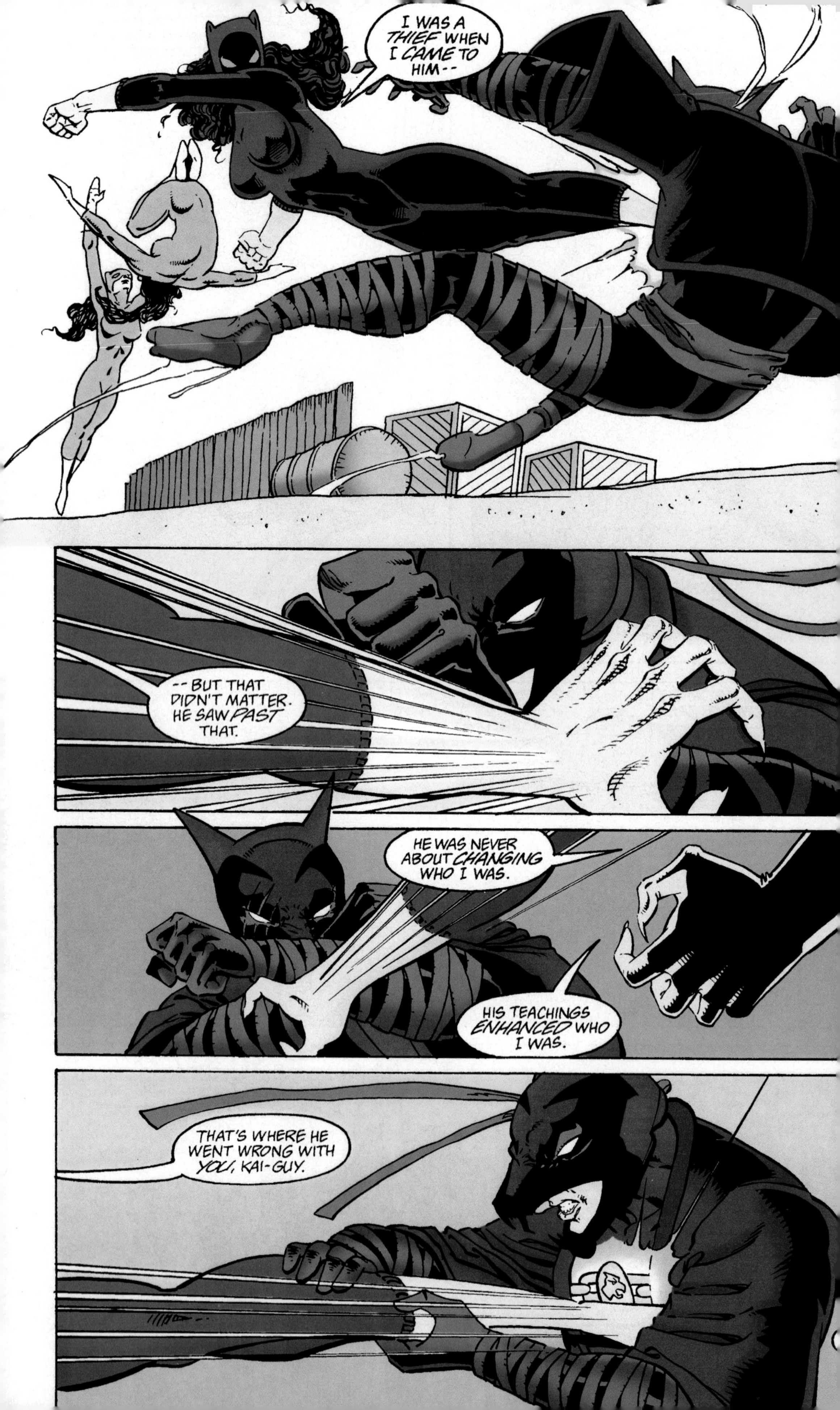
I WAS A THIEF WHEN I CAME TO HIM--
--BUT THAT DIDN'T MATTER. HE SAW PAST THAT.
HE WAS NEVER ABOUT CHANGING WHO I WAS.
HIS TEACHINGS ENHANCED WHO I WAS.
THAT'S WHERE HE WENT WRONG WITH YOU, KAI-GUY.

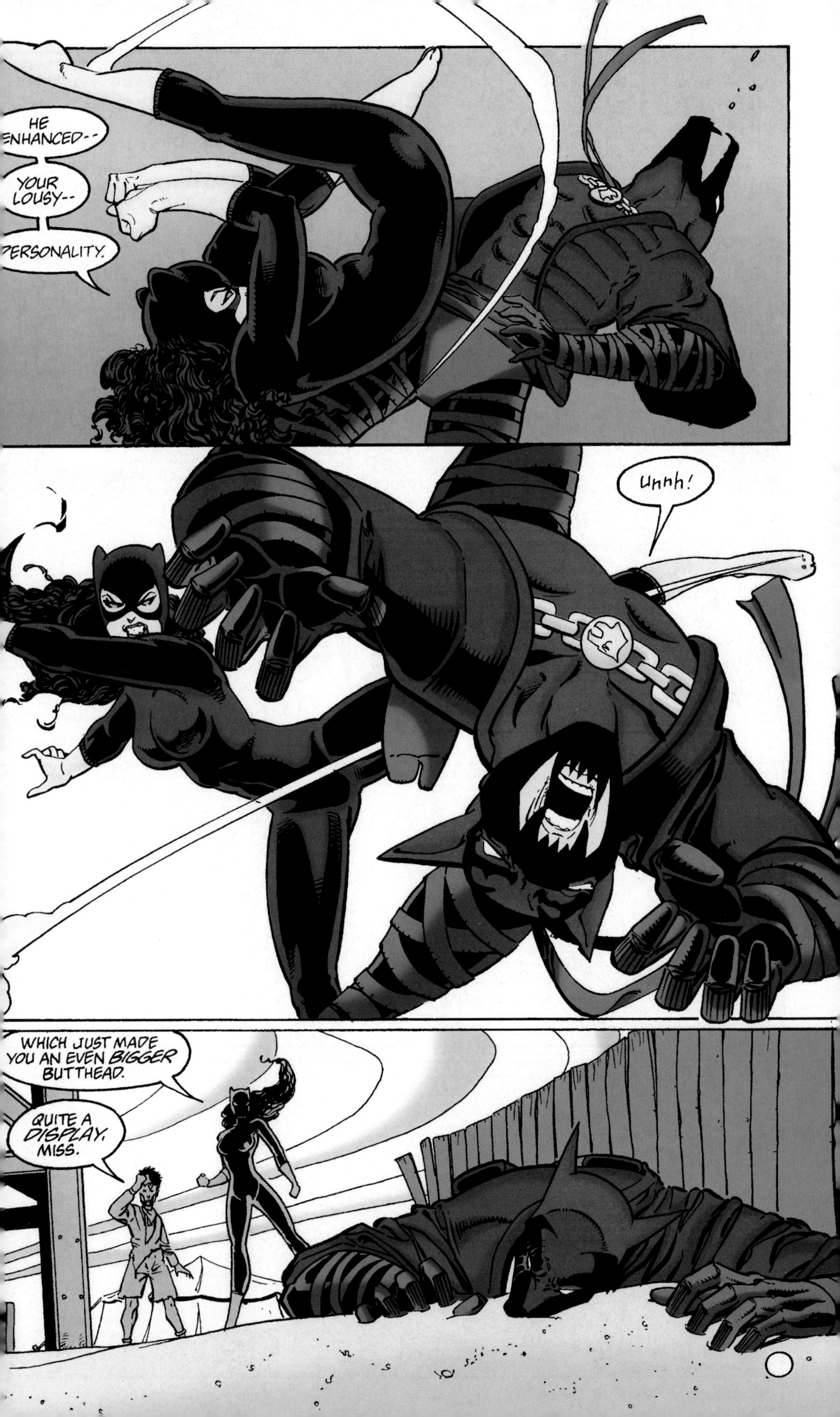
HE ENHANCED--
YOUR LOUSY--
PERSONALITY.
Unnh!
WHICH JUST MADE YOU AN EVEN BIGGER BUTTHEAD.
QUITE A DISPLAY, MISS.

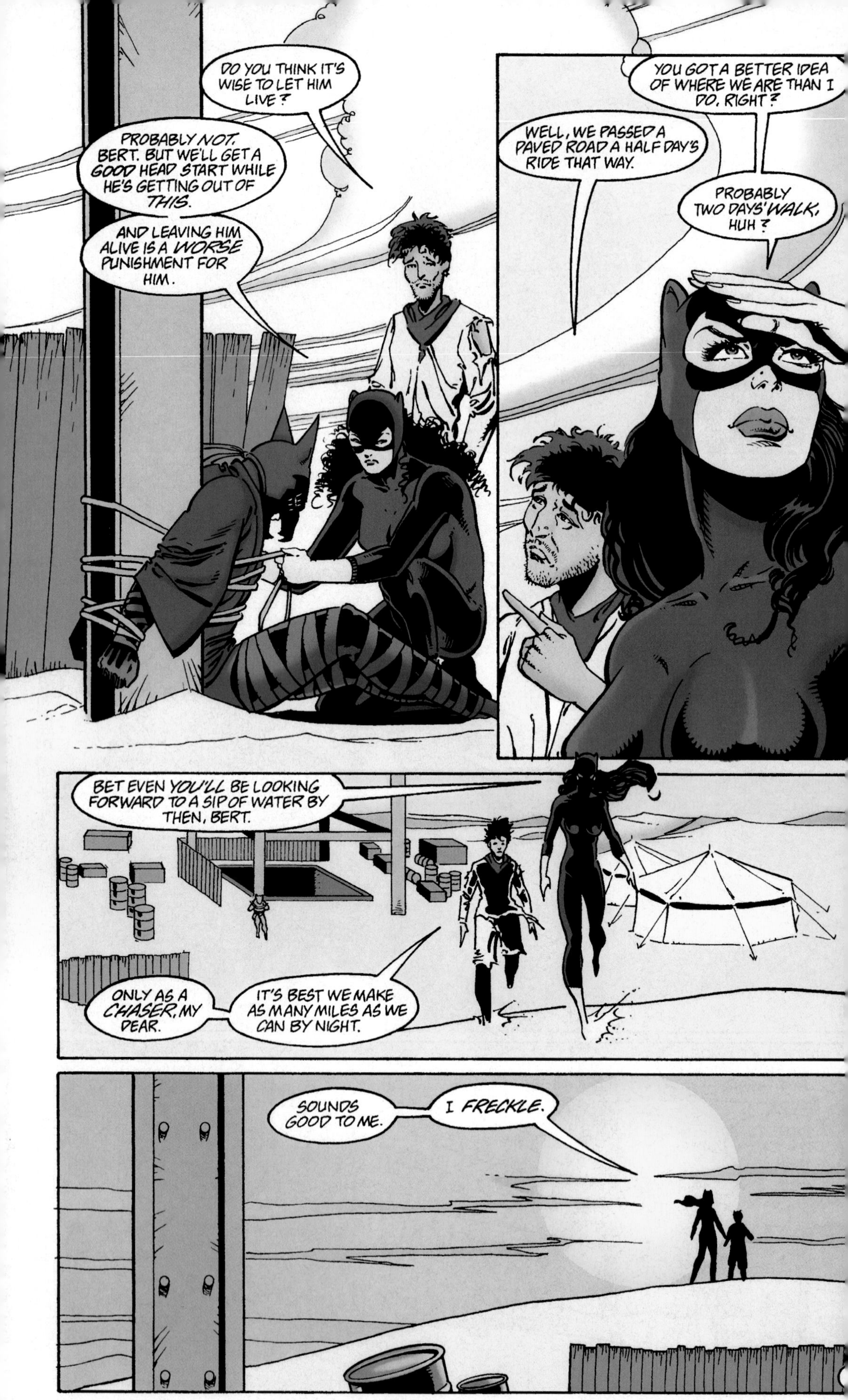
DO YOU THINK IT'S WISE TO LET HIM LIVE?
PROBABLY NOT, BERT. BUT WE'LL GET A GOOD HEAD START WHILE HE'S GETTING OUT OF THIS.
AND LEAVING HIM ALIVE IS A WORSE PUNISHMENT FOR HIM.
YOU GOT A BETTER IDEA OF WHERE WE ARE THAN I DO, RIGHT?
WELL, WE PASSED A PAVED ROAD A HALF DAY'S RIDE THAT WAY.
PROBABLY TWO DAYS' WALK, HUH?
BET EVEN YOU'LL BE LOOKING FORWARD TO A SIP OF WATER BY THEN, BERT.
ONLY AS A CHASER, MY DEAR.
IT'S BEST WE MAKE AS MANY MILES AS WE CAN BY NIGHT.
SOUNDS GOOD TO ME.
I FRECKLE.

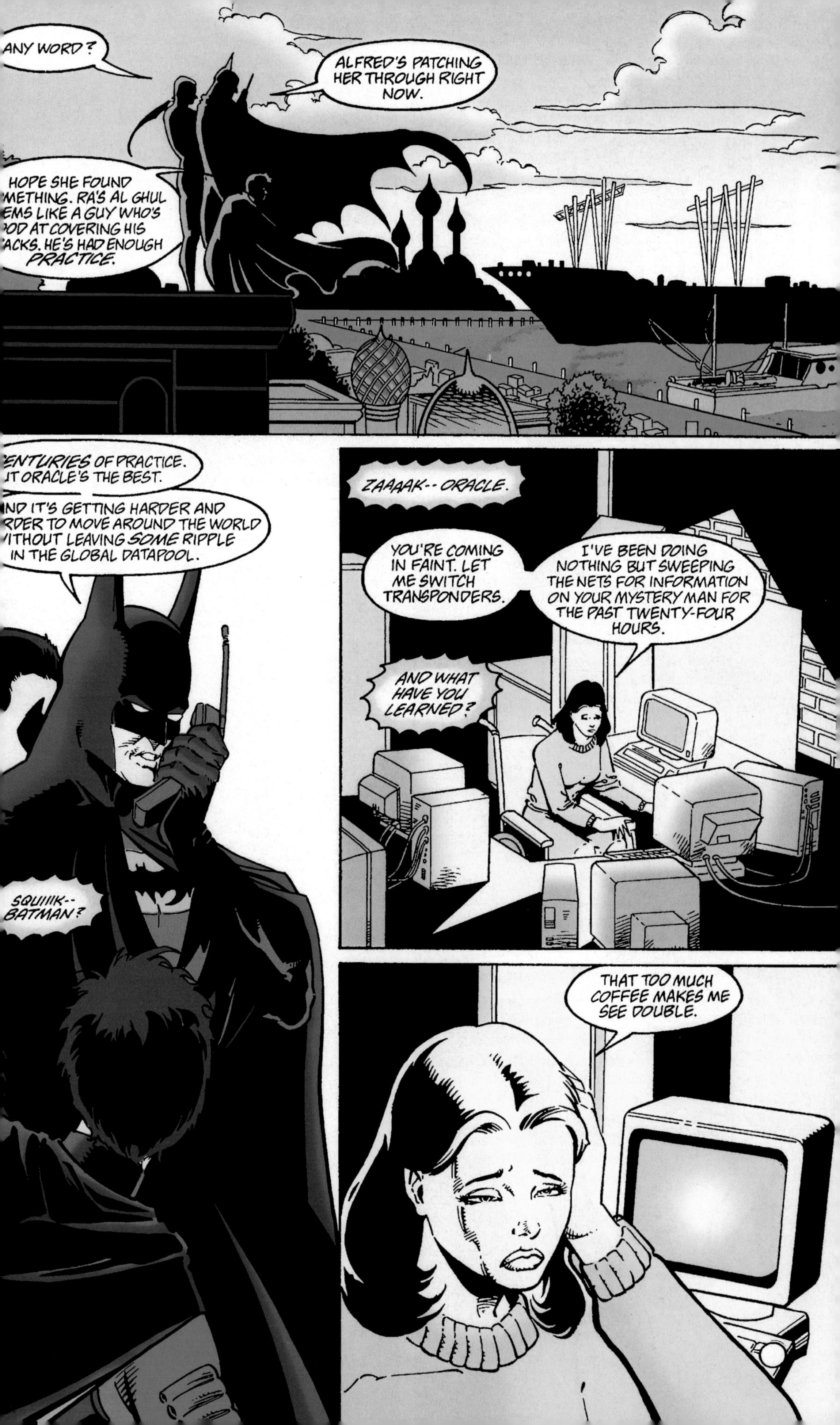

ANY WORD?
ALFRED'S PATCHING HER THROUGH RIGHT NOW.
HOPE SHE FOUND METHING. RA'S AL GHUL EMS LIKE A GUY WHO'S OD AT COVERING HIS ACKS. HE'S HAD ENOUGH PRACTICE.
ENTURIES OF PRACTICE. IT ORACLE'S THE BEST.
ND IT'S GETTING HARDER AND RDER TO MOVE AROUND THE WORLD ITHOUT LEAVING SOME RIPPLE IN THE GLOBAL DATAPOOL.
SQUIIIK-- BATMAN?
ZAAAAK-- ORACLE.
YOU'RE COMING IN FAINT. LET ME SWITCH TRANSPONDERS.
I'VE BEEN DOING NOTHING BUT SWEEPING THE NETS FOR INFORMATION ON YOUR MYSTERY MAN FOR THE PAST TWENTY-FOUR HOURS.
AND WHAT HAVE YOU LEARNED?
THAT TOO MUCH COFFEE MAKES ME SEE DOUBLE.

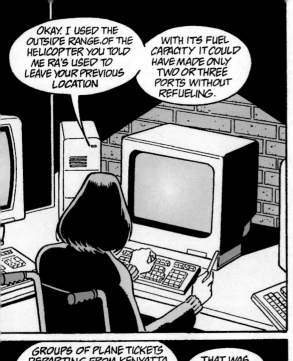

OKAY. I USED THE OUTSIDE RANGE OF THE HELICOPTER YOU TOLD ME RA'S USED TO LEAVE YOUR PREVIOUS LOCATION

WITH ITS FUEL CAPACITY IT COULD HAVE MADE ONLY TWO OR THREE PORTS WITHOUT REFUELING.

PORT MOMBASA. MOGADISHU. SAID.

WE'RE IN SAID.

HE WENT TO MOMBASA.

GROUPS OF PLANE TICKETS DEPARTING FROM KENYATTA AIRPORT WERE PURCHASED IN BLOCKS WITHIN HOURS OF ONE ANOTHER.

THAT WAS YESTERDAY.

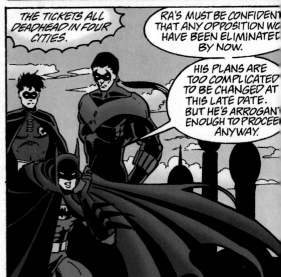

THE TICKETS ALL DEADHEAD IN FOUR CITIES.

RA'S MUST BE CONFIDENT THAT ANY OPPOSITION WOULD HAVE BEEN ELIMINATED BY NOW.

HIS PLANS ARE TOO COMPLICATED TO BE CHANGED AT THIS LATE DATE. BUT HE'S ARROGANT ENOUGH TO PROCEED ANYWAY.

WHICH CITIES, ORACLE?

PARIS. EDINBURGH.

AND GOTHAM.

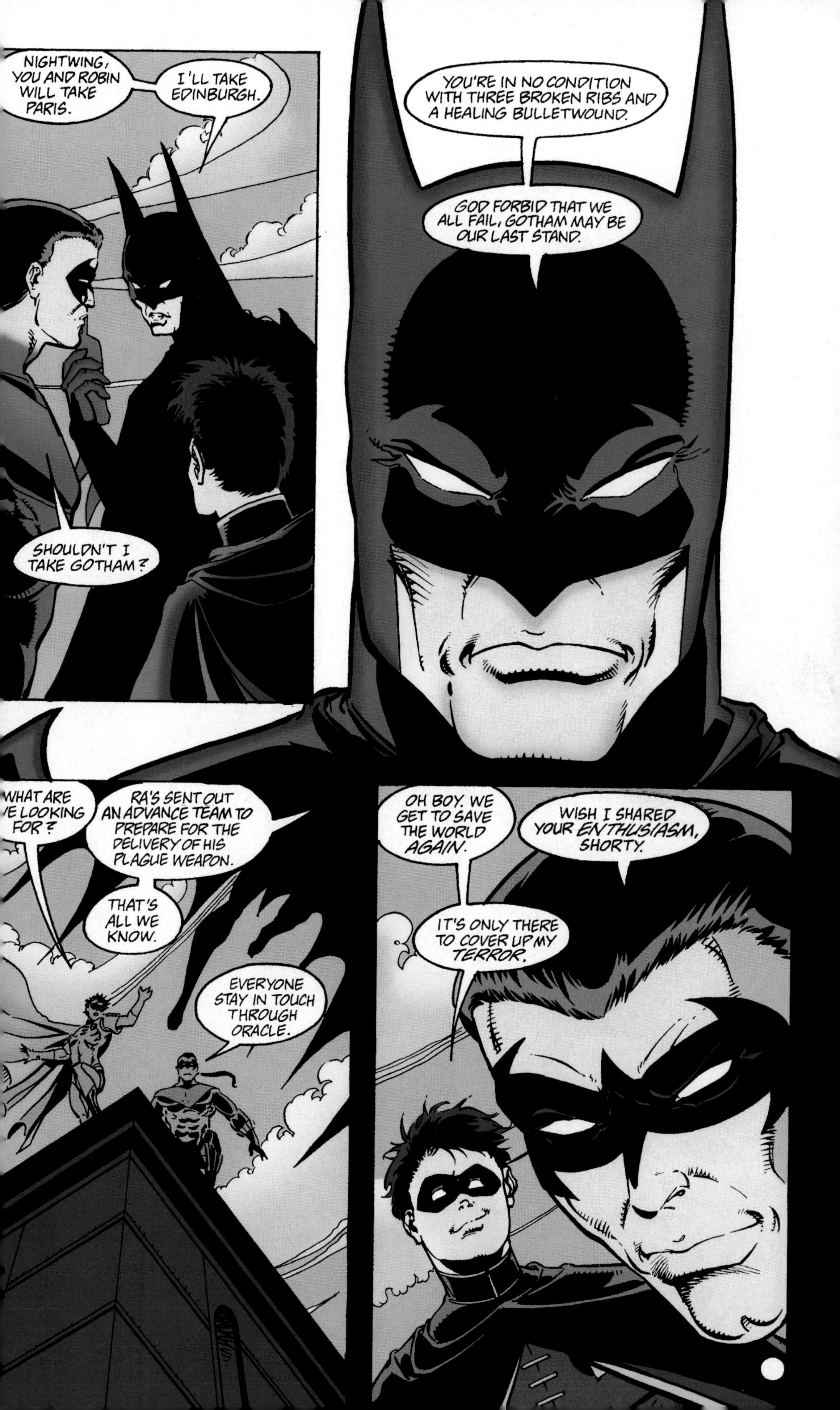
NIGHTWING, YOU AND ROBIN WILL TAKE PARIS.
I'LL TAKE EDINBURGH.
SHOULDN'T I TAKE GOTHAM?
YOU'RE IN NO CONDITION WITH THREE BROKEN RIBS AND A HEALING BULLETWOUND.
GOD FORBID THAT WE ALL FAIL, GOTHAM MAY BE OUR LAST STAND.
WHAT ARE WE LOOKING FOR?
RA'S SENT OUT AN ADVANCE TEAM TO PREPARE FOR THE DELIVERY OF HIS PLAGUE WEAPON.
THAT'S ALL WE KNOW.
EVERYONE STAY IN TOUCH THROUGH ORACLE.
OH BOY. WE GET TO SAVE THE WORLD AGAIN.
WISH I SHARED YOUR ENTHUSIASM, SHORTY.
IT'S ONLY THERE TO COVER UP MY TERROR.

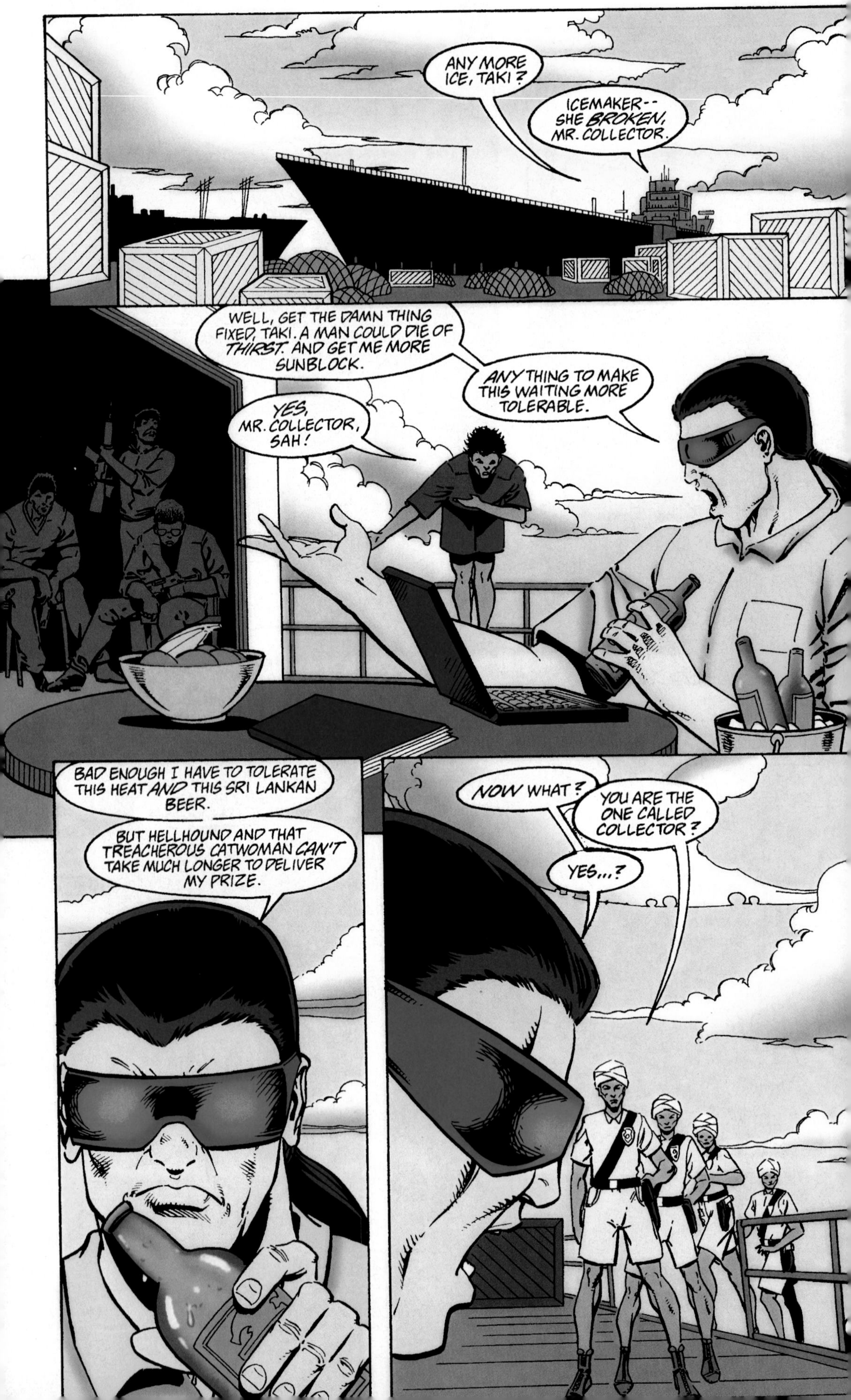

ANY MORE ICE, TAKI?
ICEMAKER-- SHE BROKEN, MR. COLLECTOR.
WELL, GET THE DAMN THING FIXED, TAKI. A MAN COULD DIE OF THIRST. AND GET ME MORE SUNBLOCK.
ANY THING TO MAKE THIS WAITING MORE TOLERABLE.
YES, MR. COLLECTOR, SAH!
BAD ENOUGH I HAVE TO TOLERATE THIS HEAT AND THIS SRI LANKAN BEER.
BUT HELLHOUND AND THAT TREACHEROUS CATWOMAN CAN'T TAKE MUCH LONGER TO DELIVER MY PRIZE.
NOW WHAT?
YOU ARE THE ONE CALLED COLLECTOR?
YES...?

YOU ARE UNDER ARREST FOR THE MOLESTATION OF ONE OF OUR FEMALE CITIZENS.

THAT'S *RIDICULOUS!* I HAVEN'T SET *FOOT* OFF THIS BOAT!

IT IS HER WORD AGAINST *YOURS.*

WHOSE WORD?

HER WORD.

I'VE NEVER SEEN HER BEFORE IN MY *LIFE!*

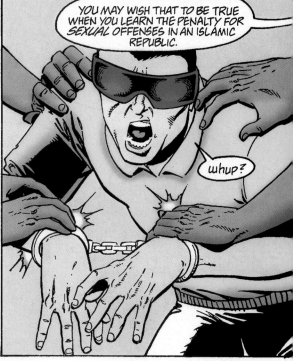

YOU MAY WISH THAT TO BE TRUE WHEN YOU LEARN THE PENALTY FOR *SEXUAL* OFFENSES IN AN ISLAMIC REPUBLIC.

whup?

BUT I'M *INNOCENT,* YOU MORONS!

YOU WILL HAVE A CHANCE TO *PROVE* THAT, SIR--

--BEFORE YOUR PUNISHMENT IS METED OUT.

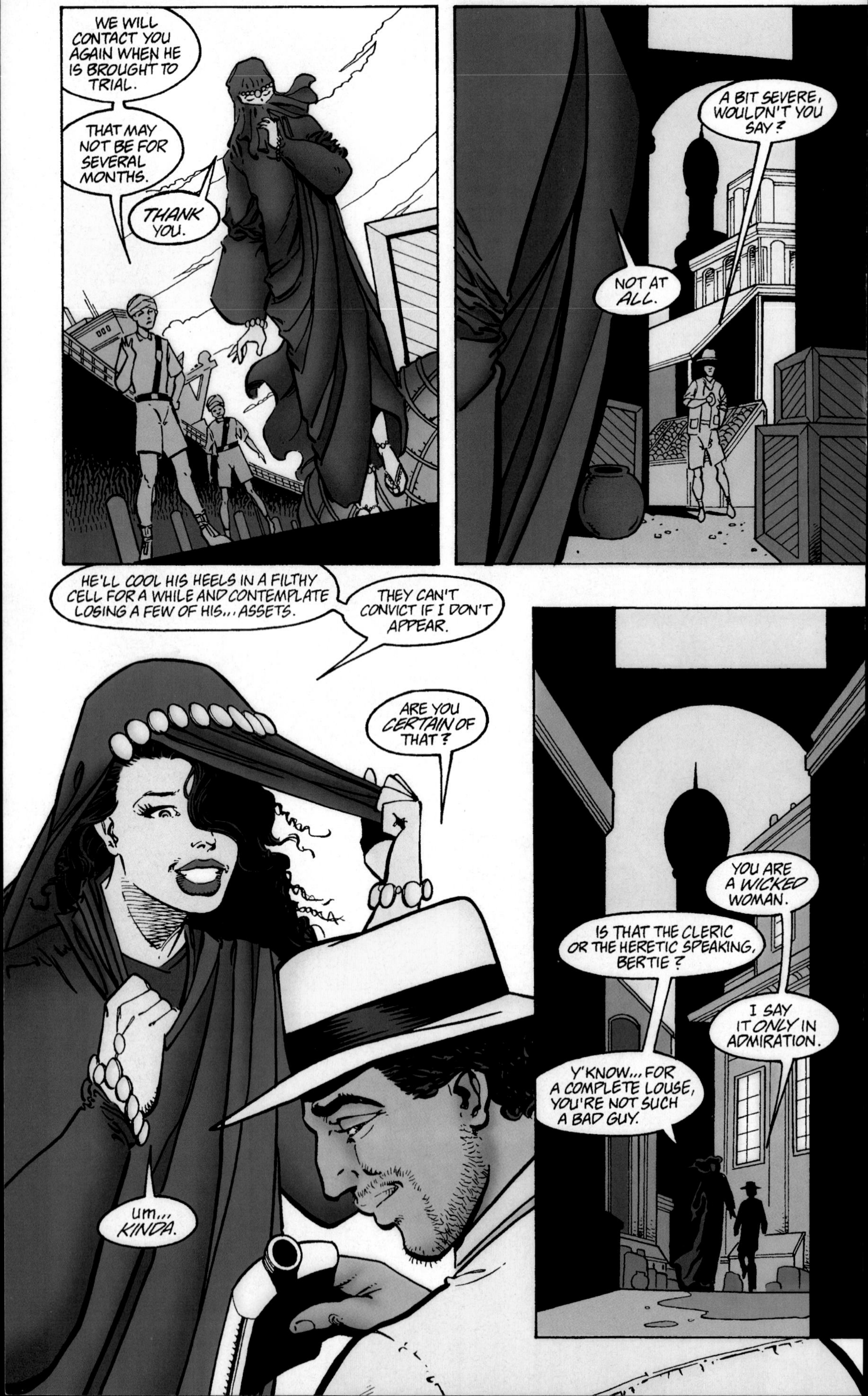
WE WILL CONTACT YOU AGAIN WHEN HE IS BROUGHT TO TRIAL.
THAT MAY NOT BE FOR SEVERAL MONTHS.
THANK YOU.
A BIT SEVERE, WOULDN'T YOU SAY?
NOT AT ALL.
HE'LL COOL HIS HEELS IN A FILTHY CELL FOR A WHILE AND CONTEMPLATE LOSING A FEW OF HIS... ASSETS.
THEY CAN'T CONVICT IF I DON'T APPEAR.
ARE YOU CERTAIN OF THAT?
UM... KINDA.
YOU ARE A WICKED WOMAN.
IS THAT THE CLERIC OR THE HERETIC SPEAKING, BERTIE?
I SAY IT ONLY IN ADMIRATION.
Y'KNOW... FOR A COMPLETE LOUSE, YOU'RE NOT SUCH A BAD GUY.

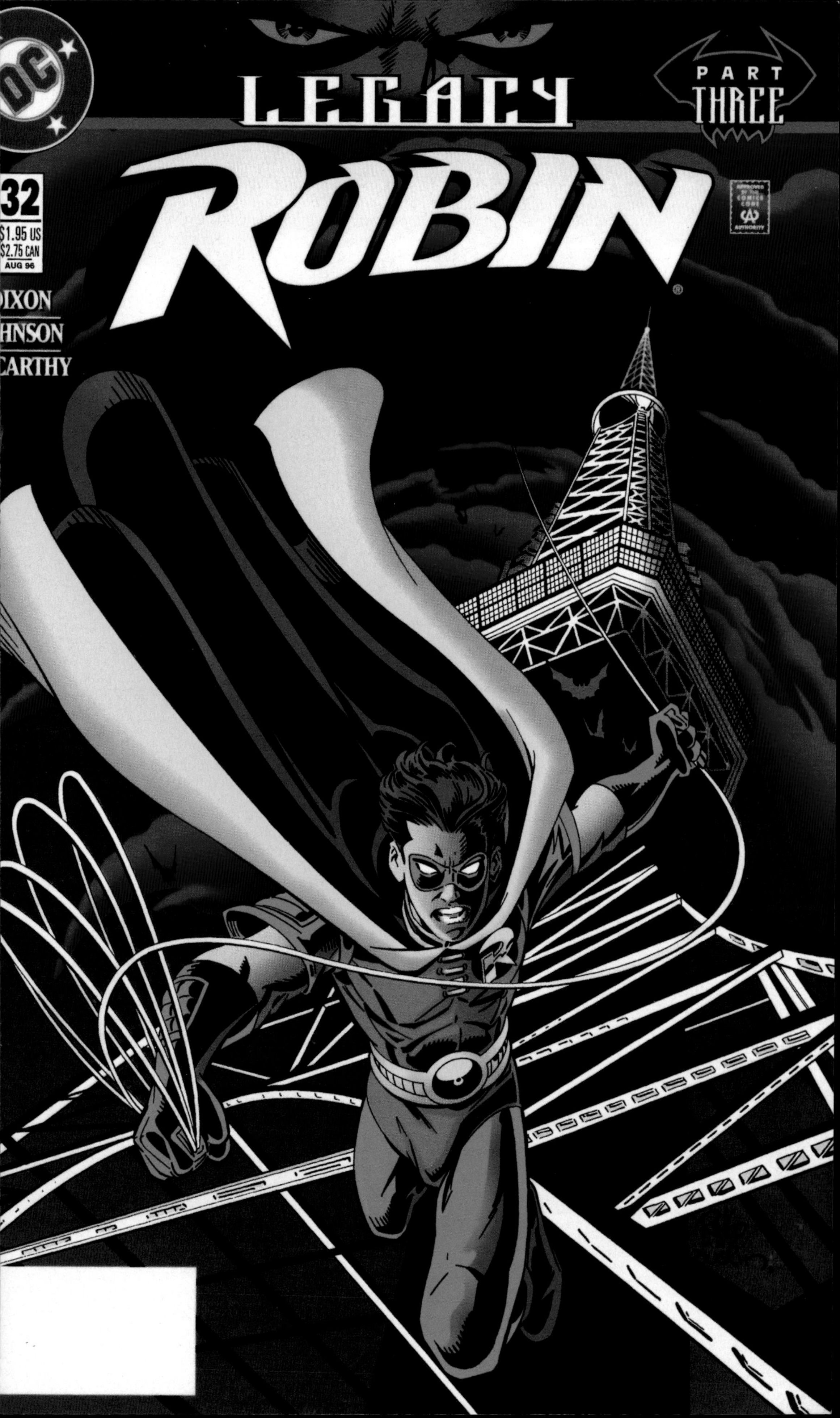
LEGACY
PART THREE
ROBIN
32
$1.95 US
$2.75 CAN
AUG 96
DIXON
HNSON
CARTHY

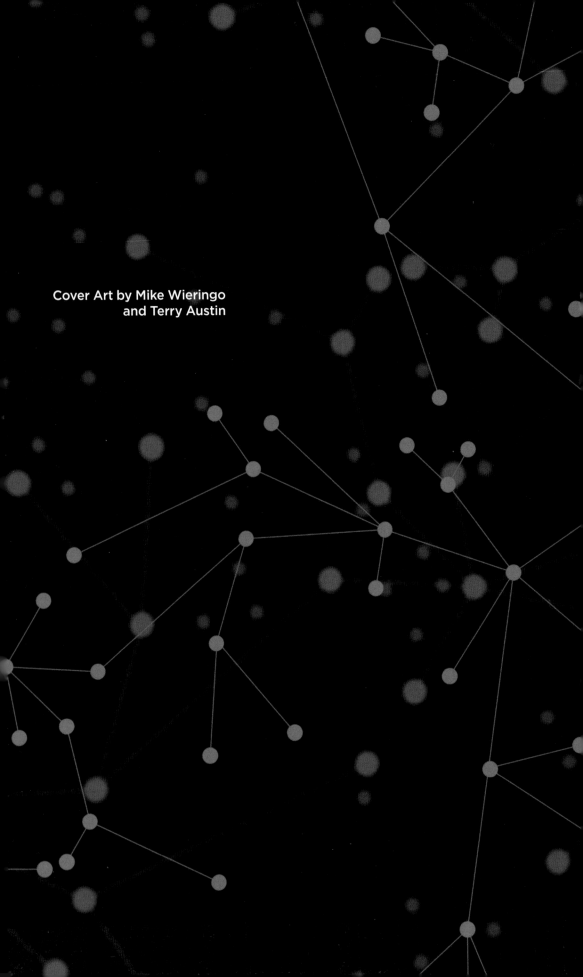

Cover Art by Mike Wieringo
and Terry Austin

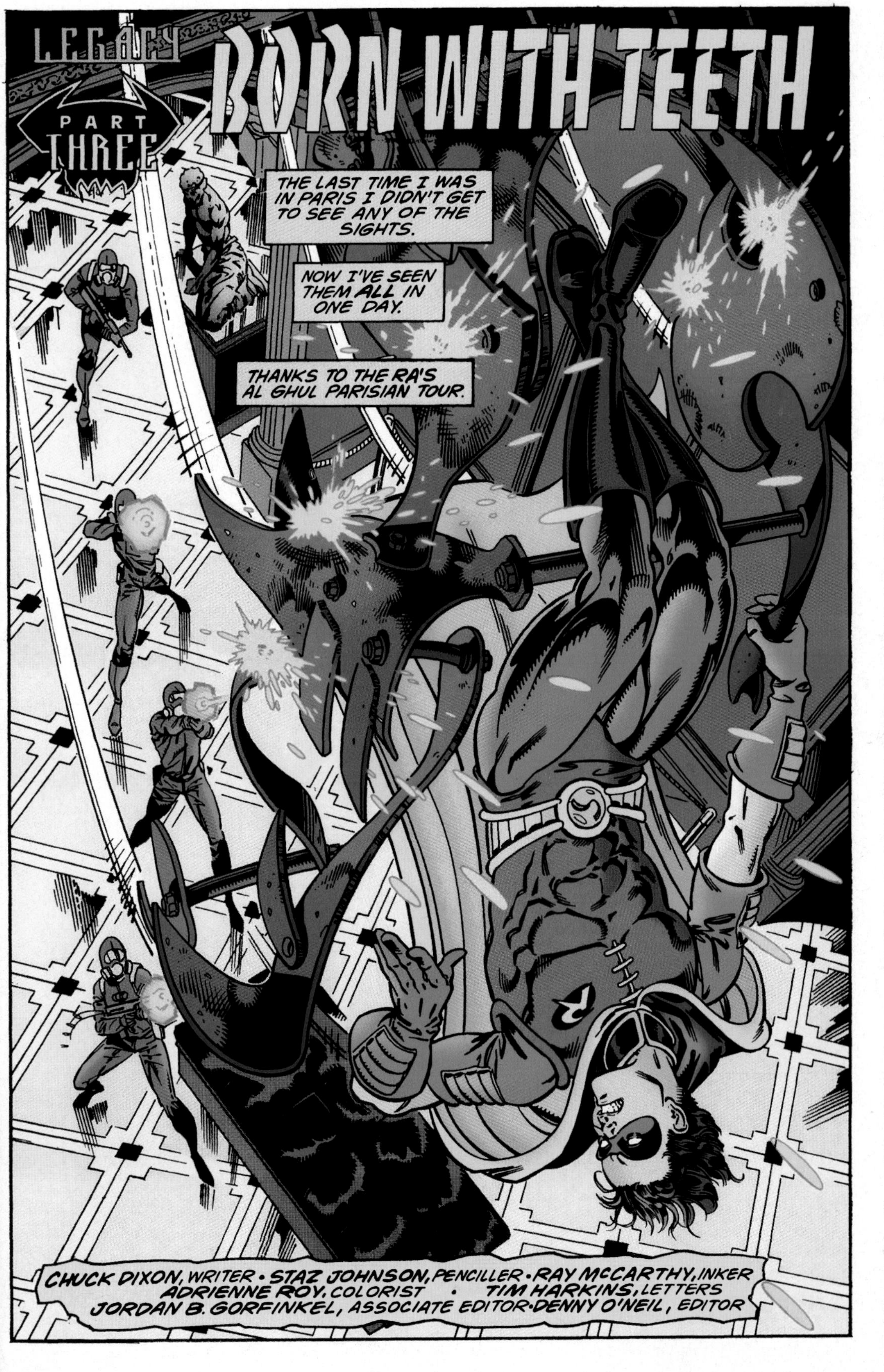
LEGACY
PART THREE
BORN WITH TEETH
THE LAST TIME I WAS IN PARIS I DIDN'T GET TO SEE ANY OF THE SIGHTS.
NOW I'VE SEEN THEM ALL IN ONE DAY.
THANKS TO THE RA'S AL GHUL PARISIAN TOUR.
CHUCK DIXON, WRITER • STAZ JOHNSON, PENCILLER • RAY MCCARTHY, INKER
ADRIENNE ROY, COLORIST • TIM HARKINS, LETTERS
JORDAN B. GORFINKEL, ASSOCIATE EDITOR • DENNY O'NEIL, EDITOR

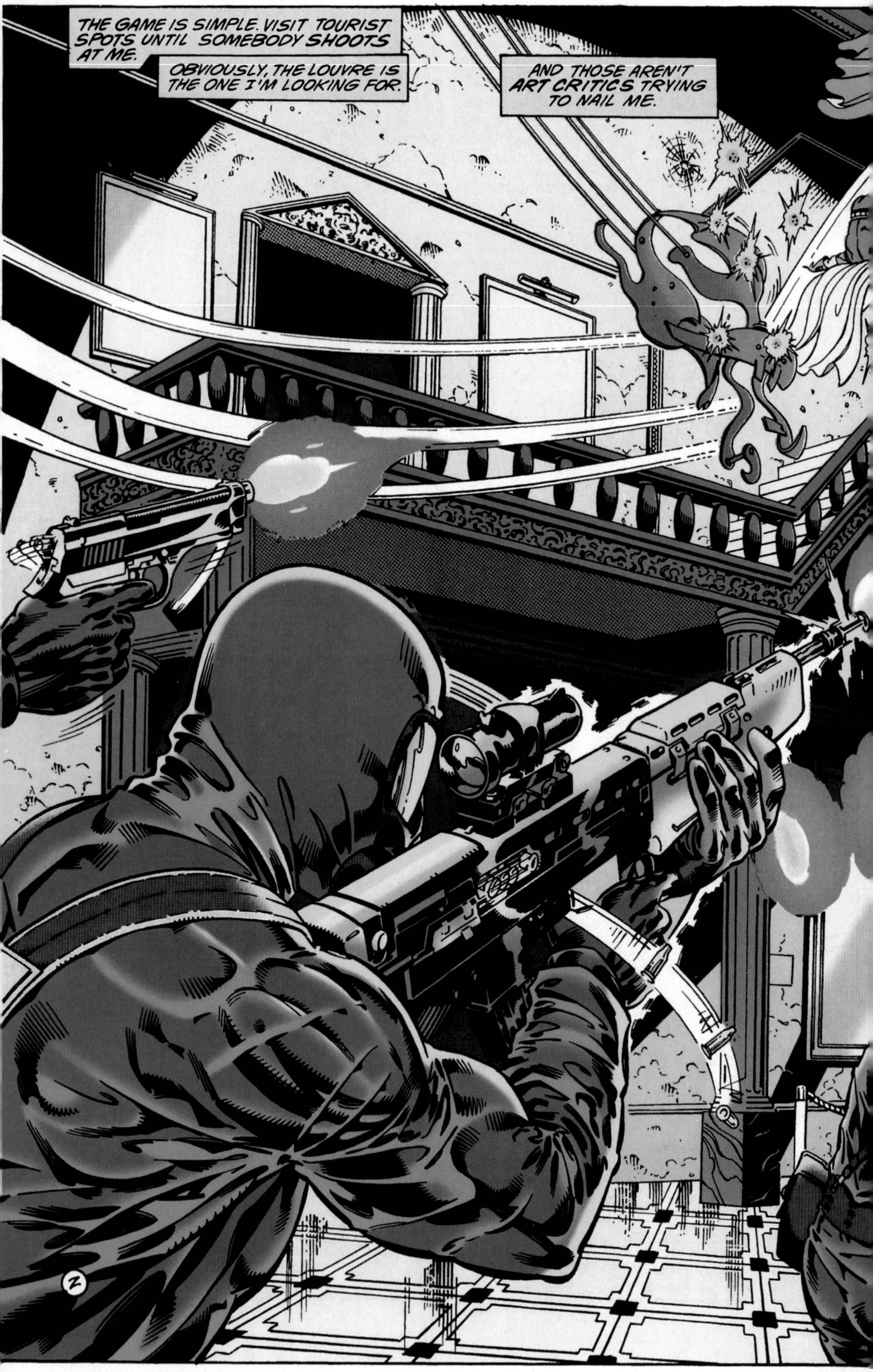
THE GAME IS SIMPLE. VISIT TOURIST SPOTS UNTIL SOMEBODY SHOOTS AT ME.
OBVIOUSLY, THE LOUVRE IS THE ONE I'M LOOKING FOR.
AND THOSE AREN'T ART CRITICS TRYING TO NAIL ME.
2

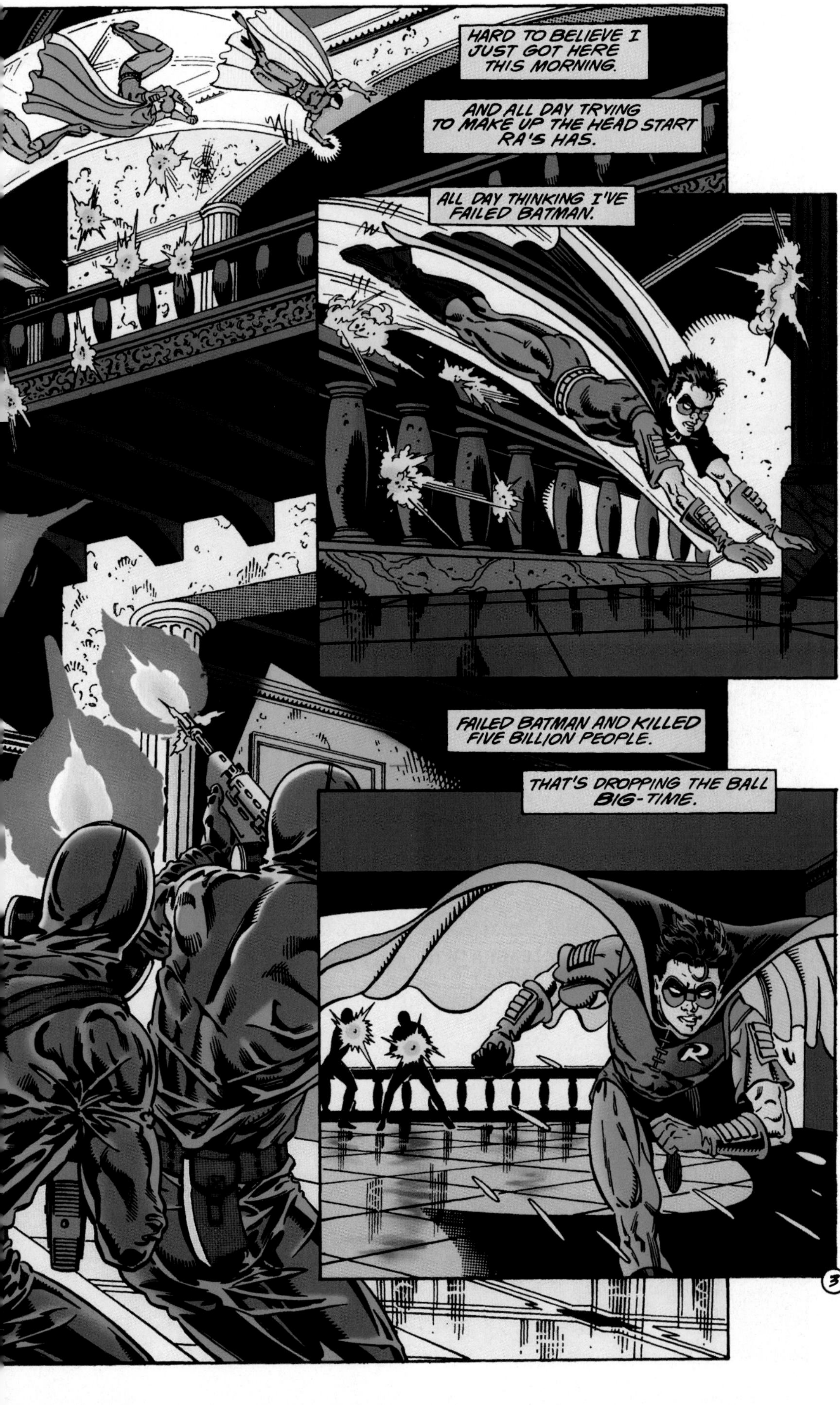
HARD TO BELIEVE I JUST GOT HERE THIS MORNING.
AND ALL DAY TRYING TO MAKE UP THE HEAD START RA'S HAS.
ALL DAY THINKING I'VE FAILED BATMAN.
FAILED BATMAN AND KILLED FIVE BILLION PEOPLE.
THAT'S DROPPING THE BALL BIG-TIME.

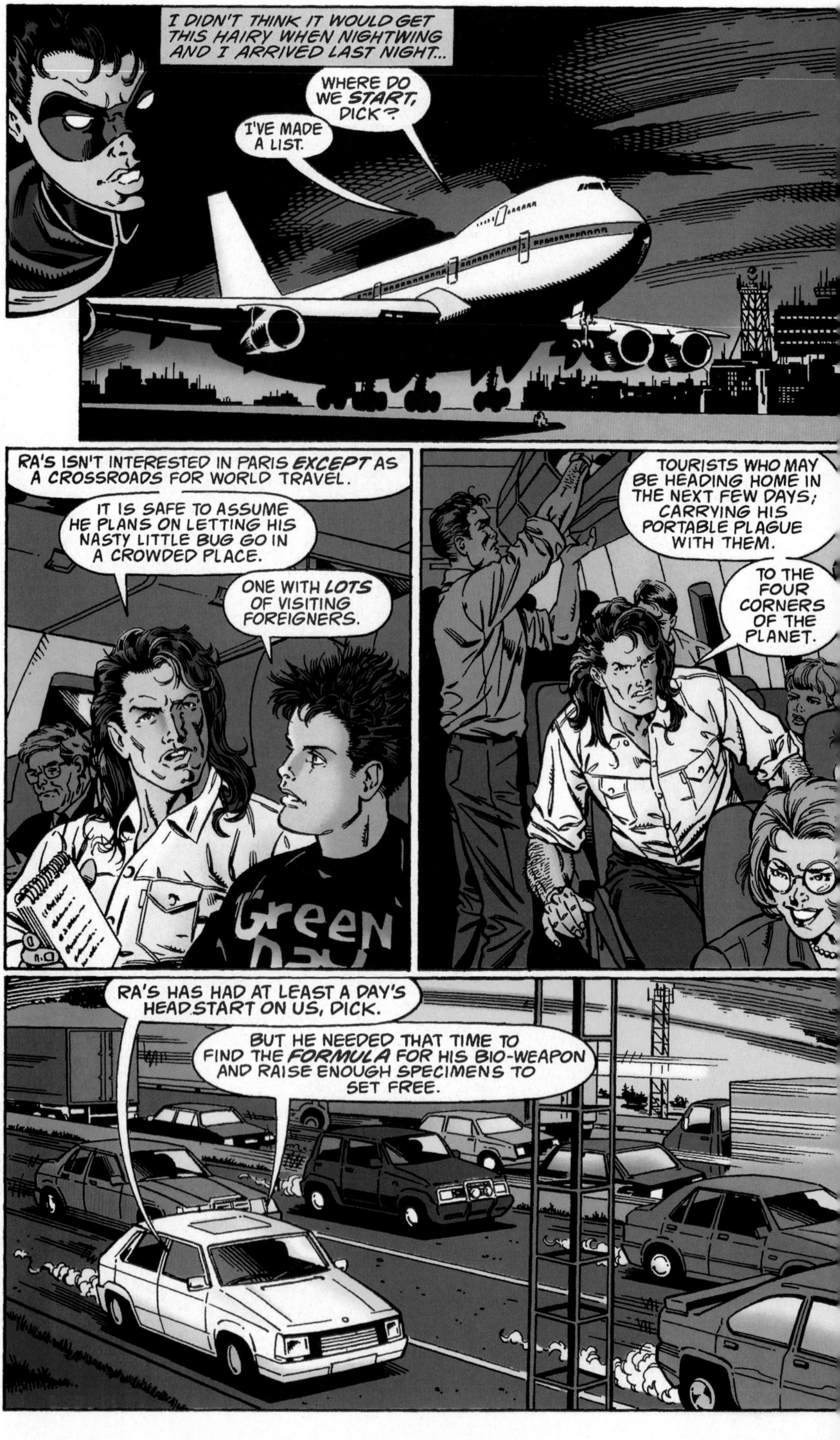
I DIDN'T THINK IT WOULD GET THIS HAIRY WHEN NIGHTWING AND I ARRIVED LAST NIGHT...
WHERE DO WE START, DICK?
I'VE MADE A LIST.
RA'S ISN'T INTERESTED IN PARIS EXCEPT AS A CROSSROADS FOR WORLD TRAVEL.
IT IS SAFE TO ASSUME HE PLANS ON LETTING HIS NASTY LITTLE BUG GO IN A CROWDED PLACE.
ONE WITH LOTS OF VISITING FOREIGNERS.
TOURISTS WHO MAY BE HEADING HOME IN THE NEXT FEW DAYS; CARRYING HIS PORTABLE PLAGUE WITH THEM.
TO THE FOUR CORNERS OF THE PLANET.
RA'S HAS HAD AT LEAST A DAY'S HEAD START ON US, DICK.
BUT HE NEEDED THAT TIME TO FIND THE FORMULA FOR HIS BIO-WEAPON AND RAISE ENOUGH SPECIMENS TO SET FREE.

THE EIFFEL TOWER. NOTRE DAME CATHEDRAL. THE CHAMPS ELYSEE. THE LEFT BANK. VERSAILLES.

I THINK WE CAN SAFELY FORGET EURO WINKYWORLD. EVEN *RA'S* HAS TO KNOW THAT PLACE WILL BE EMPTY.

I KNOW RA'S ISN'T THE SENTIMENTAL TYPE. SOME OF THE SITES I UNDERSTAND.

BUT WHY EDINBURGH?

HE'S GOT HIS OWN *PROGRAM,* I GUESS.

LIVING FOR CENTURIES CAN MAKE YOU PRETTY *TWISTED,* I GUESS.

PARIS TRAFFIC. THIS COULD TAKE *HOURS.*

HOURS WE DON'T *HAVE,* DICK.

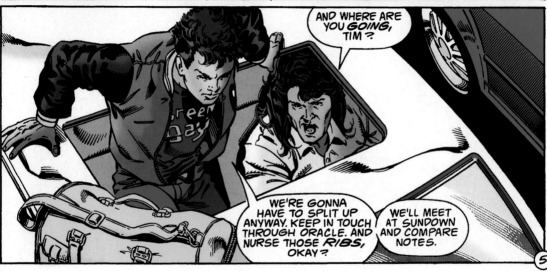

AND WHERE ARE YOU *GOING,* TIM?

WE'RE GONNA HAVE TO SPLIT UP ANYWAY. KEEP IN TOUCH THROUGH ORACLE. AND NURSE THOSE *RIBS,* OKAY?

WE'LL MEET AT SUNDOWN AND COMPARE NOTES.

5

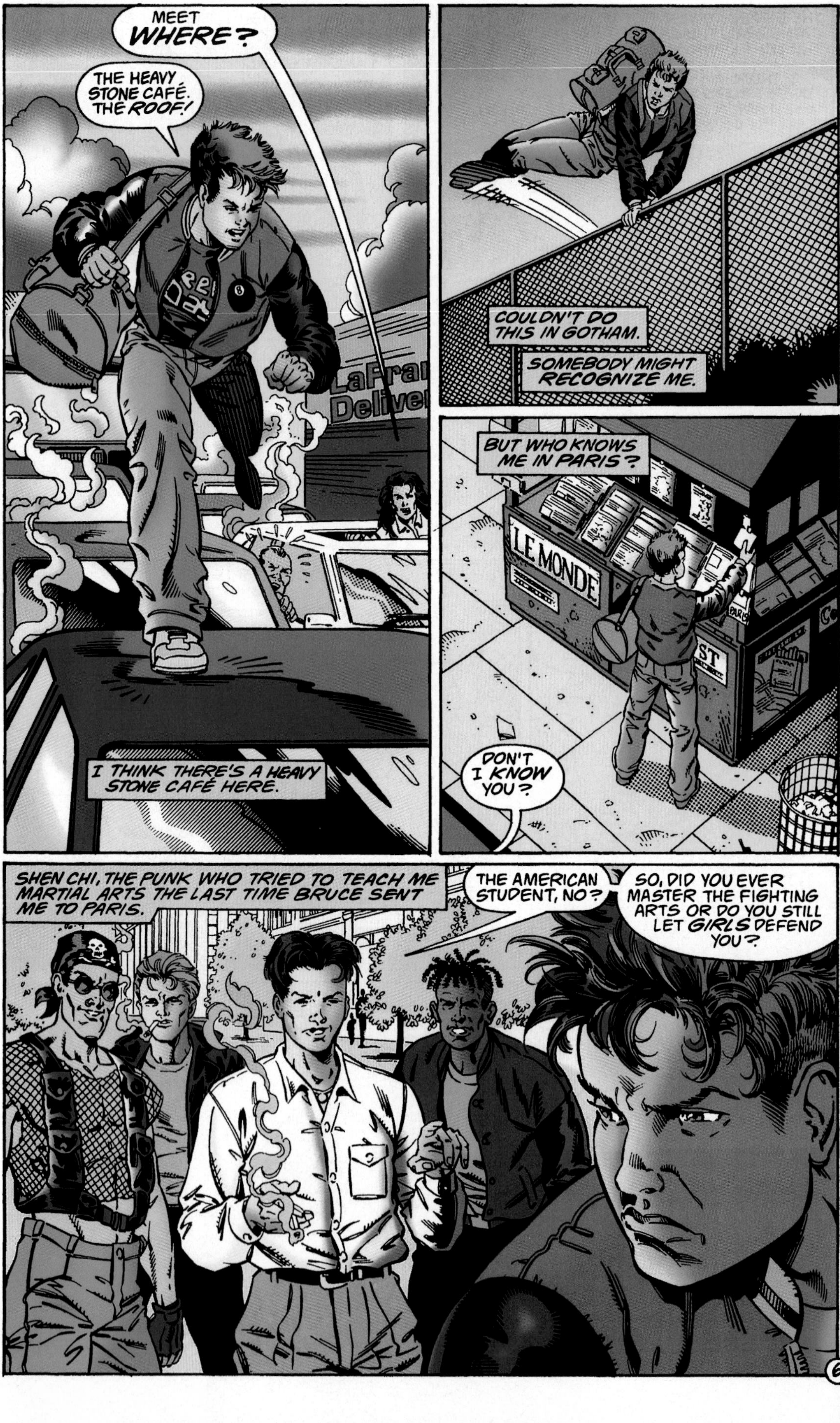
MEET WHERE?
THE HEAVY STONE CAFÉ. THE ROOF!
LaFran
Delive
I THINK THERE'S A HEAVY STONE CAFÉ HERE.
COULDN'T DO THIS IN GOTHAM.
SOMEBODY MIGHT RECOGNIZE ME.
BUT WHO KNOWS ME IN PARIS?
LE MONDE
DON'T I KNOW YOU?
SHEN CHI, THE PUNK WHO TRIED TO TEACH ME MARTIAL ARTS THE LAST TIME BRUCE SENT ME TO PARIS.
THE AMERICAN STUDENT, NO?
SO, DID YOU EVER MASTER THE FIGHTING ARTS OR DO YOU STILL LET GIRLS DEFEND YOU?

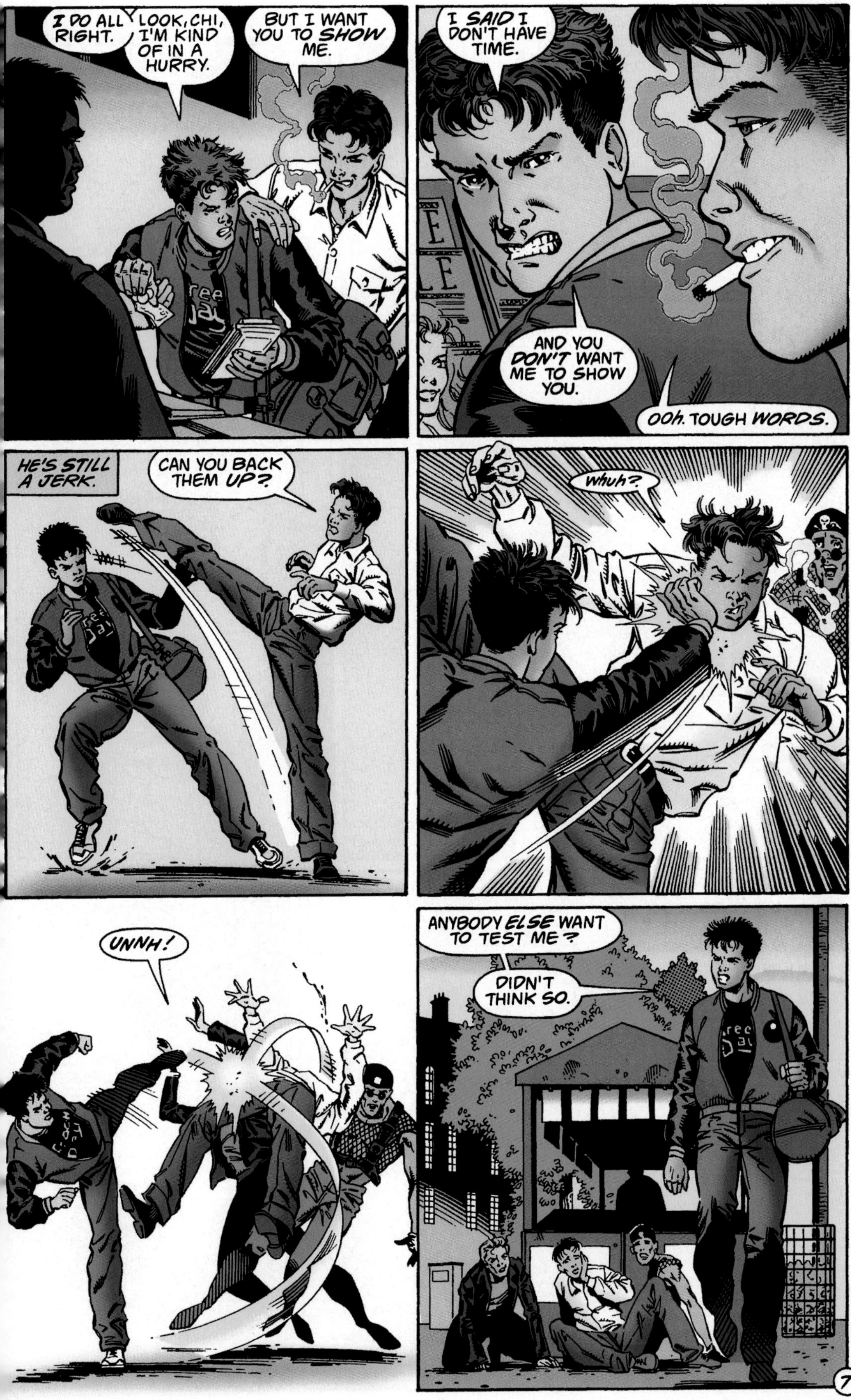

I DO ALL RIGHT.
LOOK, CHI, I'M KIND OF IN A HURRY.
BUT I WANT YOU TO SHOW ME.
I SAID I DON'T HAVE TIME.
AND YOU DON'T WANT ME TO SHOW YOU.
OOH. TOUGH WORDS.
HE'S STILL A JERK.
CAN YOU BACK THEM UP?
WHUH?
UNNH!
ANYBODY ELSE WANT TO TEST ME?
DIDN'T THINK SO.

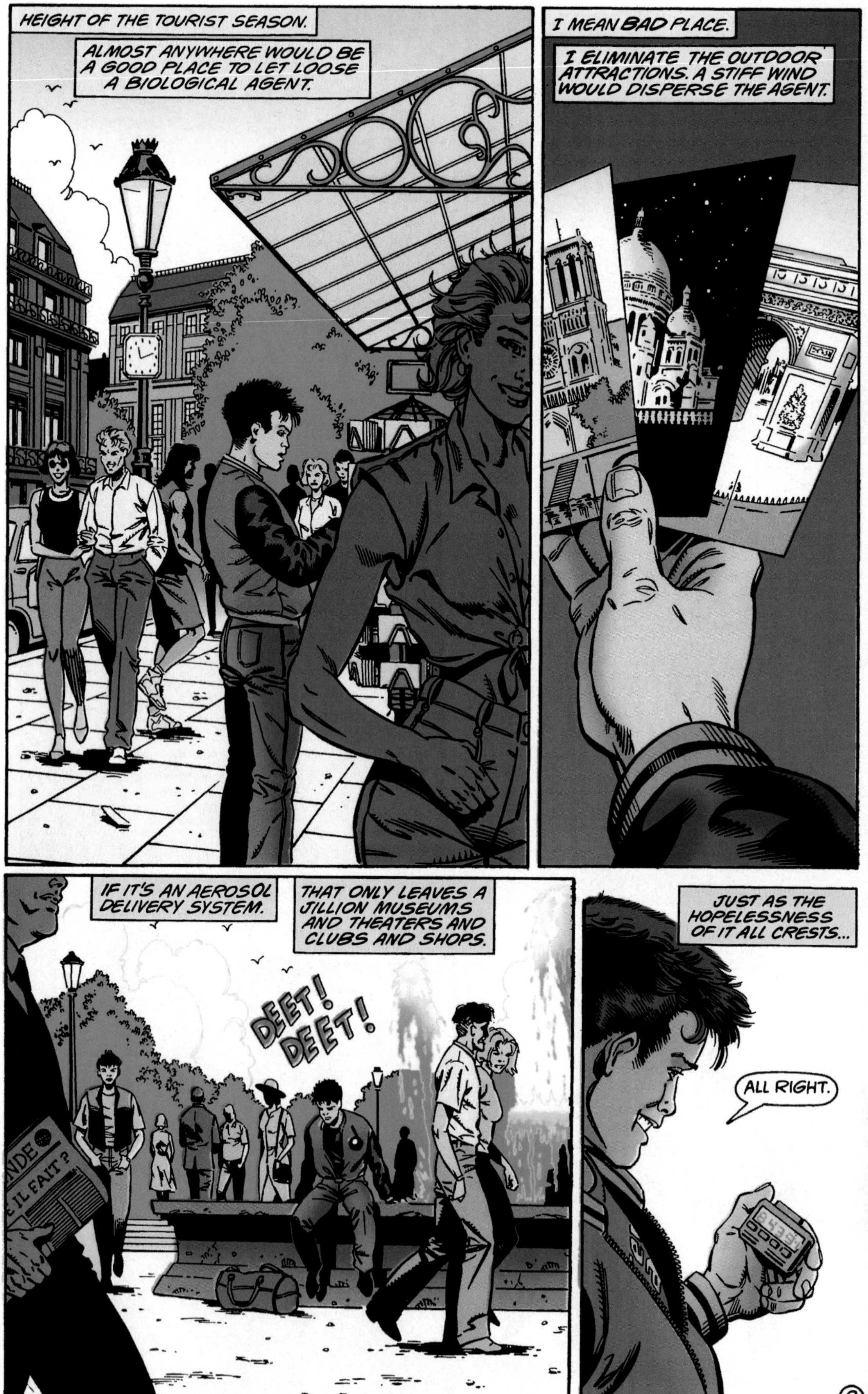
HEIGHT OF THE TOURIST SEASON.
ALMOST ANYWHERE WOULD BE A GOOD PLACE TO LET LOOSE A BIOLOGICAL AGENT.
I MEAN BAD PLACE.
I ELIMINATE THE OUTDOOR ATTRACTIONS. A STIFF WIND WOULD DISPERSE THE AGENT.
IF IT'S AN AEROSOL DELIVERY SYSTEM.
THAT ONLY LEAVES A JILLION MUSEUMS AND THEATERS AND CLUBS AND SHOPS.
DEET! DEET!
JUST AS THE HOPELESSNESS OF IT ALL CRESTS...
ALL RIGHT.

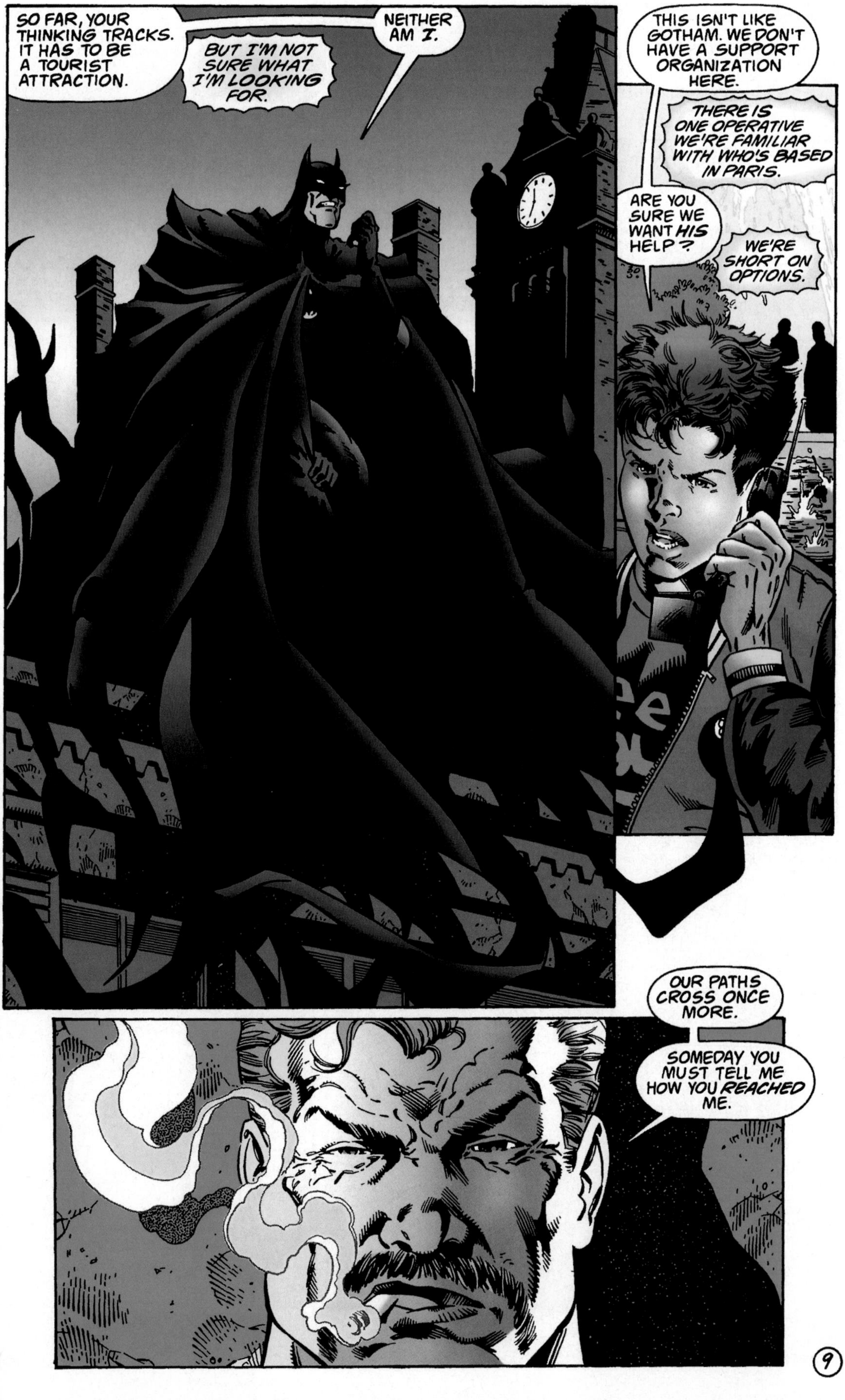

SO FAR, YOUR THINKING TRACKS. IT HAS TO BE A TOURIST ATTRACTION.
BUT I'M NOT SURE WHAT I'M LOOKING FOR.
NEITHER AM I.
THIS ISN'T LIKE GOTHAM. WE DON'T HAVE A SUPPORT ORGANIZATION HERE.
THERE IS ONE OPERATIVE WE'RE FAMILIAR WITH WHO'S BASED IN PARIS.
ARE YOU SURE WE WANT HIS HELP?
WE'RE SHORT ON OPTIONS.
OUR PATHS CROSS ONCE MORE.
SOMEDAY YOU MUST TELL ME HOW YOU REACHED ME.

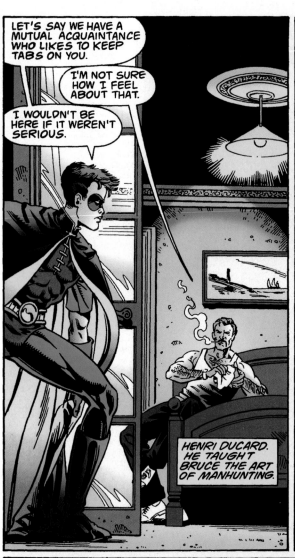

LET'S SAY WE HAVE A MUTUAL ACQUAINTANCE WHO LIKES TO KEEP TABS ON YOU.

I'M NOT SURE HOW I FEEL ABOUT THAT.

I WOULDN'T BE HERE IF IT WEREN'T SERIOUS.

HENRI DUCARD. HE TAUGHT BRUCE THE ART OF MANHUNTING.

AN EXPERT.

A PROFESSIONAL.

AN UNPRINCIPLED KILLER.

HOW SERIOUS IS THE REWARD?

NO REWARD.

THEN WE HAVE NOTHING TO TALK ABOUT.

THIS IS BIGGER THAN YOUR BANK ACCOUNT, DUCARD.

I LAY IT OUT FOR HIM.

THE PLAGUE. THE THREAT.

THE END OF THE WORLD AND EVERYTHING THAT GOES WITH IT.

JE M'EN FICHE.

MOST WHO WILL DIE ARE STRANGERS TO ME.

THE FEW I KNOW I WOULD PREFER DEAD.

10

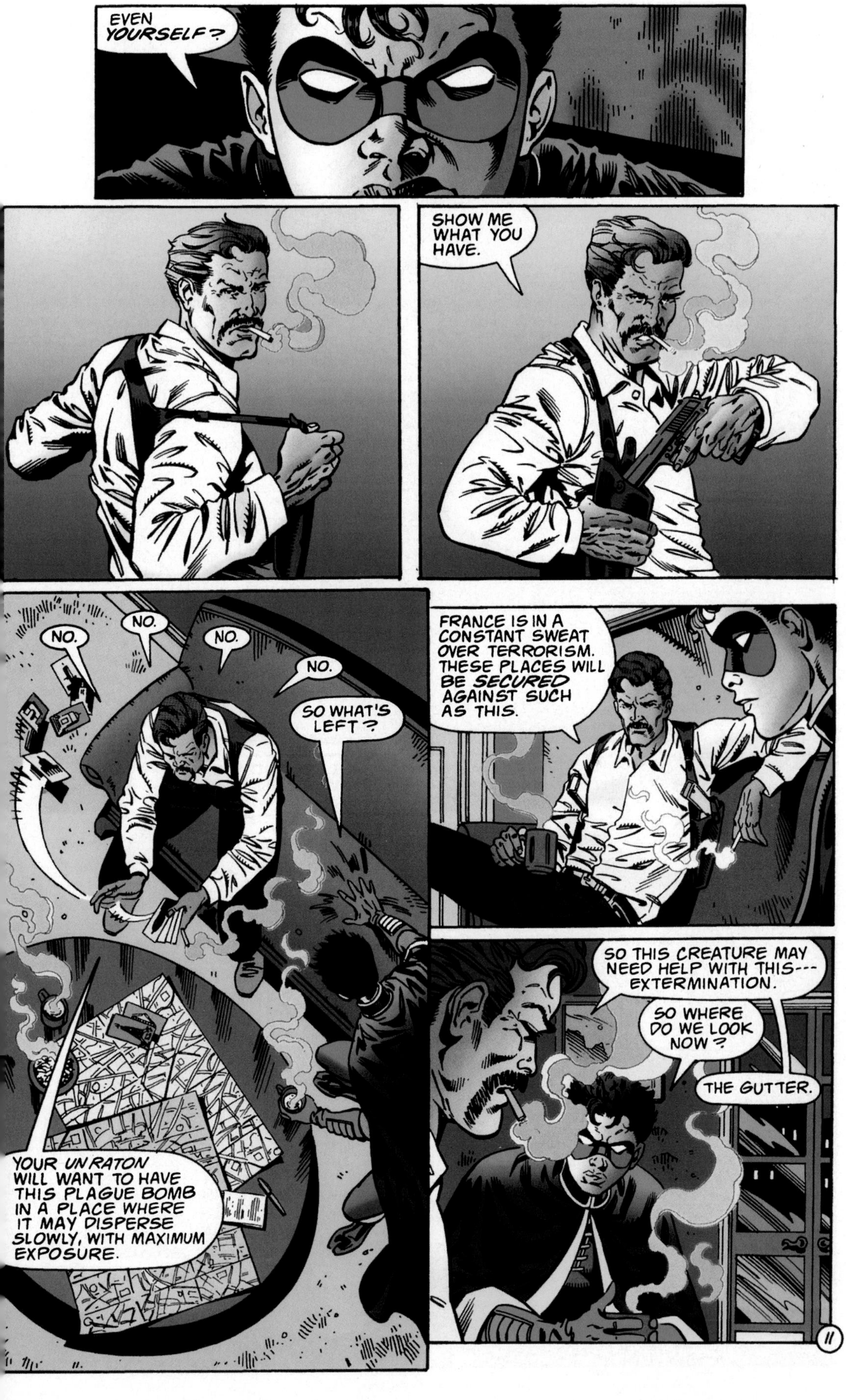

EVEN YOURSELF?
SHOW ME WHAT YOU HAVE.
NO.
NO.
NO.
NO.
SO WHAT'S LEFT?
YOUR UN RATON WILL WANT TO HAVE THIS PLAGUE BOMB IN A PLACE WHERE IT MAY DISPERSE SLOWLY, WITH MAXIMUM EXPOSURE.
FRANCE IS IN A CONSTANT SWEAT OVER TERRORISM. THESE PLACES WILL BE SECURED AGAINST SUCH AS THIS.
SO THIS CREATURE MAY NEED HELP WITH THIS--- EXTERMINATION.
SO WHERE DO WE LOOK NOW?
THE GUTTER.

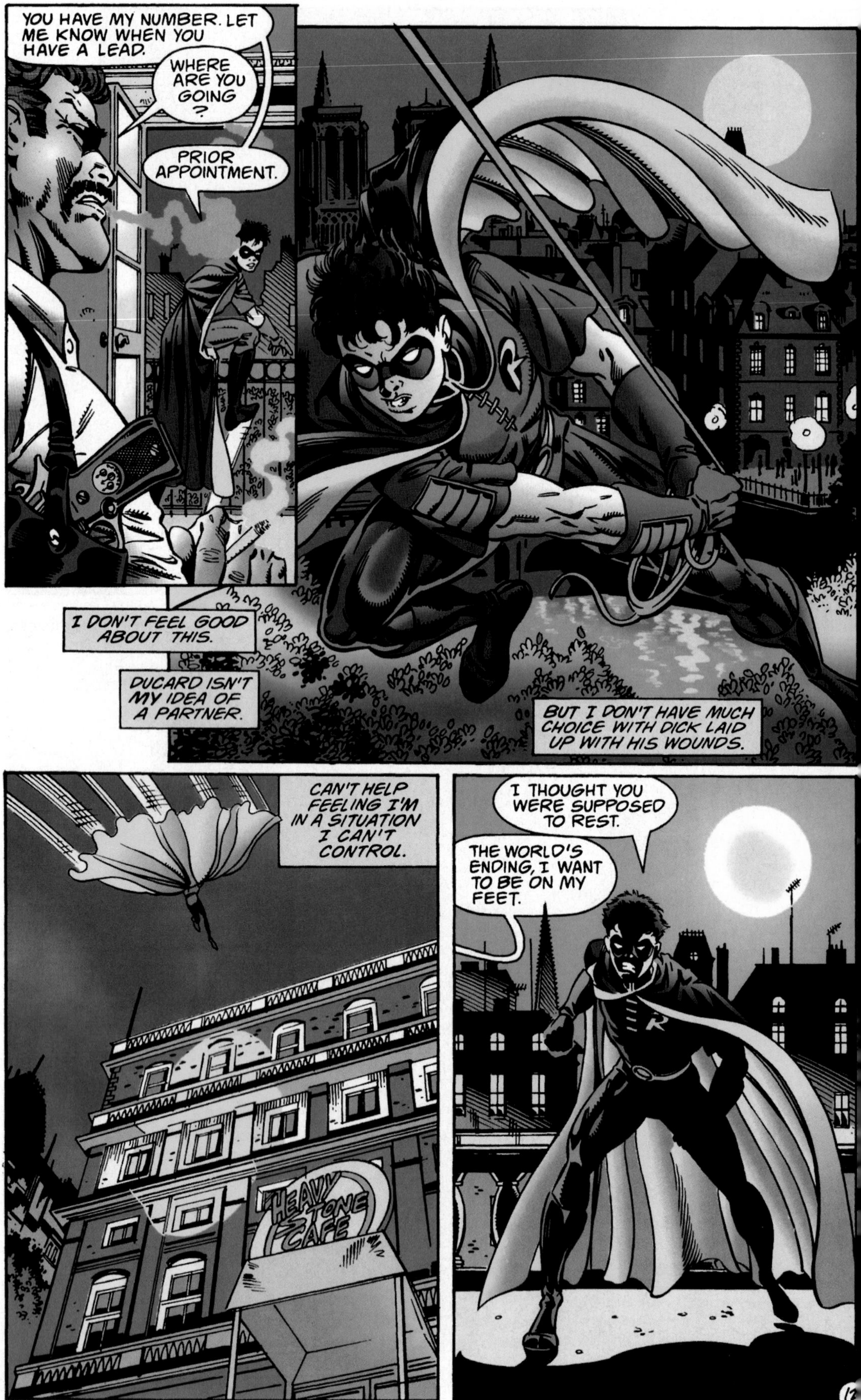
YOU HAVE MY NUMBER. LET ME KNOW WHEN YOU HAVE A LEAD.
WHERE ARE YOU GOING?
PRIOR APPOINTMENT.
I DON'T FEEL GOOD ABOUT THIS.
DUCARD ISN'T MY IDEA OF A PARTNER.
BUT I DON'T HAVE MUCH CHOICE WITH DICK LAID UP WITH HIS WOUNDS.
CAN'T HELP FEELING I'M IN A SITUATION I CAN'T CONTROL.
HEAVY STONE CAFE
I THOUGHT YOU WERE SUPPOSED TO REST.
THE WORLD'S ENDING, I WANT TO BE ON MY FEET.

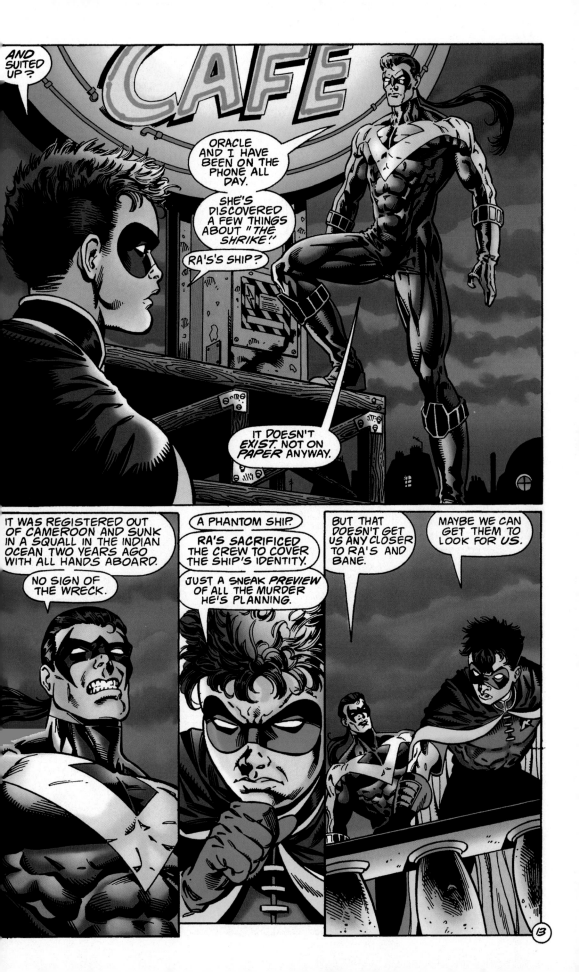

AND SUITED UP?

ORACLE AND I HAVE BEEN ON THE PHONE ALL DAY.

SHE'S DISCOVERED A FEW THINGS ABOUT "THE SHRIKE!"

RA'S'S SHIP?

IT DOESN'T EXIST. NOT ON PAPER ANYWAY.

IT WAS REGISTERED OUT OF CAMEROON AND SUNK IN A SQUALL IN THE INDIAN OCEAN TWO YEARS AGO WITH ALL HANDS ABOARD.

NO SIGN OF THE WRECK.

A PHANTOM SHIP.

RA'S SACRIFICED THE CREW TO COVER THE SHIP'S IDENTITY.

JUST A SNEAK PREVIEW OF ALL THE MURDER HE'S PLANNING.

BUT THAT DOESN'T GET US ANY CLOSER TO RA'S AND BANE.

MAYBE WE CAN GET THEM TO LOOK FOR US.

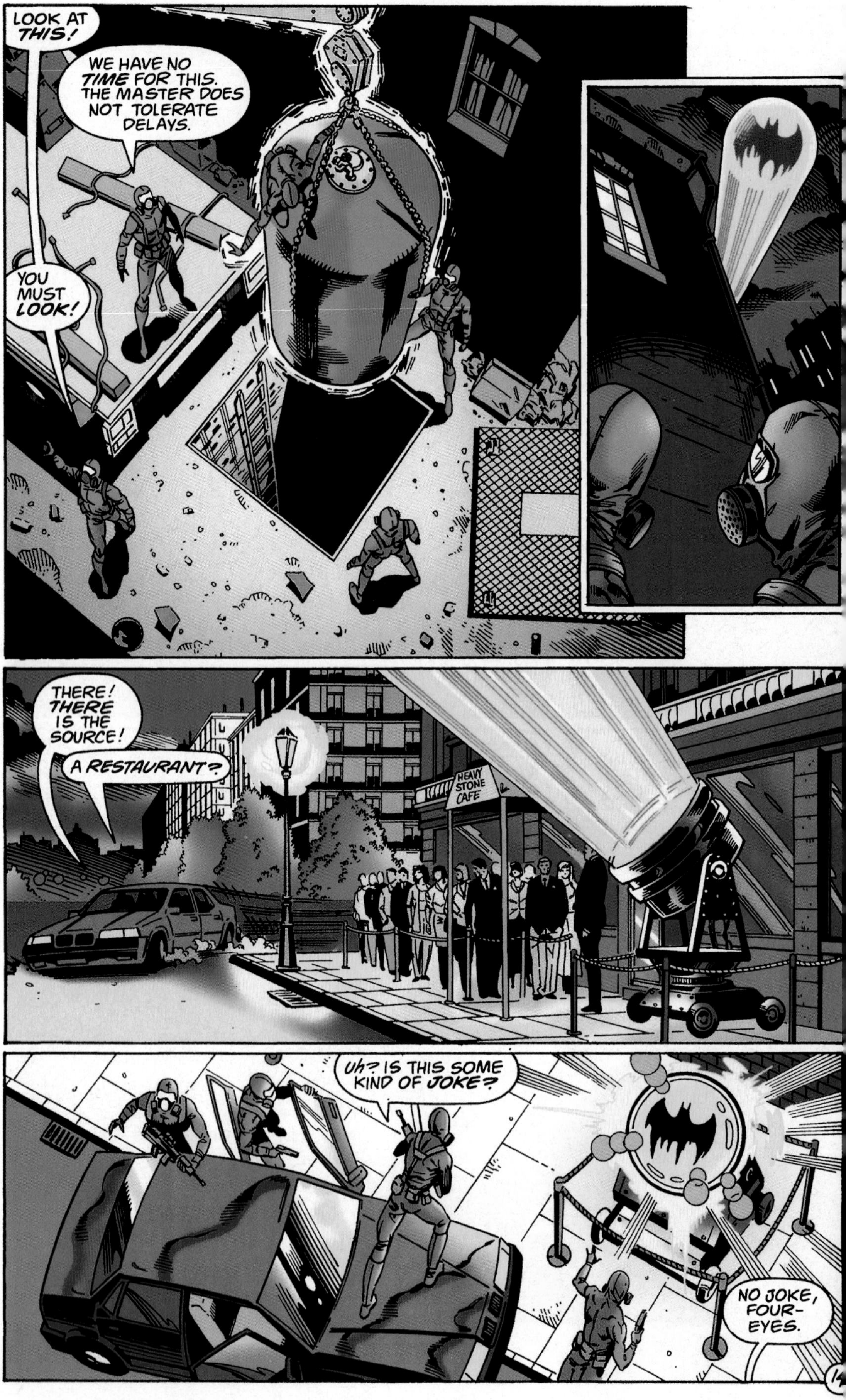
LOOK AT THIS!
WE HAVE NO TIME FOR THIS. THE MASTER DOES NOT TOLERATE DELAYS.
YOU MUST LOOK!
THERE! THERE IS THE SOURCE!
A RESTAURANT?
HEAVY STONE CAFE
Uh? IS THIS SOME KIND OF JOKE?
NO JOKE, FOUR-EYES.

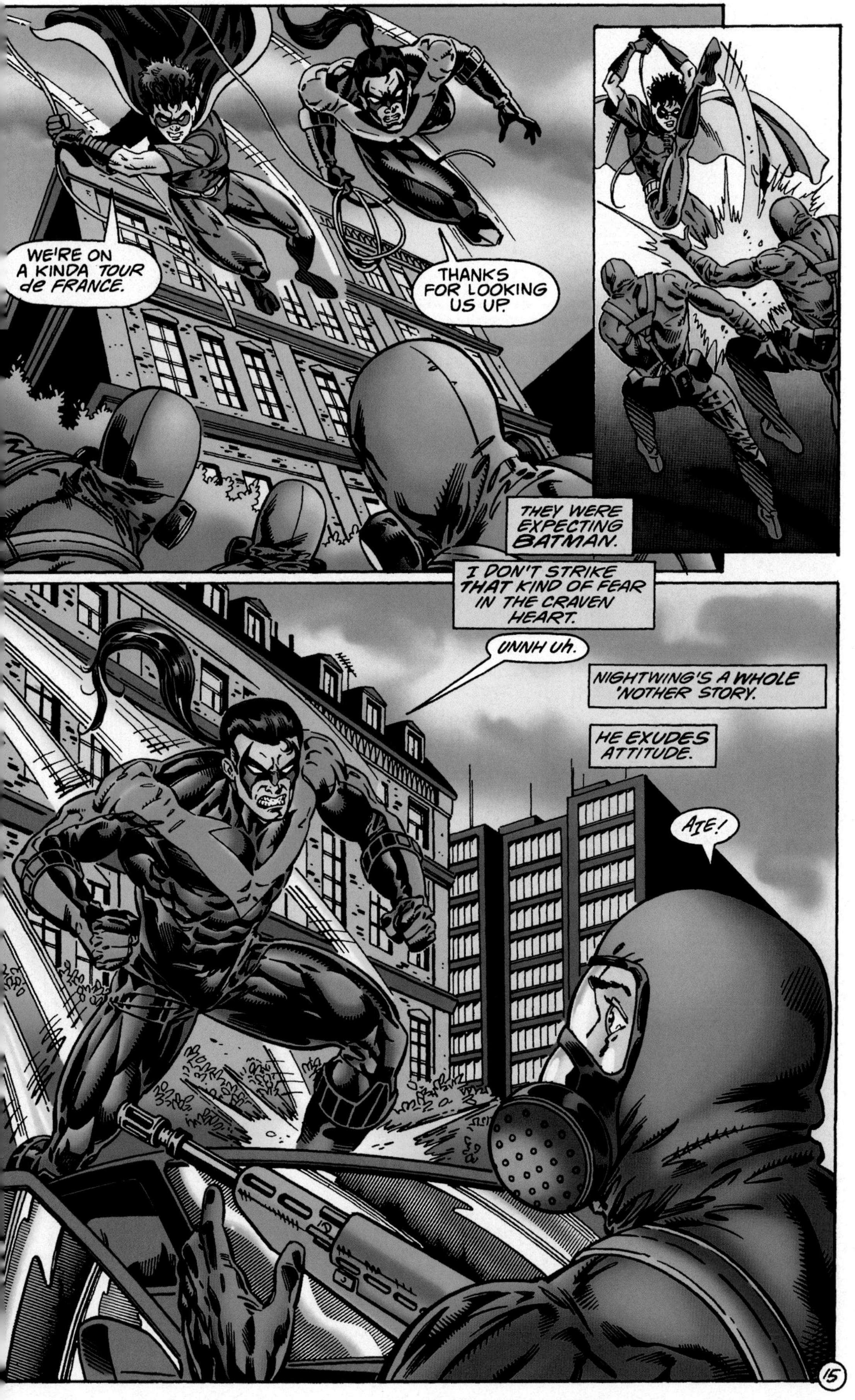
WE'RE ON A KINDA TOUR de FRANCE.
THANKS FOR LOOKING US UP.
THEY WERE EXPECTING BATMAN.
I DON'T STRIKE THAT KIND OF FEAR IN THE CRAVEN HEART.
UNNH uh.
NIGHTWING'S A WHOLE 'NOTHER STORY.
HE EXUDES ATTITUDE.
AIE!

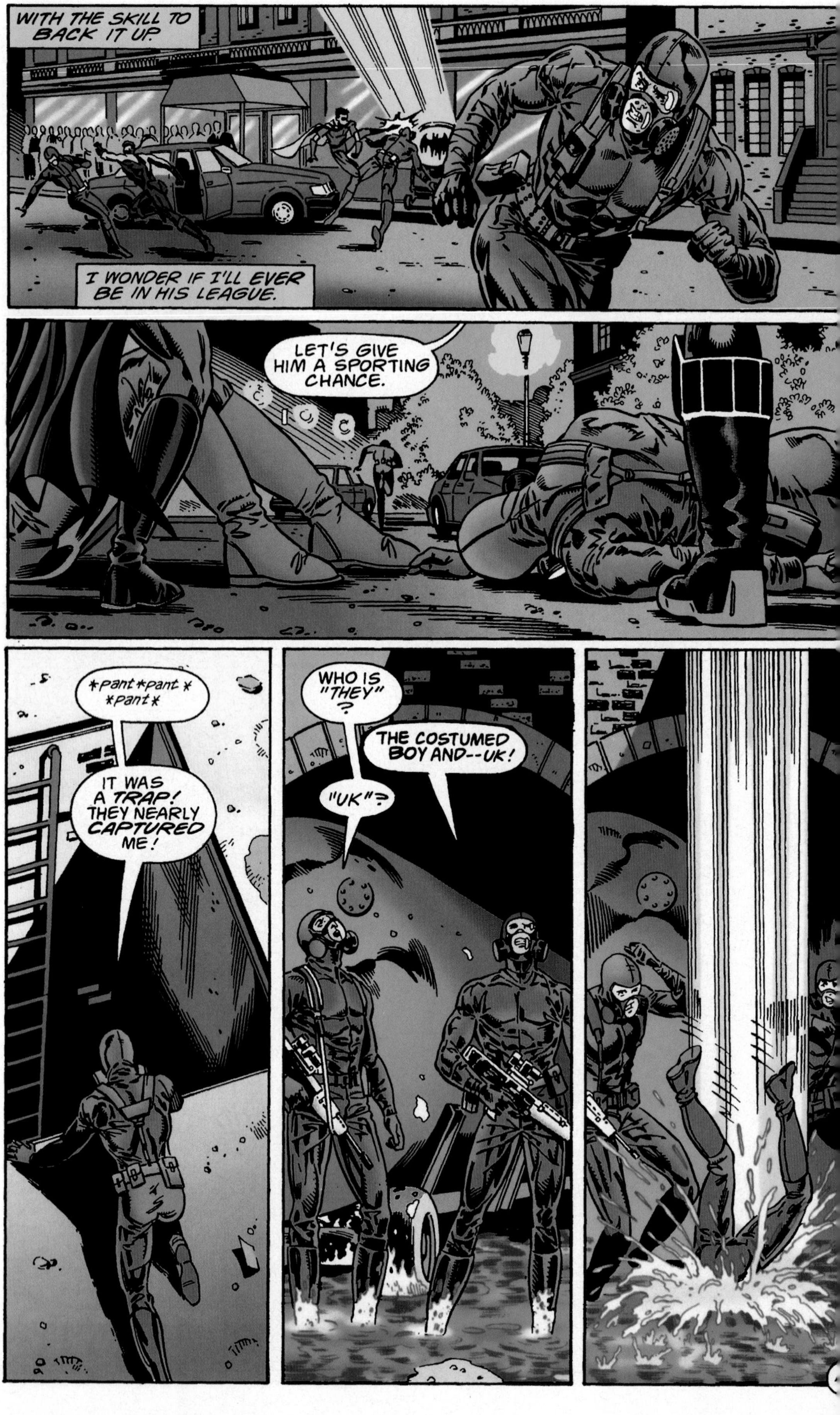

WITH THE SKILL TO BACK IT UP.
I WONDER IF I'LL EVER BE IN HIS LEAGUE.
LET'S GIVE HIM A SPORTING CHANCE.
*pant*pant* *pant*
IT WAS A TRAP! THEY NEARLY CAPTURED ME!
WHO IS "THEY"?
THE COSTUMED BOY AND--UK!
"UK"?

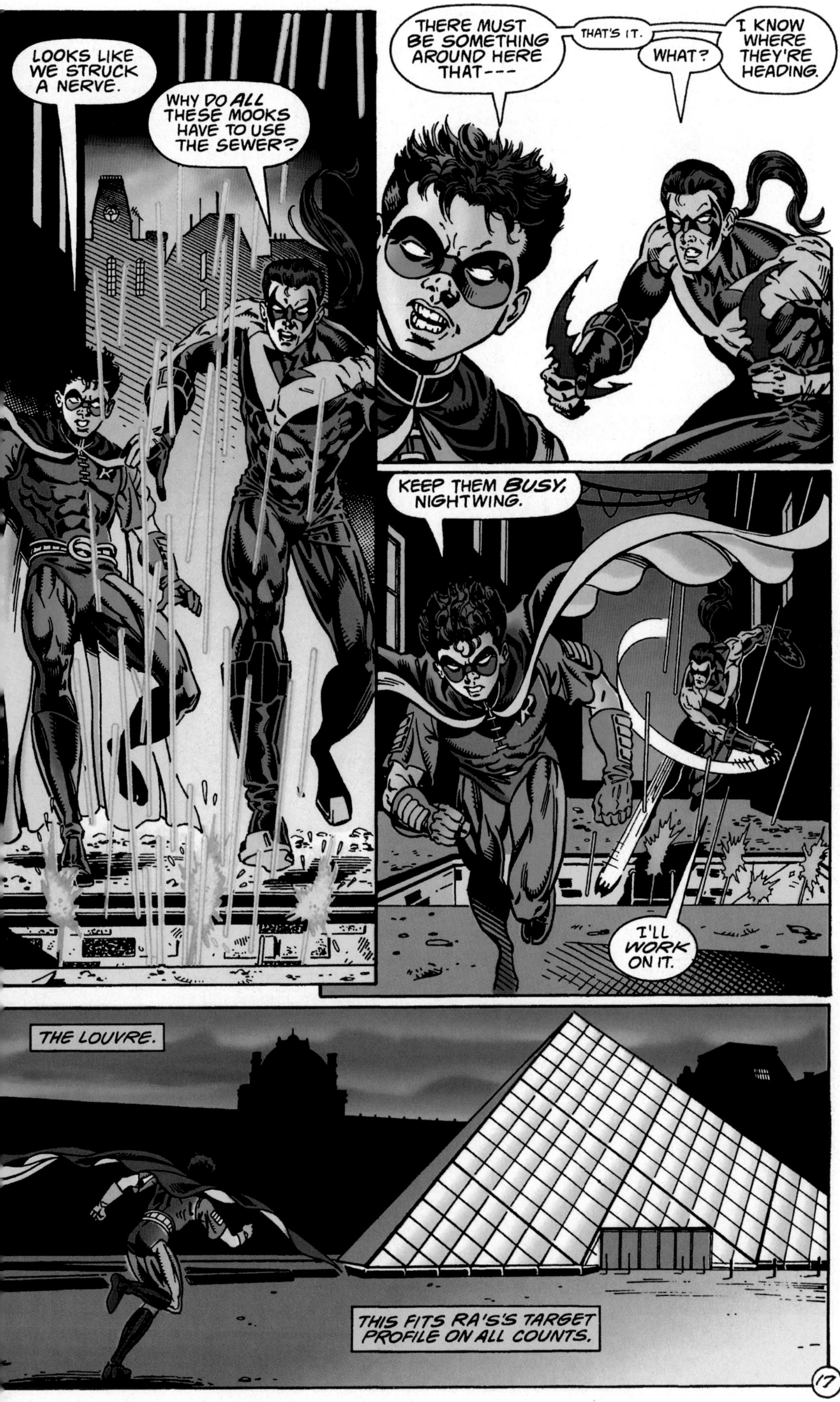

LOOKS LIKE WE STRUCK A NERVE.
WHY DO ALL THESE MOOKS HAVE TO USE THE SEWER?
THERE MUST BE SOMETHING AROUND HERE THAT---
THAT'S IT.
WHAT?
I KNOW WHERE THEY'RE HEADING.
KEEP THEM BUSY, NIGHTWING.
I'LL WORK ON IT.
THE LOUVRE.
THIS FITS RA'S'S TARGET PROFILE ON ALL COUNTS.

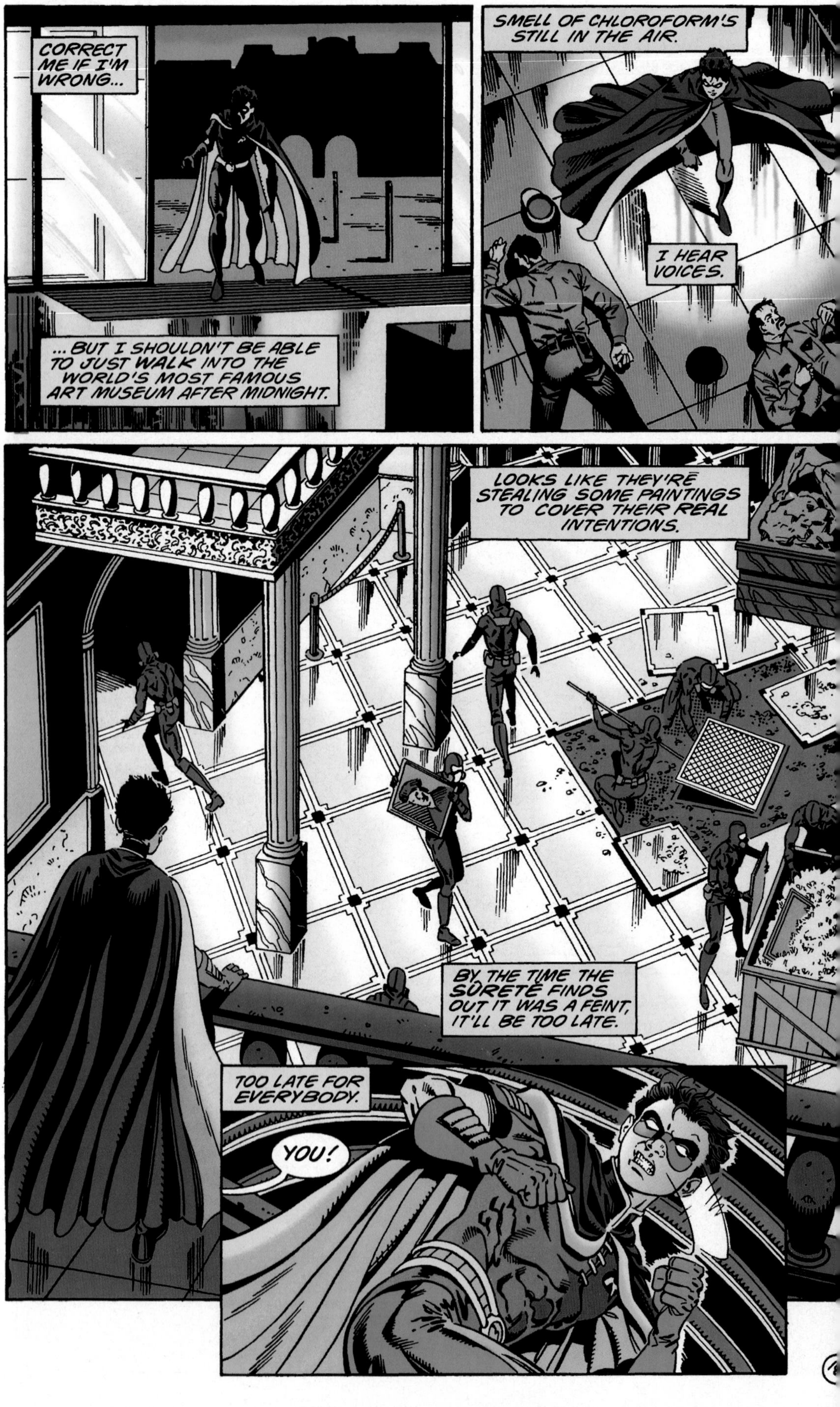
CORRECT ME IF I'M WRONG...
...BUT I SHOULDN'T BE ABLE TO JUST WALK INTO THE WORLD'S MOST FAMOUS ART MUSEUM AFTER MIDNIGHT.
SMELL OF CHLOROFORM'S STILL IN THE AIR.
I HEAR VOICES.
LOOKS LIKE THEY'RE STEALING SOME PAINTINGS TO COVER THEIR REAL INTENTIONS.
BY THE TIME THE SÛRETÉ FINDS OUT IT WAS A FEINT, IT'LL BE TOO LATE.
TOO LATE FOR EVERYBODY.
YOU!

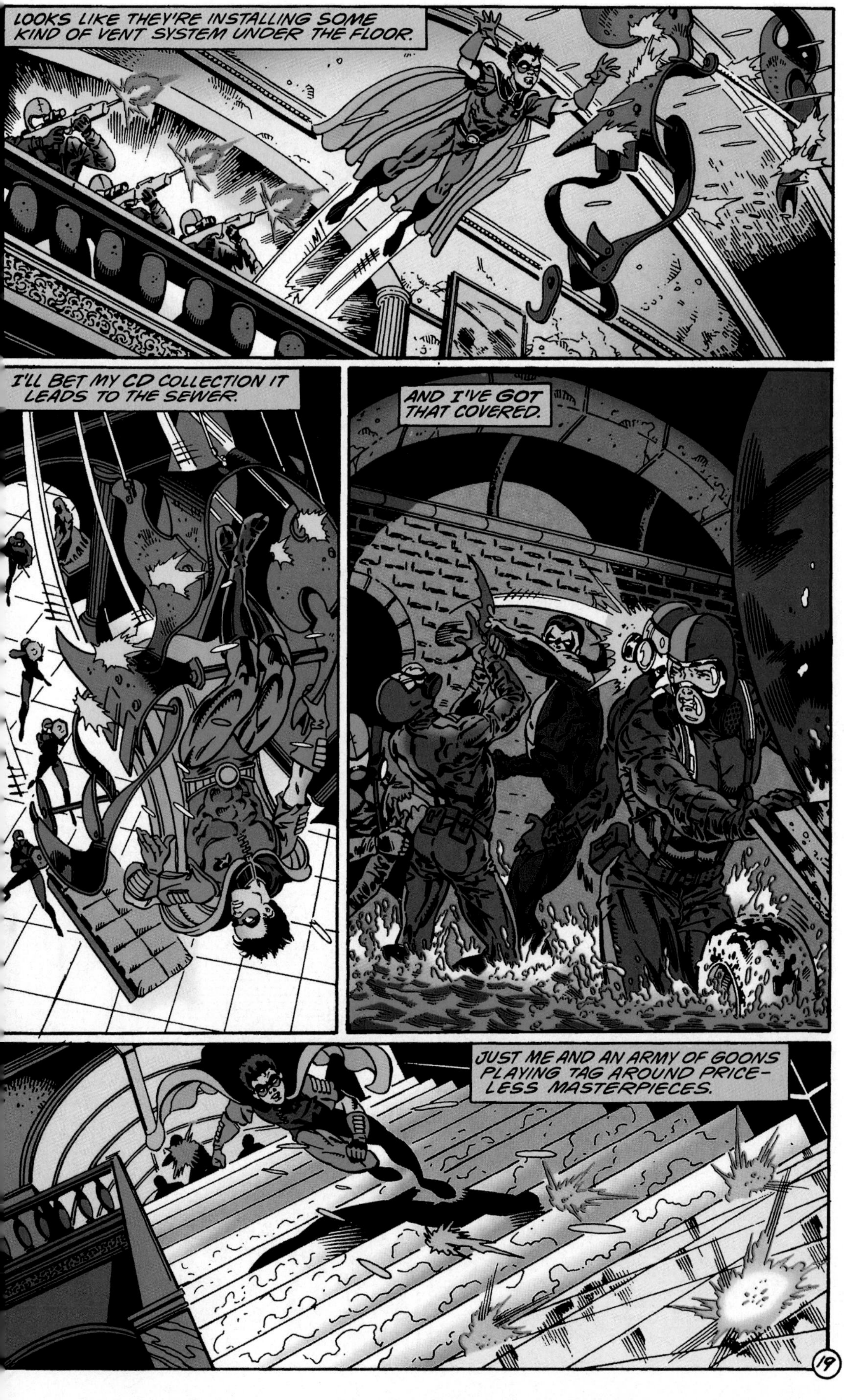
LOOKS LIKE THEY'RE INSTALLING SOME KIND OF VENT SYSTEM UNDER THE FLOOR.
I'LL BET MY CD COLLECTION IT LEADS TO THE SEWER.
AND I'VE GOT THAT COVERED.
JUST ME AND AN ARMY OF GOONS PLAYING TAG AROUND PRICE-LESS MASTERPIECES.

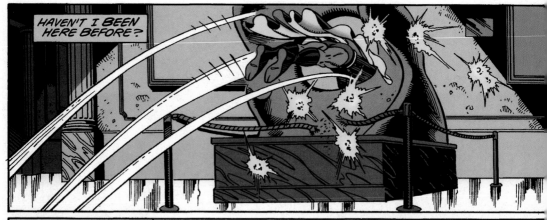

HAVEN'T I BEEN HERE BEFORE?

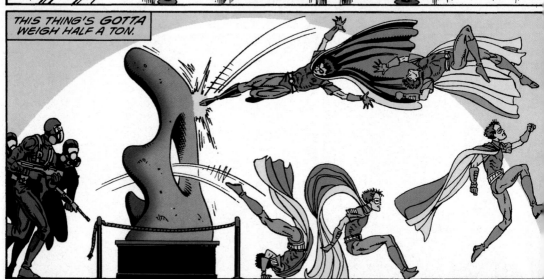

THIS THING'S GOTTA WEIGH HALF A TON.

HOPE IT WAS INSURED.

IF IT WASN'T, I CAN SAY IT WAS PERFORMANCE ART.

THE ART OF SURVIVAL.

FOR ABOUT THREE MORE SECONDS.

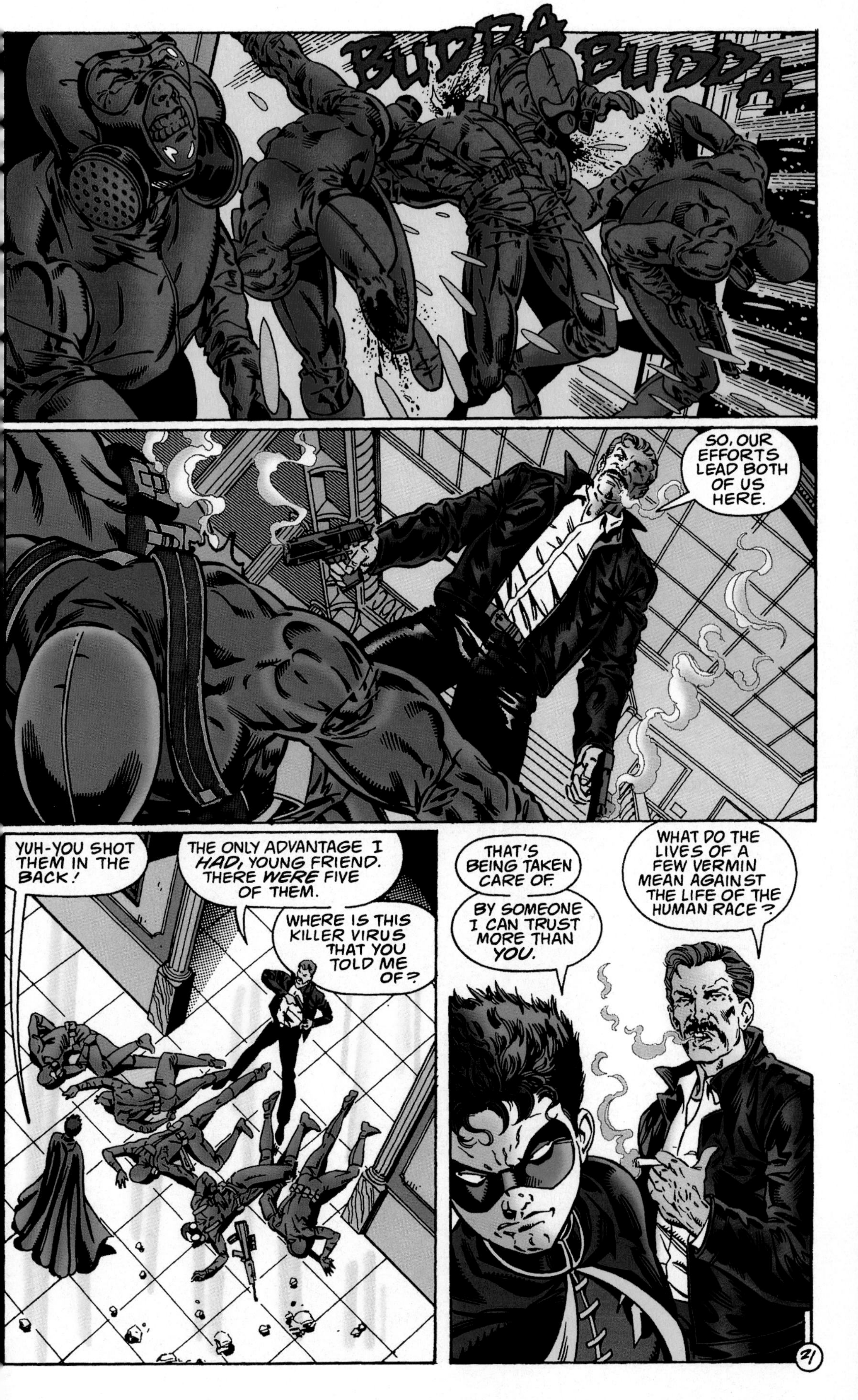

BUDDA BUDDA
SO, OUR EFFORTS LEAD BOTH OF US HERE.
YUH-YOU SHOT THEM IN THE BACK!
THE ONLY ADVANTAGE I *HAD*, YOUNG FRIEND. THERE *WERE* FIVE OF THEM.
WHERE IS THIS KILLER VIRUS THAT YOU TOLD ME OF?
THAT'S BEING TAKEN CARE OF.
BY SOMEONE I CAN TRUST MORE THAN *YOU*.
WHAT DO THE LIVES OF A FEW VERMIN MEAN AGAINST THE LIFE OF THE HUMAN RACE?

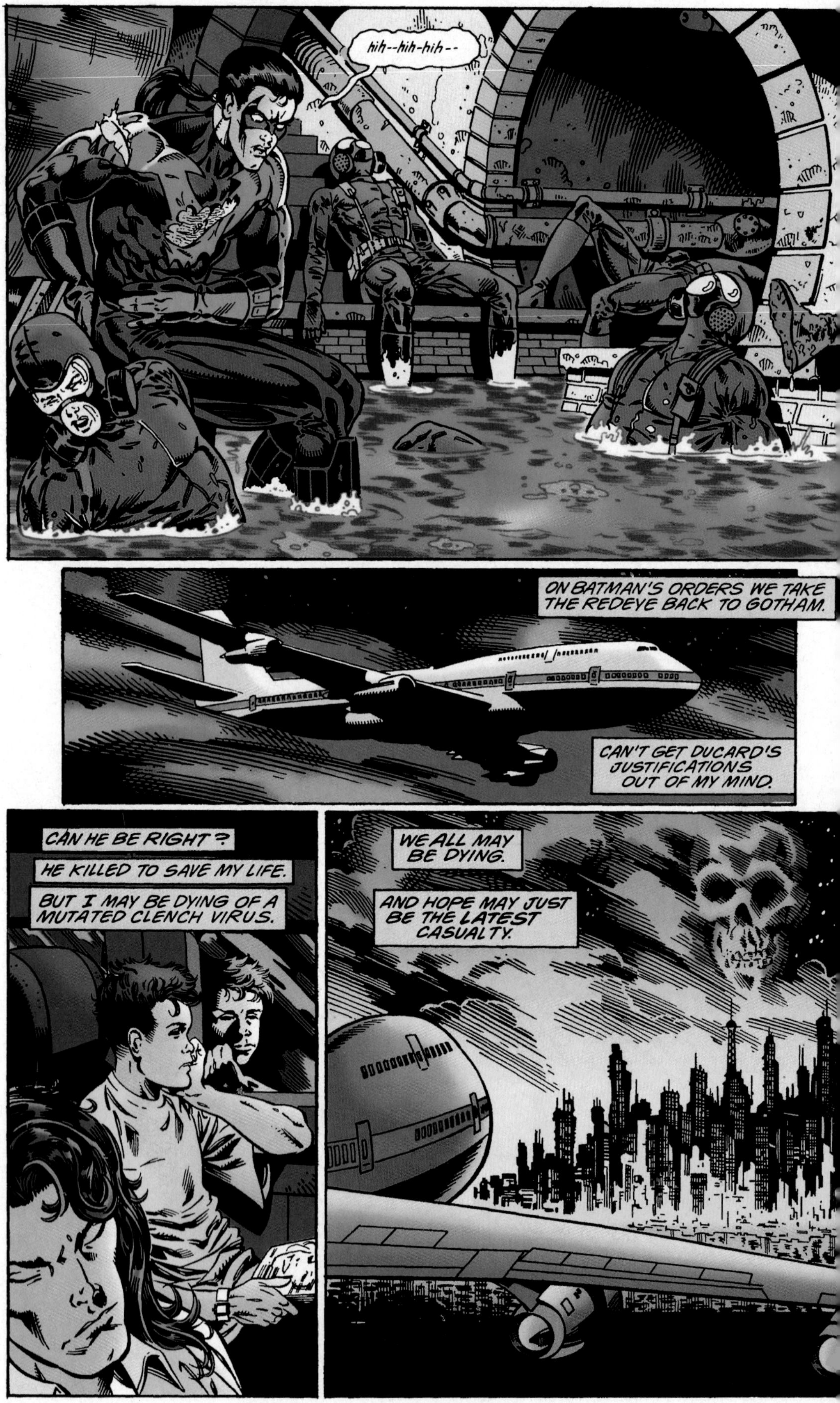
hih--hih-hih--
ON BATMAN'S ORDERS WE TAKE THE REDEYE BACK TO GOTHAM.
CAN'T GET DUCARD'S JUSTIFICATIONS OUT OF MY MIND.
CAN HE BE RIGHT?
HE KILLED TO SAVE MY LIFE.
BUT I MAY BE DYING OF A MUTATED CLENCH VIRUS.
WE ALL MAY BE DYING.
AND HOPE MAY JUST BE THE LATEST CASUALTY.

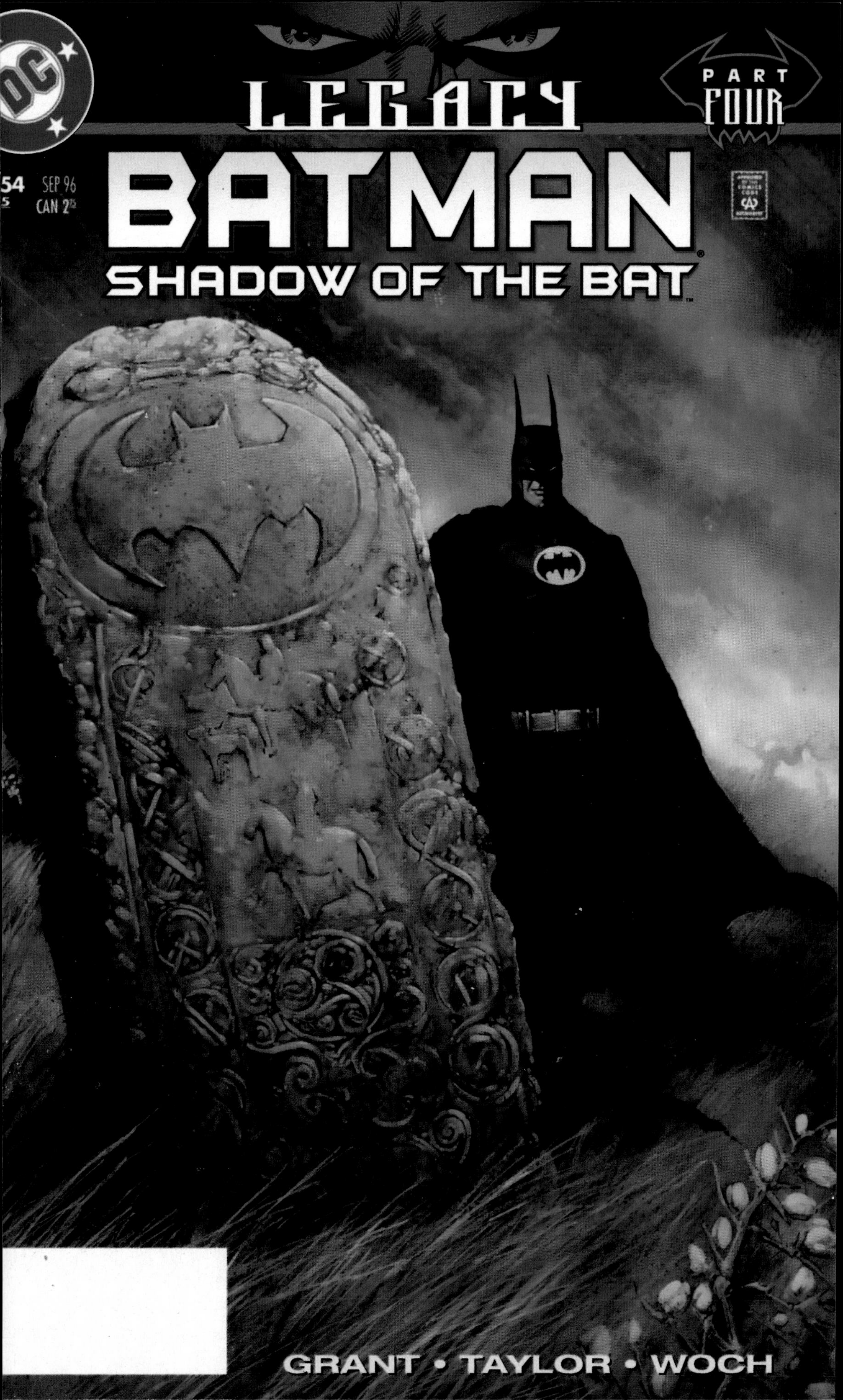
LEGACY
PART FOUR
54 SEP 96
CAN 2.75
BATMAN
SHADOW OF THE BAT
GRANT • TAYLOR • WOCH

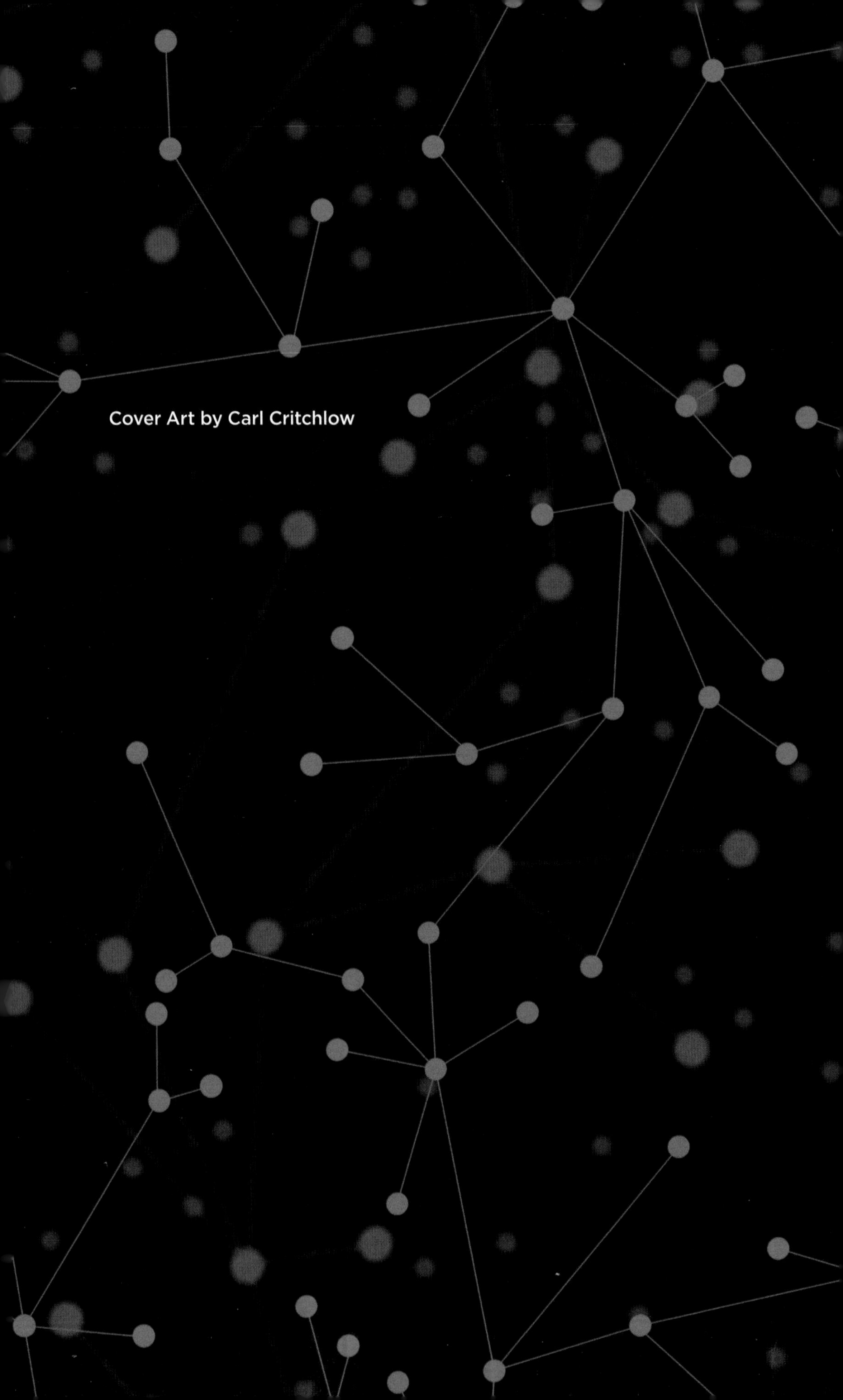

Cover Art by Carl Critchlow

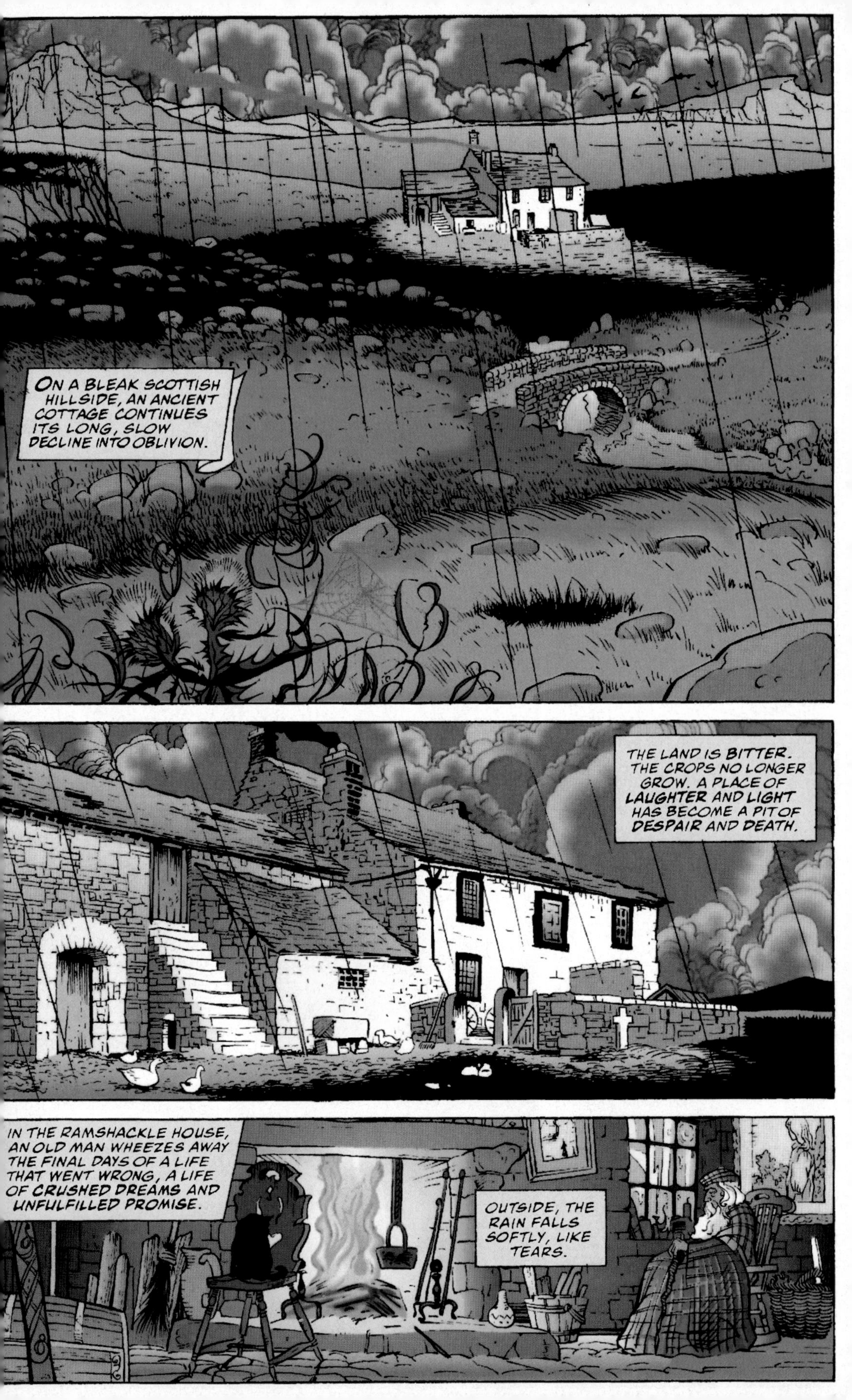
ON A BLEAK SCOTTISH HILLSIDE, AN ANCIENT COTTAGE CONTINUES ITS LONG, SLOW DECLINE INTO OBLIVION.
THE LAND IS BITTER. THE CROPS NO LONGER GROW. A PLACE OF LAUGHTER AND LIGHT HAS BECOME A PIT OF DESPAIR AND DEATH.
IN THE RAMSHACKLE HOUSE, AN OLD MAN WHEEZES AWAY THE FINAL DAYS OF A LIFE THAT WENT WRONG, A LIFE OF CRUSHED DREAMS AND UNFULFILLED PROMISE.
OUTSIDE, THE RAIN FALLS SOFTLY, LIKE TEARS.

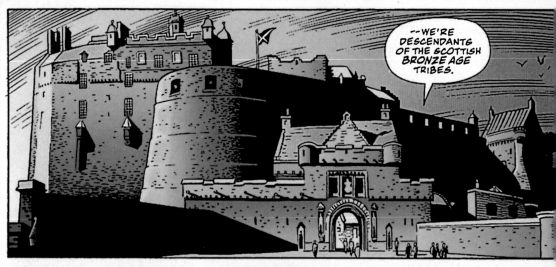

--WE'RE DESCENDANTS OF THE SCOTTISH *BRONZE AGE* TRIBES.

THE ROMAN INVADERS CALLED THEM *PICTI*-- *"THE PAINTED ONES,"* BUT NOBODY KNOWS WHAT THESE PEOPLE CALLED *THEMSELVES,* FOR *NO* WRITTEN RECORDS SURVIVE OTHER THAN THEIR UNIQUE *SYMBOL STONES.*

◄ EXHIBITION OF PICTISH CULTURE BEFORE 900AD

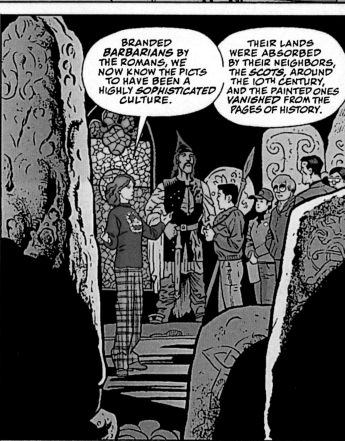

BRANDED *BARBARIANS* BY THE ROMANS, WE NOW KNOW THE PICTS TO HAVE BEEN A HIGHLY *SOPHISTICATED* CULTURE.

THEIR LANDS WERE *ABSORBED* BY THEIR NEIGHBORS, THE *SCOTS,* AROUND THE 10TH CENTURY, AND THE PAINTED ONES *VANISHED* FROM THE PAGES OF HISTORY.

AS I'M AFRAID *YOU'LL* NOW HAVE TO VANISH FROM THE EXHIBITION, LADIES AND GENTS. IT'S CLOSING TIME!

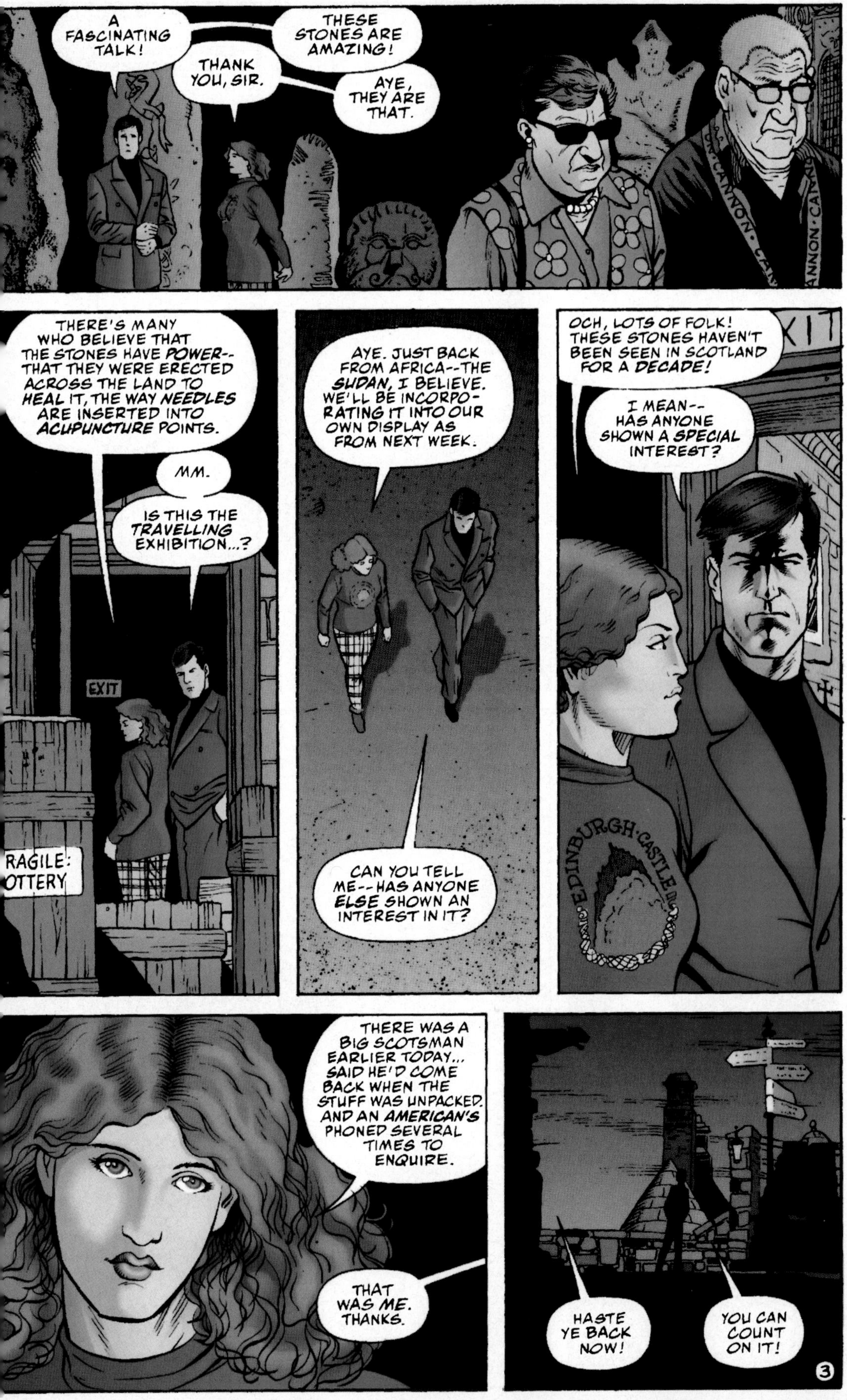
A FASCINATING TALK!
THESE STONES ARE AMAZING!
THANK YOU, SIR.
AYE, THEY ARE THAT.
CANNON
THERE'S MANY WHO BELIEVE THAT THE STONES HAVE POWER--THAT THEY WERE ERECTED ACROSS THE LAND TO HEAL IT, THE WAY NEEDLES ARE INSERTED INTO ACUPUNCTURE POINTS.
MM.
IS THIS THE TRAVELLING EXHIBITION...?
EXIT
RAGILE: OTTERY
AYE. JUST BACK FROM AFRICA--THE SUDAN, I BELIEVE. WE'LL BE INCORPORATING IT INTO OUR OWN DISPLAY AS FROM NEXT WEEK.
CAN YOU TELL ME--HAS ANYONE ELSE SHOWN AN INTEREST IN IT?
OCH, LOTS OF FOLK! THESE STONES HAVEN'T BEEN SEEN IN SCOTLAND FOR A DECADE!
I MEAN--HAS ANYONE SHOWN A SPECIAL INTEREST?
EXIT
EDINBURGH·CASTLE
THERE WAS A BIG SCOTSMAN EARLIER TODAY... SAID HE'D COME BACK WHEN THE STUFF WAS UNPACKED. AND AN AMERICAN'S PHONED SEVERAL TIMES TO ENQUIRE.
THAT WAS ME. THANKS.
HASTE YE BACK NOW!
YOU CAN COUNT ON IT!

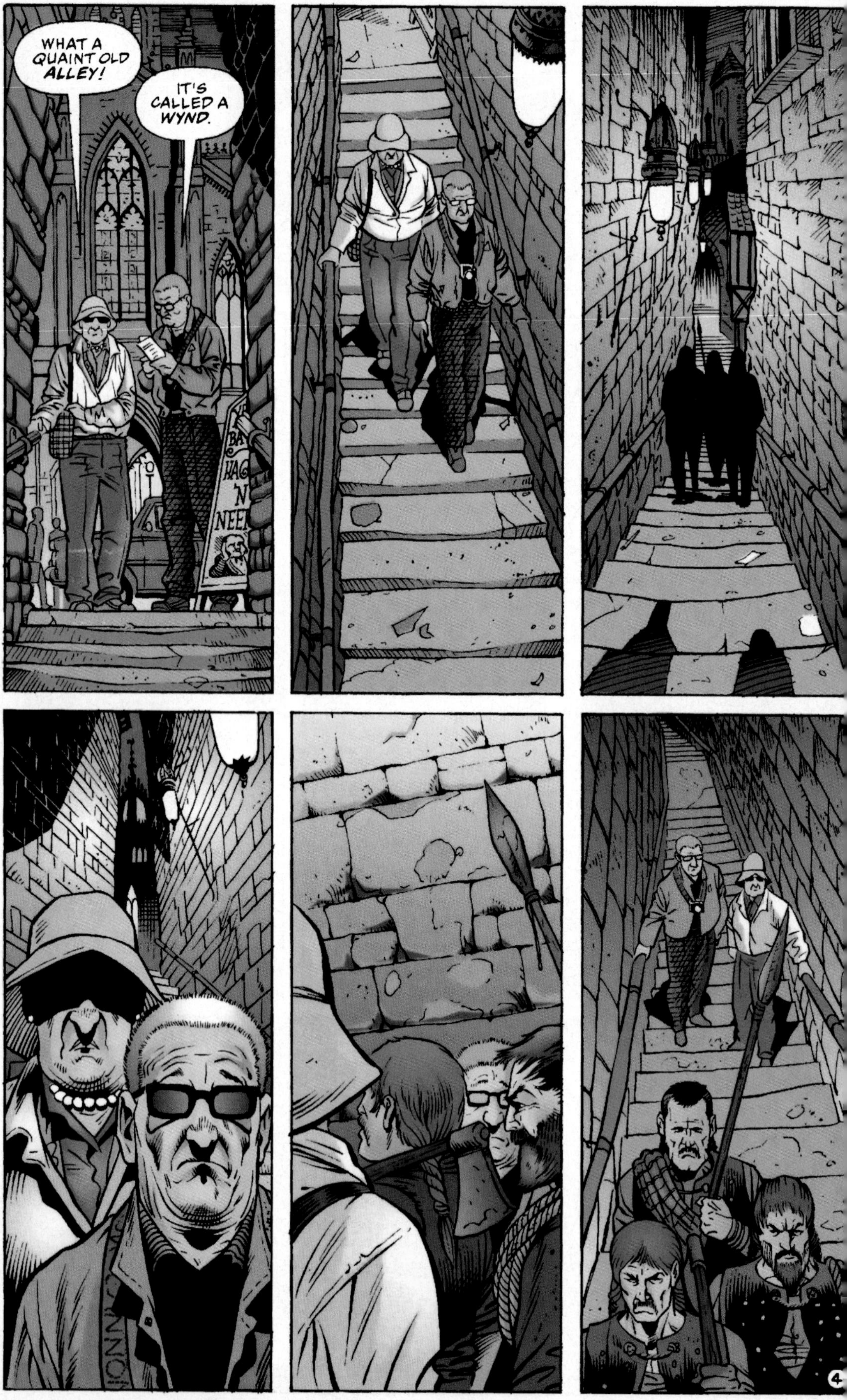
WHAT A QUAINT OLD ALLEY!
IT'S CALLED A WYND.

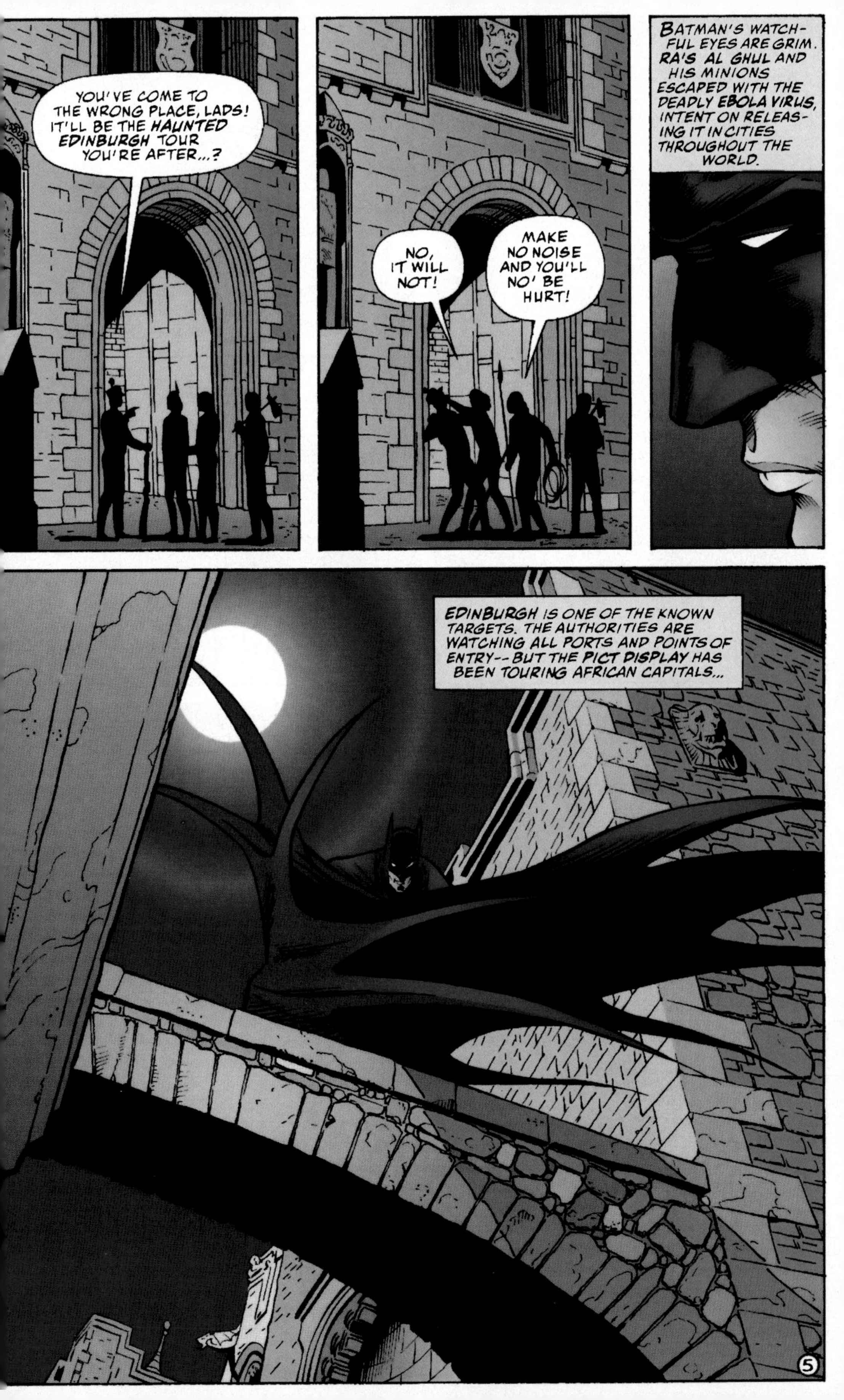
YOU'VE COME TO THE WRONG PLACE, LADS! IT'LL BE THE HAUNTED EDINBURGH TOUR YOU'RE AFTER...?
NO, IT WILL NOT!
MAKE NO NOISE AND YOU'LL NO' BE HURT!
BATMAN'S WATCHFUL EYES ARE GRIM. RA'S AL GHUL AND HIS MINIONS ESCAPED WITH THE DEADLY EBOLA VIRUS, INTENT ON RELEASING IT IN CITIES THROUGHOUT THE WORLD.
EDINBURGH IS ONE OF THE KNOWN TARGETS. THE AUTHORITIES ARE WATCHING ALL PORTS AND POINTS OF ENTRY-- BUT THE PICT DISPLAY HAS BEEN TOURING AFRICAN CAPITALS...
5

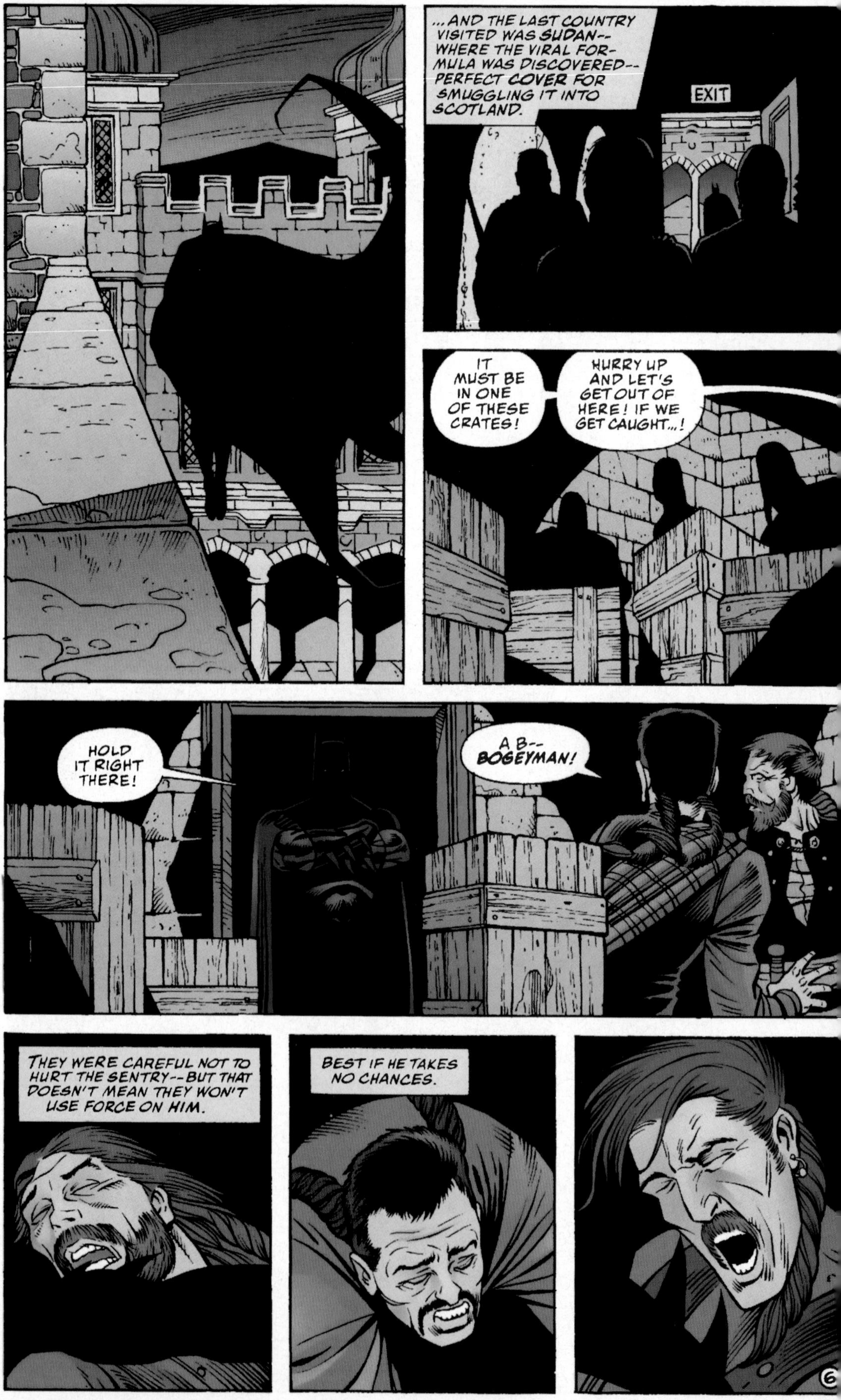
...AND THE LAST COUNTRY VISITED WAS SUDAN-- WHERE THE VIRAL FORMULA WAS DISCOVERED-- PERFECT COVER FOR SMUGGLING IT INTO SCOTLAND.
EXIT
IT MUST BE IN ONE OF THESE CRATES!
HURRY UP AND LET'S GET OUT OF HERE! IF WE GET CAUGHT...!
HOLD IT RIGHT THERE!
A B-- BOGEYMAN!
THEY WERE CAREFUL NOT TO HURT THE SENTRY--BUT THAT DOESN'T MEAN THEY WON'T USE FORCE ON HIM.
BEST IF HE TAKES NO CHANCES.
6

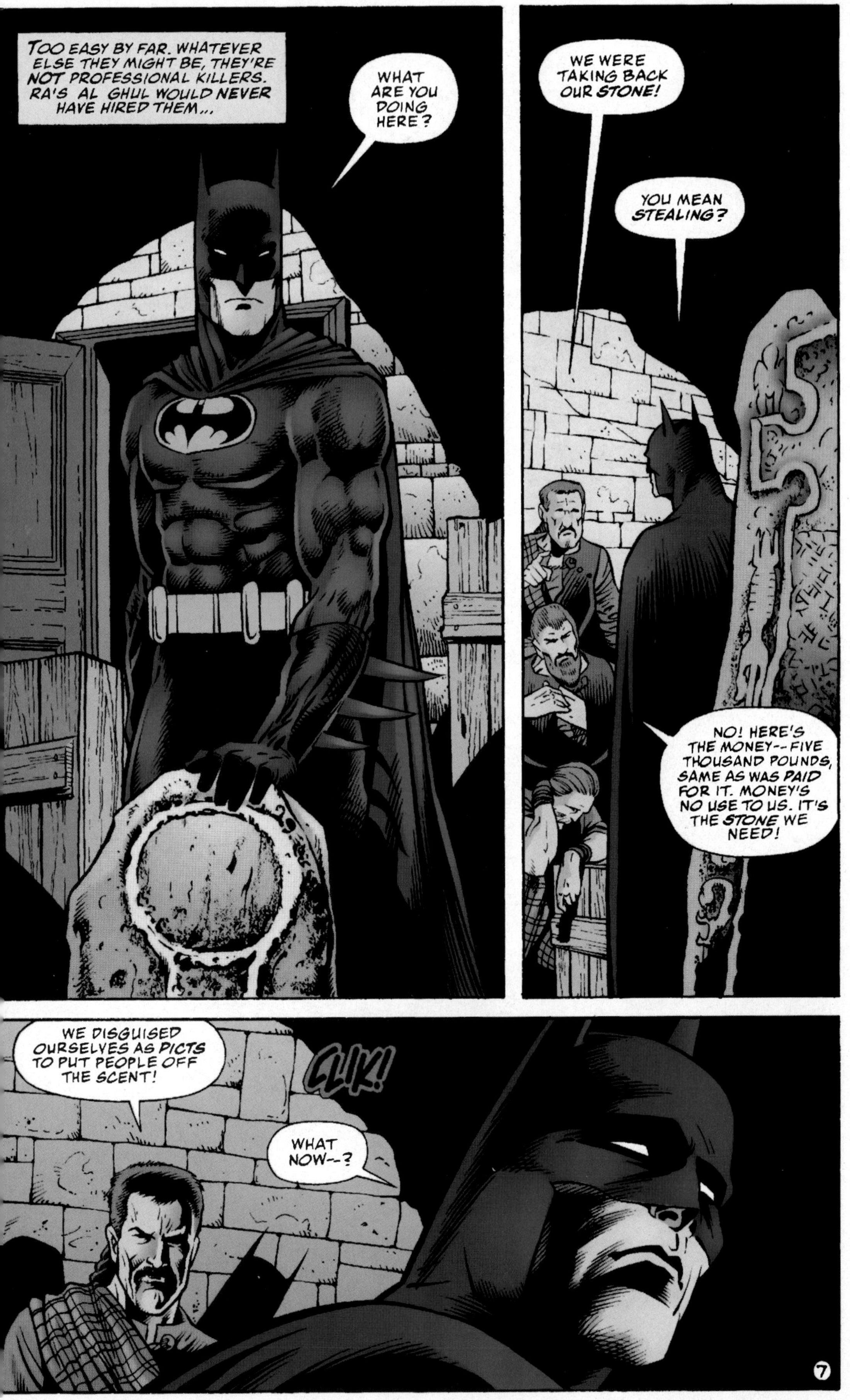
TOO EASY BY FAR. WHATEVER ELSE THEY MIGHT BE, THEY'RE NOT PROFESSIONAL KILLERS. RA'S AL GHUL WOULD NEVER HAVE HIRED THEM...
WHAT ARE YOU DOING HERE?
WE WERE TAKING BACK OUR STONE!
YOU MEAN STEALING?
NO! HERE'S THE MONEY--FIVE THOUSAND POUNDS, SAME AS WAS PAID FOR IT. MONEY'S NO USE TO US. IT'S THE STONE WE NEED!
WE DISGUISED OURSELVES AS PICTS TO PUT PEOPLE OFF THE SCENT!
CLIK!
WHAT NOW--?

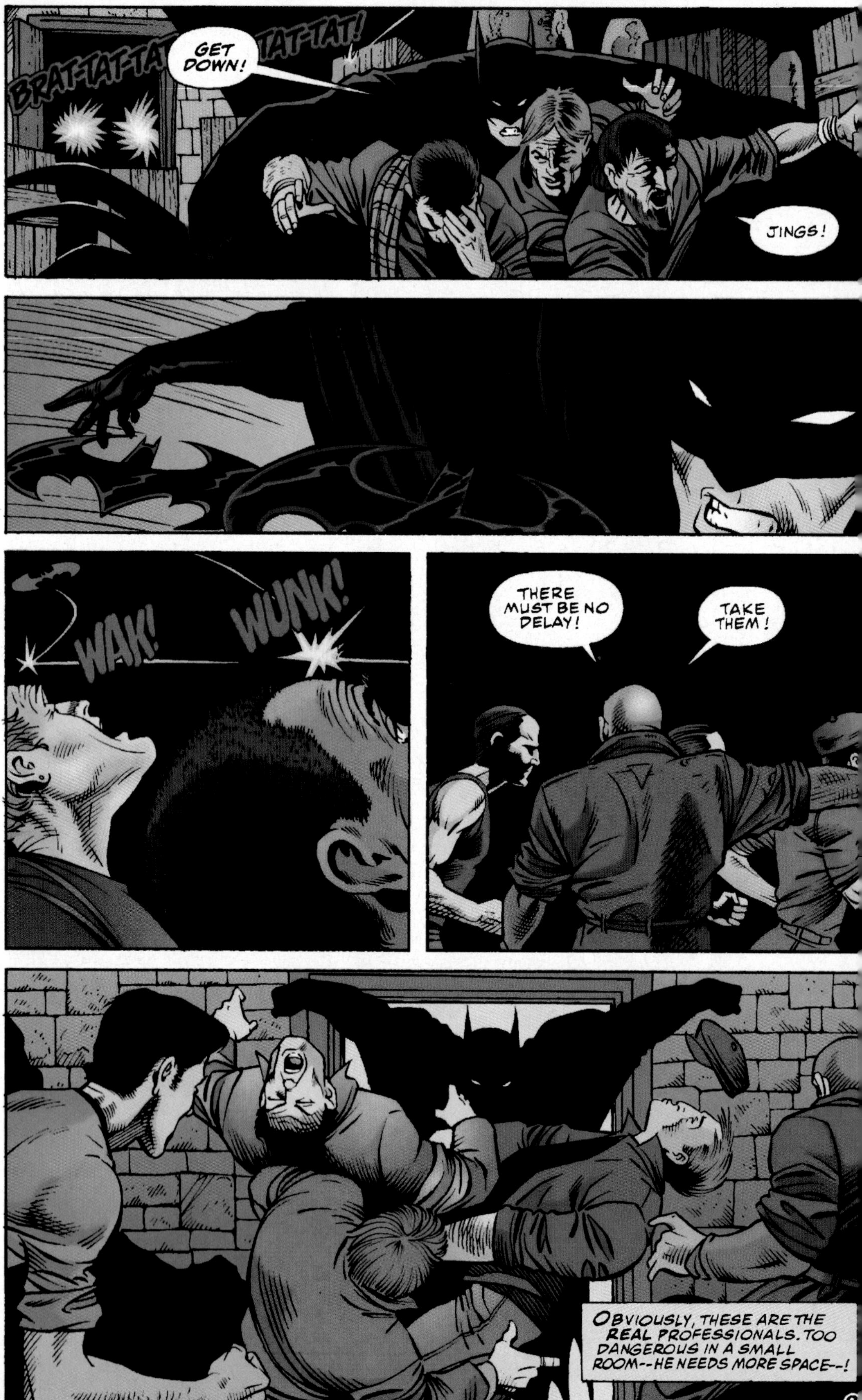
BRAT-TAT-TAT-TAT-TAT!
GET DOWN!
JINGS!
WAK!
WUNK!
THERE MUST BE NO DELAY!
TAKE THEM!
OBVIOUSLY, THESE ARE THE REAL PROFESSIONALS. TOO DANGEROUS IN A SMALL ROOM--HE NEEDS MORE SPACE--!

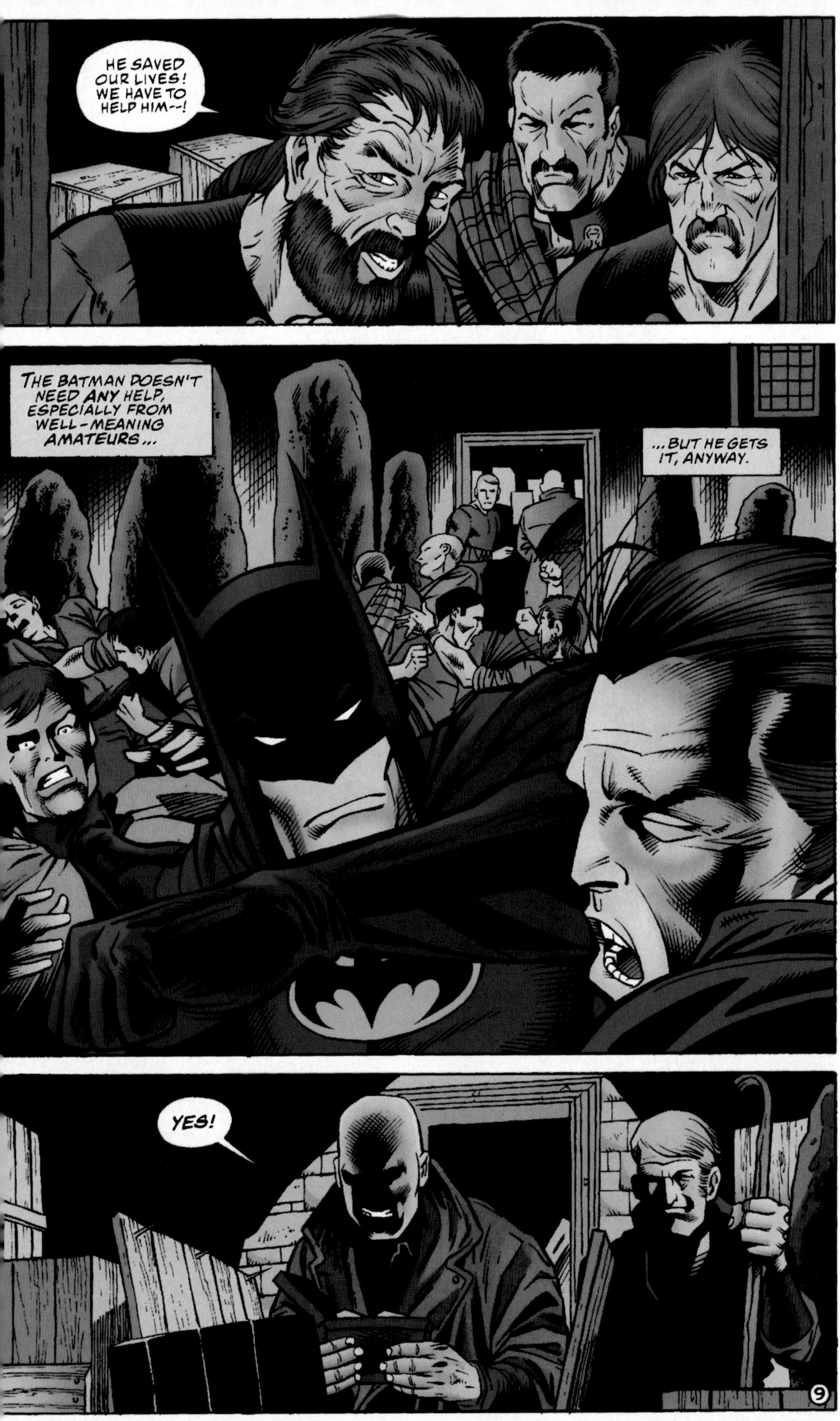

HE SAVED OUR LIVES! WE HAVE TO HELP HIM--!
THE BATMAN DOESN'T NEED ANY HELP, ESPECIALLY FROM WELL-MEANING AMATEURS...
...BUT HE GETS IT, ANYWAY.
YES!

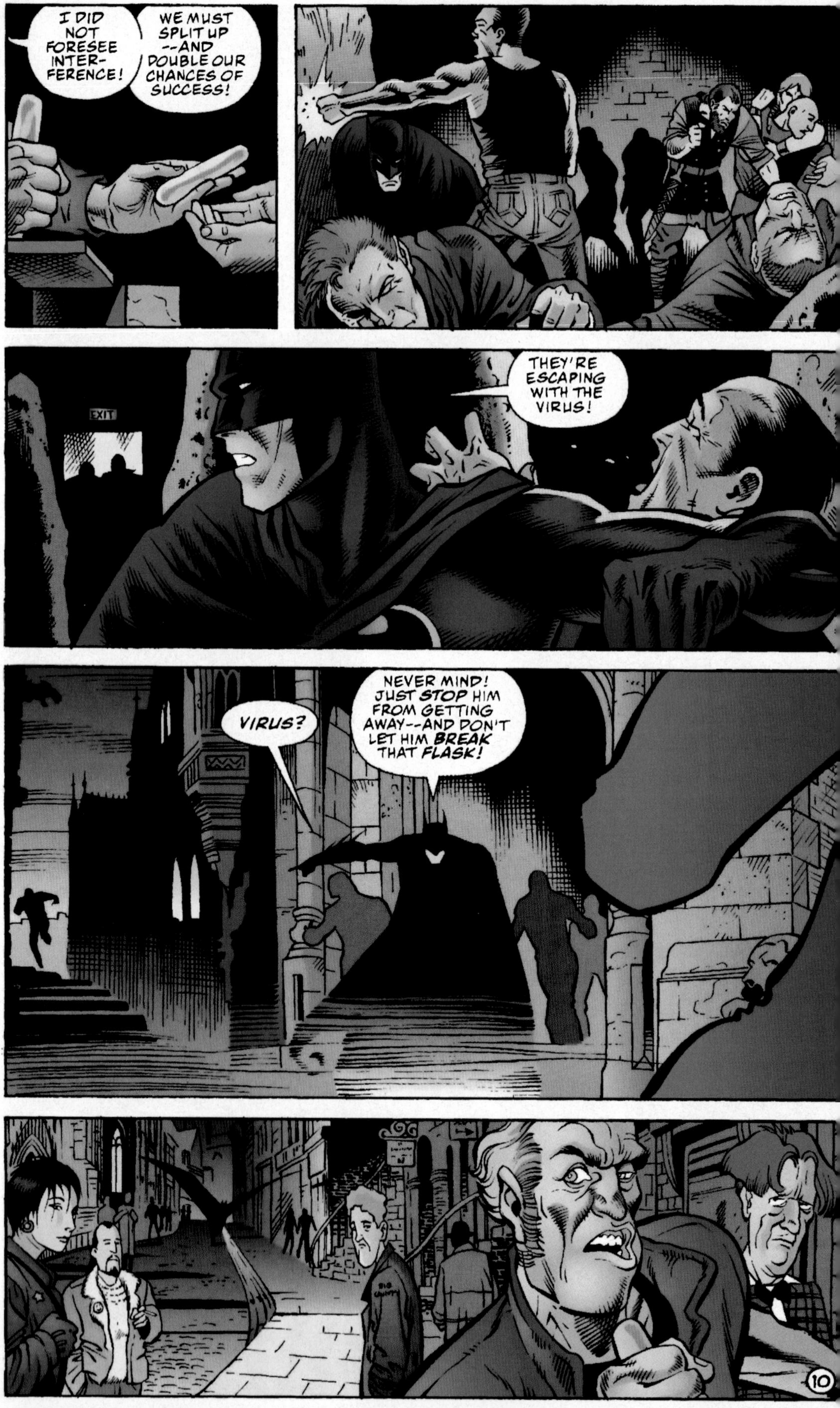
I DID NOT FORESEE INTER-FERENCE!
WE MUST SPLIT UP --AND DOUBLE OUR CHANCES OF SUCCESS!
EXIT
THEY'RE ESCAPING WITH THE VIRUS!
VIRUS?
NEVER MIND! JUST STOP HIM FROM GETTING AWAY--AND DON'T LET HIM BREAK THAT FLASK!
10

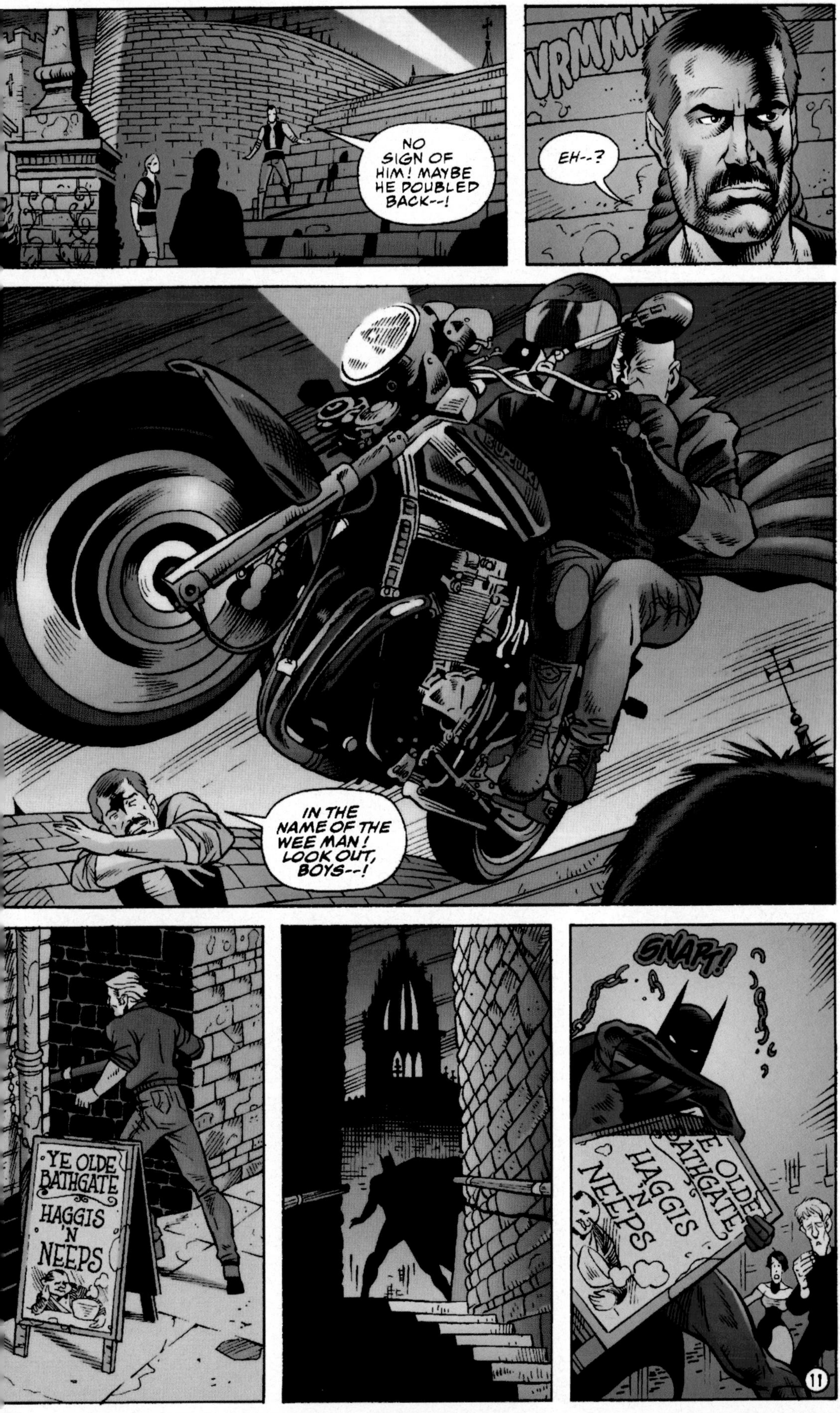
NO SIGN OF HIM! MAYBE HE DOUBLED BACK--!
VRMMMM
EH--?
IN THE NAME OF THE WEE MAN! LOOK OUT, BOYS--!
YE OLDE BATHGATE HAGGIS 'N NEEPS
SNAP!
YE OLDE BATHGATE HAGGIS 'N NEEPS
11

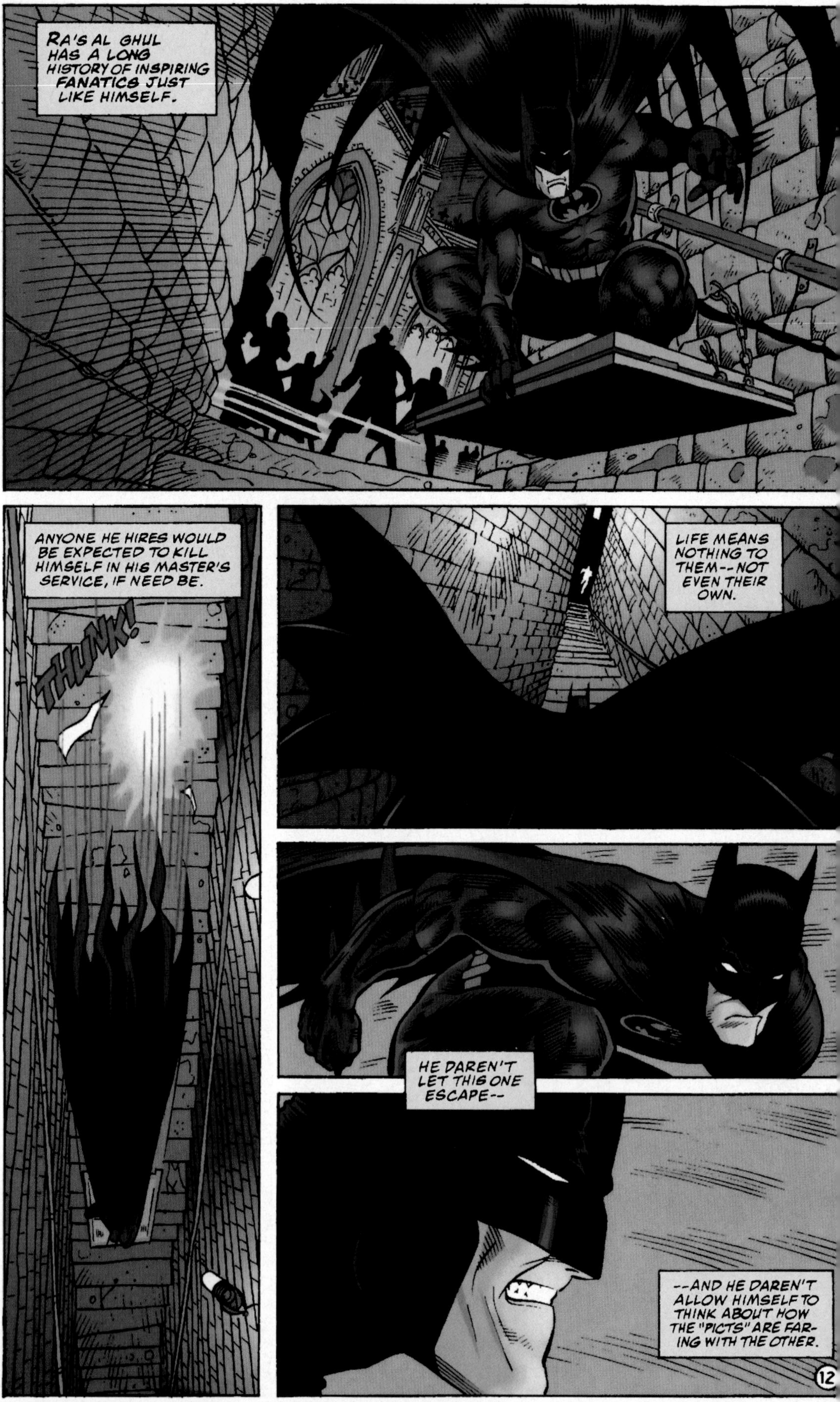

RA'S AL GHUL HAS A LONG HISTORY OF INSPIRING FANATICS JUST LIKE HIMSELF.
ANYONE HE HIRES WOULD BE EXPECTED TO KILL HIMSELF IN HIS MASTER'S SERVICE, IF NEED BE.
THUNK!
LIFE MEANS NOTHING TO THEM--NOT EVEN THEIR OWN.
HE DAREN'T LET THIS ONE ESCAPE--
--AND HE DAREN'T ALLOW HIMSELF TO THINK ABOUT HOW THE "PICTS" ARE FARING WITH THE OTHER.
12

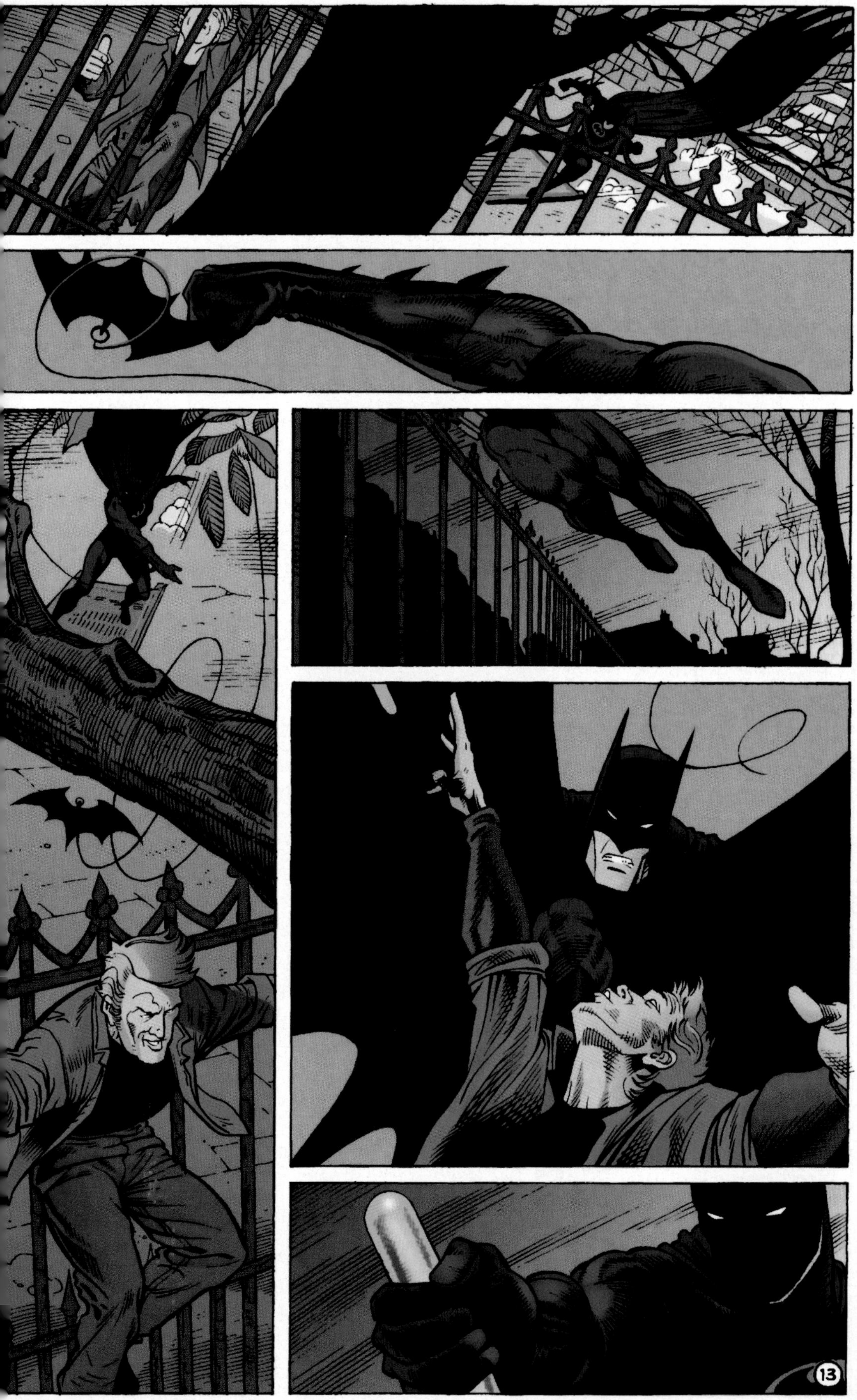

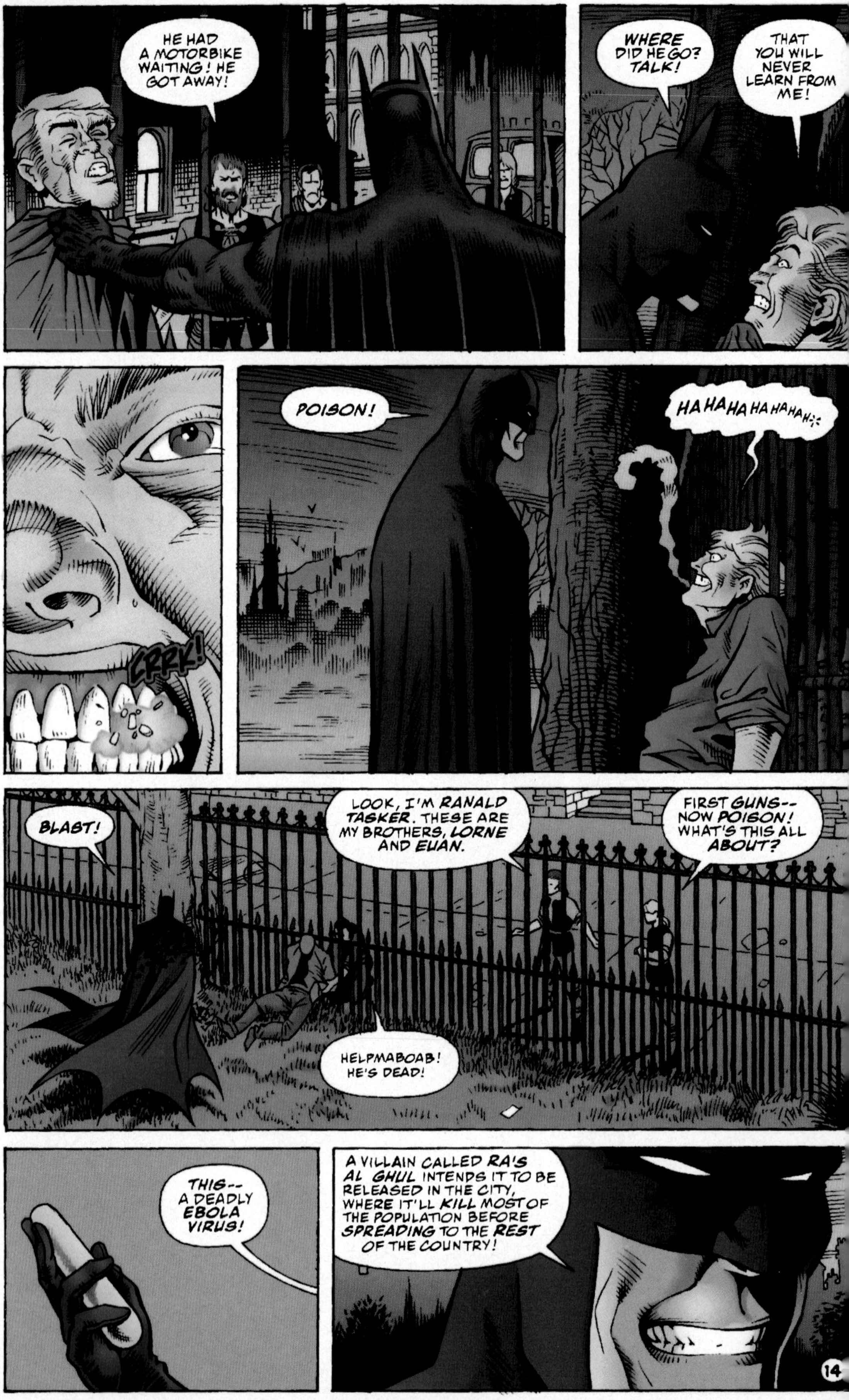
HE HAD A MOTORBIKE WAITING! HE GOT AWAY!
WHERE DID HE GO? TALK!
THAT YOU WILL NEVER LEARN FROM ME!
CRRK!
POISON!
HA HA HA HA HA HA HAH
BLAST!
LOOK, I'M RANALD TASKER. THESE ARE MY BROTHERS, LORNE AND EUAN.
FIRST GUNS-- NOW POISON! WHAT'S THIS ALL ABOUT?
HELPMABOAB! HE'S DEAD!
THIS-- A DEADLY EBOLA VIRUS!
A VILLAIN CALLED RA'S AL GHUL INTENDS IT TO BE RELEASED IN THE CITY, WHERE IT'LL KILL MOST OF THE POPULATION BEFORE SPREADING TO THE REST OF THE COUNTRY!

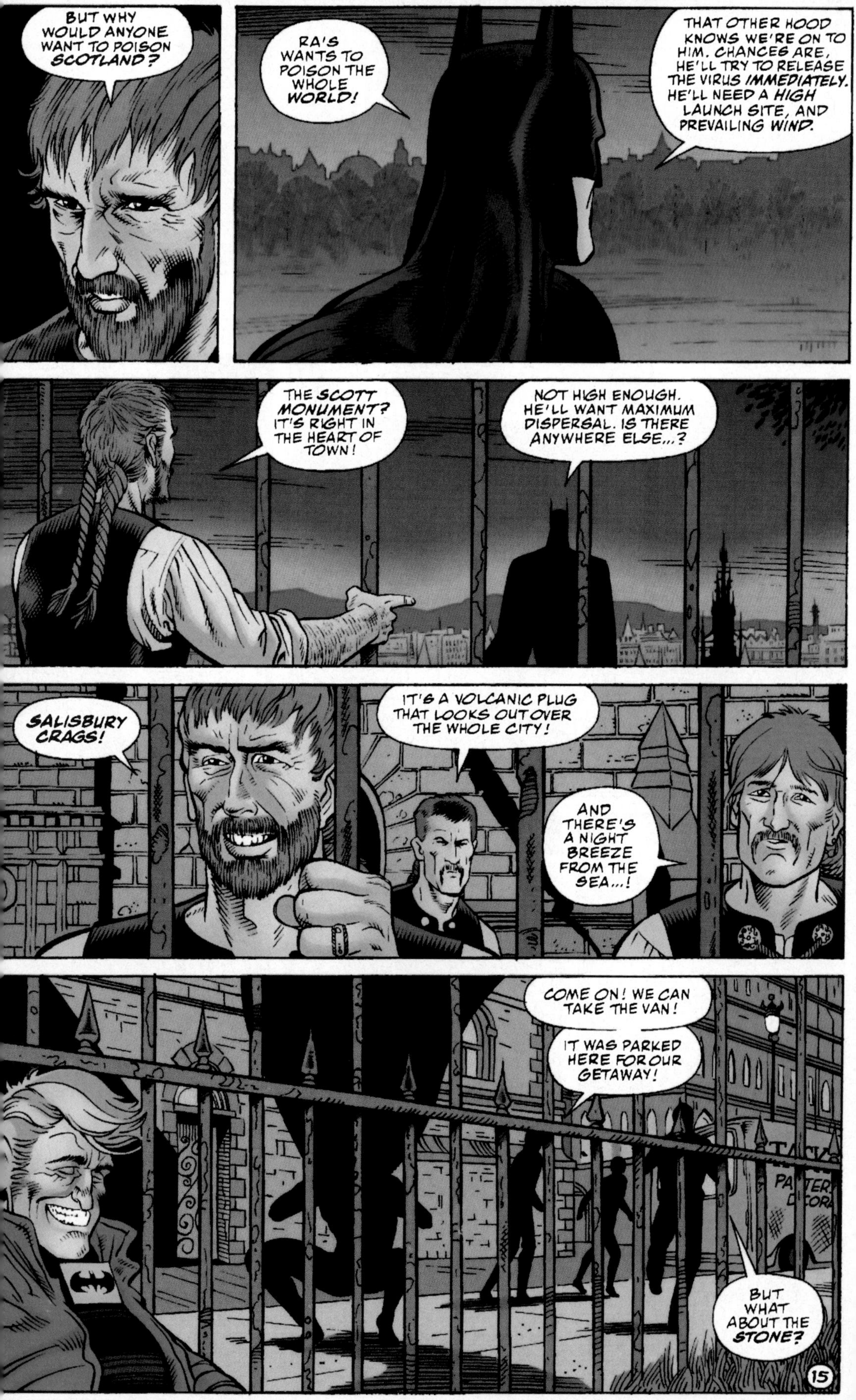
BUT WHY WOULD ANYONE WANT TO POISON SCOTLAND?
RA'S WANTS TO POISON THE WHOLE WORLD!
THAT OTHER HOOD KNOWS WE'RE ON TO HIM. CHANCES ARE, HE'LL TRY TO RELEASE THE VIRUS IMMEDIATELY. HE'LL NEED A HIGH LAUNCH SITE, AND PREVAILING WIND.
THE SCOTT MONUMENT? IT'S RIGHT IN THE HEART OF TOWN!
NOT HIGH ENOUGH. HE'LL WANT MAXIMUM DISPERSAL. IS THERE ANYWHERE ELSE...?
SALISBURY CRAGS!
IT'S A VOLCANIC PLUG THAT LOOKS OUT OVER THE WHOLE CITY!
AND THERE'S A NIGHT BREEZE FROM THE SEA...!
COME ON! WE CAN TAKE THE VAN!
IT WAS PARKED HERE FOR OUR GETAWAY!
BUT WHAT ABOUT THE STONE?
15

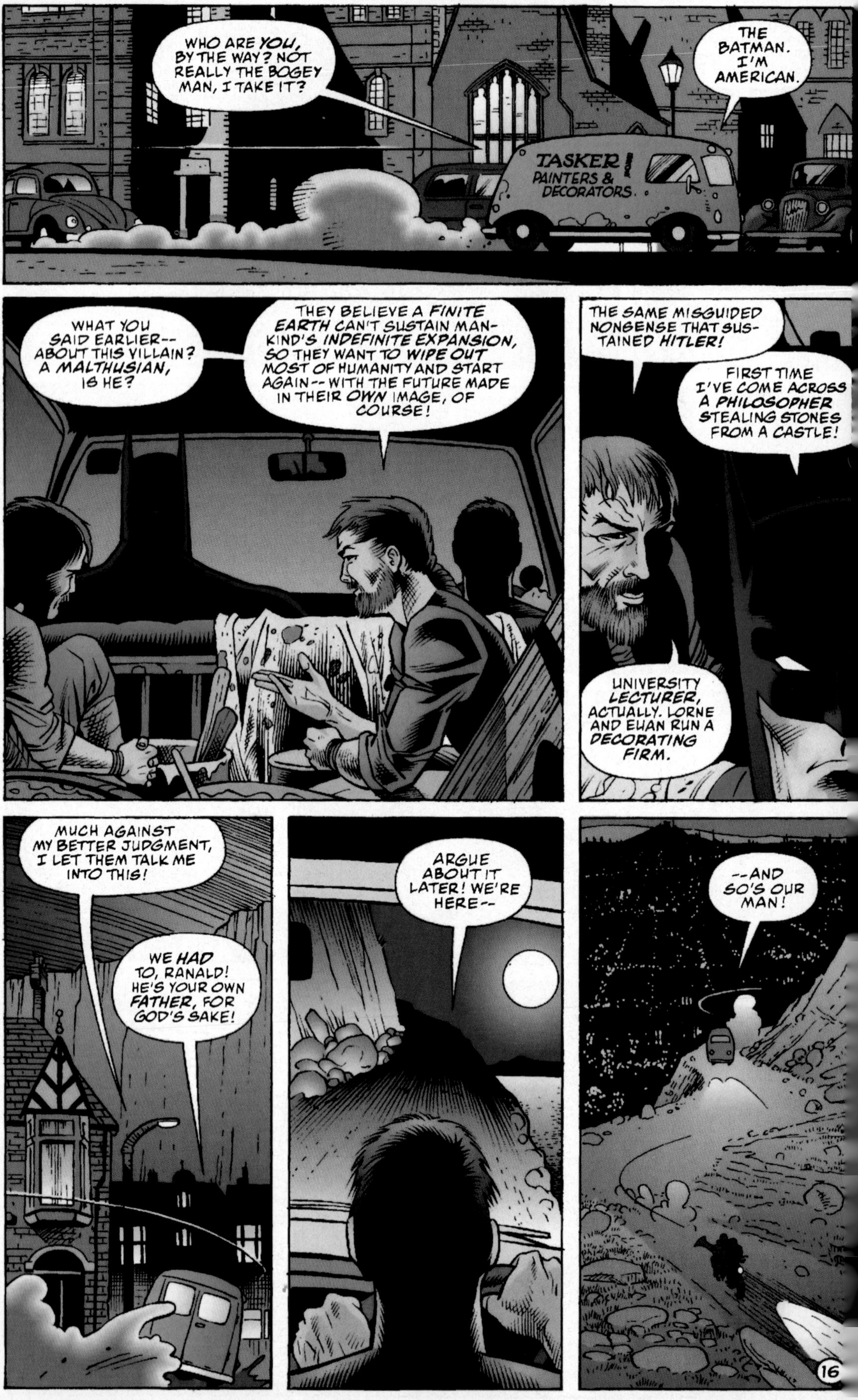
WHO ARE YOU, BY THE WAY? NOT REALLY THE BOGEY MAN, I TAKE IT?
THE BATMAN. I'M AMERICAN.
TASKER & SONS PAINTERS & DECORATORS.
WHAT YOU SAID EARLIER-- ABOUT THIS VILLAIN? A MALTHUSIAN, IS HE?
THEY BELIEVE A FINITE EARTH CAN'T SUSTAIN MANKIND'S INDEFINITE EXPANSION, SO THEY WANT TO WIPE OUT MOST OF HUMANITY AND START AGAIN--WITH THE FUTURE MADE IN THEIR OWN IMAGE, OF COURSE!
THE SAME MISGUIDED NONSENSE THAT SUSTAINED HITLER!
FIRST TIME I'VE COME ACROSS A PHILOSOPHER STEALING STONES FROM A CASTLE!
UNIVERSITY LECTURER, ACTUALLY. LORNE AND EUAN RUN A DECORATING FIRM.
MUCH AGAINST MY BETTER JUDGMENT, I LET THEM TALK ME INTO THIS!
WE HAD TO, RANALD! HE'S YOUR OWN FATHER, FOR GOD'S SAKE!
ARGUE ABOUT IT LATER! WE'RE HERE--
--AND SO'S OUR MAN!

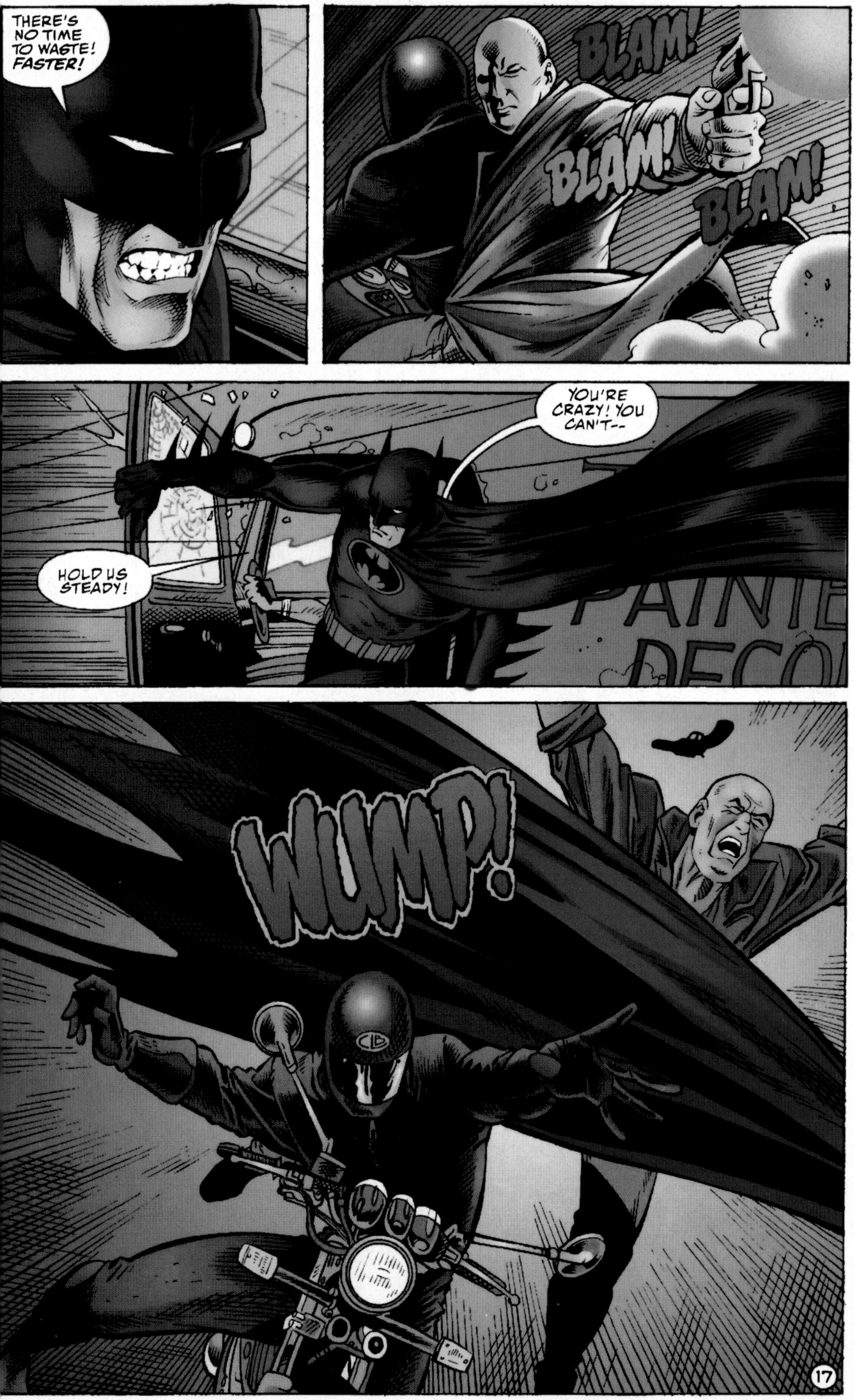
THERE'S NO TIME TO WASTE! FASTER!
BLAM!
BLAM!
BLAM!
YOU'RE CRAZY! YOU CAN'T--
HOLD US STEADY!
WUMP!

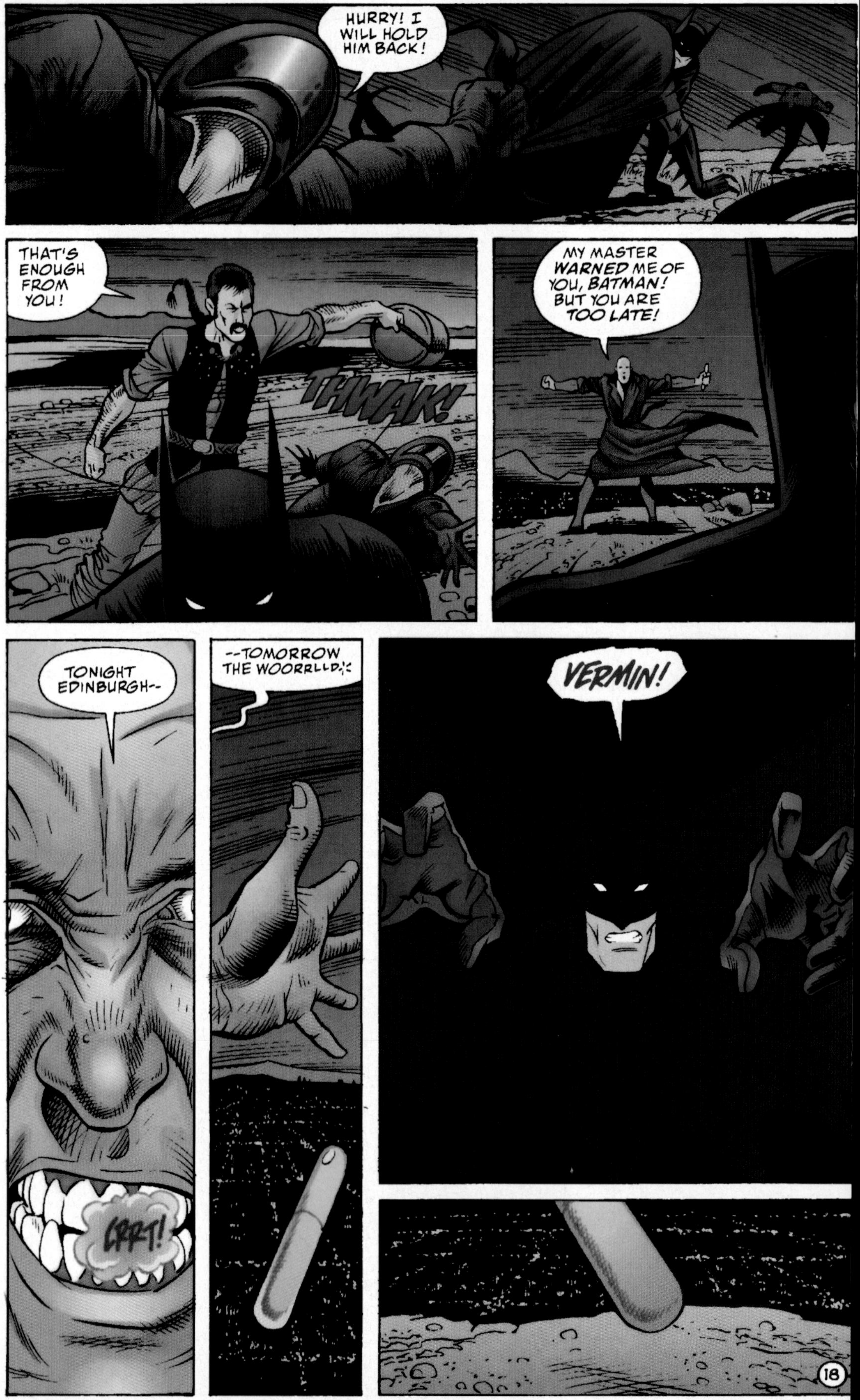
HURRY! I WILL HOLD HIM BACK!
THAT'S ENOUGH FROM YOU!
THWAK!
MY MASTER WARNED ME OF YOU, BATMAN! BUT YOU ARE TOO LATE!
TONIGHT EDINBURGH--
CRRT!
--TOMORROW THE WOORRLLD!
VERMIN!

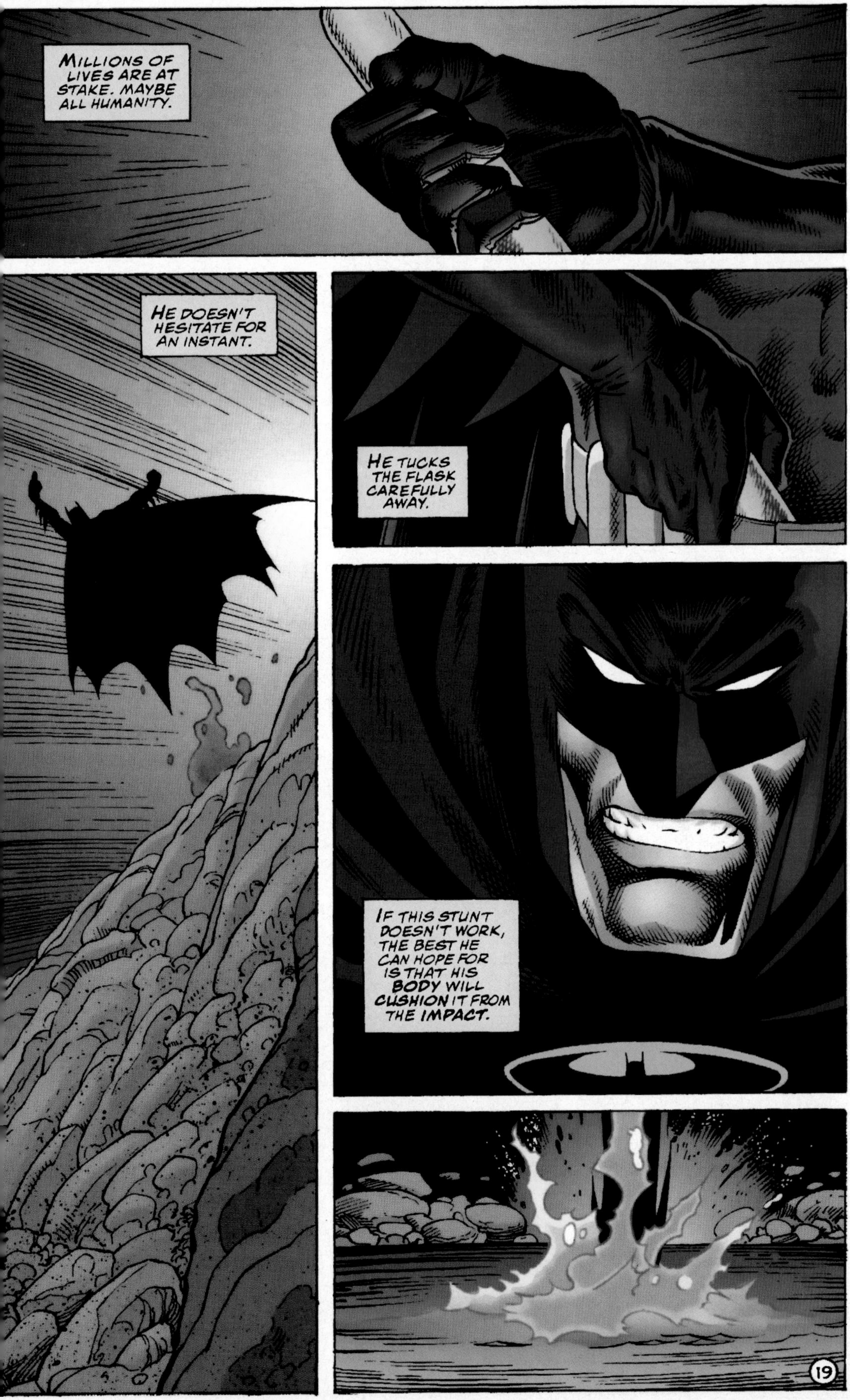
MILLIONS OF LIVES ARE AT STAKE. MAYBE ALL HUMANITY.
HE DOESN'T HESITATE FOR AN INSTANT.
HE TUCKS THE FLASK CAREFULLY AWAY.
IF THIS STUNT DOESN'T WORK, THE BEST HE CAN HOPE FOR IS THAT HIS BODY WILL CUSHION IT FROM THE IMPACT.
19

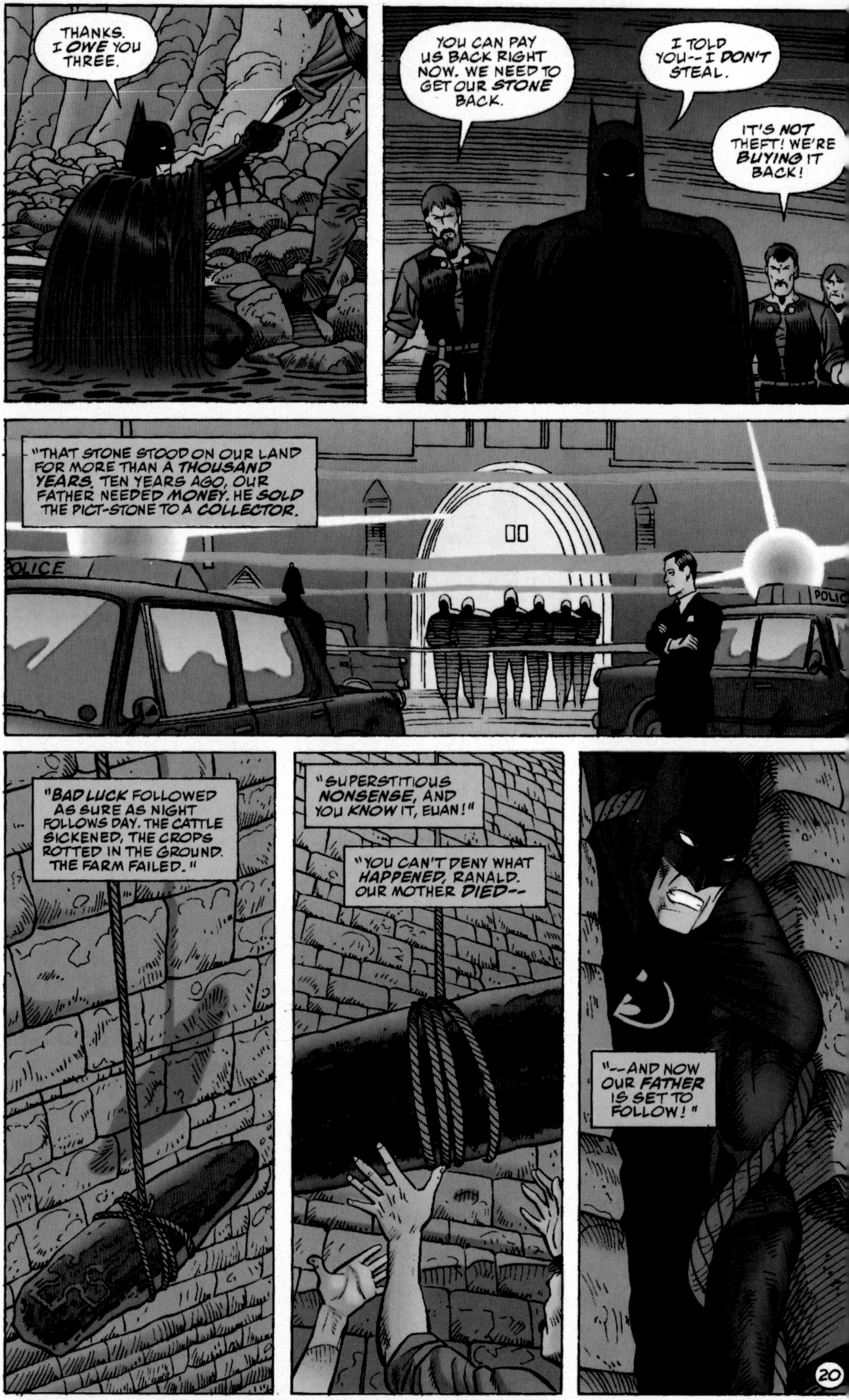
THANKS. I OWE YOU THREE.
YOU CAN PAY US BACK RIGHT NOW. WE NEED TO GET OUR STONE BACK.
I TOLD YOU-- I DON'T STEAL.
IT'S NOT THEFT! WE'RE BUYING IT BACK!
"THAT STONE STOOD ON OUR LAND FOR MORE THAN A THOUSAND YEARS. TEN YEARS AGO, OUR FATHER NEEDED MONEY. HE SOLD THE PICT-STONE TO A COLLECTOR.
POLICE
"BAD LUCK FOLLOWED AS SURE AS NIGHT FOLLOWS DAY. THE CATTLE SICKENED, THE CROPS ROTTED IN THE GROUND. THE FARM FAILED."
"SUPERSTITIOUS NONSENSE, AND YOU KNOW IT, EUAN!"
"YOU CAN'T DENY WHAT HAPPENED, RANALD. OUR MOTHER DIED--
"--AND NOW OUR FATHER IS SET TO FOLLOW!"
20

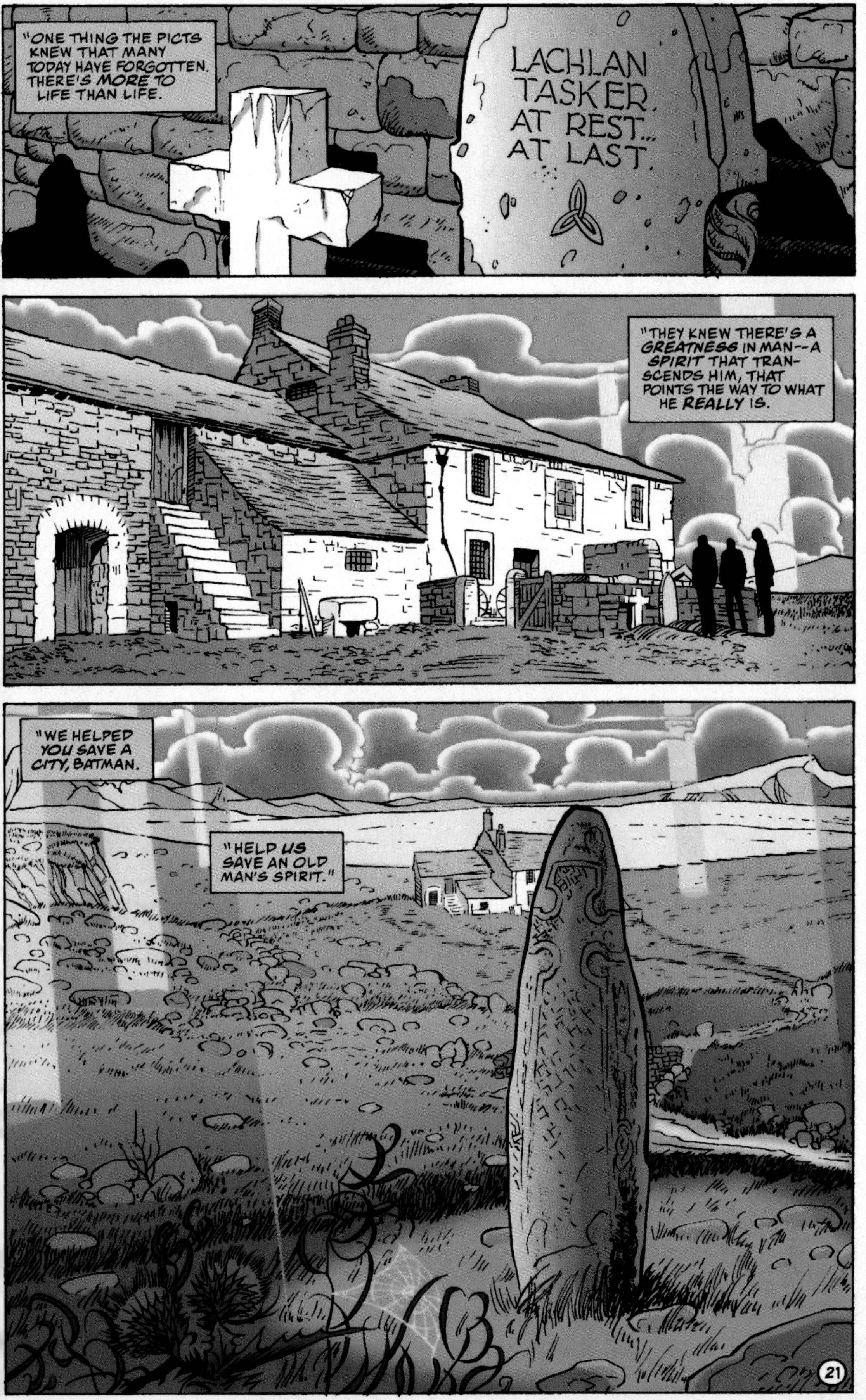
"ONE THING THE PICTS KNEW THAT MANY TODAY HAVE FORGOTTEN. THERE'S MORE TO LIFE THAN LIFE.
LACHLAN TASKER. AT REST... AT LAST.
"THEY KNEW THERE'S A GREATNESS IN MAN--A SPIRIT THAT TRANSCENDS HIM, THAT POINTS THE WAY TO WHAT HE REALLY IS.
"WE HELPED YOU SAVE A CITY, BATMAN.
"HELP US SAVE AN OLD MAN'S SPIRIT."

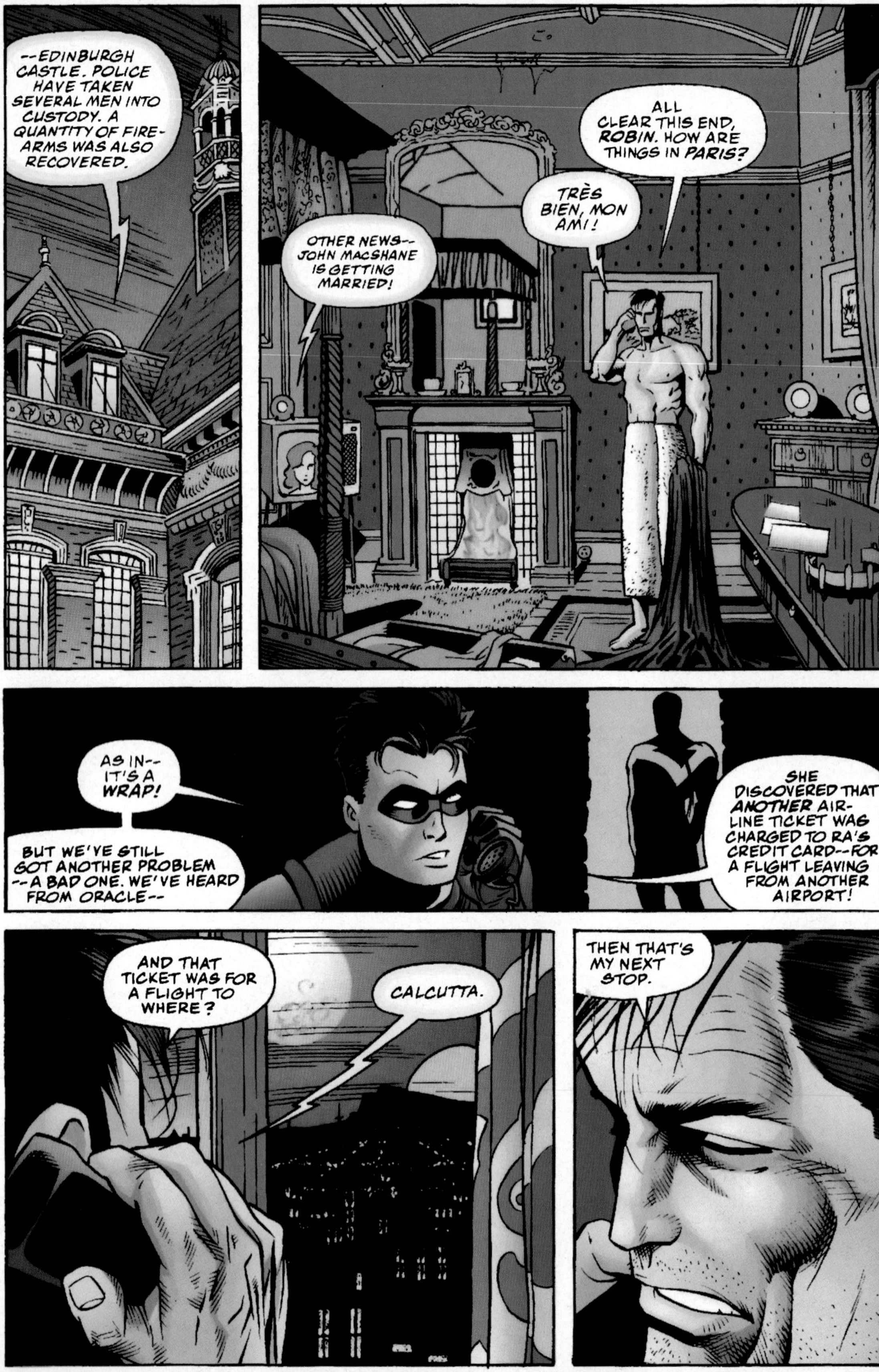
--EDINBURGH CASTLE. POLICE HAVE TAKEN SEVERAL MEN INTO CUSTODY. A QUANTITY OF FIRE-ARMS WAS ALSO RECOVERED.
ALL CLEAR THIS END, ROBIN. HOW ARE THINGS IN PARIS?
TRÈS BIEN, MON AMI!
OTHER NEWS--JOHN MACSHANE IS GETTING MARRIED!
AS IN--IT'S A WRAP!
BUT WE'VE STILL GOT ANOTHER PROBLEM --A BAD ONE. WE'VE HEARD FROM ORACLE--
SHE DISCOVERED THAT ANOTHER AIR-LINE TICKET WAS CHARGED TO RA'S CREDIT CARD--FOR A FLIGHT LEAVING FROM ANOTHER AIRPORT!
AND THAT TICKET WAS FOR A FLIGHT TO WHERE?
CALCUTTA.
THEN THAT'S MY NEXT STOP.

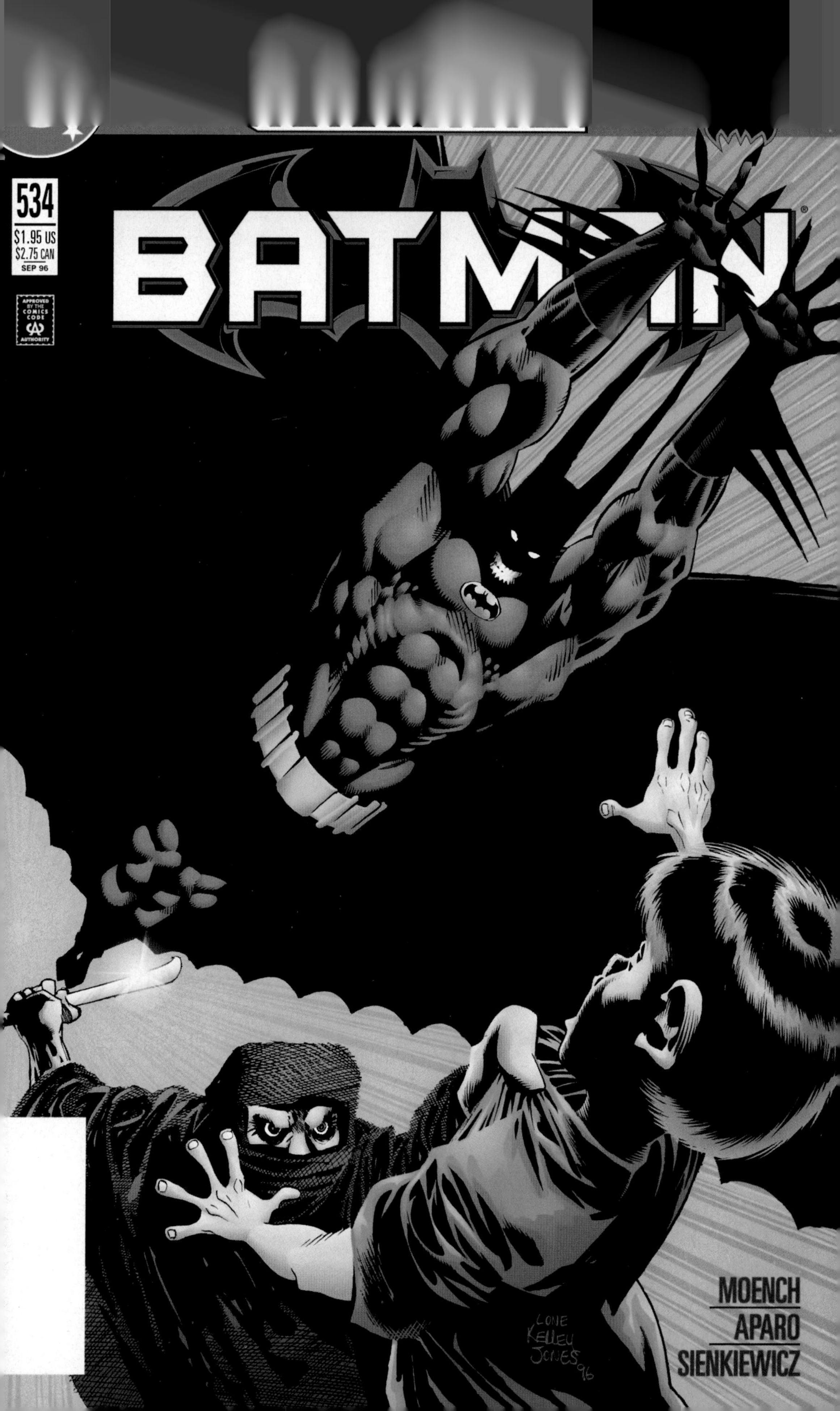
534
$1.95 US
$2.75 CAN
SEP 96
APPROVED BY THE COMICS CODE AUTHORITY
BATMAN
MOENCH
APARO
SIENKIEWICZ

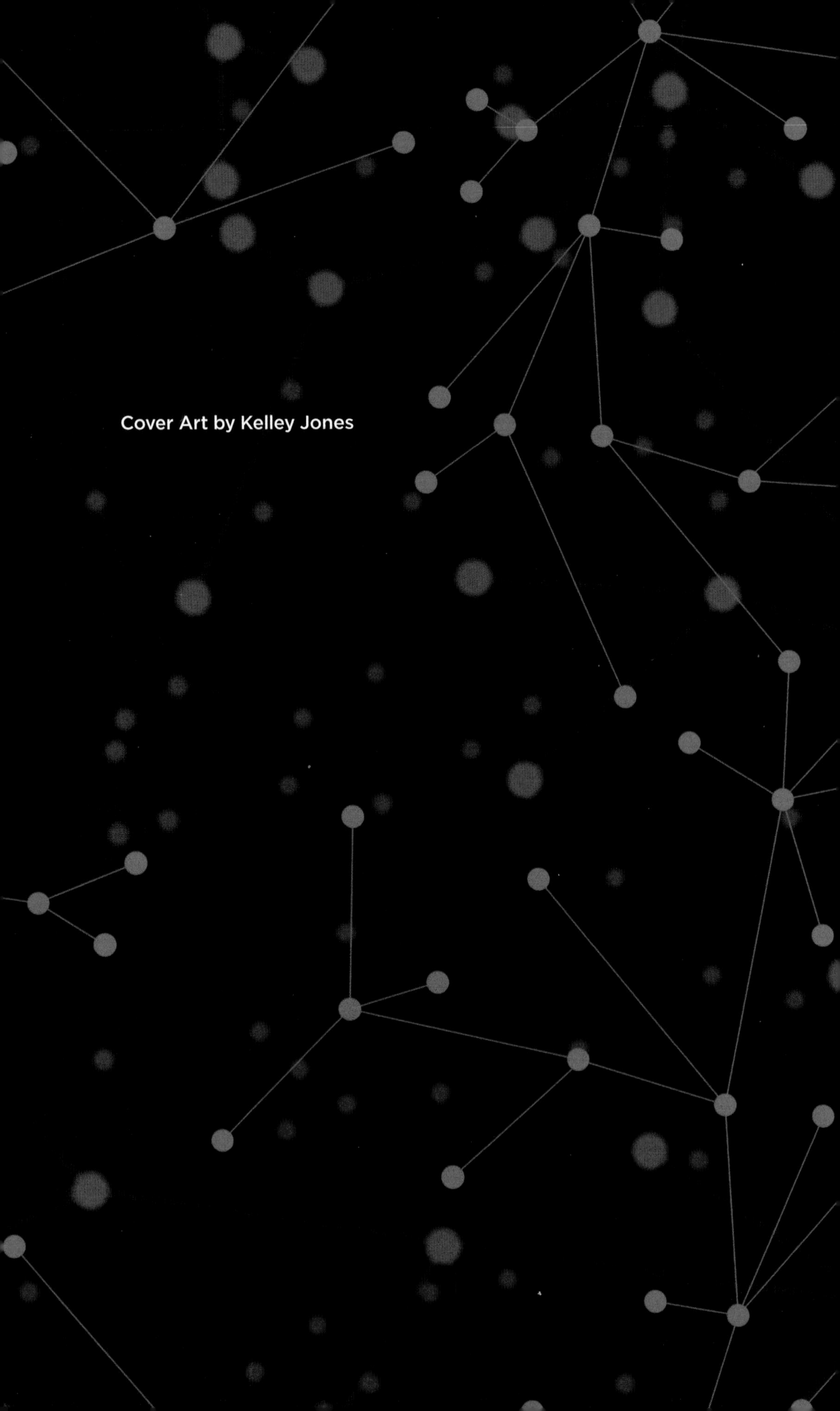

Cover Art by Kelley Jones

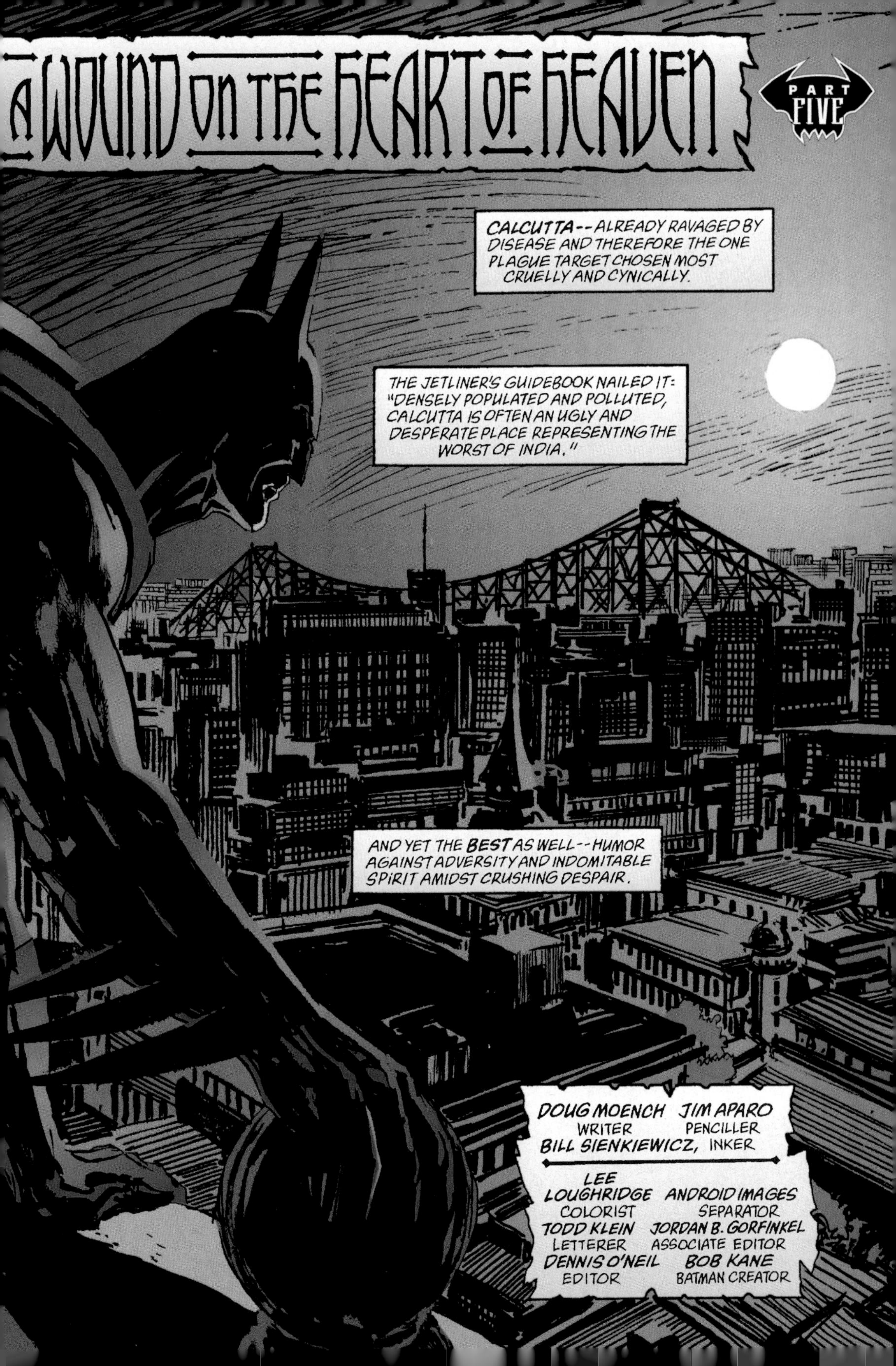

A WOUND ON THE HEART OF HEAVEN
PART FIVE
CALCUTTA--ALREADY RAVAGED BY DISEASE AND THEREFORE THE ONE PLAGUE TARGET CHOSEN MOST CRUELLY AND CYNICALLY.
THE JETLINER'S GUIDEBOOK NAILED IT: "DENSELY POPULATED AND POLLUTED, CALCUTTA IS OFTEN AN UGLY AND DESPERATE PLACE REPRESENTING THE WORST OF INDIA."
AND YET THE BEST AS WELL--HUMOR AGAINST ADVERSITY AND INDOMITABLE SPIRIT AMIDST CRUSHING DESPAIR.
DOUG MOENCH WRITER
JIM APARO PENCILLER
BILL SIENKIEWICZ, INKER
LEE LOUGHRIDGE COLORIST
ANDROID IMAGES SEPARATOR
TODD KLEIN LETTERER
JORDAN B. GORFINKEL ASSOCIATE EDITOR
DENNIS O'NEIL EDITOR
BOB KANE BATMAN CREATOR

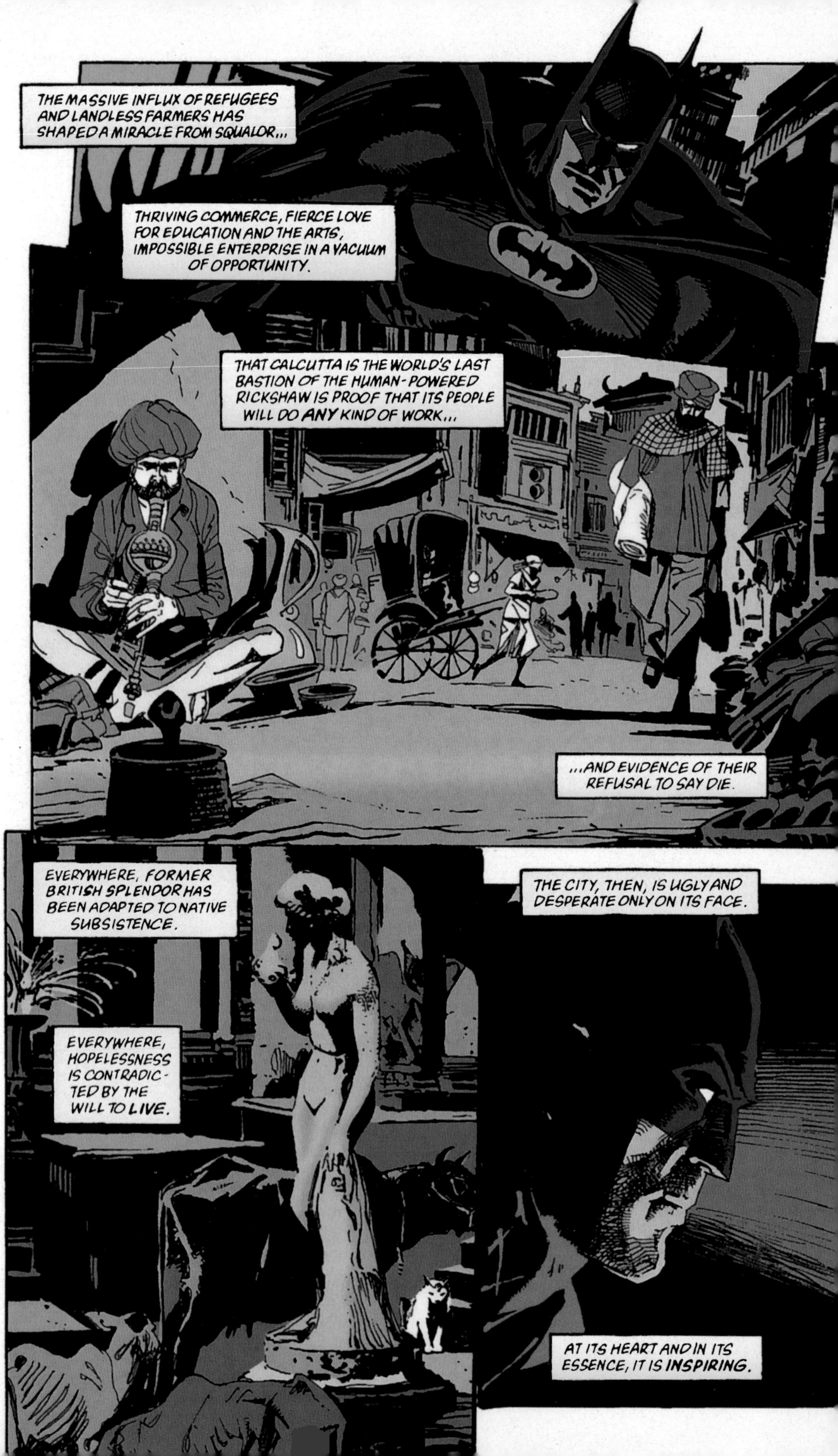
THE MASSIVE INFLUX OF REFUGEES AND LANDLESS FARMERS HAS SHAPED A MIRACLE FROM SQUALOR...
THRIVING COMMERCE, FIERCE LOVE FOR EDUCATION AND THE ARTS, IMPOSSIBLE ENTERPRISE IN A VACUUM OF OPPORTUNITY.
THAT CALCUTTA IS THE WORLD'S LAST BASTION OF THE HUMAN-POWERED RICKSHAW IS PROOF THAT ITS PEOPLE WILL DO ANY KIND OF WORK...
...AND EVIDENCE OF THEIR REFUSAL TO SAY DIE.
EVERYWHERE, FORMER BRITISH SPLENDOR HAS BEEN ADAPTED TO NATIVE SUBSISTENCE.
EVERYWHERE, HOPELESSNESS IS CONTRADIC-TED BY THE WILL TO LIVE.
THE CITY, THEN, IS UGLY AND DESPERATE ONLY ON ITS FACE.
AT ITS HEART AND IN ITS ESSENCE, IT IS INSPIRING.

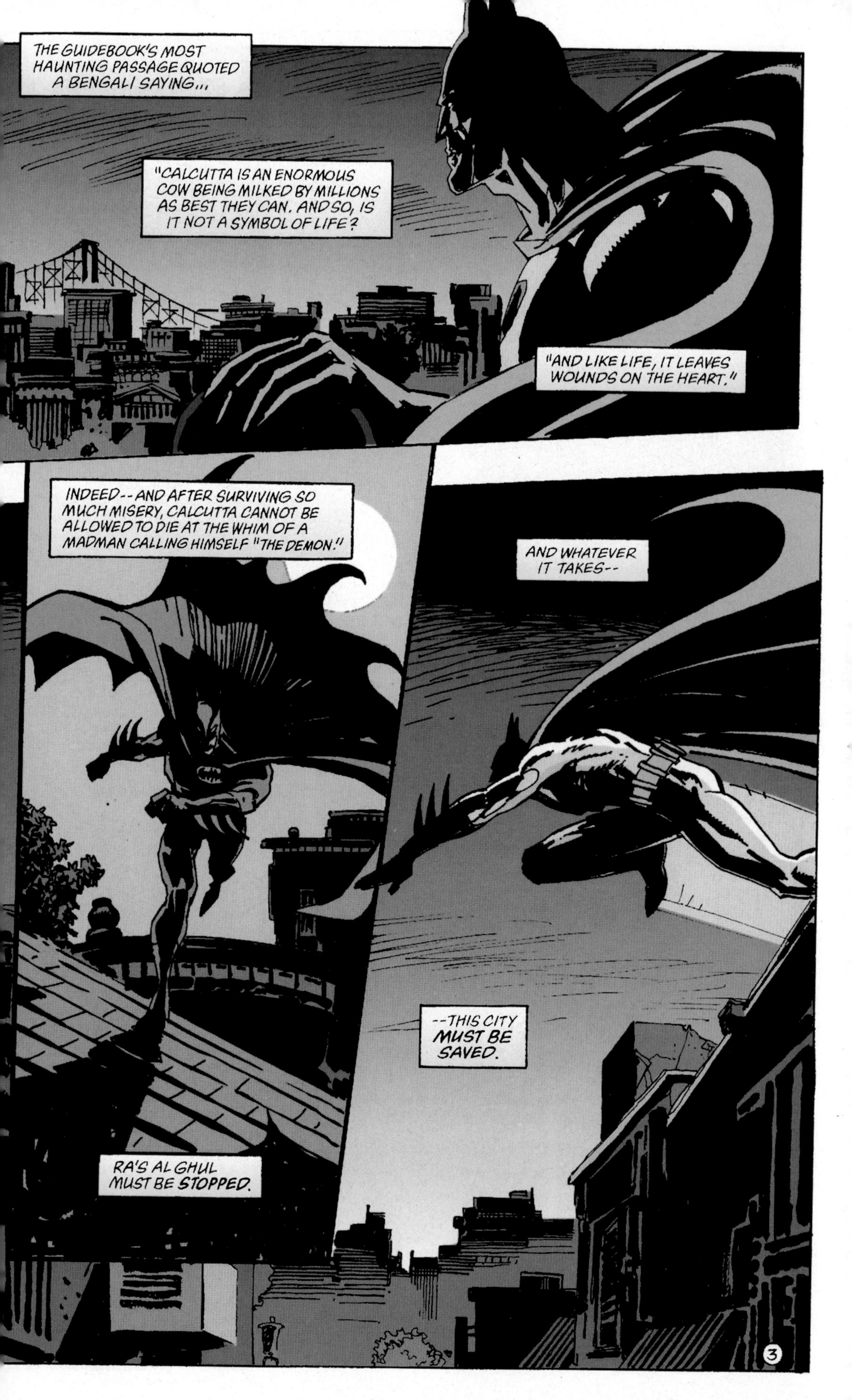
THE GUIDEBOOK'S MOST HAUNTING PASSAGE QUOTED A BENGALI SAYING...
"CALCUTTA IS AN ENORMOUS COW BEING MILKED BY MILLIONS AS BEST THEY CAN. AND SO, IS IT NOT A SYMBOL OF LIFE?
"AND LIKE LIFE, IT LEAVES WOUNDS ON THE HEART."
INDEED--AND AFTER SURVIVING SO MUCH MISERY, CALCUTTA CANNOT BE ALLOWED TO DIE AT THE WHIM OF A MADMAN CALLING HIMSELF "THE DEMON."
RA'S AL GHUL MUST BE STOPPED.
AND WHATEVER IT TAKES--
--THIS CITY MUST BE SAVED.

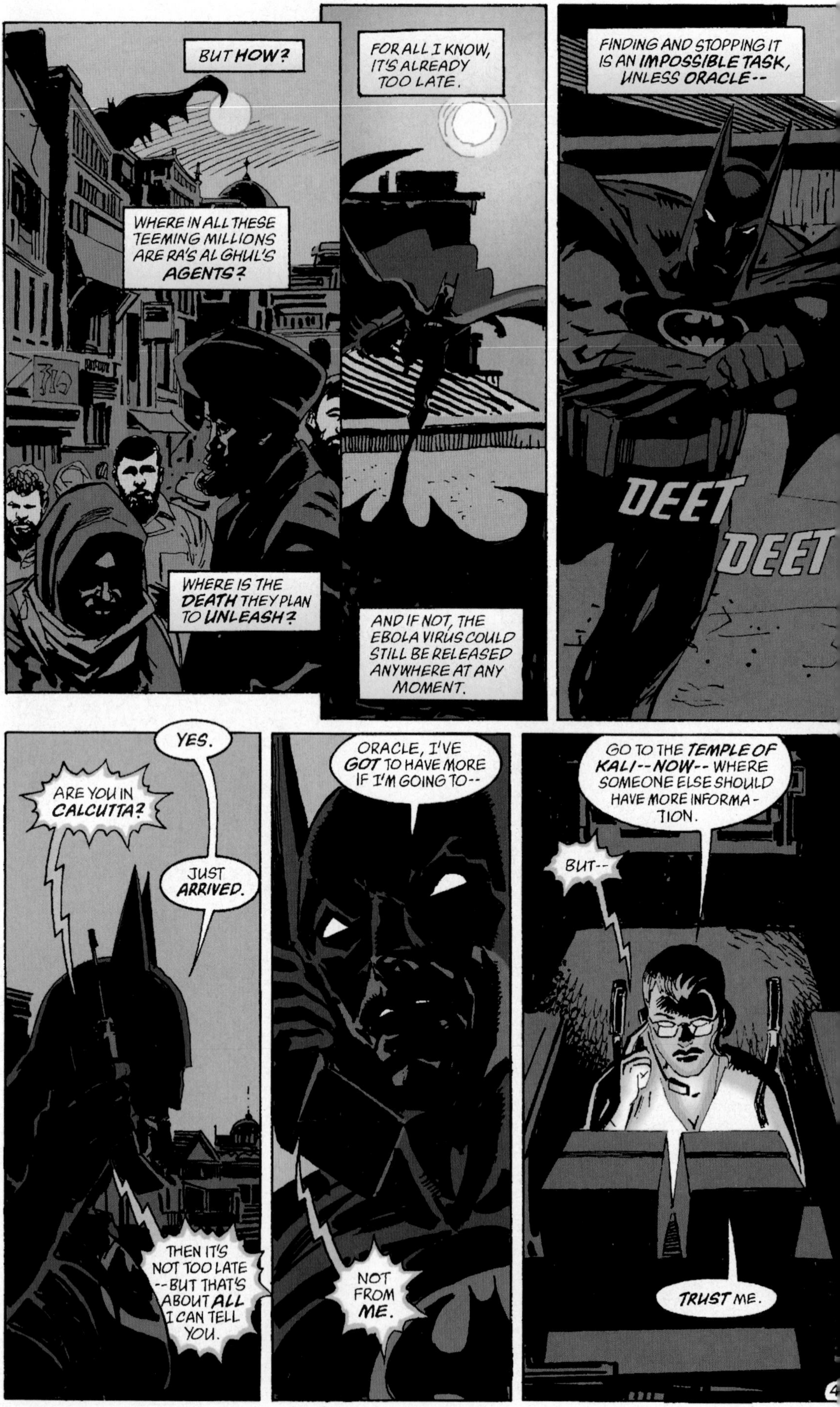

BUT HOW?
WHERE IN ALL THESE TEEMING MILLIONS ARE RA'S AL GHUL'S AGENTS?
WHERE IS THE DEATH THEY PLAN TO UNLEASH?
FOR ALL I KNOW, IT'S ALREADY TOO LATE.
AND IF NOT, THE EBOLA VIRUS COULD STILL BE RELEASED ANYWHERE AT ANY MOMENT.
FINDING AND STOPPING IT IS AN IMPOSSIBLE TASK, UNLESS ORACLE--
DEET
DEET
ARE YOU IN CALCUTTA?
YES.
JUST ARRIVED.
THEN IT'S NOT TOO LATE --BUT THAT'S ABOUT ALL I CAN TELL YOU.
ORACLE, I'VE GOT TO HAVE MORE IF I'M GOING TO--
NOT FROM ME.
GO TO THE TEMPLE OF KALI--NOW-- WHERE SOMEONE ELSE SHOULD HAVE MORE INFORMA-TION.
BUT--
TRUST ME.

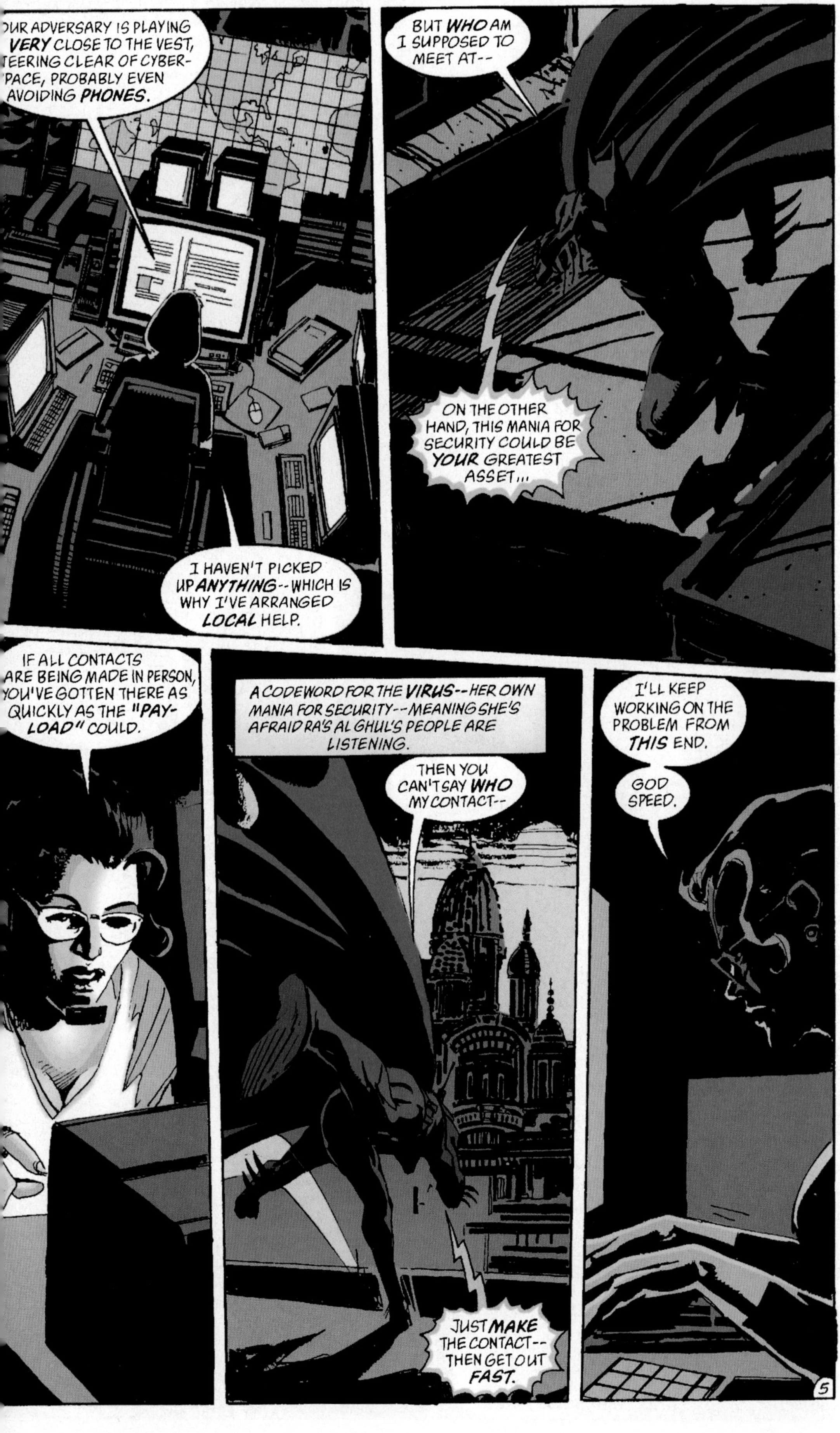
OUR ADVERSARY IS PLAYING VERY CLOSE TO THE VEST, STEERING CLEAR OF CYBERSPACE, PROBABLY EVEN AVOIDING PHONES.
I HAVEN'T PICKED UP ANYTHING--WHICH IS WHY I'VE ARRANGED LOCAL HELP.
BUT WHO AM I SUPPOSED TO MEET AT--
ON THE OTHER HAND, THIS MANIA FOR SECURITY COULD BE YOUR GREATEST ASSET...
IF ALL CONTACTS ARE BEING MADE IN PERSON, YOU'VE GOTTEN THERE AS QUICKLY AS THE "PAYLOAD" COULD.
A CODEWORD FOR THE VIRUS--HER OWN MANIA FOR SECURITY--MEANING SHE'S AFRAID RA'S AL GHUL'S PEOPLE ARE LISTENING.
THEN YOU CAN'T SAY WHO MY CONTACT--
JUST MAKE THE CONTACT--THEN GET OUT FAST.
I'LL KEEP WORKING ON THE PROBLEM FROM THIS END.
GOD SPEED.
5

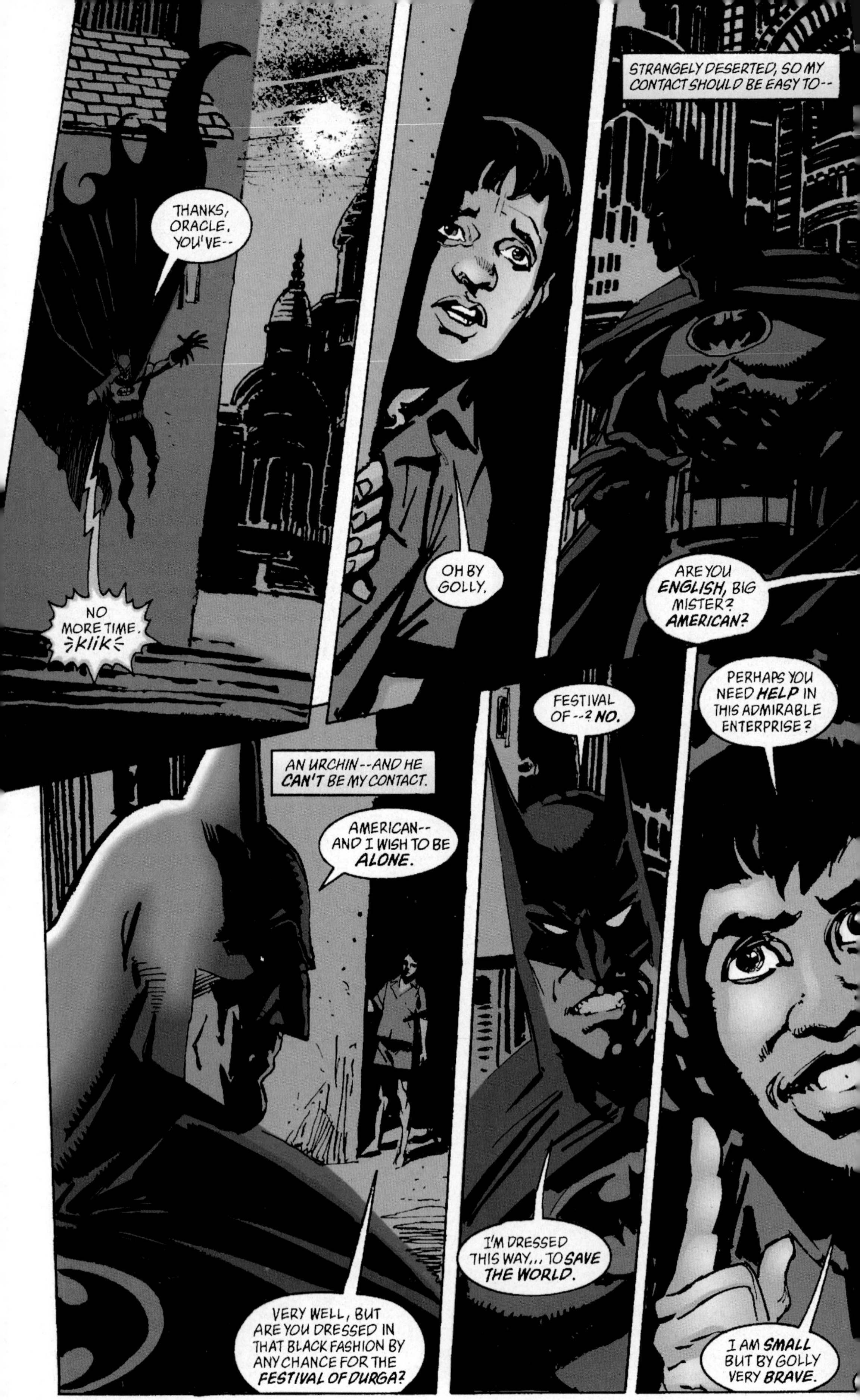
THANKS, ORACLE. YOU'VE--
NO MORE TIME. ≶KLIK≷
OH BY GOLLY.
STRANGELY DESERTED, SO MY CONTACT SHOULD BE EASY TO--
ARE YOU ENGLISH, BIG MISTER? AMERICAN?
AN URCHIN--AND HE CAN'T BE MY CONTACT.
AMERICAN-- AND I WISH TO BE ALONE.
VERY WELL, BUT ARE YOU DRESSED IN THAT BLACK FASHION BY ANY CHANCE FOR THE FESTIVAL OF DURGA?
FESTIVAL OF--? NO.
I'M DRESSED THIS WAY... TO SAVE THE WORLD.
PERHAPS YOU NEED HELP IN THIS ADMIRABLE ENTERPRISE?
I AM SMALL BUT BY GOLLY VERY BRAVE.

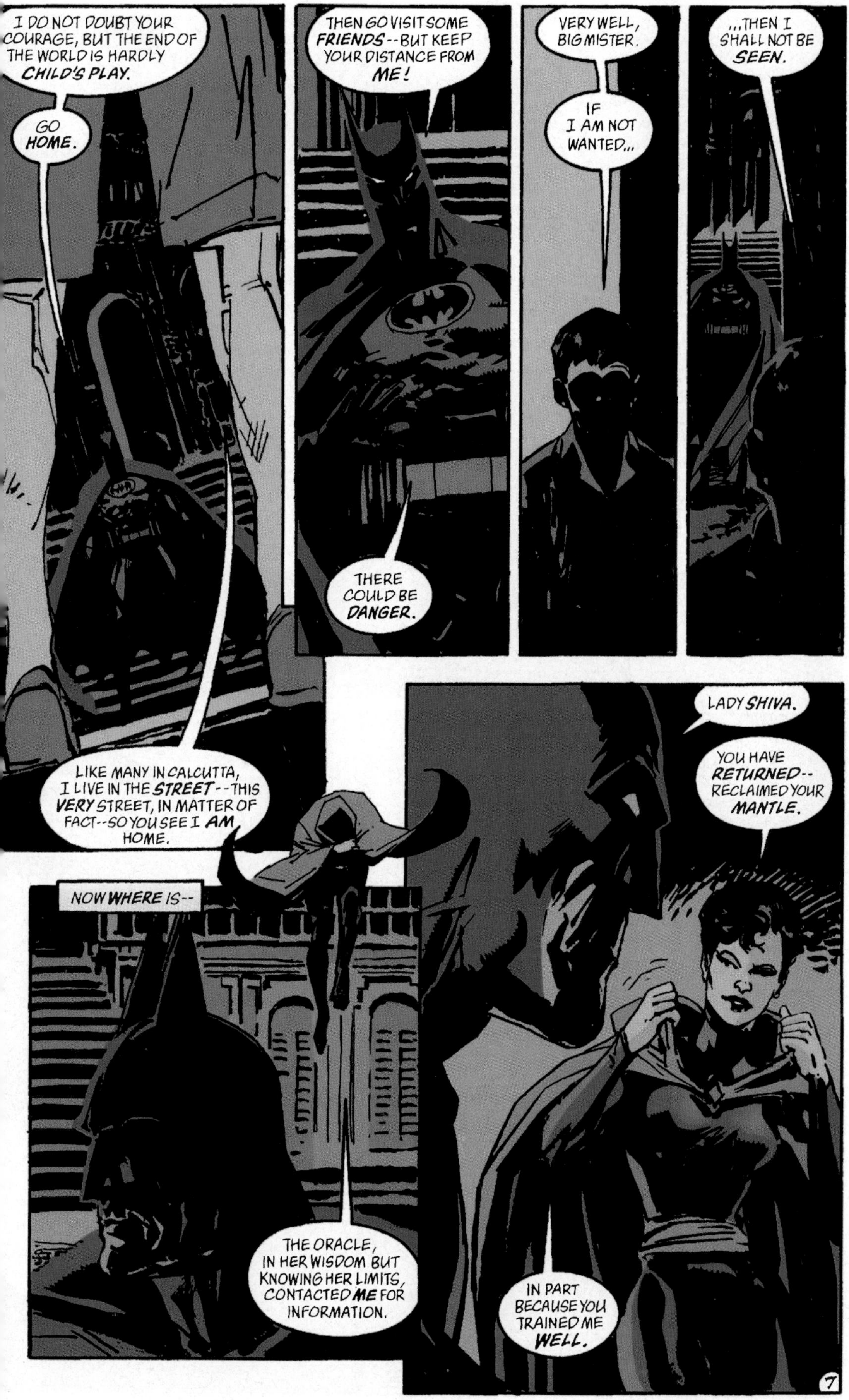

I DO NOT DOUBT YOUR COURAGE, BUT THE END OF THE WORLD IS HARDLY CHILD'S PLAY.
GO HOME.
LIKE MANY IN CALCUTTA, I LIVE IN THE STREET--THIS VERY STREET, IN MATTER OF FACT--SO YOU SEE I AM HOME.
THEN GO VISIT SOME FRIENDS--BUT KEEP YOUR DISTANCE FROM ME!
THERE COULD BE DANGER.
VERY WELL, BIG MISTER.
IF I AM NOT WANTED...
...THEN I SHALL NOT BE SEEN.
NOW WHERE IS--
LADY SHIVA.
YOU HAVE RETURNED--RECLAIMED YOUR MANTLE.
THE ORACLE, IN HER WISDOM BUT KNOWING HER LIMITS, CONTACTED ME FOR INFORMATION.
IN PART BECAUSE YOU TRAINED ME WELL.
7

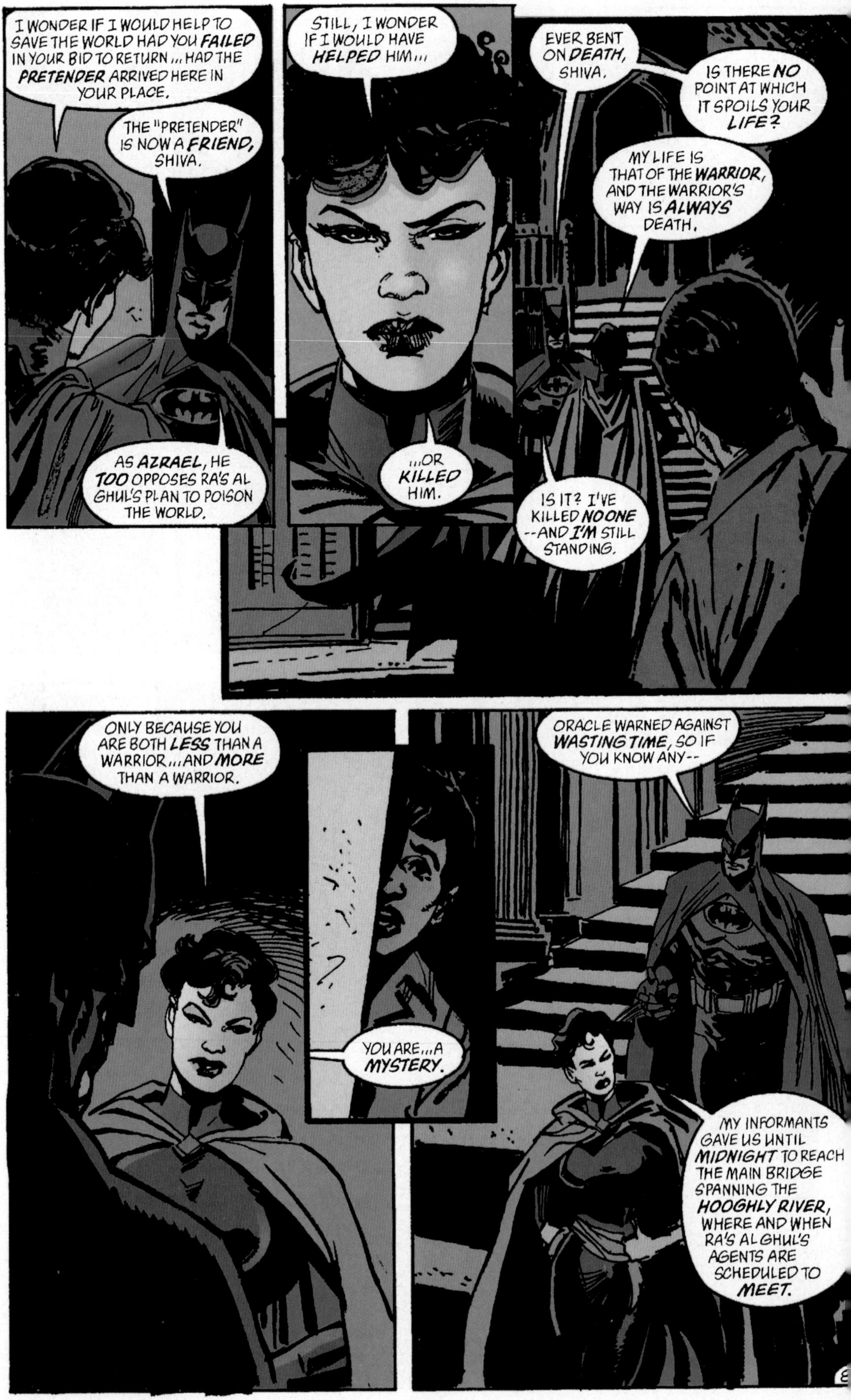

I WONDER IF I WOULD HELP TO SAVE THE WORLD HAD YOU FAILED IN YOUR BID TO RETURN... HAD THE PRETENDER ARRIVED HERE IN YOUR PLACE.
THE "PRETENDER" IS NOW A FRIEND, SHIVA.
AS AZRAEL, HE TOO OPPOSES RA'S AL GHUL'S PLAN TO POISON THE WORLD.
STILL, I WONDER IF I WOULD HAVE HELPED HIM...
...OR KILLED HIM.
EVER BENT ON DEATH, SHIVA.
IS THERE NO POINT AT WHICH IT SPOILS YOUR LIFE?
MY LIFE IS THAT OF THE WARRIOR, AND THE WARRIOR'S WAY IS ALWAYS DEATH.
IS IT? I'VE KILLED NO ONE --AND I'M STILL STANDING.
ONLY BECAUSE YOU ARE BOTH LESS THAN A WARRIOR... AND MORE THAN A WARRIOR.
YOU ARE... A MYSTERY.
ORACLE WARNED AGAINST WASTING TIME, SO IF YOU KNOW ANY--
MY INFORMANTS GAVE US UNTIL MIDNIGHT TO REACH THE MAIN BRIDGE SPANNING THE HOOGHLY RIVER, WHERE AND WHEN RA'S AL GHUL'S AGENTS ARE SCHEDULED TO MEET.

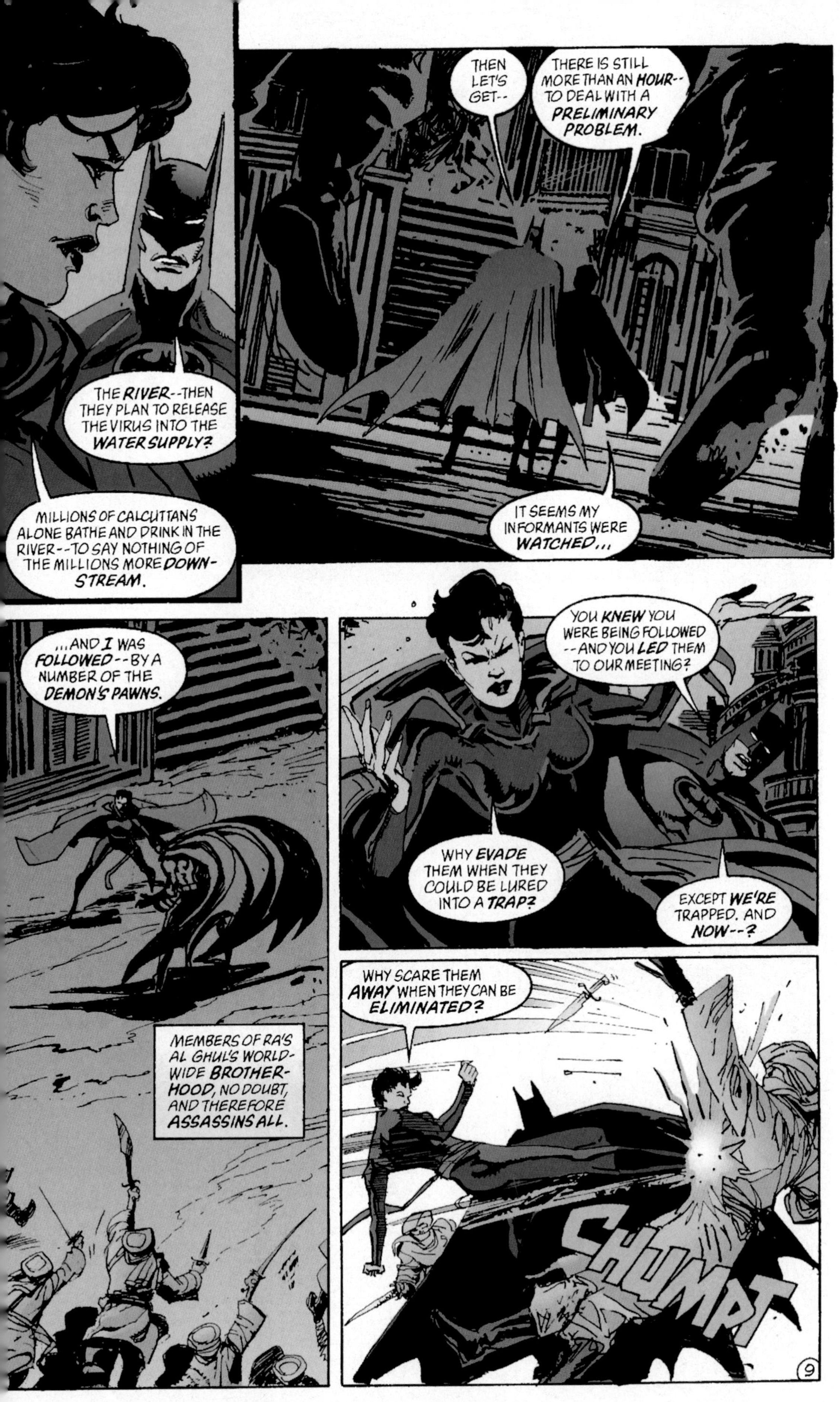
THE RIVER--THEN THEY PLAN TO RELEASE THE VIRUS INTO THE WATER SUPPLY?
MILLIONS OF CALCUTTANS ALONE BATHE AND DRINK IN THE RIVER--TO SAY NOTHING OF THE MILLIONS MORE DOWN-STREAM.
THEN LET'S GET--
THERE IS STILL MORE THAN AN HOUR--TO DEAL WITH A PRELIMINARY PROBLEM.
IT SEEMS MY INFORMANTS WERE WATCHED...
...AND I WAS FOLLOWED--BY A NUMBER OF THE DEMON'S PAWNS.
YOU KNEW YOU WERE BEING FOLLOWED--AND YOU LED THEM TO OUR MEETING?
WHY EVADE THEM WHEN THEY COULD BE LURED INTO A TRAP?
EXCEPT WE'RE TRAPPED. AND NOW--?
MEMBERS OF RA'S AL GHUL'S WORLD-WIDE BROTHER-HOOD, NO DOUBT, AND THEREFORE ASSASSINS ALL.
WHY SCARE THEM AWAY WHEN THEY CAN BE ELIMINATED?
SHUMPT
9

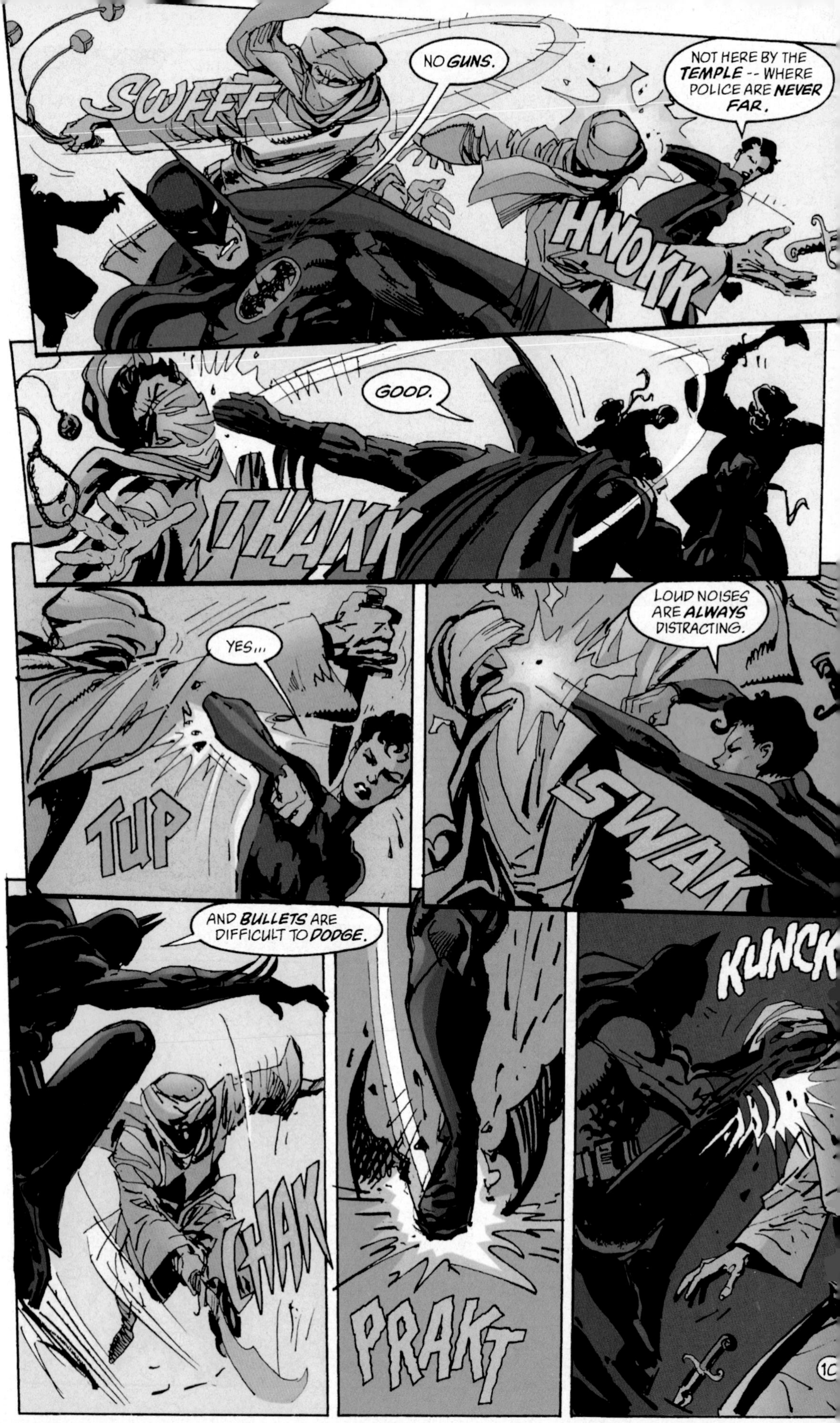
SWFFF
NO GUNS.
NOT HERE BY THE TEMPLE -- WHERE POLICE ARE NEVER FAR.
HWOKK
GOOD.
THAKK
YES...
TUP
LOUD NOISES ARE ALWAYS DISTRACTING.
SWAK
AND BULLETS ARE DIFFICULT TO DODGE.
CHAK
PRAKT
KUNCK

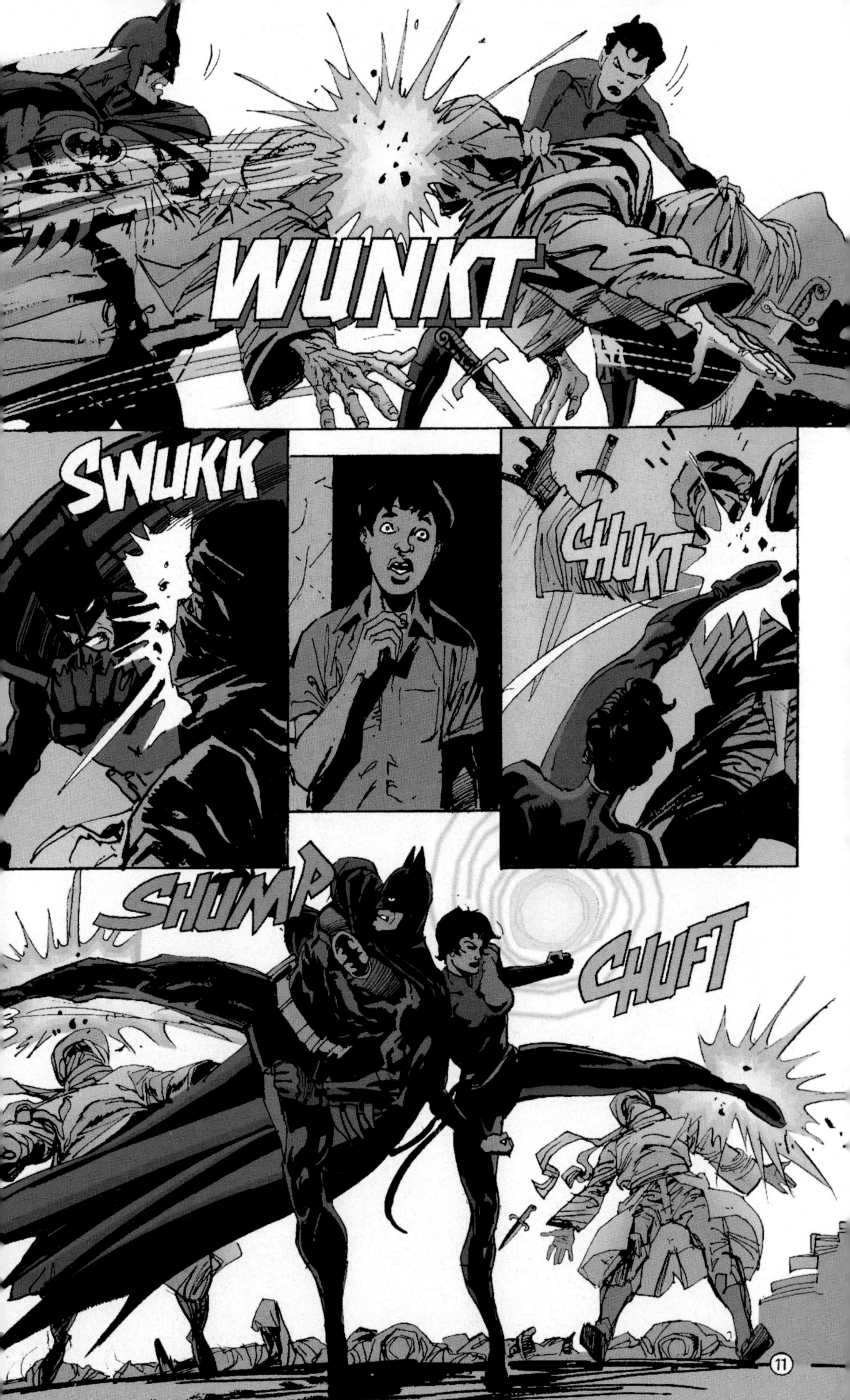
WUNKT
SWUKK
CHUKT
SHUMP
CHUFT

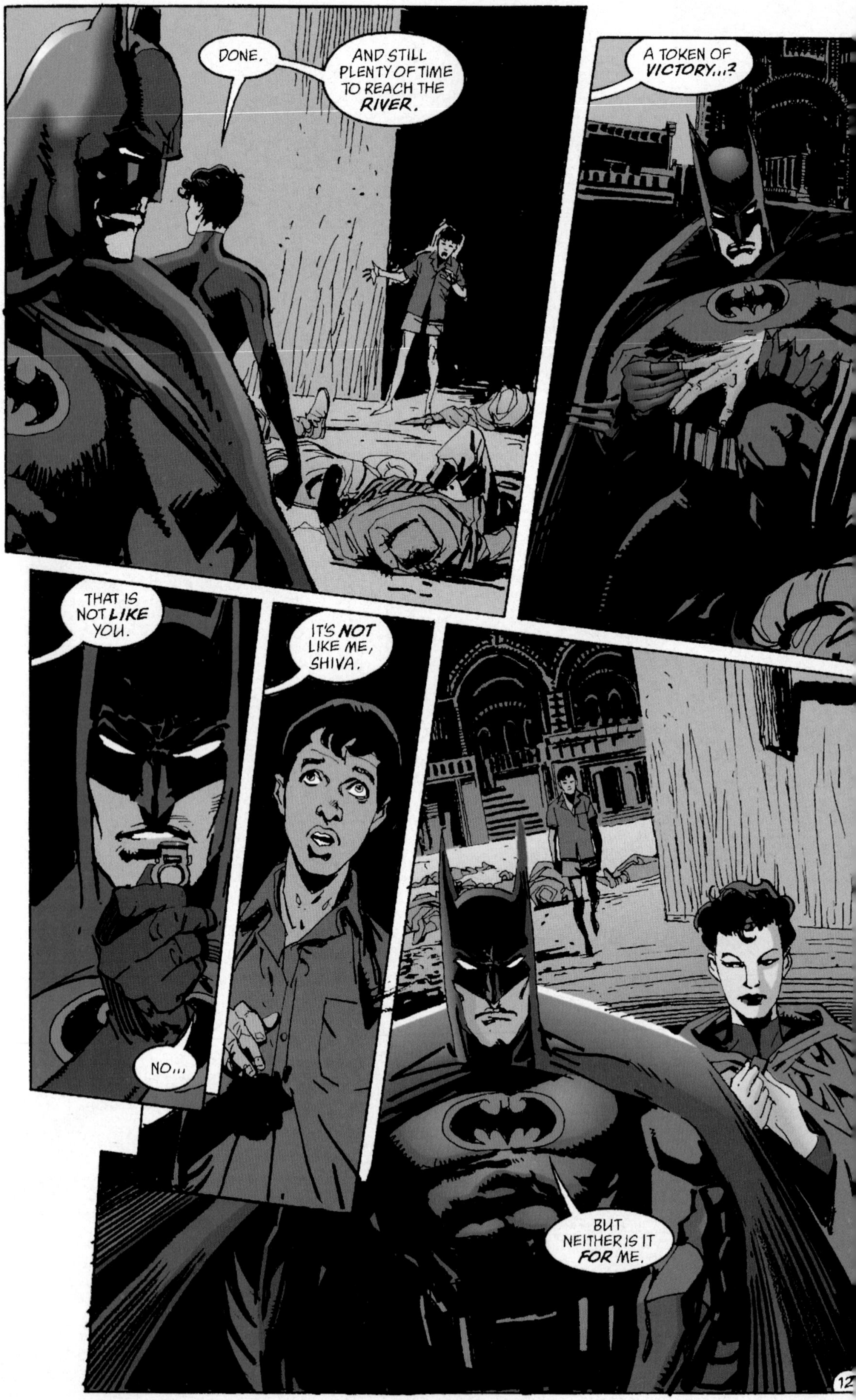
DONE.
AND STILL PLENTY OF TIME TO REACH THE RIVER.
A TOKEN OF VICTORY...?
THAT IS NOT LIKE YOU.
NO...
IT'S NOT LIKE ME, SHIVA.
BUT NEITHER IS IT FOR ME.

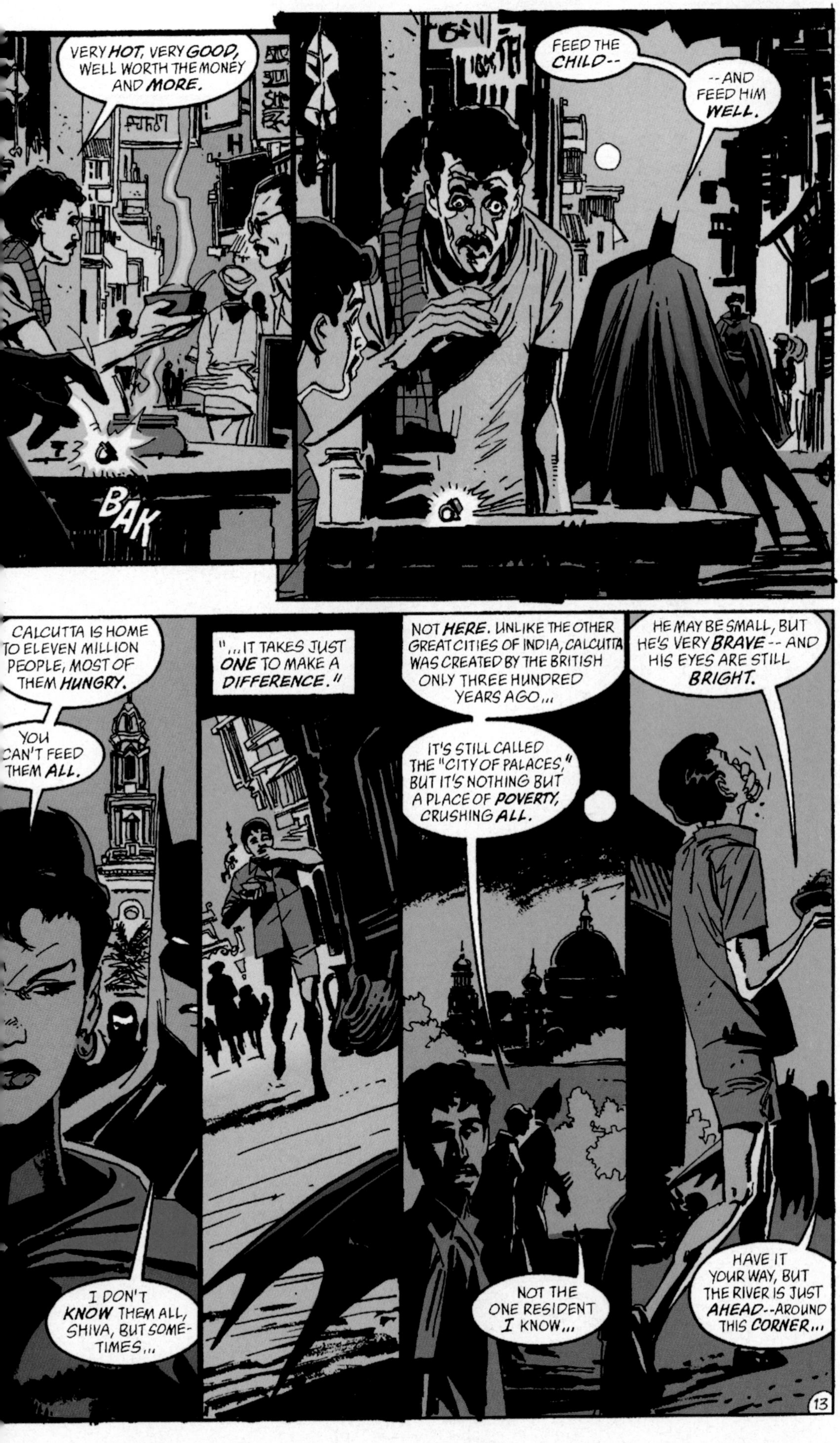

VERY HOT, VERY GOOD, WELL WORTH THE MONEY AND MORE.
BAK
FEED THE CHILD--
--AND FEED HIM WELL.
CALCUTTA IS HOME TO ELEVEN MILLION PEOPLE, MOST OF THEM HUNGRY.
YOU CAN'T FEED THEM ALL.
I DON'T KNOW THEM ALL, SHIVA, BUT SOMETIMES...
"...IT TAKES JUST ONE TO MAKE A DIFFERENCE."
NOT HERE. UNLIKE THE OTHER GREAT CITIES OF INDIA, CALCUTTA WAS CREATED BY THE BRITISH ONLY THREE HUNDRED YEARS AGO...
IT'S STILL CALLED THE "CITY OF PALACES," BUT IT'S NOTHING BUT A PLACE OF POVERTY, CRUSHING ALL.
NOT THE ONE RESIDENT I KNOW...
HE MAY BE SMALL, BUT HE'S VERY BRAVE -- AND HIS EYES ARE STILL BRIGHT.
HAVE IT YOUR WAY, BUT THE RIVER IS JUST AHEAD--AROUND THIS CORNER...

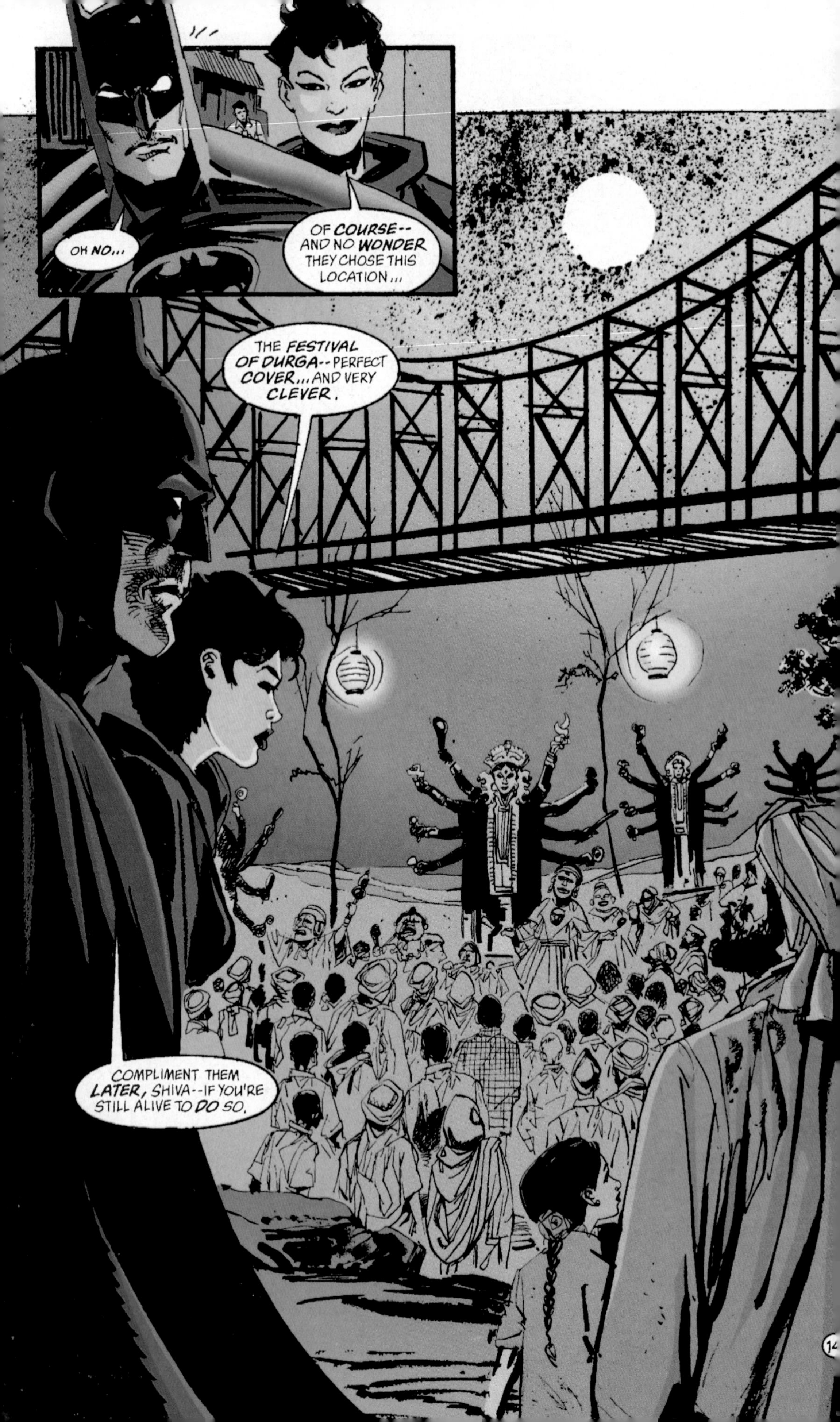
OH NO...
OF COURSE-- AND NO WONDER THEY CHOSE THIS LOCATION...
THE FESTIVAL OF DURGA-- PERFECT COVER... AND VERY CLEVER.
COMPLIMENT THEM LATER, SHIVA--IF YOU'RE STILL ALIVE TO DO SO.

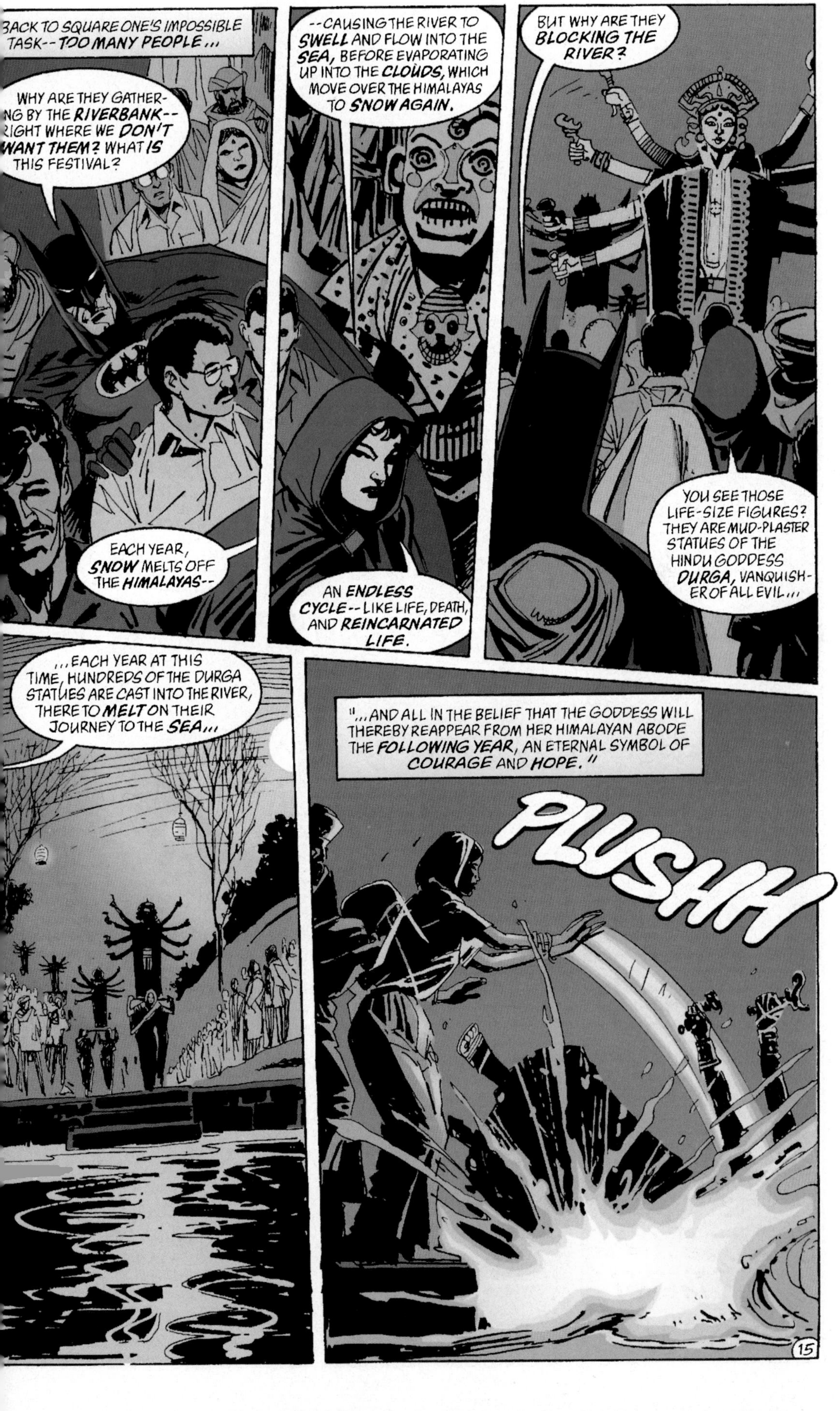
BACK TO SQUARE ONE'S IMPOSSIBLE TASK--TOO MANY PEOPLE...
WHY ARE THEY GATHERING BY THE RIVERBANK--RIGHT WHERE WE DON'T WANT THEM? WHAT IS THIS FESTIVAL?
EACH YEAR, SNOW MELTS OFF THE HIMALAYAS--
--CAUSING THE RIVER TO SWELL AND FLOW INTO THE SEA, BEFORE EVAPORATING UP INTO THE CLOUDS, WHICH MOVE OVER THE HIMALAYAS TO SNOW AGAIN.
AN ENDLESS CYCLE--LIKE LIFE, DEATH, AND REINCARNATED LIFE.
BUT WHY ARE THEY BLOCKING THE RIVER?
YOU SEE THOSE LIFE-SIZE FIGURES? THEY ARE MUD-PLASTER STATUES OF THE HINDU GODDESS DURGA, VANQUISHER OF ALL EVIL...
...EACH YEAR AT THIS TIME, HUNDREDS OF THE DURGA STATUES ARE CAST INTO THE RIVER, THERE TO MELT ON THEIR JOURNEY TO THE SEA...
"...AND ALL IN THE BELIEF THAT THE GODDESS WILL THEREBY REAPPEAR FROM HER HIMALAYAN ABODE THE FOLLOWING YEAR, AN ETERNAL SYMBOL OF COURAGE AND HOPE."
PLUSHH

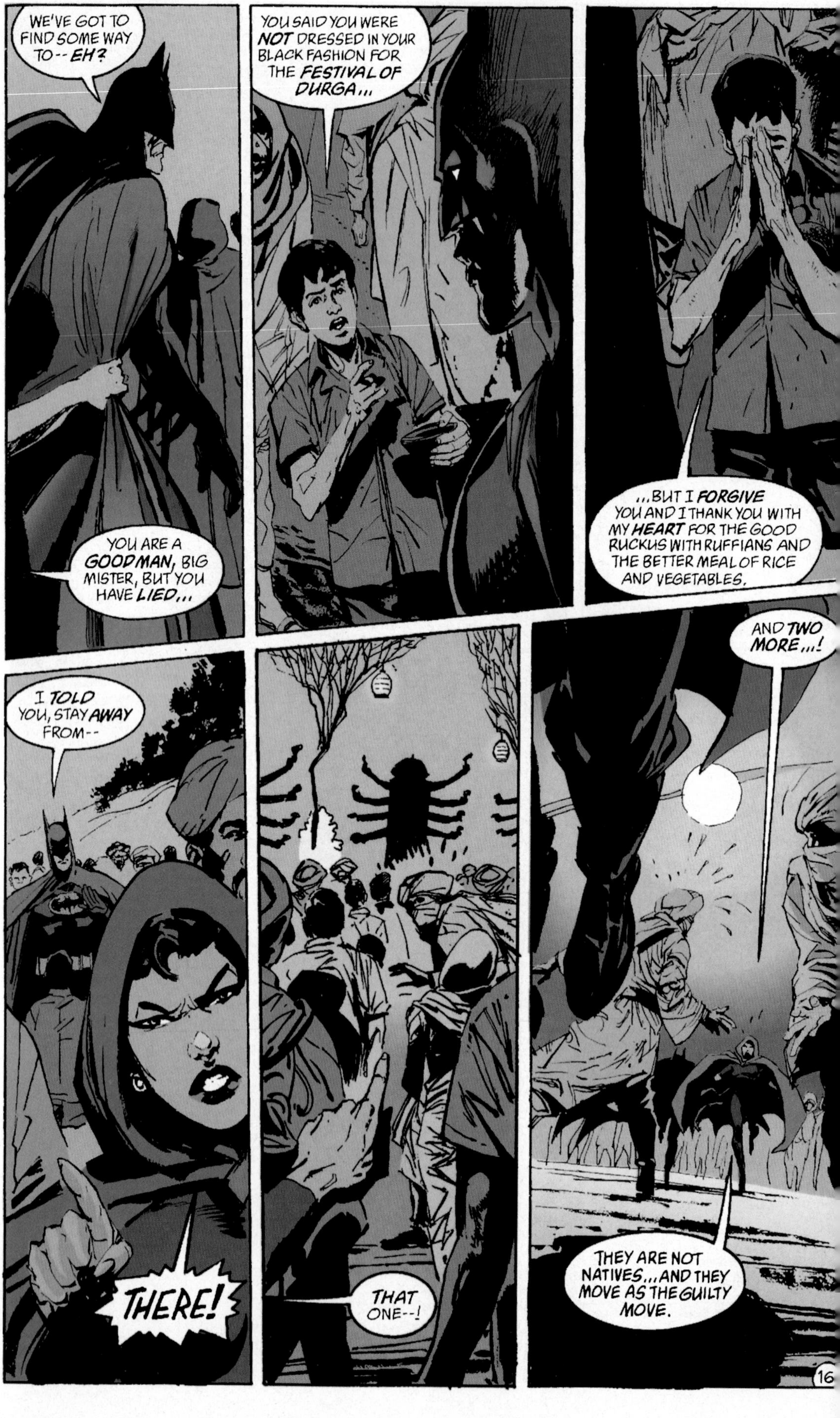
WE'VE GOT TO FIND SOME WAY TO-- EH?
YOU ARE A GOOD MAN, BIG MISTER, BUT YOU HAVE LIED...
YOU SAID YOU WERE NOT DRESSED IN YOUR BLACK FASHION FOR THE FESTIVAL OF DURGA...
...BUT I FORGIVE YOU AND I THANK YOU WITH MY HEART FOR THE GOOD RUCKUS WITH RUFFIANS AND THE BETTER MEAL OF RICE AND VEGETABLES.
I TOLD YOU, STAY AWAY FROM--
THERE!
THAT ONE--!
AND TWO MORE...!
THEY ARE NOT NATIVES... AND THEY MOVE AS THE GUILTY MOVE.
16

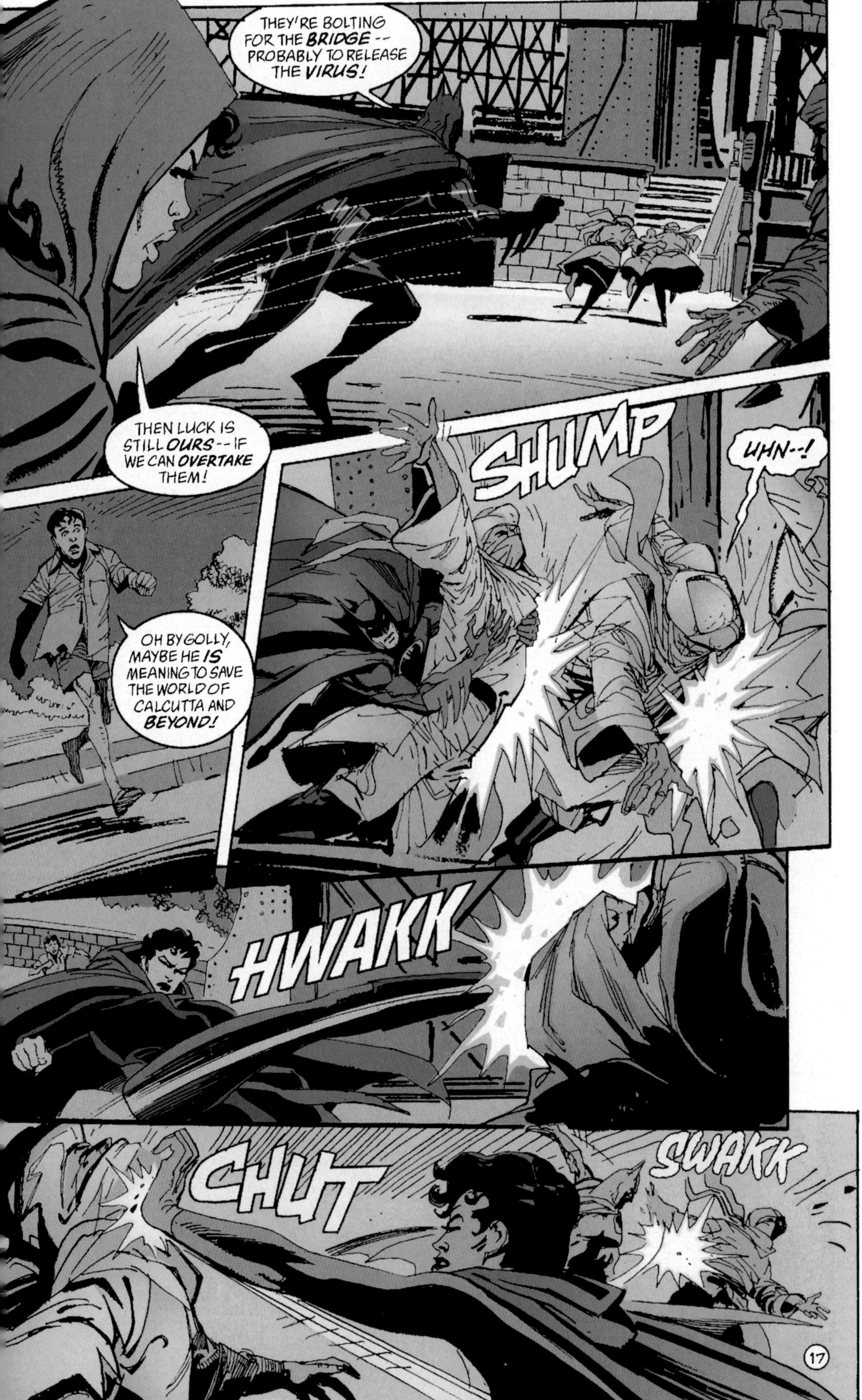
THEY'RE BOLTING FOR THE BRIDGE -- PROBABLY TO RELEASE THE VIRUS!
THEN LUCK IS STILL OURS -- IF WE CAN OVERTAKE THEM!
SHUMP
UHN--!
OH BY GOLLY, MAYBE HE IS MEANING TO SAVE THE WORLD OF CALCUTTA AND BEYOND!
HWAKK
CHUT
SWAKK

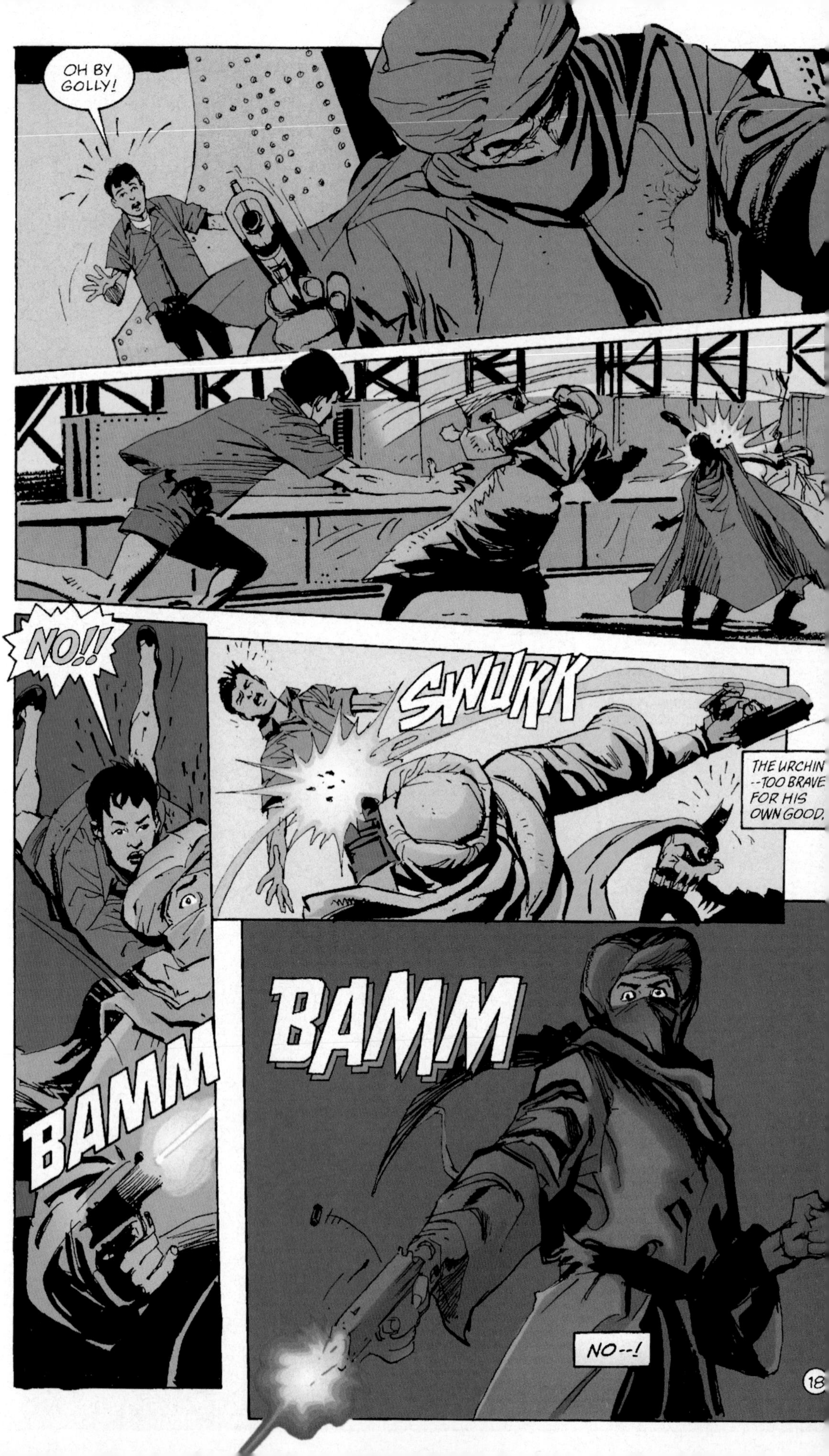
OH BY GOLLY!
NO!!
SWUKK
THE URCHIN --TOO BRAVE FOR HIS OWN GOOD.
BAMM
BAMM
NO--!

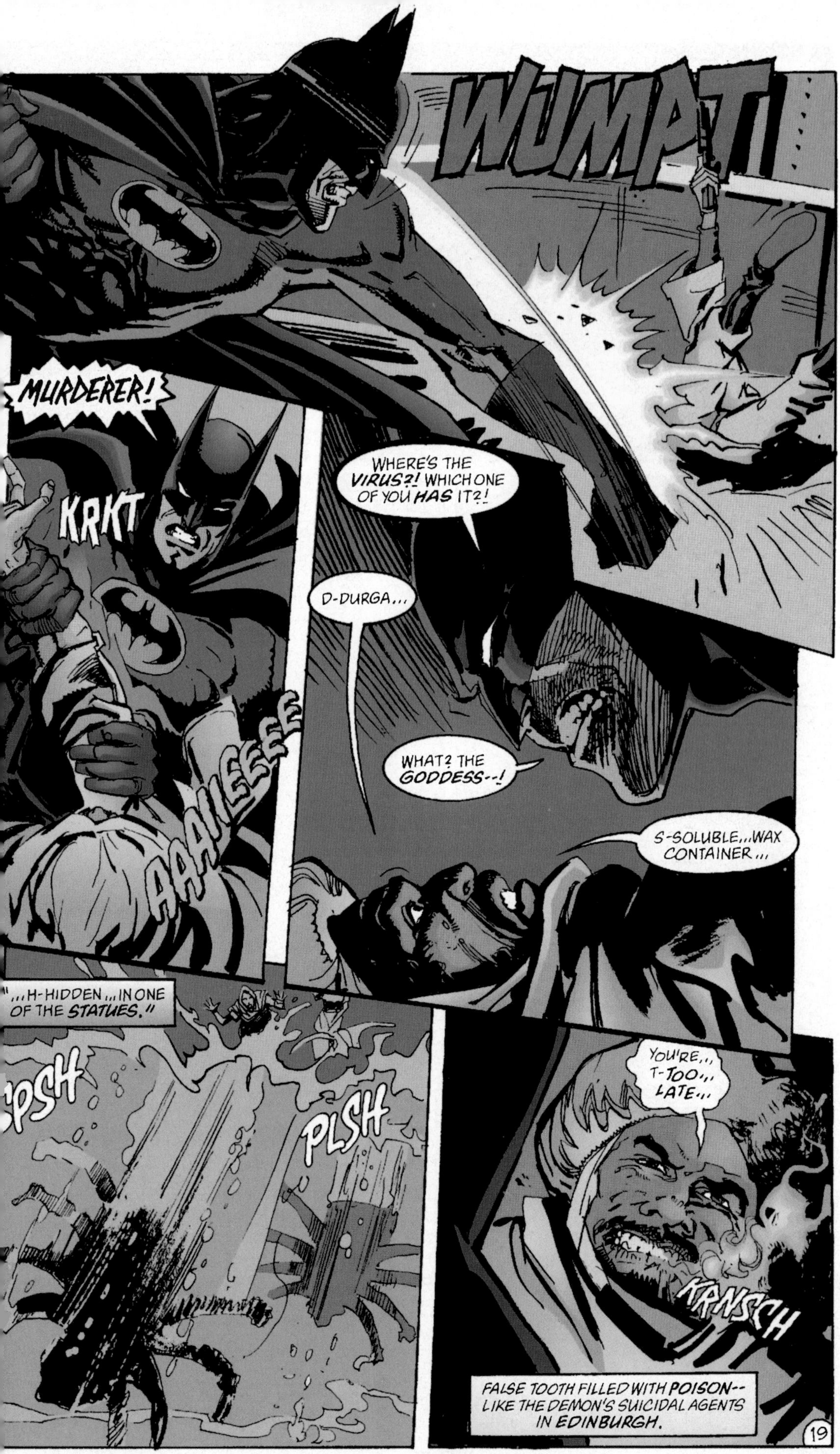
WUMP!
MURDERER!
KRKT
AAAIEEEE
WHERE'S THE VIRUS?! WHICH ONE OF YOU HAS IT?!
D-DURGA...
WHAT? THE GODDESS--!
S-SOLUBLE...WAX CONTAINER...
"...H-HIDDEN...IN ONE OF THE STATUES."
PSH
PLSH
YOU'RE... T-TOO... LATE...
KRNSCH
FALSE TOOTH FILLED WITH POISON-- LIKE THE DEMON'S SUICIDAL AGENTS IN EDINBURGH.
19

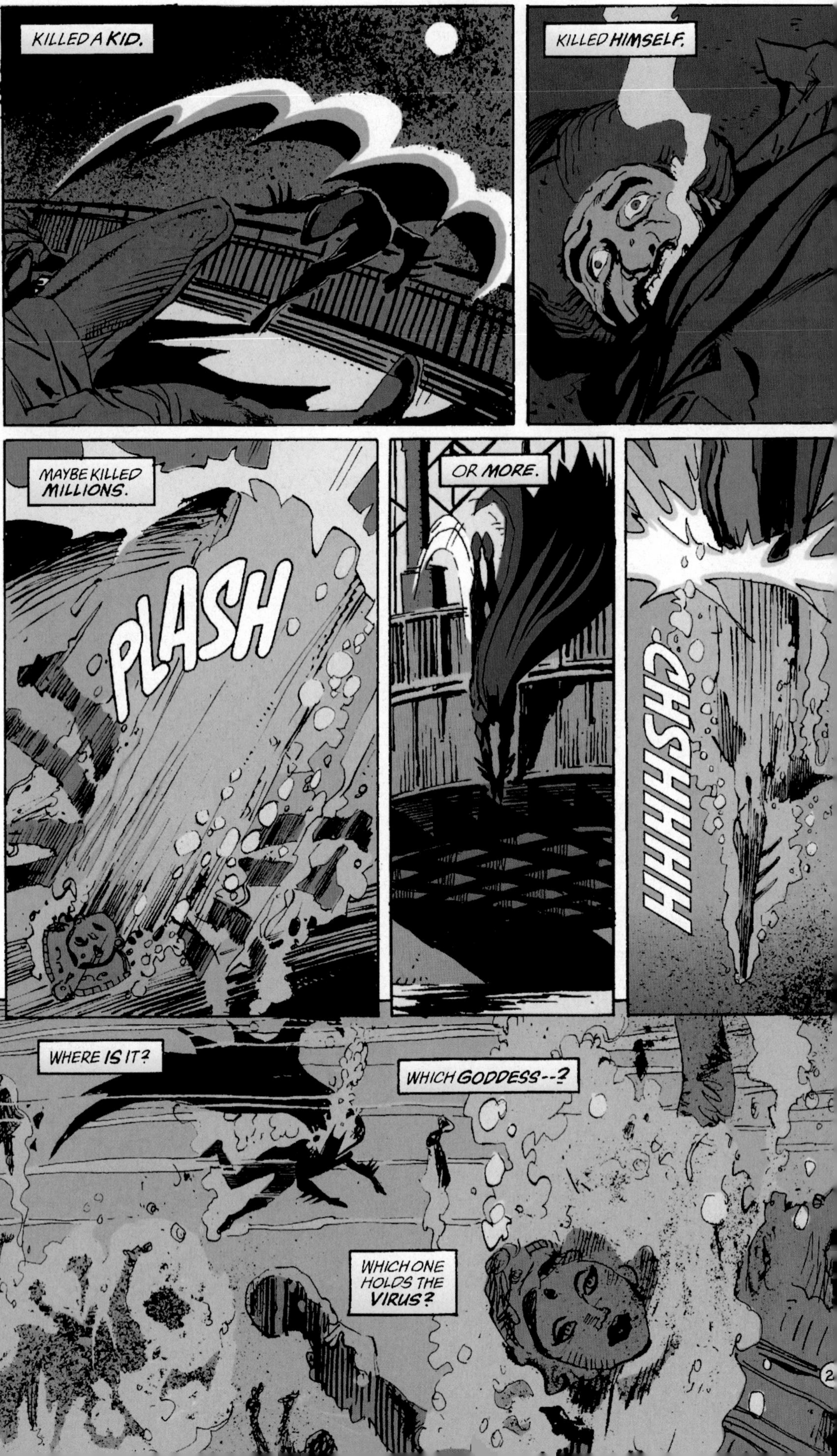
KILLED A KID.
KILLED HIMSELF.
MAYBE KILLED MILLIONS.
PLASH
OR MORE.
CHSHHHHH
WHERE IS IT?
WHICH GODDESS--?
WHICH ONE HOLDS THE VIRUS?

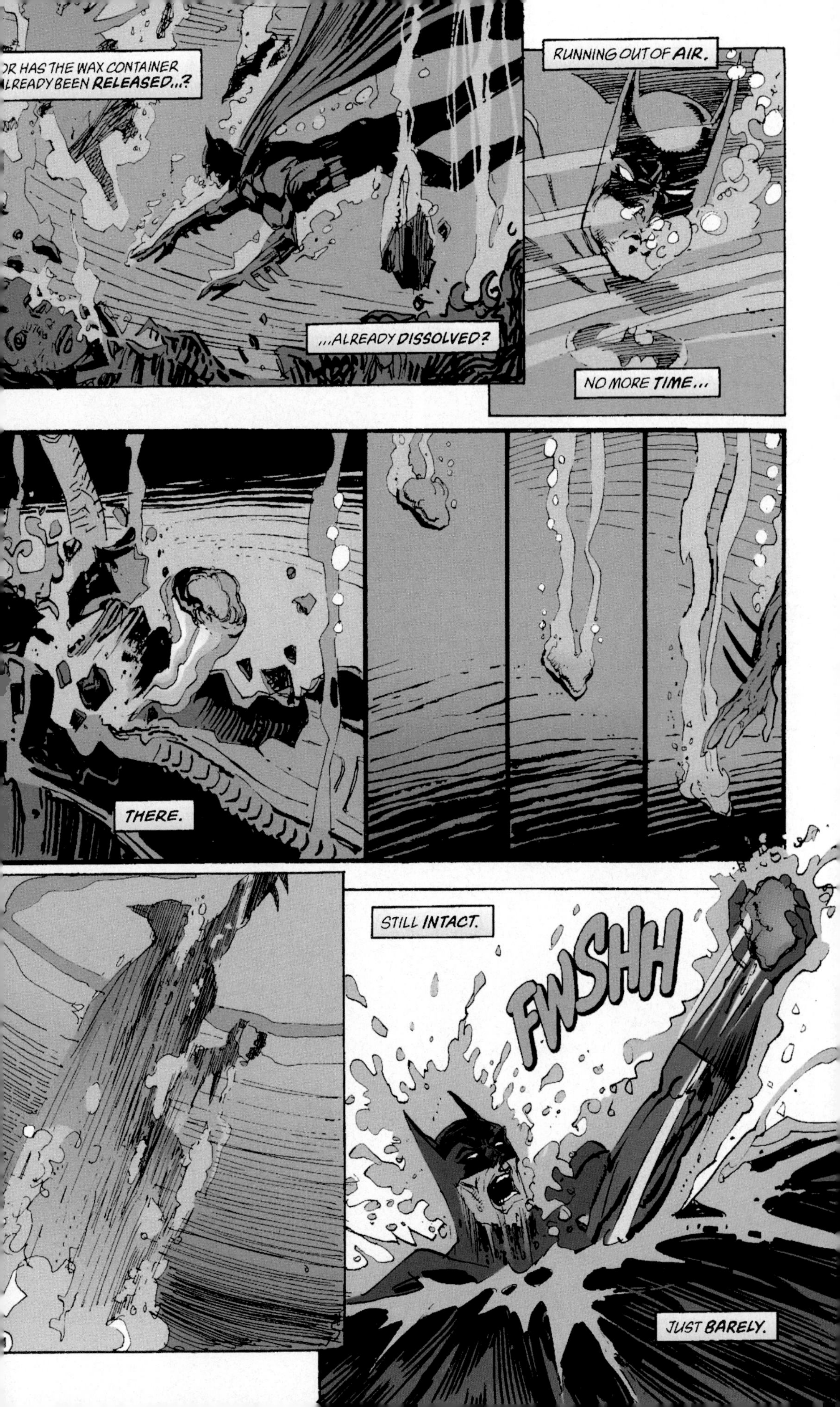

OR HAS THE WAX CONTAINER ALREADY BEEN RELEASED...?
...ALREADY DISSOLVED?
RUNNING OUT OF AIR.
NO MORE TIME...
THERE.
STILL INTACT.
FWSHH
JUST BARELY.

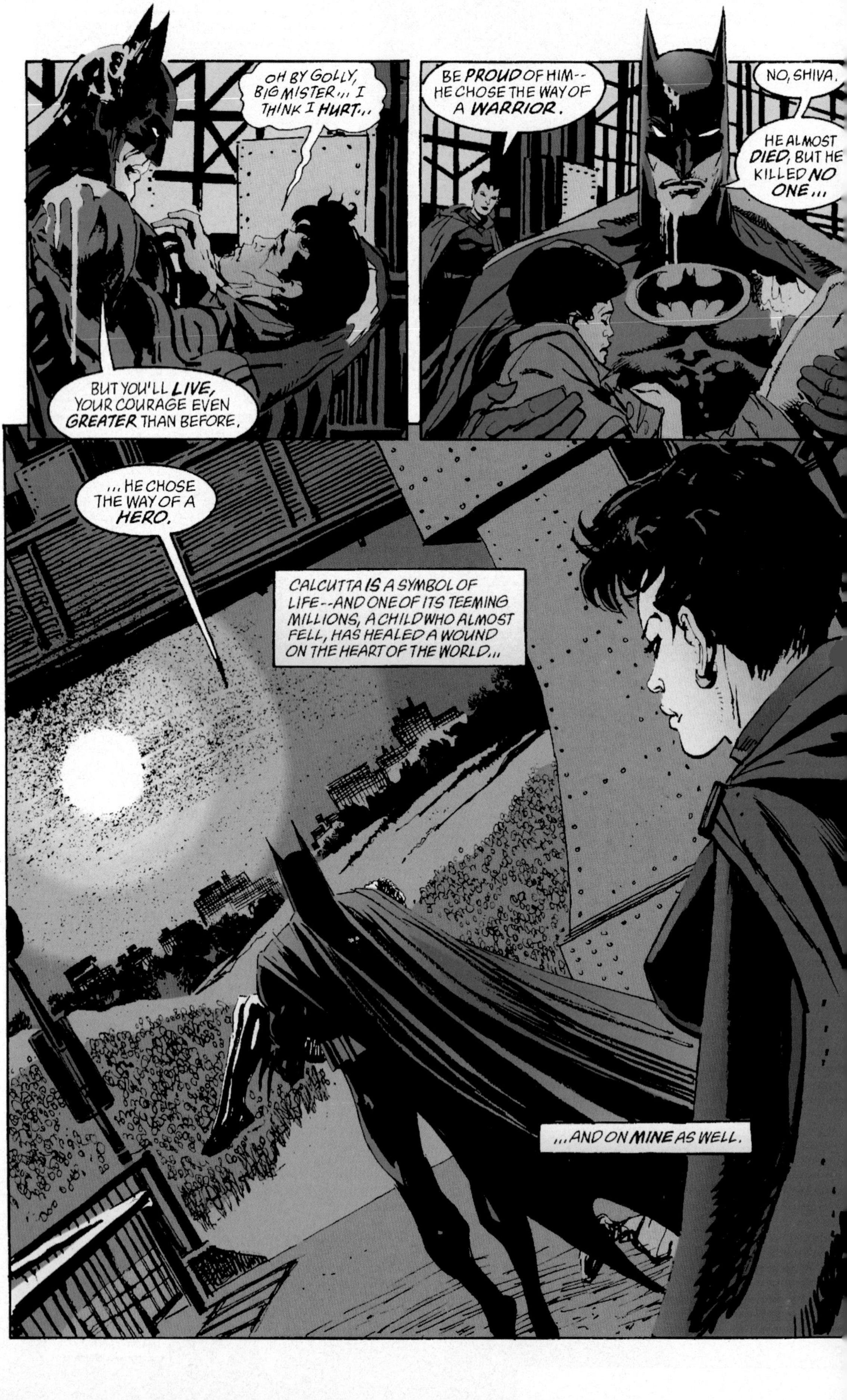
OH BY GOLLY, BIG MISTER... I THINK I HURT...
BUT YOU'LL LIVE, YOUR COURAGE EVEN GREATER THAN BEFORE.
BE PROUD OF HIM-- HE CHOSE THE WAY OF A WARRIOR.
NO, SHIVA.
HE ALMOST DIED, BUT HE KILLED NO ONE...
...HE CHOSE THE WAY OF A HERO.
CALCUTTA IS A SYMBOL OF LIFE--AND ONE OF ITS TEEMING MILLIONS, A CHILD WHO ALMOST FELL, HAS HEALED A WOUND ON THE HEART OF THE WORLD...
...AND ON MINE AS WELL.

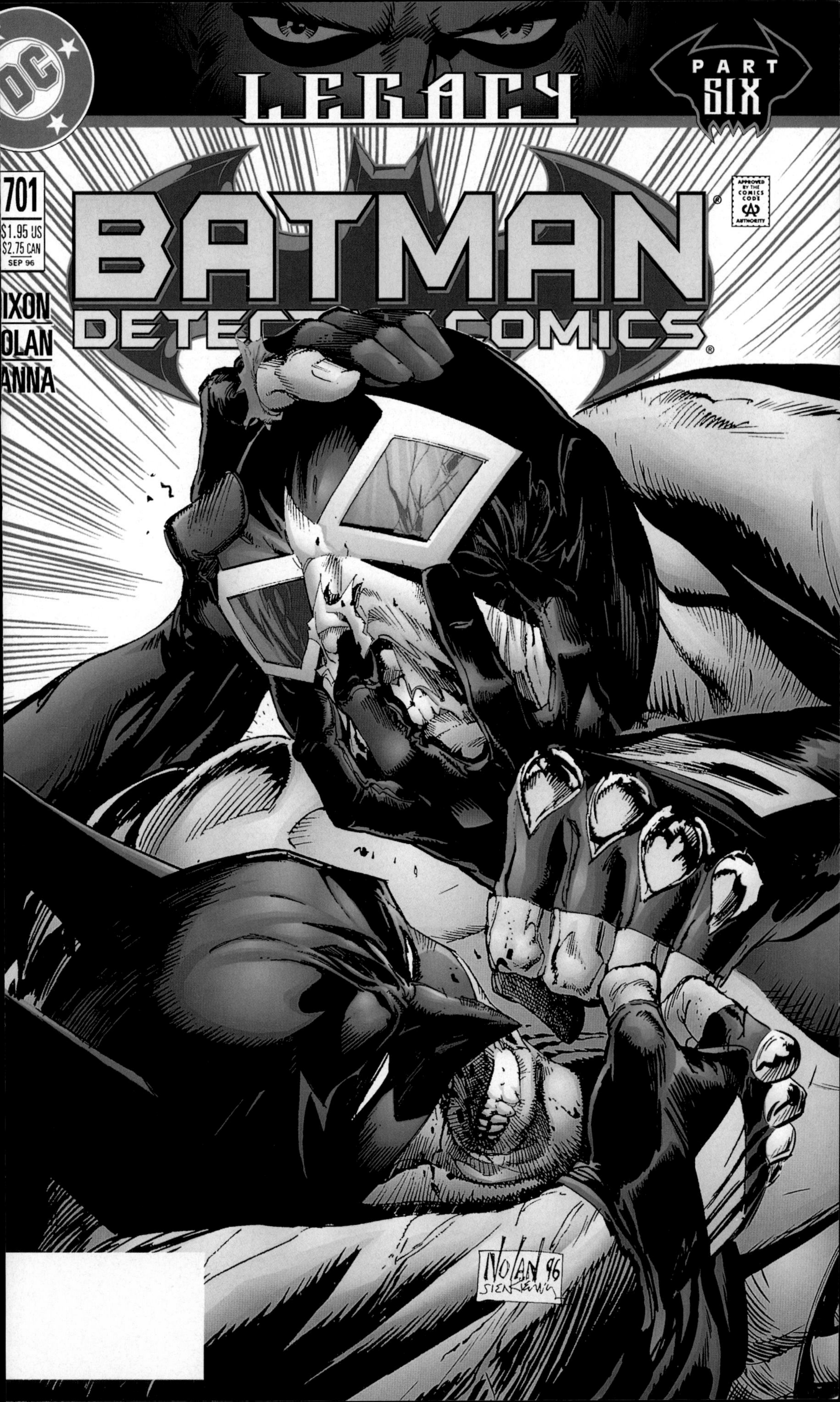

LEGACY
PART SIX
701
$1.95 US
$2.75 CAN
SEP 96
BATMAN
DETECTIVE COMICS
APPROVED BY THE COMICS CODE AUTHORITY
IXON
OLAN
ANNA
NOLAN 96
SIENKIEWICZ

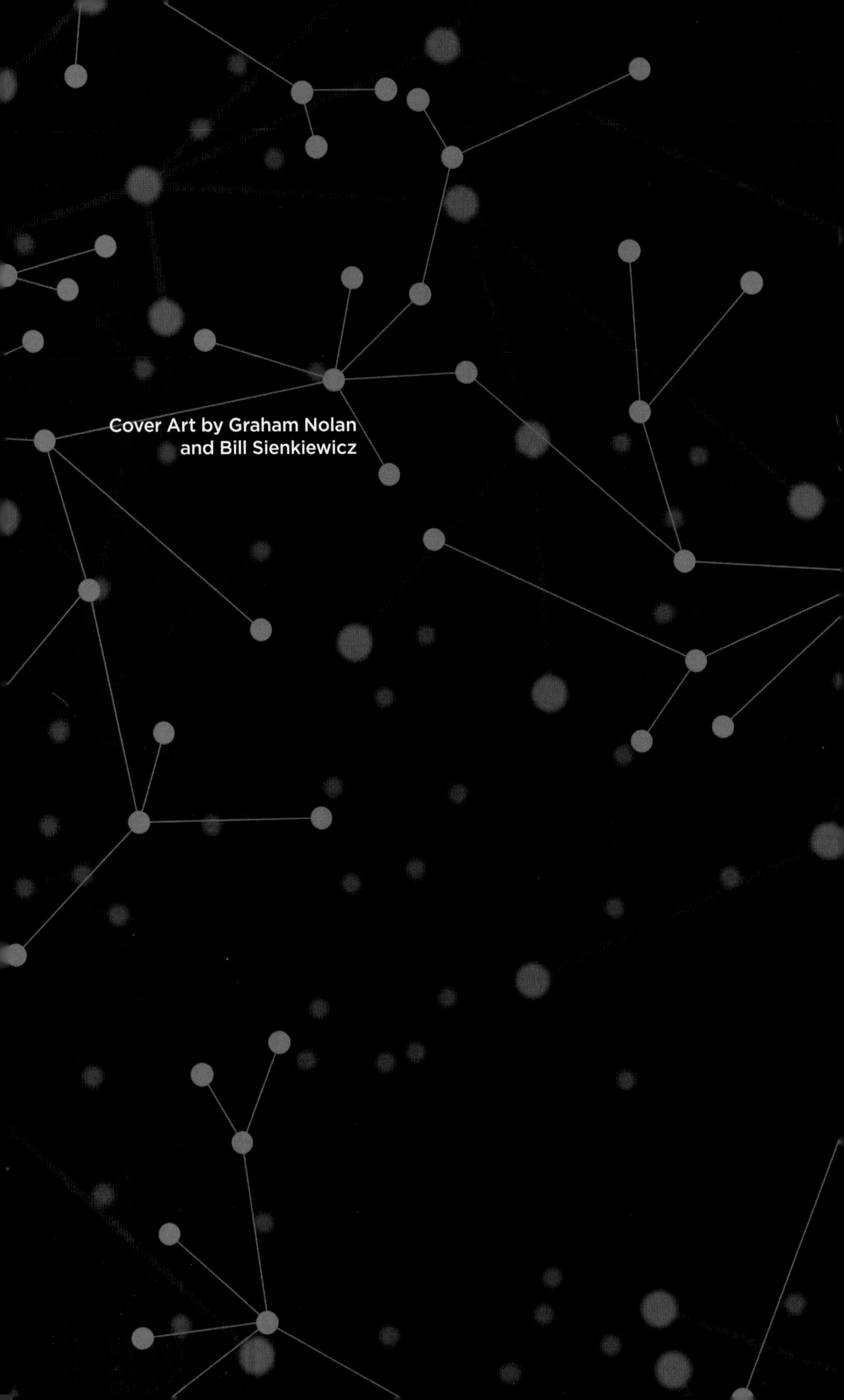

Cover Art by Graham Nolan
and Bill Sienkiewicz

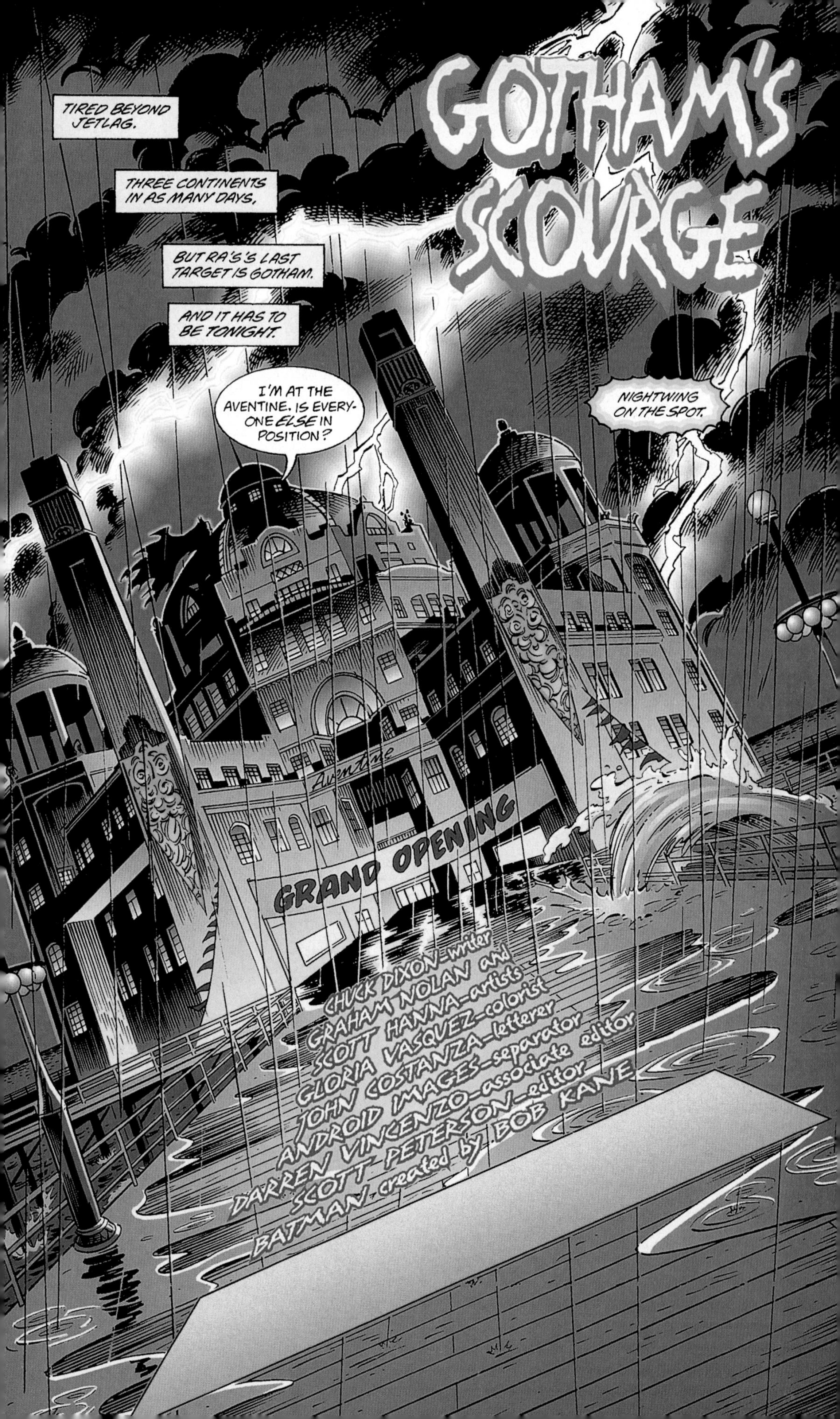
GOTHAM'S SCOURGE
TIRED BEYOND JETLAG.
THREE CONTINENTS IN AS MANY DAYS.
BUT RA'S'S LAST TARGET IS GOTHAM.
AND IT HAS TO BE TONIGHT.
I'M AT THE AVENTINE. IS EVERY-ONE ELSE IN POSITION?
NIGHTWING ON THE SPOT.
Aventine
GRAND OPENING
CHUCK DIXON-writer
GRAHAM NOLAN and
SCOTT HANNA-artists
GLORIA VASQUEZ-colorist
JOHN COSTANZA-letterer
ANDROID IMAGES-separator
DARREN VINCENZO-associate editor
SCOTT PETERSON-editor
BATMAN created by BOB KANE

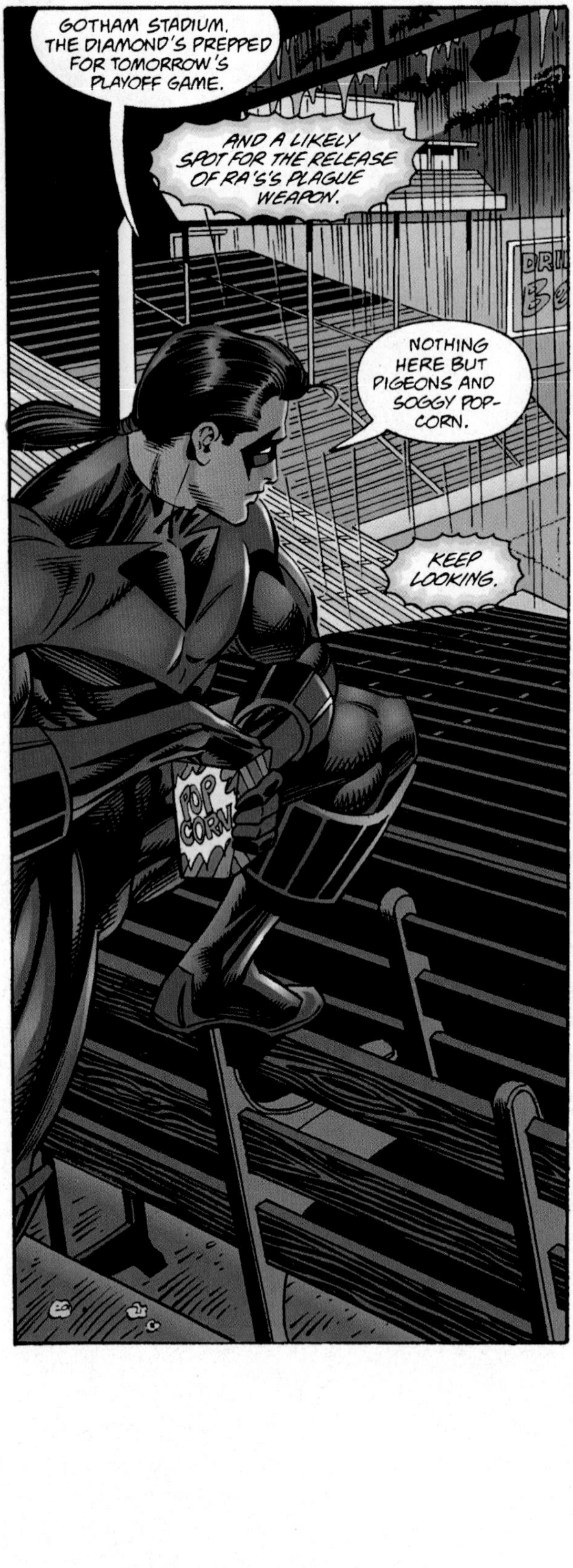
GOTHAM STADIUM. THE DIAMOND'S PREPPED FOR TOMORROW'S PLAYOFF GAME.
AND A LIKELY SPOT FOR THE RELEASE OF RA'S'S PLAGUE WEAPON.
NOTHING HERE BUT PIGEONS AND SOGGY POP-CORN.
KEEP LOOKING.
POP CORN

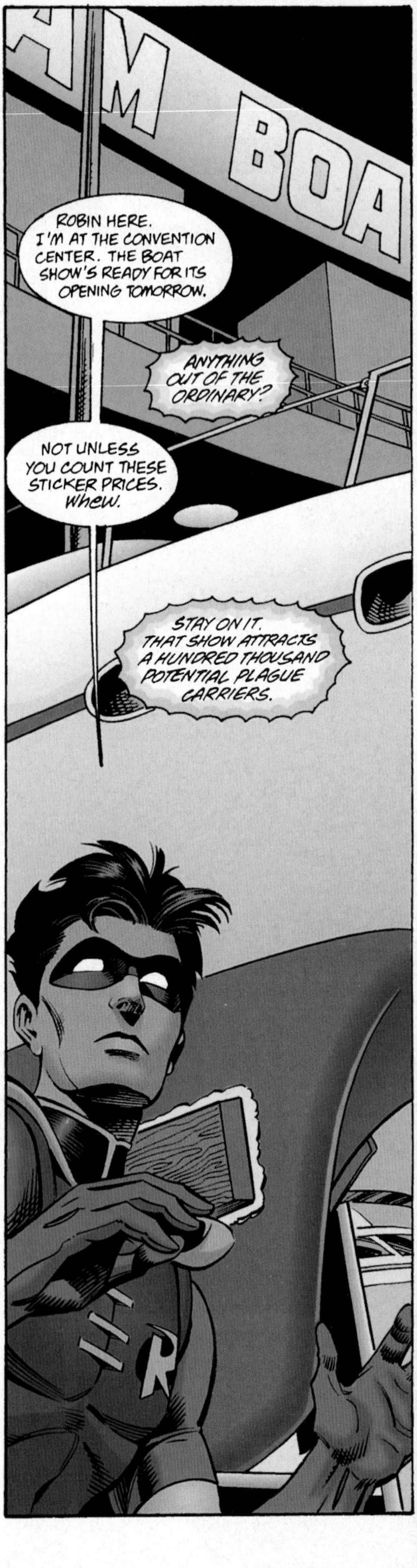
BOA
ROBIN HERE. I'M AT THE CONVENTION CENTER. THE BOAT SHOW'S READY FOR ITS OPENING TOMORROW.
ANYTHING OUT OF THE ORDINARY?
NOT UNLESS YOU COUNT THESE STICKER PRICES. Whew.
STAY ON IT. THAT SHOW ATTRACTS A HUNDRED THOUSAND POTENTIAL PLAGUE CARRIERS.

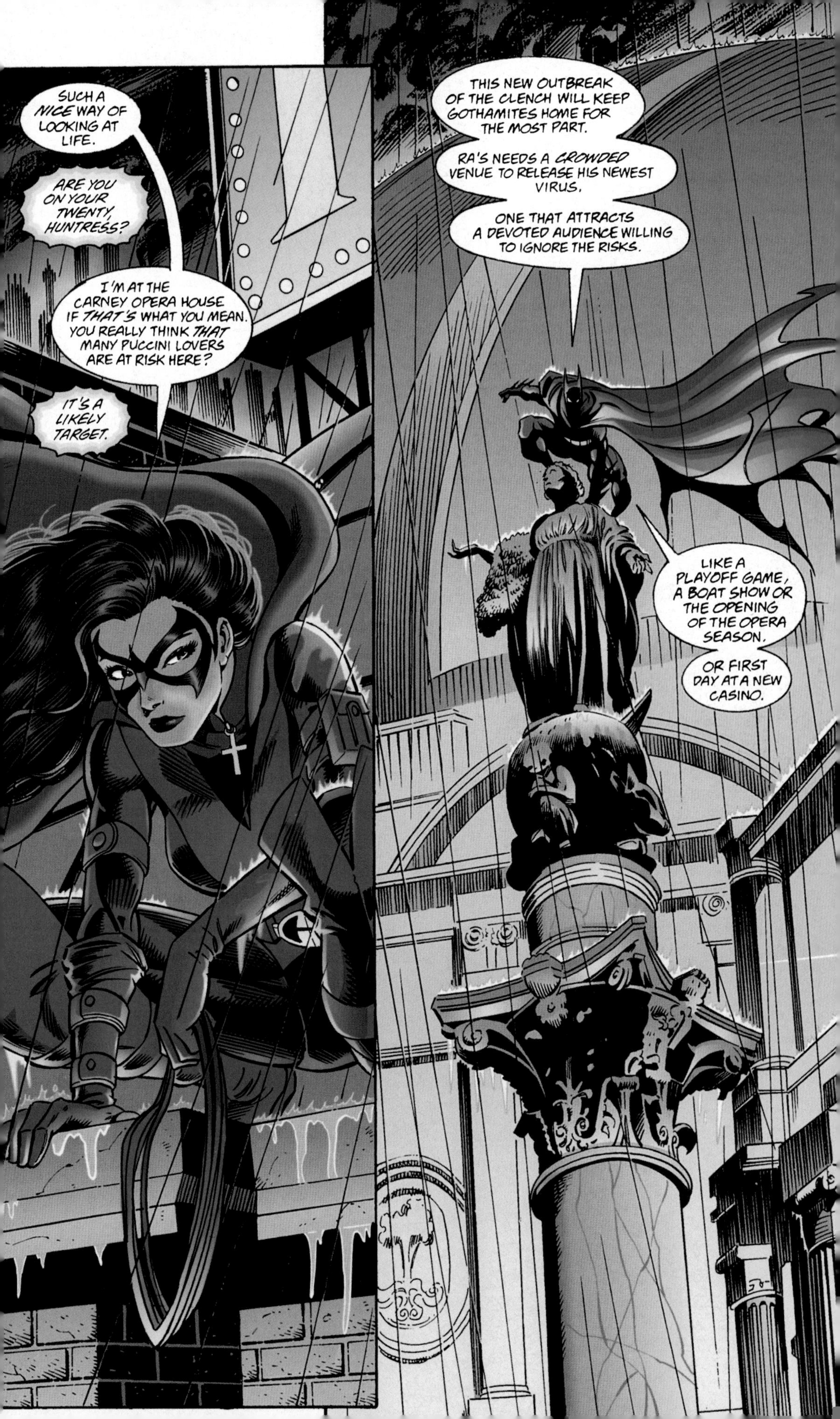

SUCH A *NICE* WAY OF LOOKING AT LIFE.
ARE YOU ON YOUR TWENTY, HUNTRESS?
I'M AT THE CARNEY OPERA HOUSE IF *THAT'S* WHAT YOU MEAN. YOU REALLY THINK *THAT* MANY PUCCINI LOVERS ARE AT RISK HERE?
IT'S A LIKELY TARGET.
THIS NEW OUTBREAK OF THE CLENCH WILL KEEP GOTHAMITES HOME FOR THE MOST PART.
RA'S NEEDS A *CROWDED* VENUE TO RELEASE HIS NEWEST VIRUS.
ONE THAT ATTRACTS A DEVOTED AUDIENCE WILLING TO IGNORE THE RISKS.
LIKE A PLAYOFF GAME, A BOAT SHOW OR THE OPENING OF THE OPERA SEASON.
OR FIRST DAY AT A NEW CASINO.

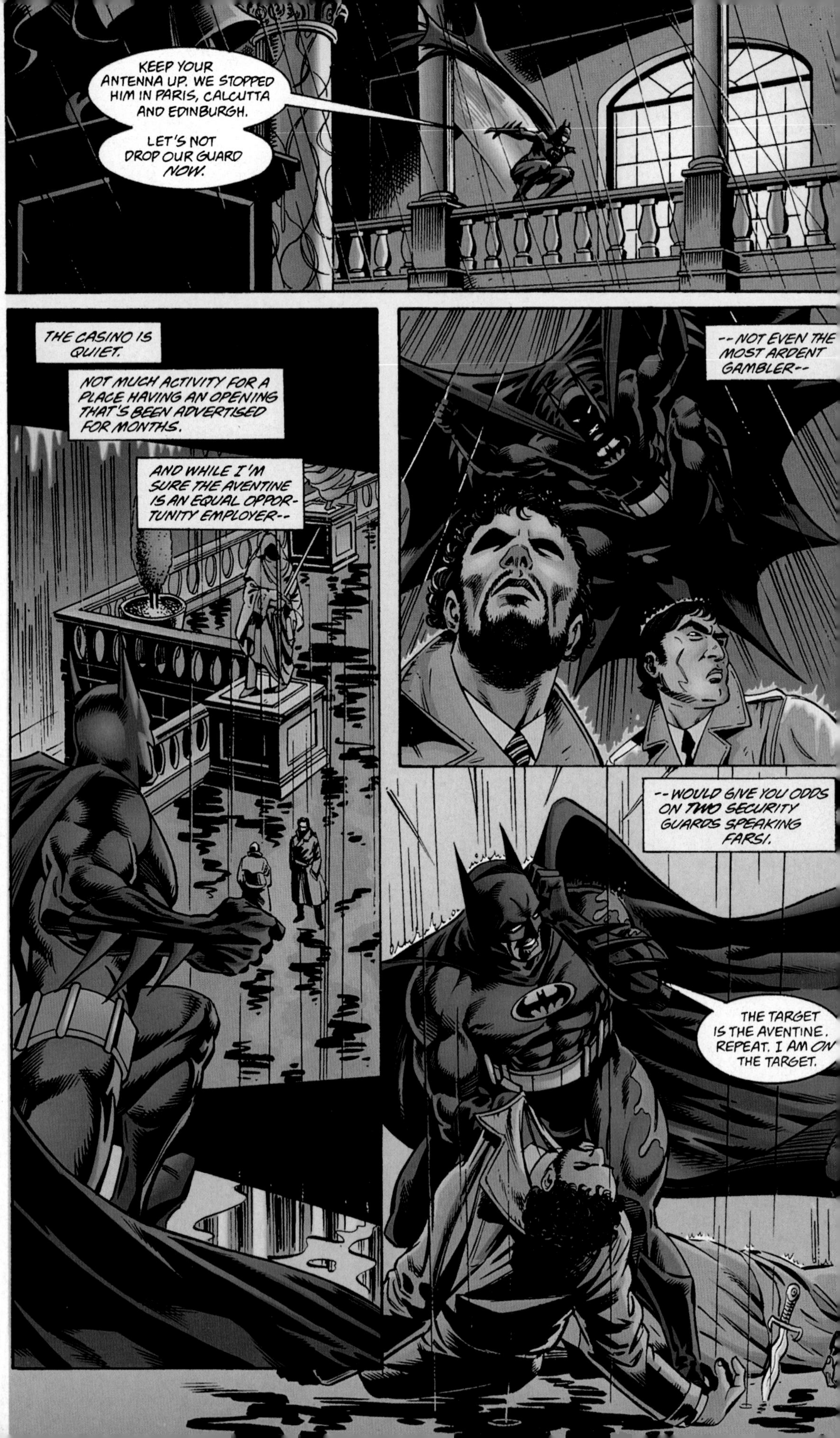

KEEP YOUR ANTENNA UP. WE STOPPED HIM IN PARIS, CALCUTTA AND EDINBURGH.
LET'S NOT DROP OUR GUARD NOW.
THE CASINO IS QUIET.
NOT MUCH ACTIVITY FOR A PLACE HAVING AN OPENING THAT'S BEEN ADVERTISED FOR MONTHS.
AND WHILE I'M SURE THE AVENTINE IS AN EQUAL OPPOR-TUNITY EMPLOYER--
--NOT EVEN THE MOST ARDENT GAMBLER--
--WOULD GIVE YOU ODDS ON TWO SECURITY GUARDS SPEAKING FARSI.
THE TARGET IS THE AVENTINE. REPEAT. I AM ON THE TARGET.

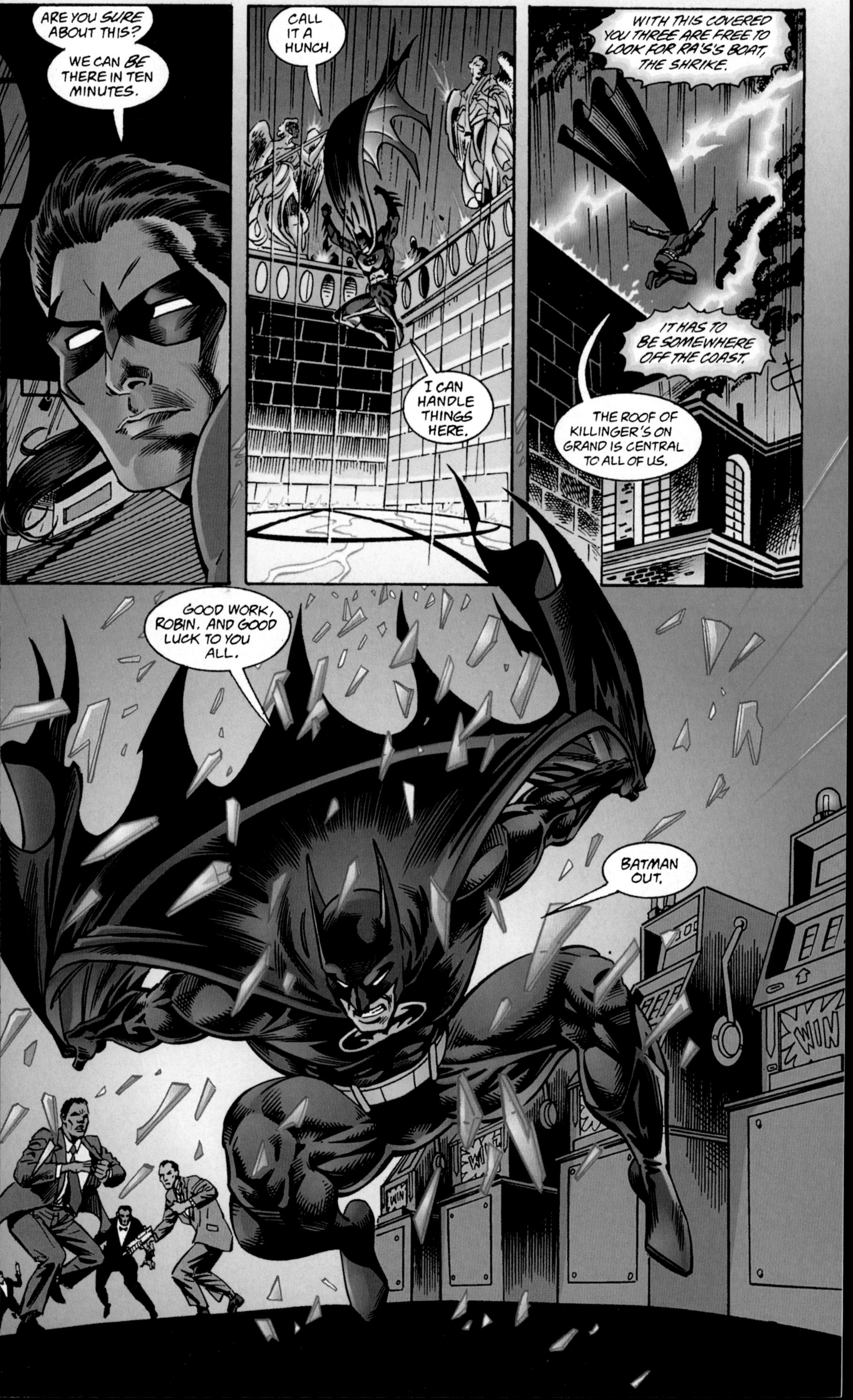
ARE YOU SURE ABOUT THIS?
WE CAN BE THERE IN TEN MINUTES.
CALL IT A HUNCH.
I CAN HANDLE THINGS HERE.
WITH THIS COVERED YOU THREE ARE FREE TO LOOK FOR RA'S'S BOAT, THE SHRIKE.
IT HAS TO BE SOMEWHERE OFF THE COAST.
THE ROOF OF KILLINGER'S ON GRAND IS CENTRAL TO ALL OF US.
GOOD WORK, ROBIN. AND GOOD LUCK TO YOU ALL.
BATMAN OUT.
WIN

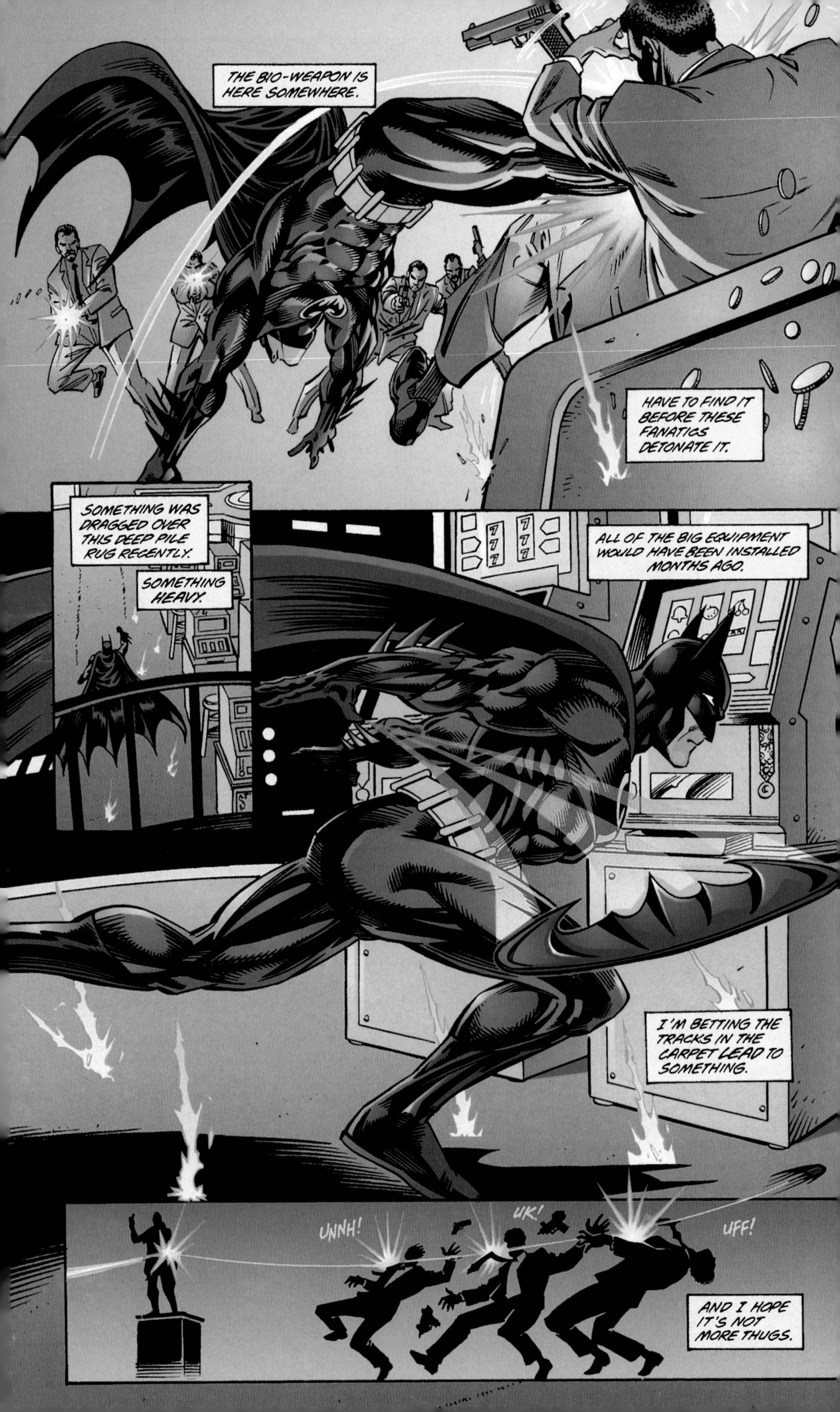
THE BIO-WEAPON IS HERE SOMEWHERE.
HAVE TO FIND IT BEFORE THESE FANATICS DETONATE IT.
SOMETHING WAS DRAGGED OVER THIS DEEP PILE RUG RECENTLY.
SOMETHING HEAVY.
ALL OF THE BIG EQUIPMENT WOULD HAVE BEEN INSTALLED MONTHS AGO.
I'M BETTING THE TRACKS IN THE CARPET LEAD TO SOMETHING.
UNNH!
UK!
UFF!
AND I HOPE IT'S NOT MORE THUGS.

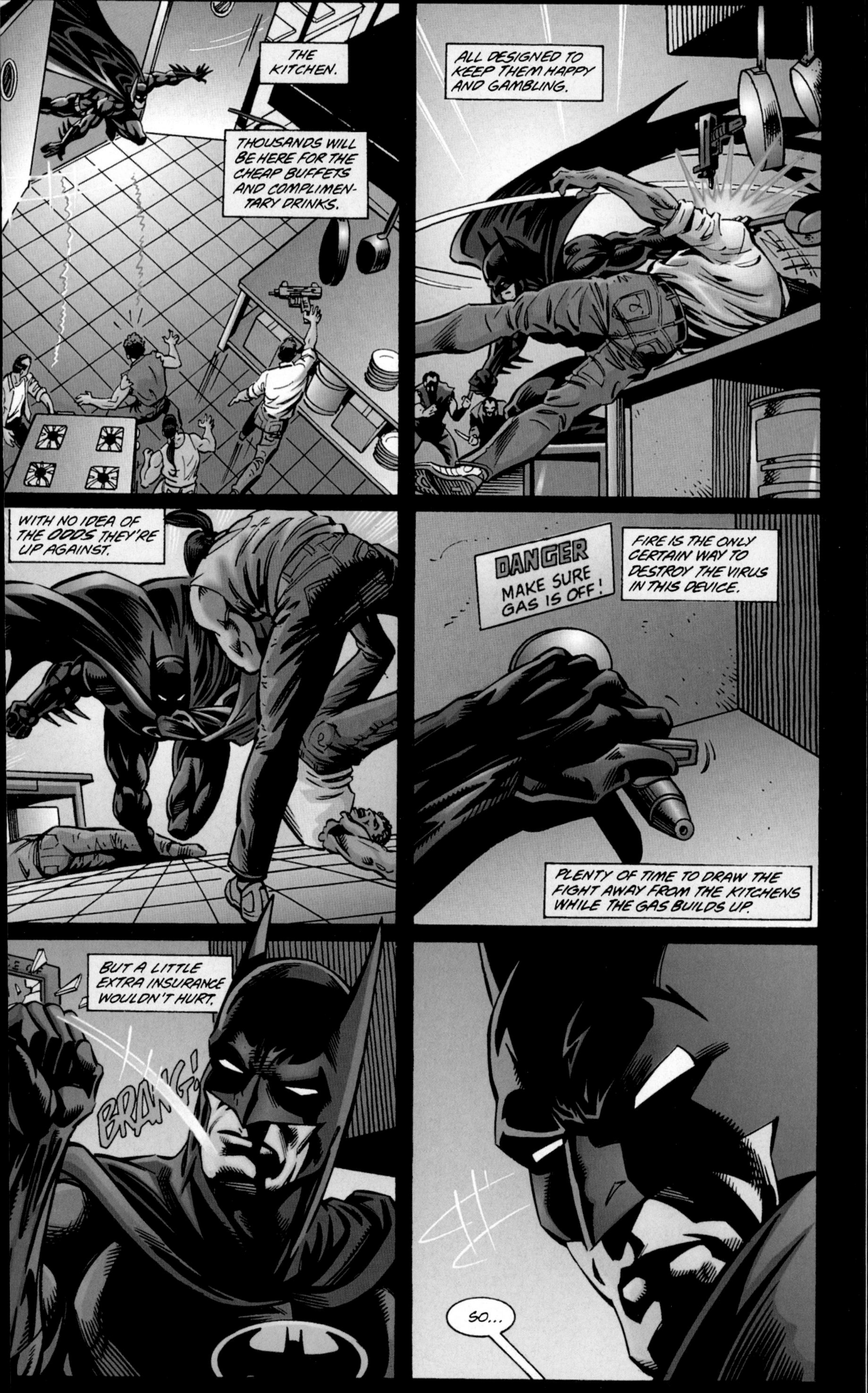
THE KITCHEN.
THOUSANDS WILL BE HERE FOR THE CHEAP BUFFETS AND COMPLIMENTARY DRINKS.
ALL DESIGNED TO KEEP THEM HAPPY AND GAMBLING.
WITH NO IDEA OF THE ODDS THEY'RE UP AGAINST.
DANGER
MAKE SURE GAS IS OFF!
FIRE IS THE ONLY CERTAIN WAY TO DESTROY THE VIRUS IN THIS DEVICE.
PLENTY OF TIME TO DRAW THE FIGHT AWAY FROM THE KITCHENS WHILE THE GAS BUILDS UP.
BUT A LITTLE EXTRA INSURANCE WOULDN'T HURT.
BRANG!
SO...

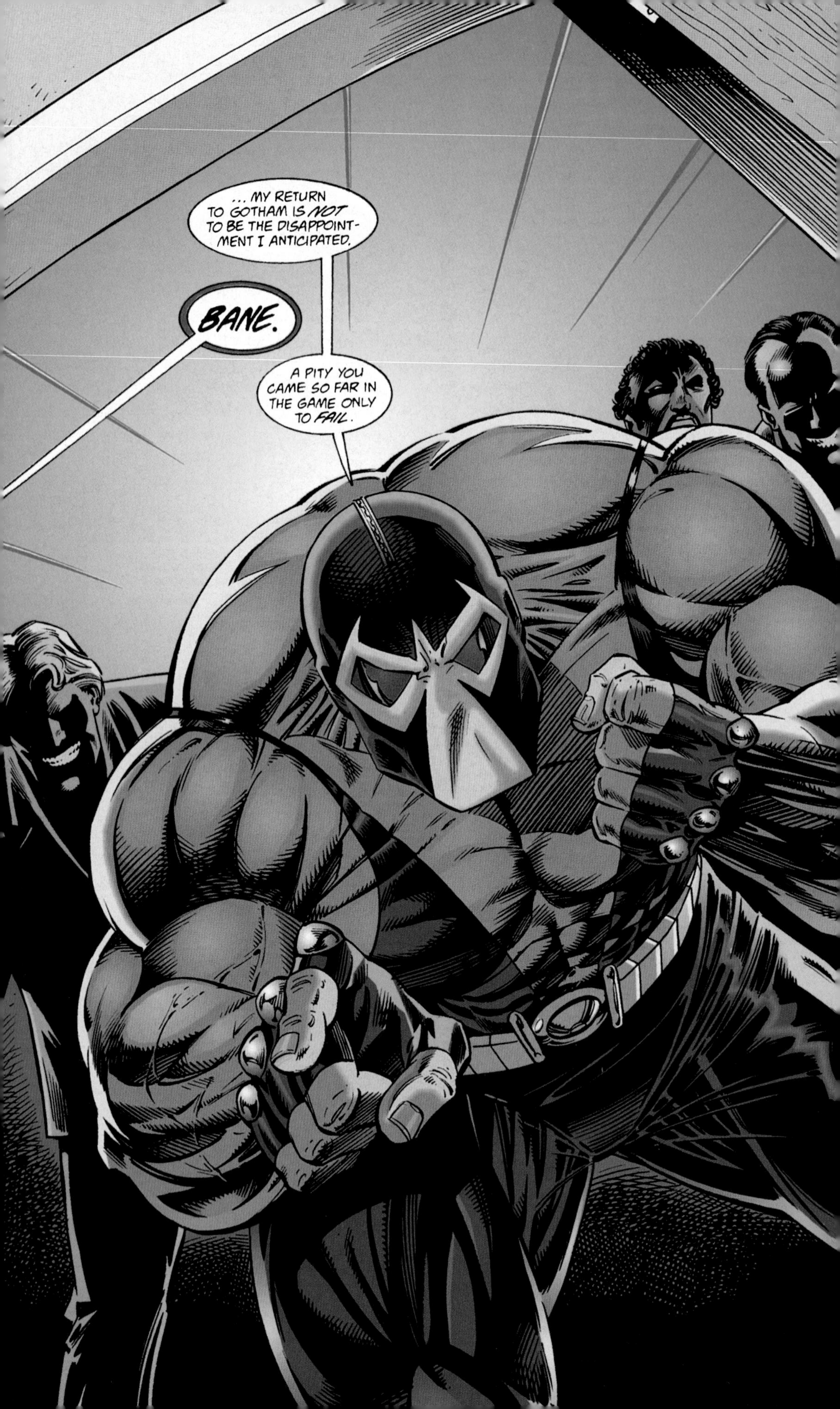
BANE.
... MY RETURN TO GOTHAM IS NOT TO BE THE DISAPPOINTMENT I ANTICIPATED.
A PITY YOU CAME SO FAR IN THE GAME ONLY TO FAIL.

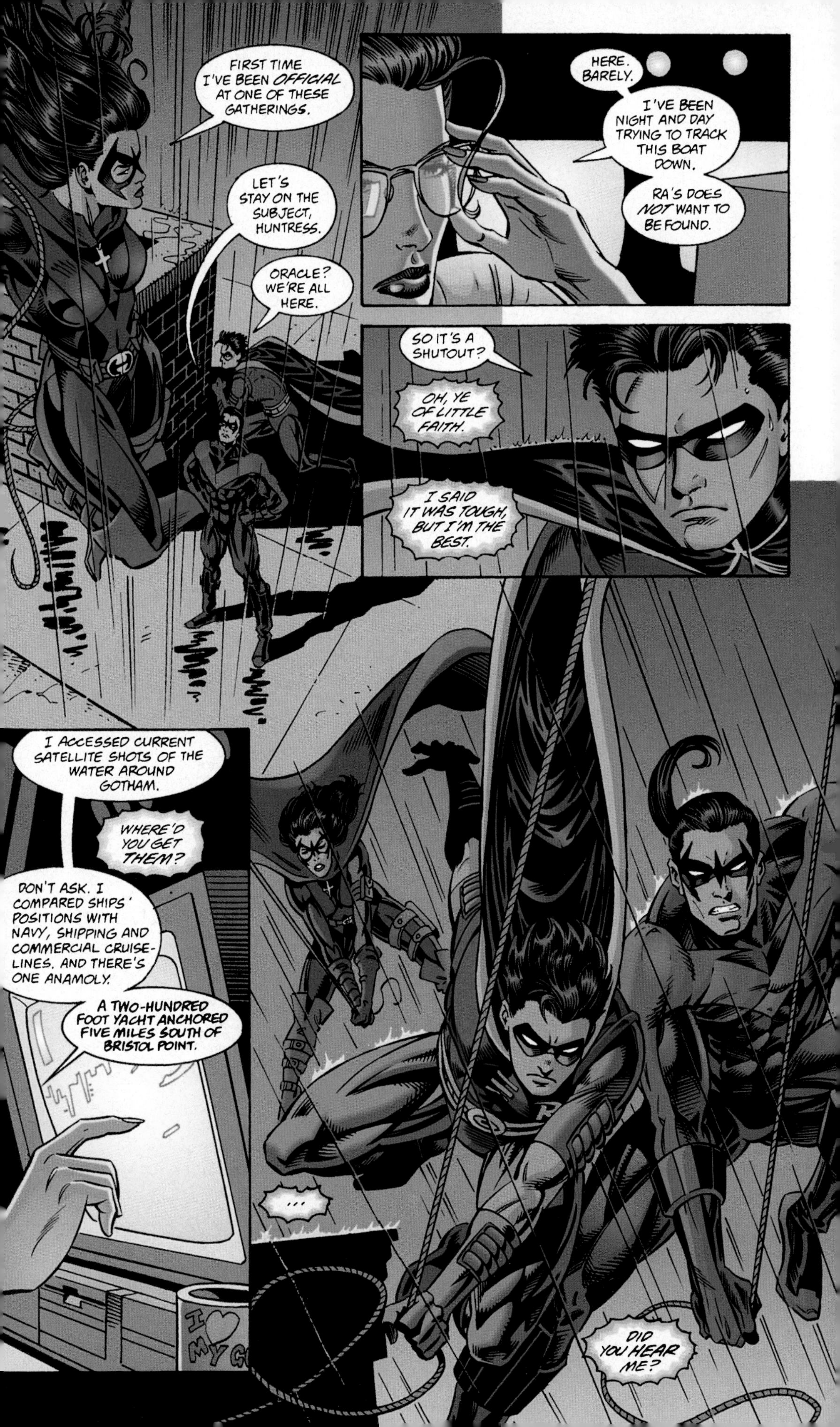
FIRST TIME I'VE BEEN OFFICIAL AT ONE OF THESE GATHERINGS.
LET'S STAY ON THE SUBJECT, HUNTRESS.
ORACLE? WE'RE ALL HERE.
HERE. BARELY.
I'VE BEEN NIGHT AND DAY TRYING TO TRACK THIS BOAT DOWN.
RA'S DOES NOT WANT TO BE FOUND.
SO IT'S A SHUTOUT?
OH, YE OF LITTLE FAITH.
I SAID IT WAS TOUGH, BUT I'M THE BEST.
I ACCESSED CURRENT SATELLITE SHOTS OF THE WATER AROUND GOTHAM.
WHERE'D YOU GET THEM?
DON'T ASK. I COMPARED SHIPS' POSITIONS WITH NAVY, SHIPPING AND COMMERCIAL CRUISE-LINES. AND THERE'S ONE ANAMOLY.
A TWO-HUNDRED FOOT YACHT ANCHORED FIVE MILES SOUTH OF BRISTOL POINT.
...
DID YOU HEAR ME?

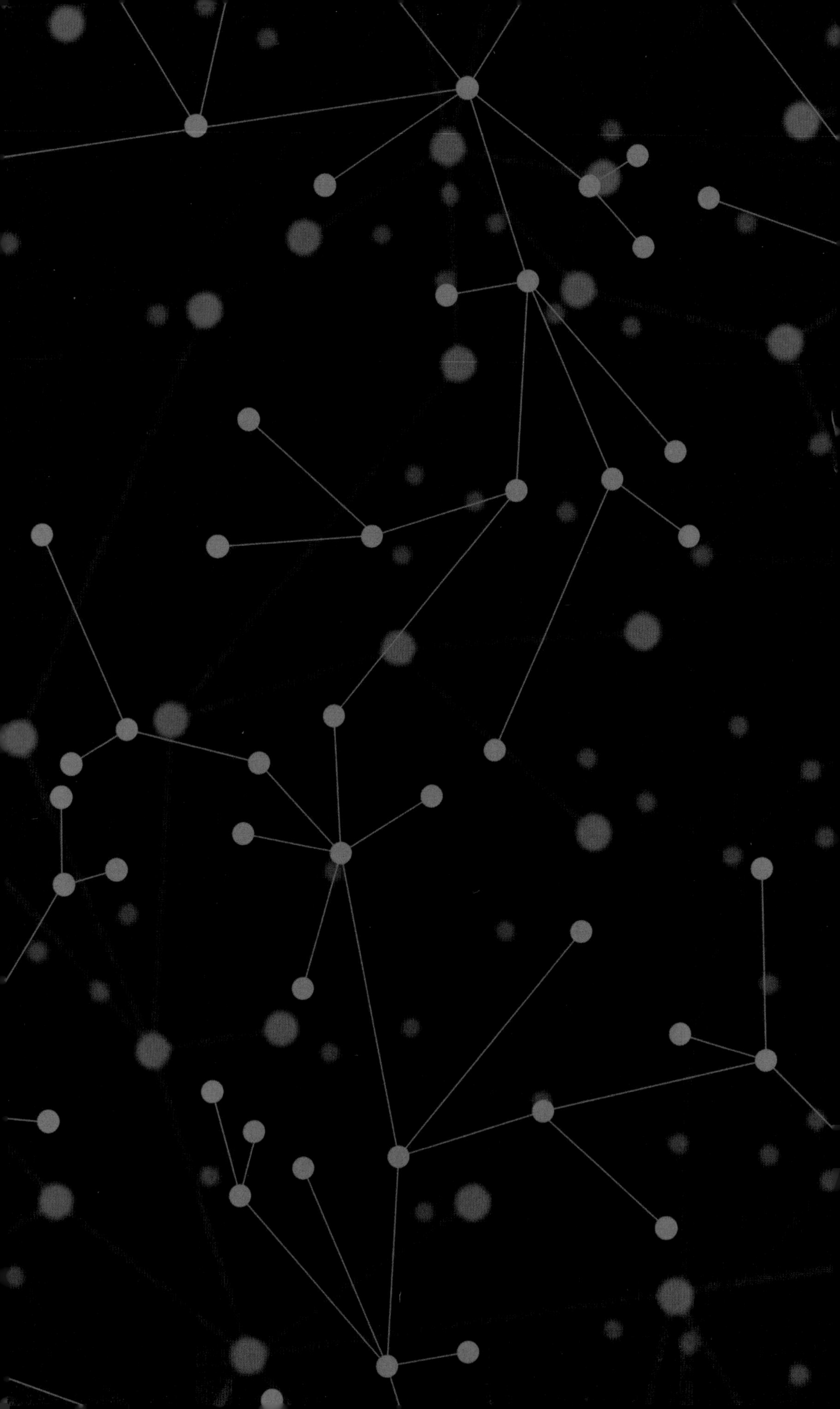

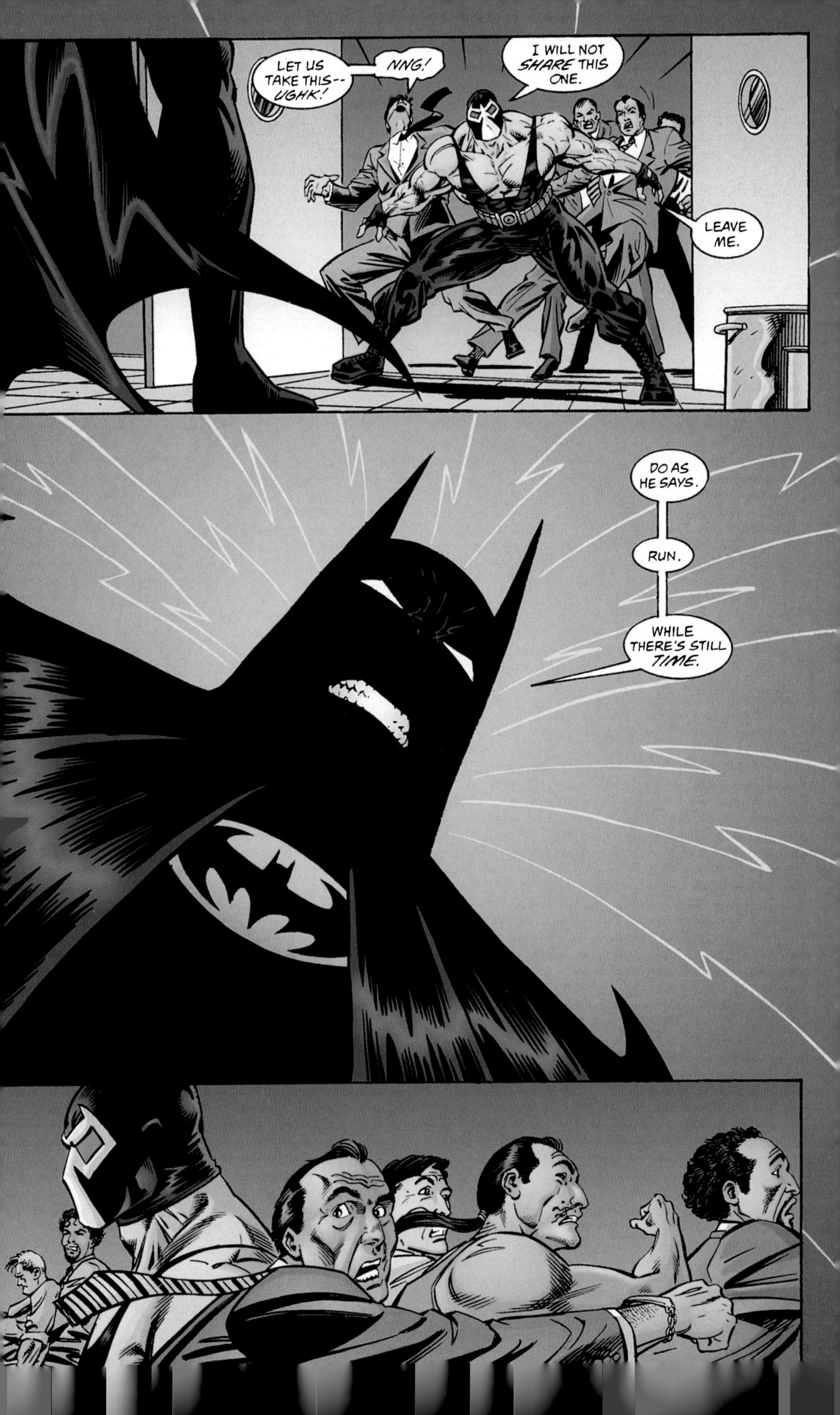
LET US TAKE THIS-- UGHK!
NNG!
I WILL NOT SHARE THIS ONE.
LEAVE ME.
DO AS HE SAYS.
RUN.
WHILE THERE'S STILL TIME.

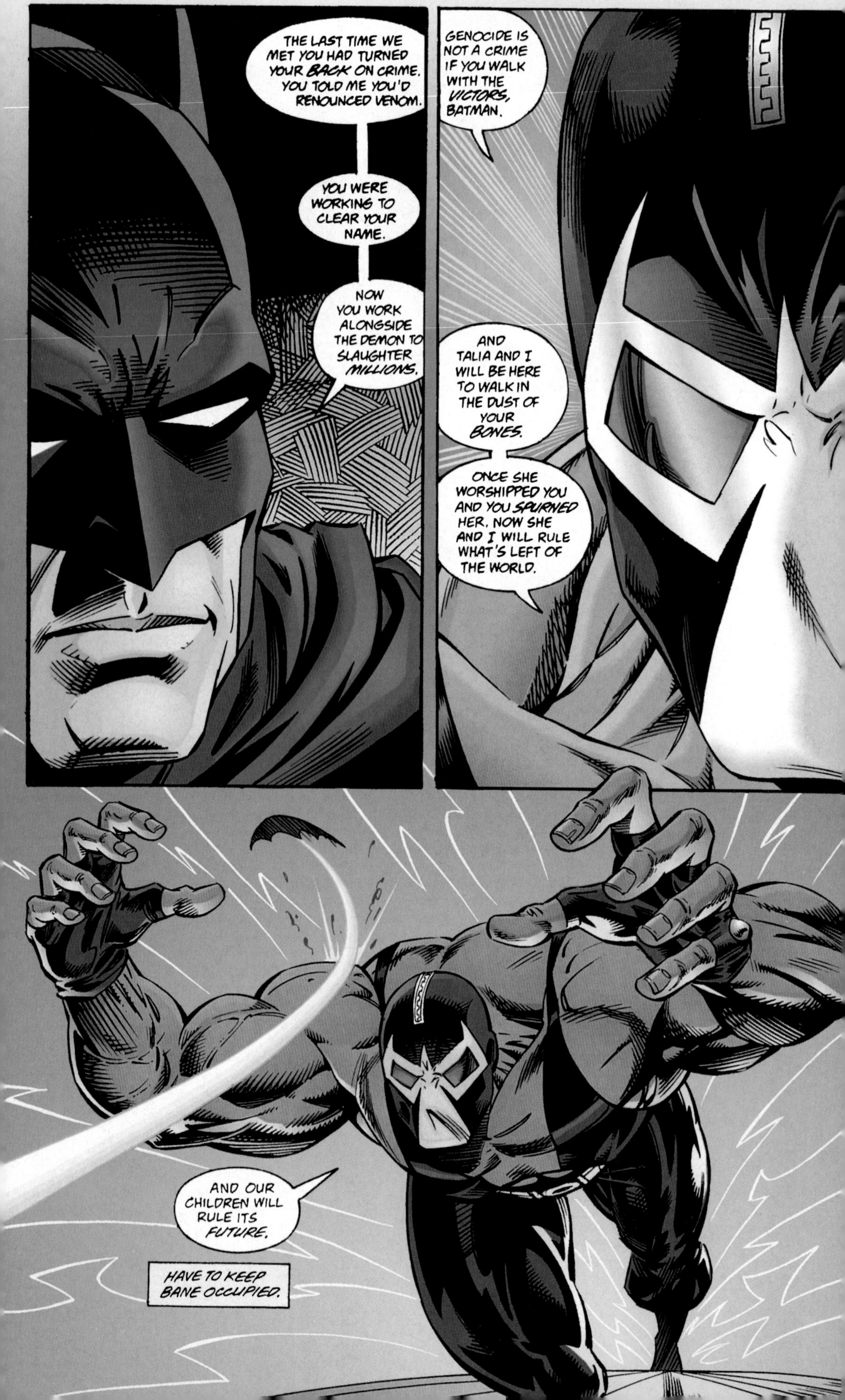

THE LAST TIME WE MET YOU HAD TURNED YOUR BACK ON CRIME. YOU TOLD ME YOU'D RENOUNCED VENOM.
YOU WERE WORKING TO CLEAR YOUR NAME.
NOW YOU WORK ALONGSIDE THE DEMON TO SLAUGHTER MILLIONS.
GENOCIDE IS NOT A CRIME IF YOU WALK WITH THE VICTORS, BATMAN.
AND TALIA AND I WILL BE HERE TO WALK IN THE DUST OF YOUR BONES.
ONCE SHE WORSHIPPED YOU AND YOU SPURNED HER. NOW SHE AND I WILL RULE WHAT'S LEFT OF THE WORLD.
AND OUR CHILDREN WILL RULE ITS FUTURE.
HAVE TO KEEP BANE OCCUPIED.

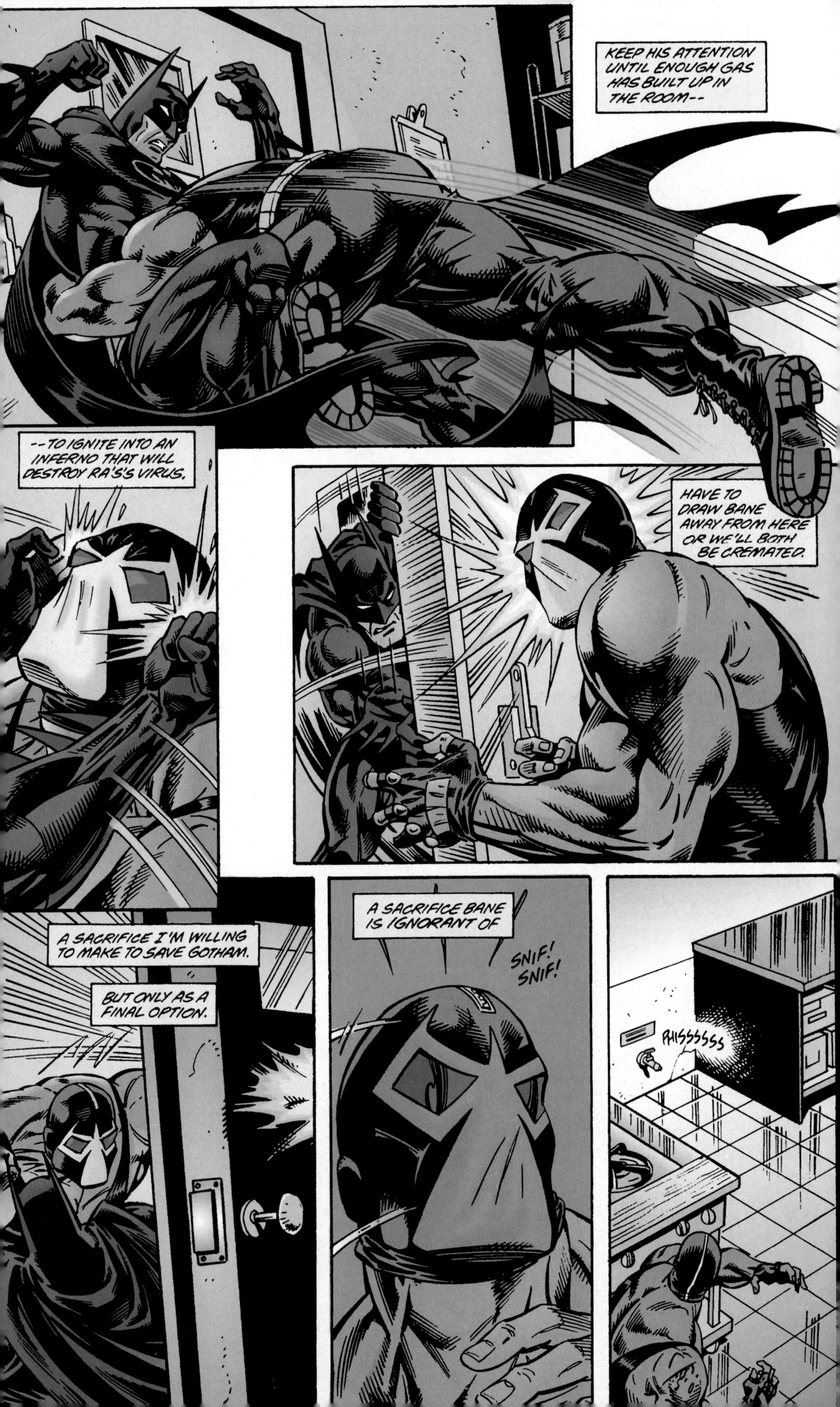
KEEP HIS ATTENTION UNTIL ENOUGH GAS HAS BUILT UP IN THE ROOM--
--TO IGNITE INTO AN INFERNO THAT WILL DESTROY RA'S'S VIRUS.
HAVE TO DRAW BANE AWAY FROM HERE OR WE'LL BOTH BE CREMATED.
A SACRIFICE I'M WILLING TO MAKE TO SAVE GOTHAM.
BUT ONLY AS A FINAL OPTION.
A SACRIFICE BANE IS IGNORANT OF
SNIF! SNIF!
RHISSSSSS

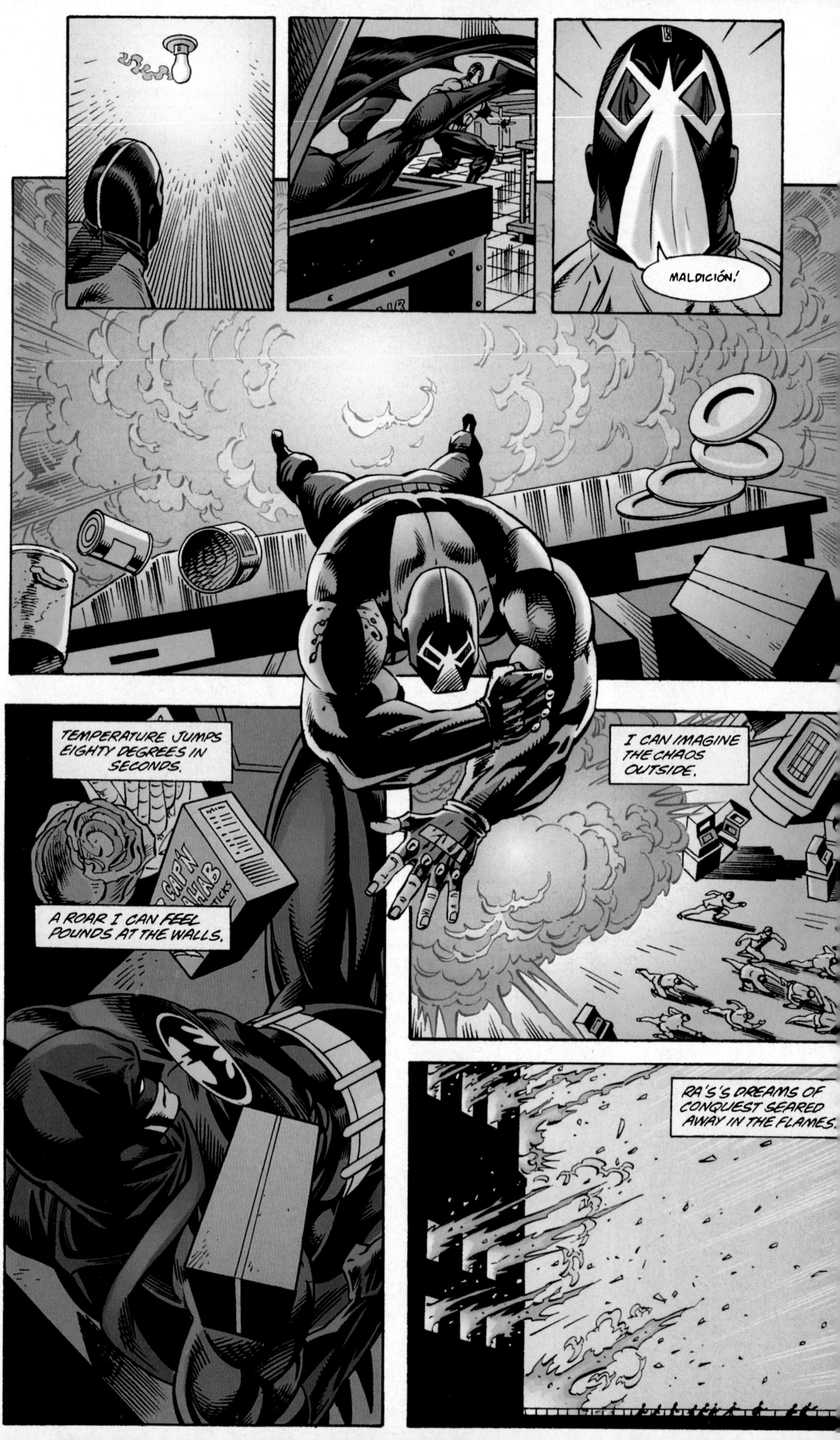
MALDICIÓN!
TEMPERATURE JUMPS EIGHTY DEGREES IN SECONDS.
A ROAR I CAN FEEL POUNDS AT THE WALLS.
I CAN IMAGINE THE CHAOS OUTSIDE.
RA'S'S DREAMS OF CONQUEST SEARED AWAY IN THE FLAMES.

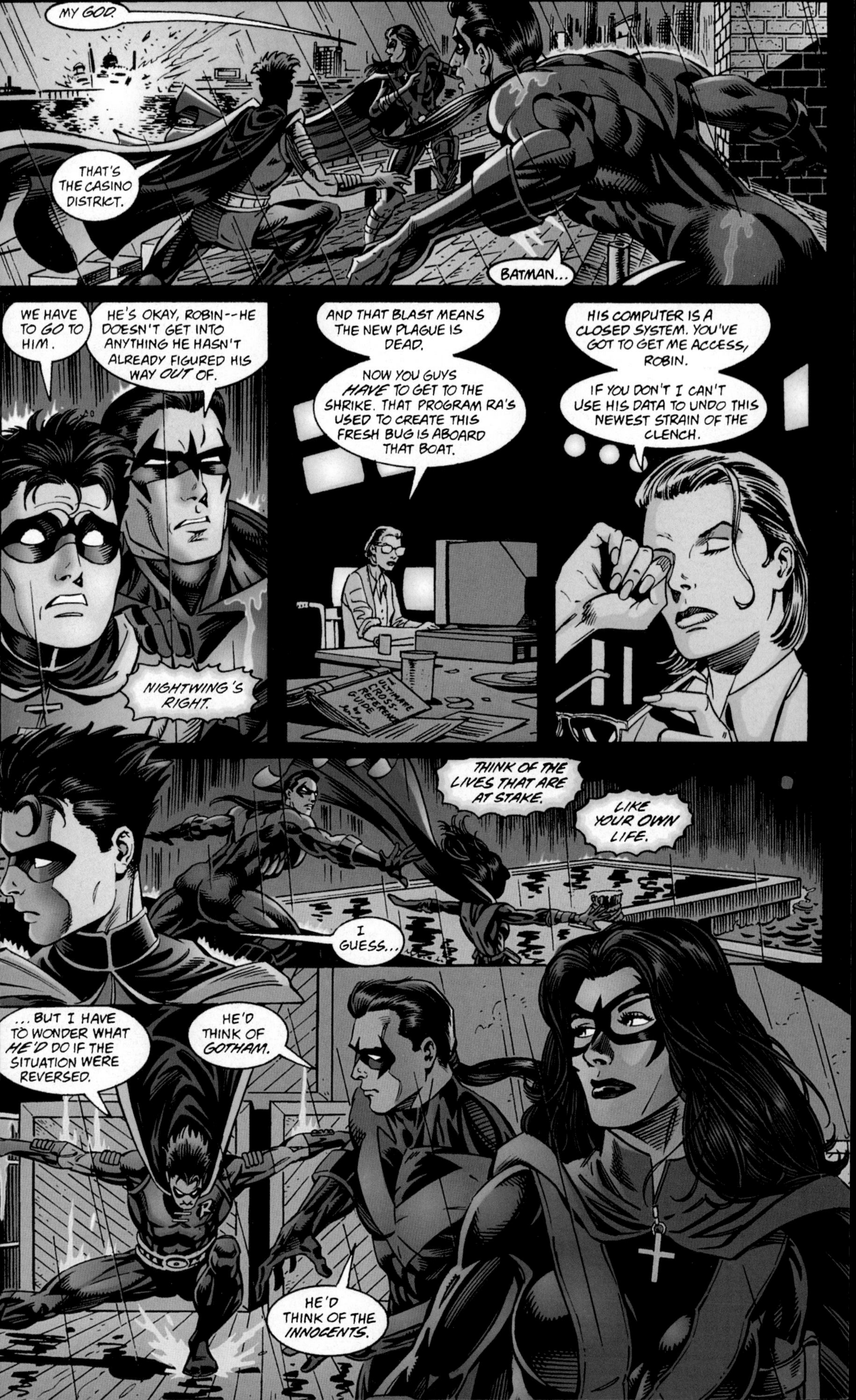
MY GOD.
THAT'S THE CASINO DISTRICT.
BATMAN...
WE HAVE TO GO TO HIM.
HE'S OKAY, ROBIN--HE DOESN'T GET INTO ANYTHING HE HASN'T ALREADY FIGURED HIS WAY OUT OF.
NIGHTWING'S RIGHT.
AND THAT BLAST MEANS THE NEW PLAGUE IS DEAD.
NOW YOU GUYS HAVE TO GET TO THE SHRIKE. THAT PROGRAM RA'S USED TO CREATE THIS FRESH BUG IS ABOARD THAT BOAT.
THE ULTIMATE CROSS-REFERENCE GUIDE
HIS COMPUTER IS A CLOSED SYSTEM. YOU'VE GOT TO GET ME ACCESS, ROBIN.
IF YOU DON'T I CAN'T USE HIS DATA TO UNDO THIS NEWEST STRAIN OF THE CLENCH.
THINK OF THE LIVES THAT ARE AT STAKE.
LIKE YOUR OWN LIFE.
I GUESS...
...BUT I HAVE TO WONDER WHAT HE'D DO IF THE SITUATION WERE REVERSED.
HE'D THINK OF GOTHAM.
HE'D THINK OF THE INNOCENTS.

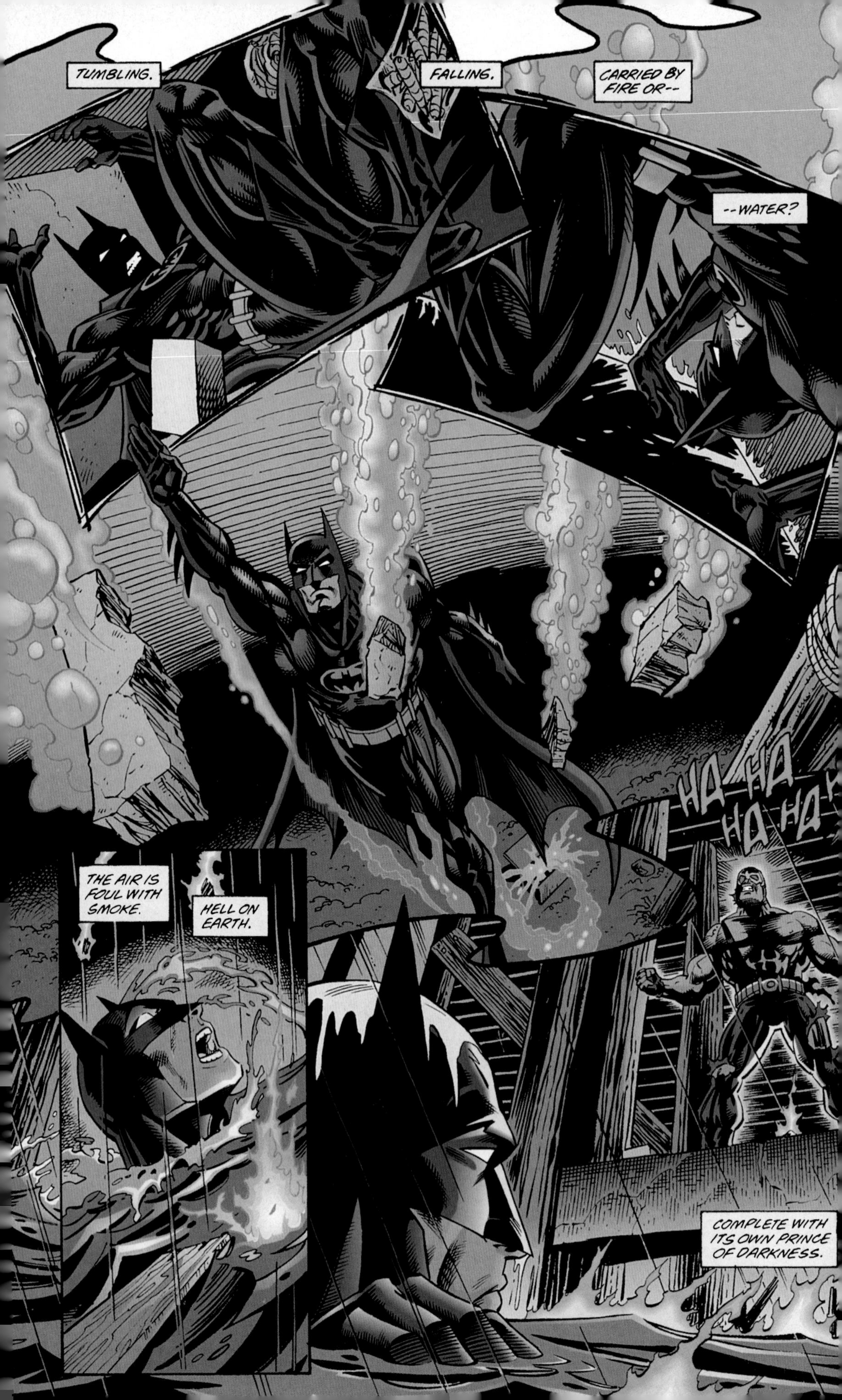
TUMBLING.
FALLING.
CARRIED BY FIRE OR--
--WATER?
HA HA HA HA!
THE AIR IS FOUL WITH SMOKE.
HELL ON EARTH.
COMPLETE WITH ITS OWN PRINCE OF DARKNESS.

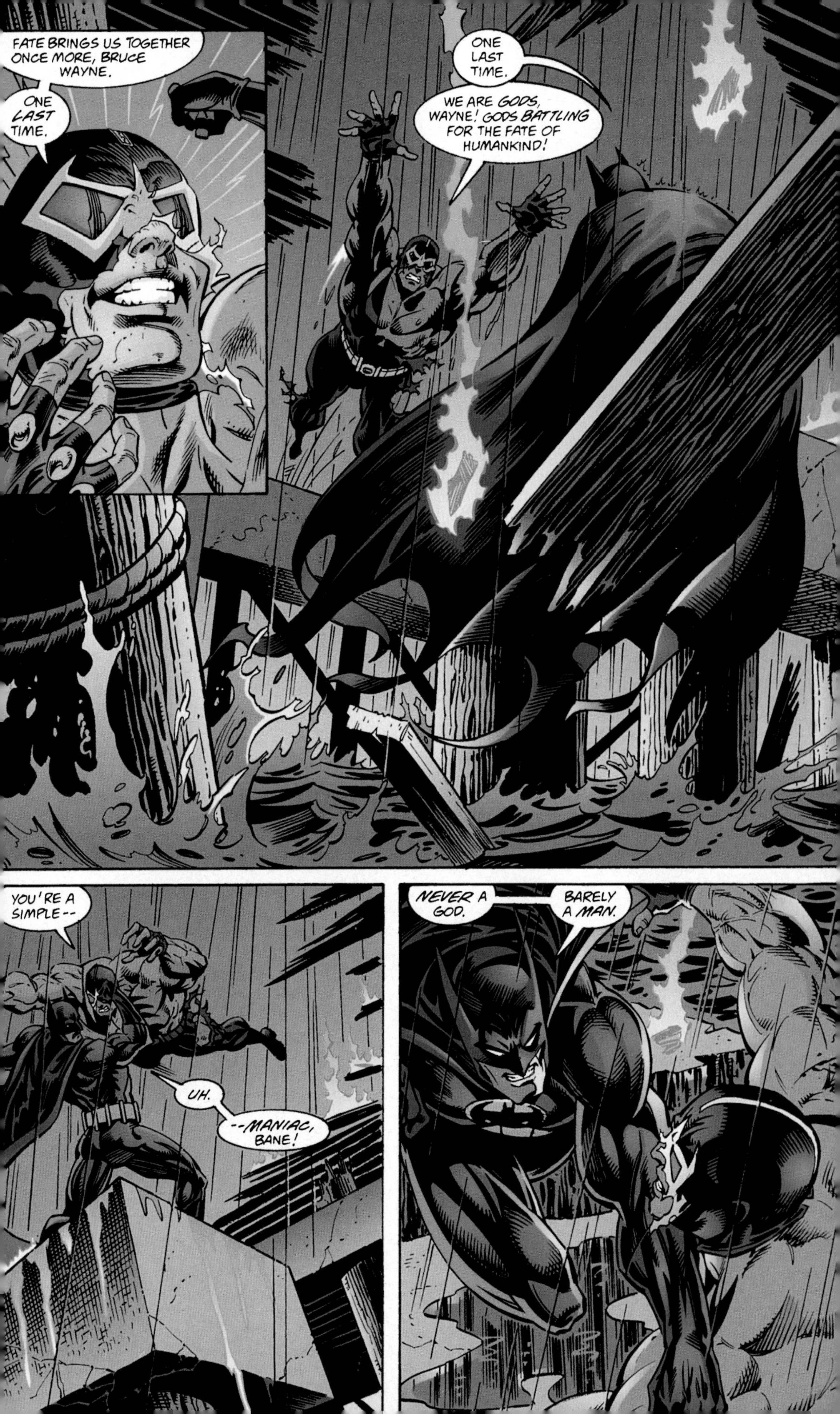
FATE BRINGS US TOGETHER ONCE MORE, BRUCE WAYNE.
ONE LAST TIME.
ONE LAST TIME.
WE ARE GODS, WAYNE! GODS BATTLING FOR THE FATE OF HUMANKIND!
YOU'RE A SIMPLE--
UH.
--MANIAC, BANE!
NEVER A GOD.
BARELY A MAN.

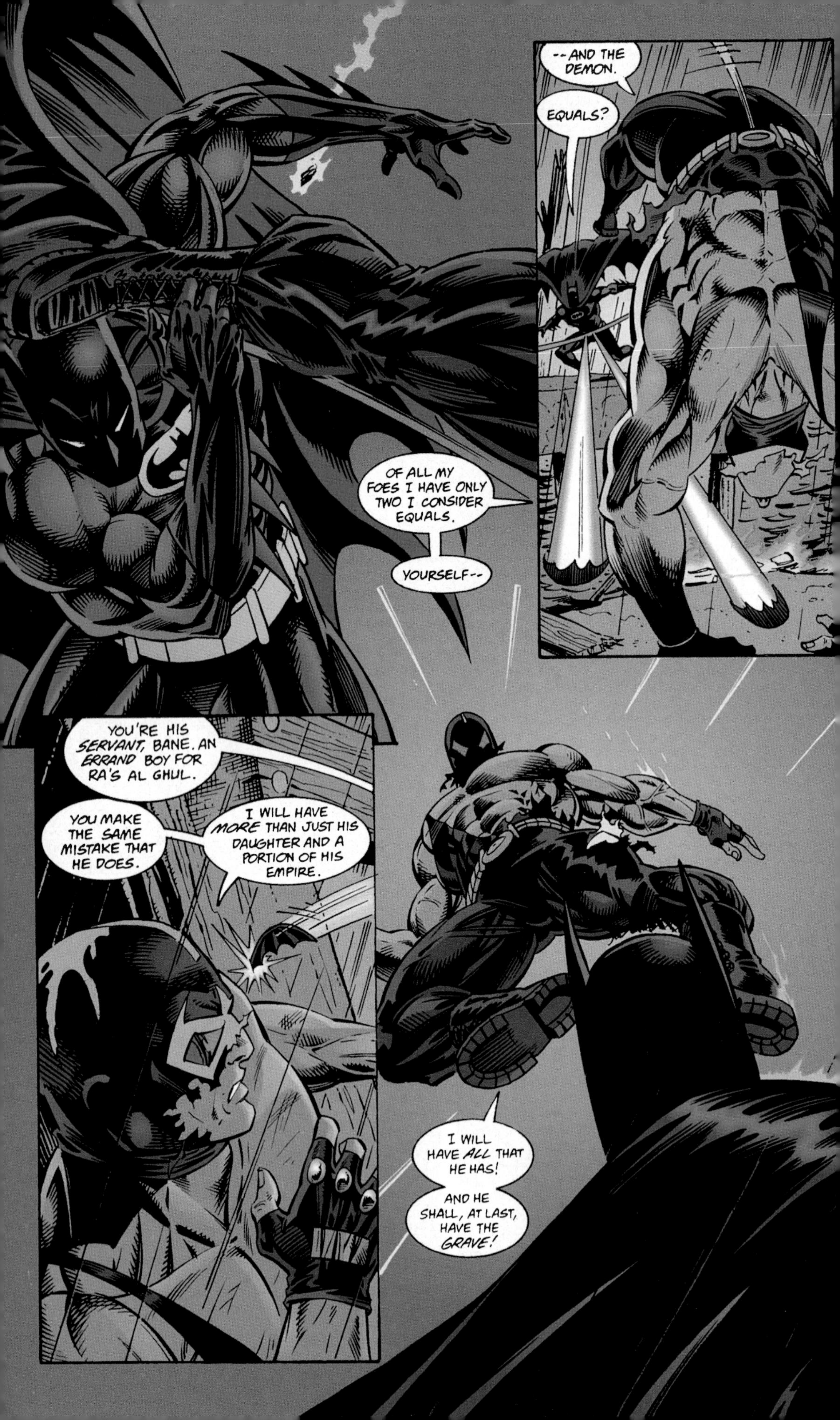
OF ALL MY FOES I HAVE ONLY TWO I CONSIDER EQUALS.
YOURSELF--
--AND THE DEMON.
EQUALS?
YOU'RE HIS SERVANT, BANE. AN ERRAND BOY FOR RA'S AL GHUL.
YOU MAKE THE SAME MISTAKE THAT HE DOES.
I WILL HAVE MORE THAN JUST HIS DAUGHTER AND A PORTION OF HIS EMPIRE.
I WILL HAVE ALL THAT HE HAS!
AND HE SHALL, AT LAST, HAVE THE GRAVE!

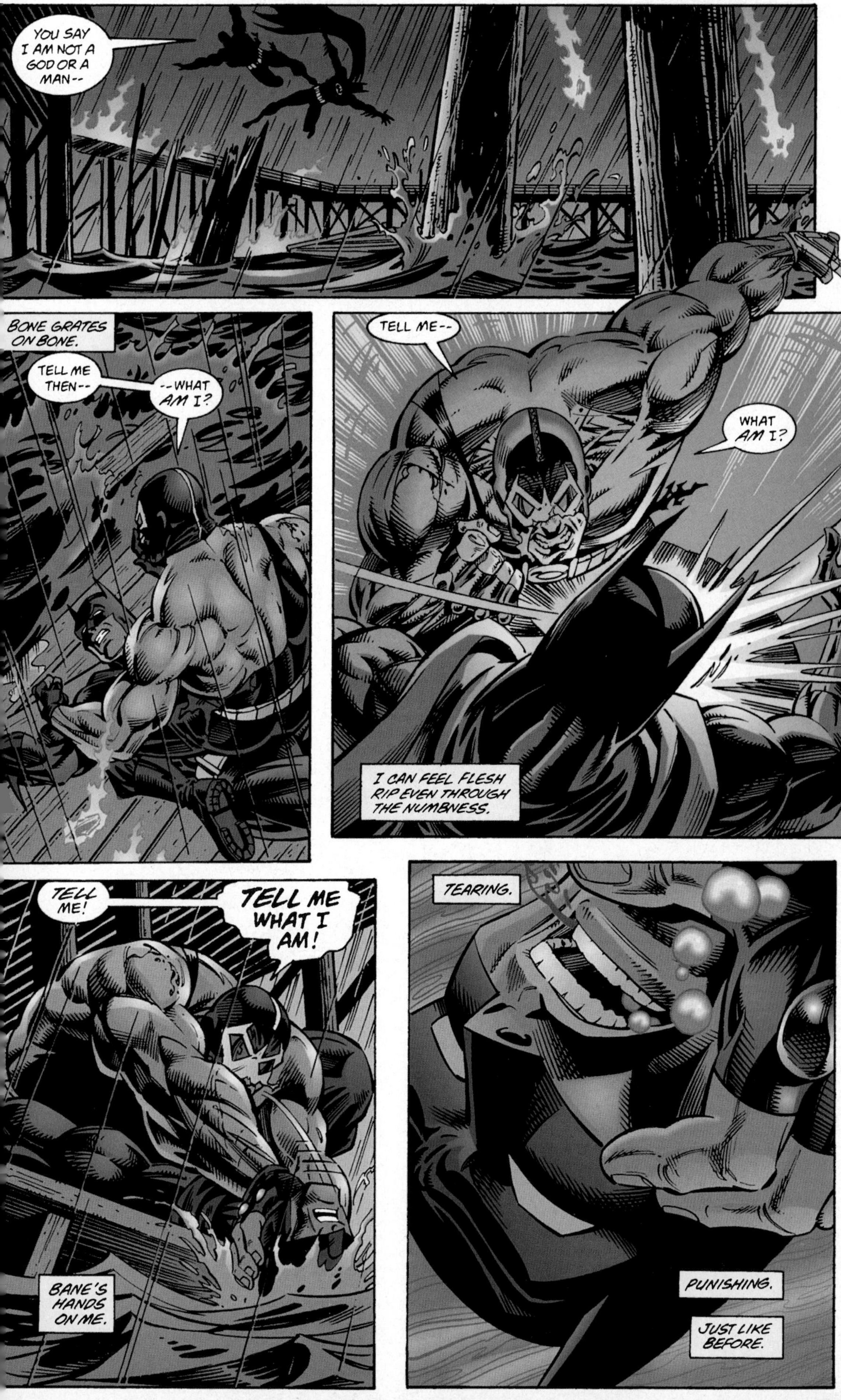

YOU SAY I AM NOT A GOD OR A MAN--
BONE GRATES ON BONE.
TELL ME THEN--
--WHAT AM I?
TELL ME--
WHAT AM I?
I CAN FEEL FLESH RIP EVEN THROUGH THE NUMBNESS.
TELL ME!
TELL ME WHAT I AM!
BANE'S HANDS ON ME.
TEARING.
PUNISHING.
JUST LIKE BEFORE.

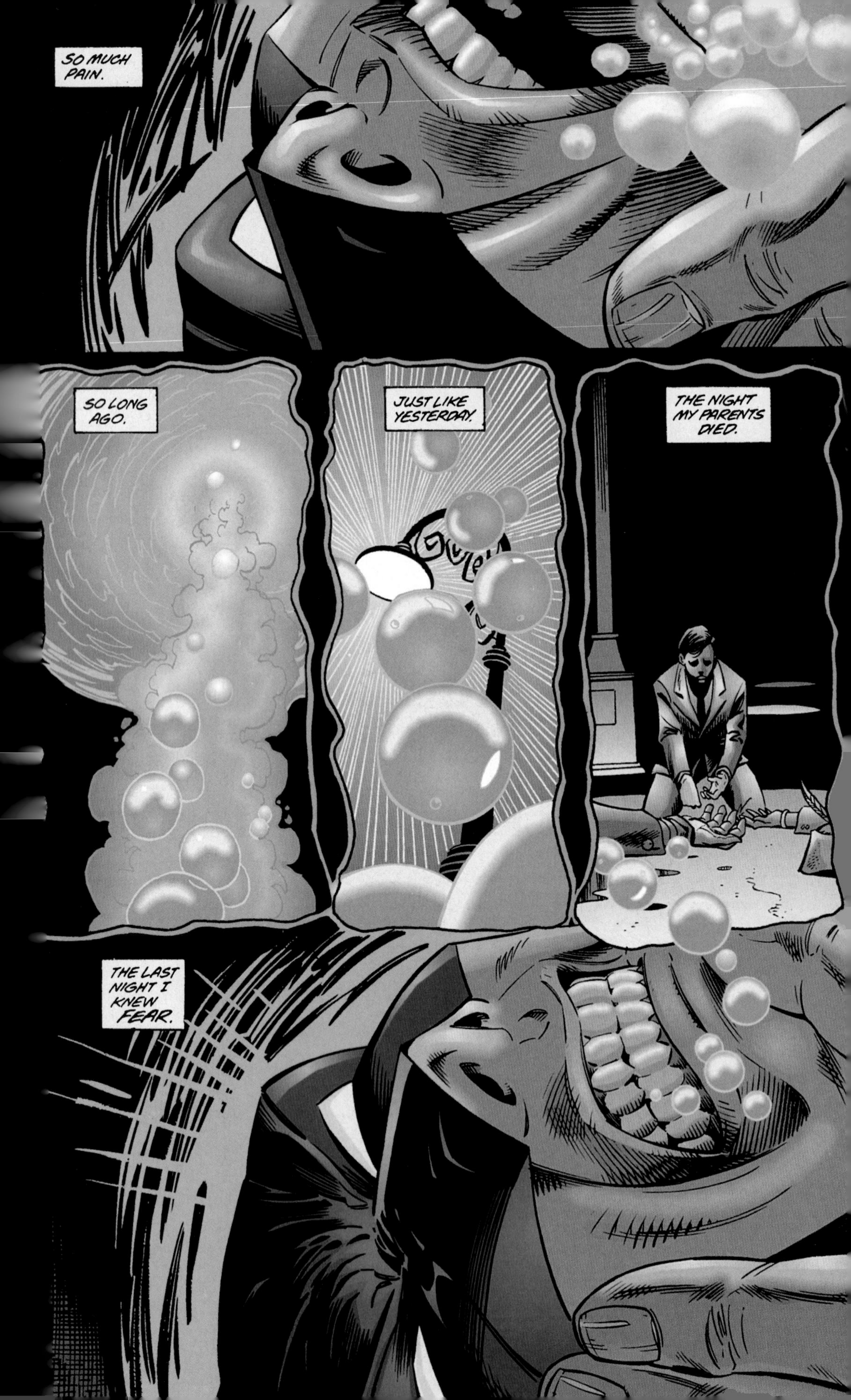

SO MUCH PAIN.
SO LONG AGO.
JUST LIKE YESTERDAY.
THE NIGHT MY PARENTS DIED.
THE LAST NIGHT I KNEW FEAR.

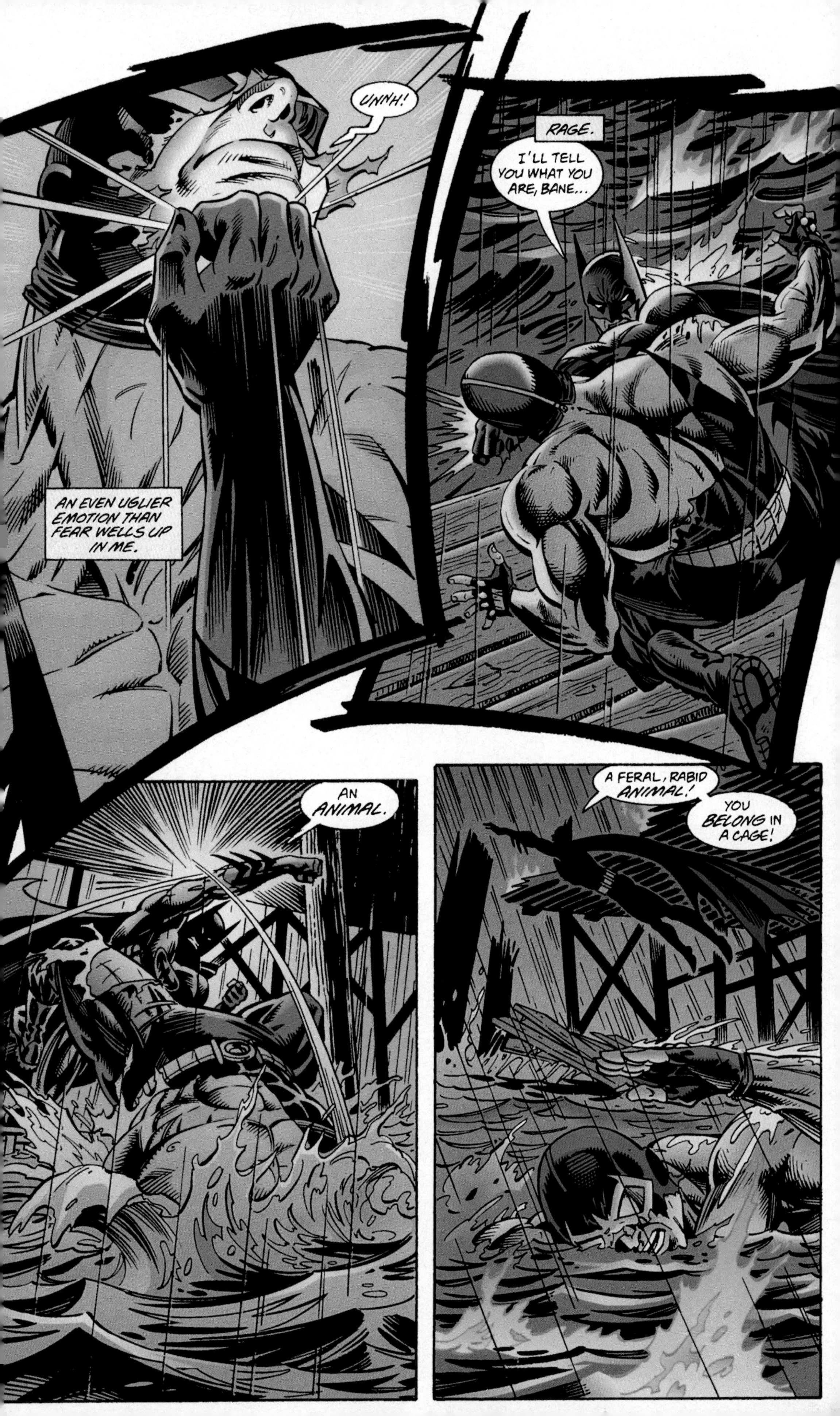
UNNH!
AN EVEN UGLIER EMOTION THAN FEAR WELLS UP IN ME.
RAGE.
I'LL TELL YOU WHAT YOU ARE, BANE...
AN ANIMAL.
A FERAL, RABID ANIMAL!
YOU BELONG IN A CAGE!

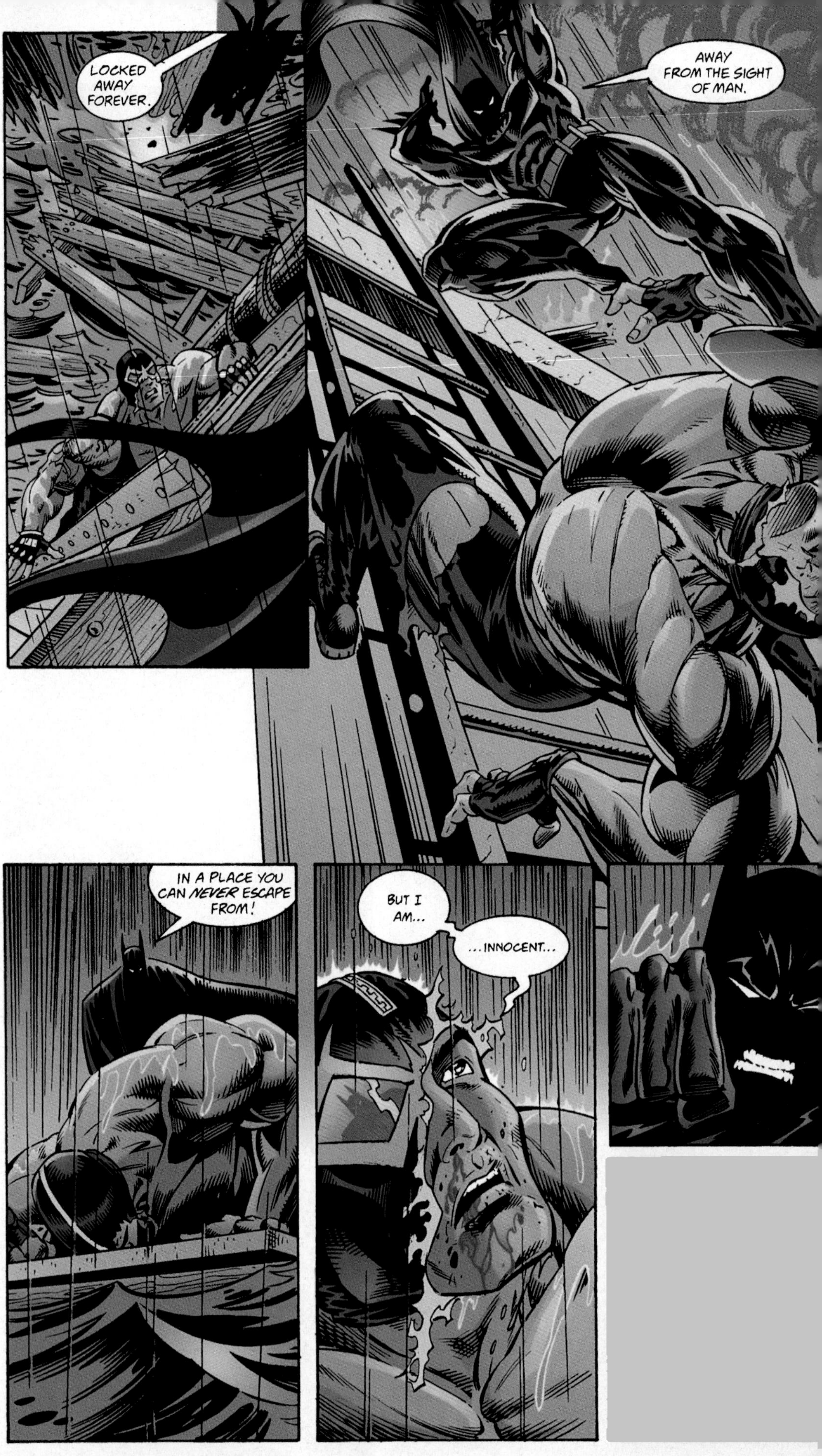
LOCKED AWAY FOREVER.
AWAY FROM THE SIGHT OF MAN.
IN A PLACE YOU CAN *NEVER* ESCAPE FROM!
BUT I AM...
...INNOCENT...

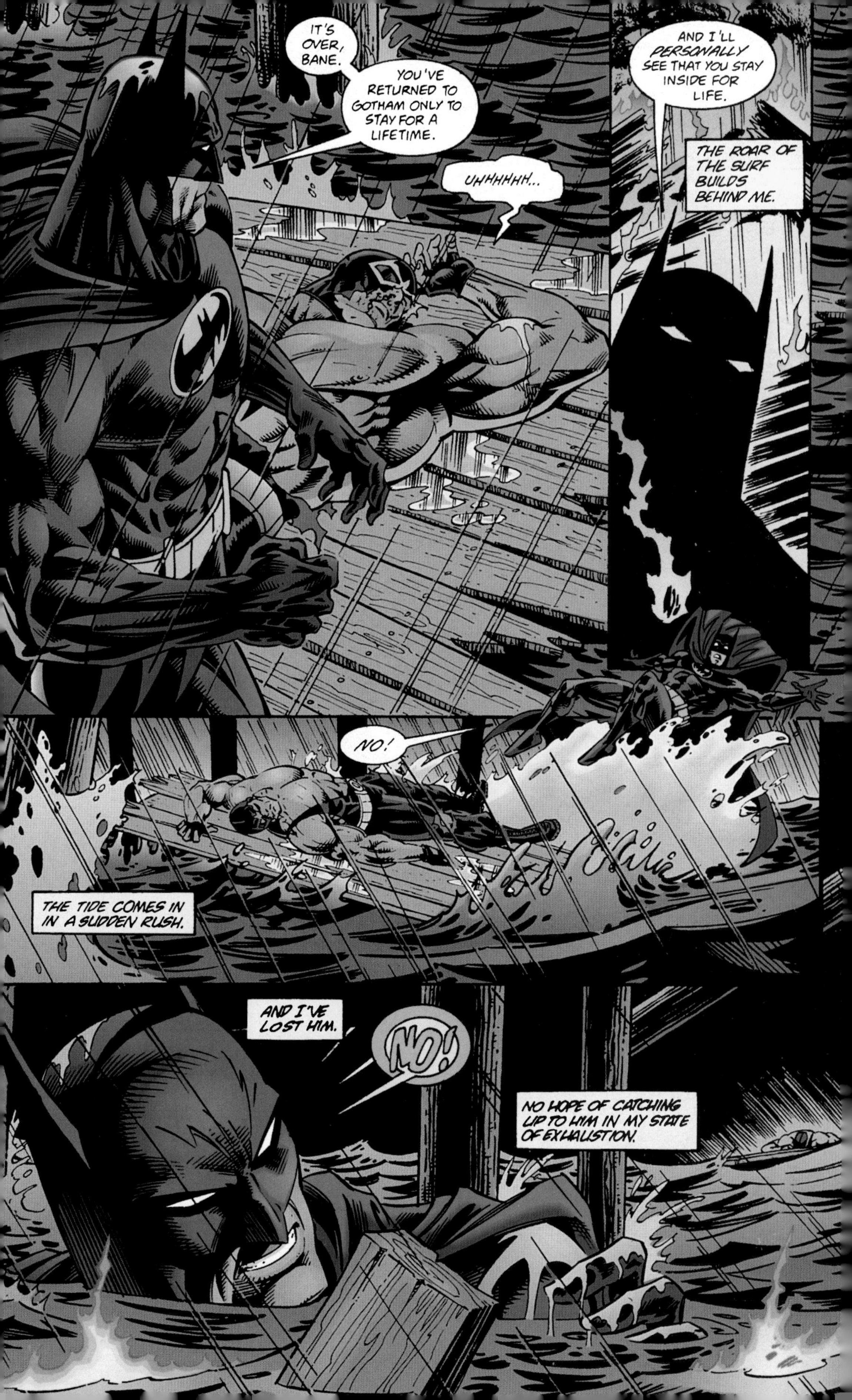
IT'S OVER, BANE.
YOU'VE RETURNED TO GOTHAM ONLY TO STAY FOR A LIFETIME.
UHHHHHH...
AND I'LL PERSONALLY SEE THAT YOU STAY INSIDE FOR LIFE.
THE ROAR OF THE SURF BUILDS BEHIND ME.
NO!
THE TIDE COMES IN IN A SUDDEN RUSH.
AND I'VE LOST HIM.
NO!
NO HOPE OF CATCHING UP TO HIM IN MY STATE OF EXHAUSTION.

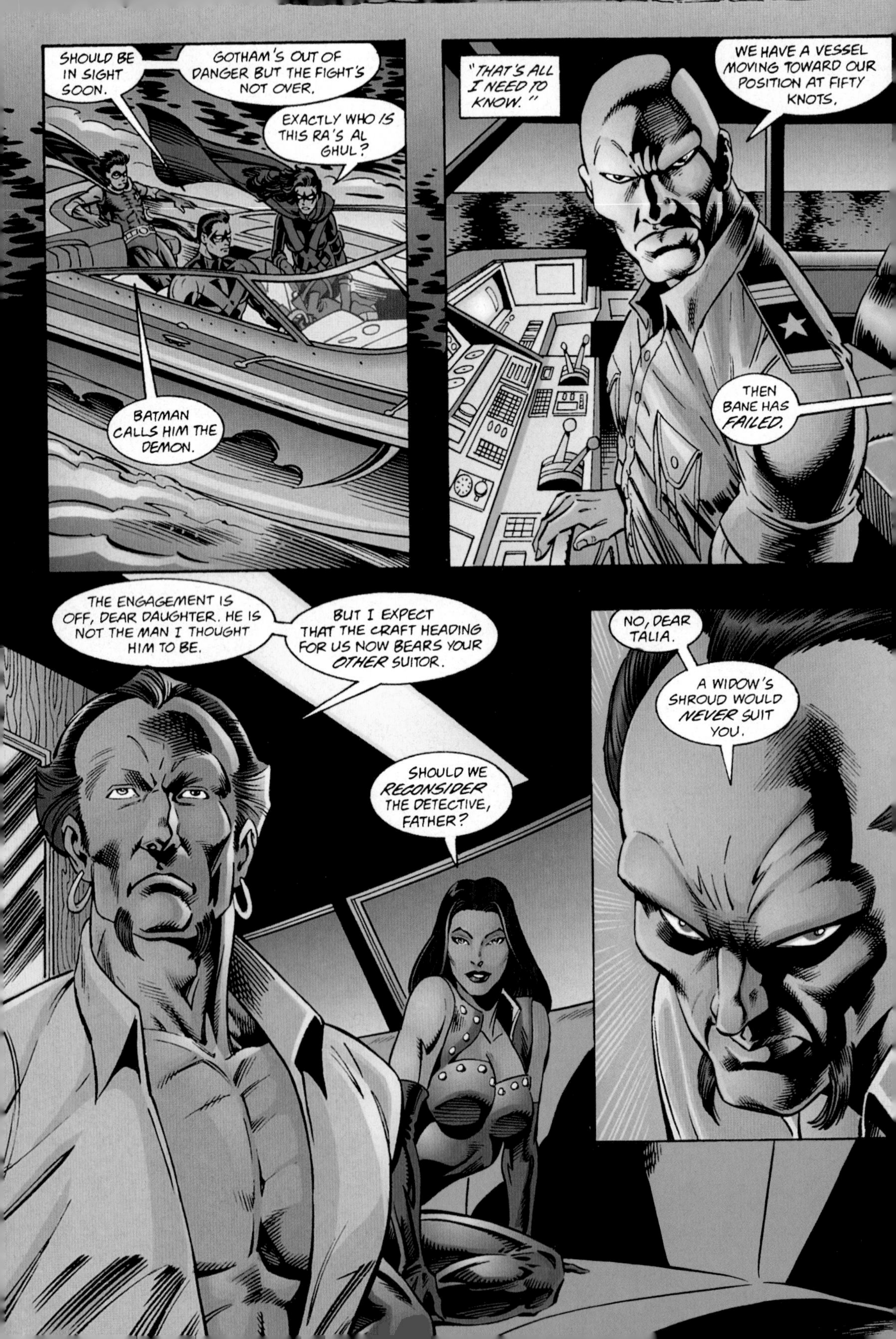
SHOULD BE IN SIGHT SOON.
GOTHAM'S OUT OF DANGER BUT THE FIGHT'S NOT OVER.
EXACTLY WHO IS THIS RA'S AL GHUL?
BATMAN CALLS HIM THE DEMON.
"THAT'S ALL I NEED TO KNOW."
WE HAVE A VESSEL MOVING TOWARD OUR POSITION AT FIFTY KNOTS.
THEN BANE HAS FAILED.
THE ENGAGEMENT IS OFF, DEAR DAUGHTER. HE IS NOT THE MAN I THOUGHT HIM TO BE.
BUT I EXPECT THAT THE CRAFT HEADING FOR US NOW BEARS YOUR OTHER SUITOR.
SHOULD WE RECONSIDER THE DETECTIVE, FATHER?
NO, DEAR TALIA.
A WIDOW'S SHROUD WOULD NEVER SUIT YOU.

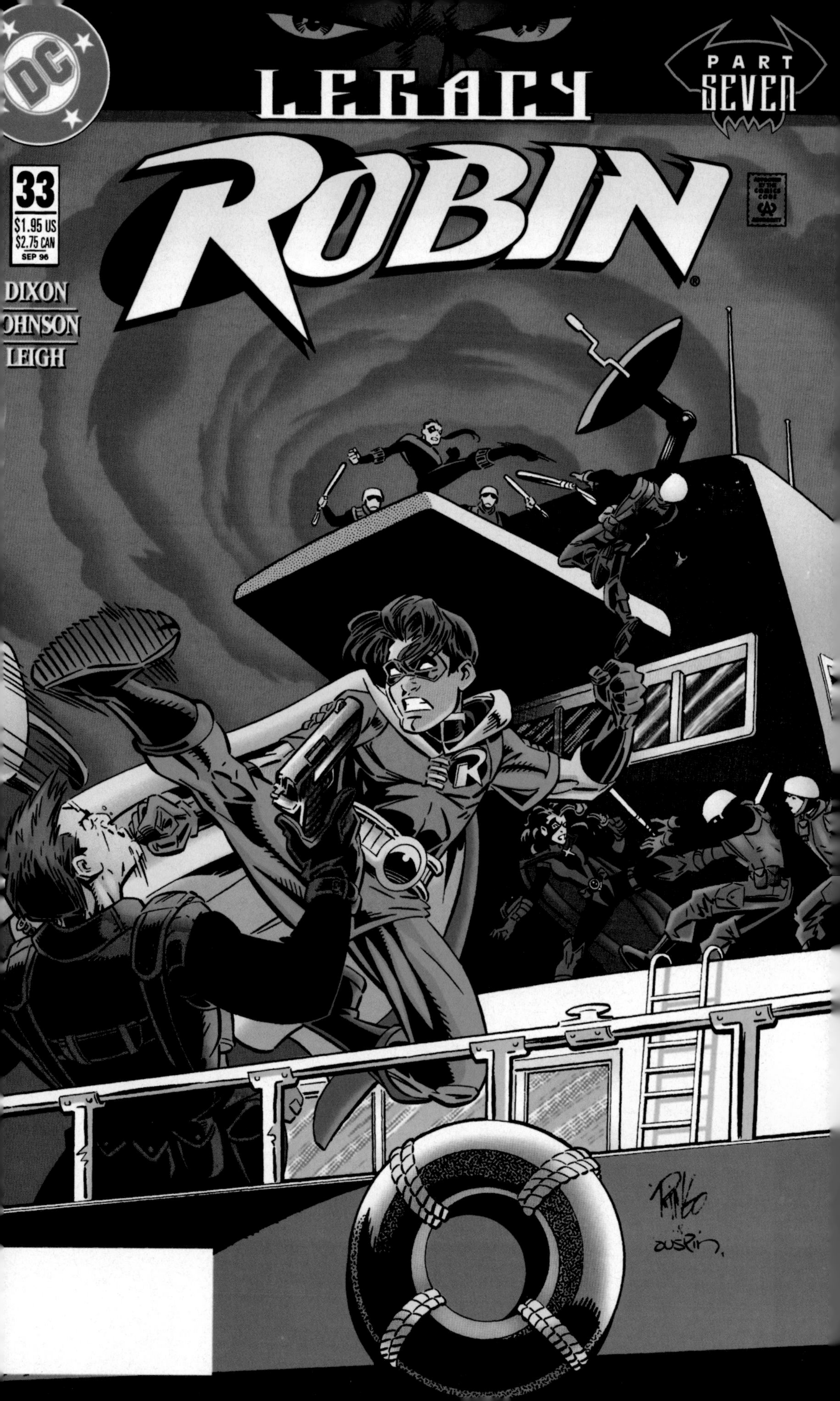

LEGACY
PART SEVEN
33
$1.95 US
$2.75 CAN
SEP 96
ROBIN
DIXON
JOHNSON
LEIGH

Cover Art by Mike Wieringo
and Terry Austin

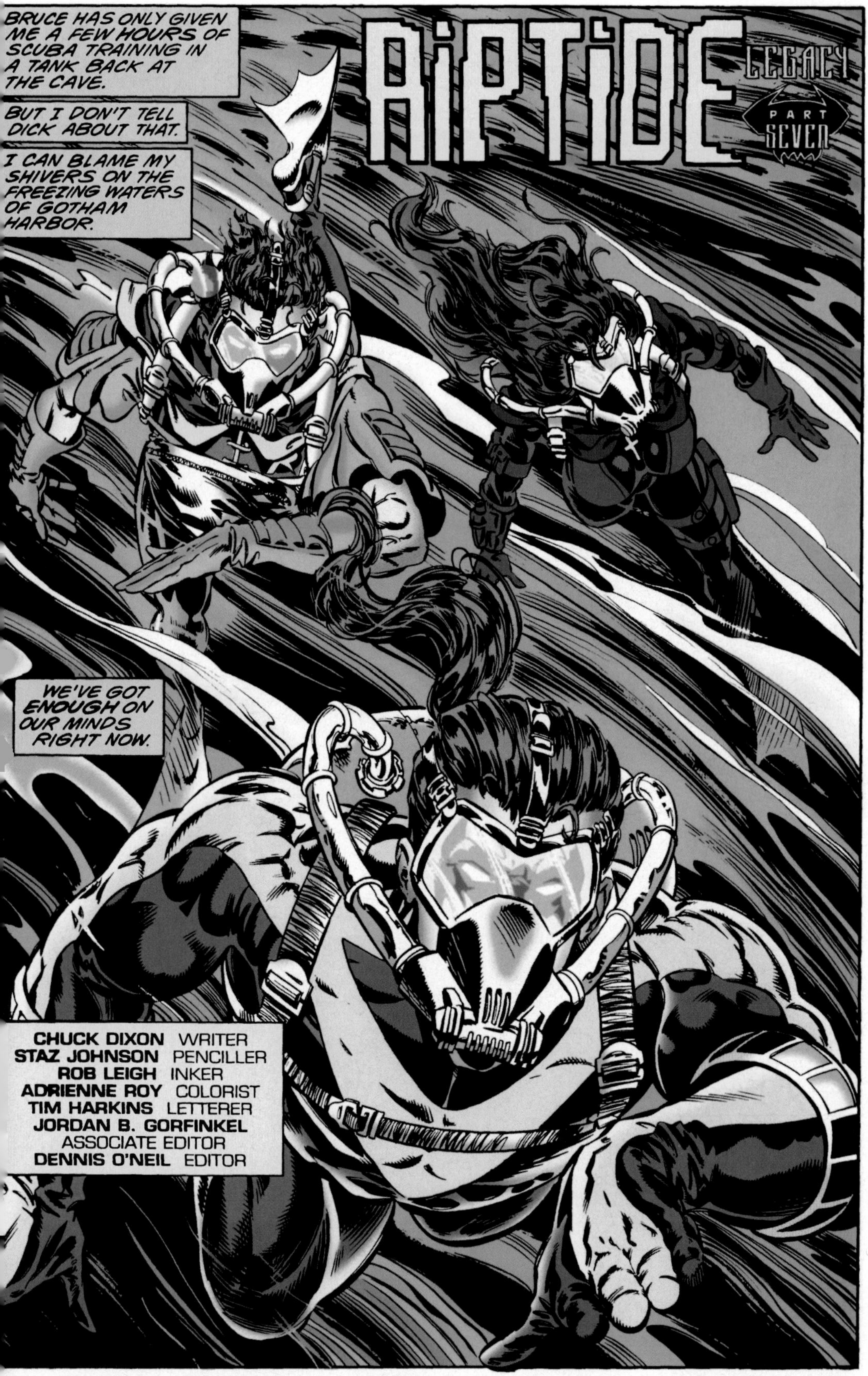
BRUCE HAS ONLY GIVEN ME A FEW HOURS OF SCUBA TRAINING IN A TANK BACK AT THE CAVE.
BUT I DON'T TELL DICK ABOUT THAT.
I CAN BLAME MY SHIVERS ON THE FREEZING WATERS OF GOTHAM HARBOR.
RIPTIDE
LEGACY PART SEVEN
WE'VE GOT ENOUGH ON OUR MINDS RIGHT NOW.
CHUCK DIXON WRITER
STAZ JOHNSON PENCILLER
ROB LEIGH INKER
ADRIENNE ROY COLORIST
TIM HARKINS LETTERER
JORDAN B. GORFINKEL ASSOCIATE EDITOR
DENNIS O'NEIL EDITOR

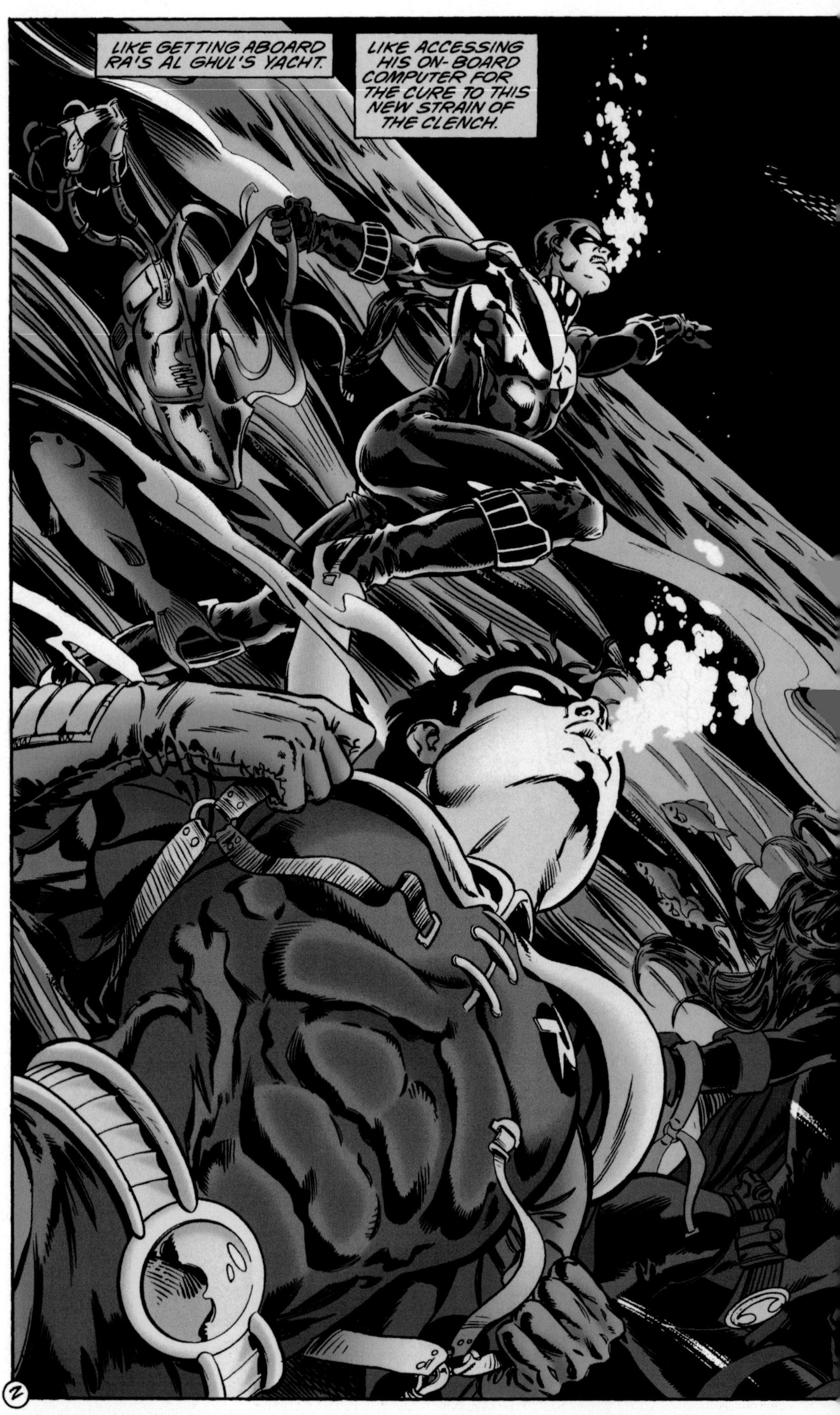
LIKE GETTING ABOARD RA'S AL GHUL'S YACHT.
LIKE ACCESSING HIS ON-BOARD COMPUTER FOR THE CURE TO THIS NEW STRAIN OF THE CLENCH.

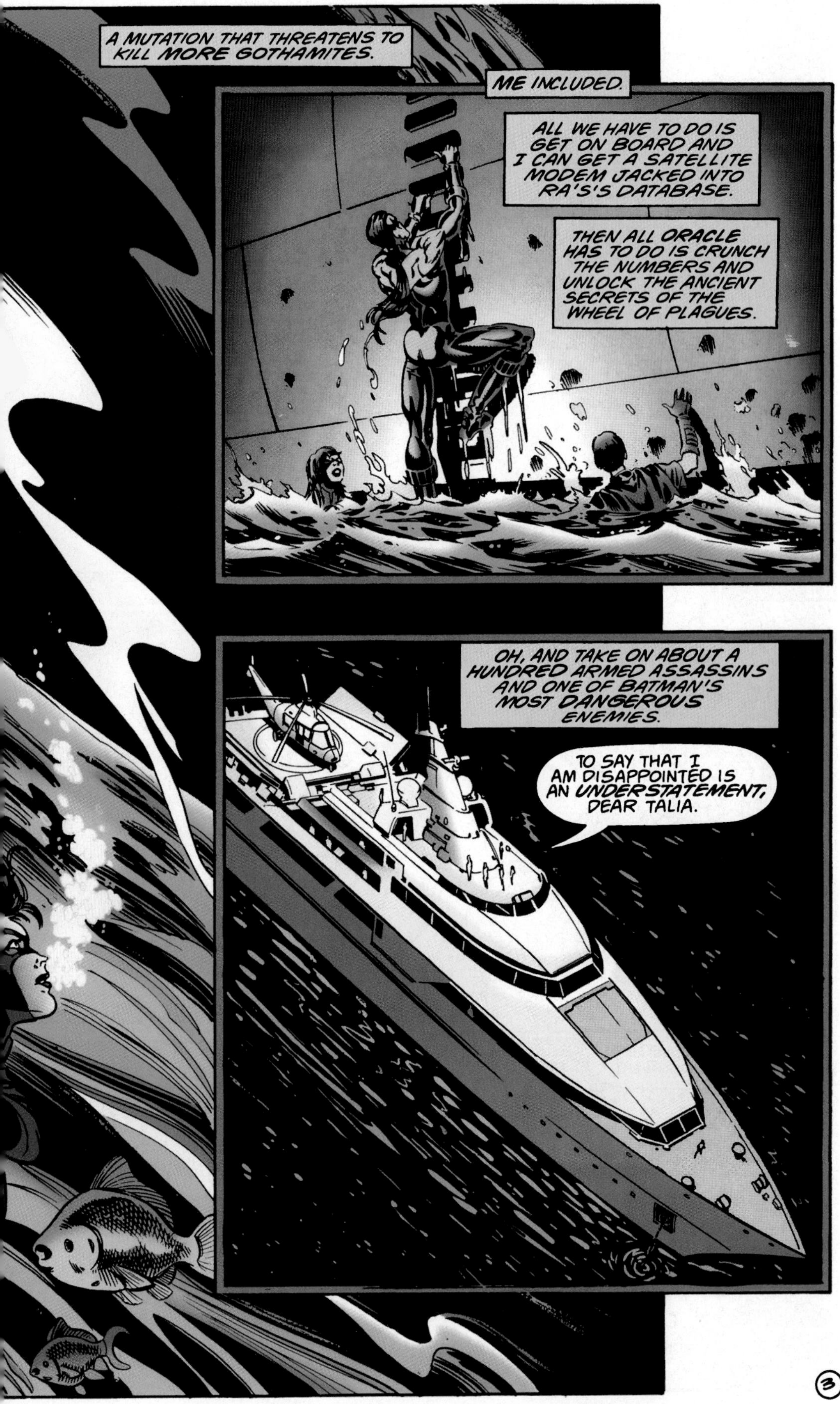

A MUTATION THAT THREATENS TO KILL MORE GOTHAMITES.
ME INCLUDED.
ALL WE HAVE TO DO IS GET ON BOARD AND I CAN GET A SATELLITE MODEM JACKED INTO RA'S'S DATABASE.
THEN ALL ORACLE HAS TO DO IS CRUNCH THE NUMBERS AND UNLOCK THE ANCIENT SECRETS OF THE WHEEL OF PLAGUES.
OH, AND TAKE ON ABOUT A HUNDRED ARMED ASSASSINS AND ONE OF BATMAN'S MOST DANGEROUS ENEMIES.
TO SAY THAT I AM DISAPPOINTED IS AN UNDERSTATEMENT, DEAR TALIA.

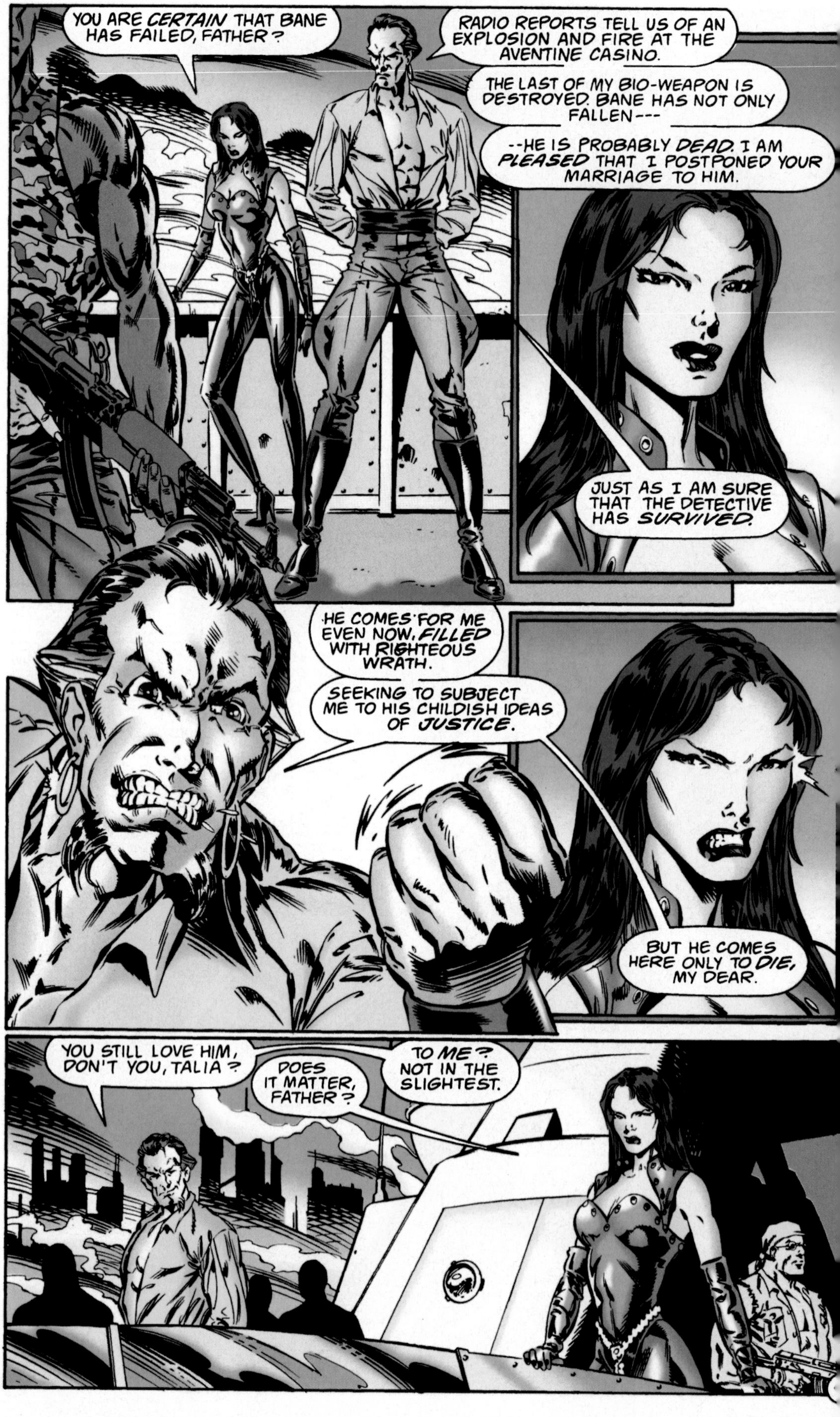
YOU ARE CERTAIN THAT BANE HAS FAILED, FATHER?
RADIO REPORTS TELL US OF AN EXPLOSION AND FIRE AT THE AVENTINE CASINO.
THE LAST OF MY BIO-WEAPON IS DESTROYED. BANE HAS NOT ONLY FALLEN---
--HE IS PROBABLY DEAD. I AM PLEASED THAT I POSTPONED YOUR MARRIAGE TO HIM.
JUST AS I AM SURE THAT THE DETECTIVE HAS SURVIVED.
HE COMES FOR ME EVEN NOW, FILLED WITH RIGHTEOUS WRATH.
SEEKING TO SUBJECT ME TO HIS CHILDISH IDEAS OF JUSTICE.
BUT HE COMES HERE ONLY TO DIE, MY DEAR.
YOU STILL LOVE HIM, DON'T YOU, TALIA?
DOES IT MATTER, FATHER?
TO ME? NOT IN THE SLIGHTEST.

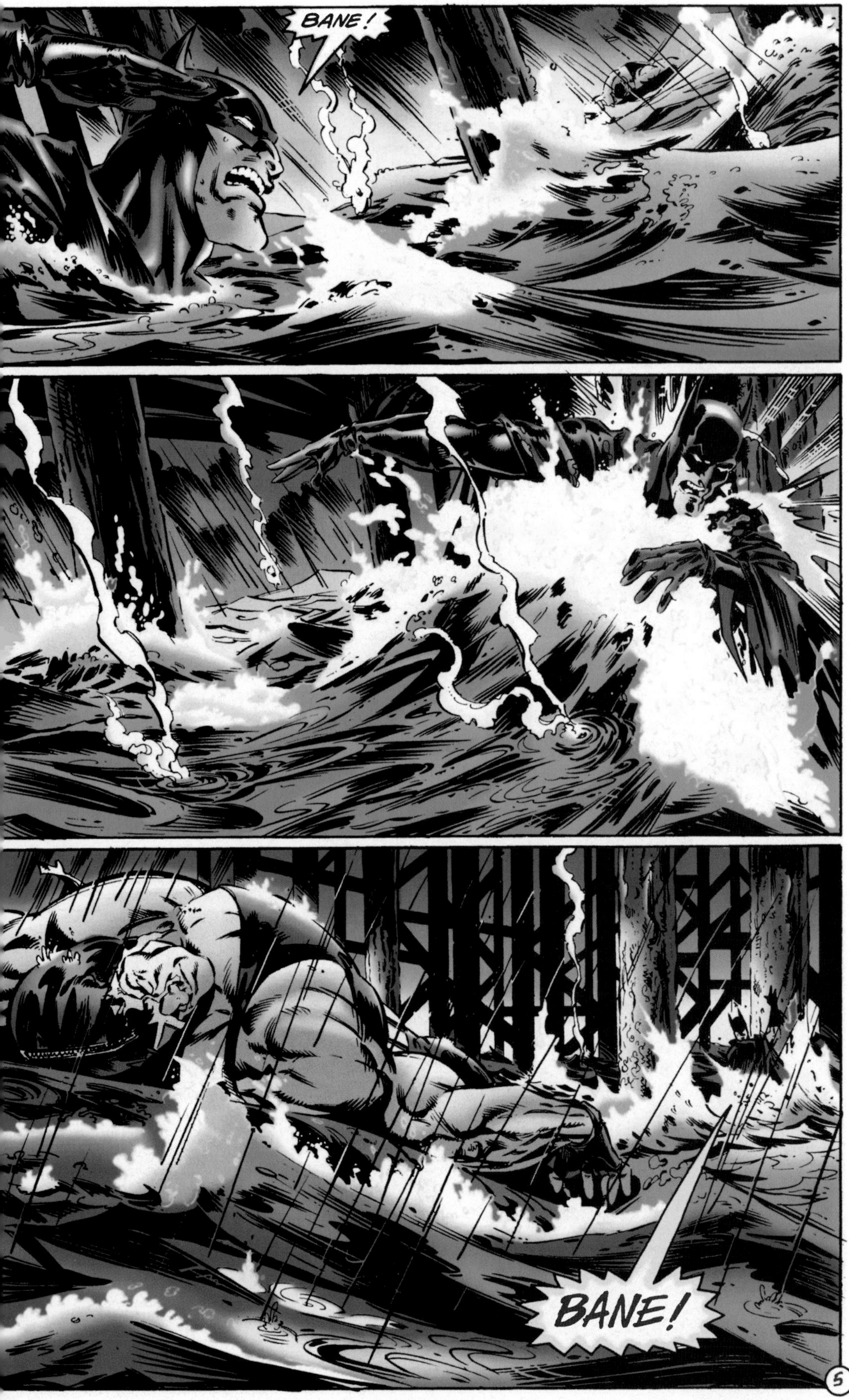
BANE!
BANE!

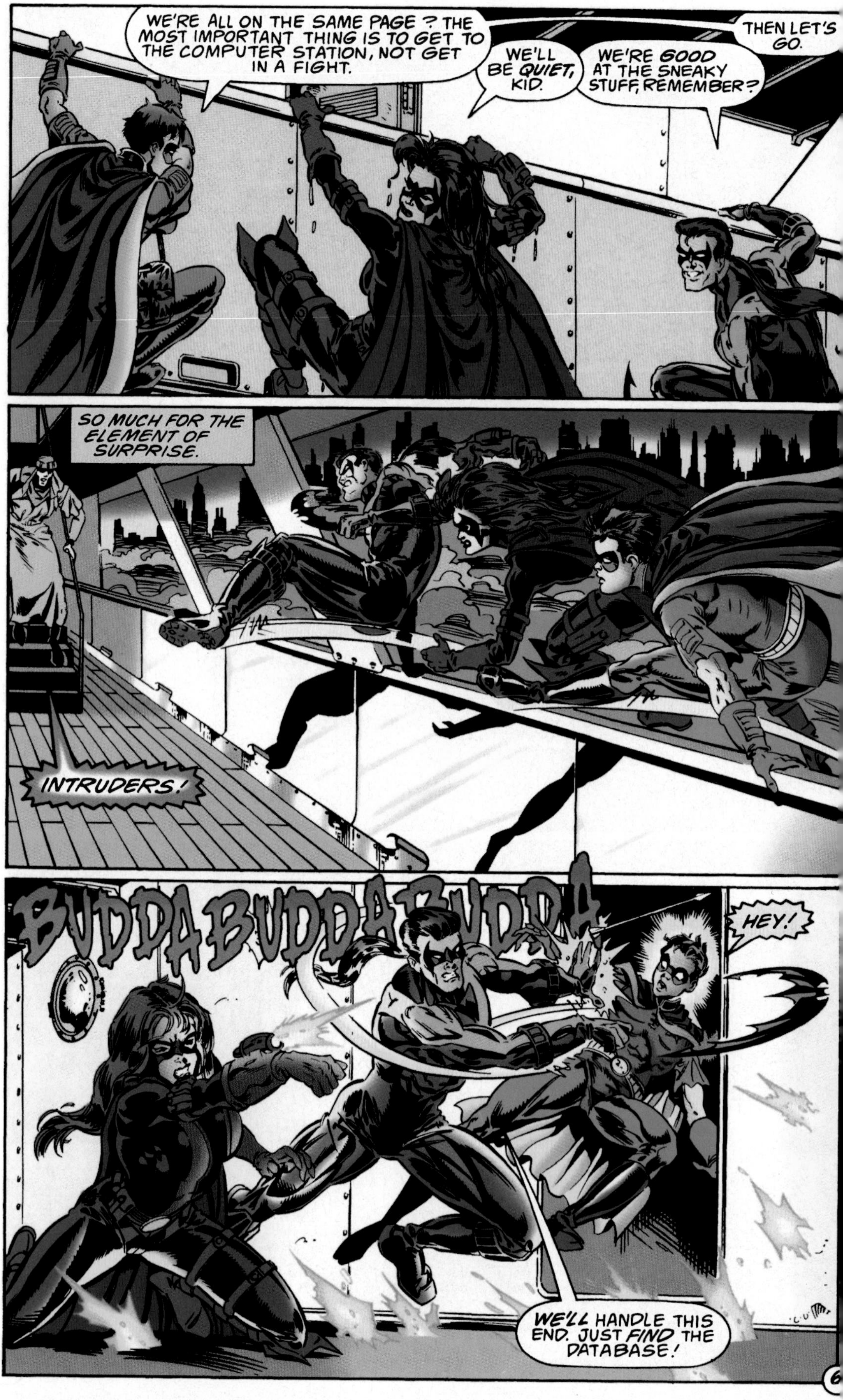
WE'RE ALL ON THE SAME PAGE? THE MOST IMPORTANT THING IS TO GET TO THE COMPUTER STATION, NOT GET IN A FIGHT.
WE'LL BE QUIET, KID.
WE'RE GOOD AT THE SNEAKY STUFF, REMEMBER?
THEN LET'S GO.
SO MUCH FOR THE ELEMENT OF SURPRISE.
INTRUDERS!
BUDDABUDDABUDDA
HEY!
WE'LL HANDLE THIS END. JUST FIND THE DATABASE!

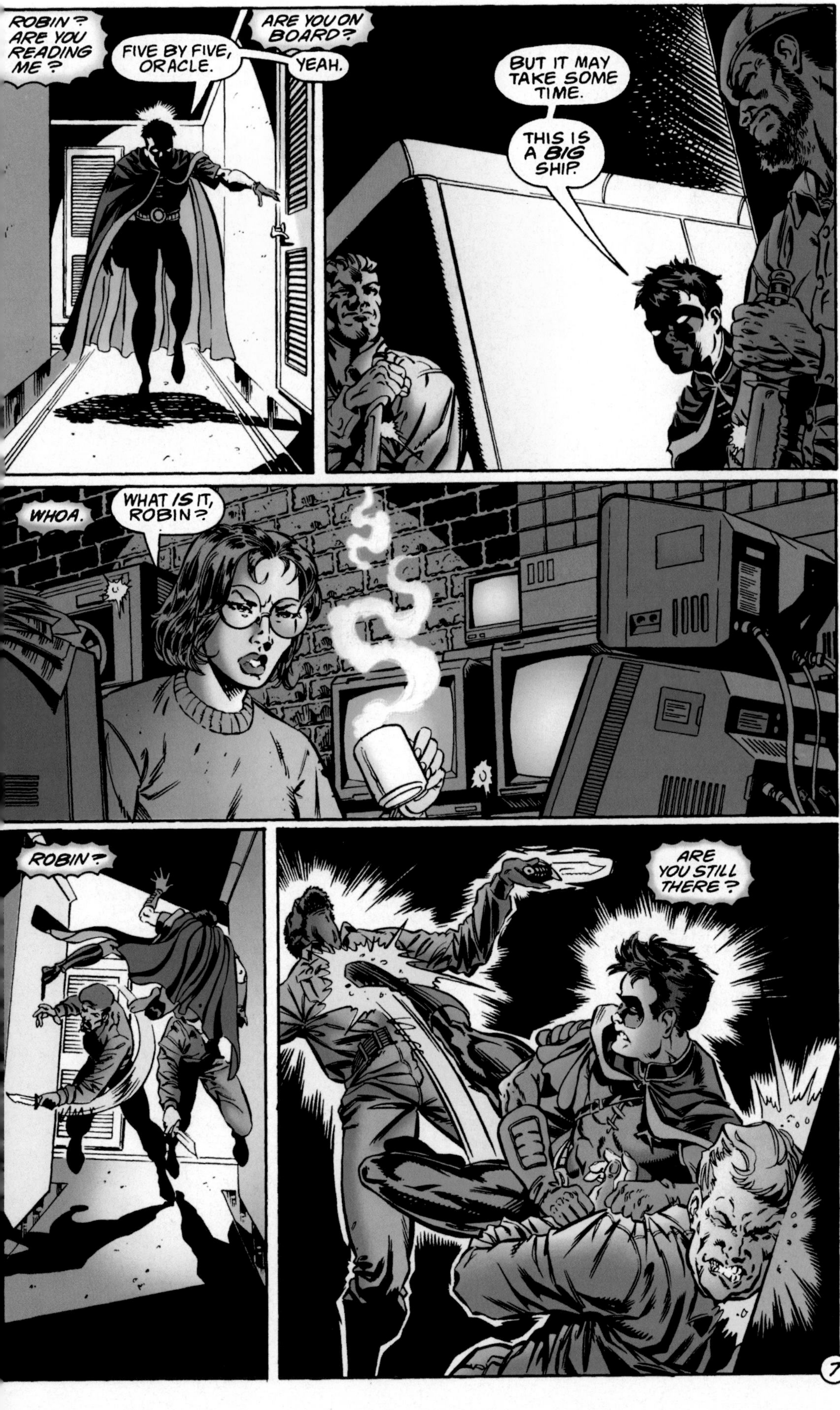
ROBIN? ARE YOU READING ME?
FIVE BY FIVE, ORACLE.
ARE YOU ON BOARD?
YEAH.
BUT IT MAY TAKE SOME TIME.
THIS IS A *BIG* SHIP.
WHOA.
WHAT *IS* IT, ROBIN?
ROBIN?
ARE YOU STILL THERE?

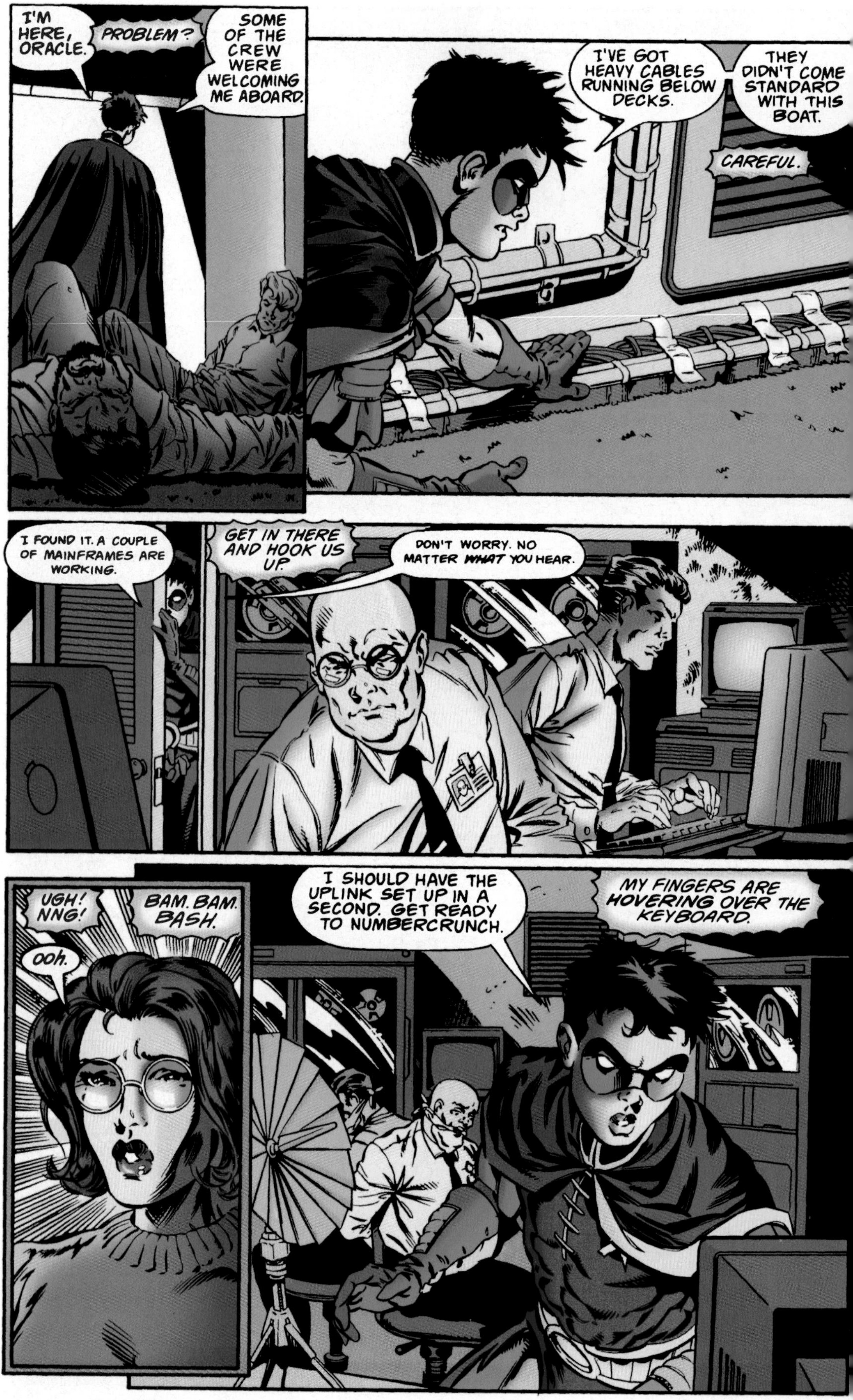
I'M HERE, ORACLE.
PROBLEM?
SOME OF THE CREW WERE WELCOMING ME ABOARD.
I'VE GOT HEAVY CABLES RUNNING BELOW DECKS.
THEY DIDN'T COME STANDARD WITH THIS BOAT.
CAREFUL.
I FOUND IT. A COUPLE OF MAINFRAMES ARE WORKING.
GET IN THERE AND HOOK US UP.
DON'T WORRY. NO MATTER WHAT YOU HEAR.
UGH! NNG!
BAM. BAM. BASH.
ooh.
I SHOULD HAVE THE UPLINK SET UP IN A SECOND. GET READY TO NUMBERCRUNCH.
MY FINGERS ARE HOVERING OVER THE KEYBOARD.

YOU ANY *GOOD* WITH THAT THING, HUNTRESS?

I CAN'T SHOOT AROUND *CORNERS* IF THAT'S WHAT YOU MEAN.

ALL I NEED IS A SECOND OR TWO.

NICE SHOT. YOU CUT THEIR ROPE.

ROBIN DIDN'T TELL ME YOU WERE A *NAG!*

WHAT *DID* HE TELL YOU?

LATER FOR THAT.

COVER ME!

UNNH!

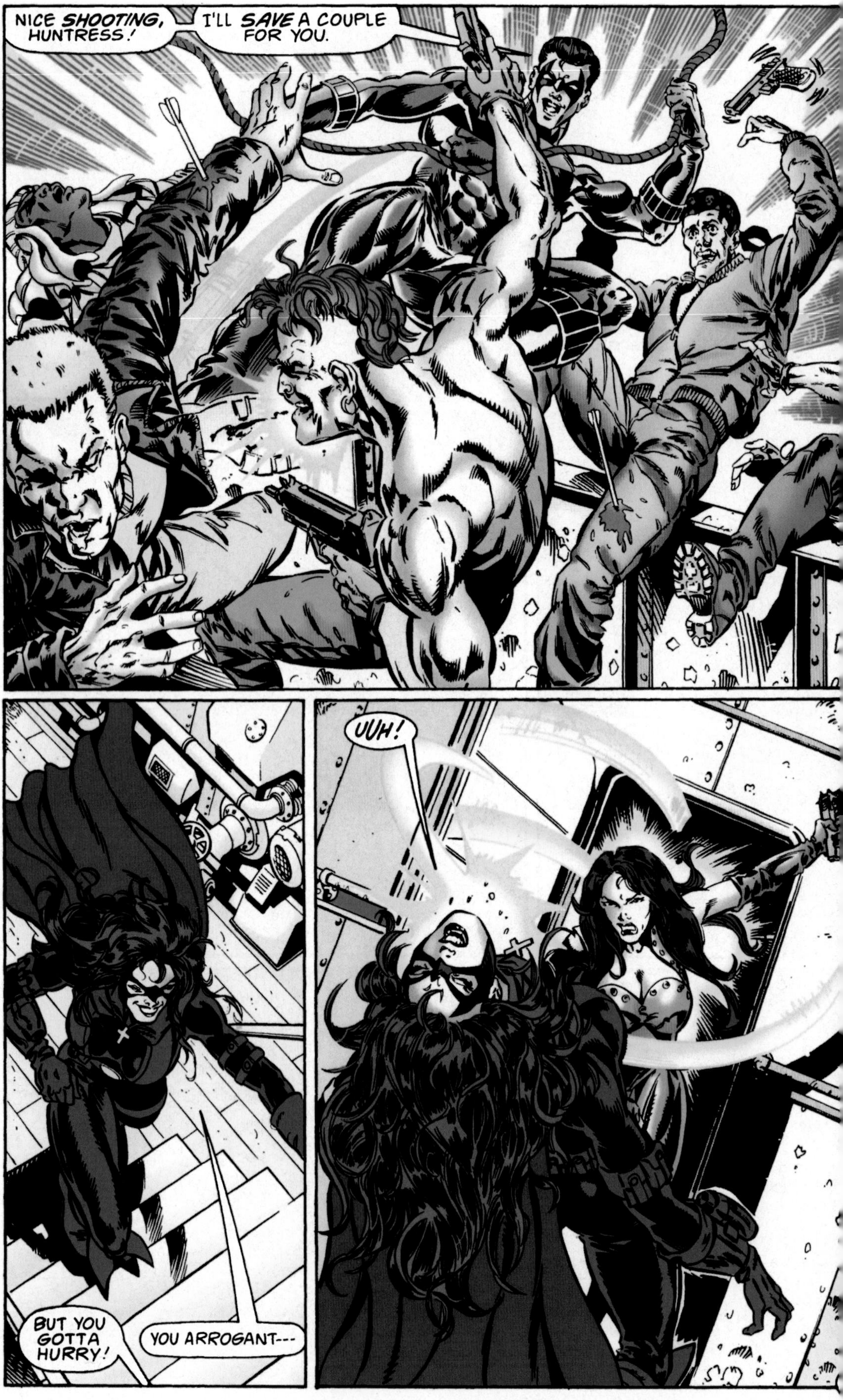

NICE SHOOTING, HUNTRESS!
I'LL SAVE A COUPLE FOR YOU.
UUH!
BUT YOU GOTTA HURRY!
YOU ARROGANT---

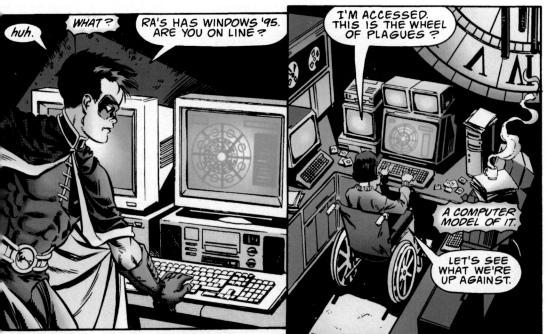

huh.

WHAT?

RA'S HAS WINDOWS '95. ARE YOU ON LINE?

I'M ACCESSED. THIS IS THE WHEEL OF PLAGUES?

A COMPUTER MODEL OF IT.

LET'S SEE WHAT WE'RE UP AGAINST.

JEEZE.

THIS DOESN'T LOOK GOOD.

THERE MUST BE MILLIONS OF POSSIBLE COMBINATIONS ON THIS WHEEL.

HARD TO BELIEVE THIS THING IS THREE THOUSAND YEARS OLD.

WELL, THEY HAD GENERATIONS TO CONFIGURE IT.

WE HAVE HOURS.

CAN YOU DO IT?

I CAN TRY.

JUST KEEP THE LINE OPEN.

11

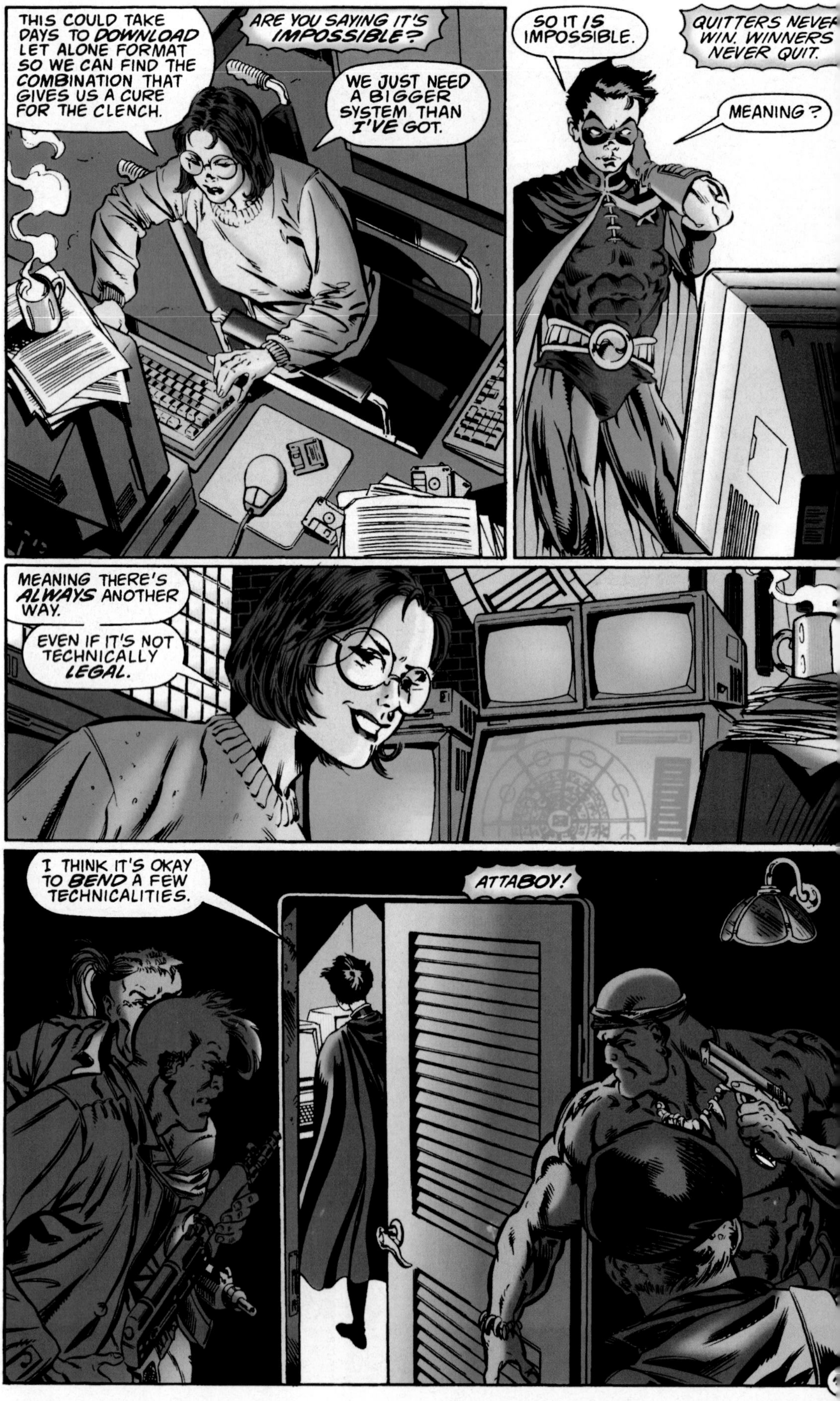

THIS COULD TAKE DAYS TO *DOWNLOAD* LET ALONE FORMAT SO WE CAN FIND THE *COMBINATION* THAT GIVES US A CURE FOR THE CLENCH.
ARE YOU SAYING IT'S IMPOSSIBLE?
WE JUST NEED A BIGGER SYSTEM THAN *I'VE* GOT.
SO IT *IS* IMPOSSIBLE.
QUITTERS NEVER WIN. WINNERS NEVER QUIT.
MEANING?
MEANING THERE'S *ALWAYS* ANOTHER WAY.
EVEN IF IT'S NOT TECHNICALLY *LEGAL*.
I THINK IT'S OKAY TO *BEND* A FEW TECHNICALITIES.
ATTABOY!

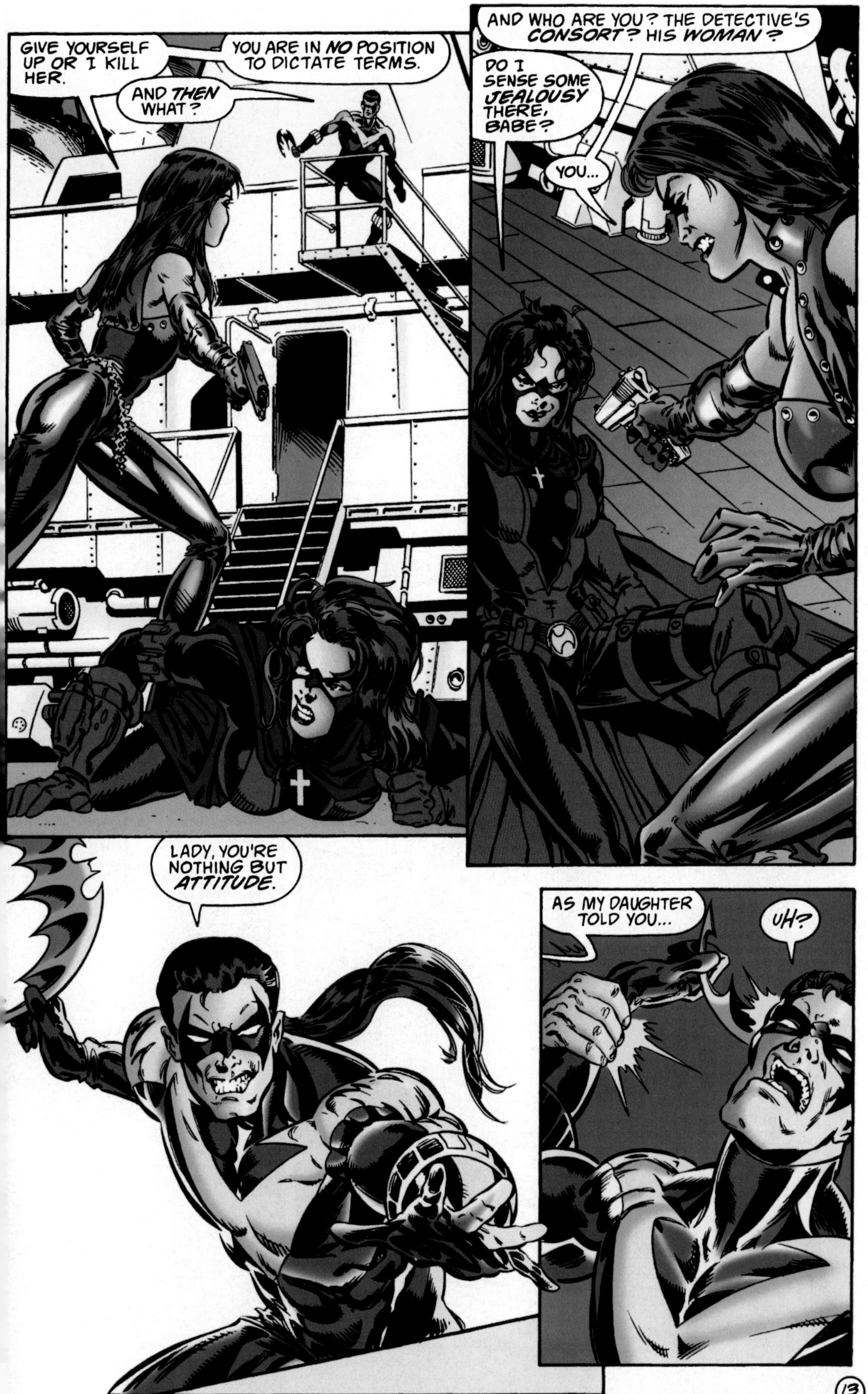
GIVE YOURSELF UP OR I KILL HER.
YOU ARE IN NO POSITION TO DICTATE TERMS.
AND THEN WHAT?
AND WHO ARE YOU? THE DETECTIVE'S CONSORT? HIS WOMAN?
DO I SENSE SOME JEALOUSY THERE, BABE?
YOU...
LADY, YOU'RE NOTHING BUT ATTITUDE.
AS MY DAUGHTER TOLD YOU...
UH?

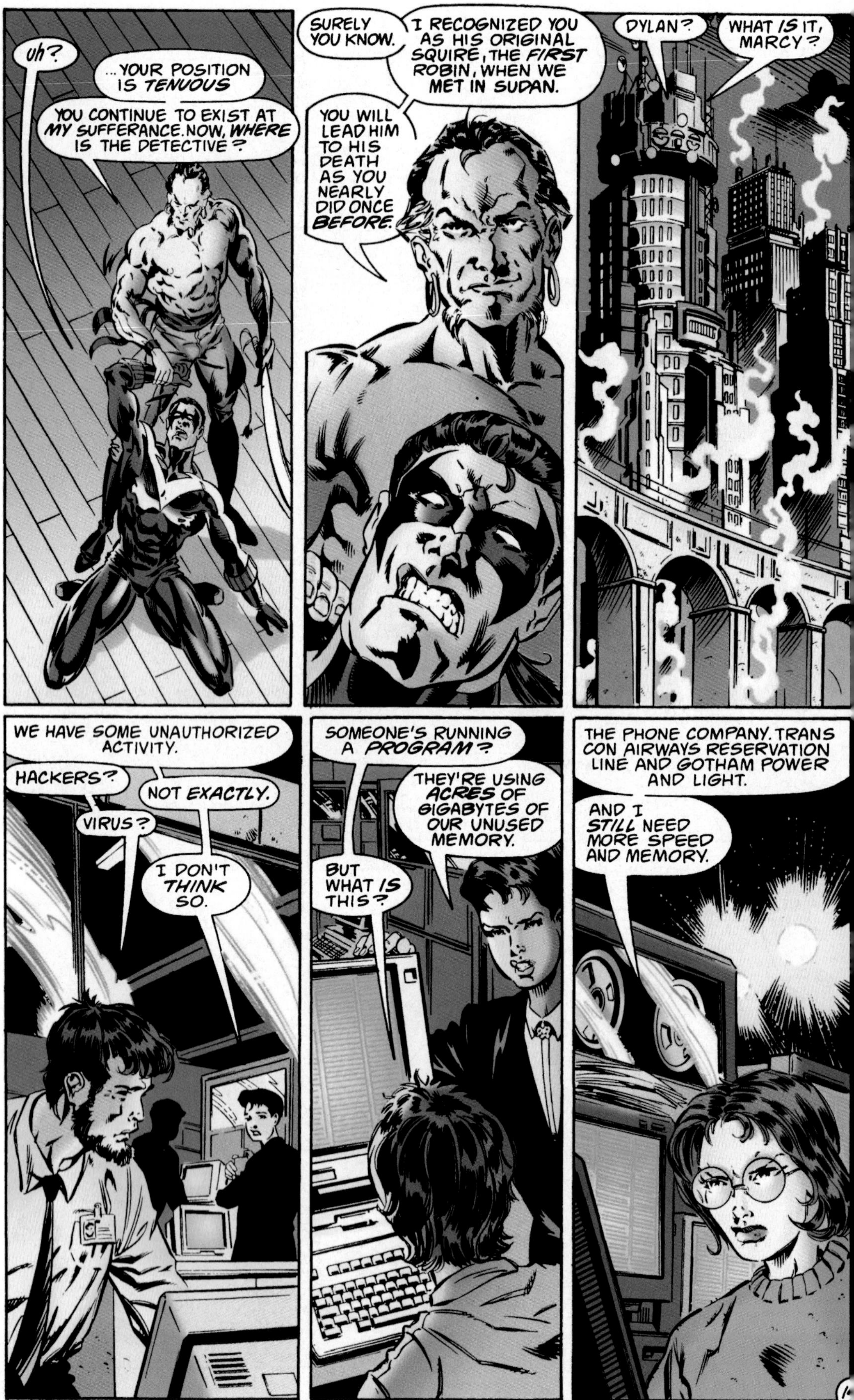
uh?
...YOUR POSITION IS TENUOUS
YOU CONTINUE TO EXIST AT MY SUFFERANCE. NOW, WHERE IS THE DETECTIVE?
SURELY YOU KNOW.
I RECOGNIZED YOU AS HIS ORIGINAL SQUIRE, THE FIRST ROBIN, WHEN WE MET IN SUDAN.
YOU WILL LEAD HIM TO HIS DEATH AS YOU NEARLY DID ONCE BEFORE.
DYLAN?
WHAT IS IT, MARCY?
WE HAVE SOME UNAUTHORIZED ACTIVITY.
HACKERS?
NOT EXACTLY.
VIRUS?
I DON'T THINK SO.
SOMEONE'S RUNNING A PROGRAM?
THEY'RE USING ACRES OF GIGABYTES OF OUR UNUSED MEMORY.
BUT WHAT IS THIS?
THE PHONE COMPANY. TRANS CON AIRWAYS RESERVATION LINE AND GOTHAM POWER AND LIGHT.
AND I STILL NEED MORE SPEED AND MEMORY.

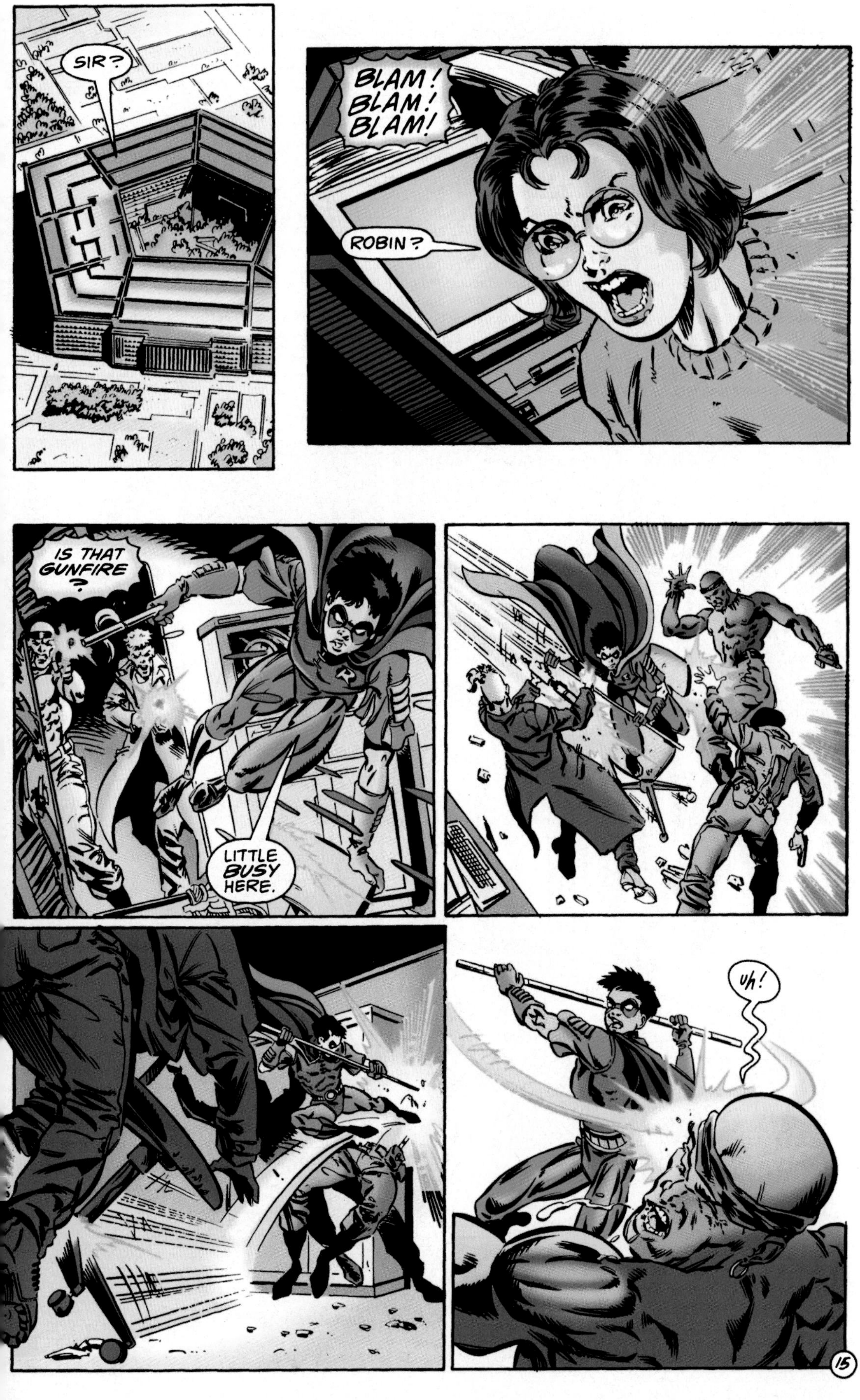
SIR?
BLAM! BLAM! BLAM!
ROBIN?
IS THAT GUNFIRE?
LITTLE BUSY HERE.
Uh!

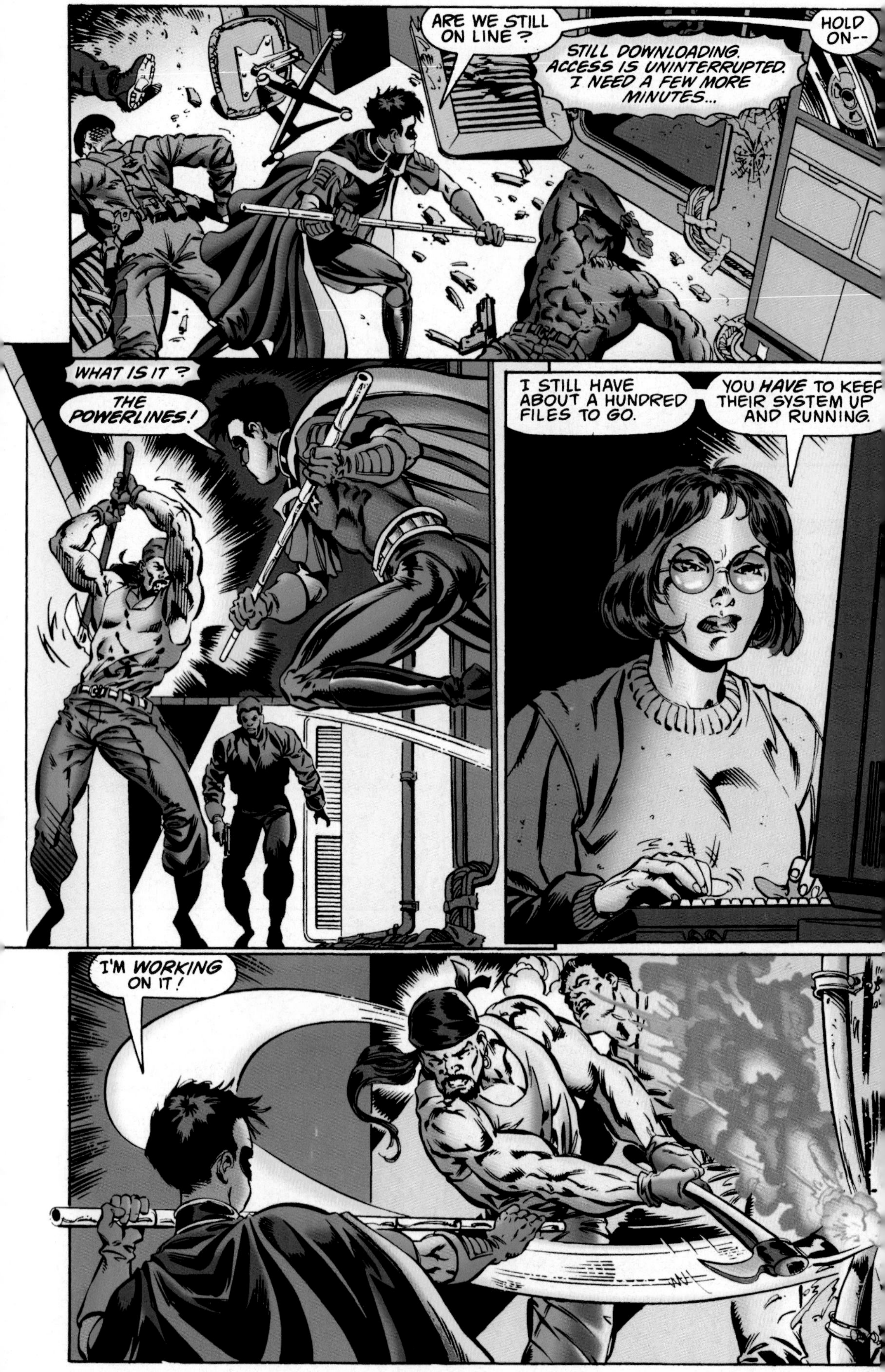
ARE WE STILL ON LINE?
STILL DOWNLOADING. ACCESS IS UNINTERRUPTED. I NEED A FEW MORE MINUTES...
HOLD ON--
WHAT IS IT?
THE POWERLINES!
I STILL HAVE ABOUT A HUNDRED FILES TO GO.
YOU HAVE TO KEEP THEIR SYSTEM UP AND RUNNING.
I'M WORKING ON IT!

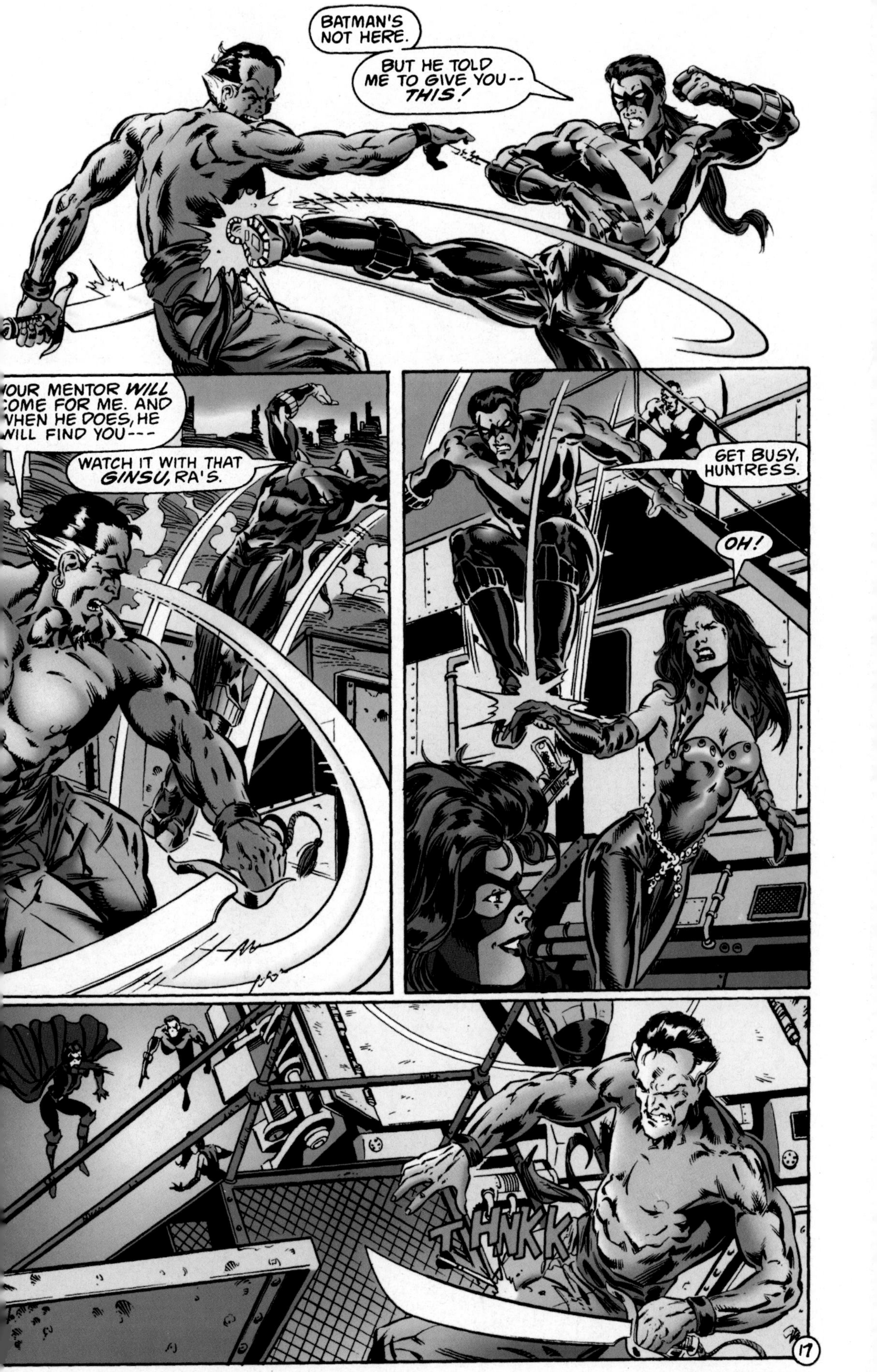

BATMAN'S NOT HERE.
BUT HE TOLD ME TO GIVE YOU-- THIS!
YOUR MENTOR WILL COME FOR ME. AND WHEN HE DOES, HE WILL FIND YOU---
WATCH IT WITH THAT GINSU, RA'S.
GET BUSY, HUNTRESS.
OH!
THNKK!
17

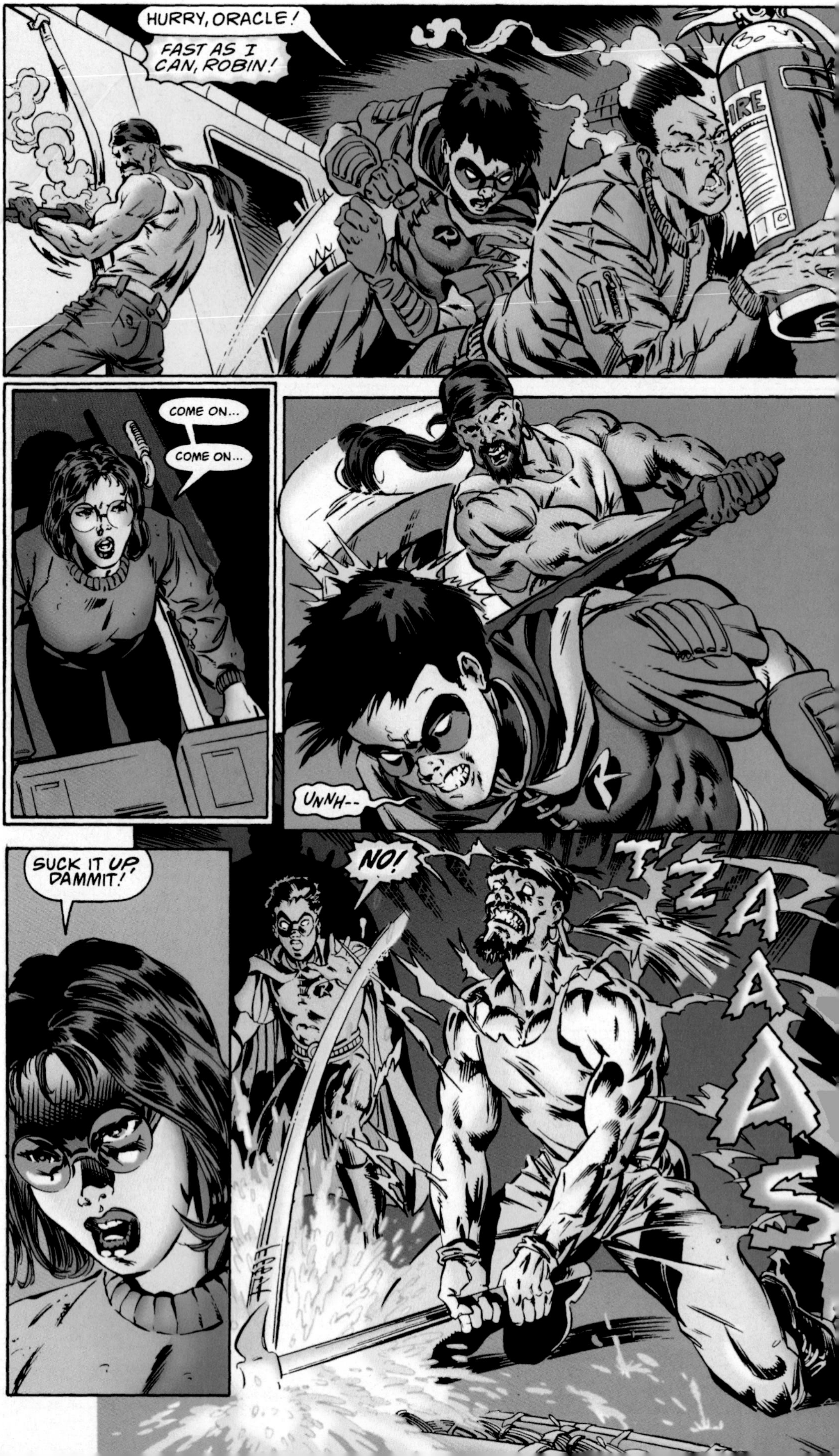
HURRY, ORACLE!
FAST AS I CAN, ROBIN!
COME ON...
COME ON...
UNNH--
SUCK IT UP, DAMMIT!
NO!
TZAAAS

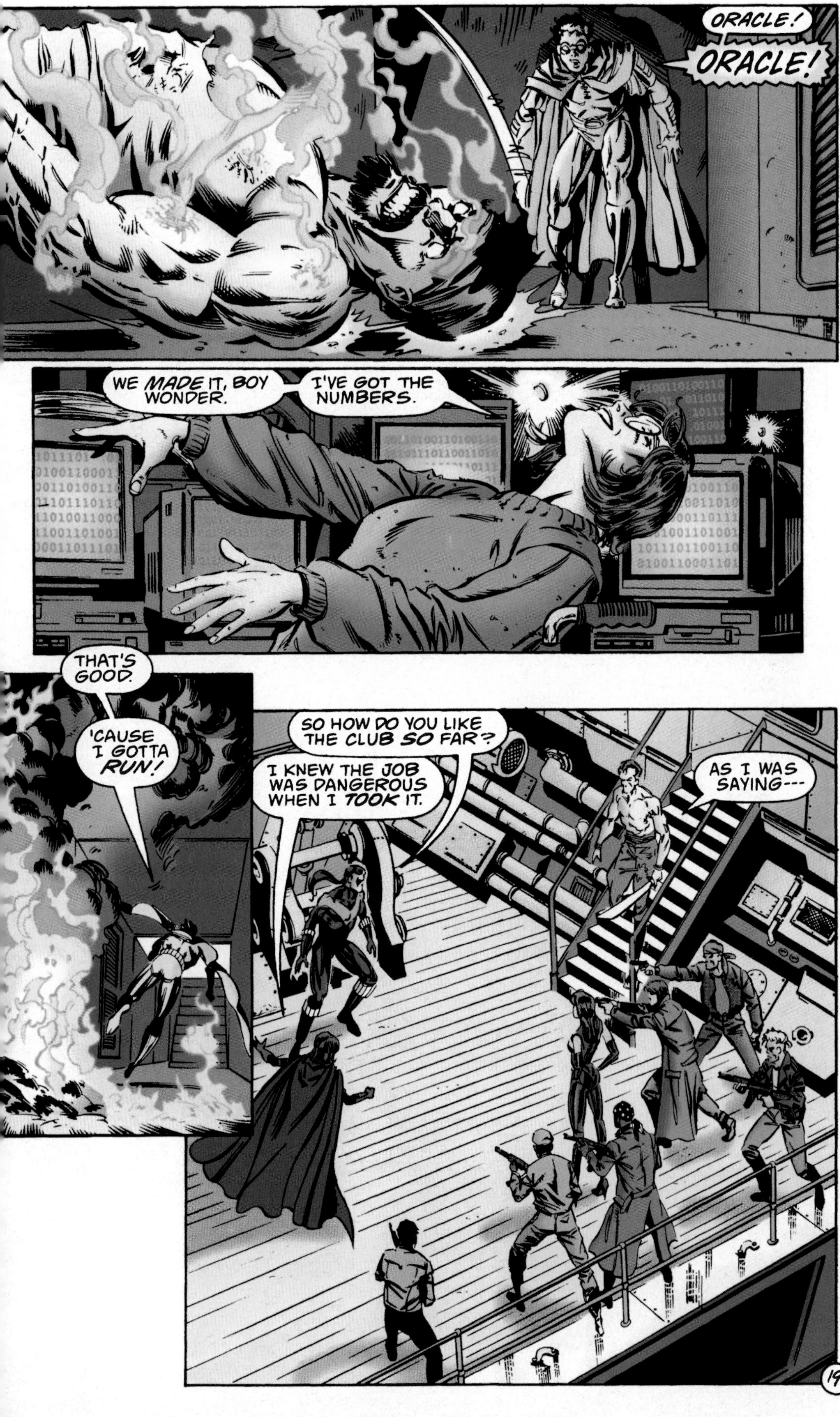
ORACLE!
ORACLE!
WE MADE IT, BOY WONDER.
I'VE GOT THE NUMBERS.
THAT'S GOOD.
'CAUSE I GOTTA RUN!
SO HOW DO YOU LIKE THE CLUB SO FAR?
I KNEW THE JOB WAS DANGEROUS WHEN I TOOK IT.
AS I WAS SAYING---

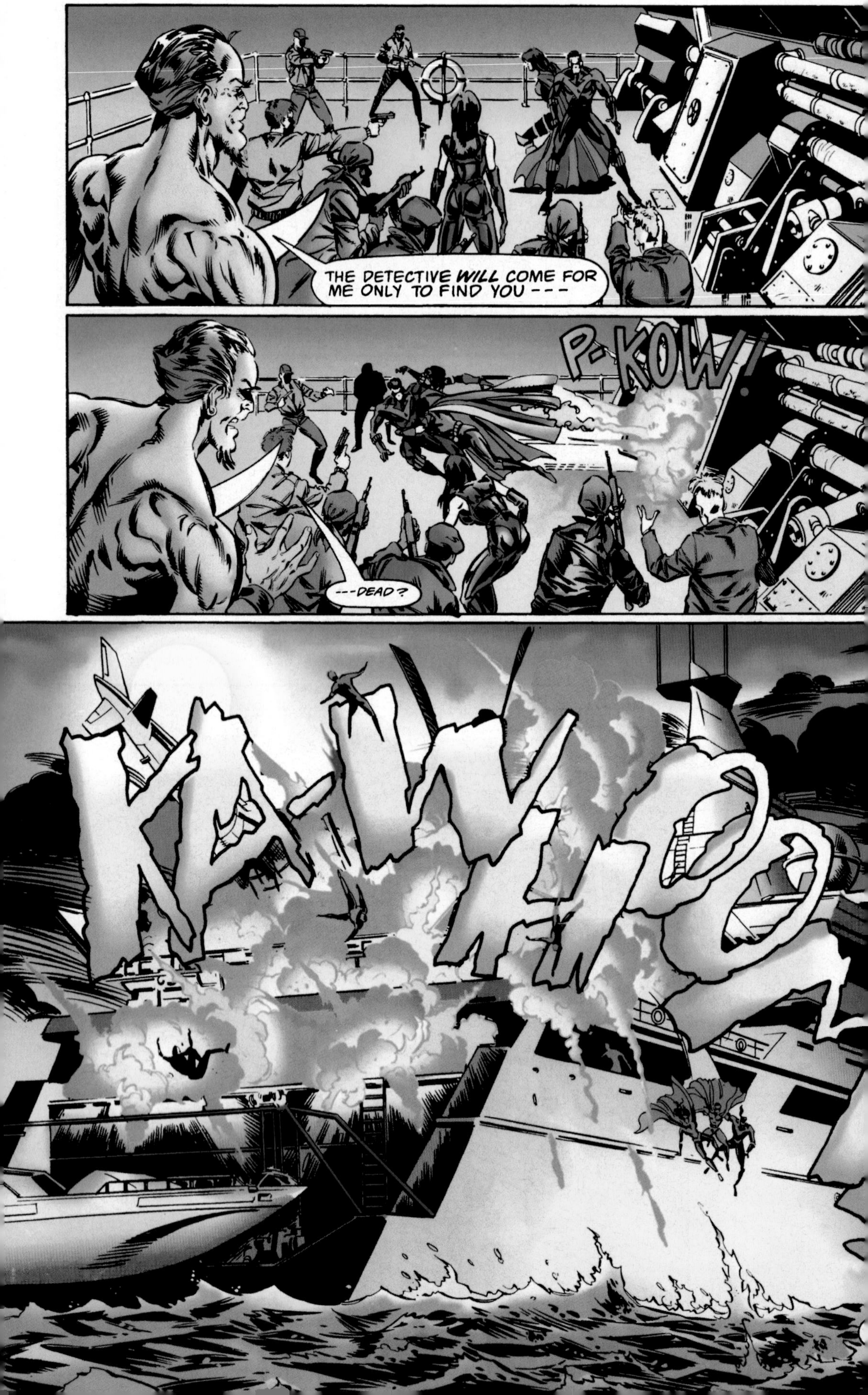

THE DETECTIVE WILL COME FOR ME ONLY TO FIND YOU---
P-KOW!
---DEAD?
KA-WHOOM

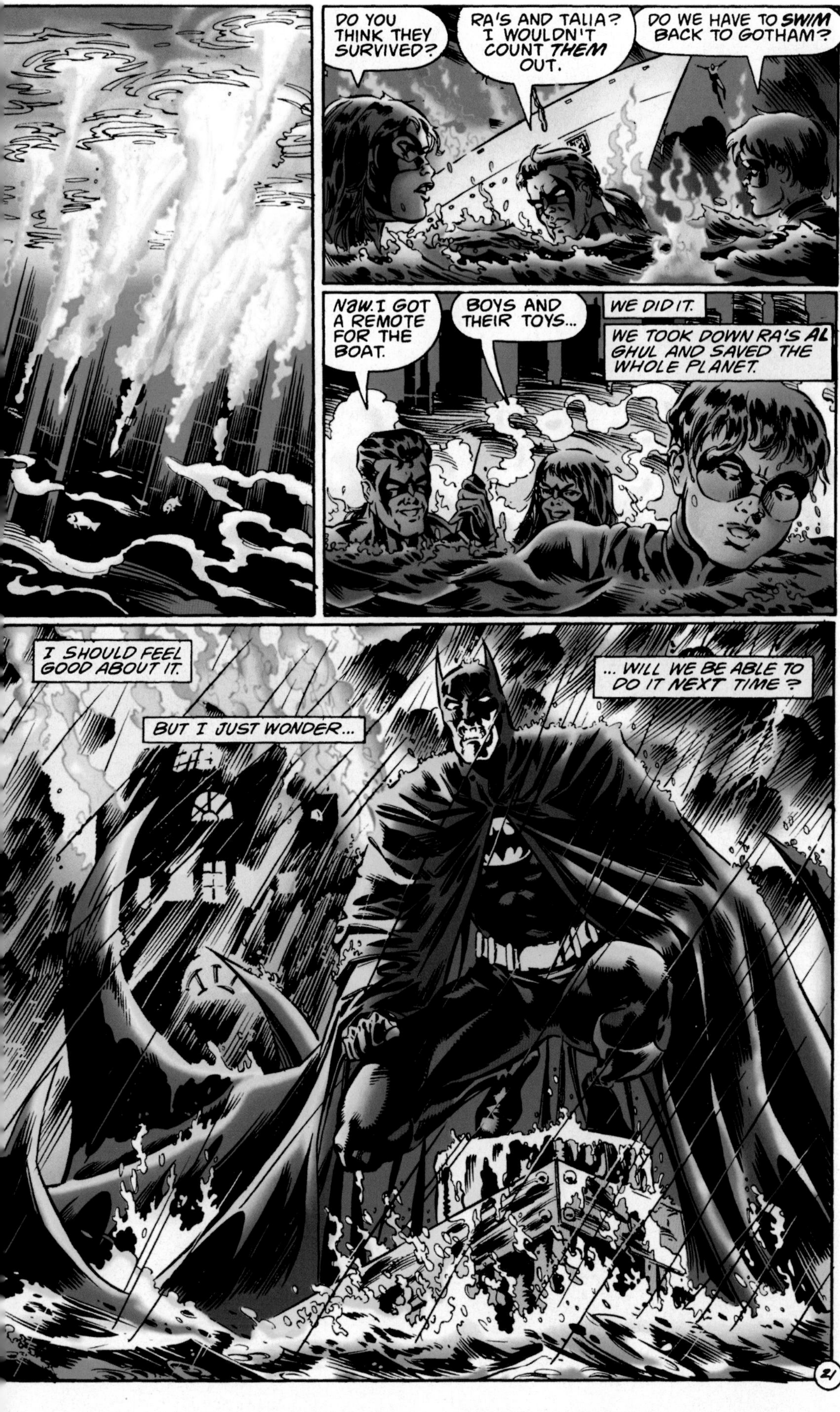

DO YOU THINK THEY SURVIVED?
RA'S AND TALIA? I WOULDN'T COUNT THEM OUT.
DO WE HAVE TO SWIM BACK TO GOTHAM?
NAW. I GOT A REMOTE FOR THE BOAT.
BOYS AND THEIR TOYS...
WE DID IT.
WE TOOK DOWN RA'S AL GHUL AND SAVED THE WHOLE PLANET.
I SHOULD FEEL GOOD ABOUT IT.
BUT I JUST WONDER...
... WILL WE BE ABLE TO DO IT NEXT TIME?

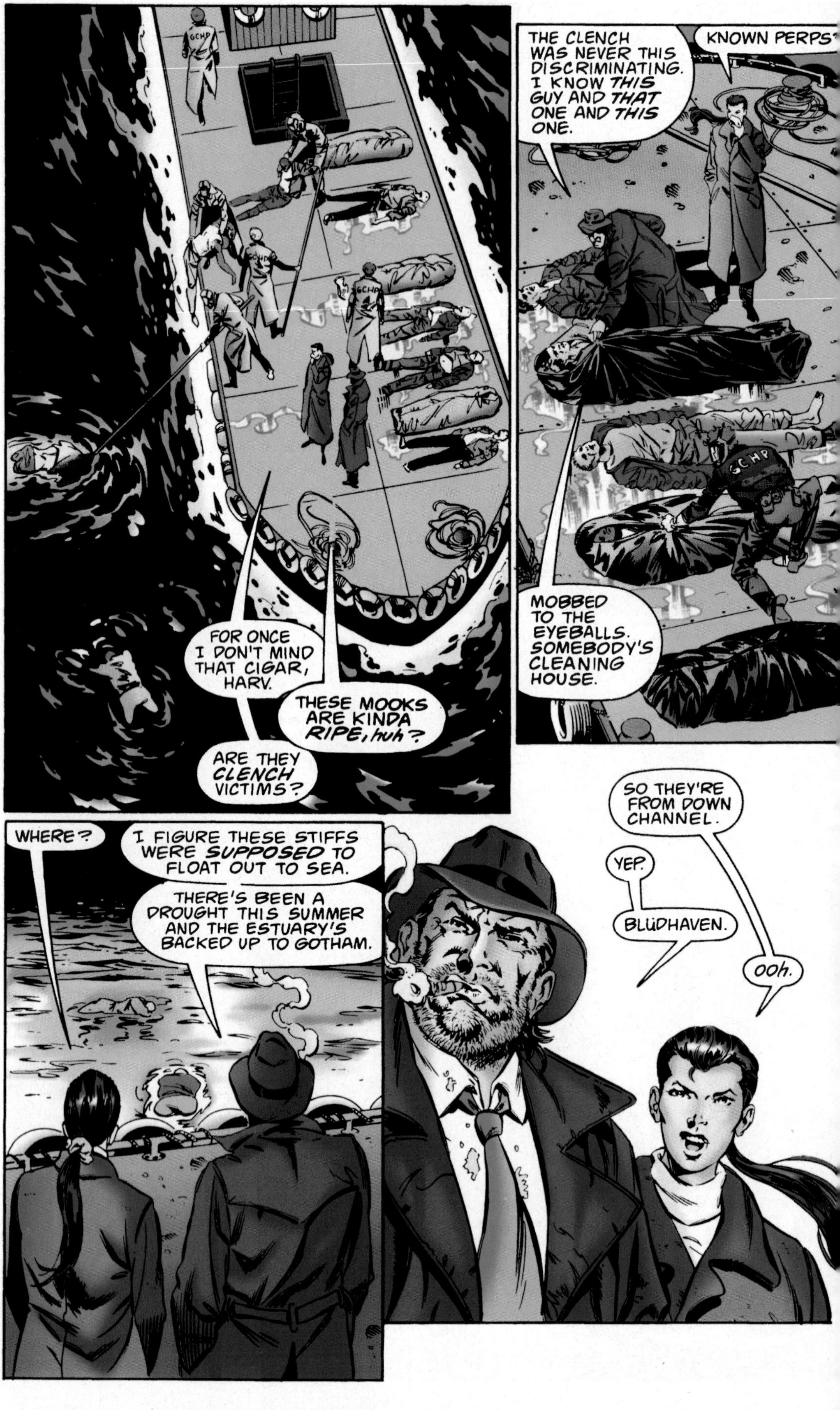
FOR ONCE I DON'T MIND THAT CIGAR, HARV.
THESE MOOKS ARE KINDA RIPE, huh?
ARE THEY CLENCH VICTIMS?
THE CLENCH WAS NEVER THIS DISCRIMINATING. I KNOW THIS GUY AND THAT ONE AND THIS ONE.
KNOWN PERPS?
MOBBED TO THE EYEBALLS. SOMEBODY'S CLEANING HOUSE.
GCHP
WHERE?
I FIGURE THESE STIFFS WERE SUPPOSED TO FLOAT OUT TO SEA.
THERE'S BEEN A DROUGHT THIS SUMMER AND THE ESTUARY'S BACKED UP TO GOTHAM.
SO THEY'RE FROM DOWN CHANNEL.
YEP.
BLÜDHAVEN.
OOH.

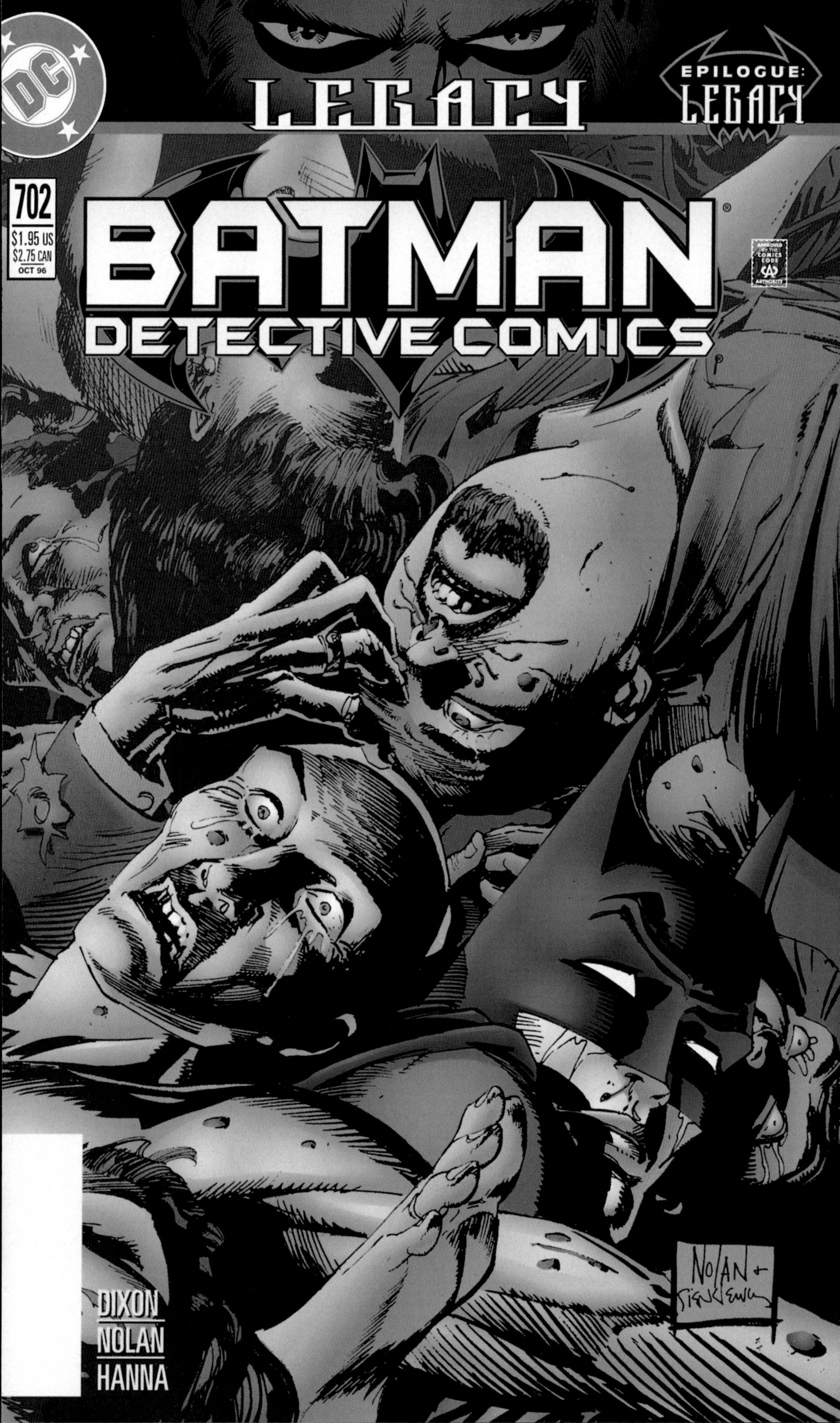
LEGACY
EPILOGUE: LEGACY
702
$1.95 US
$2.75 CAN
OCT 96
BATMAN
DETECTIVE COMICS
APPROVED BY THE COMICS CODE AUTHORITY
DIXON
NOLAN
HANNA

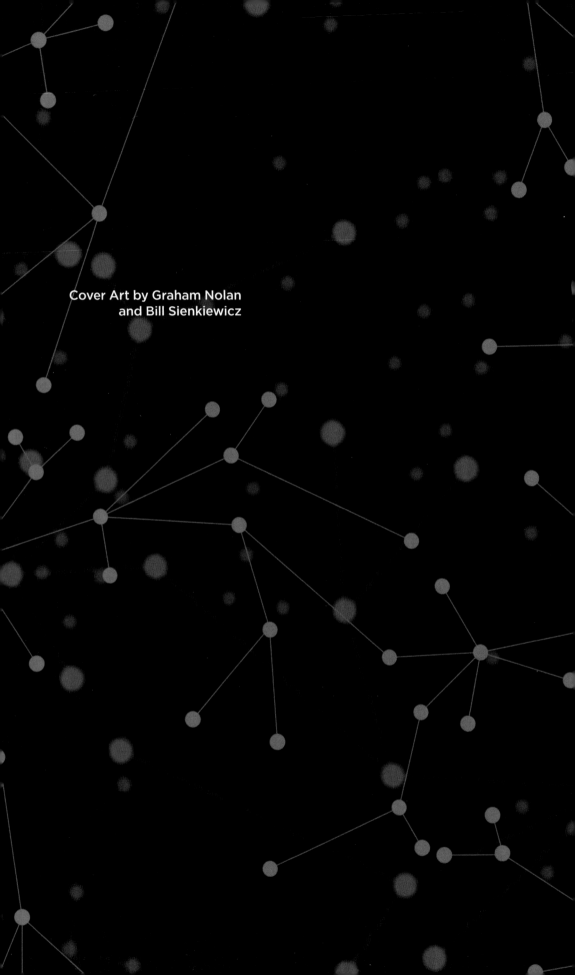

Cover Art by Graham Nolan
and Bill Sienkiewicz

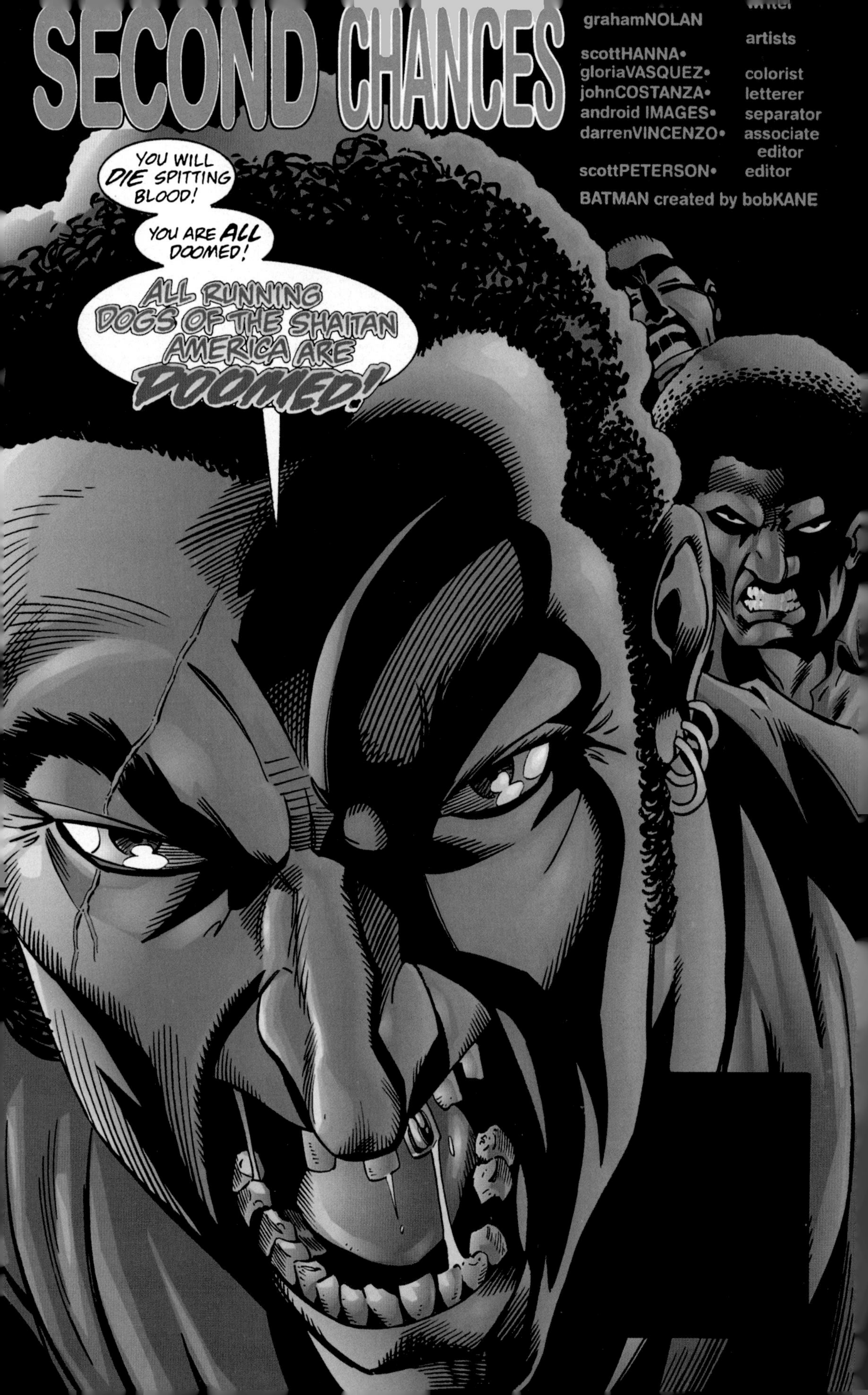
SECOND CHANCES
grahamNOLAN writer
scottHANNA• artists
gloriaVASQUEZ• colorist
johnCOSTANZA• letterer
android IMAGES• separator
darrenVINCENZO• associate editor
scottPETERSON• editor
BATMAN created by bobKANE
YOU WILL DIE SPITTING BLOOD!
YOU ARE ALL DOOMED!
ALL RUNNING DOGS OF THE SHAITAN AMERICA ARE DOOMED!

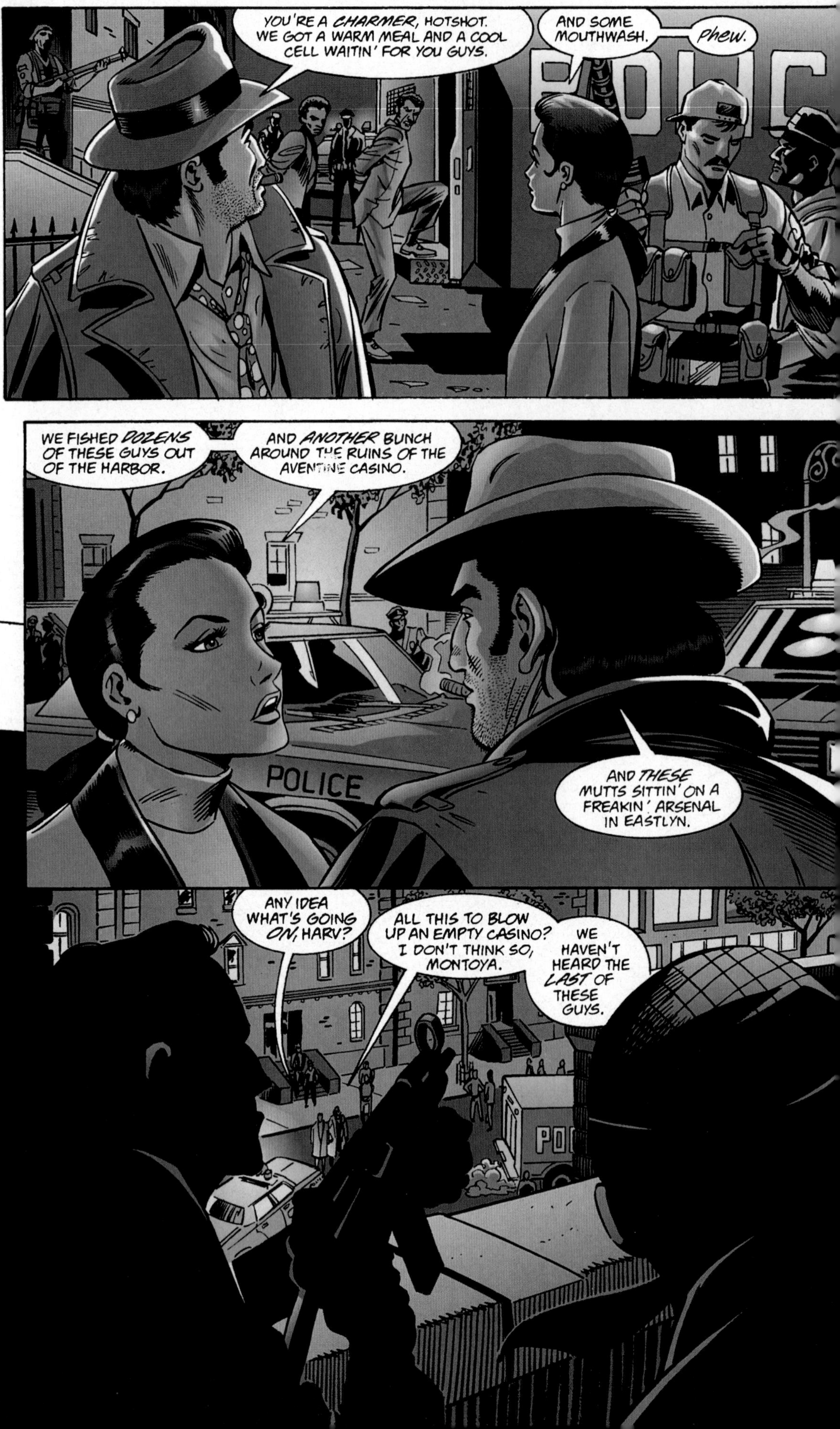

YOU'RE A CHARMER, HOTSHOT. WE GOT A WARM MEAL AND A COOL CELL WAITIN' FOR YOU GUYS.
AND SOME MOUTHWASH.
Phew.
POLIC
WE FISHED DOZENS OF THESE GUYS OUT OF THE HARBOR.
AND ANOTHER BUNCH AROUND THE RUINS OF THE AVENTINE CASINO.
POLICE
AND THESE MUTTS SITTIN' ON A FREAKIN' ARSENAL IN EASTLYN.
ANY IDEA WHAT'S GOING ON, HARV?
ALL THIS TO BLOW UP AN EMPTY CASINO? I DON'T THINK SO, MONTOYA.
WE HAVEN'T HEARD THE LAST OF THESE GUYS.
PO

--A MONUMENTAL EFFORT AS MEDICAL, POLICE, FIRE AND CITY SERVICES COME TOGETHER TO DELIVER A RARE COMMODITY.

HOPE.

ALL OVER GOTHAM THE CITIZENS FORM ORDERLY LINES--

--TO RECEIVE EITHER TREATMENT OR VACCINATIONS FOR THE EPIDEMIC THAT'S COME TO BE KNOWN AS THE CLENCH.

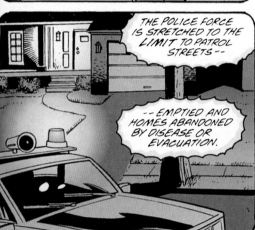

THE POLICE FORCE IS STRETCHED TO THE LIMIT TO PATROL STREETS--

--EMPTIED AND HOMES ABANDONED BY DISEASE OR EVACUATION.

A CURFEW IS IN EFFECT FOR ALL BOROUGHS OF THE CITY AND COUNTY.

ANYONE ON THE STREETS AFTER TEN P.M. WITHOUT VALID AUTHORITY WILL BE ARRESTED.

"GOTHAM AFTER DARK IS OFF LIMITS TO ALL BUT ESSENTIAL PERSONNEL."

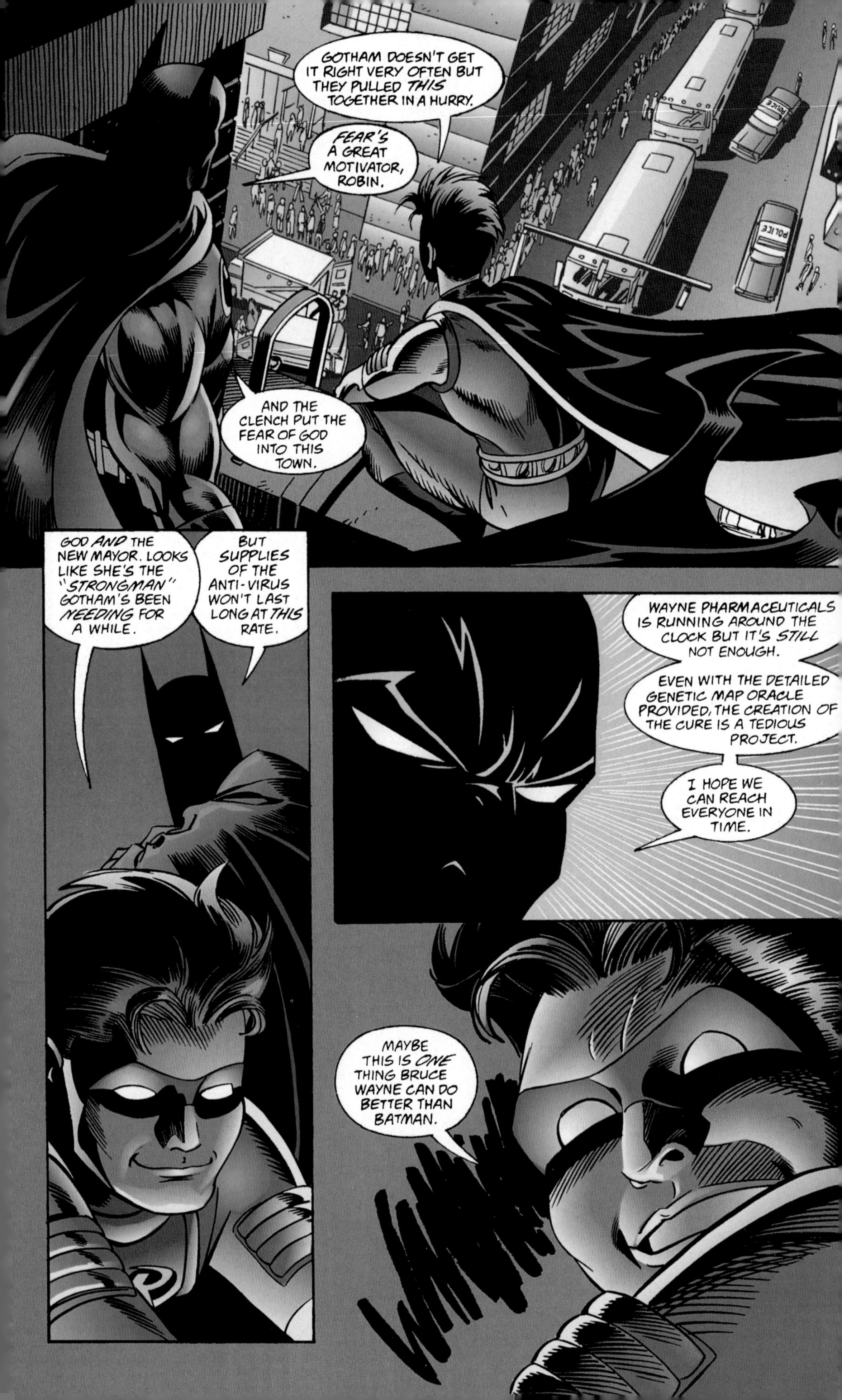
GOTHAM DOESN'T GET IT RIGHT VERY OFTEN BUT THEY PULLED THIS TOGETHER IN A HURRY.
FEAR'S A GREAT MOTIVATOR, ROBIN.
AND THE CLENCH PUT THE FEAR OF GOD INTO THIS TOWN.
POLICE
GOD AND THE NEW MAYOR. LOOKS LIKE SHE'S THE "STRONGMAN" GOTHAM'S BEEN NEEDING FOR A WHILE.
BUT SUPPLIES OF THE ANTI-VIRUS WON'T LAST LONG AT THIS RATE.
WAYNE PHARMACEUTICALS IS RUNNING AROUND THE CLOCK BUT IT'S STILL NOT ENOUGH.
EVEN WITH THE DETAILED GENETIC MAP ORACLE PROVIDED, THE CREATION OF THE CURE IS A TEDIOUS PROJECT.
I HOPE WE CAN REACH EVERYONE IN TIME.
MAYBE THIS IS ONE THING BRUCE WAYNE CAN DO BETTER THAN BATMAN.

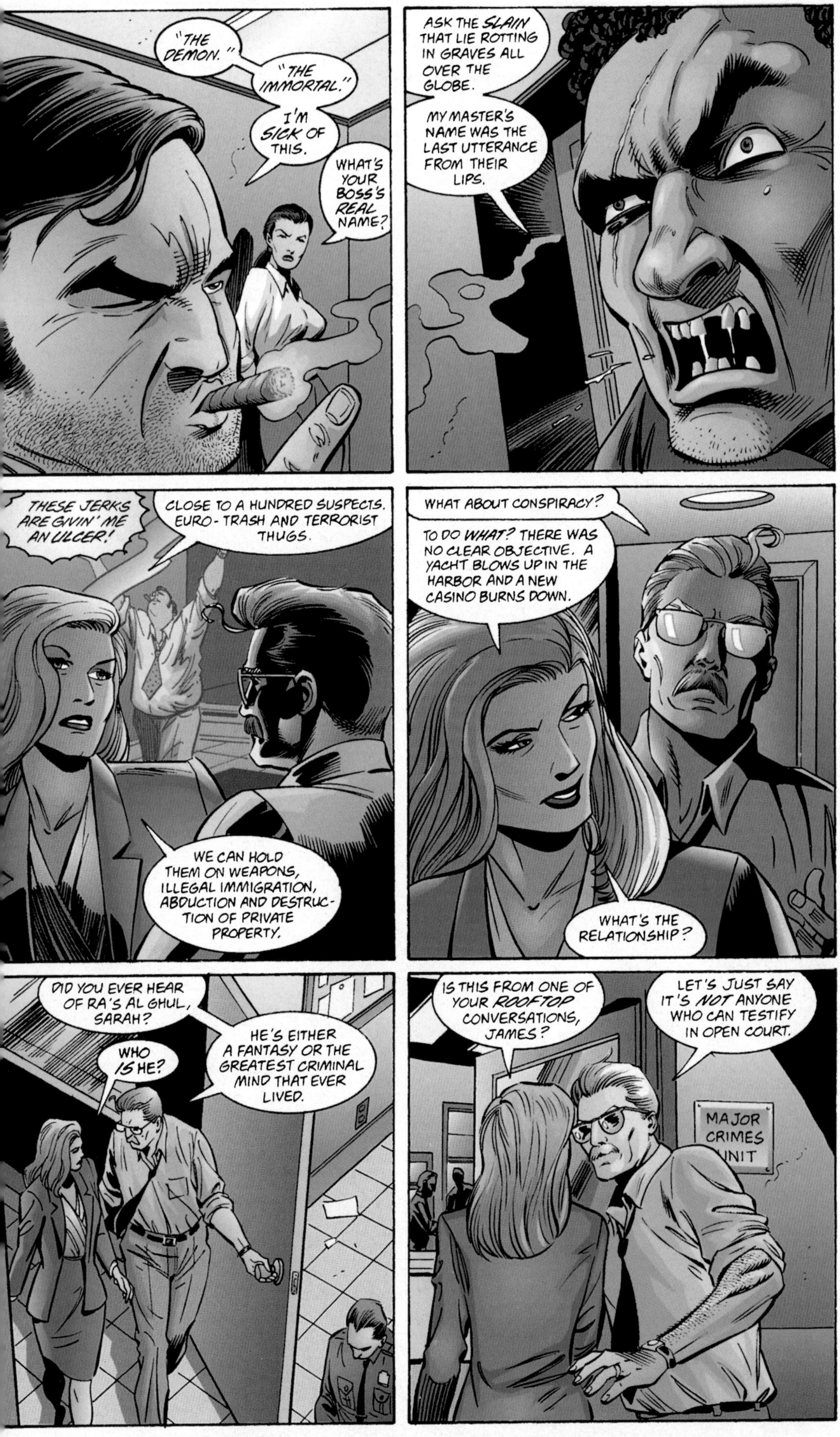
"THE DEMON."
"THE IMMORTAL."
I'M SICK OF THIS.
WHAT'S YOUR BOSS'S REAL NAME?
ASK THE SLAIN THAT LIE ROTTING IN GRAVES ALL OVER THE GLOBE.
MY MASTER'S NAME WAS THE LAST UTTERANCE FROM THEIR LIPS.
THESE JERKS ARE GIVIN' ME AN ULCER!
CLOSE TO A HUNDRED SUSPECTS. EURO-TRASH AND TERRORIST THUGS.
WE CAN HOLD THEM ON WEAPONS, ILLEGAL IMMIGRATION, ABDUCTION AND DESTRUC-TION OF PRIVATE PROPERTY.
WHAT ABOUT CONSPIRACY?
TO DO WHAT? THERE WAS NO CLEAR OBJECTIVE. A YACHT BLOWS UP IN THE HARBOR AND A NEW CASINO BURNS DOWN.
WHAT'S THE RELATIONSHIP?
DID YOU EVER HEAR OF RA'S AL GHUL, SARAH?
WHO IS HE?
HE'S EITHER A FANTASY OR THE GREATEST CRIMINAL MIND THAT EVER LIVED.
IS THIS FROM ONE OF YOUR ROOFTOP CONVERSATIONS, JAMES?
LET'S JUST SAY IT'S NOT ANYONE WHO CAN TESTIFY IN OPEN COURT.
MAJOR CRIMES UNIT

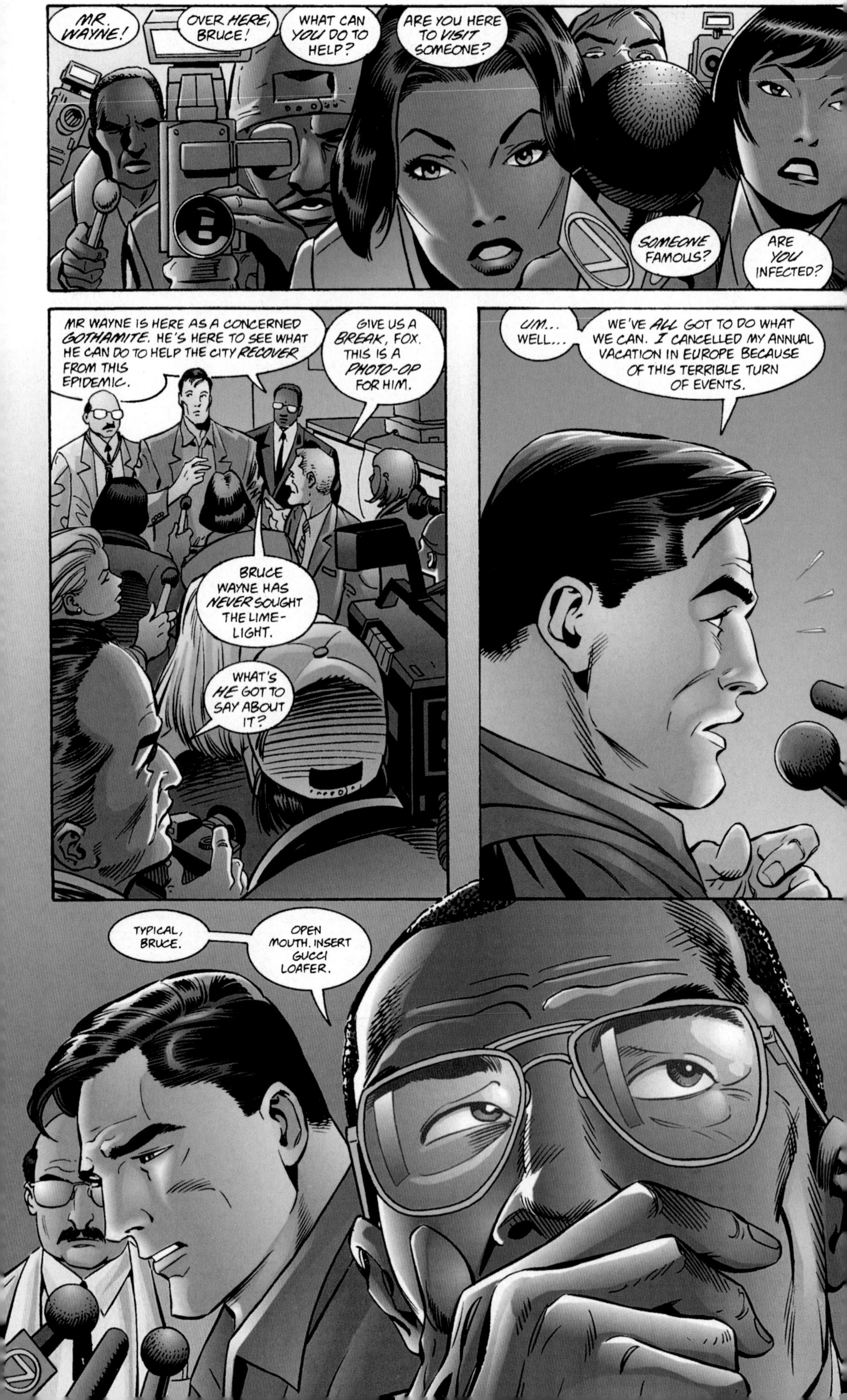
MR. WAYNE!
OVER HERE, BRUCE!
WHAT CAN YOU DO TO HELP?
ARE YOU HERE TO VISIT SOMEONE?
SOMEONE FAMOUS?
ARE YOU INFECTED?
MR WAYNE IS HERE AS A CONCERNED GOTHAMITE. HE'S HERE TO SEE WHAT HE CAN DO TO HELP THE CITY RECOVER FROM THIS EPIDEMIC.
GIVE US A BREAK, FOX. THIS IS A PHOTO-OP FOR HIM.
BRUCE WAYNE HAS NEVER SOUGHT THE LIME-LIGHT.
WHAT'S HE GOT TO SAY ABOUT IT?
UM... WELL...
WE'VE ALL GOT TO DO WHAT WE CAN. I CANCELLED MY ANNUAL VACATION IN EUROPE BECAUSE OF THIS TERRIBLE TURN OF EVENTS.
TYPICAL, BRUCE.
OPEN MOUTH. INSERT GUCCI LOAFER.

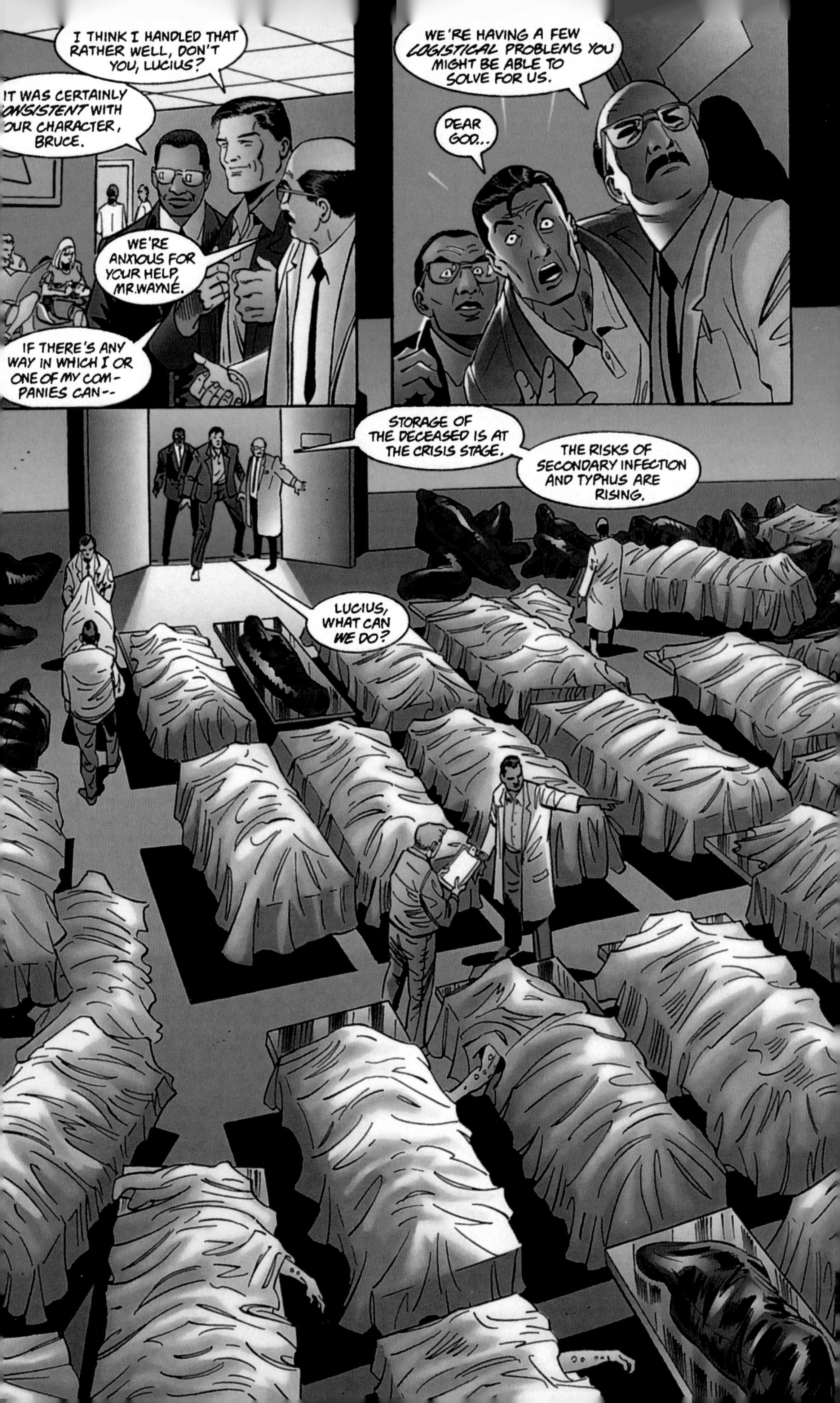
I THINK I HANDLED THAT RATHER WELL, DON'T YOU, LUCIUS?
IT WAS CERTAINLY CONSISTENT WITH YOUR CHARACTER, BRUCE.
WE'RE ANXIOUS FOR YOUR HELP, MR.WAYNE.
IF THERE'S ANY WAY IN WHICH I OR ONE OF MY COMPANIES CAN--
WE'RE HAVING A FEW LOGISTICAL PROBLEMS YOU MIGHT BE ABLE TO SOLVE FOR US.
DEAR GOD...
STORAGE OF THE DECEASED IS AT THE CRISIS STAGE.
THE RISKS OF SECONDARY INFECTION AND TYPHUS ARE RISING.
LUCIUS, WHAT CAN WE DO?

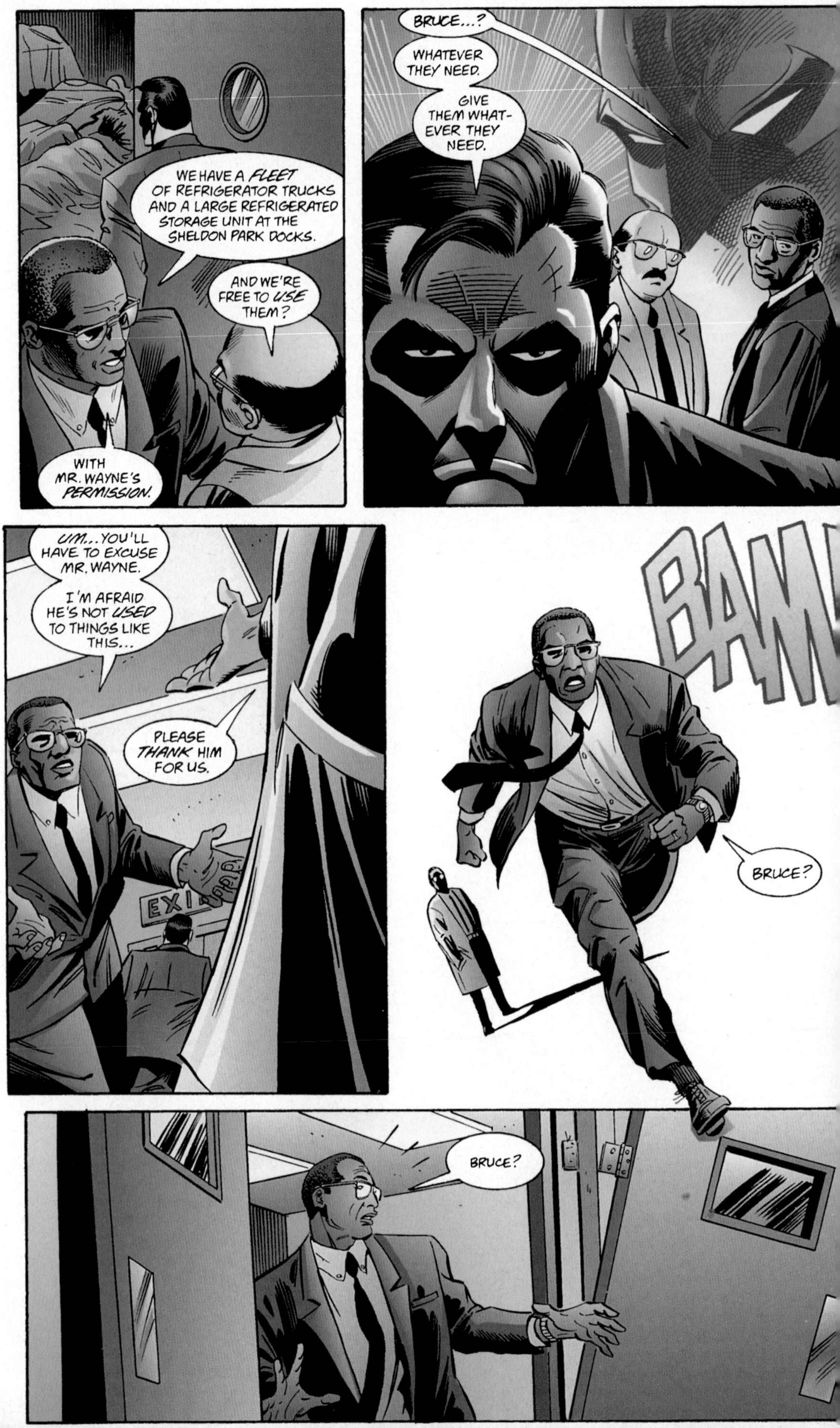
WE HAVE A FLEET OF REFRIGERATOR TRUCKS AND A LARGE REFRIGERATED STORAGE UNIT AT THE SHELDON PARK DOCKS.
AND WE'RE FREE TO USE THEM?
WITH MR. WAYNE'S PERMISSION.
BRUCE...?
WHATEVER THEY NEED.
GIVE THEM WHAT-EVER THEY NEED.
UM... YOU'LL HAVE TO EXCUSE MR. WAYNE.
I'M AFRAID HE'S NOT USED TO THINGS LIKE THIS...
PLEASE THANK HIM FOR US.
BAM
BRUCE?
BRUCE?

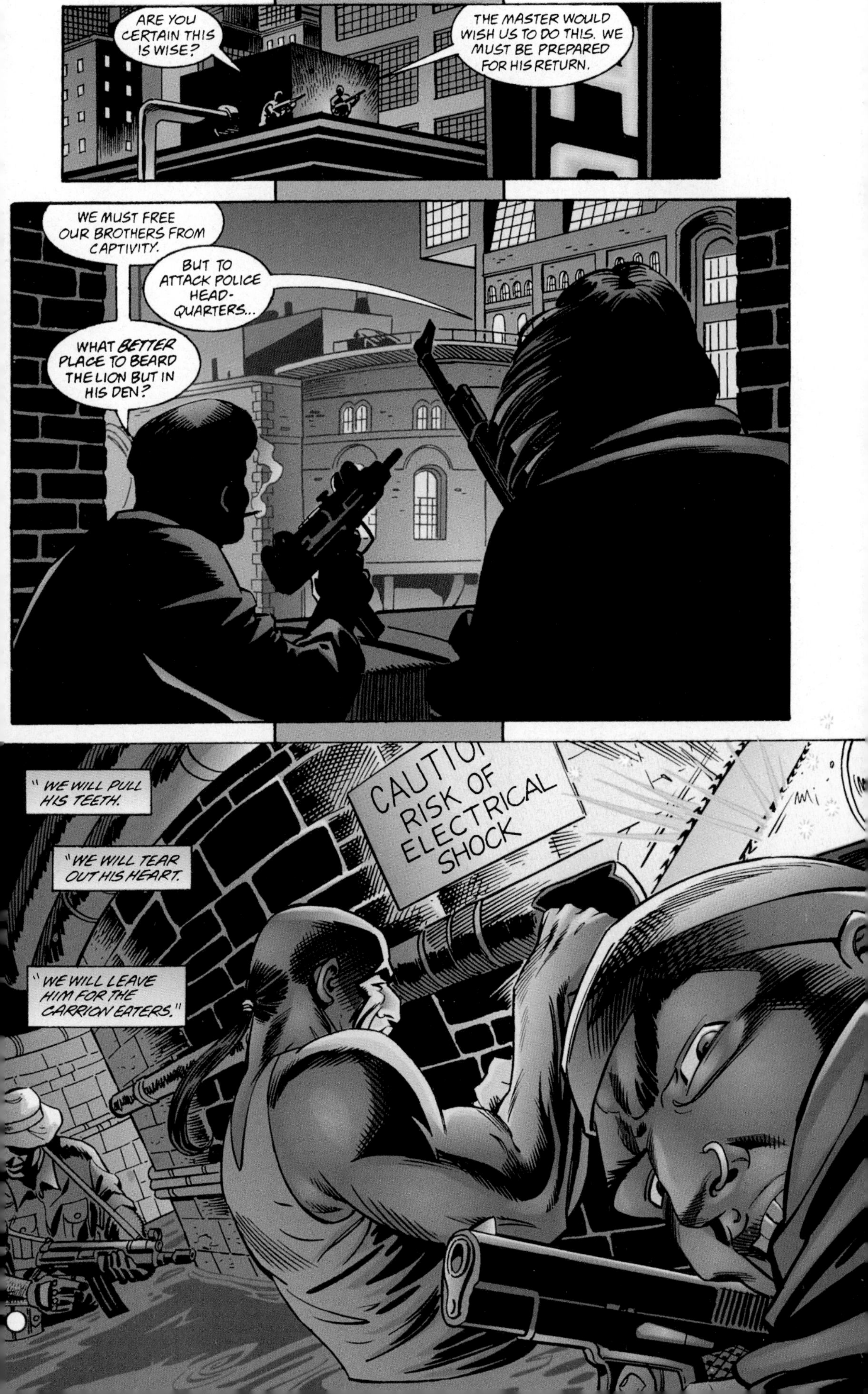
ARE YOU CERTAIN THIS IS WISE?
THE MASTER WOULD WISH US TO DO THIS. WE MUST BE PREPARED FOR HIS RETURN.
WE MUST FREE OUR BROTHERS FROM CAPTIVITY.
BUT TO ATTACK POLICE HEAD-QUARTERS...
WHAT BETTER PLACE TO BEARD THE LION BUT IN HIS DEN?
"WE WILL PULL HIS TEETH.
"WE WILL TEAR OUT HIS HEART.
"WE WILL LEAVE HIM FOR THE CARRION EATERS."
CAUTIO RISK OF ELECTRICAL SHOCK

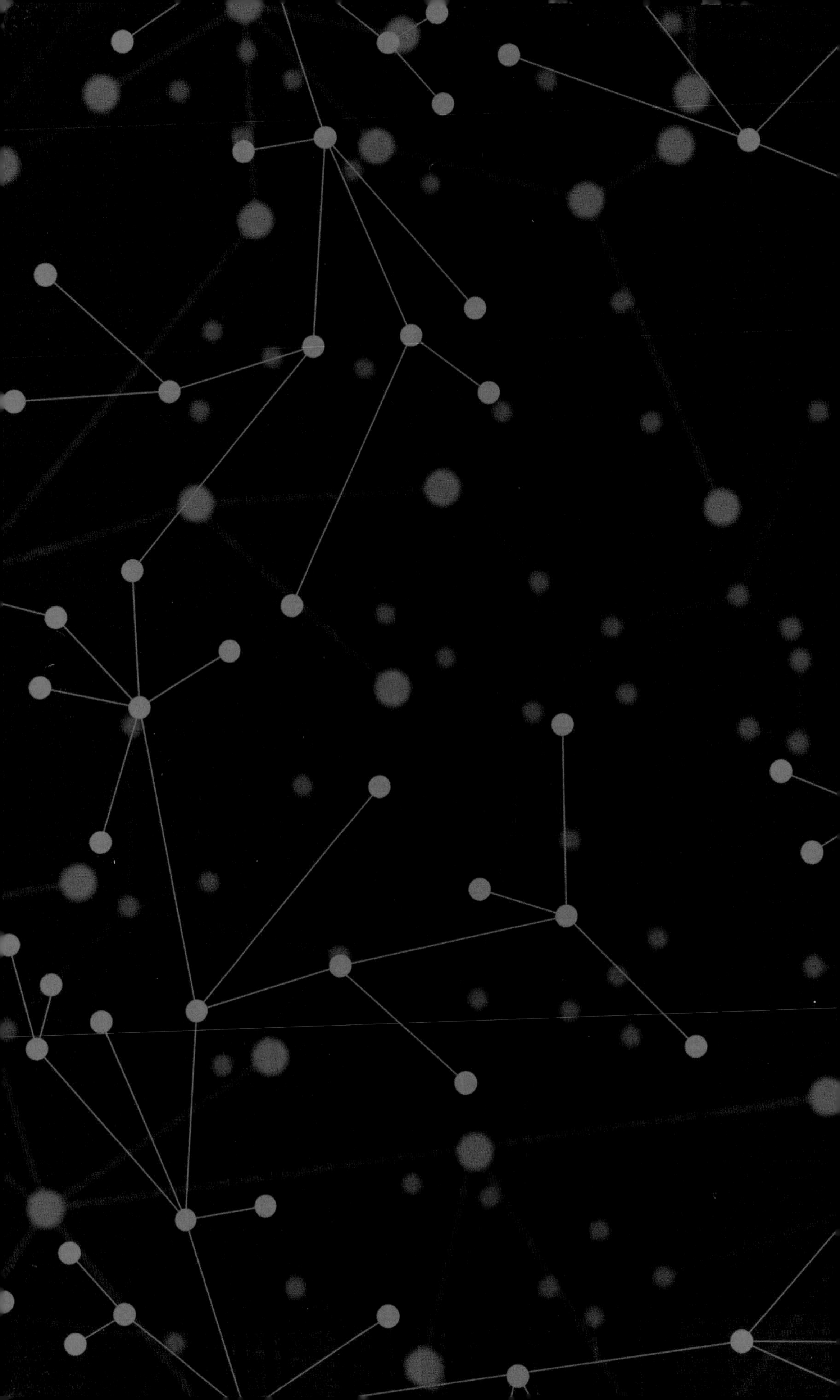

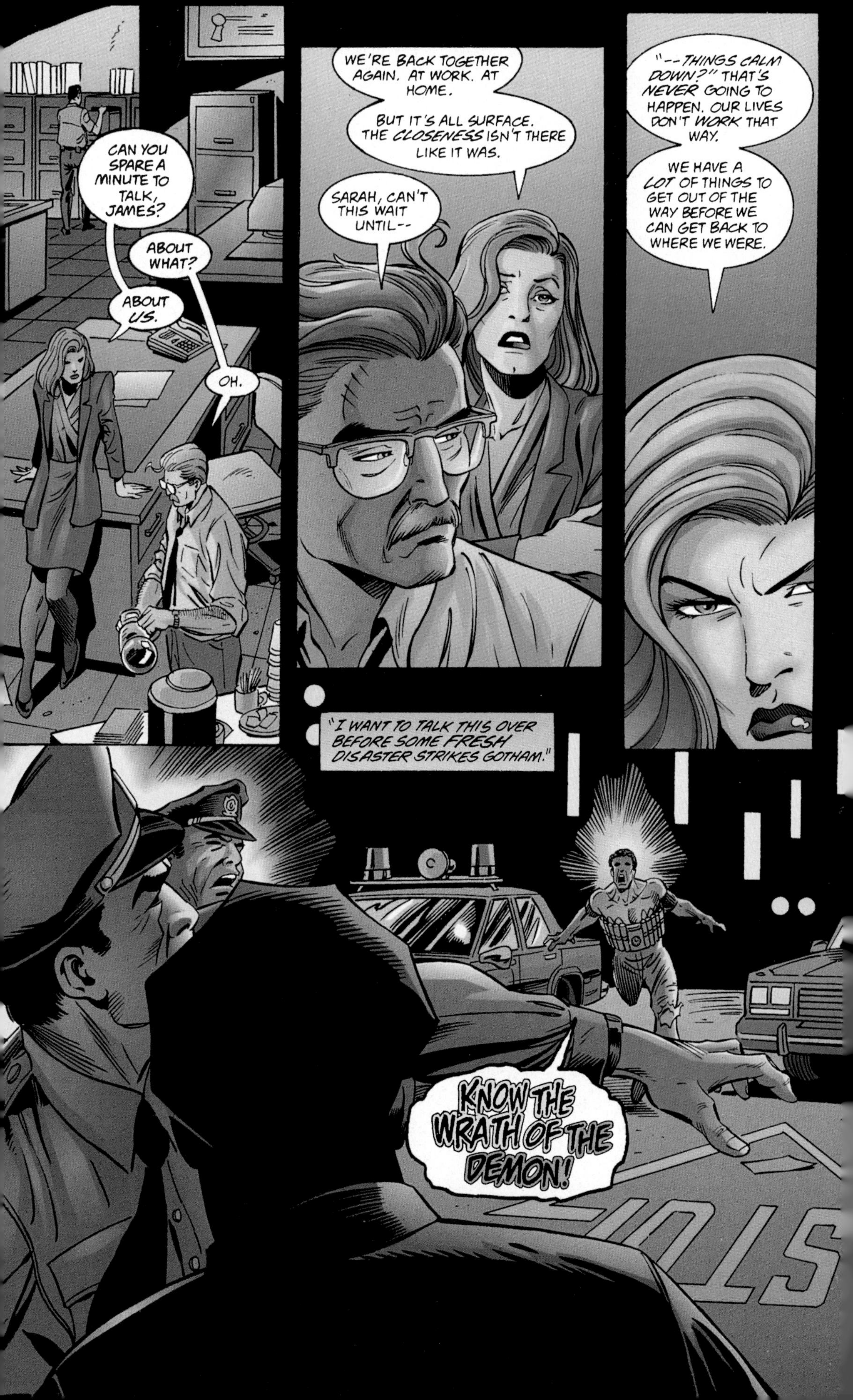
CAN YOU SPARE A MINUTE TO TALK, JAMES?
ABOUT WHAT?
ABOUT US.
OH.
WE'RE BACK TOGETHER AGAIN. AT WORK. AT HOME.
BUT IT'S ALL SURFACE. THE CLOSENESS ISN'T THERE LIKE IT WAS.
SARAH, CAN'T THIS WAIT UNTIL--
"--THINGS CALM DOWN?" THAT'S NEVER GOING TO HAPPEN. OUR LIVES DON'T WORK THAT WAY.
WE HAVE A LOT OF THINGS TO GET OUT OF THE WAY BEFORE WE CAN GET BACK TO WHERE WE WERE.
"I WANT TO TALK THIS OVER BEFORE SOME FRESH DISASTER STRIKES GOTHAM."
KNOW THE WRATH OF THE DEMON!

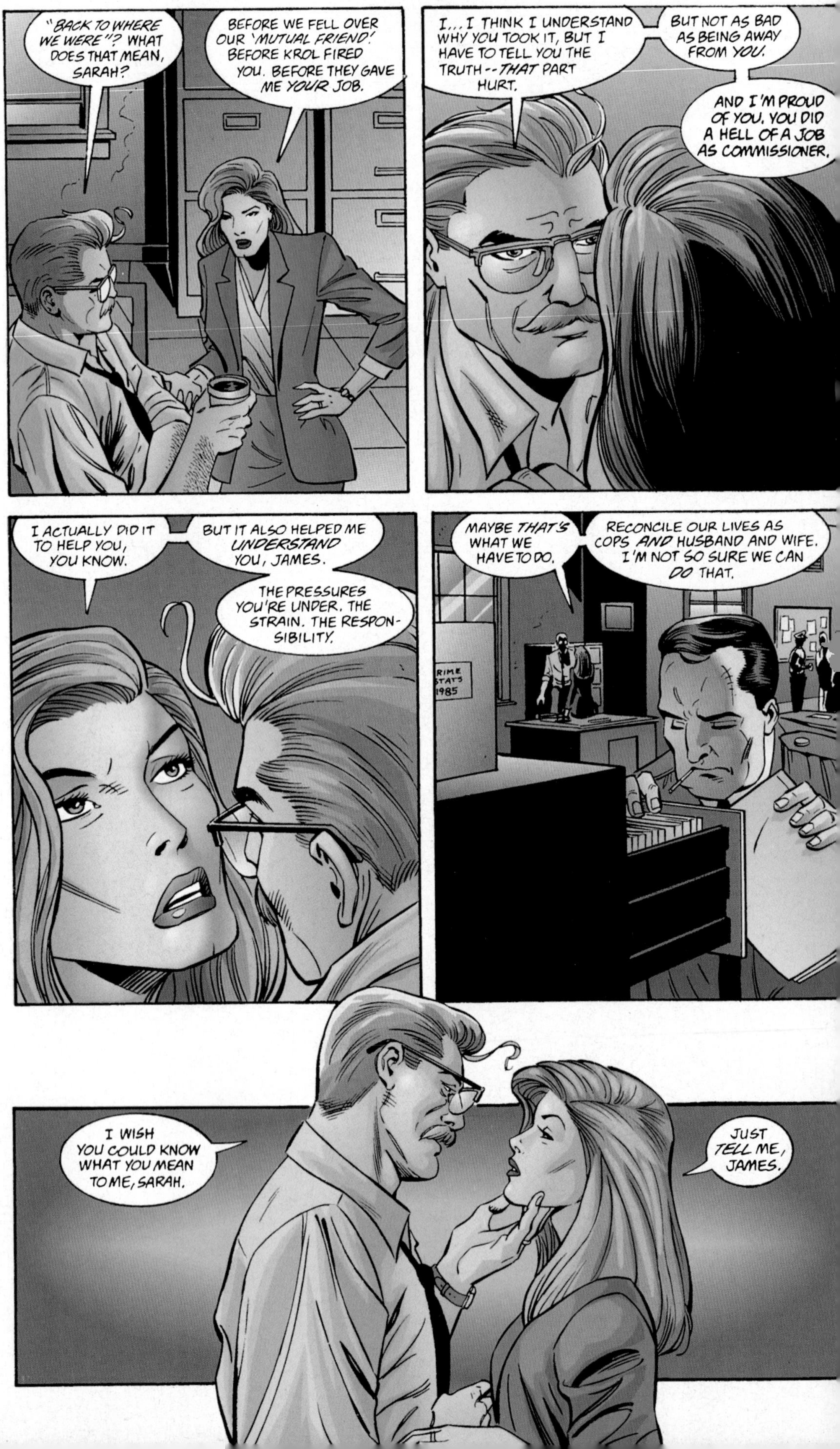
"BACK TO WHERE WE WERE"? WHAT DOES THAT MEAN, SARAH?
BEFORE WE FELL OVER OUR 'MUTUAL FRIEND.' BEFORE KROL FIRED YOU. BEFORE THEY GAVE ME YOUR JOB.
I... I THINK I UNDERSTAND WHY YOU TOOK IT, BUT I HAVE TO TELL YOU THE TRUTH -- THAT PART HURT.
BUT NOT AS BAD AS BEING AWAY FROM YOU.
AND I'M PROUD OF YOU. YOU DID A HELL OF A JOB AS COMMISSIONER.
I ACTUALLY DID IT TO HELP YOU, YOU KNOW.
BUT IT ALSO HELPED ME UNDERSTAND YOU, JAMES.
THE PRESSURES YOU'RE UNDER. THE STRAIN. THE RESPONSIBILITY.
MAYBE THAT'S WHAT WE HAVE TO DO.
RECONCILE OUR LIVES AS COPS AND HUSBAND AND WIFE. I'M NOT SO SURE WE CAN DO THAT.
RIME STATS 1985
I WISH YOU COULD KNOW WHAT YOU MEAN TO ME, SARAH.
JUST TELL ME, JAMES.

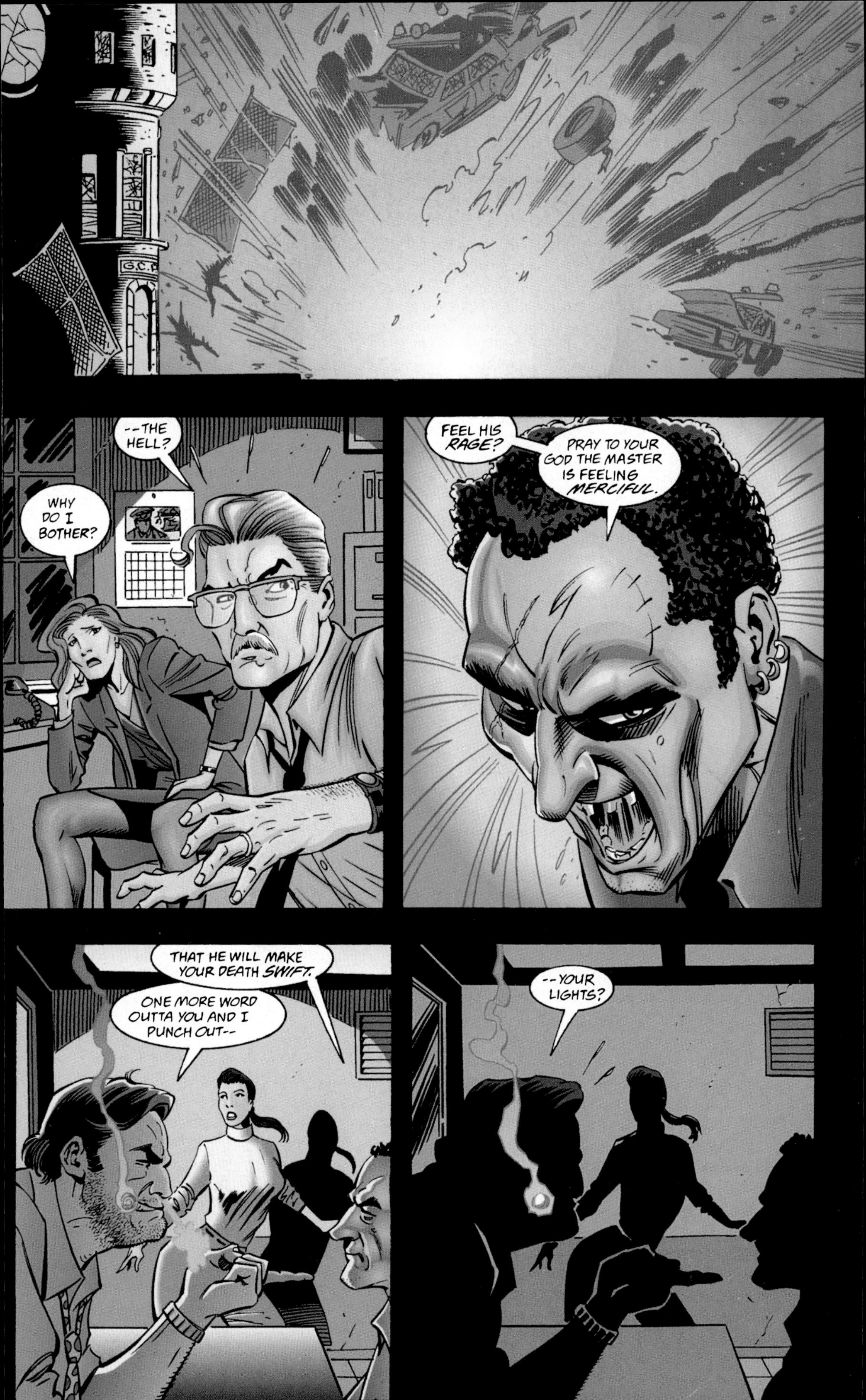
--THE HELL?
WHY DO I BOTHER?
FEEL HIS RAGE?
PRAY TO YOUR GOD THE MASTER IS FEELING MERCIFUL.
THAT HE WILL MAKE YOUR DEATH SWIFT.
ONE MORE WORD OUTTA YOU AND I PUNCH OUT--
--YOUR LIGHTS?

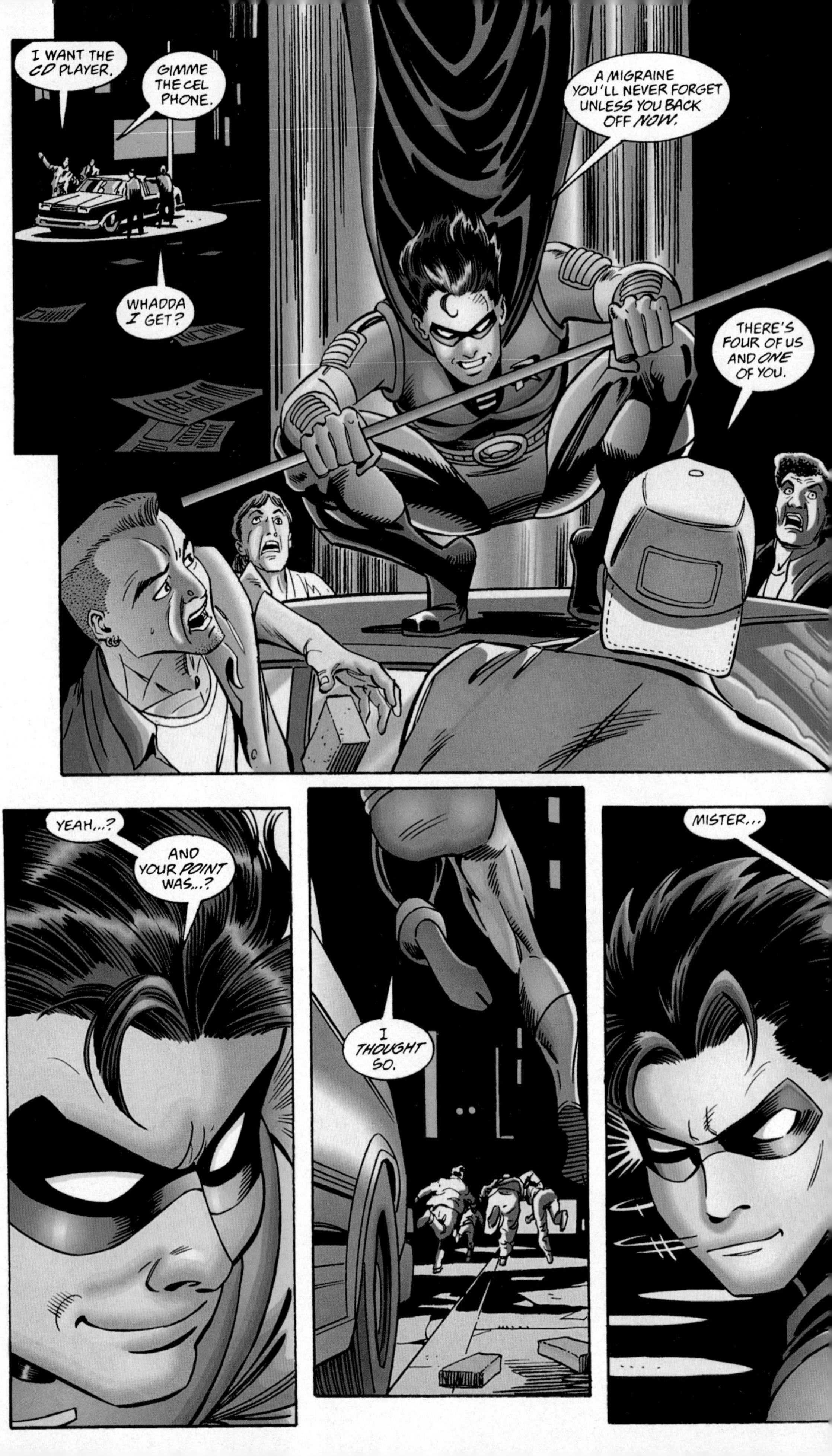
I WANT THE CD PLAYER.
GIMME THE CEL PHONE.
WHADDA I GET?
A MIGRAINE YOU'LL NEVER FORGET UNLESS YOU BACK OFF NOW.
THERE'S FOUR OF US AND ONE OF YOU.
YEAH...?
AND YOUR POINT WAS...?
I THOUGHT SO.
MISTER...

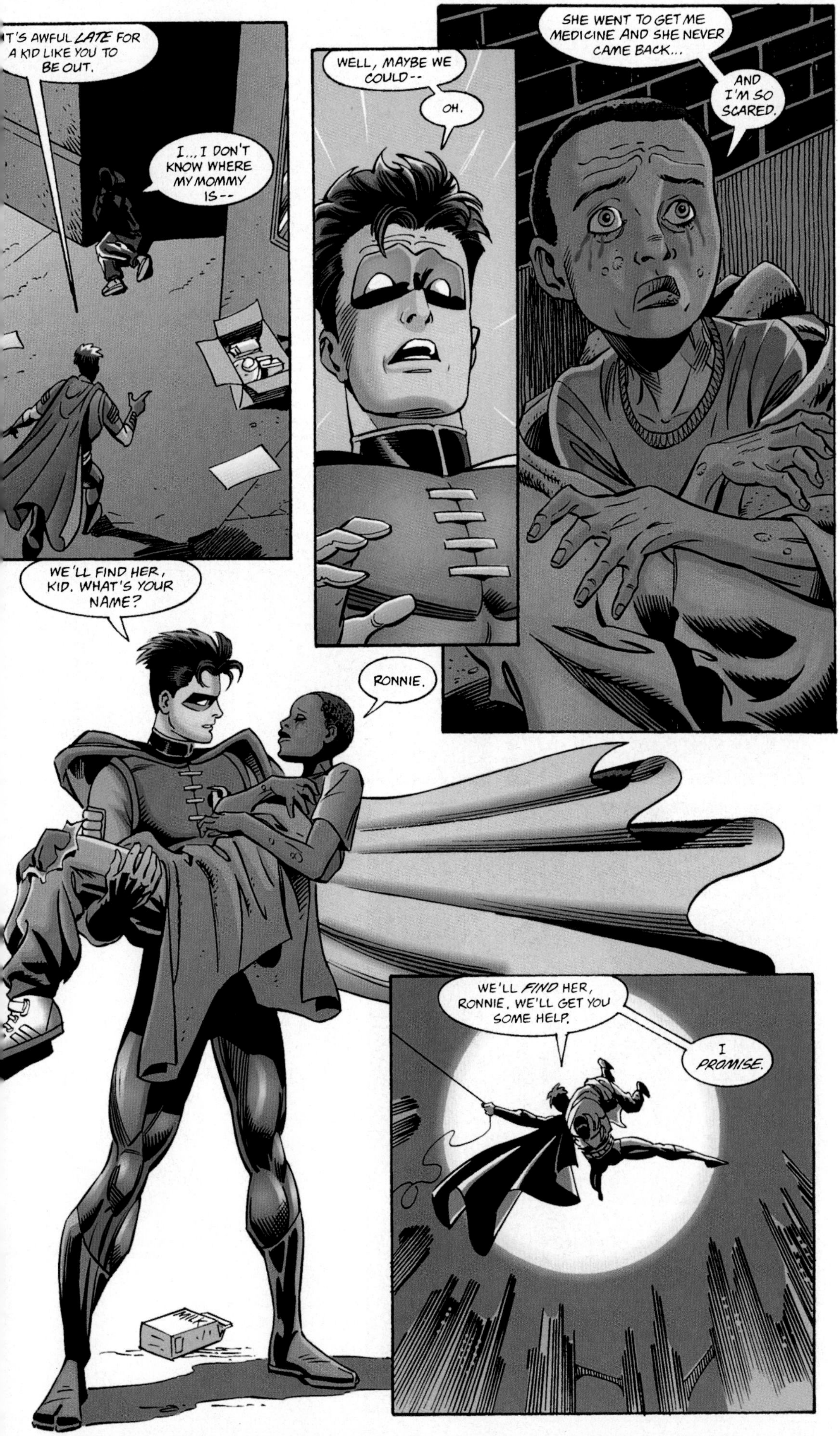
T'S AWFUL LATE FOR A KID LIKE YOU TO BE OUT.
I... I DON'T KNOW WHERE MY MOMMY IS--
WELL, MAYBE WE COULD--
OH.
SHE WENT TO GET ME MEDICINE AND SHE NEVER CAME BACK...
AND I'M SO SCARED.
WE'LL FIND HER, KID. WHAT'S YOUR NAME?
RONNIE.
MILK
WE'LL FIND HER, RONNIE. WE'LL GET YOU SOME HELP.
I PROMISE.

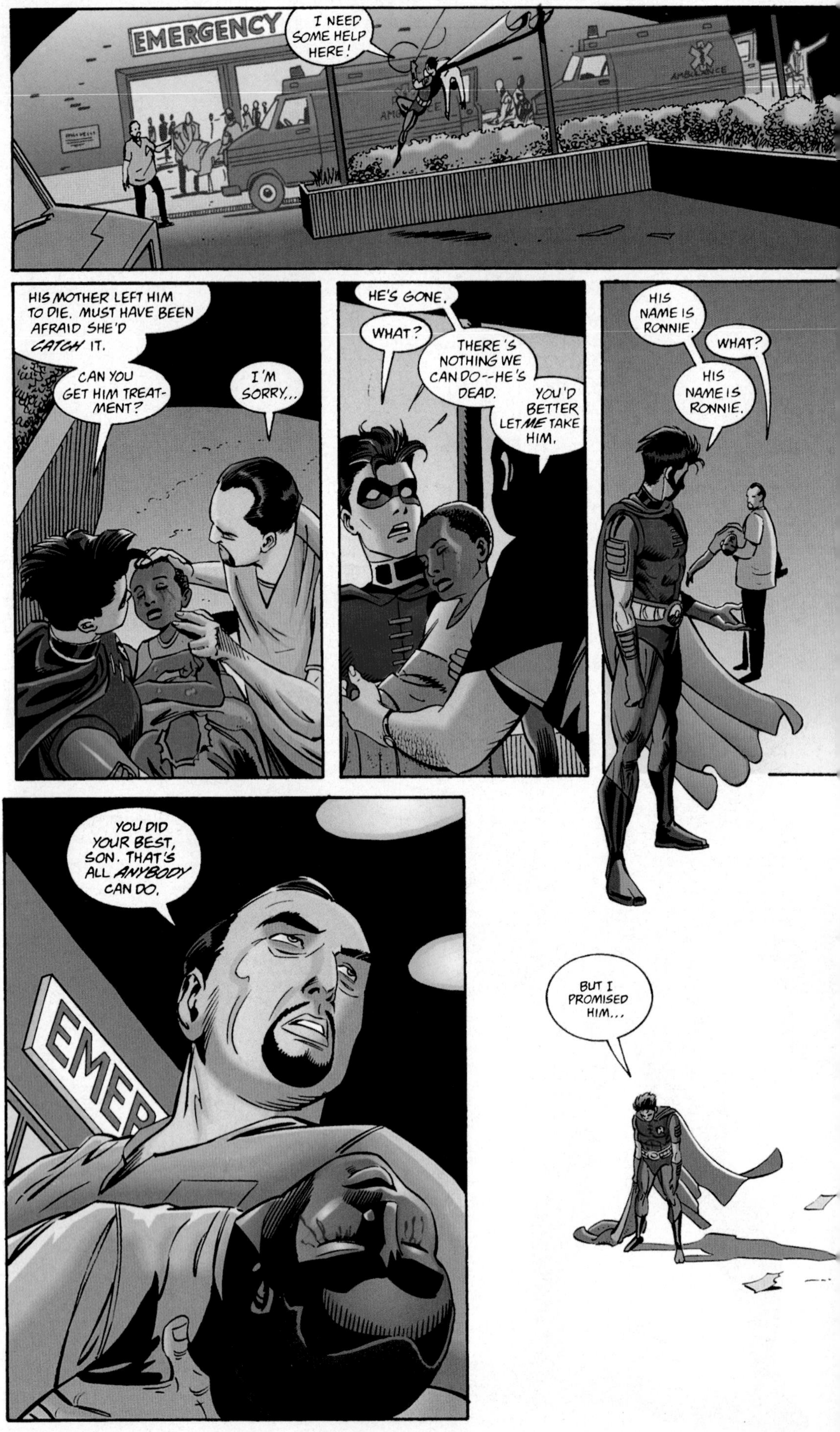
EMERGENCY
I NEED SOME HELP HERE!
HIS MOTHER LEFT HIM TO DIE. MUST HAVE BEEN AFRAID SHE'D CATCH IT.
CAN YOU GET HIM TREATMENT?
I'M SORRY...
HE'S GONE.
WHAT?
THERE'S NOTHING WE CAN DO--HE'S DEAD.
YOU'D BETTER LET ME TAKE HIM.
HIS NAME IS RONNIE.
WHAT?
HIS NAME IS RONNIE.
YOU DID YOUR BEST, SON. THAT'S ALL ANYBODY CAN DO.
EMER
BUT I PROMISED HIM...

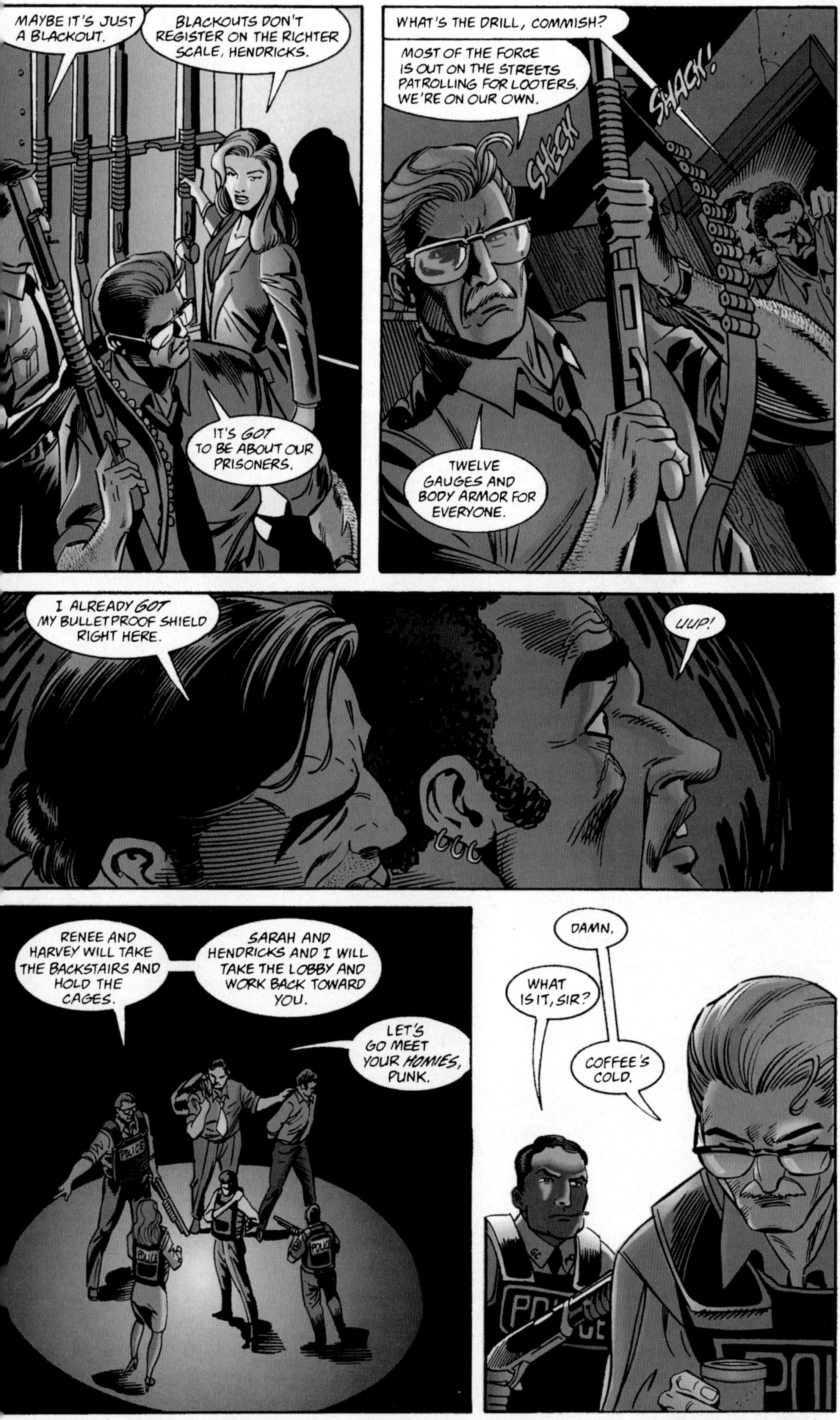
MAYBE IT'S JUST A BLACKOUT.
BLACKOUTS DON'T REGISTER ON THE RICHTER SCALE, HENDRICKS.
IT'S *GOT* TO BE ABOUT OUR PRISONERS.
WHAT'S THE DRILL, COMMISH?
MOST OF THE FORCE IS OUT ON THE STREETS PATROLLING FOR LOOTERS. WE'RE ON OUR OWN.
SHACK!
SHACK
TWELVE GAUGES AND BODY ARMOR FOR EVERYONE.
I ALREADY *GOT* MY BULLETPROOF SHIELD RIGHT HERE.
UUP!
RENEE AND HARVEY WILL TAKE THE BACKSTAIRS AND HOLD THE CAGES.
SARAH AND HENDRICKS AND I WILL TAKE THE LOBBY AND WORK BACK TOWARD YOU.
LET'S GO MEET YOUR *HOMIES*, PUNK.
POLICE
DAMN.
WHAT IS IT, SIR?
COFFEE'S COLD.

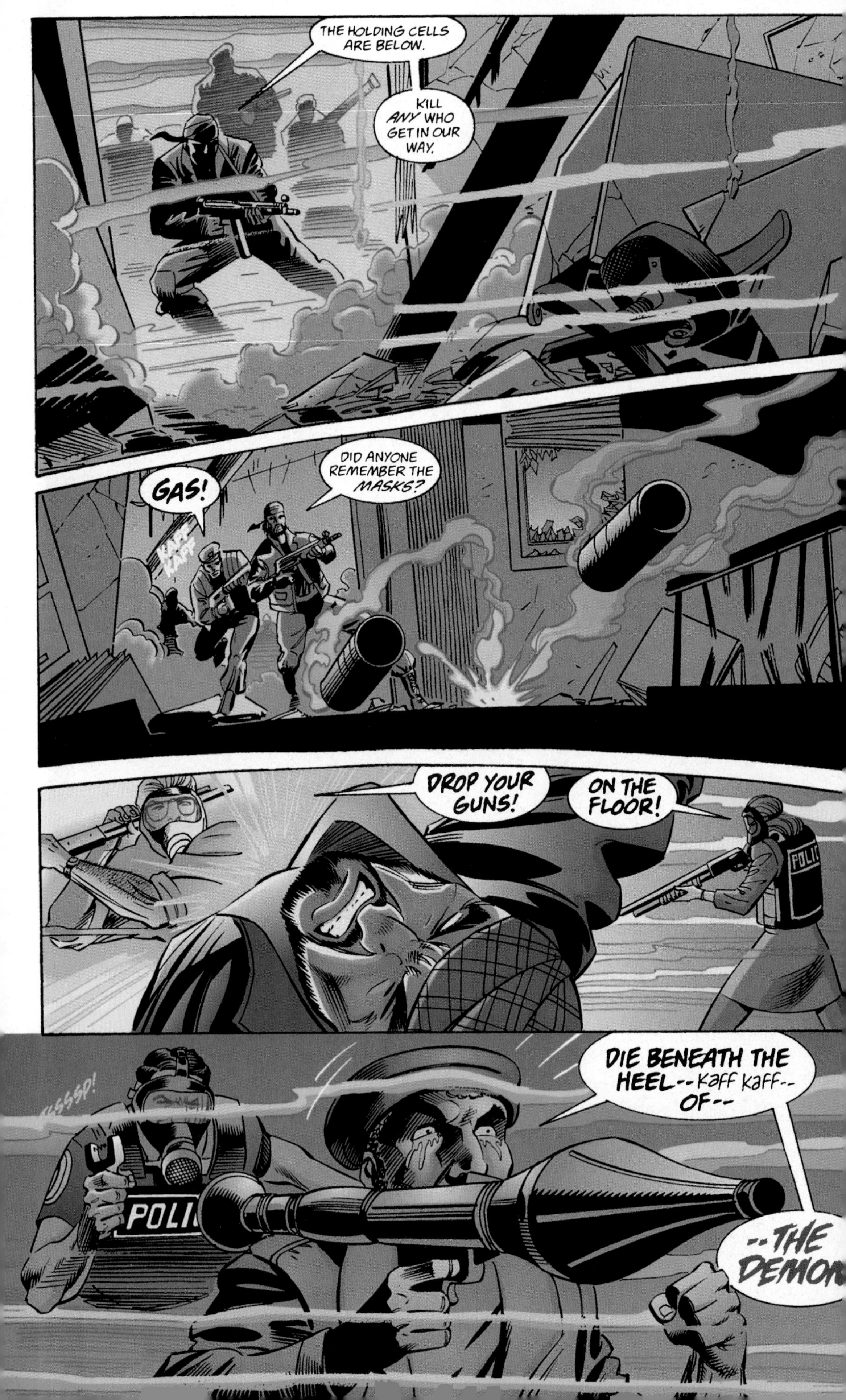
THE HOLDING CELLS ARE BELOW.
KILL ANY WHO GET IN OUR WAY.
GAS!
KAFF KAFF
DID ANYONE REMEMBER THE MASKS?
DROP YOUR GUNS!
ON THE FLOOR!
POLIC
RSSSP!
POLIC
DIE BENEATH THE HEEL--kaff kaff--OF--
--THE DEMON

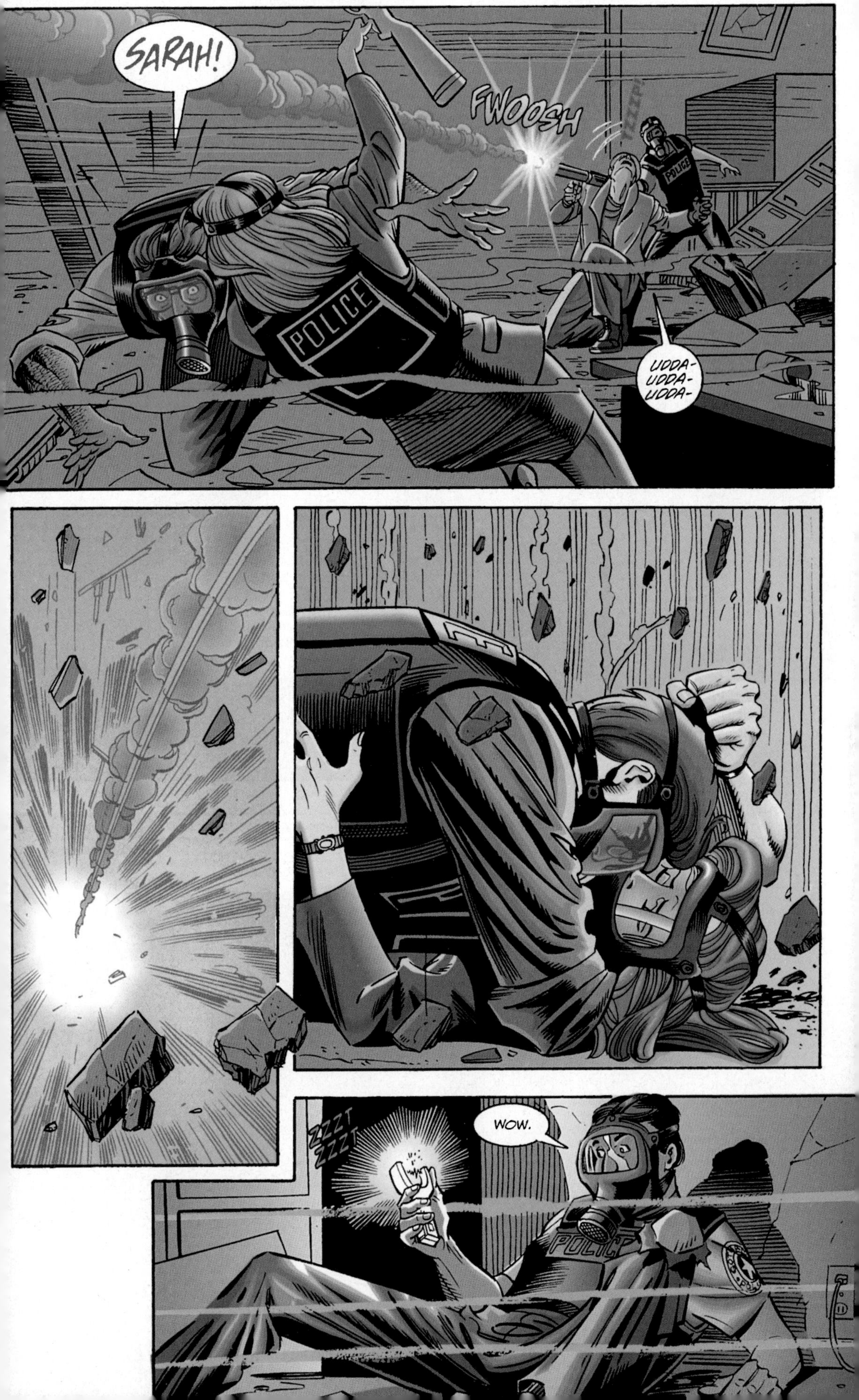
SARAH!
FWOOSH
UDDA-
UDDA-
UDDA-
ZZZT
ZZZT
WOW.

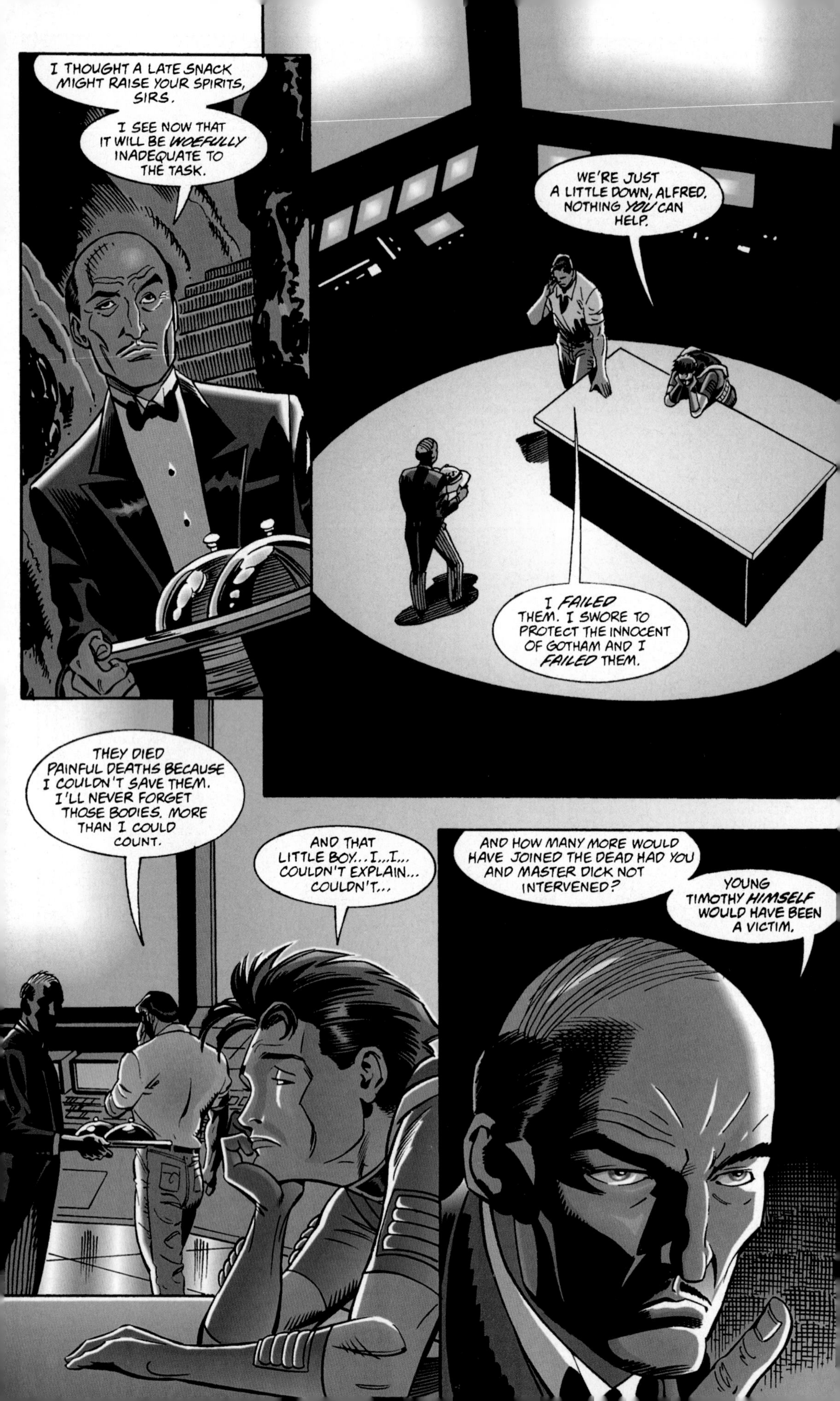
I THOUGHT A LATE SNACK MIGHT RAISE YOUR SPIRITS, SIRS.
I SEE NOW THAT IT WILL BE WOEFULLY INADEQUATE TO THE TASK.
WE'RE JUST A LITTLE DOWN, ALFRED. NOTHING YOU CAN HELP.
I FAILED THEM. I SWORE TO PROTECT THE INNOCENT OF GOTHAM AND I FAILED THEM.
THEY DIED PAINFUL DEATHS BECAUSE I COULDN'T SAVE THEM. I'LL NEVER FORGET THOSE BODIES. MORE THAN I COULD COUNT.
AND THAT LITTLE BOY... I...I... COULDN'T EXPLAIN... COULDN'T...
AND HOW MANY MORE WOULD HAVE JOINED THE DEAD HAD YOU AND MASTER DICK NOT INTERVENED?
YOUNG TIMOTHY HIMSELF WOULD HAVE BEEN A VICTIM.

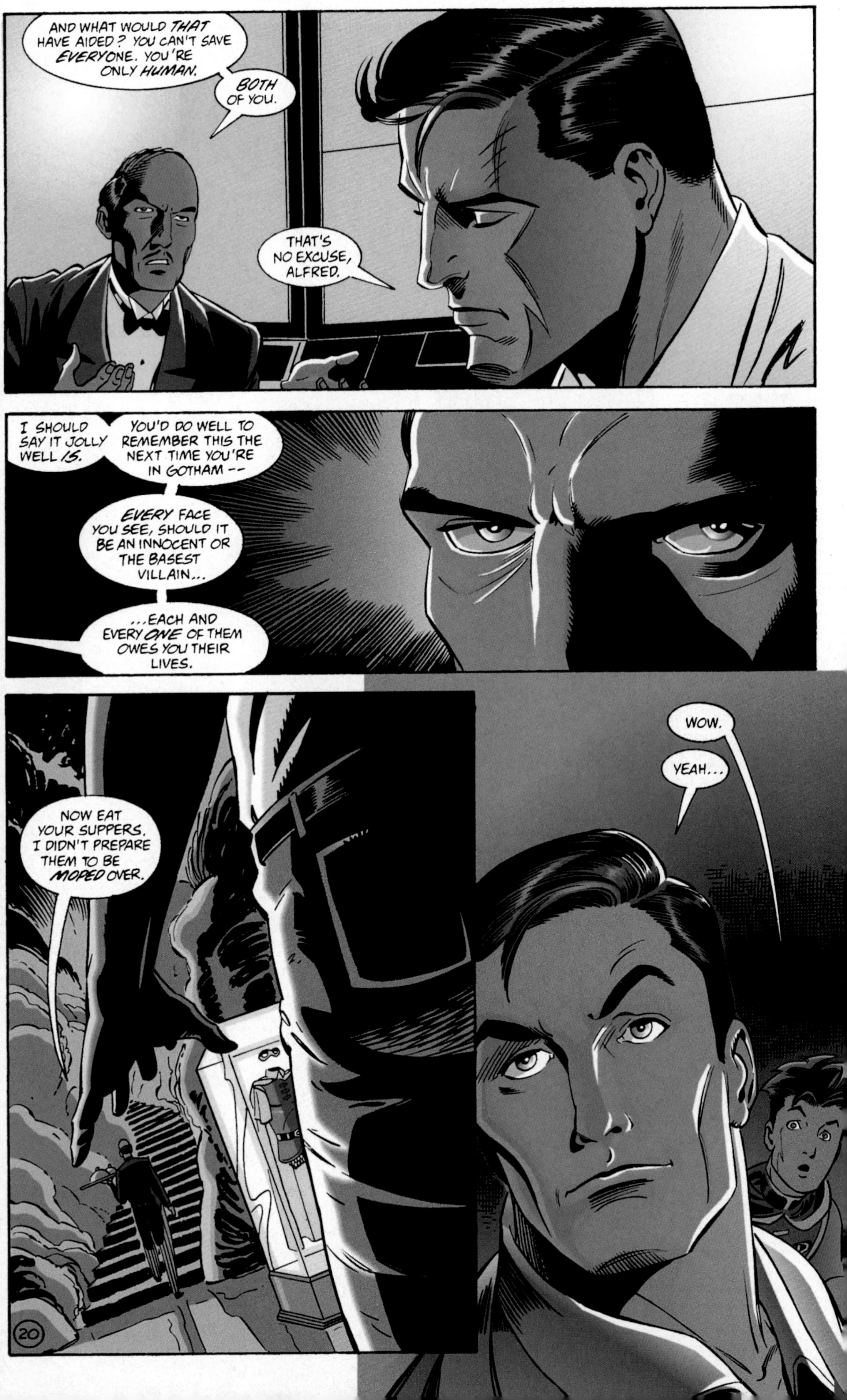
AND WHAT WOULD THAT HAVE AIDED? YOU CAN'T SAVE EVERYONE. YOU'RE ONLY HUMAN.
BOTH OF YOU.
THAT'S NO EXCUSE, ALFRED.
I SHOULD SAY IT JOLLY WELL IS.
YOU'D DO WELL TO REMEMBER THIS THE NEXT TIME YOU'RE IN GOTHAM --
EVERY FACE YOU SEE, SHOULD IT BE AN INNOCENT OR THE BASEST VILLAIN...
...EACH AND EVERY ONE OF THEM OWES YOU THEIR LIVES.
NOW EAT YOUR SUPPERS. I DIDN'T PREPARE THEM TO BE MOPED OVER.
WOW.
YEAH...
20

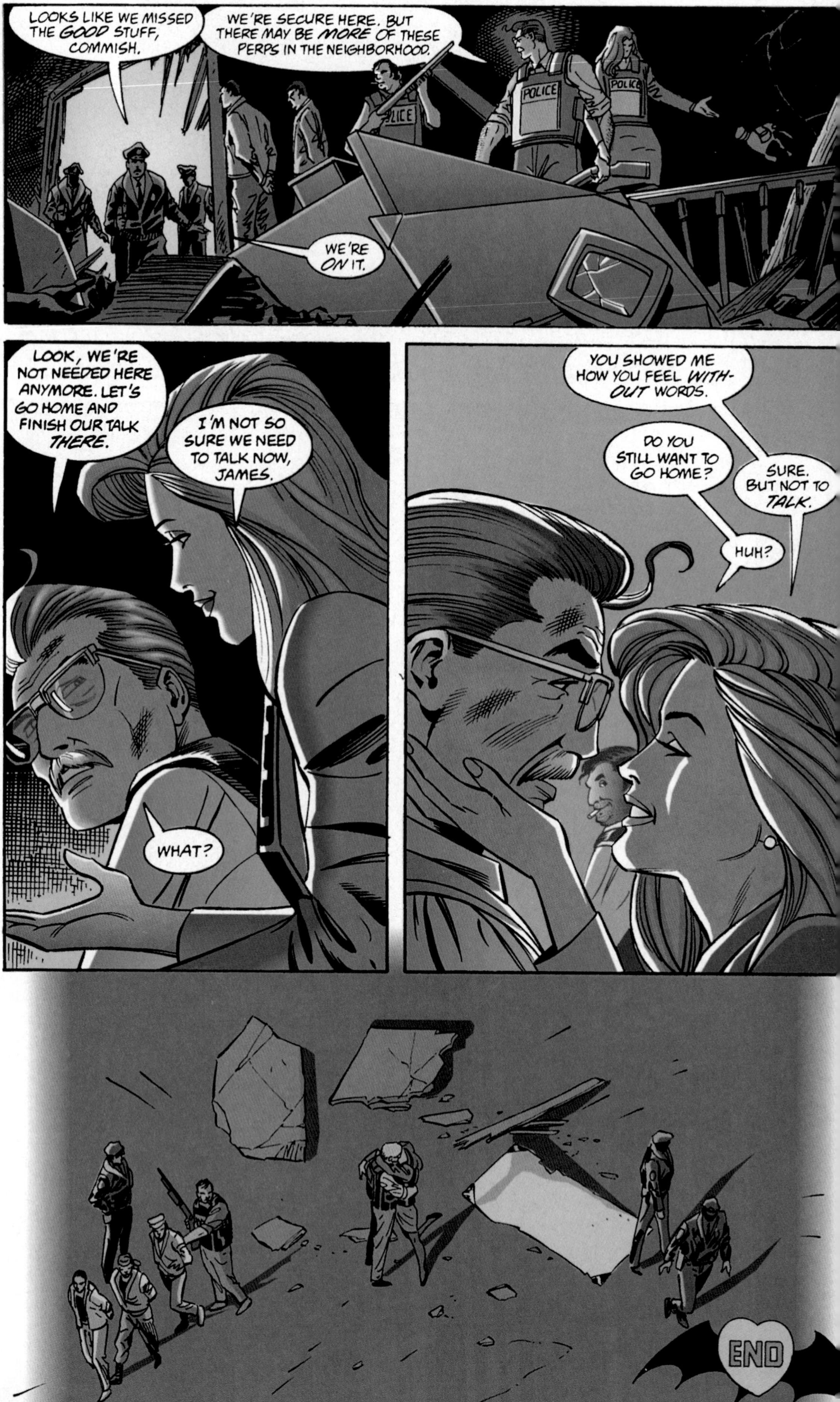
LOOKS LIKE WE MISSED THE *GOOD* STUFF, COMMISH.
WE'RE SECURE HERE. BUT THERE MAY BE *MORE* OF THESE PERPS IN THE NEIGHBORHOOD.
POLICE
POLICE
POLICE
WE'RE *ON* IT.
LOOK, WE'RE NOT NEEDED HERE ANYMORE. LET'S GO HOME AND FINISH OUR TALK *THERE*.
I'M NOT SO SURE WE NEED TO TALK NOW, JAMES.
WHAT?
YOU SHOWED ME HOW YOU FEEL *WITH-OUT* WORDS.
DO YOU STILL WANT TO GO HOME?
SURE. BUT NOT TO *TALK*.
HUH?
END

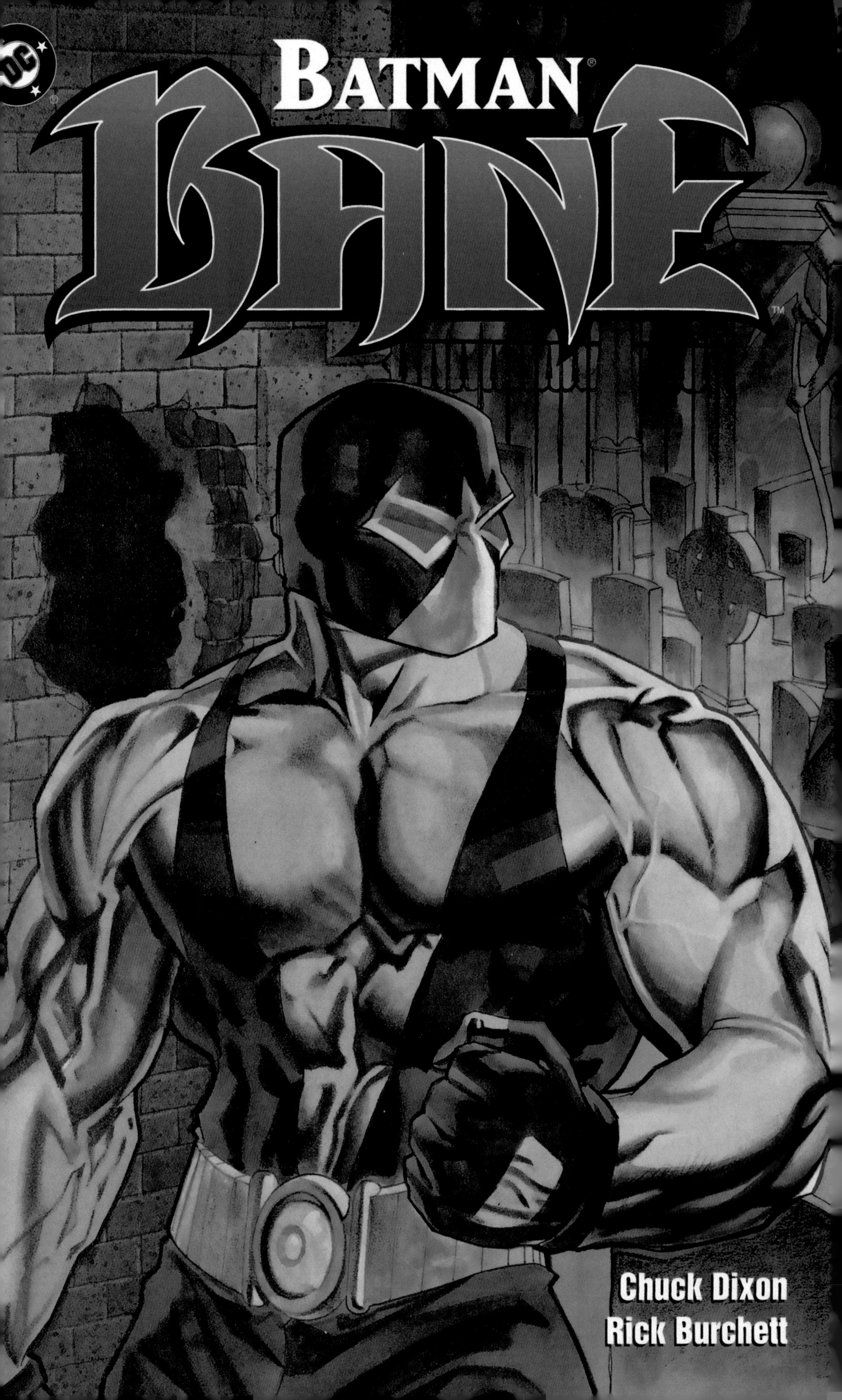
BATMAN
BANE
Chuck Dixon
Rick Burchett

Cover Art by Brian Stelfreeze

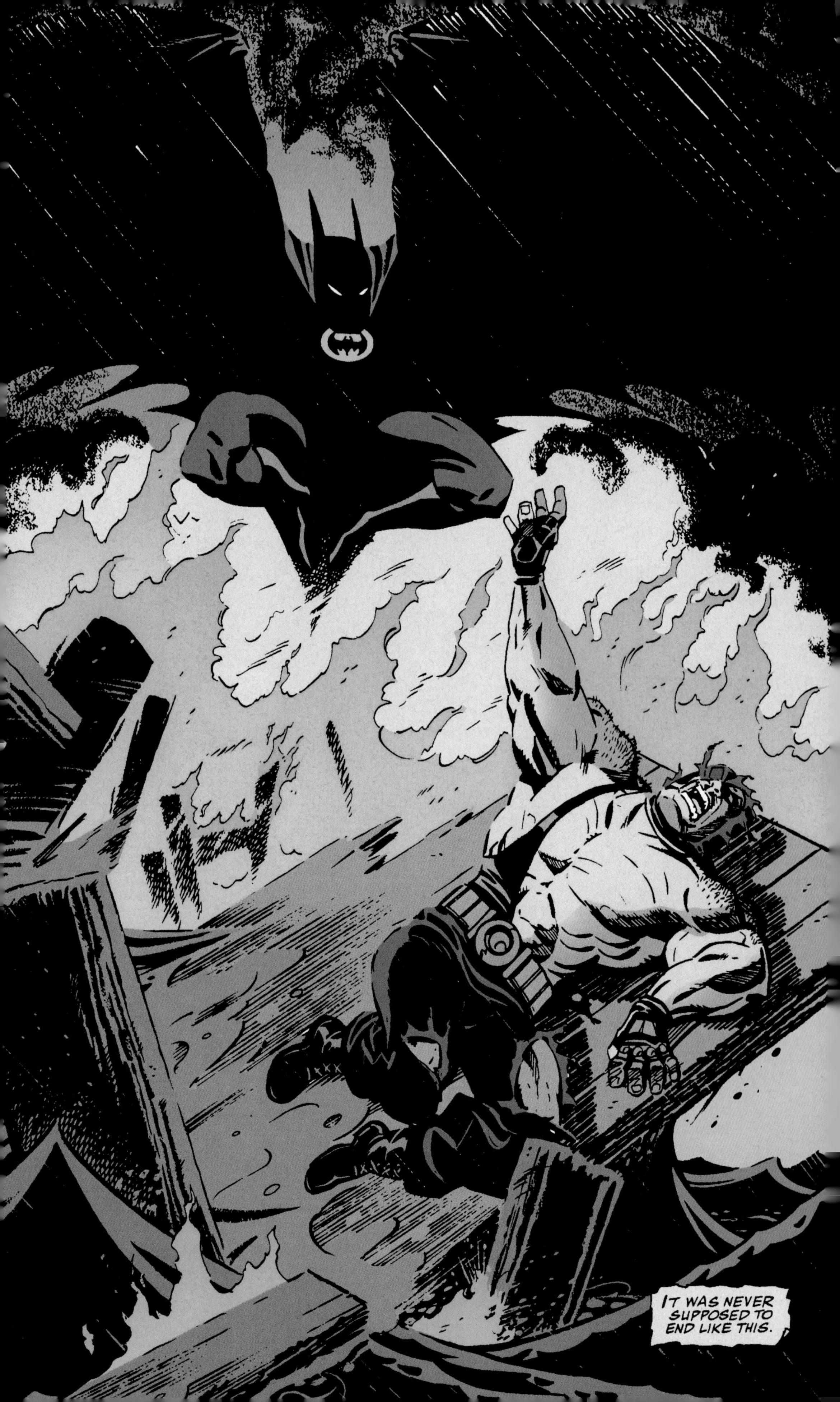
IT WAS NEVER SUPPOSED TO END LIKE THIS.

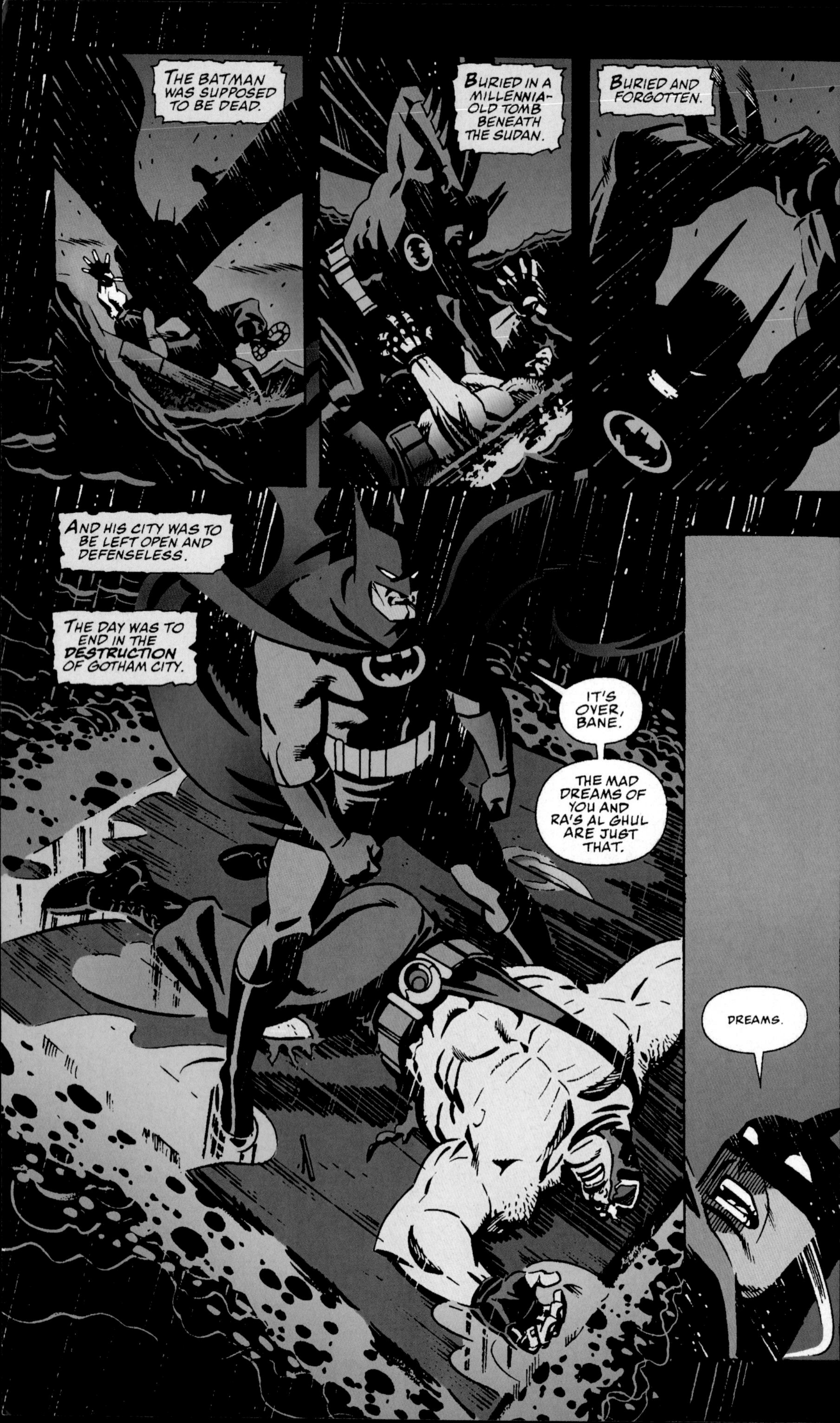

THE BATMAN WAS SUPPOSED TO BE DEAD.
BURIED IN A MILLENNIA-OLD TOMB BENEATH THE SUDAN.
BURIED AND FORGOTTEN.
AND HIS CITY WAS TO BE LEFT OPEN AND DEFENSELESS.
THE DAY WAS TO END IN THE DESTRUCTION OF GOTHAM CITY.
IT'S OVER, BANE.
THE MAD DREAMS OF YOU AND RA'S AL GHUL ARE JUST THAT.
DREAMS.

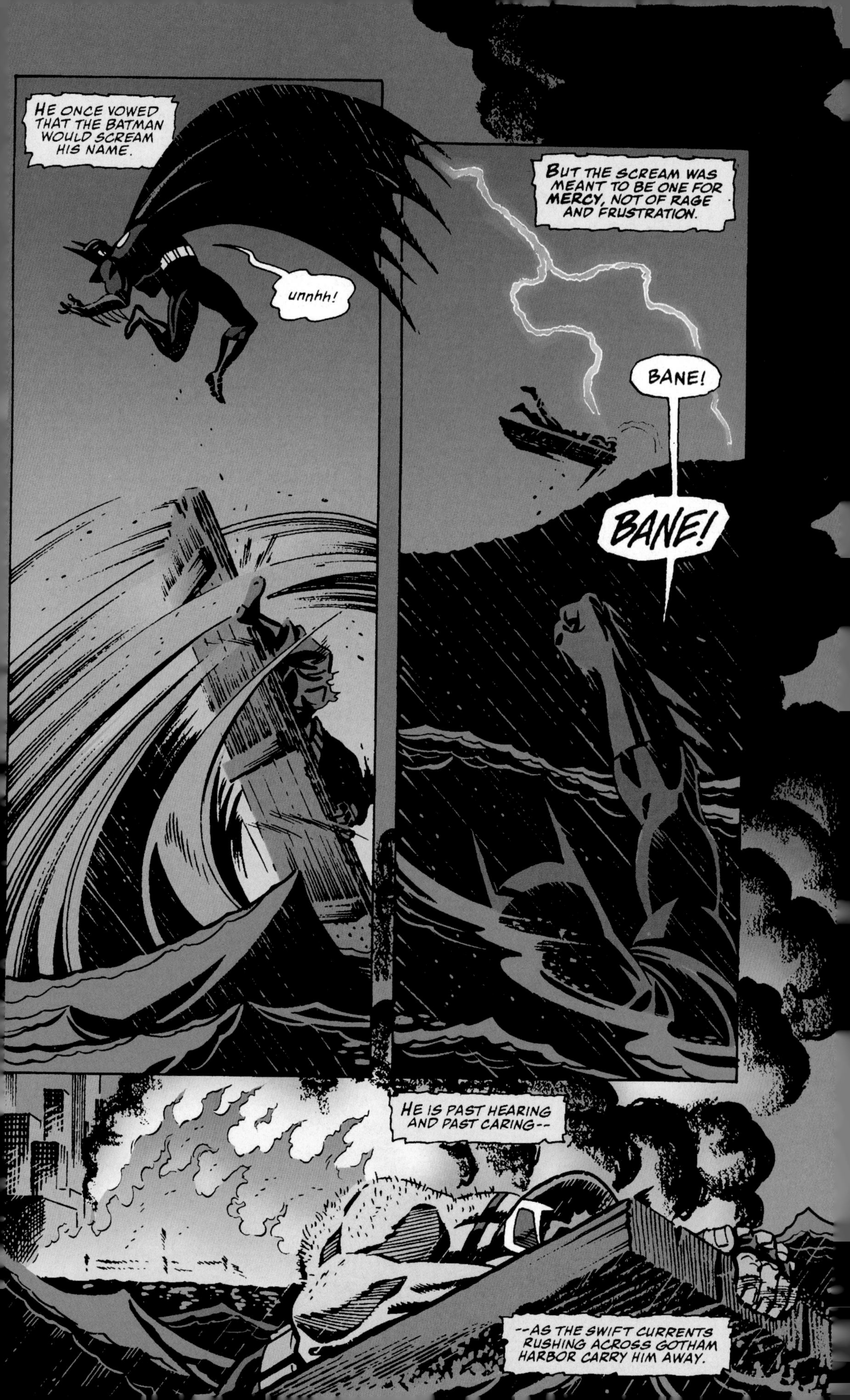

HE ONCE VOWED THAT THE BATMAN WOULD SCREAM HIS NAME.
unnhh!
BUT THE SCREAM WAS MEANT TO BE ONE FOR MERCY, NOT OF RAGE AND FRUSTRATION.
BANE!
BANE!
HE IS PAST HEARING AND PAST CARING--
--AS THE SWIFT CURRENTS RUSHING ACROSS GOTHAM HARBOR CARRY HIM AWAY.

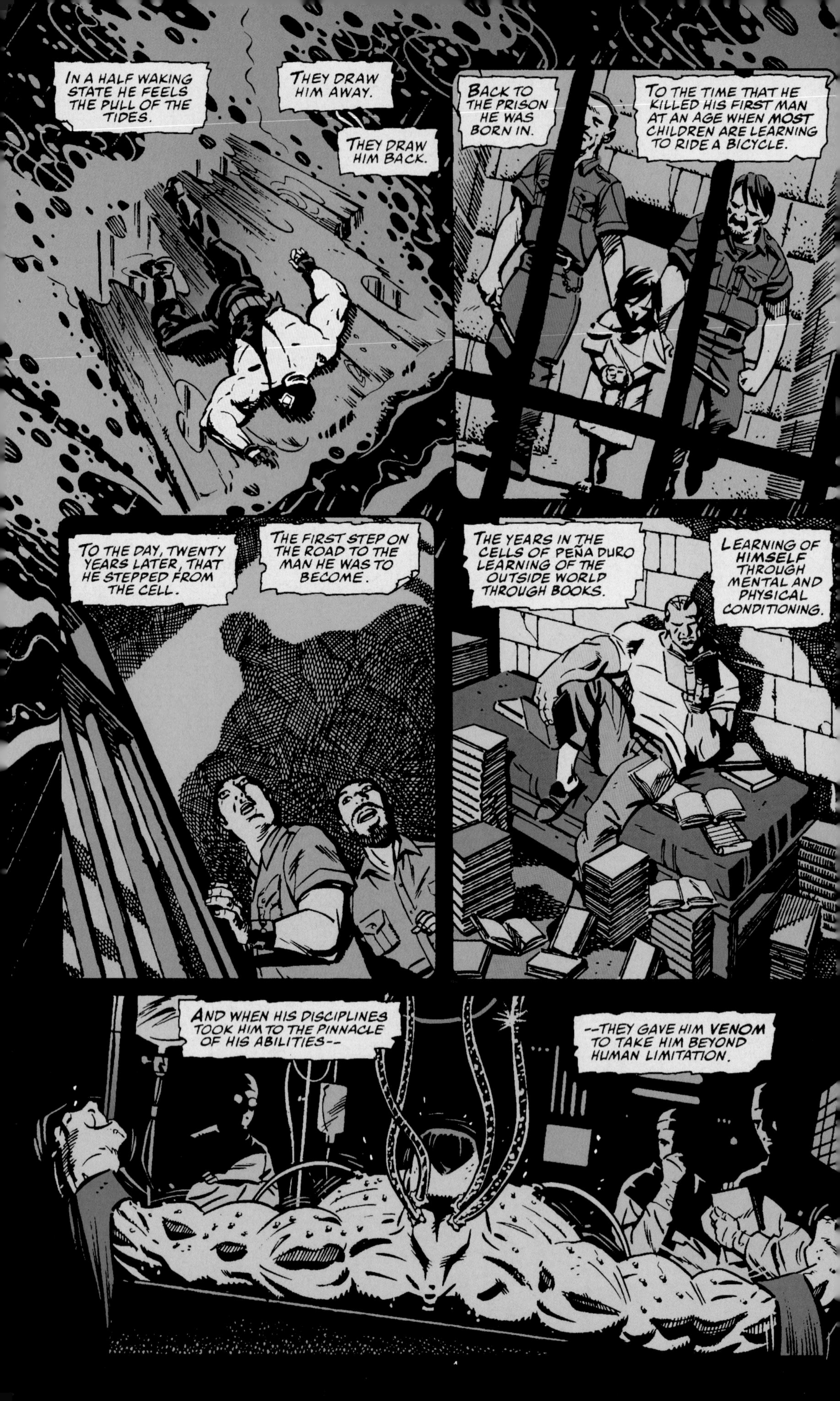
IN A HALF WAKING STATE HE FEELS THE PULL OF THE TIDES.
THEY DRAW HIM AWAY.
THEY DRAW HIM BACK.
BACK TO THE PRISON HE WAS BORN IN.
TO THE TIME THAT HE KILLED HIS FIRST MAN AT AN AGE WHEN MOST CHILDREN ARE LEARNING TO RIDE A BICYCLE.
TO THE DAY, TWENTY YEARS LATER, THAT HE STEPPED FROM THE CELL.
THE FIRST STEP ON THE ROAD TO THE MAN HE WAS TO BECOME.
THE YEARS IN THE CELLS OF PEÑA DURO LEARNING OF THE OUTSIDE WORLD THROUGH BOOKS.
LEARNING OF HIMSELF THROUGH MENTAL AND PHYSICAL CONDITIONING.
AND WHEN HIS DISCIPLINES TOOK HIM TO THE PINNACLE OF HIS ABILITIES--
--THEY GAVE HIM VENOM TO TAKE HIM BEYOND HUMAN LIMITATION.

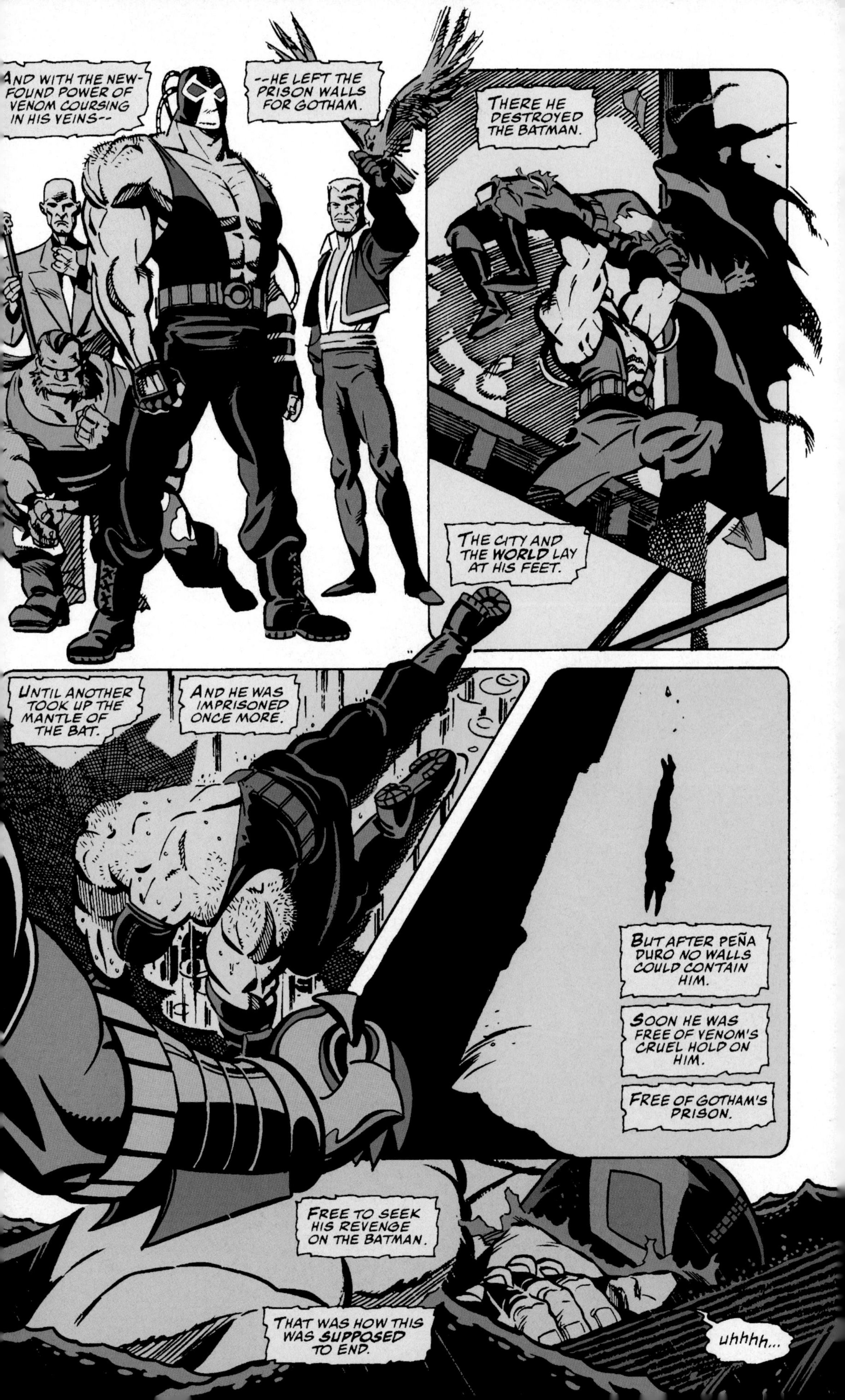
AND WITH THE NEW-FOUND POWER OF VENOM COURSING IN HIS VEINS--
--HE LEFT THE PRISON WALLS FOR GOTHAM.
THERE HE DESTROYED THE BATMAN.
THE CITY AND THE WORLD LAY AT HIS FEET.
UNTIL ANOTHER TOOK UP THE MANTLE OF THE BAT.
AND HE WAS IMPRISONED ONCE MORE.
BUT AFTER PEÑA DURO NO WALLS COULD CONTAIN HIM.
SOON HE WAS FREE OF VENOM'S CRUEL HOLD ON HIM.
FREE OF GOTHAM'S PRISON.
FREE TO SEEK HIS REVENGE ON THE BATMAN.
THAT WAS HOW THIS WAS SUPPOSED TO END.
uhhhh...

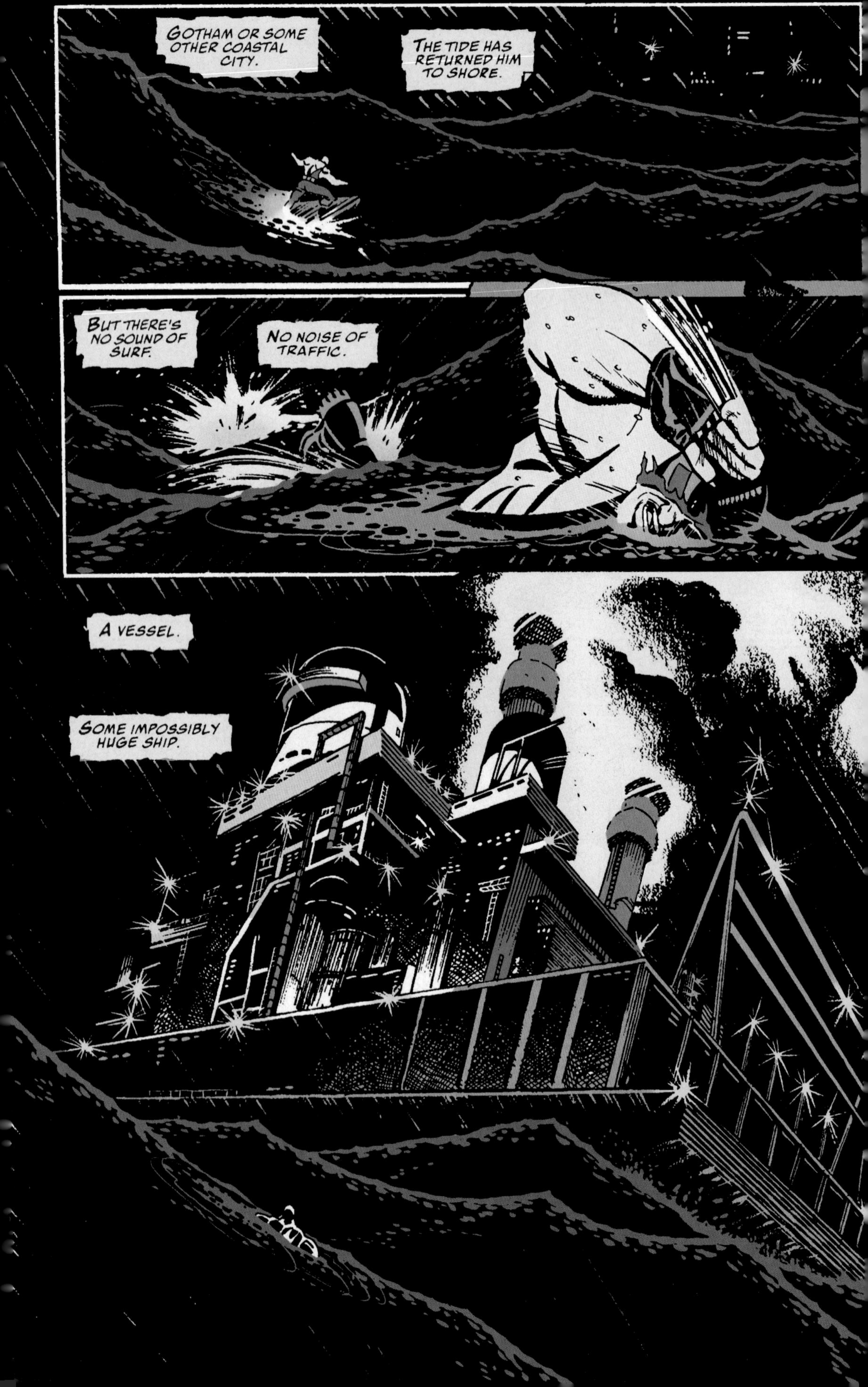
GOTHAM OR SOME OTHER COASTAL CITY.
THE TIDE HAS RETURNED HIM TO SHORE.
BUT THERE'S NO SOUND OF SURF.
NO NOISE OF TRAFFIC.
A VESSEL.
SOME IMPOSSIBLY HUGE SHIP.

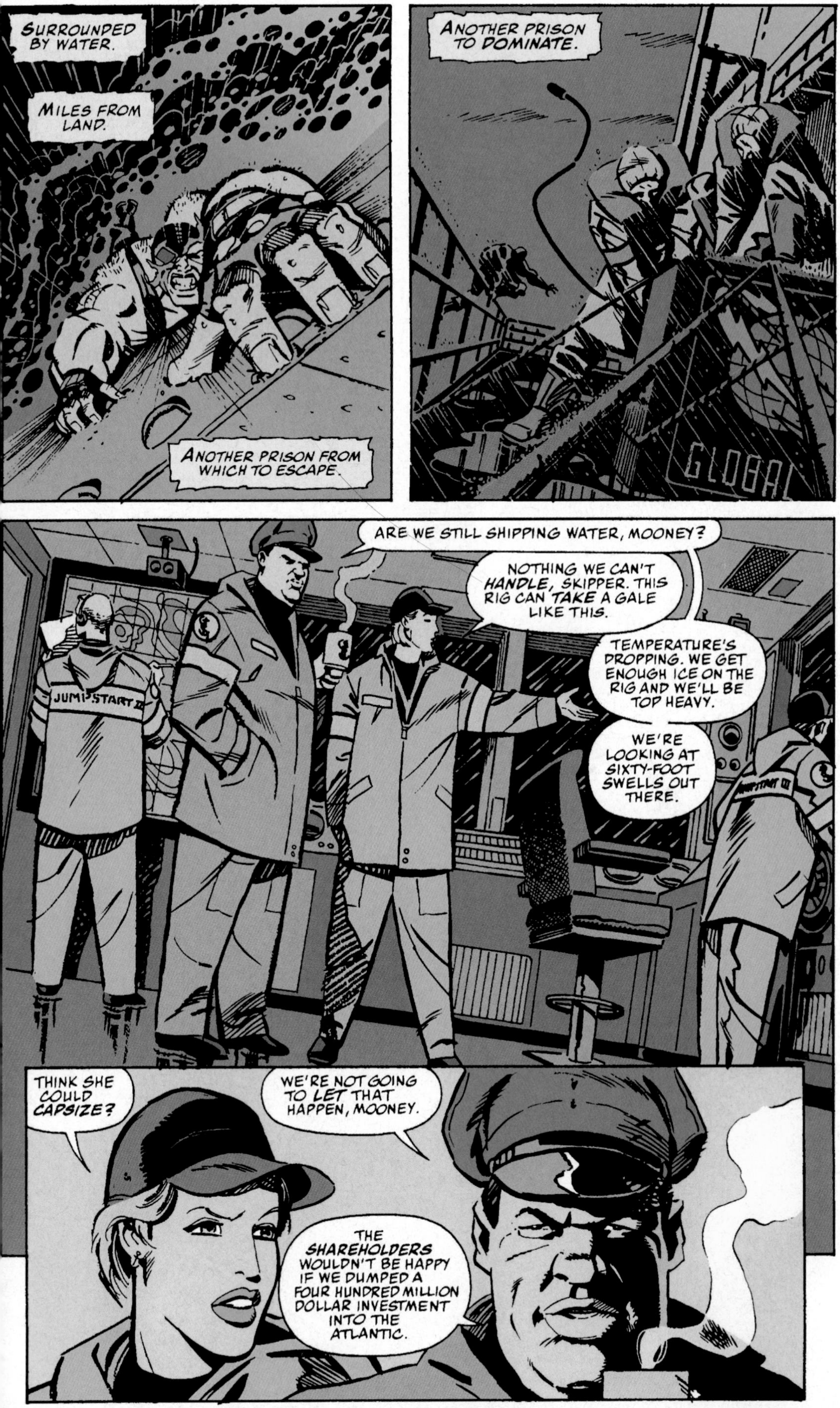
SURROUNDED BY WATER.
MILES FROM LAND.
ANOTHER PRISON FROM WHICH TO ESCAPE.
ANOTHER PRISON TO DOMINATE.
GLOBA
ARE WE STILL SHIPPING WATER, MOONEY?
NOTHING WE CAN'T HANDLE, SKIPPER. THIS RIG CAN TAKE A GALE LIKE THIS.
TEMPERATURE'S DROPPING. WE GET ENOUGH ICE ON THE RIG AND WE'LL BE TOP HEAVY.
WE'RE LOOKING AT SIXTY-FOOT SWELLS OUT THERE.
JUMPSTART III
THINK SHE COULD CAPSIZE?
WE'RE NOT GOING TO LET THAT HAPPEN, MOONEY.
THE SHAREHOLDERS WOULDN'T BE HAPPY IF WE DUMPED A FOUR HUNDRED MILLION DOLLAR INVESTMENT INTO THE ATLANTIC.

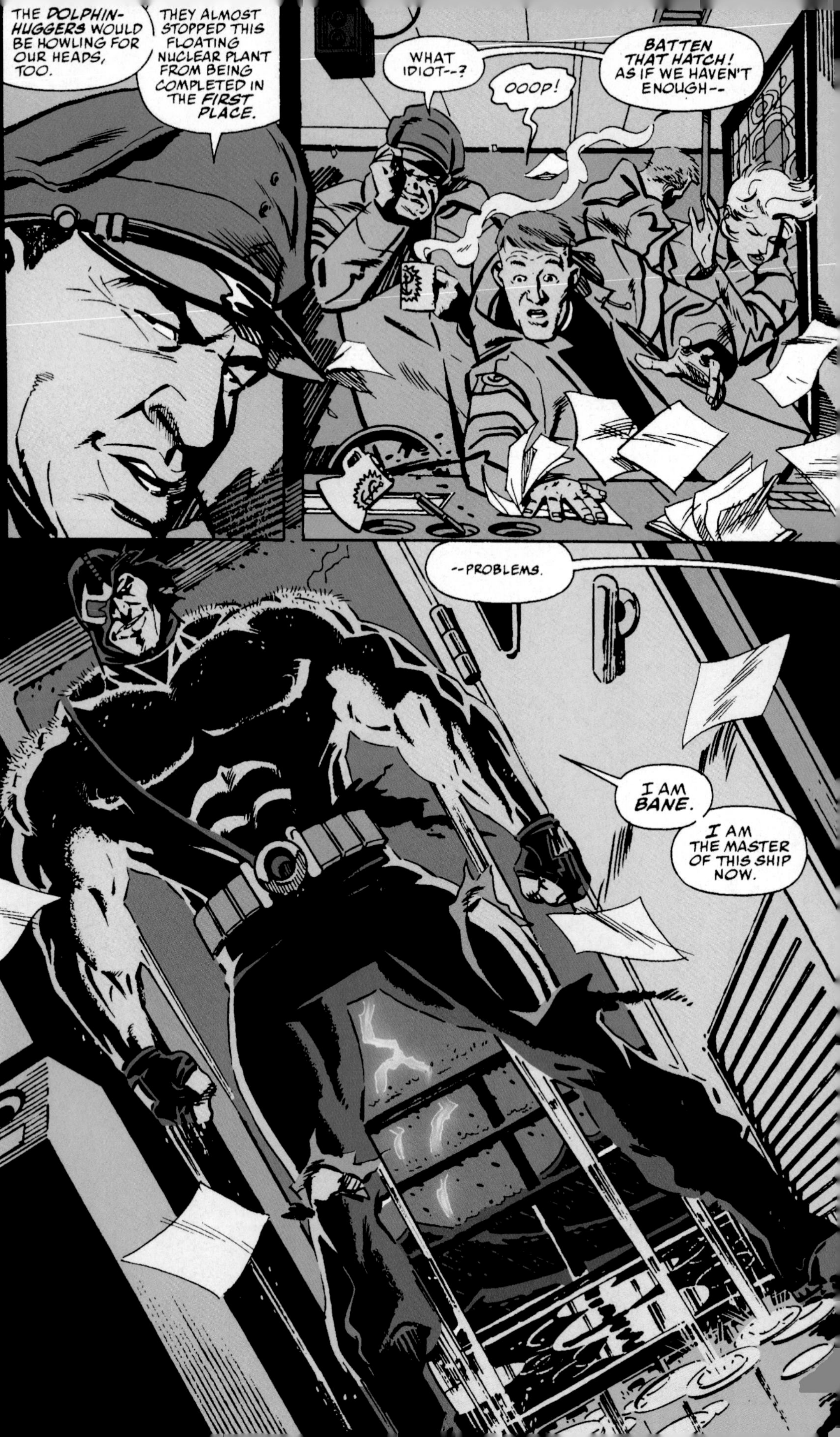
THE DOLPHIN-HUGGERS WOULD BE HOWLING FOR OUR HEADS, TOO.
THEY ALMOST STOPPED THIS FLOATING NUCLEAR PLANT FROM BEING COMPLETED IN THE FIRST PLACE.
WHAT IDIOT--?
OOOP!
BATTEN THAT HATCH! AS IF WE HAVEN'T ENOUGH--
--PROBLEMS.
I AM BANE.
I AM THE MASTER OF THIS SHIP NOW.

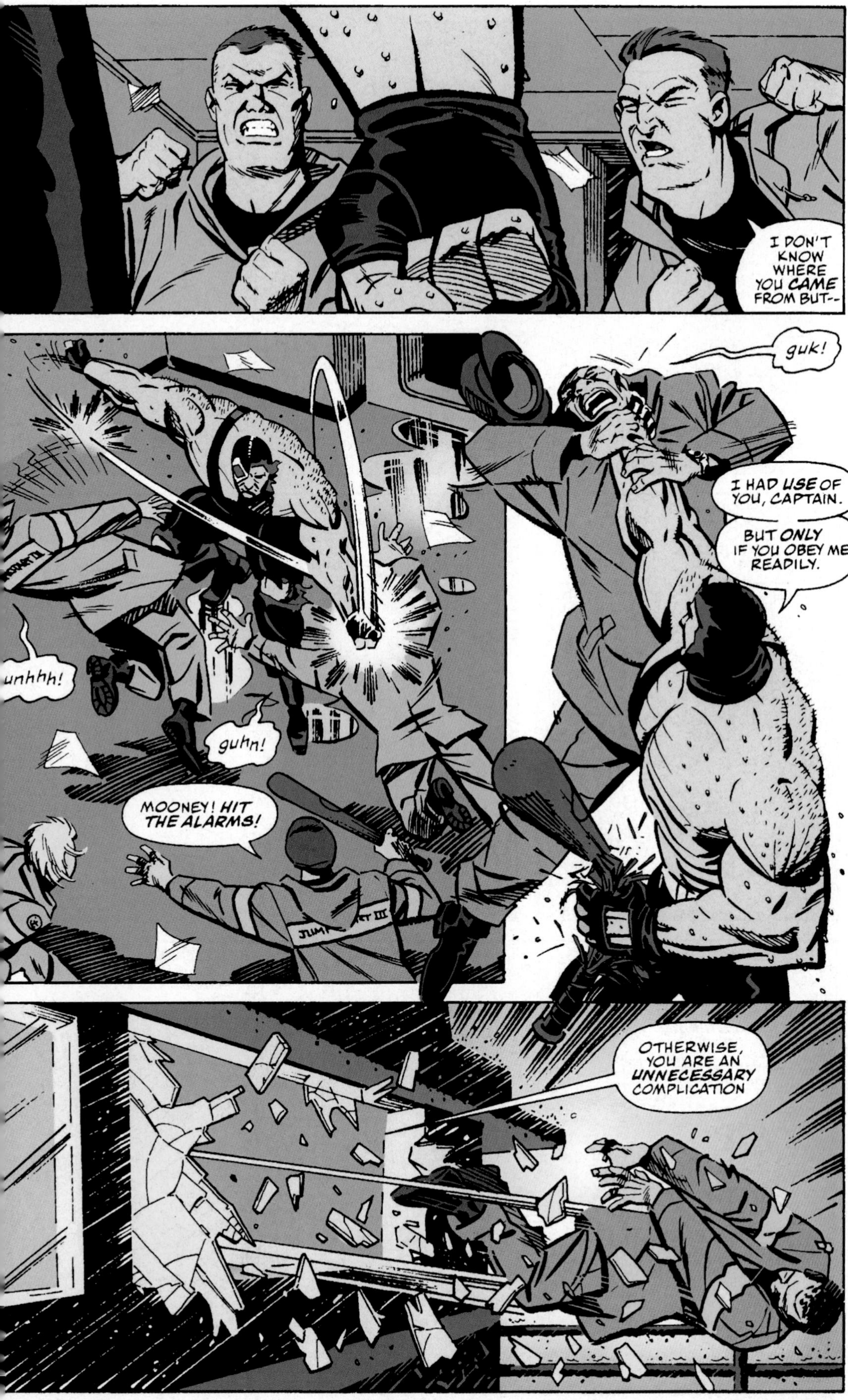

I DON'T KNOW WHERE YOU CAME FROM BUT--
guk!
I HAD USE OF YOU, CAPTAIN.
BUT ONLY IF YOU OBEY ME READILY.
unhhh!
guhn!
MOONEY! HIT THE ALARMS!
OTHERWISE, YOU ARE AN UNNECESSARY COMPLICATION

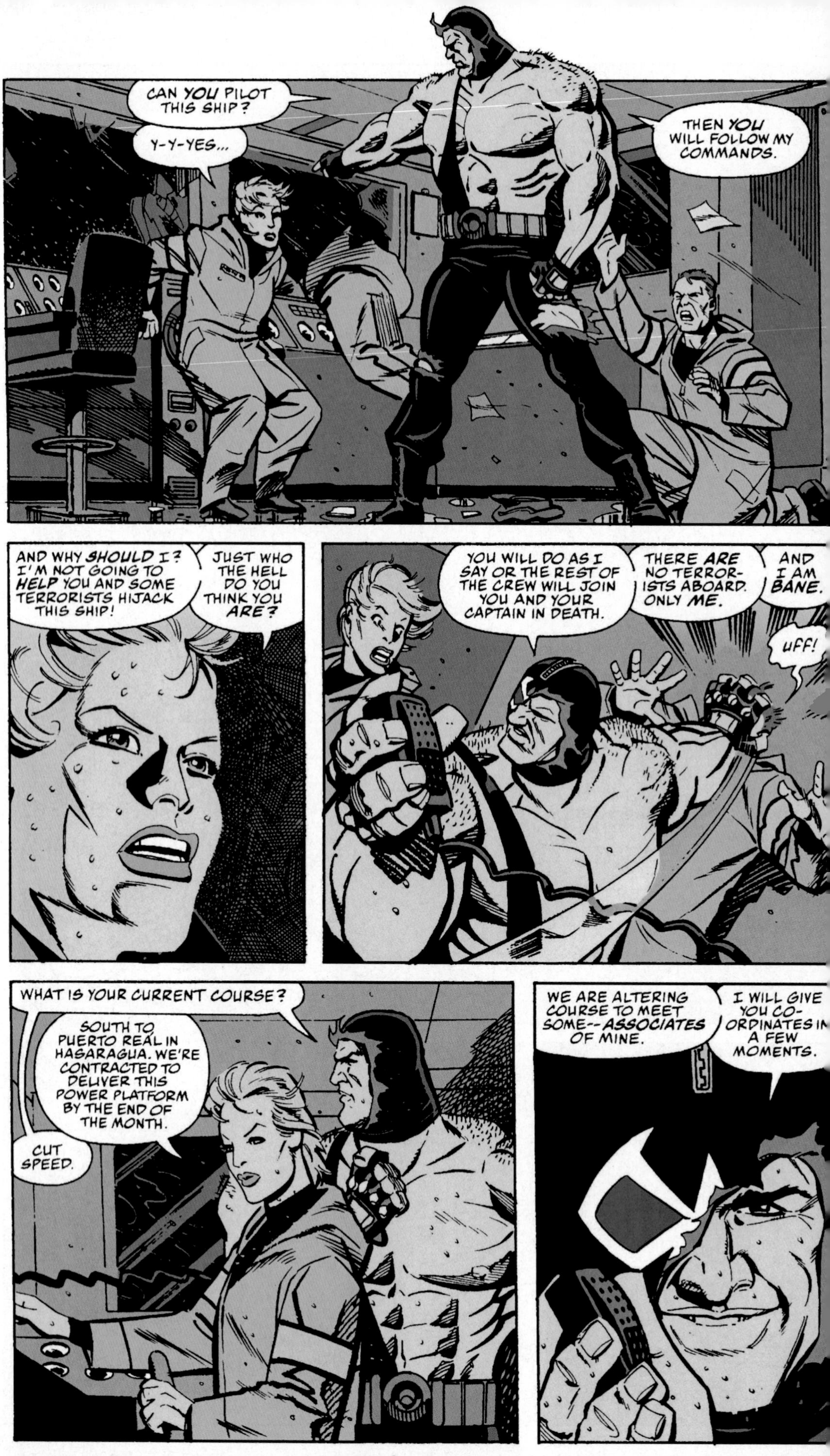
CAN YOU PILOT THIS SHIP?
Y-Y-YES...
THEN YOU WILL FOLLOW MY COMMANDS.
AND WHY SHOULD I? I'M NOT GOING TO HELP YOU AND SOME TERRORISTS HIJACK THIS SHIP!
JUST WHO THE HELL DO YOU THINK YOU ARE?
YOU WILL DO AS I SAY OR THE REST OF THE CREW WILL JOIN YOU AND YOUR CAPTAIN IN DEATH.
THERE ARE NO TERRORISTS ABOARD. ONLY ME.
AND I AM BANE.
UFF!
WHAT IS YOUR CURRENT COURSE?
SOUTH TO PUERTO REAL IN HASARAGUA. WE'RE CONTRACTED TO DELIVER THIS POWER PLATFORM BY THE END OF THE MONTH.
CUT SPEED.
WE ARE ALTERING COURSE TO MEET SOME--ASSOCIATES OF MINE.
I WILL GIVE YOU CO-ORDINATES IN A FEW MOMENTS.

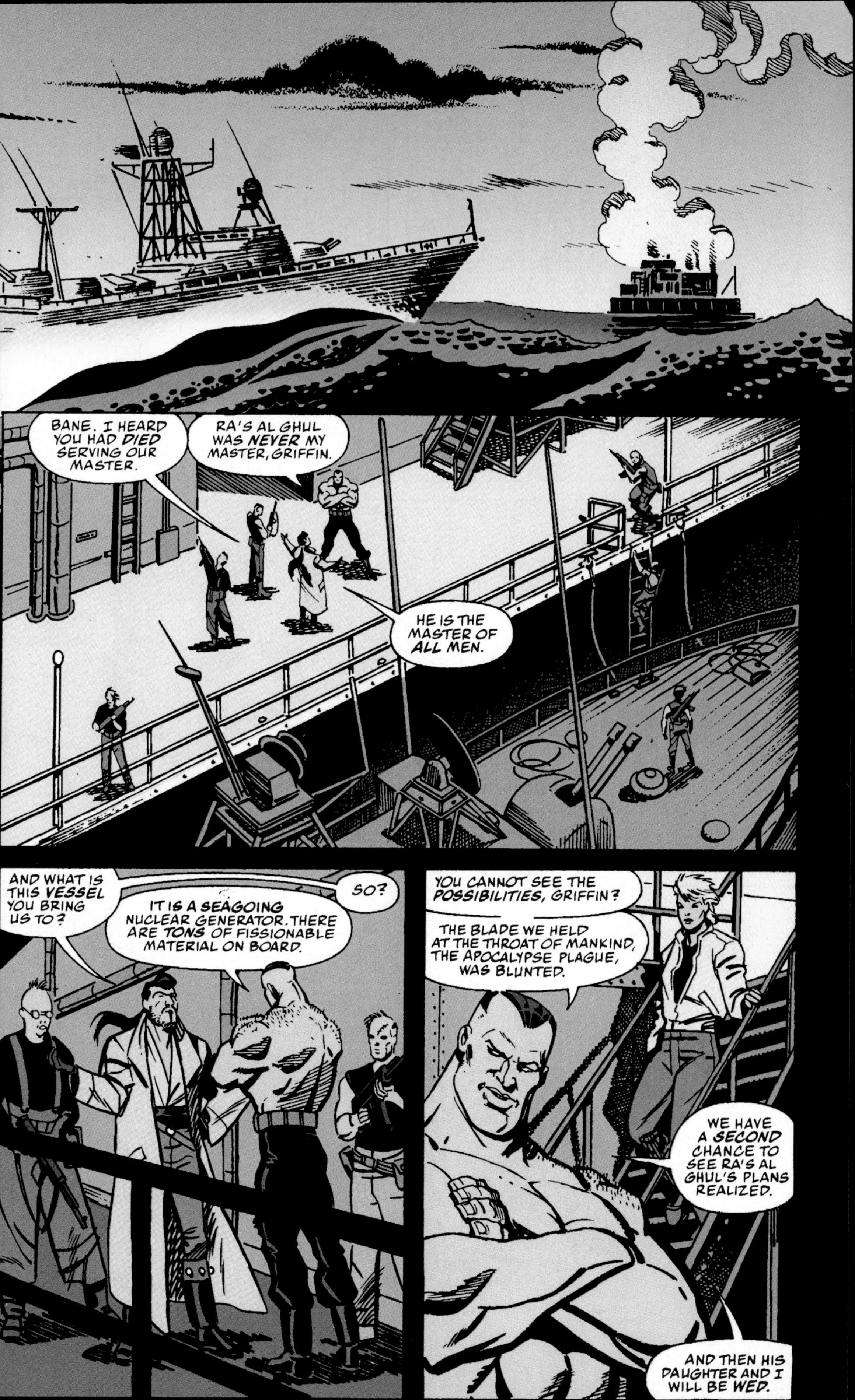
BANE. I HEARD YOU HAD DIED SERVING OUR MASTER.
RA'S AL GHUL WAS NEVER MY MASTER, GRIFFIN.
HE IS THE MASTER OF ALL MEN.
SO?
AND WHAT IS THIS VESSEL YOU BRING US TO?
IT IS A SEAGOING NUCLEAR GENERATOR. THERE ARE TONS OF FISSIONABLE MATERIAL ON BOARD.
YOU CANNOT SEE THE POSSIBILITIES, GRIFFIN?
THE BLADE WE HELD AT THE THROAT OF MANKIND, THE APOCALYPSE PLAGUE, WAS BLUNTED.
WE HAVE A SECOND CHANCE TO SEE RA'S AL GHUL'S PLANS REALIZED.
AND THEN HIS DAUGHTER AND I WILL BE WED.

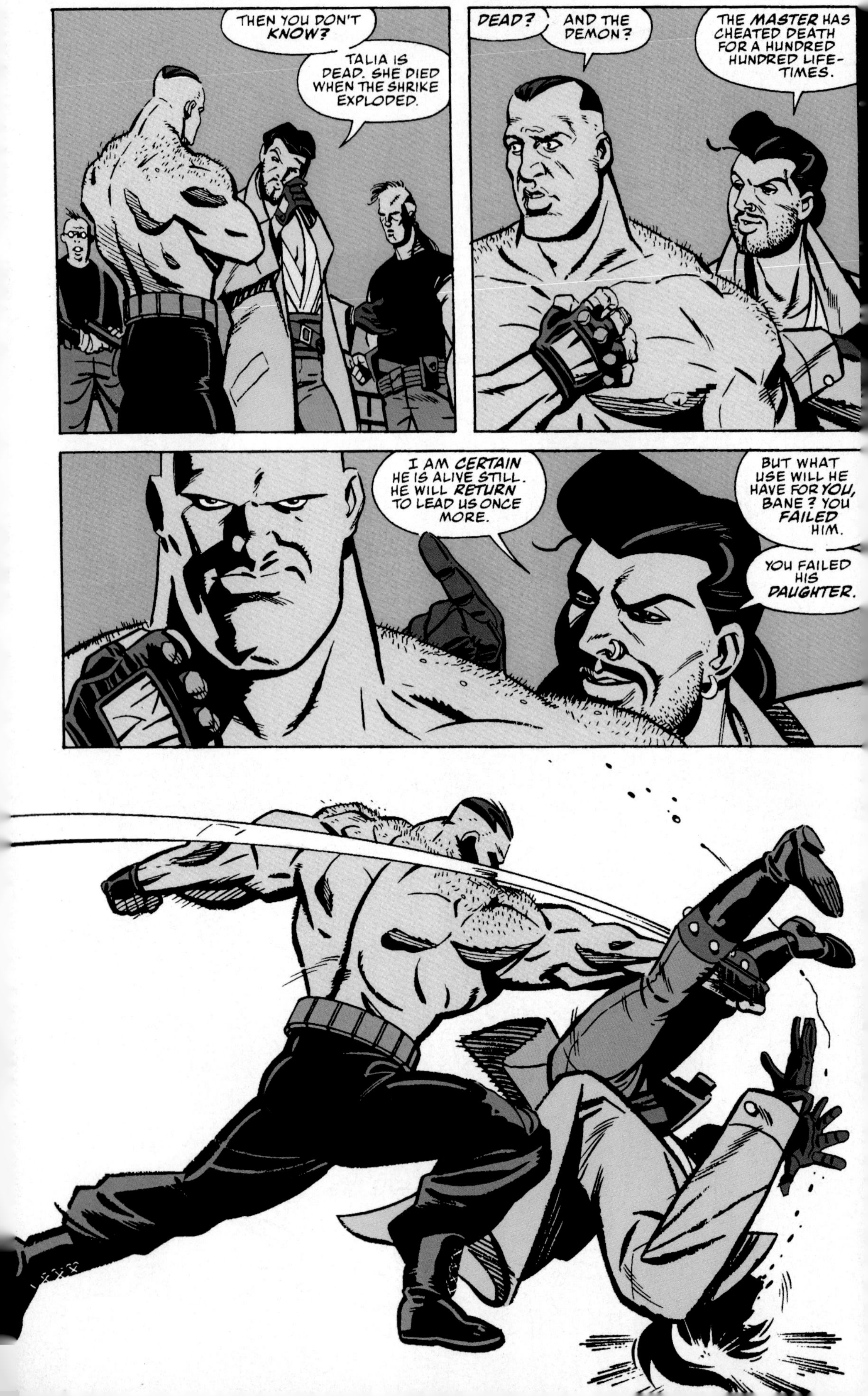
THEN YOU DON'T KNOW?
TALIA IS DEAD. SHE DIED WHEN THE SHRIKE EXPLODED.
DEAD?
AND THE DEMON?
THE MASTER HAS CHEATED DEATH FOR A HUNDRED HUNDRED LIFE-TIMES.
I AM CERTAIN HE IS ALIVE STILL. HE WILL RETURN TO LEAD US ONCE MORE.
BUT WHAT USE WILL HE HAVE FOR YOU, BANE? YOU FAILED HIM.
YOU FAILED HIS DAUGHTER.

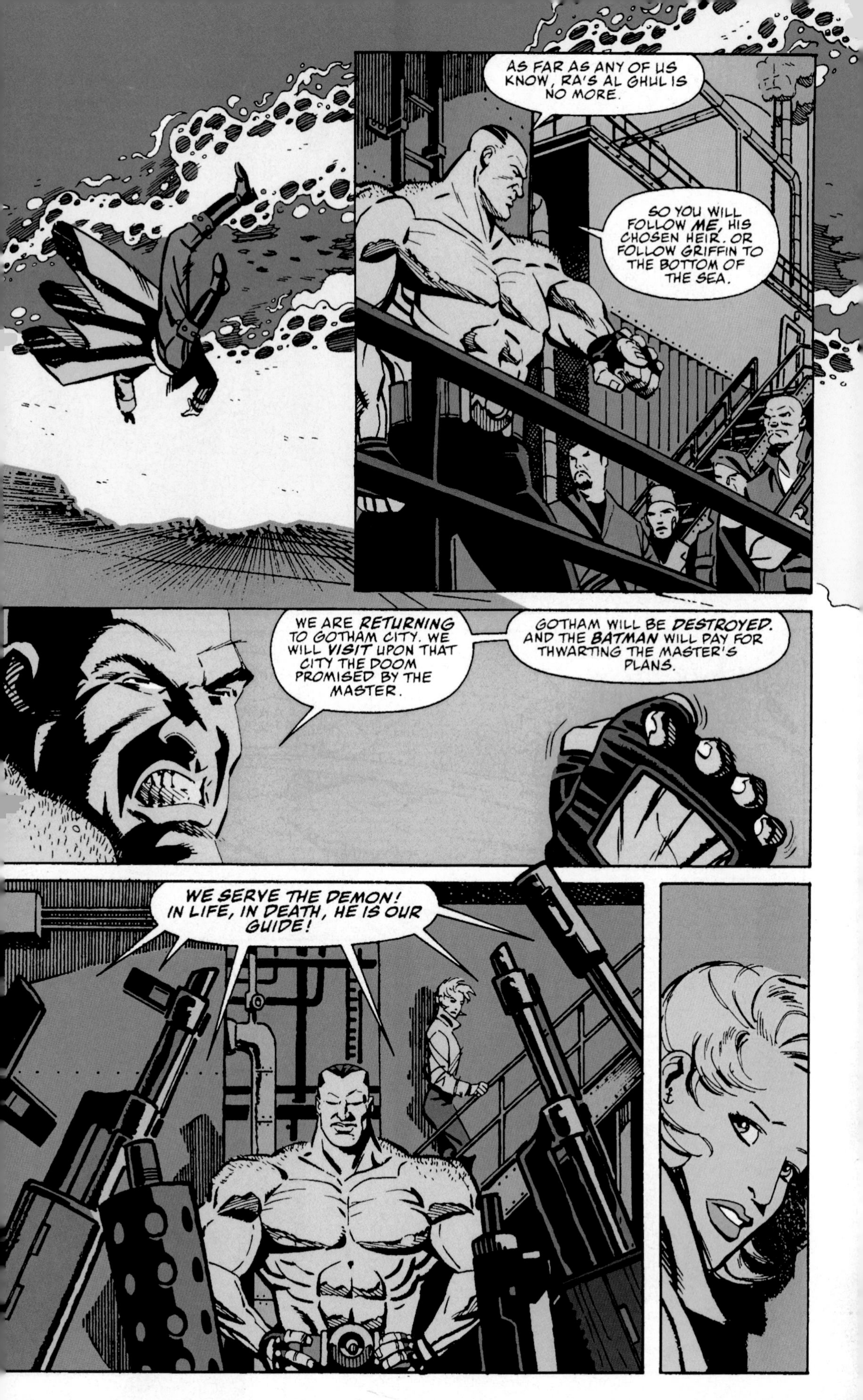
AS FAR AS ANY OF US KNOW, RA'S AL GHUL IS NO MORE.
SO YOU WILL FOLLOW ME, HIS CHOSEN HEIR. OR FOLLOW GRIFFIN TO THE BOTTOM OF THE SEA.
WE ARE RETURNING TO GOTHAM CITY. WE WILL VISIT UPON THAT CITY THE DOOM PROMISED BY THE MASTER.
GOTHAM WILL BE DESTROYED. AND THE BATMAN WILL PAY FOR THWARTING THE MASTER'S PLANS.
WE SERVE THE DEMON! IN LIFE, IN DEATH, HE IS OUR GUIDE!

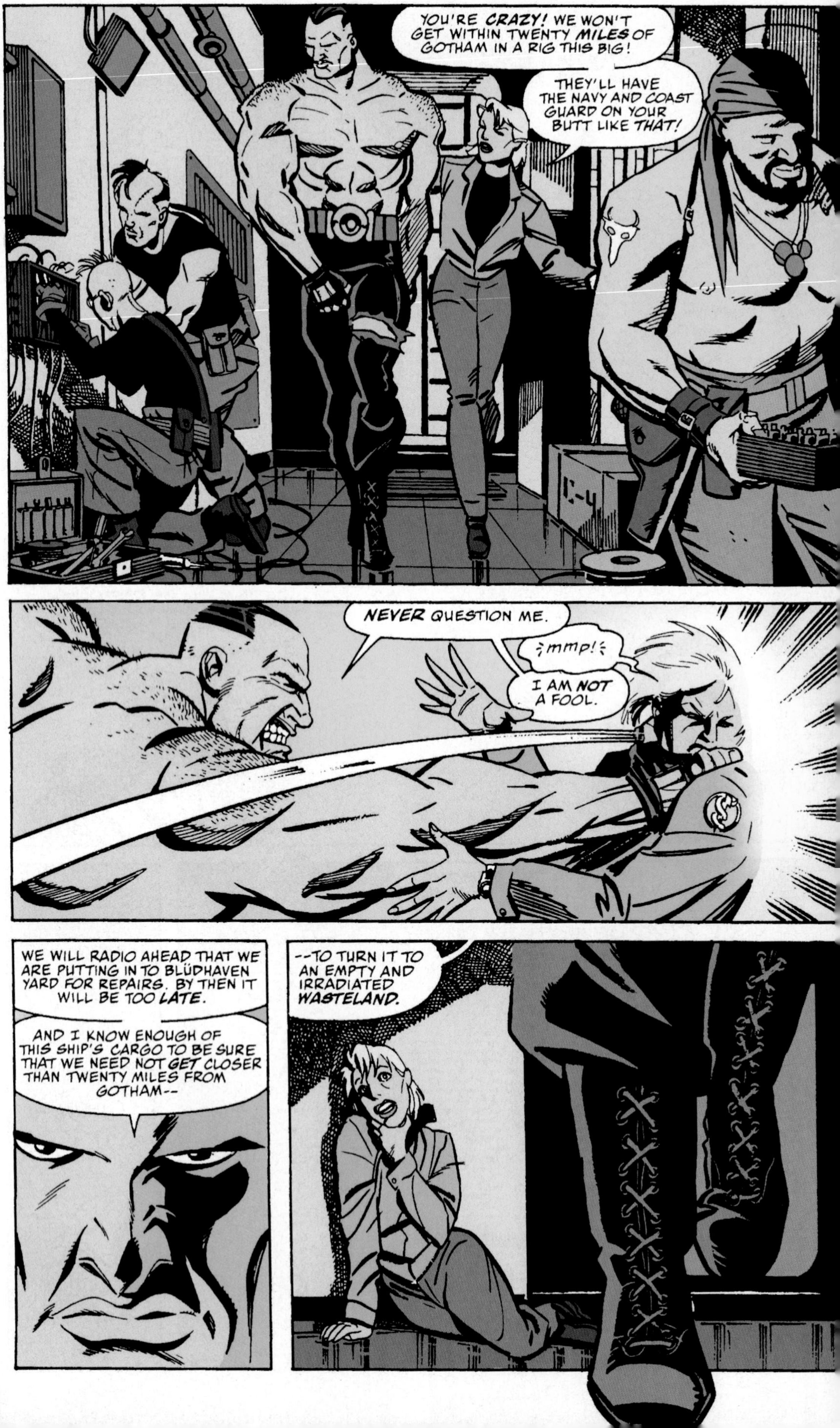
YOU'RE CRAZY! WE WON'T GET WITHIN TWENTY MILES OF GOTHAM IN A RIG THIS BIG!
THEY'LL HAVE THE NAVY AND COAST GUARD ON YOUR BUTT LIKE THAT!
C-4
NEVER QUESTION ME.
mmp!
I AM NOT A FOOL.
WE WILL RADIO AHEAD THAT WE ARE PUTTING IN TO BLÜDHAVEN YARD FOR REPAIRS. BY THEN IT WILL BE TOO LATE.
AND I KNOW ENOUGH OF THIS SHIP'S CARGO TO BE SURE THAT WE NEED NOT GET CLOSER THAN TWENTY MILES FROM GOTHAM--
--TO TURN IT TO AN EMPTY AND IRRADIATED WASTELAND.

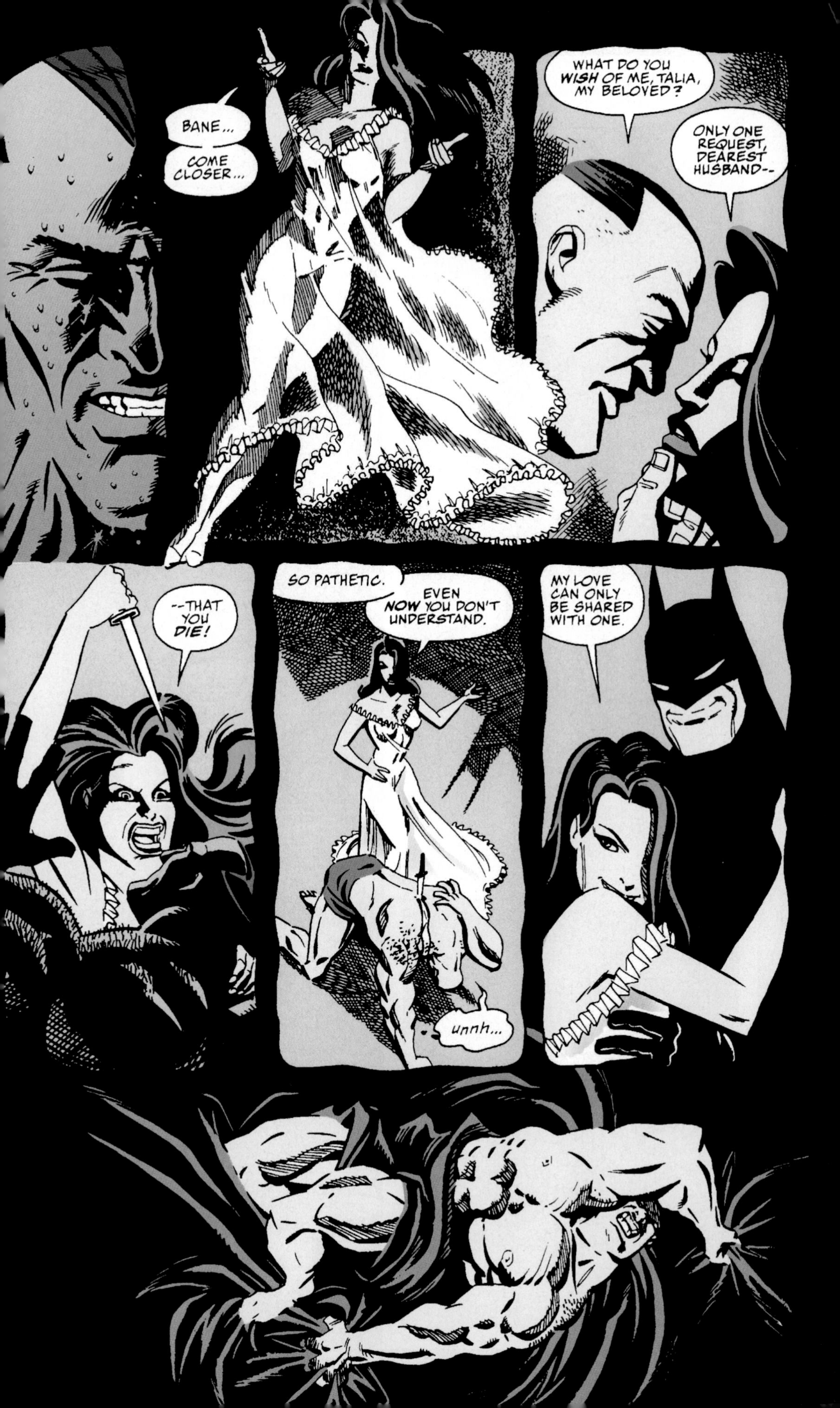
BANE...
COME CLOSER...
WHAT DO YOU WISH OF ME, TALIA, MY BELOVED?
ONLY ONE REQUEST, DEAREST HUSBAND--
--THAT YOU DIE!
SO PATHETIC.
EVEN NOW YOU DON'T UNDERSTAND.
unnh...
MY LOVE CAN ONLY BE SHARED WITH ONE.

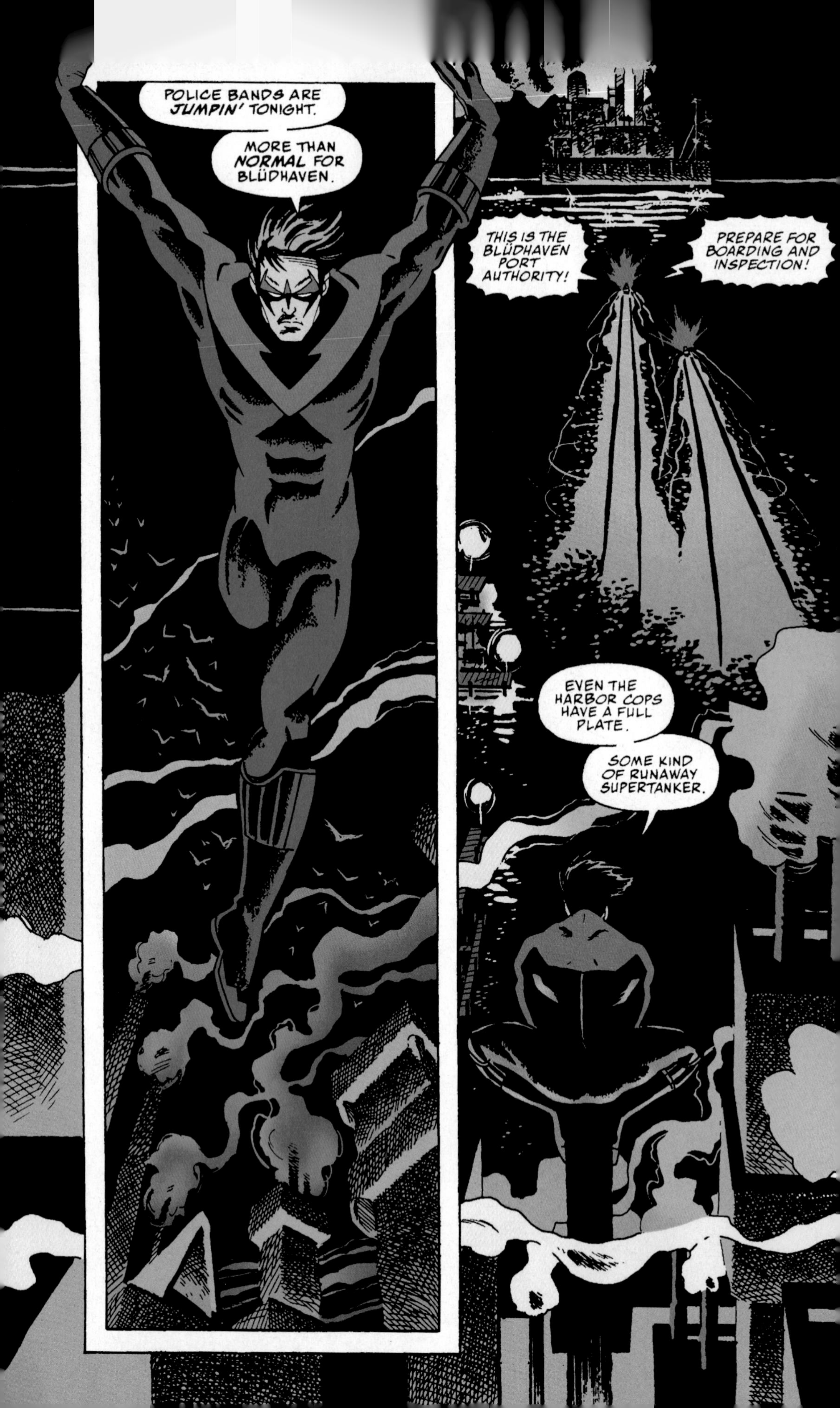

POLICE BANDS ARE JUMPIN' TONIGHT.
MORE THAN NORMAL FOR BLÜDHAVEN.
THIS IS THE BLÜDHAVEN PORT AUTHORITY!
PREPARE FOR BOARDING AND INSPECTION!
EVEN THE HARBOR COPS HAVE A FULL PLATE.
SOME KIND OF RUNAWAY SUPERTANKER.

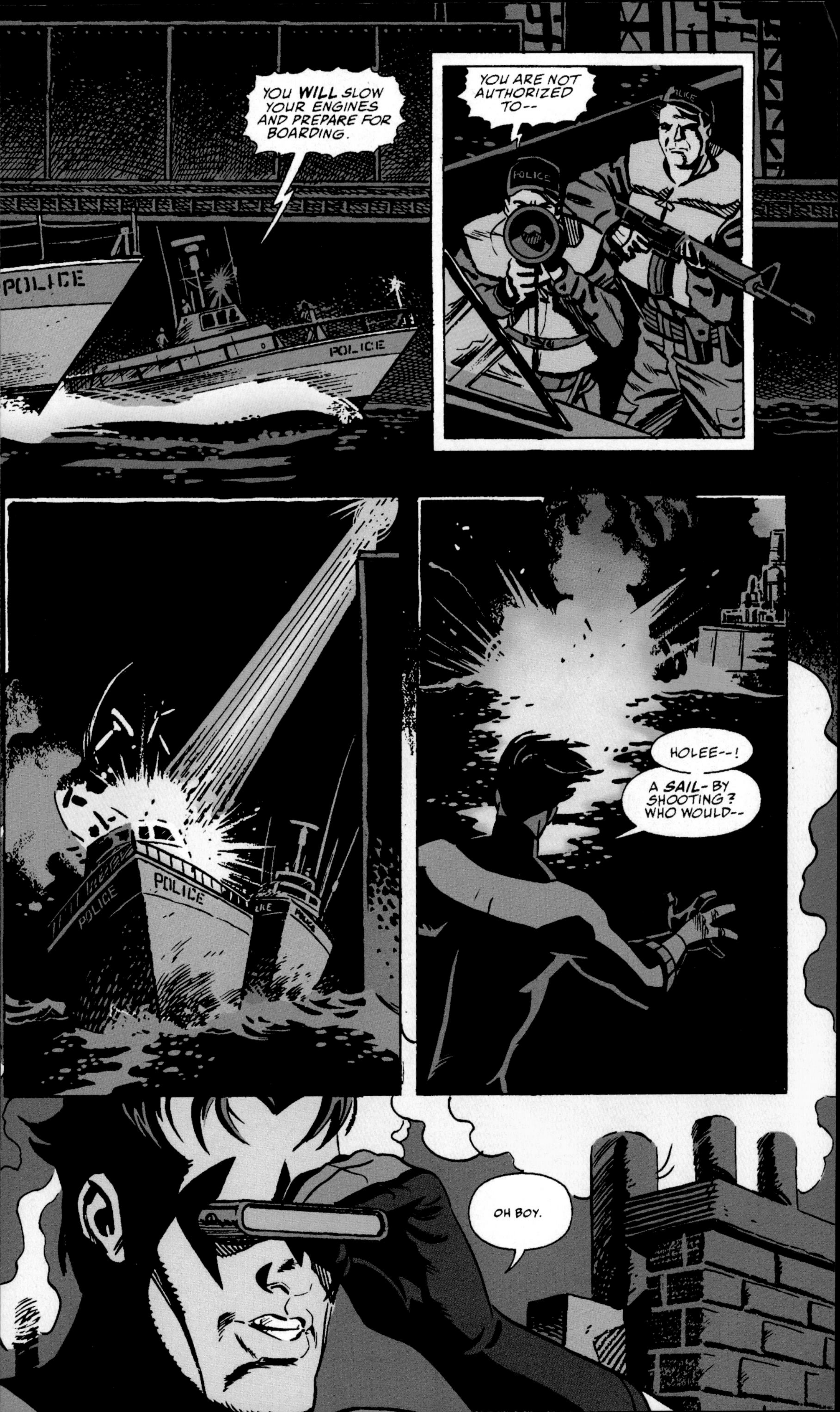
YOU WILL SLOW YOUR ENGINES AND PREPARE FOR BOARDING.
POLICE
POLICE
YOU ARE NOT AUTHORIZED TO--
POLICE
POLICE
POLICE
HOLEE--!
A SAIL-BY SHOOTING? WHO WOULD--
OH BOY.

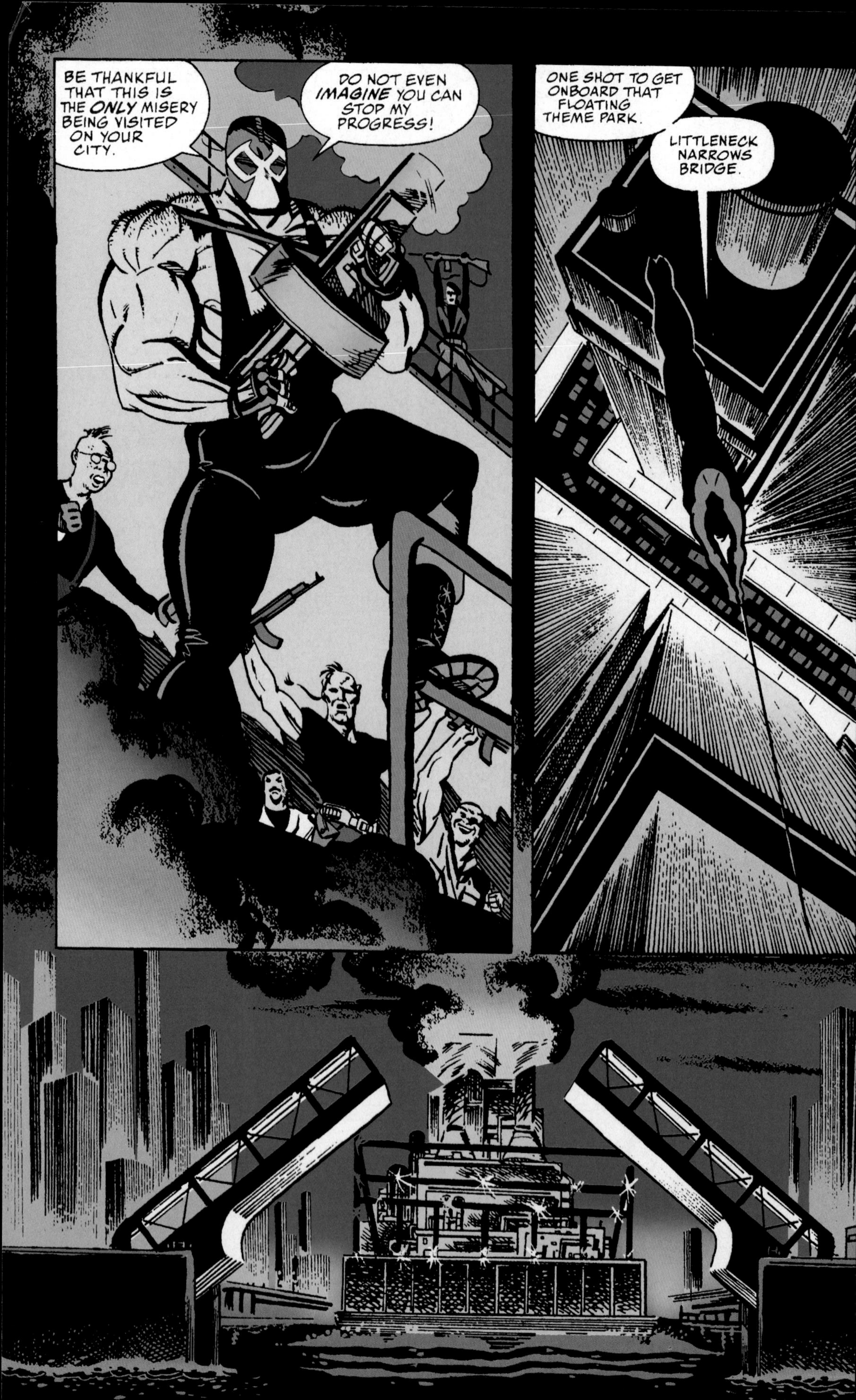
BE THANKFUL THAT THIS IS THE ONLY MISERY BEING VISITED ON YOUR CITY.
DO NOT EVEN IMAGINE YOU CAN STOP MY PROGRESS!
ONE SHOT TO GET ONBOARD THAT FLOATING THEME PARK.
LITTLENECK NARROWS BRIDGE.

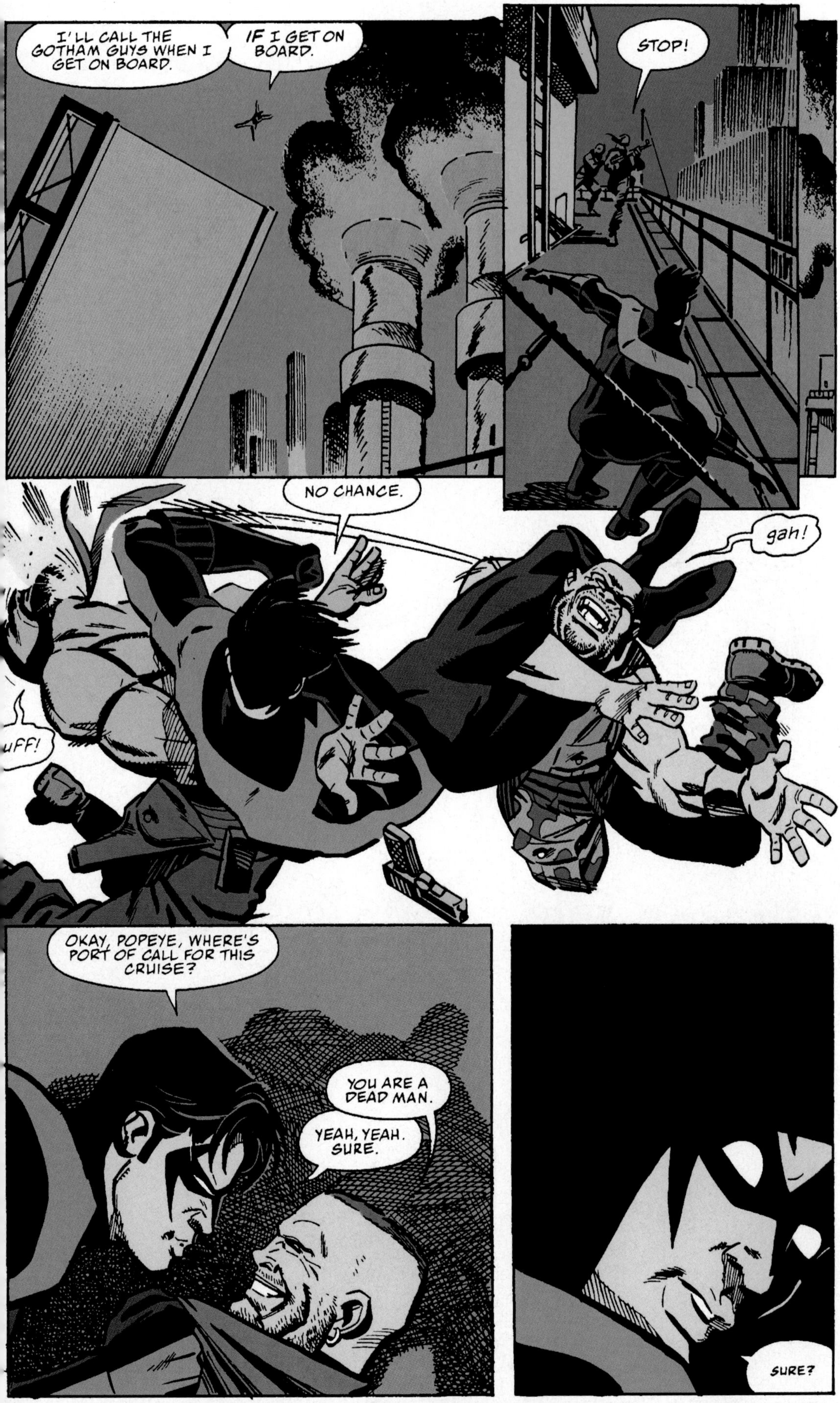
I'LL CALL THE GOTHAM GUYS WHEN I GET ON BOARD.
IF I GET ON BOARD.
STOP!
NO CHANCE.
gah!
uFF!
OKAY, POPEYE, WHERE'S PORT OF CALL FOR THIS CRUISE?
YOU ARE A DEAD MAN.
YEAH, YEAH. SURE.
SURE?

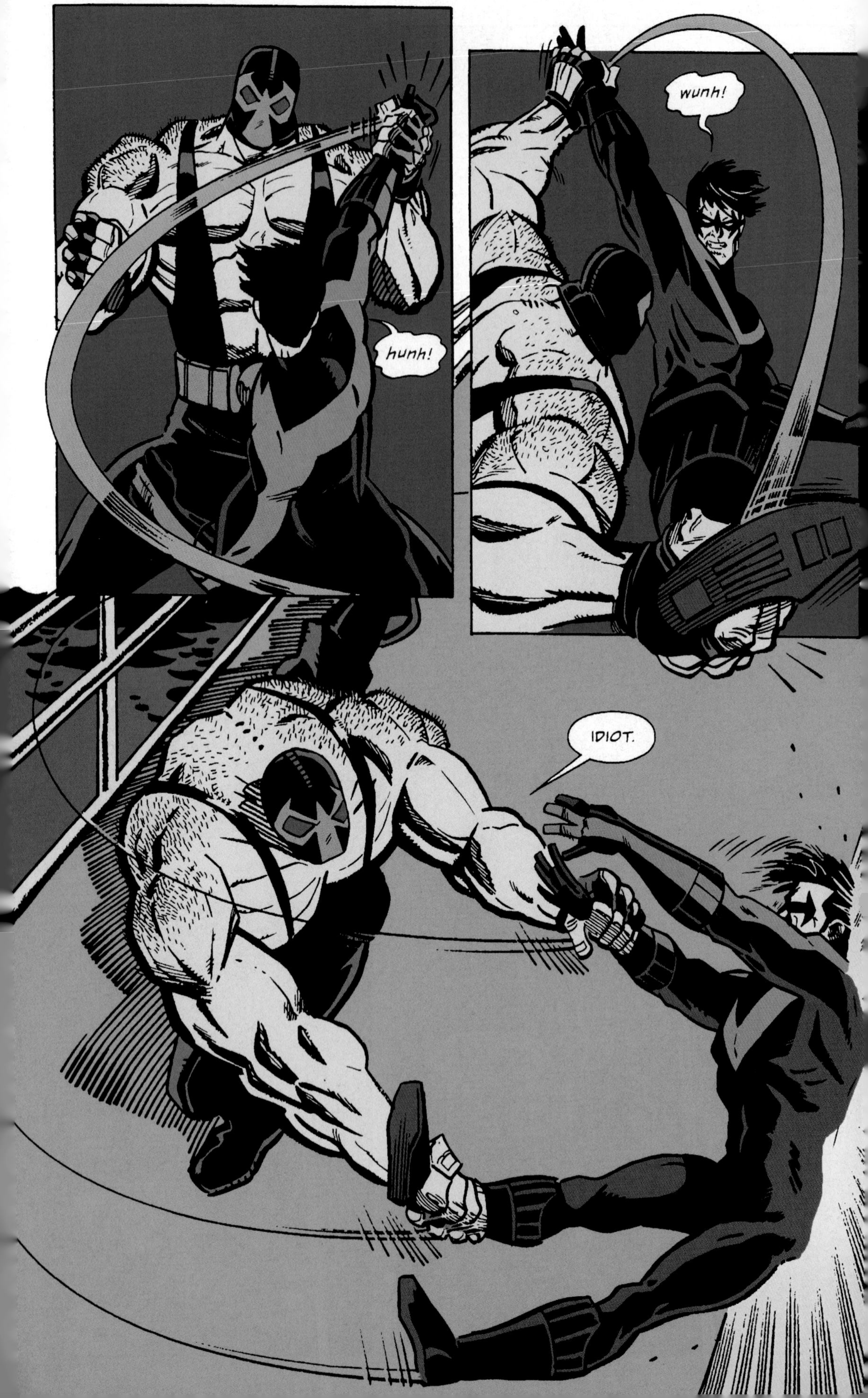
hunh!
wunh!
IDIOT.

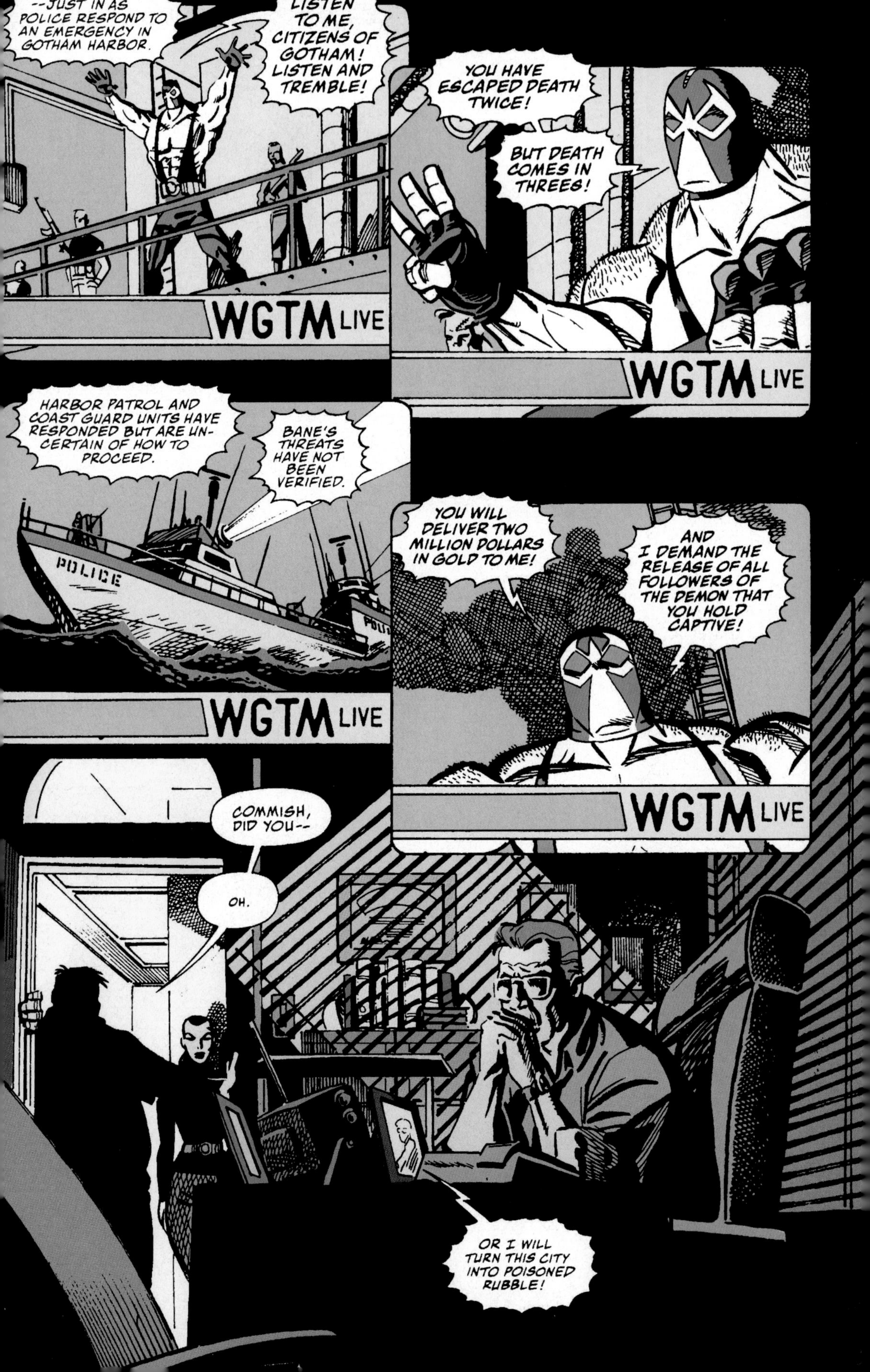
--JUST IN AS POLICE RESPOND TO AN EMERGENCY IN GOTHAM HARBOR.
LISTEN TO ME, CITIZENS OF GOTHAM! LISTEN AND TREMBLE!
WGTM LIVE
YOU HAVE ESCAPED DEATH TWICE!
BUT DEATH COMES IN THREES!
WGTM LIVE
HARBOR PATROL AND COAST GUARD UNITS HAVE RESPONDED BUT ARE UNCERTAIN OF HOW TO PROCEED.
BANE'S THREATS HAVE NOT BEEN VERIFIED.
POLICE
WGTM LIVE
YOU WILL DELIVER TWO MILLION DOLLARS IN GOLD TO ME!
AND I DEMAND THE RELEASE OF ALL FOLLOWERS OF THE DEMON THAT YOU HOLD CAPTIVE!
WGTM LIVE
COMMISH, DID YOU--
OH.
OR I WILL TURN THIS CITY INTO POISONED RUBBLE!

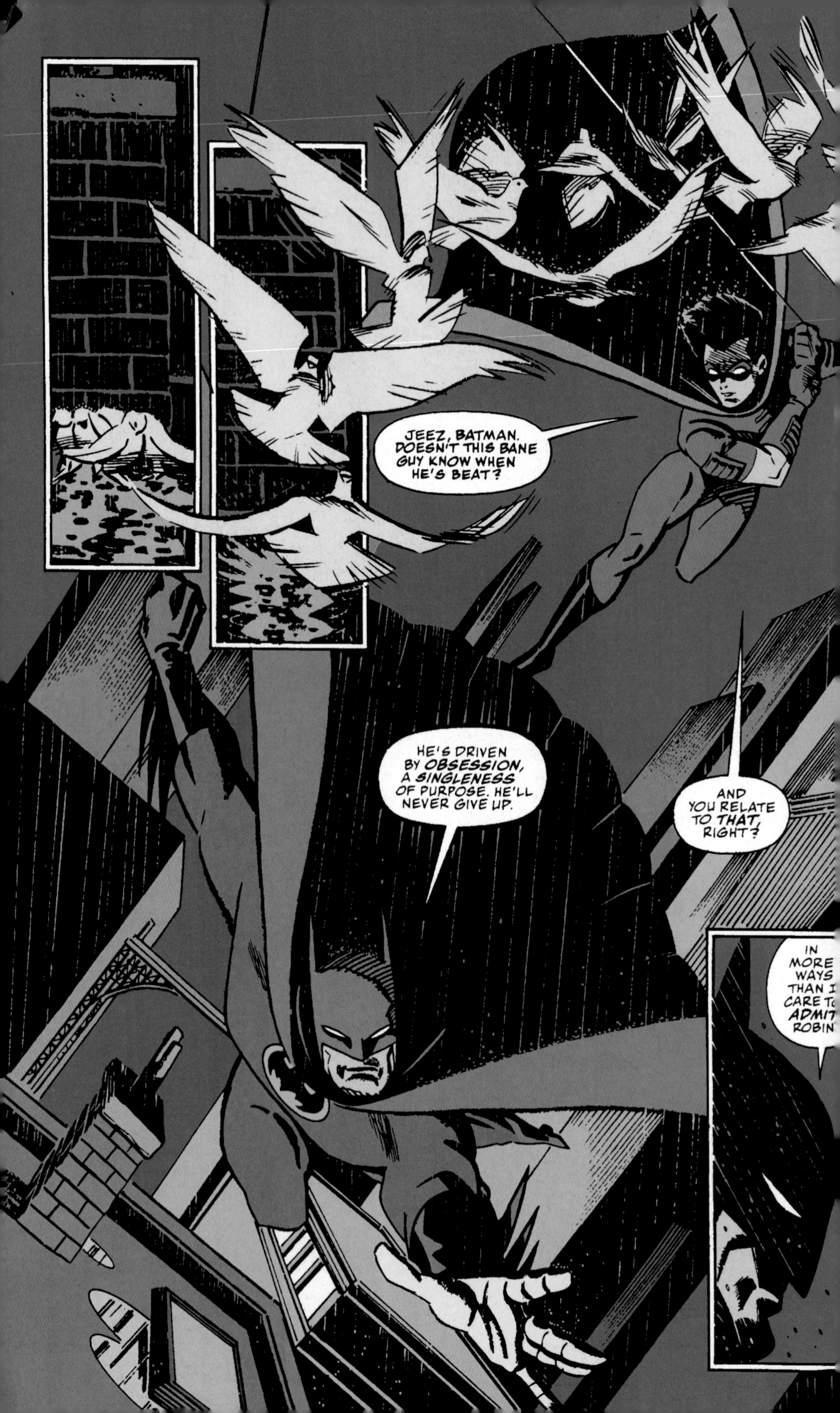
JEEZ, BATMAN. DOESN'T THIS BANE GUY KNOW WHEN HE'S BEAT?
HE'S DRIVEN BY OBSESSION, A SINGLENESS OF PURPOSE. HE'LL NEVER GIVE UP.
AND YOU RELATE TO THAT, RIGHT?

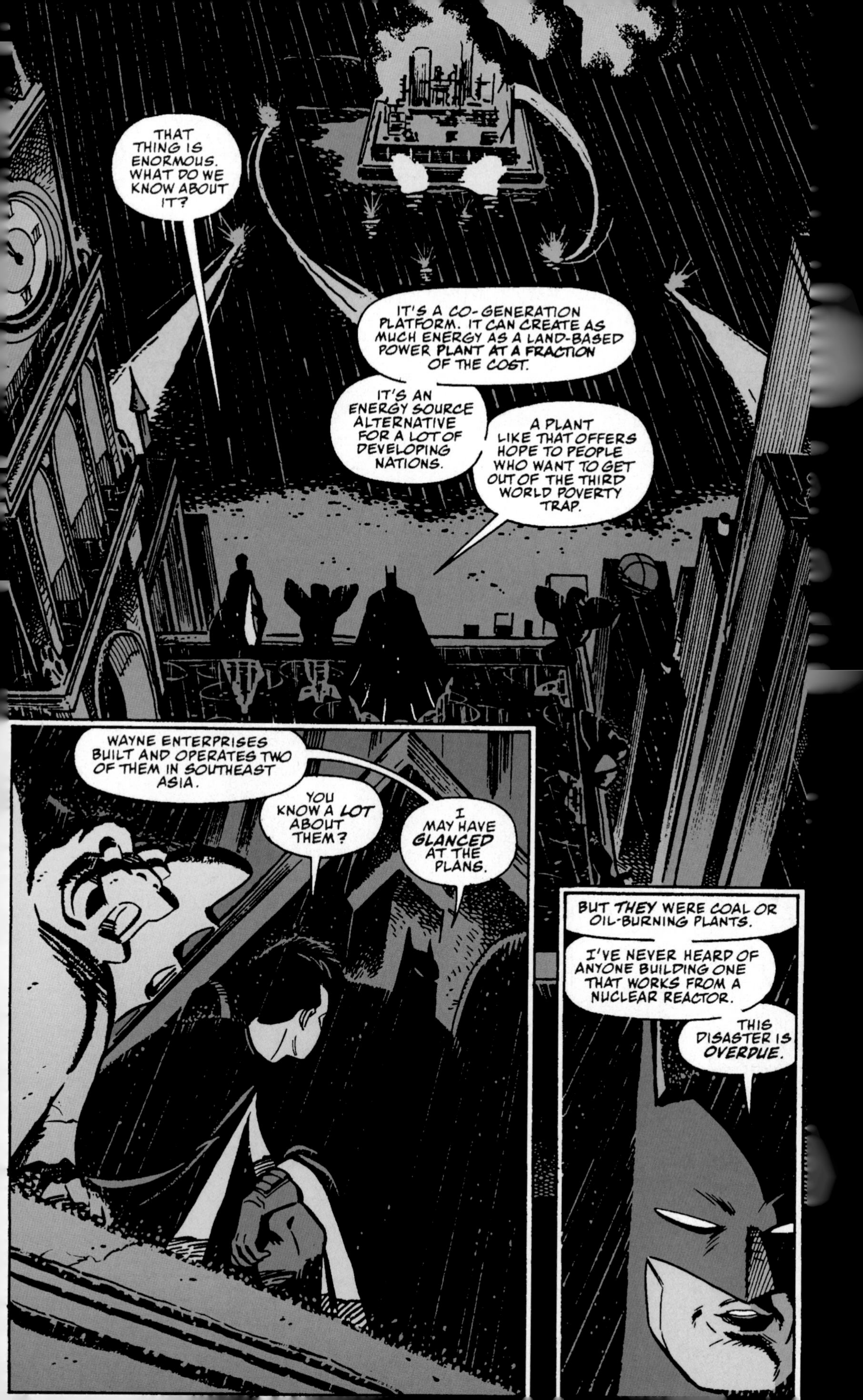
THAT THING IS ENORMOUS. WHAT DO WE KNOW ABOUT IT?
IT'S A CO-GENERATION PLATFORM. IT CAN CREATE AS MUCH ENERGY AS A LAND-BASED POWER PLANT AT A FRACTION OF THE COST.
IT'S AN ENERGY SOURCE ALTERNATIVE FOR A LOT OF DEVELOPING NATIONS.
A PLANT LIKE THAT OFFERS HOPE TO PEOPLE WHO WANT TO GET OUT OF THE THIRD WORLD POVERTY TRAP.
WAYNE ENTERPRISES BUILT AND OPERATES TWO OF THEM IN SOUTHEAST ASIA.
YOU KNOW A *LOT* ABOUT THEM?
I MAY HAVE *GLANCED* AT THE PLANS.
BUT *THEY* WERE COAL OR OIL-BURNING PLANTS.
I'VE NEVER HEARD OF ANYONE BUILDING ONE THAT WORKS FROM A NUCLEAR REACTOR.
THIS DISASTER IS *OVERDUE*.

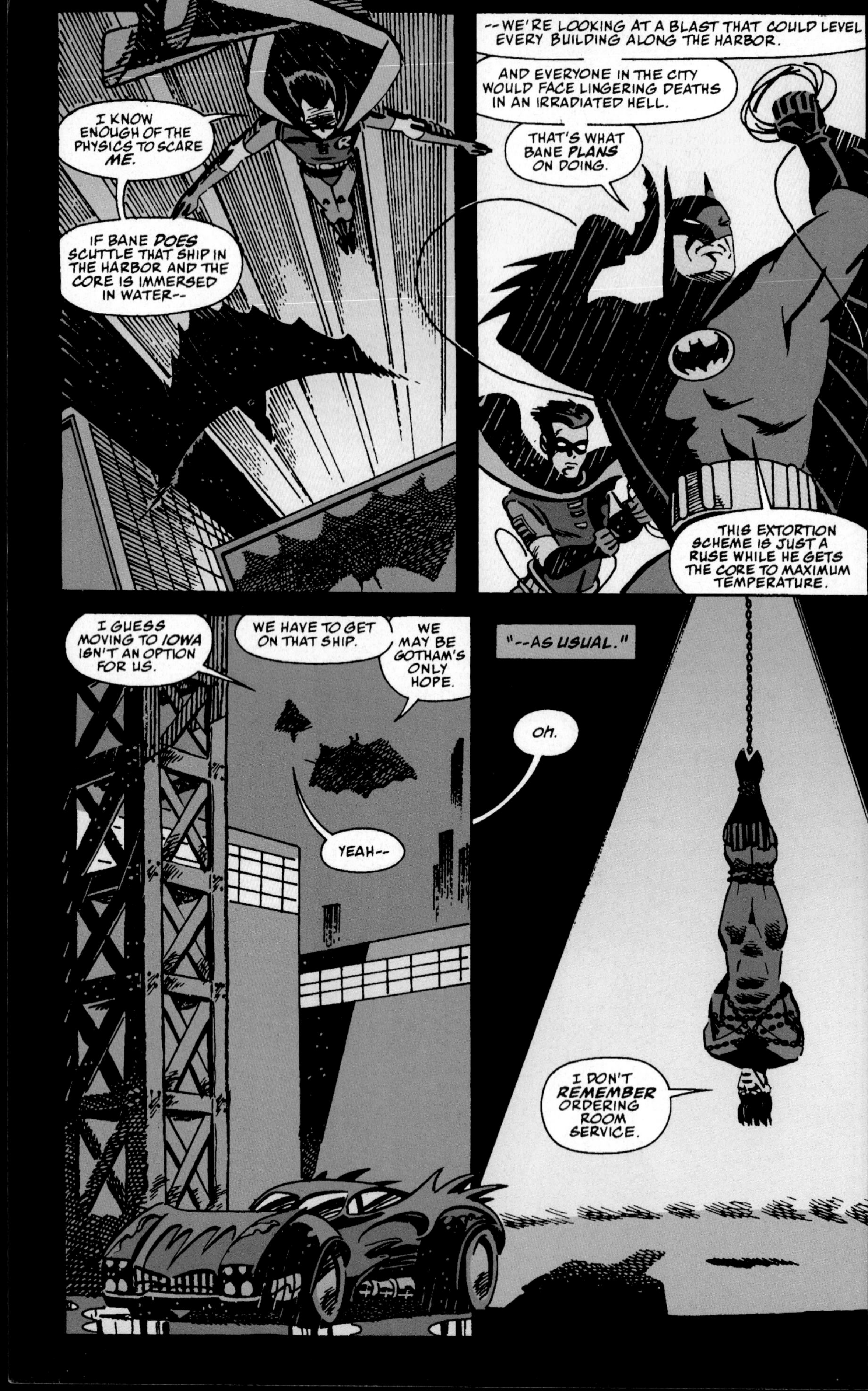
I KNOW ENOUGH OF THE PHYSICS TO SCARE *ME.*
IF BANE *DOES* SCUTTLE THAT SHIP IN THE HARBOR AND THE CORE IS IMMERSED IN WATER--
--WE'RE LOOKING AT A BLAST THAT COULD LEVEL EVERY BUILDING ALONG THE HARBOR.
AND EVERYONE IN THE CITY WOULD FACE LINGERING DEATHS IN AN IRRADIATED HELL.
THAT'S WHAT BANE *PLANS* ON DOING.
THIS EXTORTION SCHEME IS JUST A RUSE WHILE HE GETS THE CORE TO MAXIMUM TEMPERATURE.
I GUESS MOVING TO *IOWA* ISN'T AN OPTION FOR US.
WE HAVE TO GET ON THAT SHIP.
WE MAY BE GOTHAM'S ONLY HOPE.
YEAH--
"--AS *USUAL.*"
OH.
I DON'T *REMEMBER* ORDERING ROOM SERVICE.

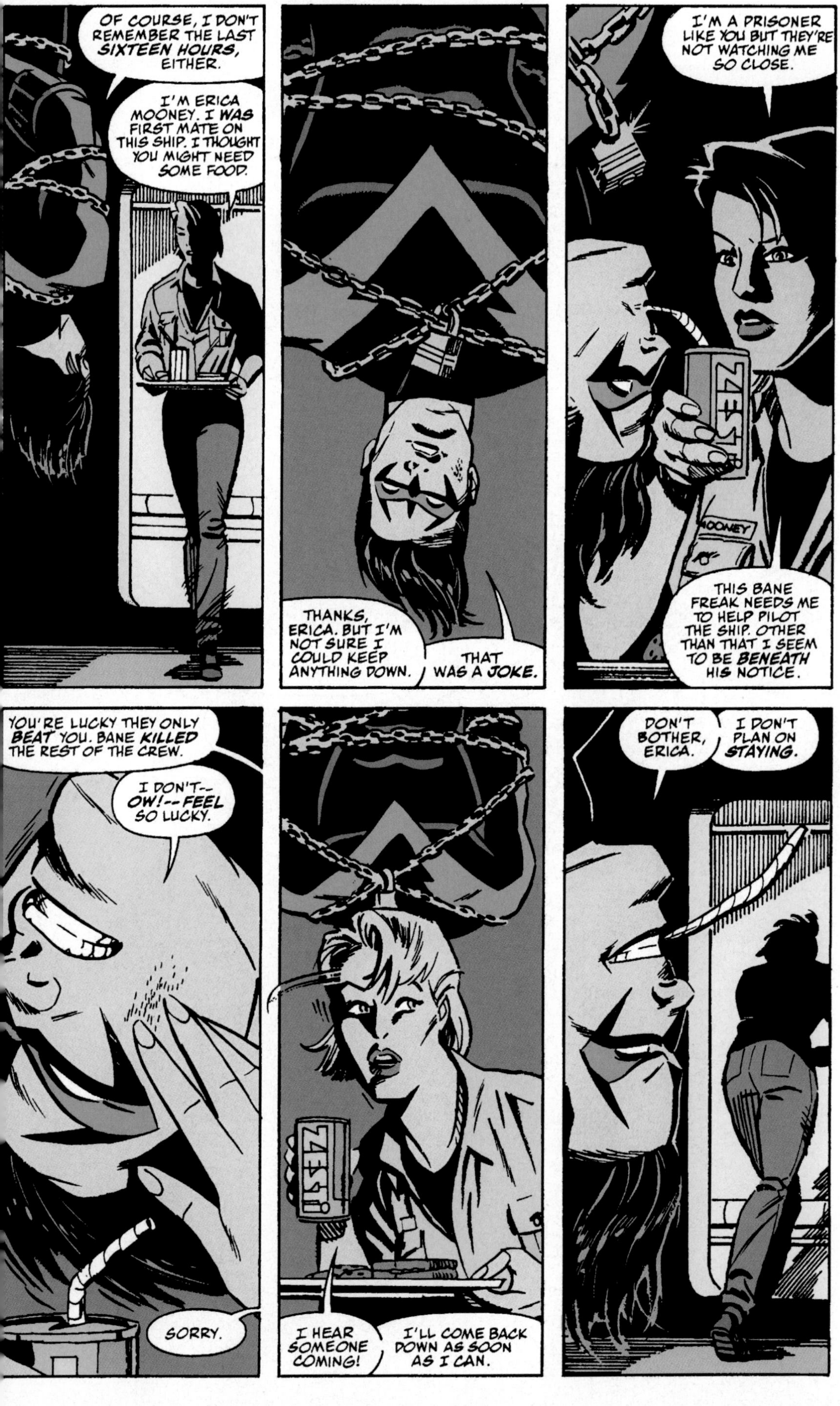
OF COURSE, I DON'T REMEMBER THE LAST SIXTEEN HOURS, EITHER.
I'M ERICA MOONEY. I WAS FIRST MATE ON THIS SHIP. I THOUGHT YOU MIGHT NEED SOME FOOD.
THANKS, ERICA. BUT I'M NOT SURE I COULD KEEP ANYTHING DOWN.
THAT WAS A JOKE.
I'M A PRISONER LIKE YOU BUT THEY'RE NOT WATCHING ME SO CLOSE.
ZEST
MOONEY
THIS BANE FREAK NEEDS ME TO HELP PILOT THE SHIP. OTHER THAN THAT I SEEM TO BE BENEATH HIS NOTICE.
YOU'RE LUCKY THEY ONLY BEAT YOU. BANE KILLED THE REST OF THE CREW.
I DON'T-- OW!--FEEL SO LUCKY.
SORRY.
ZEST
I HEAR SOMEONE COMING!
I'LL COME BACK DOWN AS SOON AS I CAN.
DON'T BOTHER, ERICA.
I DON'T PLAN ON STAYING.

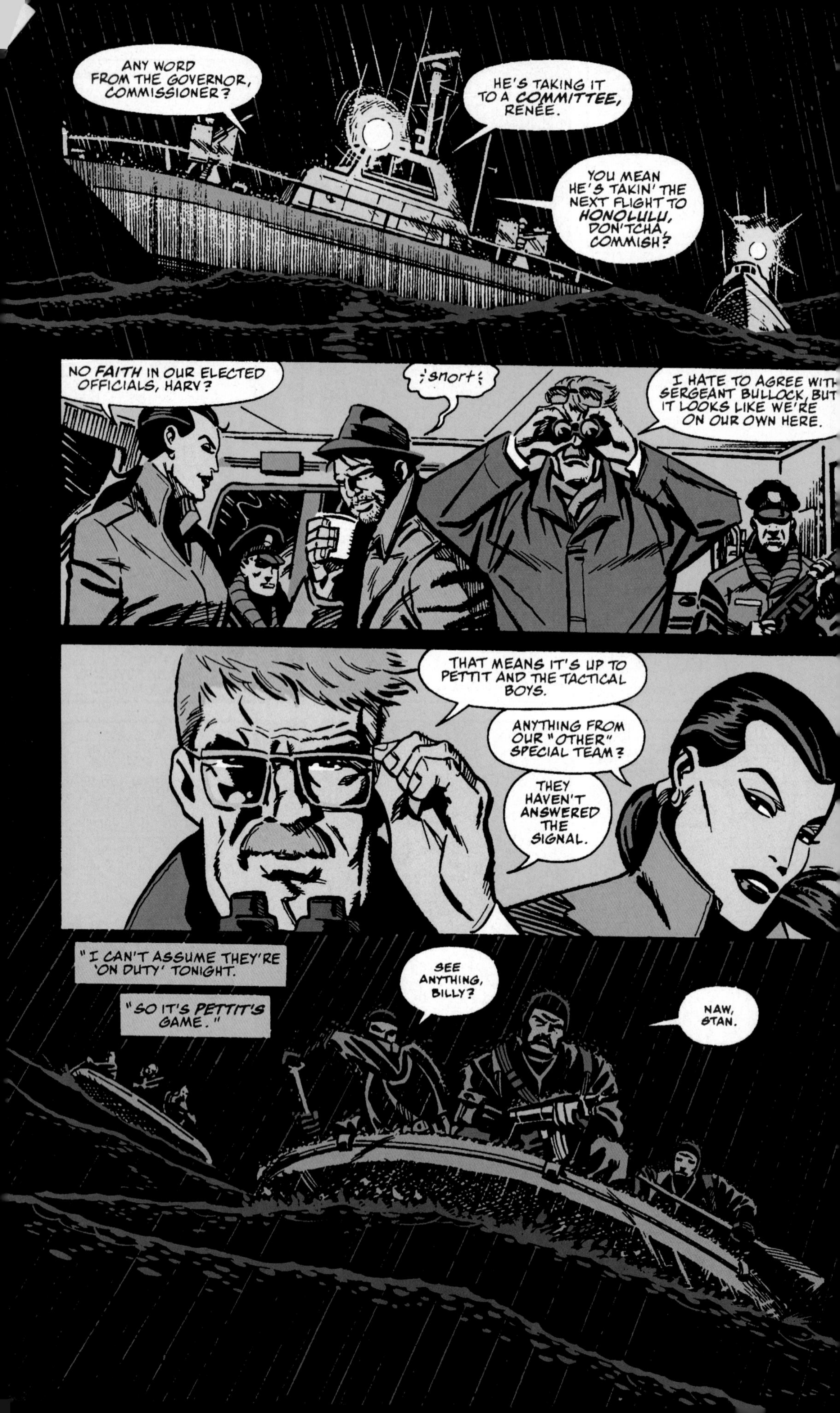

ANY WORD FROM THE GOVERNOR, COMMISSIONER?
HE'S TAKING IT TO A COMMITTEE, RENÉE.
YOU MEAN HE'S TAKIN' THE NEXT FLIGHT TO HONOLULU, DON'TCHA, COMMISH?
NO FAITH IN OUR ELECTED OFFICIALS, HARV?
snort
I HATE TO AGREE WITH SERGEANT BULLOCK, BUT IT LOOKS LIKE WE'RE ON OUR OWN HERE.
THAT MEANS IT'S UP TO PETTIT AND THE TACTICAL BOYS.
ANYTHING FROM OUR "OTHER" SPECIAL TEAM?
THEY HAVEN'T ANSWERED THE SIGNAL.
"I CAN'T ASSUME THEY'RE 'ON DUTY' TONIGHT.
"SO IT'S PETTIT'S GAME."
SEE ANYTHING, BILLY?
NAW, STAN.

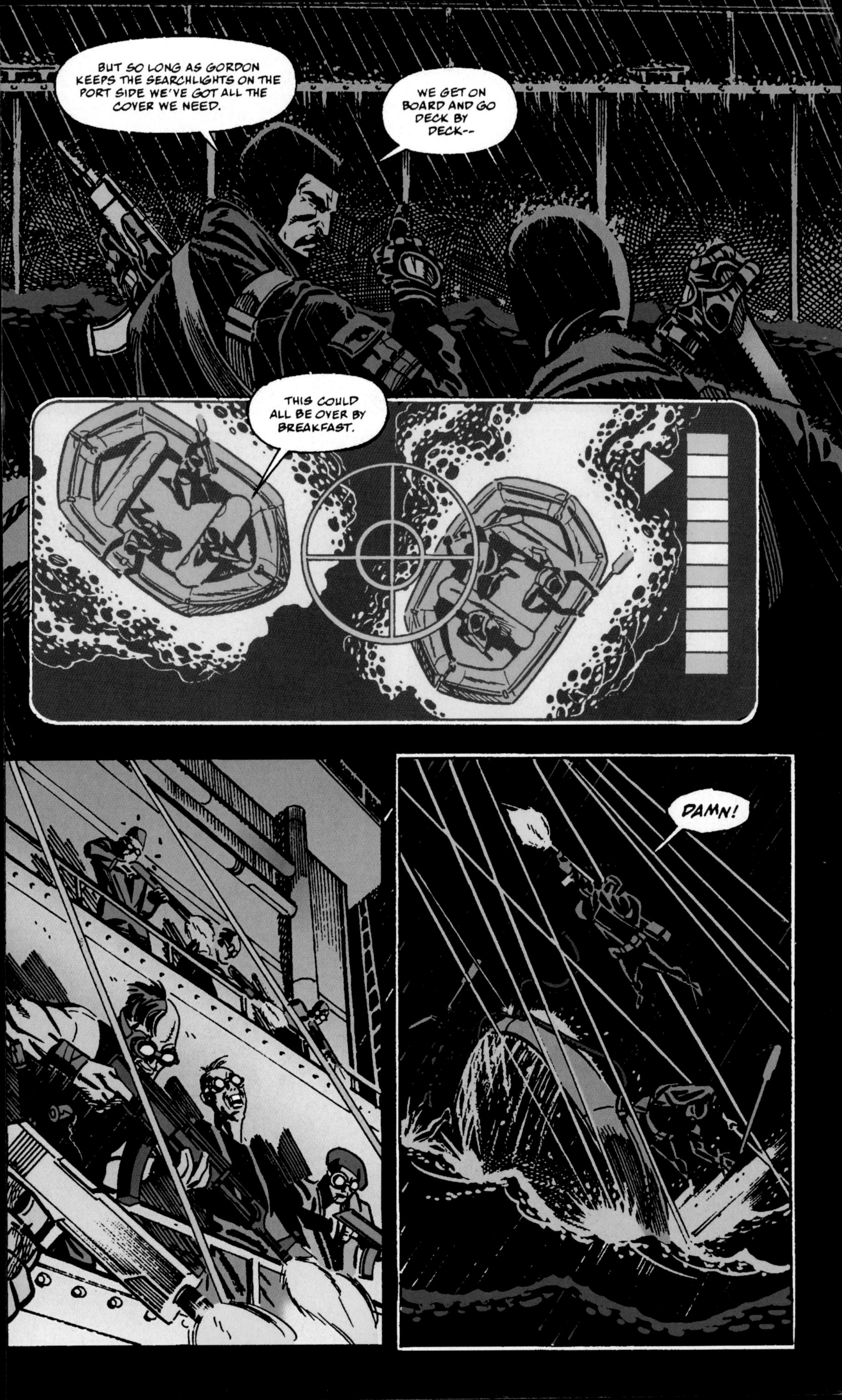
BUT SO LONG AS GORDON KEEPS THE SEARCHLIGHTS ON THE PORT SIDE WE'VE GOT ALL THE COVER WE NEED.
WE GET ON BOARD AND GO DECK BY DECK--
THIS COULD ALL BE OVER BY BREAKFAST.
DAMN!

MAKE FOR THE SHORE! HELP ANY WOUNDED!

I THINK THOSE GUYS ARE TRYING TO ;glug; KILL US!

I DON'T MIND DYING, STAN--

"--I JUST HATE LOSING."

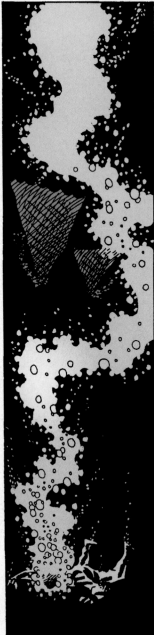

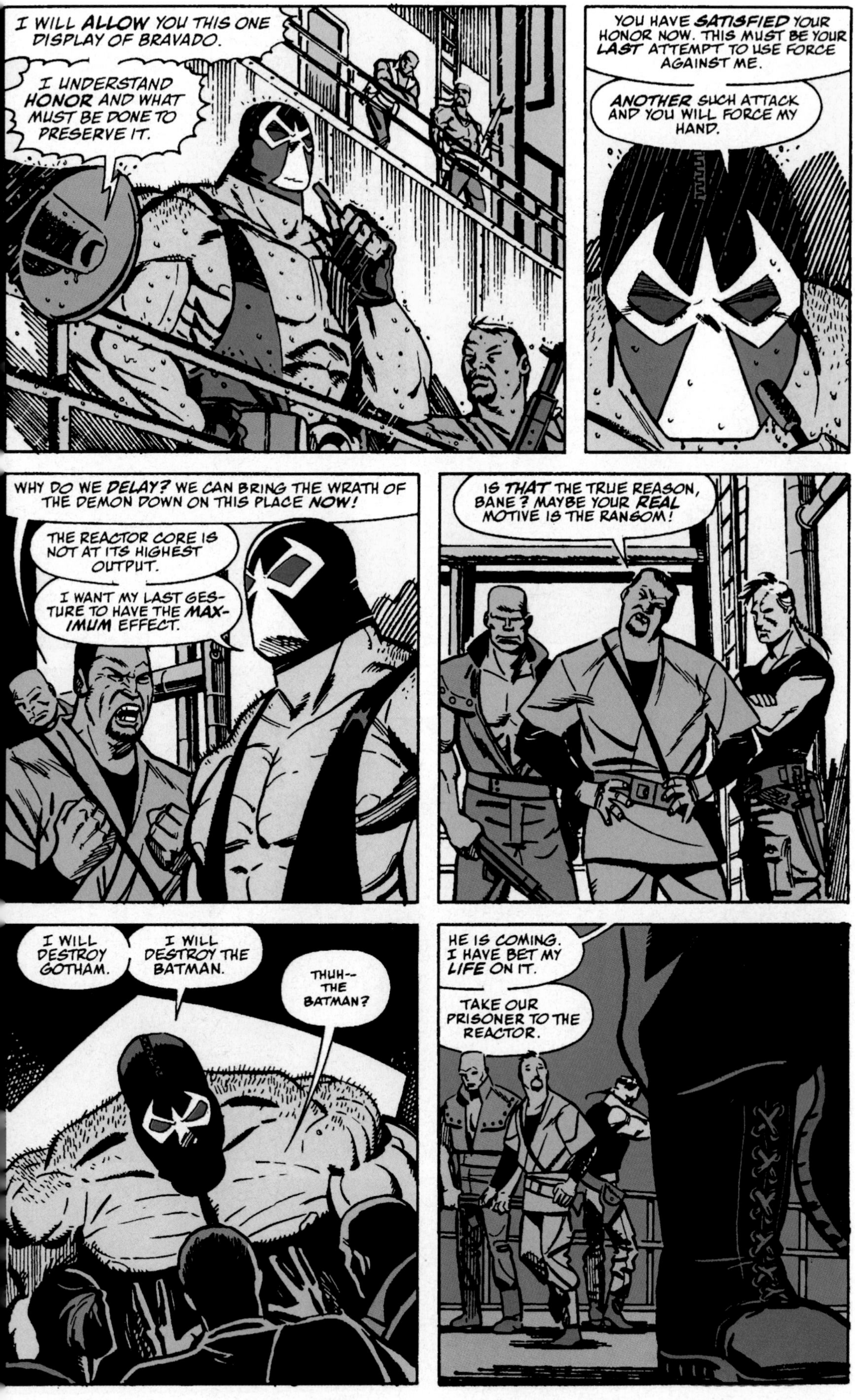
I WILL ALLOW YOU THIS ONE DISPLAY OF BRAVADO.
I UNDERSTAND HONOR AND WHAT MUST BE DONE TO PRESERVE IT.
YOU HAVE SATISFIED YOUR HONOR NOW. THIS MUST BE YOUR LAST ATTEMPT TO USE FORCE AGAINST ME.
ANOTHER SUCH ATTACK AND YOU WILL FORCE MY HAND.
WHY DO WE DELAY? WE CAN BRING THE WRATH OF THE DEMON DOWN ON THIS PLACE NOW!
THE REACTOR CORE IS NOT AT ITS HIGHEST OUTPUT.
I WANT MY LAST GESTURE TO HAVE THE MAXIMUM EFFECT.
IS THAT THE TRUE REASON, BANE? MAYBE YOUR REAL MOTIVE IS THE RANSOM!
I WILL DESTROY GOTHAM.
I WILL DESTROY THE BATMAN.
THUH-- THE BATMAN?
HE IS COMING. I HAVE BET MY LIFE ON IT.
TAKE OUR PRISONER TO THE REACTOR.

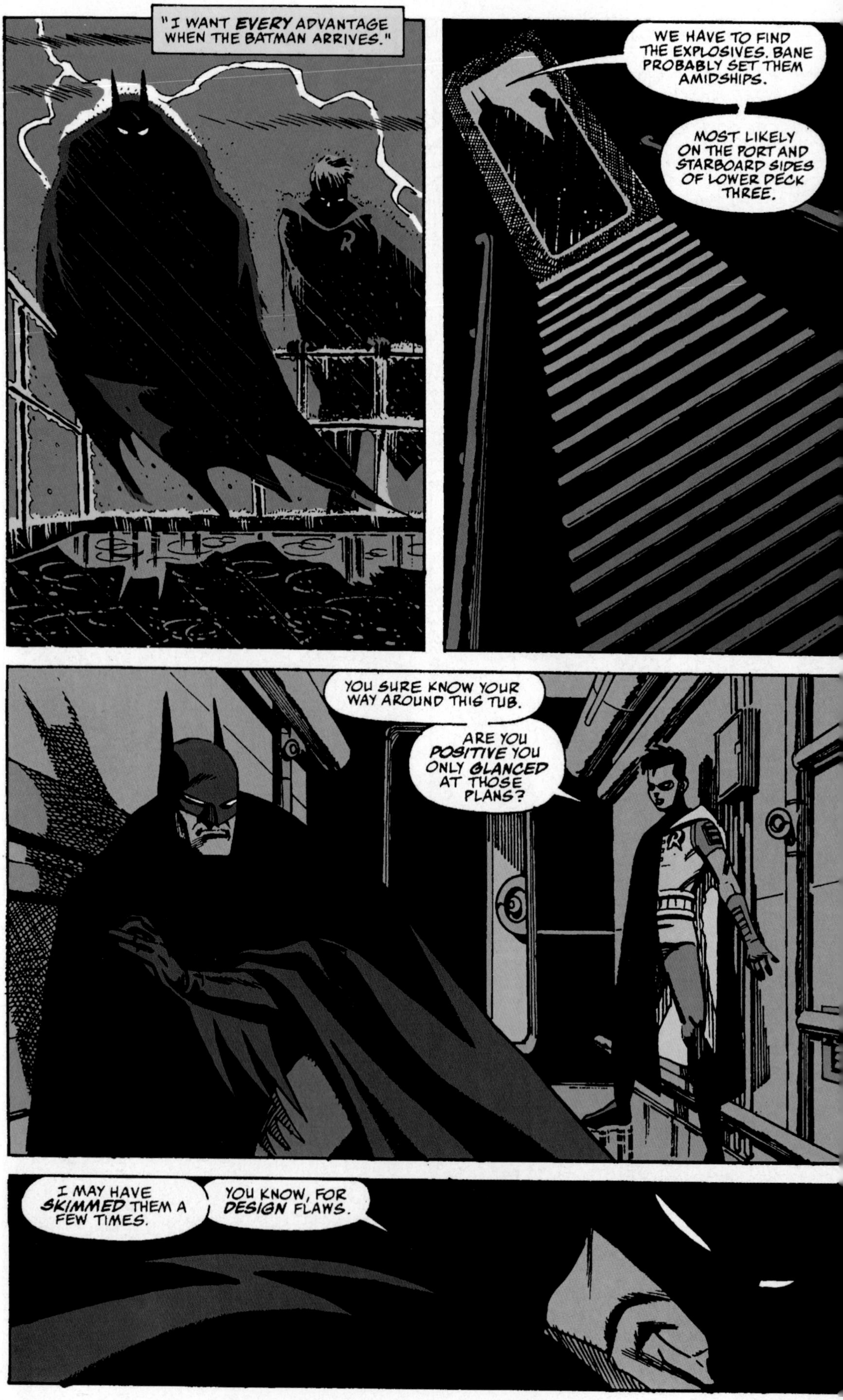
"I WANT EVERY ADVANTAGE WHEN THE BATMAN ARRIVES."
WE HAVE TO FIND THE EXPLOSIVES. BANE PROBABLY SET THEM AMIDSHIPS.
MOST LIKELY ON THE PORT AND STARBOARD SIDES OF LOWER DECK THREE.
YOU SURE KNOW YOUR WAY AROUND THIS TUB.
ARE YOU POSITIVE YOU ONLY GLANCED AT THOSE PLANS?
I MAY HAVE SKIMMED THEM A FEW TIMES.
YOU KNOW, FOR DESIGN FLAWS.

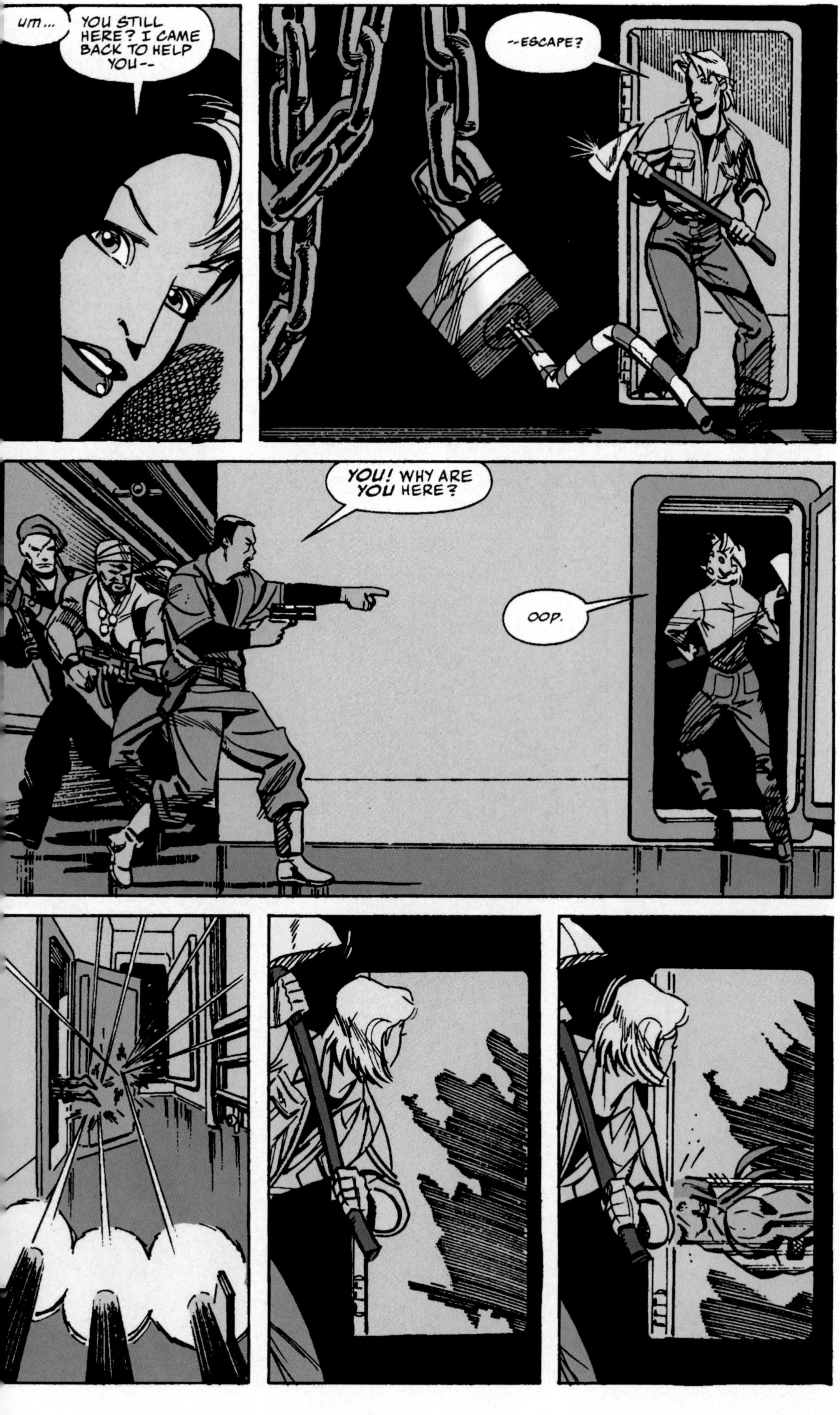
um...
YOU STILL HERE? I CAME BACK TO HELP YOU--
--ESCAPE?
YOU! WHY ARE YOU HERE?
OOP.

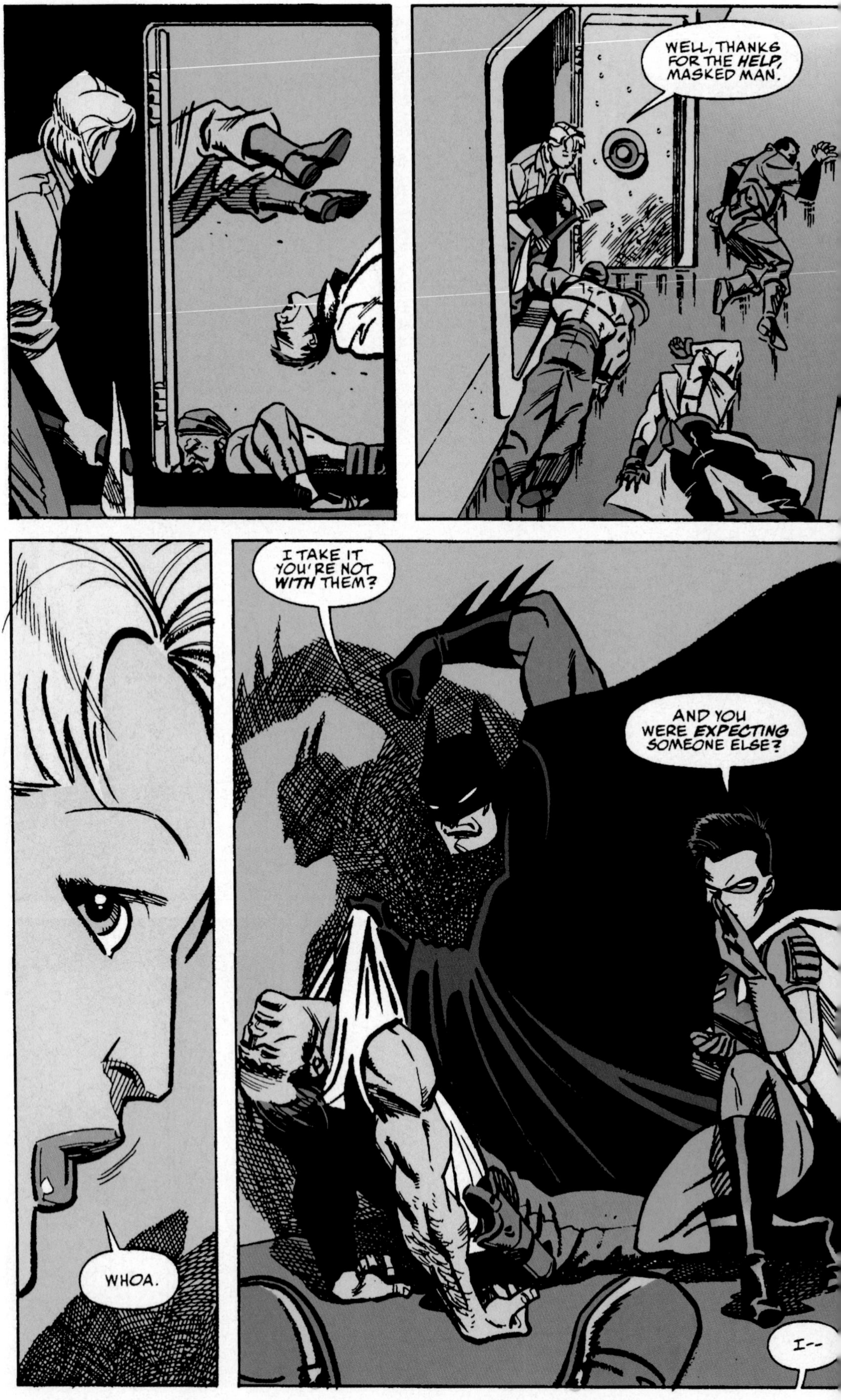
WELL, THANKS FOR THE *HELP*, MASKED MAN.
I TAKE IT YOU'RE NOT *WITH* THEM?
AND YOU WERE *EXPECTING* SOMEONE ELSE?
WHOA.
I--

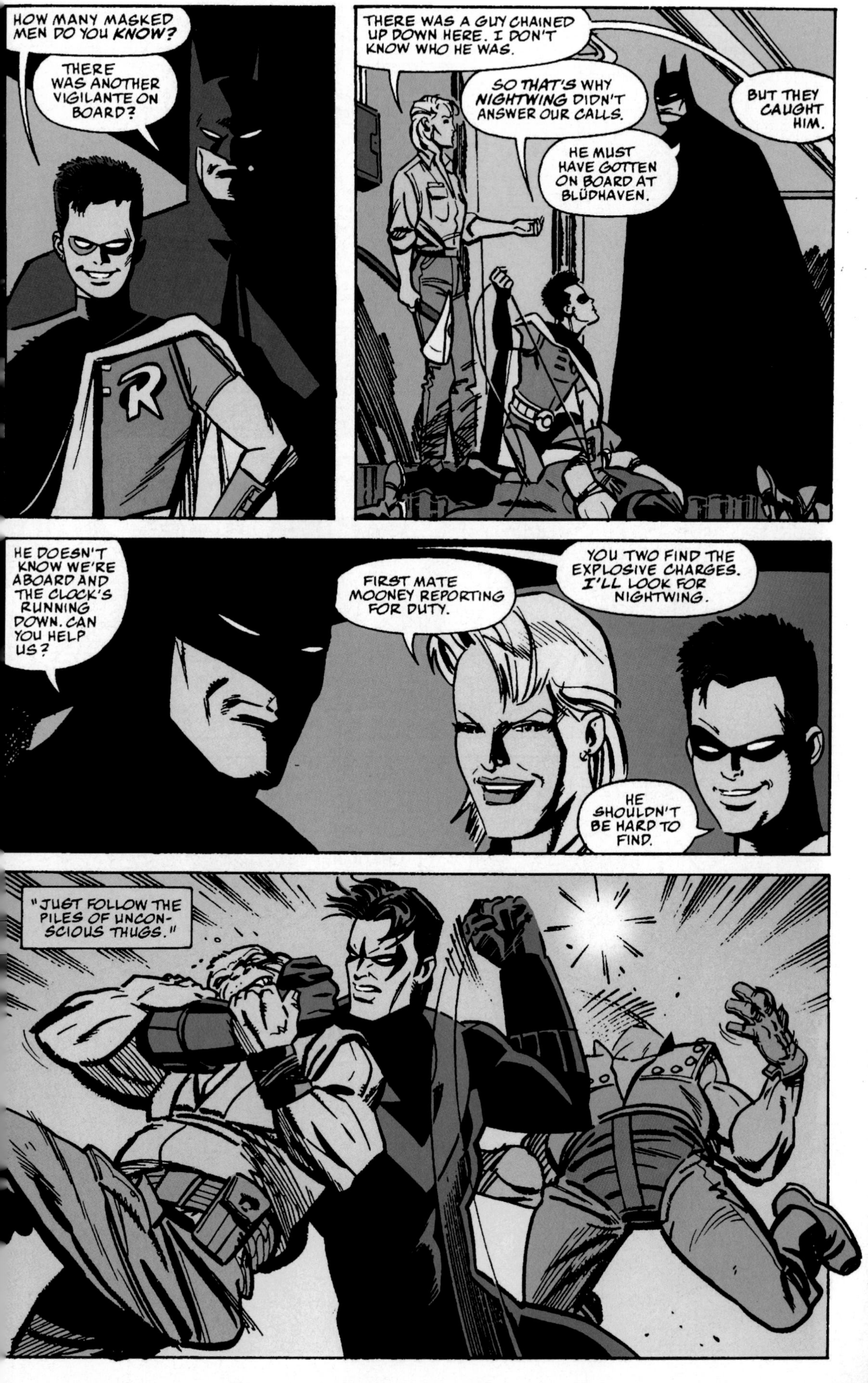
HOW MANY MASKED MEN DO YOU KNOW?
THERE WAS ANOTHER VIGILANTE ON BOARD?
THERE WAS A GUY CHAINED UP DOWN HERE. I DON'T KNOW WHO HE WAS.
SO THAT'S WHY NIGHTWING DIDN'T ANSWER OUR CALLS.
BUT THEY CAUGHT HIM.
HE MUST HAVE GOTTEN ON BOARD AT BLÜDHAVEN.
HE DOESN'T KNOW WE'RE ABOARD AND THE CLOCK'S RUNNING DOWN. CAN YOU HELP US?
FIRST MATE MOONEY REPORTING FOR DUTY.
YOU TWO FIND THE EXPLOSIVE CHARGES. I'LL LOOK FOR NIGHTWING.
HE SHOULDN'T BE HARD TO FIND.
"JUST FOLLOW THE PILES OF UNCONSCIOUS THUGS."

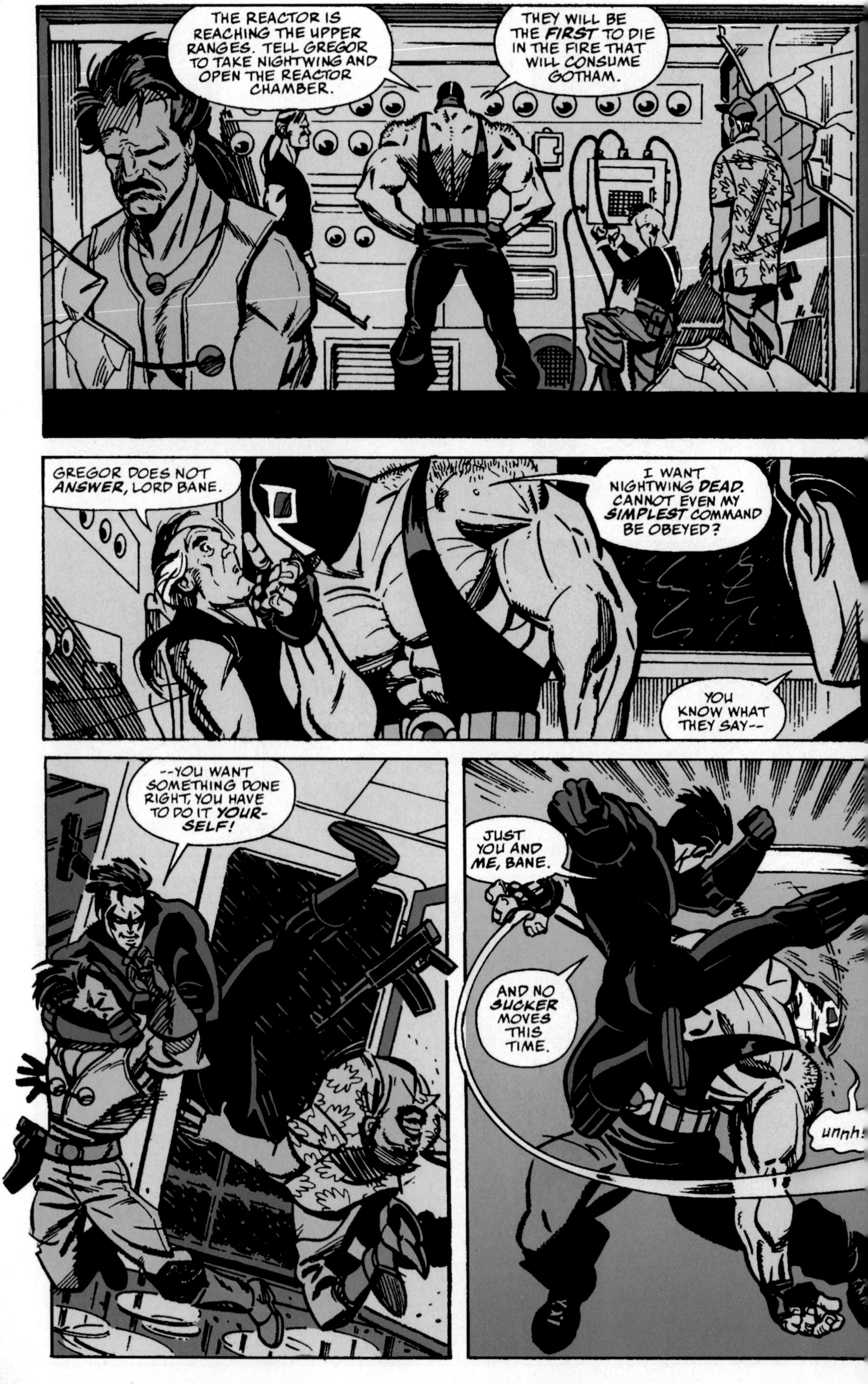
THE REACTOR IS REACHING THE UPPER RANGES. TELL GREGOR TO TAKE NIGHTWING AND OPEN THE REACTOR CHAMBER.
THEY WILL BE THE FIRST TO DIE IN THE FIRE THAT WILL CONSUME GOTHAM.
GREGOR DOES NOT ANSWER, LORD BANE.
I WANT NIGHTWING DEAD. CANNOT EVEN MY SIMPLEST COMMAND BE OBEYED?
YOU KNOW WHAT THEY SAY--
--YOU WANT SOMETHING DONE RIGHT, YOU HAVE TO DO IT YOURSELF!
JUST YOU AND ME, BANE.
AND NO SUCKER MOVES THIS TIME.
unnh!

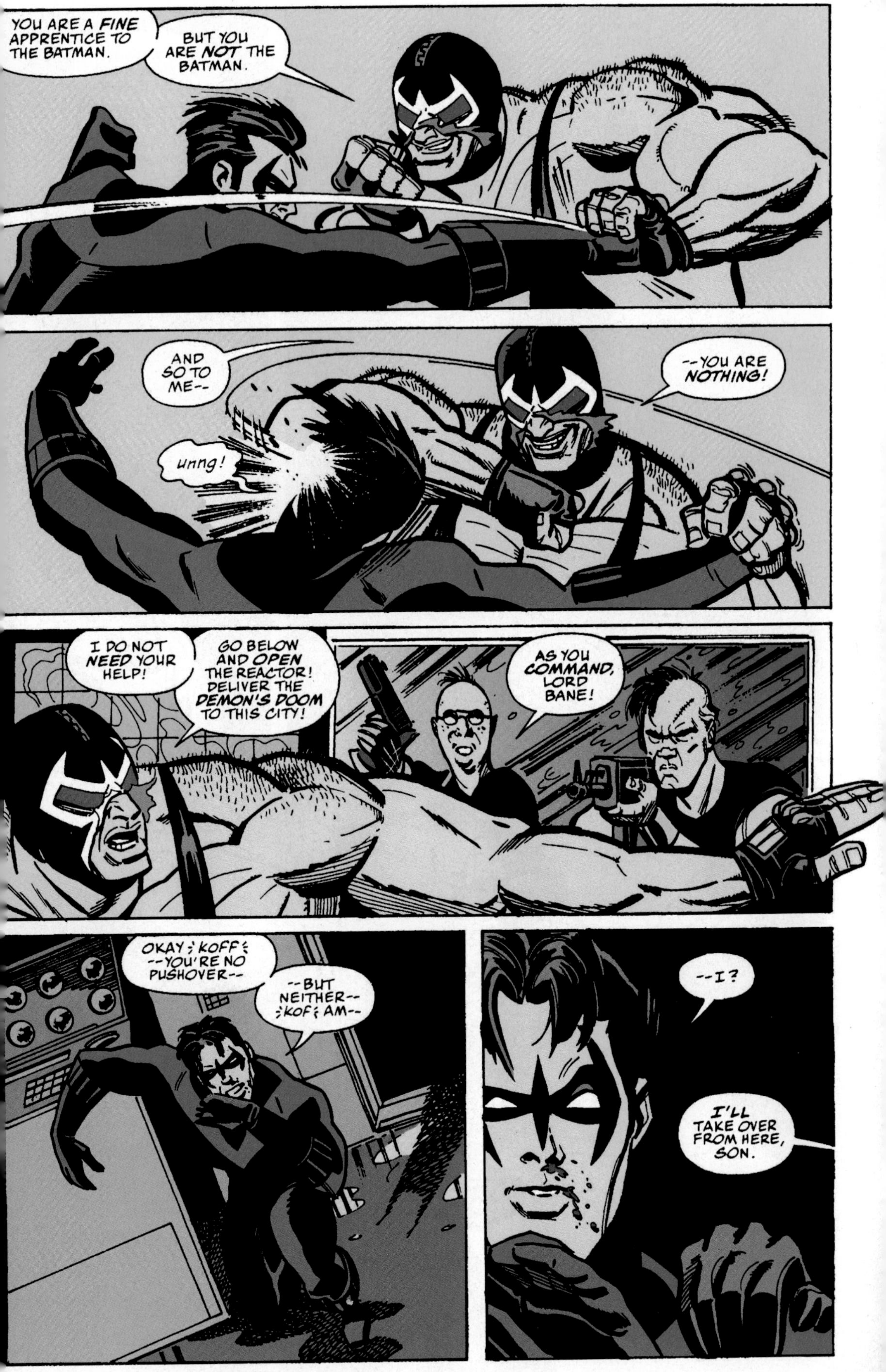
YOU ARE A FINE APPRENTICE TO THE BATMAN.
BUT YOU ARE NOT THE BATMAN.
AND SO TO ME--
--YOU ARE NOTHING!
unng!
I DO NOT NEED YOUR HELP!
GO BELOW AND OPEN THE REACTOR! DELIVER THE DEMON'S DOOM TO THIS CITY!
AS YOU COMMAND, LORD BANE!
OKAY ;KOFF; --YOU'RE NO PUSHOVER--
--BUT NEITHER-- ;KOF; AM--
--I?
I'LL TAKE OVER FROM HERE, SON.

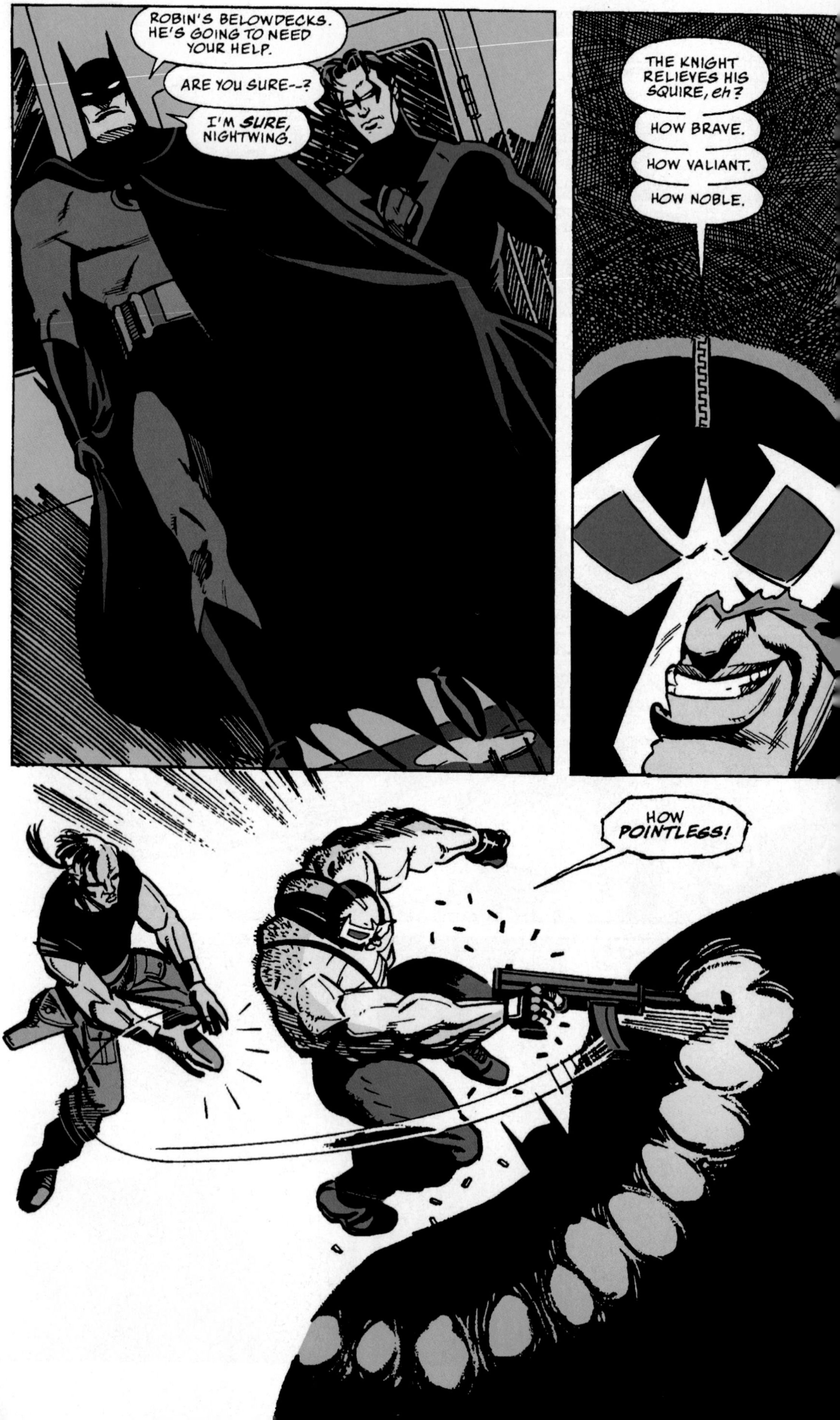
ROBIN'S BELOWDECKS. HE'S GOING TO NEED YOUR HELP.
ARE YOU SURE--?
I'M SURE, NIGHTWING.
THE KNIGHT RELIEVES HIS SQUIRE, eh?
HOW BRAVE.
HOW VALIANT.
HOW NOBLE.
HOW POINTLESS!

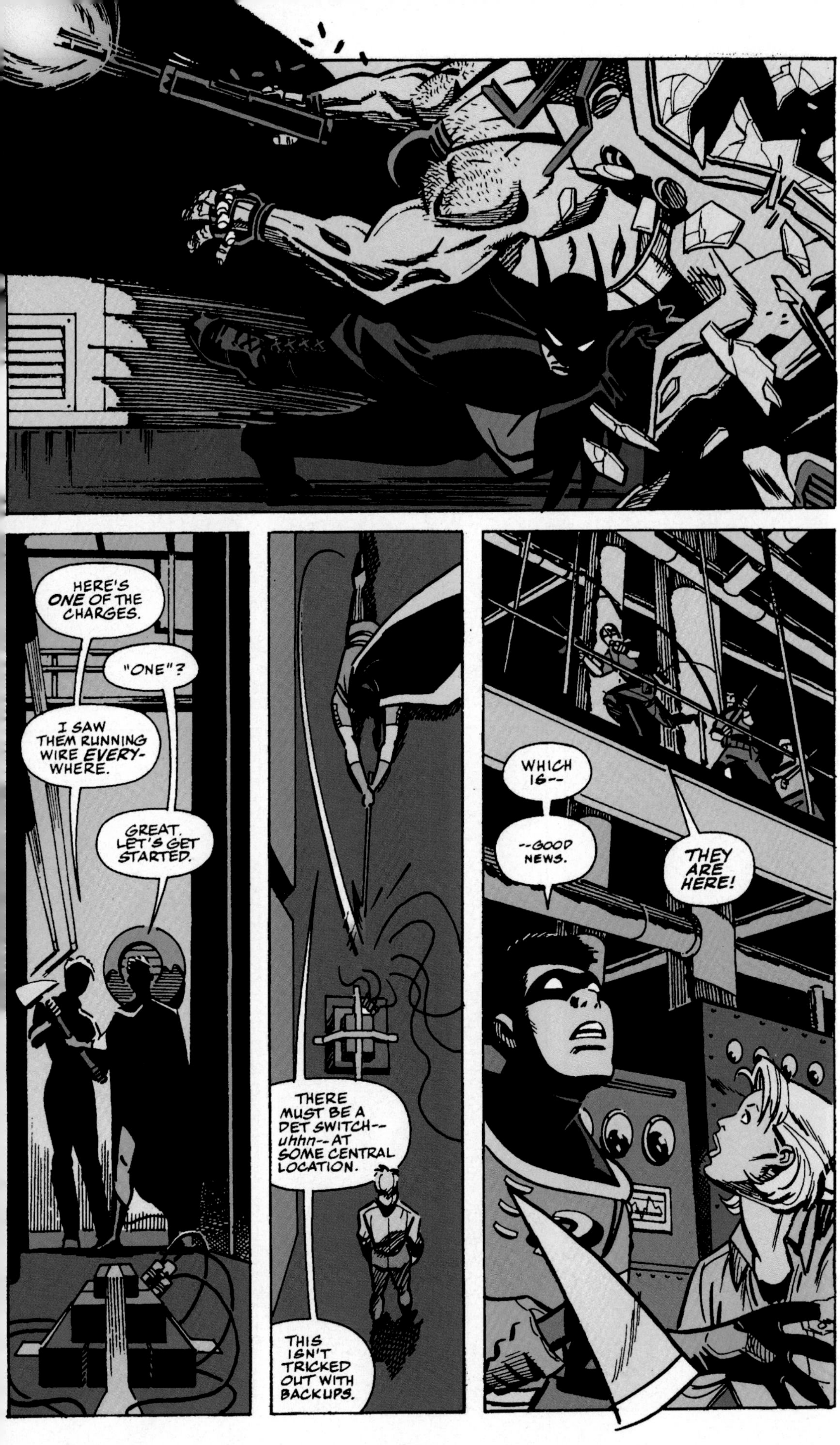
HERE'S ONE OF THE CHARGES.
"ONE"?
I SAW THEM RUNNING WIRE EVERY-WHERE.
GREAT. LET'S GET STARTED.
THERE MUST BE A DET SWITCH-- uhhn--AT SOME CENTRAL LOCATION.
THIS ISN'T TRICKED OUT WITH BACKUPS.
WHICH IS--
--GOOD NEWS.
THEY ARE HERE!

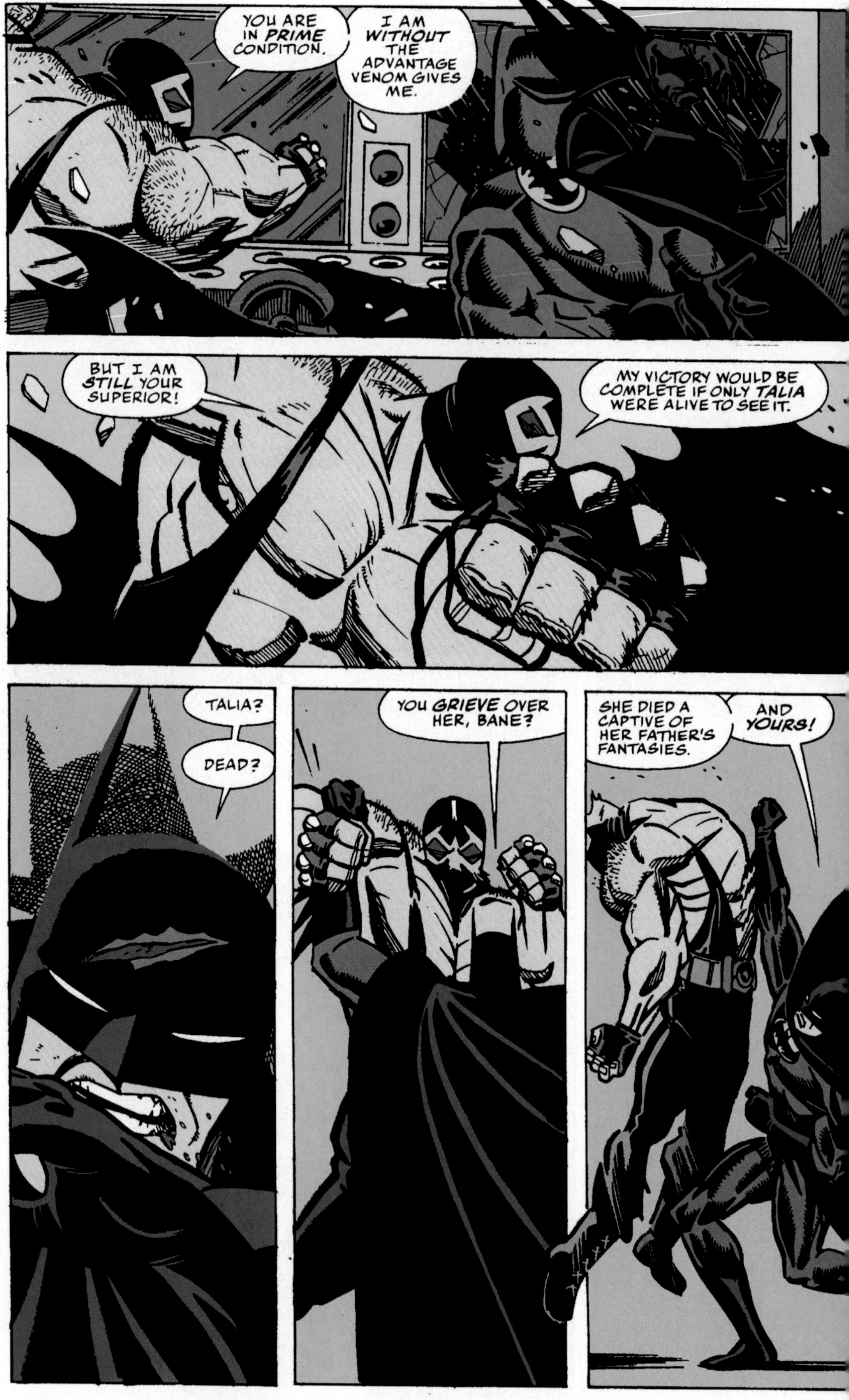
YOU ARE IN PRIME CONDITION.
I AM WITHOUT THE ADVANTAGE VENOM GIVES ME.
BUT I AM STILL YOUR SUPERIOR!
MY VICTORY WOULD BE COMPLETE IF ONLY TALIA WERE ALIVE TO SEE IT.
TALIA?
DEAD?
YOU GRIEVE OVER HER, BANE?
SHE DIED A CAPTIVE OF HER FATHER'S FANTASIES.
AND YOURS!

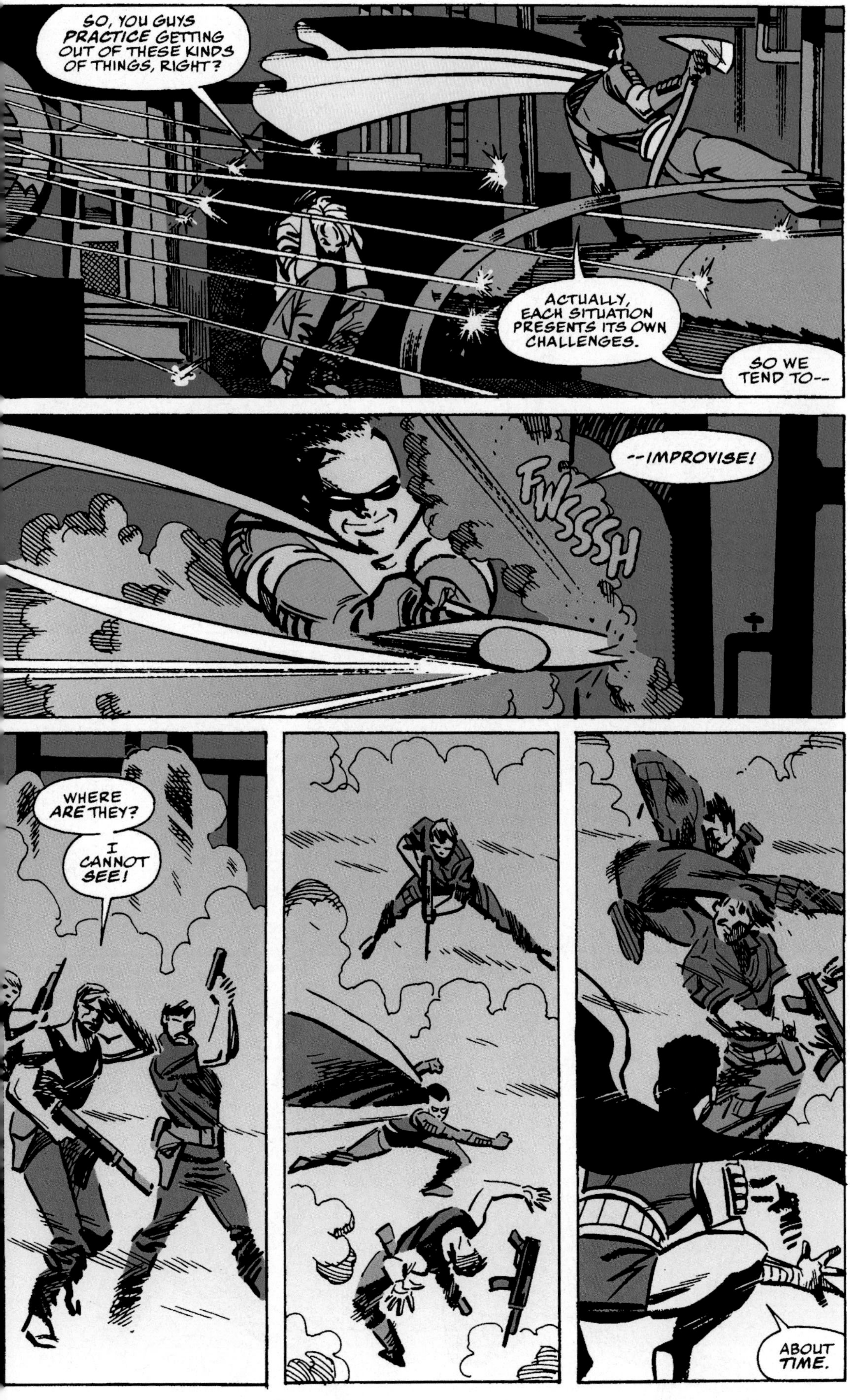
SO, YOU GUYS PRACTICE GETTING OUT OF THESE KINDS OF THINGS, RIGHT?
ACTUALLY, EACH SITUATION PRESENTS ITS OWN CHALLENGES.
SO WE TEND TO--
--IMPROVISE!
FWSSSH
WHERE ARE THEY?
I CANNOT SEE!
ABOUT TIME.

HEY, IT'S *HARD* TO FIND YOUR WAY AROUND A SHIP. THE SCENERY'S ALWAYS CHANGING.

HO, HO.

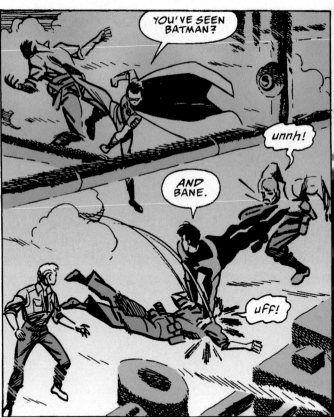

YOU'VE SEEN BATMAN?

unnh!

AND BANE.

uff!

THERE'S THREE OF BANE'S BUDDIES HEADING FOR THE FUEL CHAMBER TO OPEN IT UP.

WE HAVE TO GET THERE *BEFORE* THEM.

WHAT ABOUT THE EXPLOSIVES?

WE HAVE TO TRUST BATMAN TO KEEP BANE AWAY FROM THE DETONATOR.

CAN YOU SHOW US THE WAY TO THE REACTOR, ERICA?

FOLLOW ME.

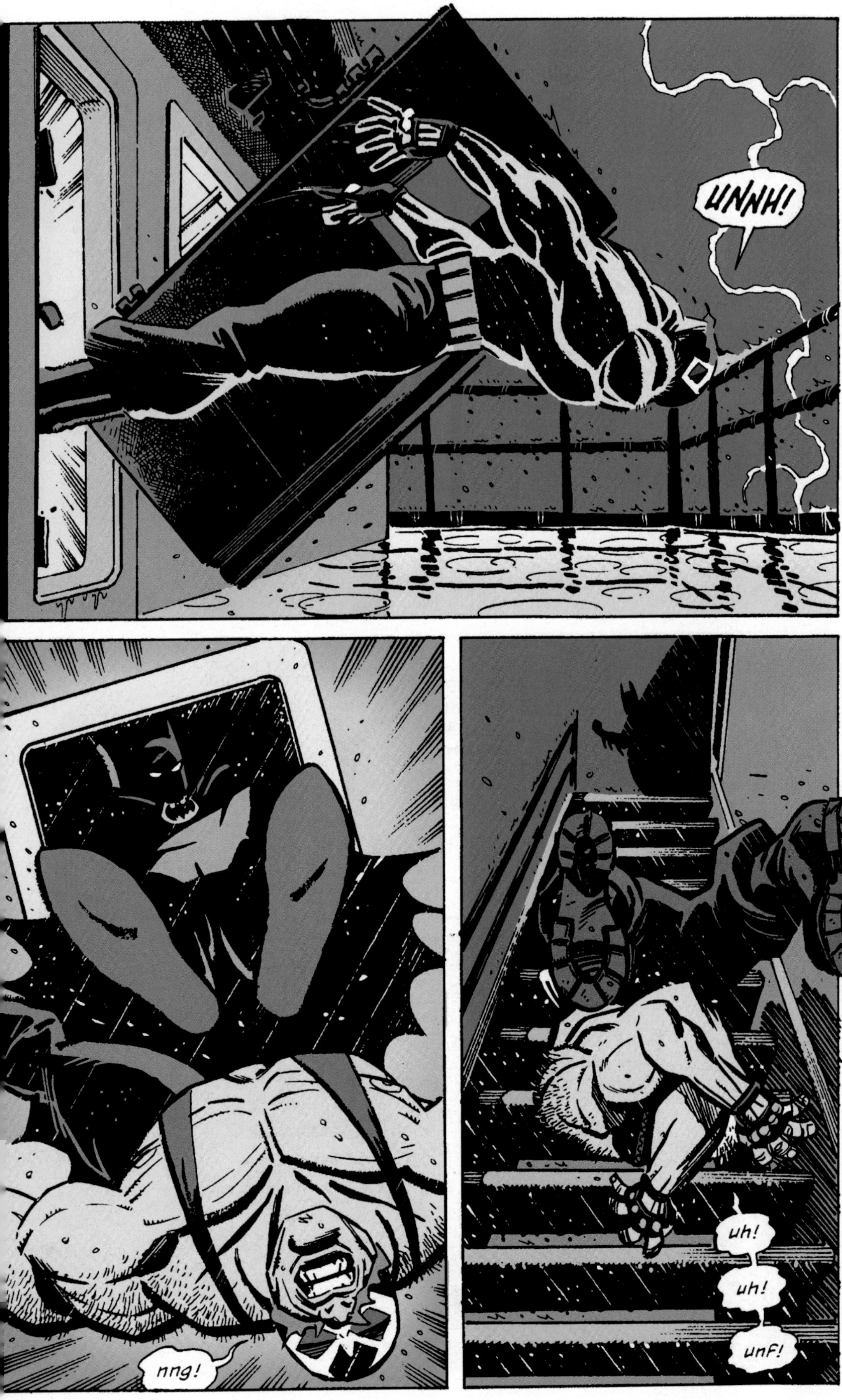
UNNH!
nng!
uh!
uh!
unf!

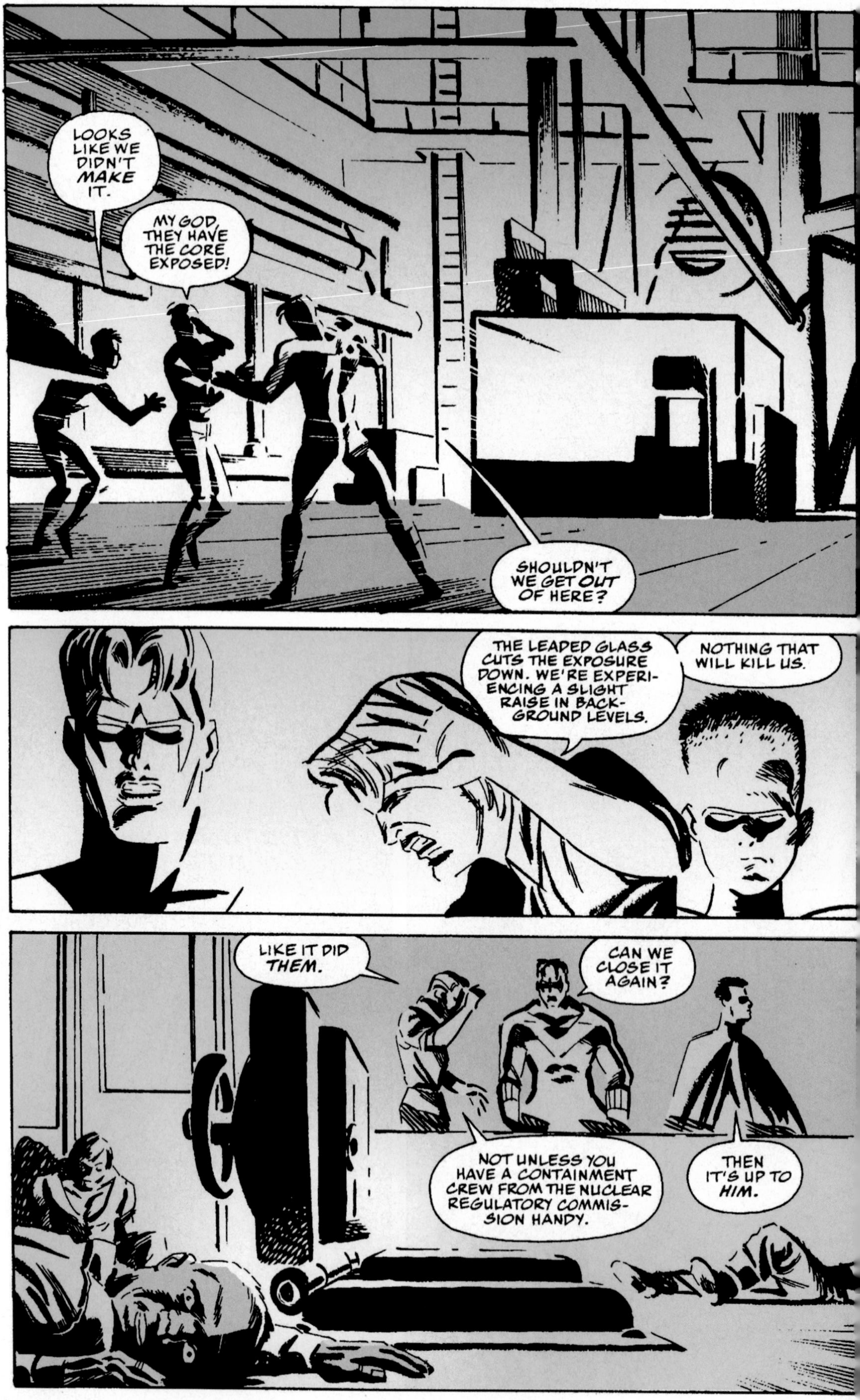
LOOKS LIKE WE DIDN'T MAKE IT.
MY GOD, THEY HAVE THE CORE EXPOSED!
SHOULDN'T WE GET OUT OF HERE?
THE LEADED GLASS CUTS THE EXPOSURE DOWN. WE'RE EXPERIENCING A SLIGHT RAISE IN BACKGROUND LEVELS.
NOTHING THAT WILL KILL US.
LIKE IT DID THEM.
CAN WE CLOSE IT AGAIN?
NOT UNLESS YOU HAVE A CONTAINMENT CREW FROM THE NUCLEAR REGULATORY COMMISSION HANDY.
THEN IT'S UP TO HIM.

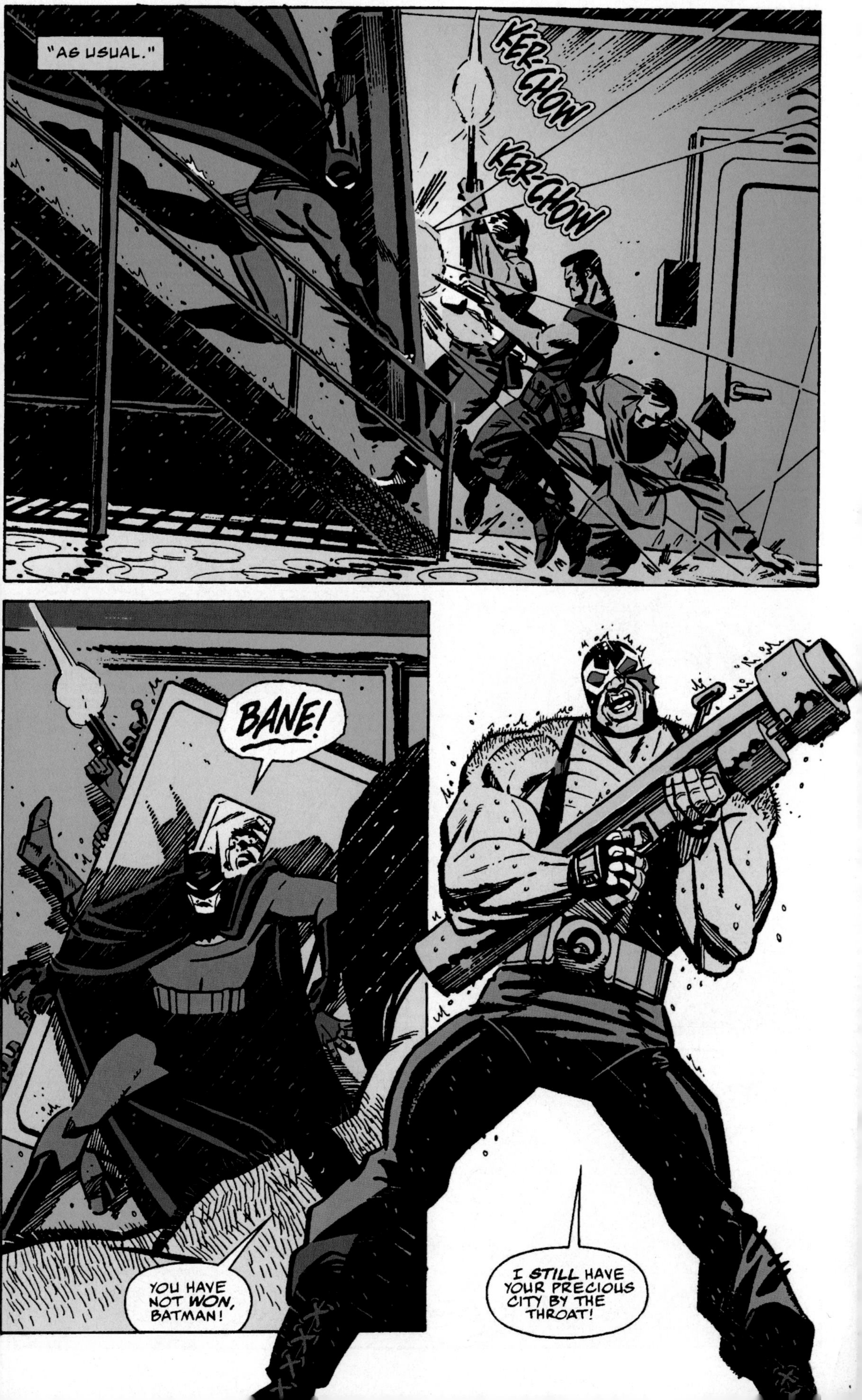
"AS USUAL."
KER-CHOW
KER-CHOW
BANE!
YOU HAVE NOT WON, BATMAN!
I STILL HAVE YOUR PRECIOUS CITY BY THE THROAT!

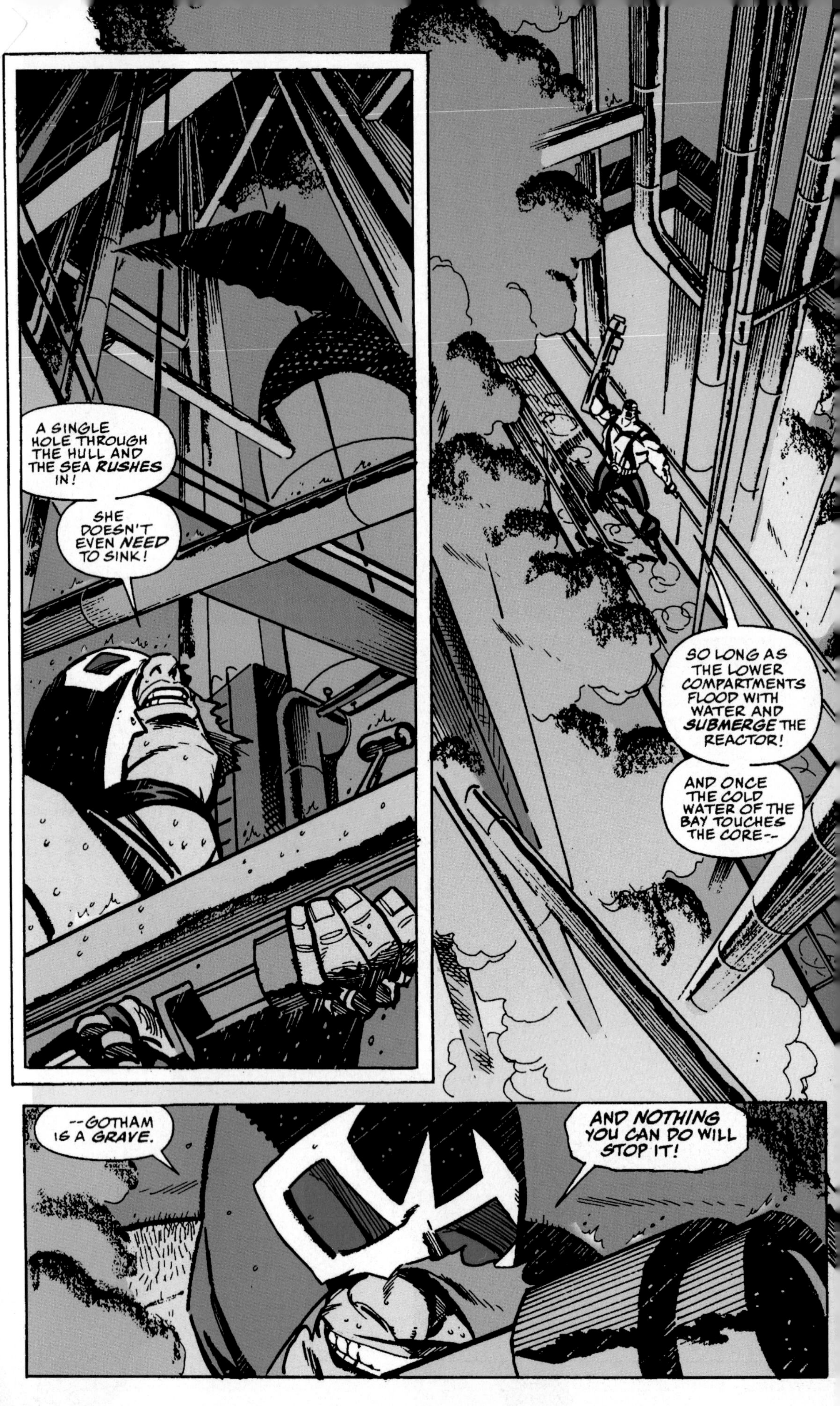
A SINGLE HOLE THROUGH THE HULL AND THE SEA RUSHES IN!
SHE DOESN'T EVEN NEED TO SINK!
SO LONG AS THE LOWER COMPARTMENTS FLOOD WITH WATER AND SUBMERGE THE REACTOR!
AND ONCE THE COLD WATER OF THE BAY TOUCHES THE CORE--
--GOTHAM IS A GRAVE.
AND NOTHING YOU CAN DO WILL STOP IT!

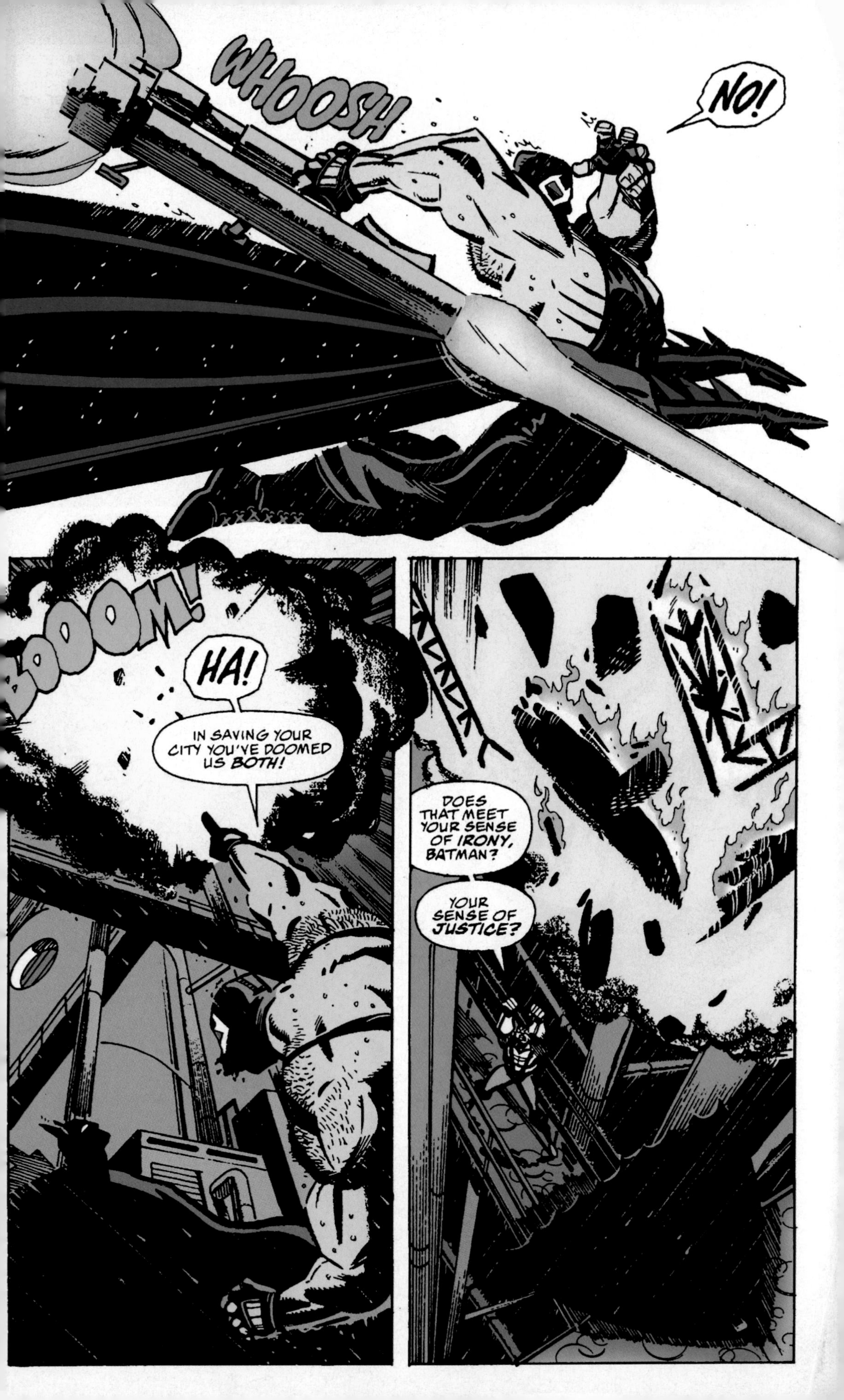
WHOOSH
NO!
BOOOM!
HA!
IN SAVING YOUR CITY YOU'VE DOOMED US BOTH!
DOES THAT MEET YOUR SENSE OF IRONY, BATMAN?
YOUR SENSE OF JUSTICE?

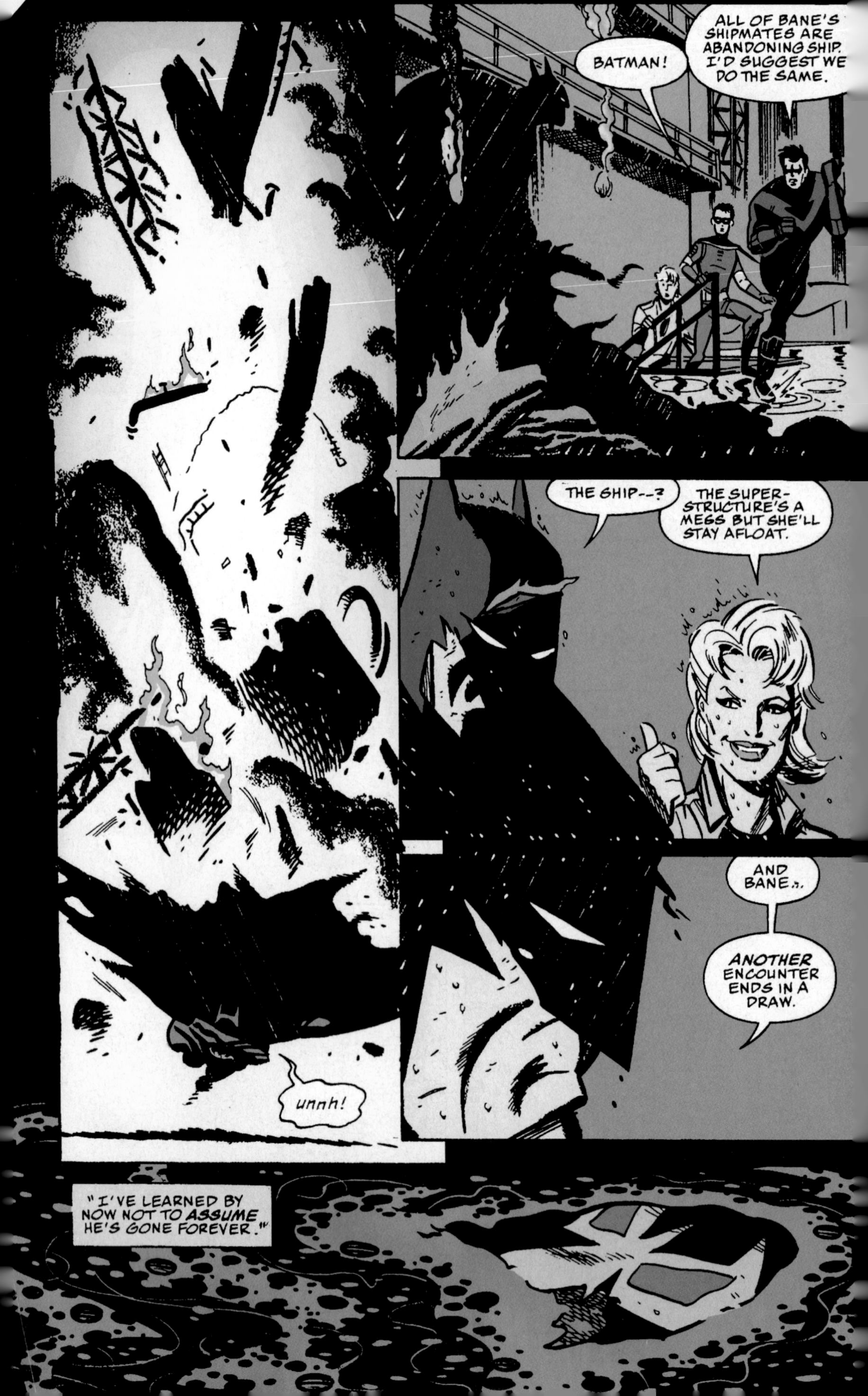
BATMAN!
ALL OF BANE'S SHIPMATES ARE ABANDONING SHIP. I'D SUGGEST WE DO THE SAME.
unnh!
THE SHIP--?
THE SUPER-STRUCTURE'S A MESS BUT SHE'LL STAY AFLOAT.
AND BANE...
ANOTHER ENCOUNTER ENDS IN A DRAW.
"I'VE LEARNED BY NOW NOT TO ASSUME HE'S GONE FOREVER."

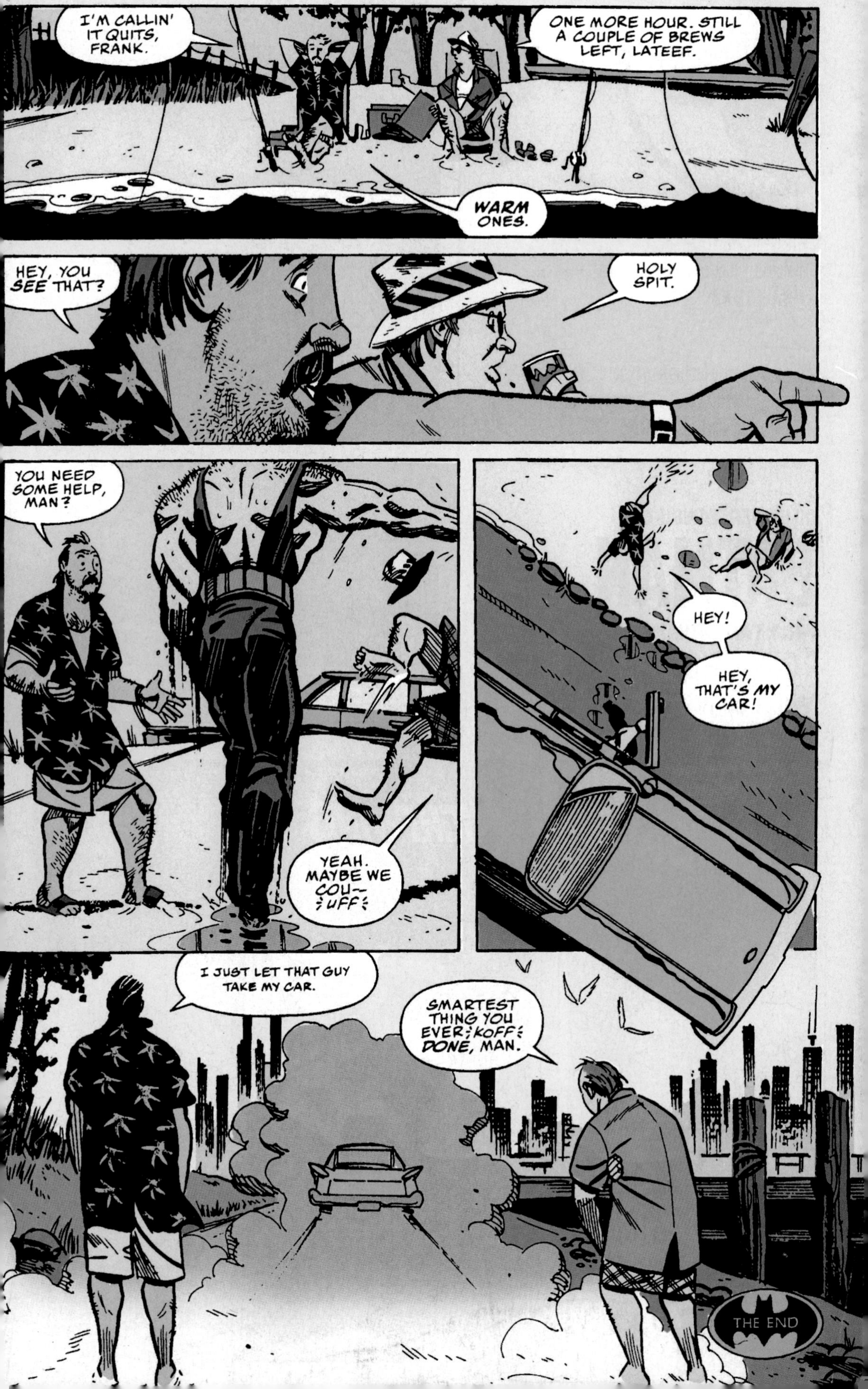
I'M CALLIN' IT QUITS, FRANK.
ONE MORE HOUR. STILL A COUPLE OF BREWS LEFT, LATEEF.
WARM ONES.
HEY, YOU SEE THAT?
HOLY SPIT.
YOU NEED SOME HELP, MAN?
YEAH. MAYBE WE COU-- UFF
HEY!
HEY, THAT'S MY CAR!
I JUST LET THAT GUY TAKE MY CAR.
SMARTEST THING YOU EVER KOFF DONE, MAN.
THE END

DC UNIVERSE REBIRTH

VOL.1 I AM GOTHAM
TOM KING • DAVID FINCH

DC UNIVERSE REBIRTH

BATMAN

VOL. 1: I AM GOTHAM
TOM KING
with DAVID FINCH

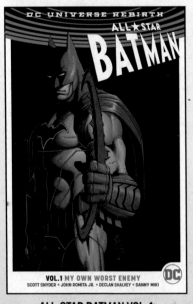

**ALL-STAR BATMAN VOL. 1:
MY OWN WORST ENEMY**

**NIGHTWING VOL. 1:
BETTER THAN BATMAN**

**DETECTIVE COMICS VOL. 1:
RISE OF THE BATMEN**